MORE PRAISE FOR JIM CARLTON'S *APPLE*

"Thoroughly researched and superbly written, *Apple* sheds light on the vexing question of how a company with such a spectacular start and great promise could in the end fail to become an enduring great company, indeed perhaps even to survive. Failure teaches at least as much as success, and Jim Carlton brings us a detailed and authoritative telling of one of the most fascinating and instructive failure stories of the century."

—Jim Collins, coauthor of *Built to Last*

"Carlton . . . provides vivid, previously unpublicized accounts of the management infighting that paralyzed the company."

—*Washington Post*

"This is the story of a true American tragedy, and Carlton's telling makes it impossible to put down. There are lessons here for everyone."

—Jeff Bezos, founder and CEO, *Amazon.com*

"If you want the full story of what happened, it's hard to imagine anyone improving on *Apple*."

—*Red Herring*

"Jim Carlton puts Apple through the Cuisinart. He captures the social anthropology of Silicon Valley during its boom and bust years. Tribalism, cultural variations, and not-invented-here syndrome all contribute to this compelling cautionary tale of a brilliant American icon gone wrong."

—Jeff Berg, chairman and CEO, ICM

"An impressive, thorough history. . . . Carlton's reporting is stellar."

—*San Francisco Examiner*

"Anyone who ever worked for Apple or loved the ease of use of a Macintosh computer should put this book on a 'must read' list."

—*Amazon.com*

"A remarkable job. . . . Carlton deftly details Apple's ignominious fall."

—*Booklist*

"The author is such a skilled reporter that he gives the impression of having worked at Apple, rather than the *Journal*'s San Francisco Bureau."

—*Boston Book Review*

"Jim Carlton's book reads more like a novel, although it would be hard for even the best fiction writer to come up with a story as amazing as this. . . . A most fascinating and accurate account of what really happened behind closed doors to make Apple Computer what it once was and what it is today. Anyone who has even the slightest interest in Apple or the personal computer should read this book."

—Tim Bajarin, president, Creative Strategies

"Jim Carlton's book is a must-read for any technology investor. He weaves together a rich fabric of behind-the-scenes detail of how a company with the best products can avoid success by undermining its own development efforts, mismanaging investments, disenchanting employees, and damaging relationships with partners. One can't help but walk away with greater insight into the 'business' of technology."

—Michael Kwatinetz, managing director, DMG Technology Group

APPLE

The Inside Story
of Intrigue, Egomania,
and Business Blunders

JIM CARLTON

HarperBusiness
A Division of HarperCollinsPublishers

To Adriana
For her love and patience

This book was originally published in 1997 by Times Books, a division of Random House, Inc. It is here reprinted by arrangement with Random House, Inc.

HarperCollins books may be purchased for educational, business, or sales promotional use. For information please write: Special Markets Department, HarperCollins Publishers, Inc., 10 East 53rd Street, New York, NY 10022.

First paperback edition published 1998.

Designed by Mina Greenstein

Library of Congress Cataloging-in-Publication Data
Carlton, Jim, 1955–
    Apple: the inside story of intrigue, egomania, and business blunders / Jim Carlton.
      p. cm.
    Originally published: New York : Times Business/Random House, 1997
    ISBN 0–88730–965–8
    1. Apple Computer, Inc.—Management. 2. Computer industry—United States—Management—Case studies. I. Carlton, Jim, 1955– Apple. II. Title
HD9696.C64A8633 1998
338.7'61004'65—dc21
                                                        98–39061

98 99 00 01 02 ❖/RRD 10 9 8 7 6 5 4 3 2 1

CONTENTS

FOREWORD

Silence gives consent.
—OLIVER GOLDSMITH, *The Good Natur'd Man*

In order to help soldiers learn from training exercises, the U.S. Army conducts after-action reviews (AAR). The goal is to answer three questions:

What happened?
Why did it happen?
How do we sustain strengths and improve weaknesses?

Every business that wants to stay in business should adopt the AAR model. In order to learn from the past and turn failures into opportunities, it is essential to ask and answer these questions—as painful as that might be. So, while much of what follows in these pages may be painful reading for an Apple aficionado, we are fortunate because *Apple* is the definitive AAR for the first twenty years of Apple Computer's existence. (To be fair, it would be difficult to characterize competing with Microsoft as a training exercise.)

I cannot vouch for the accuracy of every story in this book, but it seems that Jim Carlton has answered the first two AAR questions: What happened? and Why did it happen? The third question, How do we sustain strengths and improve weaknesses?, is beyond the scope of this book, but what the hell, I'll take a shot at it:

- Build an executive team and board whose goal is to either serve customers or serve employees—either can work. These executives must be comfortable with what they are, deep in specific knowledge, and broad in perspective. As you will see, Apple's history is littered with executives who were primarily concerned with personal agendas. This team of executives has to, frankly, add up to Bill Gates's astonishing ability to be deep and wide without giving up Apple's idealistic goal of making the world a better place.
- Eat like a bird and poop like an elephant. A bird eats 50 percent of its body weight per day, and an elephant poops 165 pounds per day. Apple needs to eat like a bird and gain knowledge constantly: listening to

customers, running list servers, attending trade shows, using competitive products, etc. It also needs to poop like an elephant: spreading out this knowledge, creating open standards, and aggressively licensing technology. I've never seen a company fail because it was too open.

- Seize segments, not share. Imagine a graph with a vertical axis that measures Apple's unique ability to provide something and a horizontal axis that measures the value of that something to customers. Apple needs to seize segments where it is uniquely providing something of great value. Examples abound: education, publishing, multimedia, and other forms of digital content creation. If Apple does a great job in these segments, then its overall market share will increase—but it can't go after market share by trying to be all things to all people.

- Don't let the bozos grind you down. Or, as better said by General Joe Stillwell (in fake Latin), "*Illegitimi non carborundum*"—Don't let the bastards grind you down. For example, I continue to operate on the naïve belief that there are many people who can happily appreciate (and pay for) deep, indulgent, complete, and elegant products. Apple's role is to lead, not fit in; to innovate, not follow; and do the right things, not the acceptable ones.

One might ask how an Apple employee (and Apple's chief evangelist, no less) could write the foreword for a book that reveals the inner workings of Apple—warts and all. I counter and ask, How could Apple's chief evangelist and an employee who loves Apple *not* write the foreword for this book?

The soul of evangelism is catalyzing positive change. Thus, these embarrassing, frustrating, and sometimes frightening stories must be exposed because this crap has to stop for Apple to return to a leadership position. In this sense, Carlton has done Apple and its customers a big favor.

This is not to say that only Apple and computer-industry aficionados should read this book—that would be selling the book far short. Anyone in a high-growth industry can reap vast benefits by observing what Apple did right and did wrong. You can pay $27.50 for this book now or millions later in golden parachutes.

And, while there are bad guys in this book, there are also heroes. Let us celebrate them too because no matter what anyone says, Apple did change the world. While it should be obvious to anyone who reads this book with a close eye who these heroes are, I offer my interpretation of this list:

- the rank-and-file Apple employees who created great products, programs, and services
- the third-party developers who provided the real reasons to use a personal computer at all

- the loyal Apple customers who knew that there must be a better way because they saw a better way.

These folks are the strength of Apple Computer—in the past, now, and ever more. As for the future, to quote the Army, let us "practice the task again." *

Guy Kawasaki
Former Chief Evangelist
Apple Computer, Inc.

---

* "The environment and climate surrounding an AAR must be one in which the soldiers and leaders openly and honestly discuss what actually transpired in sufficient detail and clarity that not only will everyone understand what did and did not occur and why, but most importantly will have a strong desire to seek the opportunity to practice the task again."
— "A Leader's Guide to After-Action Reviews" (TC-25-20)

ACKNOWLEDGMENTS

This is my very first book, and it proved to be a mammoth undertaking that would not have been possible without the help of many people. I wish to thank them all.

My gratitude is extended, first, to my dear wife, Adriana, to whom this book is dedicated and who deserves a perseverance medal of the highest order for having stood by through her writer husband's inevitable bouts with insecurity and paranoia. Besides acting as a sounding board for many ideas and offering her keen insight on the manuscript as it progressed, she provided me with unwavering faith and devotion through a difficult period for both of us. For this I will forever be grateful.

My parents, Bob and Joan Carlton, have also proven a source of strength and inspiration my entire life and helped encourage me to pursue a writing career that ultimately resulted in this book. I camped out at their home in Kansas City several times during this venture, hammering away at the manuscript as they offered support and helpful input, along with my brother Richard Carlton and sister, Janice Barbosa, and their families. Another brother, Robert Carlton, and his family live in Pennsylvania, and I used their home as a port in the storm during the book-reporting process. I also wish to thank my wife's family for their support.

In my professional life, it was a veteran journalist named Greg Hill who put me onto the path to this book. Greg, a longtime reporter and editor for *The Wall Street Journal*, hired me as a reporter in the *Journal*'s San Francisco bureau. Greg was one of the first business journalists who understood the severity of Apple Computer's business situation, and in 1993 he asked me to begin covering the company with a sharp eye to that. Greg, who is now the *Journal*'s senior technology editor in San Francisco, proved dead right in his early skepticism about Apple as the company hurtled toward self-destruction through the events chronicled in this book.

My other colleagues and editors at *The Wall Street Journal* have also offered me invaluable advice and support in this project. Charlie McCoy, the *Journal's* San Francisco bureau chief and my immediate boss, was gracious enough to allow me to take a one-year leave of absence to write this book, as was Paul Steiger, the *Journal's* venerable managing editor. Colleagues in the San Francisco bureau also helped out, including Don Clark, who provided some internal documents; Lee Gomes, who helped flesh out the details of an anecdote; and Sharon Massey, who helped amass a library of news clippings. To all at the *Journal*, a heartfelt thanks, as well as to friends and colleagues from other parts of the news industry who have helped over my career.

As for the actual book development process, I wish to first express my deep gratitude to the management of Times Books for entrusting the great responsibility of chronicling the decline of an American icon to a novice author. At Times, my highest appreciation goes to executive editor Tracy Smith, whose superb editing work guided this manuscript to fruition. As Apple fell into crisis in January 1996, Tracy approached my fine literary agent, Peter Ginsberg, about the possibility of someone writing a book about the tragic turn of events for this great American company. Coincidentally, I had called Peter a few days later with the same idea. Peter demonstrated patience and foresight in working with me for several years prior to this toward the possibility of my writing a business book.

At Peter's suggestion, I cranked out a book proposal that he helped edit before it was sent to Tracy and the other editors at Times. Once a contract was finalized, it was pretty much left to Tracy and me to work through the book alone. I could not have been placed in more competent hands. Every time I hit a writing obstacle, she was there to point the way out. Each time I sent in a crude draft, Tracy used her magical editing skills to make the copy sing. Through it all, she proved a pillar of support, a beacon of hope in a sometimes stormy night. Without Tracy, this book would not have been possible. Special appreciation goes also to John Mahaney, for his managerial support of the project early on; Lynn Anderson, for her long hours of painstaking copyediting work; and Mary Beth Roche, for her adroit coordination of the book's publicity. I also wish to thank all the other people at Times who assisted in other aspects, including the artwork, legal review, and marketing.

The story of what happened to Apple could not have been told without the cooperation of the people who either worked there or had a close relationship to the company. I wish to express my gratitude to the more than 160 of these people who agreed to be interviewed for this book, in many cases for two or more hours at a time as well as two, three, and even four follow-up sessions. The vast majority of my interviews were with current and former Apple employees and executives, who entrusted me with their stories in the hope that I would write as accurate and balanced an account of Apple as I could.

At the top of the list of those I wish to thank is John Sculley, Apple's most famous CEO. After his ignominious fall from power, Sculley had refused to discuss his experiences at Apple with anyone from the press. Sculley, as outlined in the book, made many mistakes as CEO. But he always chafed at the fact that no one seemed to remember the good he had done for Apple. Sculley was most wary when I first approached him to participate in the book but finally agreed to tell his story after I promised to give him a fair hearing. I hope I have accomplished that.

The others who helped include: Dennis Adler, Al Alcorn, Gil Amelio, Fred Anderson, Tim Bajarin, Phil Baker, Peter Barrett, Gaston Bastiaens, Andy Bose, Greg Branche, Jim Buckley, Dave Burnard, Gifford Calenda, Charlie Carinalli, Satjiv Chahil, Andy Chang, Robert Charlton, Cary Clark, Kirby Coryell, Bill Curley, Gary Davidian, Ian Diery, Phil Dixon, Al Eisenstat, Cheryl England, George Everhart, Elaine Fellenbaum, Jon Fitch, Fred Forsyth, Terry Fowler, Greg Galanos, Jean-Louis Gassée, Bill Gates, Aaron Goldberg, Phil Goldman, Mark Gonzales, Joe Graziano, Adam Grosser, Ellen Hancock, Jeff Harbers, Trip Hawkins, Ruth Hennigar, Marty Hess, Carl Hewitt, Pete Higgins, Peter Hirshberg, Bob Hollyer, Mike Homer, Frank Huang, Fred Huxham, Russ Irwin, Subrah Iyar, Dave Johnson, Steve Kahng, Peter Kavanaugh, Guy Kawasaki, Barbara Krause, Jack Kuehler, Mark Kvamme, Allan Loren, Lee Lorenzen, Peter Lycurgus, Mark Macgillivray, Hugh Martin, Roger McNamee, Paul Mercer, Nobuo Mii, Jeff Miller, Lonnie Millett, Mike Murray, Dave Nagel, David Neal, Konstantin Othmer, Steve Perlman, Jean Proulx, Bob Puette, Jeff Raikes, Erich Ringewald, Heidi Roizen, Tom Rolander, Steve Roskowski, Tom Ryan, Steve Sakoman, Bob Saltmarsh, George Scalise, Duane Schulz, John Scull, Neil Selvin, Richard Shaffer, Charles Simonyi, Rick Spitz, Peter Sprague, Andy Stadler, Carl Stork, Don Strickland, Kevin Sullivan, Michael Tchao, Larry Tesler, Cheryl Vedoe, John Vito, Ted Waitt, Ben Waldman, John Warnock, Camilo Wilson, Del Yocam, David Yoffie, Mansoor Zakaria, and John Ziel.

Some other people I cannot mention, because they agreed to provide information on the condition they remain anonymous. To all of these, I also offer thanks.

Finally, I offer thanks to Marianne Allison at the public relations firm of Waggener Edstrom for her diligence in coordinating my many requests for information and interviews from Microsoft, and to Kristin Brownstone and Katie Cotton, who performed the same efficient duty on my behalf while working in Apple Computer's public relations department. And Nancy Montgomery in San Francisco saved me much time by transcribing many hours of taped interviews.

APPLE

1

In the Beginning

By the afternoon of June 17, 1993, the temperature in the asphalt flat-lands that sprawl across California's Silicon Valley had climbed to a sizzling ninety-six degrees. This was nearly twenty degrees higher than normal, since the Valley, near San Francisco, lies on the ocean side of a towering mountain range that holds in moist, cool Pacific air.

Infrequently, a heat wave such as this bakes the entire San Francisco Bay area, when the high-pressure system that is usually parked over the Pacific and is responsible for generating those delicious marine breezes shifts over to nearby Nevada and funnels hot, dry air down that same mountain range in a reverse flow. The effect is known locally as a "Diablo wind," because the range those winds pour down is called the Diablo. "Diablo" is a Spanish word mean-ing "devil," so these are devil winds and appropriately named because they can spark wicked firestorms that wreak destruction and havoc across the region.

That same afternoon, a devil's wind of another sort was whipping through the air-conditioned corridors of the worldwide headquarters of Apple Com-puter Inc. in the Silicon Valley community of Cupertino. The 1980s had re-cently drawn to a close, capping a decade of dizzying growth for a company that had rocketed out of a garage to become the symbol of America's eco-nomic renaissance, a swashbuckling pioneer at the vanguard of the new Infor-mation Age. This shining star was the progeny of Steve Jobs, the long-haired whiz kid who had teamed up with fellow college dropout Steve Wozniak to create the first computer "for the rest of us," taking the power of computing out of the stuffy corporate realm and putting it into the hands of the average person for the first time.

By now, though, Jobs was long gone, having succumbed to a coup that had left his onetime friend and mentor, John Sculley, alone at the helm. And on this day, Sculley felt more alone than ever as he sat in the office of his friend and chief financial officer, Joe Graziano, atop a gleaming four-story building called De Anza 7, wondering aloud why his own board of directors was meeting in secret in a nearby conference room. The 1990s had gotten off to a rocky start. Apple's profits were falling under fierce competition. Its outlandish research projects were not panning out. And the bottom had just fallen out of the current quarter, triggering this special board meeting.

"Joe, what do you think they're doing in there?" Sculley asked Graziano in a voice that betrayed growing unease. This from the chairman and chief executive officer of Apple Computer, a man who had become a global celebrity and confidant to presidents and movie stars. As the most visible spokesman for the world's most exciting industry, his face was on the cover of business magazines and crowds wanting to hear his speeches had to be turned away. At age fifty-three, John Sculley was still a young-thinking man, but the toll of running Apple Computer during a decade of rocketing growth and change was evident. He still retained a sleek, well-proportioned physique from a regimen of jogging for miles each day before dawn, but his hair was grayer and his face was creased with lines.

Reclining in the chair in his office, which commanded a view of the coastal Santa Cruz Mountains to the west, Graziano, a tall, dark-complected man who loved to race hot rods in his spare time, looked back at his boss and replied, "There's no way they're going to get rid of you, John. That would be really stupid."[1]

The board's meeting, which had started that morning, had dragged on for excruciatingly long hours. Finally, a board member named A. C. "Mike" Markkula Jr., a chain-smoking millionaire who had cofounded Apple with Jobs and Wozniak by backing them with money, notified a Sculley assistant to send in the CEO. Sculley walked into the conference room, called "Synergy," noticing as he closed the door behind him that nary one of the four directors present would look up to make eye contact. Aides outside strained to hear but could make out only muffled voices from the room. After only a few moments, the door reopened and Sculley shuffled out, white as a sheet. Collapsing into the chair of his own office, which like all others on the executive floor was glass-walled, Sculley broke the news to his staff: after ten years on the job, he had been summarily fired as CEO.

And that was not the only indignity. The board told Sculley he could continue to serve as Apple's chairman, but in a powerless, figurehead role in which he would have to report to, of all people, his former subordinate: Michael Spindler. A German national, Spindler before that board meeting had been Sculley's trusted lieutenant overseeing the grind of Apple's daily operations. At least, Sculley had thought he could trust Spindler, a large, gruff man known for such intensity that he was nicknamed "the Diesel." The Diesel occasionally ran out of gas, folding under apparent stress attacks that left him incapacitated on a couch or under his desk. This was the man that

Apple's board named to replace Sculley as CEO, entrusting to his meaty hands the future of Apple Computer. It was a crossroads for both Apple and a computer industry that had exploded into the world's foremost catalyst for change.

The events culminating in the ouster of John Sculley involved the kind of boardroom drama and intrigue rarely displayed in a more conventional company. But Apple had never pretended to be like any other company, and in fact it went out of its way to thumb its nose at the conventional way of doing things. This was just another day at the office, another poignant moment in a tumultuous history that had unfolded like the story line of a soap opera. Apple had never been like any other company because its leaders and employees had always believed they were working for a cause, a mission to spread the wonders of computer technology to all the corners of the globe. Apple had in fact done just that, to a degree not even Steve Jobs could have envisioned when he almost single-handedly founded the personal computer industry during America's era of disco and Jimmy Carter.

Two decades later, the world is indeed filled with personal computers that look very much like the ones Jobs helped create at Apple. Someone in San Francisco can sit down at a computer in the comfort of home and trade e-mail or even play video games with, at the same time, complete strangers in, say, Brazil, Afghanistan, and China. Office workers the world over have been liberated from the tyranny of pencils and typewriters. With a keyboard and mouse, they now use their computers to write reports, prepare presentations, access library files—and even goof off now and then with a discreet game of solitaire. And learning the "three Rs" is no longer the drudgery it used to be: children are learning how to read, write, and perform mathematical calculations by playing computer games that teach while offering fun.

The world, in short, is a much smaller and more understandable place because of the computer. It is just too bad that Apple, which started it all, did not change as it was changing the world.

Almost every personal computer on earth now has the distinctive look of Apple's legendary Macintosh computer, which was the first to bring easy-to-use graphical icons and pull-down menus to the masses. When it was first introduced in 1984, following a memorable commercial televised during the Super Bowl, the Mac held a good ten-year lead in technology over all other computers. Almost all other personal computers forced the user to type in arcane commands to open a program. With the Mac, you just used a handheld "mouse" to point a little arrow at a graphical box on the screen and then double-clicked on it. It was so simple that even a child could learn how to use a Mac within minutes, without ever having to open a manual. It was, as Jobs had promised, the computer "for the rest of us."

The Mac did go on to sweep the world, but it would be under a different name. Nine out of every ten personal computers today run on software made by Microsoft Corporation, the computer giant that replicated the look of the Mac in its enormously successful Windows operating system. By the mid-1990s, the Mac was stuck with less than a 10 percent share of the world's desktop computers, and as a consequence, Apple itself was in shocking decline. Almost overnight, it seemed, the company that had done so much to give rise to a huge, new industry that had changed the lives of so many millions of people was in danger of going out of business altogether.

By this time, Spindler had assumed his place as Apple's chief executive officer. But in January 1996, he himself was on the firing line. Although the 1980s had been high flying for Apple, in the 1990s the company became the gang that couldn't shoot straight. It would have been comical, had it not been so tragic. Everything boiled over for Spindler and Apple during the Christmas season of 1995, when Mac sales suddenly dried up and the company was left with a frightful buildup of unsold computers. In January 1996, Apple was forced to post a loss of $69 million for that period, with no return to profitability in sight. The company's share of the personal computer market dipped precipitously, as did its stock. Adding to the turbulence, a feisty computer maker named Sun Microsystems moved in to try to buy Apple at a fire-sale price. The ship was sinking, and so was its captain.

There had been signs of impending trouble many months before, to the point that in 1995 the drumbeat had been begun by a growing number of people inside and outside the company for Spindler to step down. Spindler had never been one to listen, and he was not about to begin now. But when the full toll of the financial damage to Apple became known, Spindler's job was beyond salvation. And his health was in question again, too. Expected to attend the annual Macworld trade show in San Francisco, Spindler abruptly canceled any appearance there, instead huddling in his offices in Cupertino with a heart monitor strapped to his bearlike chest.

Spindler was finally forced out—from both the desk and the office—after enraged investors howled for his head during a January 23, 1996, shareholders' meeting that had all the blood lust of a lynch mob. "Mr. Spindler, it is time to go!" one investor insisted from his seat in a theater on Apple's futuristic-looking research-and-development campus. Spindler just stood forlornly up on stage, shoulders slumped as though he were a student being scolded by the principal. A dunce hat would not have looked out of place.

Spurning an insultingly low takeover offer by Sun Microsystems in January 1996, the board turned for salvation to one of its own members, Gilbert Amelio, whose ability to revive some smaller companies in trouble had earned him a reputation in Silicon Valley as a turnaround expert. Amelio was a no-nonsense type of guy whose insistence on discipline was sorely needed. At his first appearance before the press as Apple's new CEO, he confidently proclaimed that Apple's problems were "fixable." A physics Ph.D. with sixteen patents to his credit, Amelio seemed just the medicine for the ailing company. But time was not on his side. Indeed, seventeen months into Amelio's reign, after Apple had hemorrhaged more than another $1.6 billion in cash and more share of the computer market, he was unceremoniously ousted by the board. This happened after the intrigue had built for another takeover attempt involving a cast of characters that included a flamboyant Silicon Valley billionaire and a Saudi Arabian prince.

The technology industry moves so rapidly that competitors that stumble often can never get back up. Apple, for example, embraced the explosively growing Internet only after Amelio took charge. Nearly all others in the industry had done so a good year before. And Apple's vaunted leadership in technology innovation was badly eroded. Microsoft not only had all but caught up but had jumped out in front with its Internet strategy. That would be a potentially lethal blow to Apple, since it would mean one less reason for people to buy the Mac. Apple's global share of the personal computer market had dwindled to 3.1 percent by early 1997.[2] The game was almost over.

Since Apple had epitomized the glamour and excitement of the computer revolution, its struggle for life was a painful thing to watch, almost akin to seeing one's sports hero hobbled by a life-threatening disease. *Business Week* sadly proclaimed "The Fall of an American Icon" on its front cover. In *Fortune*, a lengthy opus on Apple's decline opened with the words "It's enough to break your heart." And throughout Silicon Valley, even Apple's competitors joined with their Cupertino brethren in an emotional outpouring over what appeared to be the end of an era. Trip Hawkins, a former Apple executive who had gone on to run his own Silicon Valley companies, summed up the sentiment in this way: "It's a shame that a company that did so much for the industry may not continue to go on."

Apple's fall was so dramatic because it had come from such a great height. Through much of the 1980s, Apple had been the apple of everyone's eye, the unparalleled star of Silicon Valley. And everybody had wanted a piece of the action. Investors had lined up in droves to snap up Apple's stock. Engineers fresh out of college had spent their meager savings to make the pilgrimage to Cupertino, joining hundreds of others for a shot at working at Apple, sometimes camping out in the reception lobby in hopes of finagling an interview. The rest of the world had looked on in awe at the magic of what Apple's computers could do.

"It was the promised land," says Peter Barrett, a software entrepreneur who journeyed all the way to Cupertino from his homeland of Australia to view the Apple revolution up close. "There was this idea of a brash technology company building a business with all these opportunities. You had to make the pilgrimage to come see it."

It all went back to Steve Jobs, a dashingly handsome megalomaniac who connived and coerced to market a computer that was finally ready for the masses. Jobs was not really much of a technologist. What he did possess was charisma with a capital "C." With his shoulder-length dark hair and rock star good looks, Jobs had as smooth a stage presence as they come. Computer audiences would erupt into bedlam when Steve Jobs appeared. He would stand there onstage—sometimes in just jeans and a shirt with the sleeves rolled up, other times in a suit with the same striped bow tie—and just take it all in with a thin smile, like a potentate surveying his subjects, until he lifted his arms to quiet them down.

The mesmerizing effect Steve Jobs held over people, in small gatherings as well, was demonstrated one afternoon in the spring of 1980 at a career-day presentation by Apple Computer on the campus of nearby Stanford University. "We were sitting in a room and a guy comes in with a vest and blue jeans, looking like one of us students," recalls Mike Murray, now vice president for human resources and administration for Microsoft. "He ignores three other Apple guys doing presentations, sits on a table, and says, 'Hi, I'm Steve Jobs. What do you want to talk about?' I got so excited by this that I actually cut classes. I went back to my apartment and looked up Apple in the phone book and called the company. I said, 'There is this guy named Steve, and I want to be hired as a summer intern.' " Murray would go on to become the Macintosh division's director of marketing.

It was Steve Jobs, therefore, who popularized the personal computer and came to personify it. He did not invent it, though. The first widely used PC was the Altair, introduced as a mail-order kit in 1975 by now-defunct Micro-instrumentation and Telemetry Systems (MITS) in Albuquerque, New Mexico. It was a primitive device, unable to really do anything until a teenage hacker named Bill Gates and his pal Paul Allen came up with a programming language that enabled it to perform rudimentary tasks. They would go on to form Microsoft.

In 1975, Jobs was immersed in soul-searching, trying to figure out what to do with his life after graduating from high school in Cupertino, a bucolic suburb basking in the bright Silicon Valley sun about forty miles south of the fog banks of San Francisco. After wanderings in India and a stay on a communal farm in Oregon, Jobs had returned to the Valley to nurture his passion for electronics. Between shifts as a video-game programmer at Atari, he attended night sessions in Menlo Park, California, of a computer hobbyists' group called the Homebrew Computer Club and was there when an attendee toted in a real-life Altair. The other hobbyists looked at the crude machine as a new toy. Jobs saw dollar signs.

Lacking the skill to make a computer himself, he enlisted the help of a Homebrew buddy named Steve Wozniak, a prankster known as "Woz," who had just written a programming language for a new microprocessor called the MOS Technology 6502 and designed a computer circuit board to run it. At Homebrew, hobbyists like Woz were always bringing in parts and computer kits. Woz was a long-haired college dropout, too, but that was about the extent of the similarity between himself and Jobs. Woz was plainer in appearance, with thick eyebrows and a shaggy beard, and vastly preferred the solitude of a computer keyboard to the limelight.

Woz had taught himself enough about engineering to land a job at Hewlett-Packard, the venerable grandfather of Silicon Valley. Jobs sold his Volkswagen van and Woz his programmable calculator to raise money to get started, and the pair set up shop in the garage of Jobs's parents' home in Los Altos, California. They made fifty of the circuit boards that Woz designed, selling them to other hobbyists through a local dealer for $500 apiece. Influenced in part because he was a Beatles fan who admired that group's Apple Records label, Jobs decided to call their new venture Apple Computer. Thus was Apple Computer born, on April Fool's Day 1976.

Jobs, then twenty-one, knew that he and Woz, then twenty-six, needed a third partner with enough business experience to get the fledgling enterprise off the ground. Through contacts in Silicon Valley, Jobs was introduced to the easygoing Mike Markkula, who had retired the year before at age thirty-three. Even at that young age, Markkula looked like a middle-aged man with his receding hairline and thinning hair tucked over his ears. And even at that age, he could afford to just sit and do nothing because he had made a killing off the initial public offering in 1971 of his former employer Intel Corporation. An electrical engineer with considerable marketing savvy, Markkula had started out at Fairchild Semiconductor, the legendary maker of computer chips whose greatest claim to fame was having spawned the creation of some of Silicon Valley's hottest start-up companies, including Intel and its main competitor, Advanced Micro Devices.

The start-ups were launched by some of Fairchild's best and brightest, including Intel cofounders Robert Noyce and Gordon Moore. After those two left Fairchild to start a little company they called Intel, Markkula followed. At age twenty-six, while he was directing Intel's marketing strategy, the company went public and young Markkula was holding enough shares to make him a multimillionaire. He did not have to work another day in his life, and for a time that was his plan.

At least until he met Jobs. In manner and habit, the two men could hardly have been farther apart. Markkula was the quintessential laid-back Californian, a disarmingly courteous counterpart to the frenetic Jobs. They were opposites in other ways, too. Jobs was a health fanatic who eschewed meat and fats. Markkula, on the other hand, was a guy at home with a backyard barbecue who chain-smoked and drank whiskey with little regard for the consequences.

But Markkula knew a market opportunity when he saw one, and the crudely assembled computers he saw lined up in the Jobs family garage convinced him that these precocious youngsters were really onto something. Markkula's role would be vital to the creation of a real Apple Computer. He could infuse the fledgling venture with the business maturity that the two Steves sorely lacked. Jobs at least wanted to learn. Woz could hardly have cared less; he made computers mainly for the fun of it. Markkula helped them prepare a business plan and arrange financing through Bank of America and two venture capital firms, kicking in $91,000 of his own money. With Markkula now at the helm as third cofounder, Apple formally incorporated on January 3, 1977, with a bankroll of up to $250,000 in cash and loan commitments. The tiny company moved into new corporate headquarters, a leased building in Cupertino near which a vast Apple campus would arise.

Soon thereafter, Jobs and Woz replaced their tiny company's bare-bones Apple I circuit board with a full-fledged computer called the Apple II that for the first time encased a PC in an attractive box and included a keyboard, a power supply, and the ability to generate color graphics. Actually, almost all the technical credit for the Apple II went to Woz. Through sheer engineering genius, Woz had built the thing almost single-handedly, using tricks and shortcuts to overcome the Apple I's problems with performance and memory.

This was a truly usable computer, the first for the masses. After it was unveiled at the first West Coast Computer Faire in April 1978, the machine's popularity propelled Apple's annual sales to more than $300 million in just the company's first five years of existence. "It was almost like a World War I plane going at Mach 2," recalls Trip Hawkins, a fast-talking man with an Ivy League look who started in 1978 as Apple's employee number 68. The company raced into the *Fortune* 500 faster than any other in history, and its 1980 initial public stock offering was among the most anticipated ever on Wall Street. Jobs and Woz were instant multimillionaires. Markkula added more millions to his wealth.

Apple's success spawned a legion of competitors. There were names like Atari, Zenith, Commodore, and Tandy, most of them now gone from the PC industry. (Atari was also the inventor of Pong, the world's first video game.) Primitive by today's standards, these limited machines enabled people to perform rudimentary word processing and spreadsheet tasks, among other basic functions. By 1980, the industry had grown to more than $1 billion in annual sales, a feat that caught the attention of the men in blue suits at a corporate behemoth known as Big Blue. IBM had long been the bastion of the computer establishment, a fearsome colossus of $26 billion in annual revenues whose very name then symbolized power and domination. IBM had controlled the growing corporate market through its gigantic mainframe computers, which cost corporate customers a cool $1 million or more each. A PC for less than $5,000 was comparatively small potatoes, but IBM decided this was a growing market in which it wanted a piece of the action.

It was another watershed moment for the fledgling industry, almost as significant as Woz's invention of the Apple II, when the IBM PC made its debut in 1981, taking the personal computer revolution to a new phase. Big Blue was in the game. The desktop computer would soon move beyond the world of hobbyists, homes, schools, and small businesses into the center stage of big business and, eventually, the mass consumer market. Actually, about the only thing proprietary to the machine was the IBM name on the side of the box. This was a machine that anybody could copy shamelessly, and copy they did. What made things even easier for these copiers, or "clone" manufacturers, was that IBM had ceded control over the PC's operating system and its microprocessor to Microsoft and Intel, respectively. These were the two most critical parts of any PC, since the microprocessor acted as the "brain" of a computer and the operating system was like a central nervous system that coordinates tasks.

Since neither Microsoft nor Intel had an exclusive deal to furnish its components to IBM alone, two guys with a screwdriver in a garage could get everything they needed to assemble their very own "IBM-compatible" personal computer. This is what a company called Compaq Computer did. It started with three men sitting around a table at a House of Pies restaurant in Houston, sketching out on a place mat the concept for a company that, by the mid-1990s, would mushroom to become the biggest manufacturer of PCs in the world. In just its first year of operation, Compaq's IBM-compatibles, also sporting Microsoft's MS-DOS and the Intel chip, soared to $300 million in sales.

It had been 132 years since the California gold rush. Now a new gold rush was on, and those wacky Californians at Apple had started it all. As of 1980, when IBM was planning its entry into the PC market, Apple controlled 16 percent of all PC sales—the highest level it would ever attain—to an audience that then consisted heavily of hobbyists, schools, and small businesses. After Big Blue jumped in, with its following of clones, Apple's share began dipping precipitously, to 6.2 percent by 1982.[3] If Jobs himself was worried about all this new competition, he did not show it publicly. Jobs was all of twenty-six years old by then, a multimillionaire whose ego had swollen in tandem with Apple's growth.

Jobs's arrogance, his unwavering conviction that he knew more than almost anyone else, influenced the birth of a culture that saw fit to demean worthy competitors instead of respecting and learning from them. The insolence he imbued into Apple was manifested in an ad the company placed in major newspapers when IBM announced its first PC: "Welcome, IBM. Seriously."

Jobs demonstrated even less respect for his own workers, many of whom toiled nights and weekends for a job that had become a burning cause, only to endure insults and public ridicule. Bill Curley, a middle-aged Apple marketing manager then, remembers this incident from his very first week on the job at Apple: "I was at a meeting with Jobs and several other managers, and he is in shorts, running shoes, and no socks. He's disagreeing with a guy, so he kicks off his shoes and puts his bare feet on the table. He framed the guy's face with his feet."

Another time, Jobs was called in to address a group of about a hundred employees responsible for overseeing Apple's in-house computer system. Standing before the throng assembled at dining tables in the company cafeteria, Jobs shook his long brown hair back from his face and snapped, "You're all a bunch of bozos. If you had any guts, you'd be out there developing computers." With this kind of treatment, most people at Apple tried to avoid Jobs. "A contact with Jobs was an ass kicking," recalls Peter Kavanaugh, a former manager who was one of the bozos in the cafeteria. "You were going to come out belittled. Steve had to be right, even if he was wrong."

Though he was lacking in people skills, Jobs was the consummate visionary, a perfectionist whose insistence on quality resulted in Apple's greatest achievement of all: the Macintosh. The name of the machine came from another Apple engineer named Jef Raskin, who was inspired by the richness of the apples in New York State. But the Mac became Jobs's baby as soon as he laid eyes on it.

Man and machine. It would be the most important love affair in the history of computerdom.

The Mac was a computer, but it really had a personality all its own. In those days, the name "personal computer" was an oxymoron because a computer really was not personal at all. It came in a big box with sharp, menacing corners and looked about as appealing as the office copier. When you logged on to the thing, it was even more impersonal. Type in one wrong letter out of an arcane code to open up a file, and a stern warning such as "Invalid Command" would pop up on the monitor screen. A neophyte user who happened to be disabled saw that warning and called his computer maker's technical support line to complain that his PC had called him an "invalid." Seriously.

The Mac, on the other hand, was like a long-lost friend. For one thing, it came in a sleek little box with rounded corners that looked as good in the living room as at the office. When you fired it up, the first thing you saw on the screen was a tiny Mac with a happy face. And if you made a mistake, such as clicking the mouse button on the wrong thing, it would let you know gently, making cute sounds such as a duck's quack. "It looks cute. It's my Mac," says Cheryl England, editor of a magazine called *MacAddict* for Mac addicts like herself. "It makes me feel warm and fuzzy." You didn't hear too many people saying *that* about their IBM-compatibles.

What made the Mac so easy to use was a feature known in nerd lingo as a graphical user interface, or GUI (pronounced "gooey"). Now, as great as Jobs was at promoting Apple's technology, he never actually came up with any breakthrough inventions himself. Woz ran circles around him in actually engineering things. But Jobs was brilliant at recognizing the commercial potential of the technological advances bubbling down in the lab. The GUI, in fact, had begun bubbling in the 1970s at Xerox Corporation's Palo Alto Research Center, or PARC, as it was known. Xerox had amassed a collection of the world's finest engineers to engage in futuristic computer research aimed at protecting its hold on the copier market. Xerox could see that the world was relying more on paperless computers and wanted to maintain its leadership as an innovator in the copier market. Xerox's GUI technology was like a weapon, except that Xerox never used it.

But it was Jobs, on a tour of the facility one day in December 1979, who had instantly recognized the greatness of the technology—and its potential to make him even richer and more famous. Inspired by what he had seen, he prodded Apple's engineers to incorporate the graphical look into a new computer he dubbed the Lisa, after his toddler daughter. The Lisa was an elegant machine and truly a breakthrough, but, priced at $10,000, it was way too expensive to garner many sales. Jobs, known for his brash and unorthodox management practices, then seized Raskin's Macintosh project, which had the power and easy-to-use features of the Lisa machine at a low price of $1,000, and made it his own. He assembled a group of programmers, sequestering them in a building off Apple's main campus. A pirate flag was hoisted in tribute to Jobs's renegade spirit.

The flag was also a symbol of a growing divisiveness within Apple that would play a key role in the company's turmoil ahead. Engineers from the Apple II division, which was the bread and butter of Apple's sales, were particularly incensed at the favored treatment their colleagues were getting. Jobs pampered them with at-the-desk massages, coolers stocked with freshly squeezed orange juice, and first-class plane seats on flights of more than two hours. No other employees at Apple got to travel first class. Topping it all off was the Bösendorfer piano in the lobby of the Macintosh development building and its $10,000 speakers, put on grand display in the atrium of the building, near where Jobs would park a BMW motorcycle that he rarely had time to ride. These were the elite, the chosen few. Everyone else, in Jobs's officious vernacular, was a "bozo" who "didn't get it."

One evening at Ely McFly's, a local watering hole popular back then, tensions between Apple II engineers seated at one table and those of a Mac team at another boiled over. Aaron Goldberg, a longtime industry consultant who has tracked Apple since its infancy, watched from his bar stool nearby as the squabbling escalated. "The Mac guys were screaming, 'We're the future!' The

Apple II guys were screaming, 'We're the money!' Then there was a geek brawl. Pocket protectors and pens were flying. I was waiting for a notebook to drop, so they would stop to pick up the papers."

The discord, in fact, filtered down from the top ranks. A year before the Mac would debut in 1984, Markkula and Jobs agreed they needed to bring in a professional manager as president and CEO. The first president, Mike Scott, had been hired from National Semiconductor Corporation by Markkula and then fired by him after a scant two years on the job. A gruff man of thirty-two who would repeatedly tell Jobs, "Shut up," Scott was removed after terrorizing employees through such actions as humiliating people in meetings. (Former executives say Scott, or "Scotty," as he was known, was simply buckling under the pressure of running a company growing as fast as Apple.) Woz was off finishing an engineering degree. Markkula agreed to run the company until he and Jobs could find a replacement, preferably someone of stature on Wall Street who could convince skeptical corporate customers that Apple was not just a bunch of long-haired California hippies.

Someone like John Sculley, a middle-aged whiz at Pepsi.

It took much wooing to convince Sculley. After all, Sculley, at age forty-four, had emerged from the ranks as president of PepsiCo's giant Pepsi-Cola division and was on track to one day succeed his former father-in-law, Don Kendall, as chief executive of the whole company. A genteel easterner with a taste for eighteenth-century English landscapes and portraits, Sculley was a relentless workaholic who arose at 4:30 A.M. every day to pore over his eight morning papers and then jog several miles to maintain his sinewy build.

It was a wonder Sculley had gotten as far as he had in the business world. His biggest handicap was a stutter that had taken him many years to overcome. He was also painfully shy, even at the pinnacle of his career at Apple, when he gained renown for his ability to deliver rousing speeches in front of thousands, sometimes without notes. Sculley had become so practiced at the art of public speaking that, to him, it was a tool he could use at will. "I was determined to build a strength out of what was originally a weakness," Sculley wrote in his 1987 autobiography, Odyssey. "I went to the theater to watch how performers positioned themselves on stage. I'd practice for hours. I became obsessed with the idea that I was going to become better than anyone else as a business communicator."[4]

But deep down, Sculley had long fancied himself a technologist, though he had had no formal training. In Odyssey, he recounted how that fascination went back to his adolescence, when he had come up with an idea for a color television cathode-ray tube. He had been beaten to the punch, though, by another inventor, whose patent was used in Sony Corporation's Trinitron color TV tube. Sculley said in his book that he finally knew he could not say no to

Apple when, standing high on a Manhattan rooftop overlooking the Hudson River one afternoon, Jobs turned to him and asked, "Do you want to spend the rest of your life selling sugared water or do you want a chance to change the world?"

Sculley was one of the few people Jobs actually thought he could learn from, though they were polar opposites in personality. Jobs was especially interested in Sculley's forte of consumer marketing, since he rightly believed marketing would be a powerful tool in selling computers to the masses. Through shrewd tactics such as starring singer Michael Jackson in a Pepsi commercial and instituting the "Pepsi Challenge" taste test, Sculley had engineered such an amazing resurgence for the bottling giant that it had finally overtaken Coca-Cola as the U.S. soda industry's market share leader.

Jobs wanted Sculley to train him to be a CEO. As for Sculley, he was convinced his wide-eyed, younger partner could teach him a lot about this revolution going on out in California. And actually, yes, he did want to change the world. "The Apple job would put me on the cutting edge of technology, almost completing the loop of my childhood fascination with electronics," Sculley explained in *Odyssey*. By this time, Sculley had become completely enamored of Jobs. "There aren't many people during your lifetime that you feel you can really learn from," Sculley wrote. "I thought Steve could be one of them. I was fascinated by his mind and his vision and my place in it. I could help Steve become the Henry Ford of the computer age."

Sculley took the plunge in 1983, fully planning to return back east within five years. By then, he believed, Apple would be in the hands of an older and wiser Jobs. Since he was no longer needed in a day-to-day role, Markkula eased back into retirement and let the new team of Jobs and Sculley take over. In the beginning, the two got along famously, thinking so much alike that at public appearances they would literally finish each other's sentences. "Apple has one leader, Steve and me," Sculley said at a private dinner with fellow Apple executives celebrating his first anniversary at Apple.[5] Sculley, with his gentlemanly charm, provided the perfect counterpoint to the abrasive Jobs. Together, they seemed unstoppable.

"The combination of Steve and John was really magical," recalls Barbara Krause, who joined Apple to run public relations in almost the same month as Sculley. A veteran of political campaigns, she, too, was drawn to the cause. "It was such a wonderful philosophy they shared: giving computers to empower the people. I really felt like I was living a dream." So did a young engineer named Adam Grosser, who vividly remembers his first day on the job at Apple: "I remember seeing a bunch of scruffy-looking guys wearing T-shirts that said, 'Working 90 Hours a Week and Loving It.' It was a very emotional company, and people would arrive in the lobby and wait two days for an interview."

Snapshots from the era capture some of the magic. There is Sculley, an arm draped over Jobs's shoulder, as they stand smiling on a sandy beach. There they are again, speaking seriously to each other while clad in jogging shorts without shirts on. And in another, there are Jobs, Sculley, and members of the Macintosh team, gathered in conversation around the Bösendorfer piano. They appeared almost everywhere together, drawing cheers from thousands of employees as they spoke before sales meetings and product rollouts, accompanied by the inevitable blare of pulsating rock music. They were the Dynamic Duo, the Steve and John Show.

The pinnacle of the relationship between Jobs and Sculley came in January 1984. On Super Bowl Sunday, as the Los Angeles Raiders romped to a 38–9 victory over the Washington Redskins, Jobs and Sculley sat together in the New Orleans Superdome, watching anxiously as a sixty-second Apple TV spot broadcast over the stands and to 43 million TV viewers beyond. The ad, a teaser for the Mac's introduction the following week, showed a dingy room full of shaved-headed workers listening impassively as a menacing Big Brother lectures from a video screen. Then an athletic woman in colorful running attire dashed in and hurled a sledgehammer into the image. The screen exploded, smoke appeared, and, in an Orwellian reference to an IBM-dominated world, a male voice intoned, "On January twenty-fourth, Apple Computer will introduce Macintosh. And you'll see why 1984 won't be like 1984."

The ad marked the climax of a carefully orchestrated marketing campaign, one of the slickest in business history. In the months preceding, Mike Murray, the Macintosh division's diminutive and energetic marketing manager, had worked with Jobs to muster support for the Mac by undertaking such schemes as secretly funding a new trade magazine called Macworld to tout the new machine. Macworld lives on to this day, although its funding from Apple lasted only the first year. Another tack was to start a group called the Apple University Consortium, composed of universities entitled to volume discounts on Macintosh purchases and private audiences with Jobs. This move got Apple's foot into the door of the big higher education market, adding to the company's earlier strategic advances into the primary school market with the Apple II. The overall education market would grow to become one of Apple's greatest strongholds.

As for the Super Bowl ad itself, Murray had been working with the advertising agency of Chiat /Day Inc. for many months in 1983 to come up with a theme for the Macintosh launch. "One day, a guy at Chiat said, 'Hey, next year is 1984 and the year of Big Brother,'" Murray recalls. "They pitched that idea, which really appealed to us. After all, who was IBM? Big Brother. We needed a movement. The movement was Macintosh, the democratization of technology."

The message was so stunning and controversial that the "1984" ad became big news when it appeared at that Super Bowl. Jobs and Sculley were jubilant. The world's first commercial for a personal computer had just been aired, and in a flash Apple's message of change and nonconformity had been conveyed to the world. At the annual shareholders' meeting the following week, Jobs stood at a podium in a darkened auditorium in Cupertino, looking radiant in his dark suit and bow tie as he pulled the wraps off his Macintosh for all to see. With its screen glowing cheerily onstage, the machine for the first time spoke for itself: "Hello, I am Macintosh. It sure is great to get out of that bag . . ." The audience of more than 2,500 people roared with delight. A cult had been born.

"This place was literally shaking, and people were screaming out of their minds," recalls Mike Murray, who left Apple in 1985 to join Microsoft. "I was in the front row giving a thumbs-up to Steve." Adds another former Apple manager, "You'd look around, and it was almost a religion."

It was Jobs's finest hour, and Sculley watched proudly from the wings. At that moment, Jobs was master of the universe.

But Jobs's day in the sun was about to fade. The Mac was impressive enough, but it was hard for people to use. In his quest to make the Mac an aesthetic masterpiece, Jobs had sacrificed functional essentials such as enough memory to run big programs and a hard disk drive to store things. In fact, there were almost no programs for the Mac when it first came out. Sales were terrible. The company's mainstay line of Apple IIs, meanwhile, was beginning to wither under the onslaught of competition and an industry slump. By 1985, Apple's sales peaked at $2 billion and began a year-long ebb, the first in the company's brief history, while the IBM PC and PC-compatibles grew in market share. Apple was in trouble, and it was time for an adult to take charge.

Sculley was adult enough, but Jobs had him under his seductive spell. Apple had to get its new products out faster than the two-year intervals it maintained as a result of delays caused in large part by Jobs's insistence on perfection. Jobs was also interfering more and more with other parts of the company outside the Macintosh division. Managers from all over Apple deluged Sculley with complaints. Contain Jobs fast, they said, or the ship might sink.

Contain Steve Jobs? This was the cofounder of Apple Computer, the young man who had started a revolution, the techno guru who had led Sculley to the promised land out west. Yet Sculley knew they were right. Apple had to start moving ahead again, he realized, and that was not likely to happen with Jobs remaining in a position to disrupt things. Sculley swallowed hard and decided to relegate his friend and teacher to the symbolic post of chairman, stripping him of any operating power. It would be a corporate emasculation and one requiring the endorsement of Markkula and the board. Sculley called Jobs aside before the board meeting on April 10, 1985, and told him what he planned to do. The look on Jobs's face was like that of a child being put out to a foster home against his will.

"If you do that, you're going to destroy this company!" Jobs spat at Sculley, according to Sculley's account of the episode in *Odyssey*. "I'm the only one who understands enough around here about manufacturing and operations, and I don't think you understand these things yet." Sculley refused to budge. Before the meeting, Jobs began lobbying the board members to side with him against Sculley. He was trying to launch a coup of his own. Finally, after marathon discussions that began in the late afternoon and concluded nearly twenty-four hours later, the board unanimously decided to boot Jobs upstairs and authorized Sculley to take the action.

Afterward, Jobs pleaded with Sculley to change his mind. He would be a good boy. He could change. He sounded almost like a teenager begging his father to give him back the keys to the family car he had already wrecked. Behind Sculley's back, at the same time, Jobs was working the other side of the fence. He tried to enlist support from members of Apple's managing executive staff to back him in a move to throw Sculley out of the company altogether. Warned of the plot by others, Sculley canceled a business trip to China and confronted Jobs in front of the executive staff at a meeting on May 24, 1985.

"It's come to my attention that you'd like to throw me out of the company, and I'd like to ask you if that's true," Sculley asked the sullen-faced Jobs in a boardroom as the other executives looked on nervously. Sculley sat at one end of a conference table, Jobs at the other. Glaring back at Sculley, Jobs fired back, "I think you're bad for Apple and I think you're the wrong person to run the company." Jobs continued his verbal attack as the other senior executives looked on in discomfort. Sculley became so angry that he lapsed back into his childhood stutter, retorting, "I made a mistake treating you with high esteem. I don't trust you, and I won't tolerate a lack of trust."[6]

It had come down to this: either Sculley goes or Jobs goes. Sculley looked around the room at his senior executives and, like Colonel William Travis at the Battle of the Alamo, drew a line in the sand and asked for volunteers to join him. "Do you support me or do you support Steve?" Sculley asked each person seated around the conference table. If they had supported Jobs, Sculley was quite prepared to resign. But he would not have to. One by one, they verbally stood up to cross over onto Sculley's side of the imaginary line. "I remember swinging my chair to Steve and telling him how much I loved him," recalls Del Yocam, a respected executive who had joined Apple in 1979. "But then I swung my chair the other way to Sculley and I said, 'John, I respect your experience and what you've brought to Apple.' I was swinging my vote with Sculley—literally."

That act of loyalty of Yocam's was touching—and would one day be forgotten by Sculley, to the regret of both men.

With the board and executive staff now behind him, Sculley made the demotion official the following week. Jobs stormed out of Apple a few months later, taking with him a band of engineers to help him start a new computer company, appropriately called NeXT. He remained so embittered that he and Sculley, the onetime Dynamic Duo, never made up. When interviewed a decade later for a television documentary called "Triumph of the Nerds," Jobs said of Sculley, "I hired the wrong guy." Jobs had been wrong about a lot of things, but he was ultimately proven right about that.

One day, many years down the line, Jobs would have much more to say about Apple Computer and its future.

2

The Glory Years

Steve Jobs may have been a royal pain in the neck, but he had been the heart and soul of Apple, the whiz kid pictured on the cover of *Time* magazine, the one who constantly exhorted his engineers to build something "insanely great." Many people were indeed relieved when Jobs finally quit Apple in September 1985. But there were also a good number, especially on the Macintosh team, who felt a profound loss. Indeed, some of them actually broke into tears when John Sculley broke the news during a meeting with nearly three thousand employees at the Flint Center auditorium of nearby De Anza College.

Sculley felt an acute loss, as well. Here he was, a continent away from home, in an industry that he still knew very little about, and alone at the helm of a company whose freewheeling culture was totally alien to the rigid East Coast style he had known at Pepsi. On top of all that, Sculley was left with a business that had taken on serious water almost overnight. Just the year before, amid all the hoopla of the Macintosh launch, he and Jobs had confidently predicted that Apple would sell 2 million of the machines by the end of 1985. But it was almost that date now, and so far Apple had sold less than one fourth that number. The company's eight-year-old Apple II, meanwhile, was growing mighty long in the tooth. It had fallen under vicious assault from IBM and its battalions of clones, all of which fought for a bigger slice of a market that was starting to swoon. As a result, Apple's share of the worldwide PC market had plunged, in just two years, to 11 percent from almost 20 percent. The stock price was in critical shape, too: by mid-1985, it had fallen to $14 from a 1983 peak of $63.

Sculley was shaken to his core. "I was failing, and the evidence of it surrounded me," Sculley recounted in his book *Odyssey*. "The company was in real trouble. For the first time in my life, my power, prestige, and self-assurance were in jeopardy. I had never lost my self-confidence. I had never known failure before. But now I wondered whether I was capable of leading the company through its crisis, or if Steve was right. Maybe I wasn't the best person to run Apple."[1]

The core problem at Apple was that Jobs and Sculley had bet almost everything on the success of a single product, with almost nothing in the wings to fall back on in case it failed. While it had been Jobs's brilliance that had fostered the creation of the Mac, he had considered it such a work of art that he had forbidden anyone to make the changes needed to attract more customers. The Mac, therefore, was gathering dust on store shelves. And Sculley, brought into Apple to build a major brand image, had admittedly erred by robbing money from research and development to pay for a Pepsi-like advertising campaign. As a result, only one slightly improved version had been shipped since the big launch, and development of successors had virtually ground to a halt. In other words, the cupboard was bare, and it was highly conceivable the whole company could go down the tubes if something drastic did not happen soon.

Between May of that year, when he was stripped of power, and September, when he quit altogether, Jobs was really a lame duck. That's when Sculley rolled up his sleeves and put a turnaround plan into motion. He started off by chopping out some of the fat, shutting down three plants, and laying off a fifth of the workers. Then he reorganized Apple around areas of function, such as marketing, product research, and manufacturing, as opposed to Jobs's inefficient and disruptive system of having one division in charge of Apple IIs and another in charge of Macs. In other words, the company was now centralized. "When I joined Apple, it was a feudal society," Sculley recalls. "It was the Macintosh Division versus the Apple II Division. The Apple II versus the Apple III [a failed project to create a successor to the Apple II]. They were literally at war with each other. It was like Bosnia."

Sculley's theme of unification quickly caught on with the employees, who began wearing T-shirts that proclaimed: ONE APPLE. At a company sales meeting that year, Michael Spindler, who was heading Apple's business in Europe, delivered an impassioned speech called "The Two Hearts" that reinforced the unity idea. "Apple," he said in a voice rising in the cadence of a revivalist preacher, "beats with two hearts—our California heart and the heart of the local company." It didn't matter where in the world you happened to call home. You were still all a part of a unique family called Apple.

The other important step for Sculley was to surround himself with a strong management team. He was lucky, for now at least, to have competent and loyal executives from which to choose. Del Yocam, for instance, was an extraordinary numbers guy, a man as fastidious about making sure supplies jibed with orders as he was in his neatly groomed personal appearance. A short man with a well-trimmed beard and wire-rimmed glasses, Yocam was careful to wear freshly ironed designer shirts and slacks. Yocam had organized Apple's manufacturing operation from a chaotic mess, with piles of materials strewn all over the floor, into a well-oiled machine. He had also overseen the operational aspects of the Apple II business when Jobs had gone off to do the Macintosh project. Within that first year, he would be named chief operating officer, Sculley's right-hand man.

There were four other key people in Sculley's executive suite. Debi Coleman, whom Jobs had recruited from Hewlett-Packard to oversee manufacturing for the Macintosh, had demonstrated such an acumen for overseeing operations that she was placed in charge of all production. A jovial workaholic who put in as many as sixteen hours a day at Apple, she was more up to this challenge than to her constant battle with weight. Coleman wore her dark hair in bangs and was always quick to smile and laugh. Bill Campbell had joined Apple not because of any computer expertise but because his wife had roomed with Sculley's third wife, Leezy, in college. Still, the "Coach," as he was called from having been Columbia University's football coach, was a tall, rugged, and gregarious backslapper who lifted the morale of a dispirited U.S. sales corps when Sculley put him in charge.

Then there was Spindler, selected to spearhead Apple's advances overseas. He was ideally suited for this role, unlike the larger ones he would take later. Spindler was busy transforming Apple's European market from an insignificant afterthought into what would become a thriving business. Spindler held cogent views on global strategy and how Apple fit into the overall world economy. He was a Big Picture guy who cut a truly impressive figure when onstage. The job seemed to agree with Spindler in another way, too. In a 1986 profile on Apple's international operations in *Business Week*, a photo portrayed an impressively svelte Spindler, looking healthy and dashing in his blue suit and red power tie. His ruddy complexion, thick, bushy hair, and intense eyes portrayed the image of a successful businessman working for a successful and thriving enterprise.

Finally, there was the inimitable Jean-Louis Gassée (pronounced "Gahs-*say*"). Apple's history is filled with colorful characters, but none more so than Jean-Louis, the debonair Frenchman with the diamond earring and a sexual analogy to fit almost any situation. Gassée had already enjoyed a fanciful past, having once worked as maître d' at a strip joint in Paris. A dropout from graduate school, he had also peddled a hormone-rich compound door to door in Paris to wives seeking to "reinvigorate" their husbands, as he once explained to an interviewer.[2] By age twenty-four, he had entered the computer industry, hawking products for Hewlett-Packard's business in France. An opening had come up to do the same work for an upstart company called Apple, and he had jumped at the chance to join a culture of kindred free spirits.

After having boosted Apple's business in France tremendously, Gassée had been summoned by Jobs and Sculley to Cupertino earlier that year to help out with the Mac marketing effort. Gassée comported himself with much of the same arrogance as Jobs and even walked with the same swagger. More important, he possessed the same keen eye for detail and quality in a product that had made Jobs so great. Unlike Jobs, though, Gassée lavished so much praise on all the engineers, not just a select few, that they naturally reciprocated with their affection. To him, they were *artistes*, sculpting things of beauty. And they practically worshiped him for appreciating their genius.

With Jobs out of the picture, Sculley knew that Apple needed a new charismatic leader. He also knew that it certainly could not be him. In contrast to Jean-Louis's savoir faire, Sculley had all the charisma of a grapefruit and was shy to the point of awkwardness in social settings. Hence, Sculley anointed Gassée as the leader of Apple's elite engineering corps, Jobs's de facto replacement. "I put Gassée in the job because I thought he was the closest thing to a Jobs," Sculley says. "Gassée used to say, 'You have to bleed in six colors' [in reference to Apple's multihued logo]. So Gassée became the cult leader. I was the outside spokesperson." The appointment would prove fateful to Apple's future, as well as Sculley's own.

By 1986, Sculley's new team had gotten Apple humming on all cylinders again. Their first coup was launching Apple's first truly usable Macintosh. The original Mac had contained only 128,000 bytes of memory. Although this was a lot compared to the Apple II, which then contained 48,000 bytes, it was not enough to run power-intensive graphics programs for which the Mac was designed. (A 1997 personal computer, by contrast, would contain 32 million bytes, each one of which can hold one character of text.) Under Gassée's fatherly guidance, Apple's product engineers designed a sort of Mac on steroids. When it first shipped in January 1986, this Macintosh Plus would contain 1 megabyte of memory—nearly ten times that of the original. A year later, the Macintosh SE and the Macintosh II would feature even more power.

The Mac's other fundamental problem had been that it had had almost no software programs when it came out. To remedy this, a charming but pushy marketing executive named Guy Kawasaki pestered software developers to write programs for the Mac, in an in-your-face technique that came to be known as "evangelism." The term was actually coined by Mike Murray, the Macintosh marketing manager who left the company to join Microsoft after his mentor, Steve Jobs, was pushed out of power. Murray's first "software evangelist" was a man named Mike Boich, who had once worked with him at Hewlett-Packard. Boich was an M.B.A. from Harvard who also possessed a fascination with personal computers, having used an Apple I while studying in his undergraduate work at Stanford.[3]

While at Stanford, Boich had roomed with fellow business school student Guy Kawasaki, who had grown up in Hawaii and possessed the easy laugh and radiant look of one who had spent much time in the sun and sand. The two became fast friends, to the extent that Kawasaki served as best man at Boich's wedding. So, shortly after Boich was hired as Apple's first software evangelist, he went to Mike Murray and told him he wanted to hire his friend Kawasaki to help out. "Guy had worked as a jewelry salesman," Murray remembers. "I asked him what he knew about computers. He said, 'Next to nothing.' So I told him to go work for a software developer and come back. He did, for one year."

Kawasaki joined Apple in 1983, and he would prove critical to the success of the Macintosh. Young, dynamic, and boyishly handsome, Kawasaki was a smooth talker and natural-born salesman. But all the charm in the world could get him only so far. He and Boich had to convince software developers to support a machine that was unlike any other and had no customer base. The men then decided to assume that the Macintosh would sell itself as soon as the developers laid their eyes on it. They were playing on two advantages here: One, many developers were maverick entrepreneurs, like Apple. And, two, they hated IBM as much as Apple did. "They could relate to us," Kawasaki remembers. "They were artists who we gave software to write programs they dreamed about."

Armed with a machine that developers would fall in love with, the rest of the story was shoe-leather work. Boich and Kawasaki, and a third evangelist named Alain Rossmann, fanned out across the United States, evangelizing four hundred developers over the next year and a half. Among the first developers Kawasaki managed to win over was a new company called T/Maker that had been founded by a woman in her twenties named Heidi Roizen. Roizen would become a highly influential leader in the software industry. Just then, she had recently left Stanford University with bachelor's and master's degrees.

T/Maker's main product at the time was a word processing program, and Roizen remembers Kawasaki calling her out of the blue one day to invite her over to Cupertino for lunch. "He had bought me a cup of coffee, which I don't like, and a Togo's sandwich, which I didn't like," Roizen recalls. "But Guy was the one who talked me into writing for the Mac. The Apple developers and evangelists were, like, joined at the hip. We would go to trade shows together, and they would put us in their booth for free."

Not only did Kawasaki have to convince developers to support the Mac, he also had to persuade Apple's own sales force and dealers that software was really shipping. So he reached into the Apple till and paid a cadre of developers $750,000 for thousands of copies of programs still in the testing phase, which he then distributed to salespeople and dealers. Kawasaki was nearly fired for the stunt. He had authority to disburse only up to $5,000 without higher approval and had written all the checks on his own volition. It was classic Apple chutzpah.[4]

Some developers did not need much prodding, just a little more time. In

1984, a Seattle entrepreneur named Paul Brainerd had joined with five software engineers to come up with a revolutionary way of creating business documents on a computer. (Brainerd brought the group together after their employer, Atex, a Massachusetts-based developer of publishing software for powerful minicomputers, closed the office in Redmond, Washington, where they all worked. Brainerd had managed that operation.) They developed a program called PageMaker that could incorporate text and graphics on the same computer page. A magazine, for example, could thus be designed completely by computer, eliminating the painstaking task of making a manual layout. This was truly a breakthrough, one with enormous customer appeal. Since the vast majority of other personal computers had little ability to display graphics, Brainerd's new company, Aldus, targeted its PageMaker for the Mac.

PageMaker might not have gone very far, however, if Brainerd had not had another ally within Apple to push the merits of this new form of computing. That champion was a Harvard MBA named John Scull who had worked under Jobs in the old Macintosh division. Scull saw PageMaker and instantly recognized its potential for creating a huge new market for Apple. He began the drumbeat within Apple for this new form of computing called "desktop publishing."

The notion was made all the more compelling by a revolutionary new printer Apple had just begun shipping, called the LaserWriter. At the time, almost all PC printers ran off an agonizingly slow technology called a "dot matrix." Not only were the printers annoyingly loud, generating the same clackety-clack sound as an old-fashioned typewriter, they also reproduced documents poorly. The reproductions were so unprofessional-looking that one would have been ill advised to print up a résumé on one—that is, if he or she really wanted the job. The LaserWriter, on the other hand, was based on laser technology and could produce letter-quality documents and even identical copies of graphical images created on the computer screen.

In late 1984, Jobs and Sculley had tried to push the LaserWriter as part of a package called Macintosh Office, which theoretically would solve all of a business's needs. There would be the Mac, the LaserWriter, a technology called AppleTalk that connected all the Macs together with a telephone line, and a central storage computer called a "file server" that would hold all the data that everybody in the office would need. There was one glaring problem with Macintosh Office, though: the file server would not be ready for shipping for three more years, while comparable IBM technology offered ample business productivity programs. That was enough to practically kill Office.

The needs of a desktop publishing market, which included design professionals and magazine publishers, on the other hand, could be met right then and there. All that was needed was a Mac, a LaserWriter, and PageMaker, and presto, you were an electronic publisher. It was a gonzo idea, and one that Gassée tried to shoot down. "Gassée thought it was a stupid idea," Scull recalls. "He said, 'We don't do niche marketing.' " But the idea was backed by Sculley and a Silicon Valley PR and advertising guru named Regis McKenna, whose agency had created the distinctive Apple logo. McKenna had gained renown within the Valley before going to Apple by designing a highly successful advertising campaign for Intel.

It was one of the few times Sculley stood up to Gassée, opening the way for a market that would become Apple's strongest and most profitable over time.

As his troops strengthened the product line, Sculley got to work on the strategic front. By then it had become clear to him that Apple had badly miscalculated by focusing much of its business on sales to schools, homes, and small businesses. The home and small-business market (called "SoHo," in industry vernacular, for "Small Office, Home Office") was highly unpredictable, subject to boom or bust depending on economic conditions affecting the buyer's pocketbook. And neither the SoHo nor the school market was inclined to pay top dollar for the kind of souped-up desktop computers that were in demand at large corporations. These were the computers that generated the highest profit, and it was a market dominated by IBM. Macintosh Office had been designed to crack that market, but it had been a colossal flop. Still seeing the potential for a gold mine here, Sculley repositioned Apple's selling strategy to take aim at the corporate office market.

It was time to take on Big Blue in its own backyard and forget about almost everything else.

In a 1987 interview with *Inc.* magazine, Sculley explained that he needed the high profit margins to plow back into research and development. Until 1985, he said, he had used the Pepsi formula of throwing big bucks into advertising to create a strong product brand, while keeping R-and-D spending virtually flat. The strategy had succeeded in establishing the Apple name in the minds of consumers worldwide. But what good was that if you didn't have more cool gizmos to sell? "In fact, robbing research to pay for advertising turned out to be a big, big mistake," Sculley told *Inc.* "Here we were, a new-products company in a new-products industry, and we could only turn out a new product every year or two—and then only by burning out our people."[5]

Hence, Sculley was ready to give Gassée and his engineers carte blanche to do whatever they wanted. It would be like turning kids loose in a candy store.

Big business was initially reticent to embrace Apple. One misgiving concerned the nature of Apple itself: a flaky California upstart whose products looked more like cute toys than serious instruments of office productivity. Sculley began working to polish Apple's image. In one such move, he walked into the office of junior manager Bob Saltmarsh in the fall of 1985 and named him the company treasurer. "Sculley said, 'We want you to be the Wall Street interface,'" remembers Saltmarsh, who was a midlevel finance man at the time. "When I told him I wasn't a Wall Street guy, Sculley said, 'That's okay. We need to build credibility. We need to put a flashy title behind whoever talks to Wall Street.'" Sculley chose Saltmarsh because of Saltmarsh's background in finance.

The second—and more compelling—reason for the corporate world to avoid Apple was that the original Macintosh lacked essentials such as a hard drive, which Jobs had abhorred because it required a noisy cooling fan that he thought would detract from the machine's overall attractiveness. Businesses needed the hard drive, though, to store large amounts of important data such as accounts receivable and personnel lists. They couldn't keep copying everything onto floppy disks, as Mac users were forced to do. The redesigned Macs that Gassée served up solved that problem.

One last crucial ingredient was needed for the Mac to be successful: it needed software programs, aside from those for desktop publishing, that average office workers could use to type reports and run numbers. It needed word processing and spreadsheet programs, and those were coming from William H. "Bill" Gates III—the computer industry's Great Satan himself.

Back in those days, the Microsoft kingpin was *only* a millionaire, not the popular $29 billion man he became by early 1997. When they were starting out, Gates was like the Ugly Duckling, compared to Steve Jobs. Where Jobs possessed the good looks of a rock star, with long, dark hair, a strikingly handsome face, and a tall, lean build, Gates was a gangly, mop-haired nerd with huge glasses who looked as though he were barely entering puberty. And while Jobs could captivate and enrapture a crowd, his silvery voice rising and lowering in the cadence of a revivalist preacher, Gates had all the stage demeanor of a deer caught in the headlights.

But beneath Gates's awkward exterior beat the heart of a cold-blooded killer, at least when it came to attacking business markets. Part of that instinct for going for the jugular, no doubt, came from having grown up in an upper-middle-class Seattle household headed by a father, William H. Gates Jr., who had been an accomplished trial attorney. So while Jobs was always more interested in changing the world, Gates wanted to dominate it. Coolly, methodically, Gates first secured control over the programming languages such as BASIC, COBOL, PASCAL, and eventually "C" that all developers used to write programs for the personal computer. Then he locked in control over the PC's basic operating system with MS-DOS. Finally, leveraging those dominant positions, he moved to take over the markets for the applications programs themselves, such as Microsoft Word, Excel, File, and, later, the best-selling Microsoft Office.

Yet compared to Jobs, Bill Gates was still just a peon in the industry. By 1984, for example, Apple's annual sales of $1.5 billion amounted to roughly fifteen times those of little Microsoft's $98 million. To be sure, Microsoft was growing by leaps and bounds, too; just two years before, the company's annual sales had totaled only $25 million. But Apple and Jobs were the stars of the show. So when Gates wanted to do business with Jobs, it was almost always Gates who flew down to Cupertino from his headquarters in the Seattle suburb of Bellevue. And Jobs let him know who was the boss dog.

In the year after the 1984 Mac launch, for instance, Jobs and Gates attended a New York City dinner for press and analysts at the elegant Tavern on the Green restaurant in Central Park. The restaurant, one of the finest in Manhattan with its glittery exterior illuminated by thousands of tiny white lights decorating all the trees around its periphery, its six chandeliered dining rooms, and waiters nattily attired in beige-colored uniforms, is so well regarded that it has been a lunch stop on the exclusive Deluxe Broadway Show Tour, which costs $2,000 per person. The occasion was Microsoft's announcement of its new spreadsheet, Excel, for the Macintosh. A reporter asked Gates, who was sitting at the front of the room beside Jobs, whether Microsoft would offer an IBM-compatible version of the spreadsheet and, if so, if it would feature similar performance to the one for Macintosh. Gates leaned into his microphone to say that in time that would happen. "Then Jobs grabbed the microphone from Gates and said, 'I'm sure in time we'll all be dead,' " recalls Andy Bose, an industry analyst who attended the dinner.

That drew a big laugh. But Gates, as always, would have the last one. During those early days, however, Gates was the Mac's best friend. Indeed, he and others at Microsoft fondly called it "S.A.N.D.," for "Steve's Amazing New Device," a nickname that Jeff Harbers, Microsoft's manager of Macintosh development at the time, says he coined after Jobs said he planned to "bring sand in one side of the factory for silicon and machines out the other." This may sound incongruous, since computers running Gates's Windows would go on to surround and crush Apple. But it really wasn't. Back then, no one could have predicted how rapidly and pervasively the PC business would grow. The name of the game in software was establishing beachheads for programs that served a specific function, such as creating spreadsheets. Gates, therefore, was primarily concerned with building programs such as Word, the word processor, and Excel, the spreadsheet, and putting them onto the biggest-selling computer. Seeing that the Mac was so far ahead of anything else in desktops, Gates wanted to make sure his programs would be along for the ride.

All the pieces were now in place. A strong new product line. A dynamic new market in desktop publishing. Compelling software programs from Microsoft and others. A new image that corporate America would like. And a unified management team making it all happen. With the introduction of the

Macintosh Plus, sales took off like a rocket. By the end of 1987, annual sales had almost doubled (in three years) to $2.7 billion, while profits had more than tripled to $218 million. The gross profit margin of 51 percent was the envy of the computer industry, as was the stock price, which rebounded to $58, giving Apple a market value of $7.7 billion—four times as great as in 1985.

Apple was once more flying high, and so was morale. Sculley may have convinced the outside world that this was now a serious business, but in many ways Apple was as juvenile as ever. The first tip-off was the dress code, or lack thereof. Taking a stroll on Apple's campus in those days would have been akin to walking the hallowed grounds of Stanford, just a twenty-minute drive away up nearby Interstate 280. Kids fresh out of college—many from Stanford, in fact—paraded between the clusters of low-slung buildings in jeans and T-shirts. Some even wore shorts and tank tops. It was the type of place where one employee walked around for years with a name badge that had a picture of him wearing a pirate's eye patch. The picture had been taken on his first day of work in 1983, when he had showed up for a Halloween party dressed as one of Jobs's pirates.

Even the top brass tried to get into the act. Suits were almost never worn in the executive suite, unless the honchos wanted to impress a Wall Street type coming by for the day. Sculley was so button-down, however, that for him it was hard to really adapt. The best he could manage in the dress-down category was a de facto uniform that invariably consisted of a pressed oxford-cloth shirt, khaki pants, and Docksiders. But he was just doing his thing, like everybody else in this crazy California place. What mattered was that the cult of individualism was alive and well, a cult formalized as early as 1981 by this credo in the official Apple Values: "Each person is important; each has the opportunity and the obligation to make a difference. The individual worth of each employee as a person is highly valued. We recognize that each member of Apple is important, that each can contribute to customer satisfaction. Our results come through the creativity, craftsmanship, initiative, and good work of each person as a part of a team."[6]

The work was frenetic, but so was the play. After all, most people working at Apple during this time were still in their twenties, with plenty of energy to burn after the twelve-hour workday was over. Friday afternoons were set aside for the merriment of a weekly beer bust, sponsored and paid for by the company. "A tent would be set up behind one of the buildings, and they would bring in platefuls of fresh shrimp and stuffed mushrooms, with all the beer and wine you could drink," recalls former manager Bill Curley.

The Appleites, as they came to be known, were known to wear shaggy long hair and unkempt beards, but this was about all they had in common with the real hippies who had been strung out on LSD during the 1960s in the Haight-Ashbury a little way up north. For the most part, this was a clean-living bunch. Almost no one smoked or drank much, and you could forget drugs. They liked fast cars and rock and roll, all right, but they also craved sushi, veggie burgers, and fine wine. These were really yuppie nerds, racing around in their BMWs trying to change the world.

As the chain of Apple's buildings grew to envelop both sides of De Anza Boulevard, a six-lane thoroughfare off busy I-280, so did the size of the beer bust. By the time Elaine Fellenbaum started work there in 1987 in Apple's creative services department, where she served as project manager of a team responsible for product packaging materials, she says individual buildings were sponsoring their own beer busts. Her group catered in Mexican on some Fridays, Chinese on others. "And on Friday mornings, they would bring in bagels and doughnuts," she says. "There was a very positive feeling about what was going on. Everyone was on a high. There was so much trust and belief in the product that we all thought, 'They couldn't screw it up.' "

By the late 1980s, Apple had swollen to some ten thousand employees and was getting too big to support certain traditions, such as the annual Halloween parade. Almost every Halloween through the decade, Apple employees would spill onto Bandley Drive—a side street just north of De Anza where the company's original six "Bandley" buildings were located—and parade in their costumes of pirates, clowns, ghosts, and goblins. Even the normally dour John Sculley got into the spirit. At a fall sales meeting in 1985, which happened to fall on Halloween, he showed up in long woolen underwear and a painted face as "The Spirit of Apple." A photo shows him in the outfit, sporting a wild smile uncharacteristic for the naturally subdued, intense person he was.

The money kept rolling in, as did the perks. The Christmas parties were a special extravaganza. One year, the Pointer Sisters performed for thousands of cheering employees at a hall in San Francisco. At other events, Apple was feted by the likes of rockers Huey Lewis and the News and the late jazz great Ella Fitzgerald. The Huey Lewis show took place in the nearby Santa Clara Convention Center during 1987, at a black-tie gala to commemorate Apple's tenth anniversary attended by thousands of employees. The theme was "Over the Rainbow," and the convention arena was decorated like the Emerald City from *The Wizard of Oz*, complete with actors jumping around in *Oz* costumes on a fabricated yellow brick road.

Sales conferences were held in places such as Maui, at which "Golden Apple" rewards were doled out to the year's top producers. "Once for Golden Apple, the company rented us an entire train through the Swiss Alps, with caviar, wine, and everything first class," says John Ziel, a sales manager at the time. "We were also given cruises to Cancún and Bermuda." The spending was so prolific, so outlandish, that even well-compensated executives such as Gassée, who was pulling down more than $700,000 in base salary each year, could only shake their heads in wonder. "I lived in terror that the books were cooked and that the profits had been overstated," Gassée says.

But they weren't. Sculley had executed a masterful turnaround of Apple, bringing the company from the brink of collapse to one of the most profitable enterprises on Earth. Sculley had become a millionaire many times over, as had other executives with big stock options. They worked hard, but they enjoyed the money, too, embarking on buying sprees of fancy cars and beautiful sprawling homes. And there was plenty more money to go around. Even low-level engineers were granted stock options equal to 22 percent of their annual salary, along with automatic pay hikes of 10 percent every six months. Non-engineering employees received somewhat less generous treatment, with their stock options amounting to between 5 percent and 10 percent of salary and pay raises subject to performance reviews. Apple had been completely transformed, and so had its CEO.

Even at his peak, John Sculley was never an overtly pretentious man. "Cool, disciplined, orderly and driven" were the words *Business Week* used to describe Sculley in a 1986 profile article, and they were apt ones. The son of a tough Wall Street lawyer, Sculley had been reared on Manhattan's Upper East Side and had gained his discipline and sense of orderliness from his years of attending private schools with strict codes of dress and behavior. After earning an MBA at the Wharton School, he dabbled in market analysis before signing on with Pepsi as a junior researcher.[7] Instilled with the tough competitive instincts of his father, Sculley quickly rose through the ranks, usually by leading parts of the giant company out of crisis. When marketing efforts were bogging down, he was called in to clean things up. When international operations were careening out of control, he moved in to turn things around. His turnaround of the giant Pepsi-Cola division in the United States was the most impressive achievement of all. He came onto the job in 1978 after number two Pepsi had lost share of the soft drink market for four years in a row and brought it ahead of Coca-Cola by four tenths of a percentage point.

Sculley's success at Pepsi was partly attributable to the fact that he was on known ground, with known ground rules. Pepsi's corporate culture was steeped in the mold of the eastern establishment, imbued with a clear, almost militarylike hierarchy where the consequences for failure meant a one-way ticket out of the company. "Consistent runners-up find their jobs disappear," Sculley explained about his life at Pepsi in *Odyssey*. "You must win merely to stay in place. You must devastate the competition to get ahead."[8] Sculley understood those rules and embraced them.

As demanding as this style was, Pepsi was instilled with an ethic of straightforwardness and fair play. "Pepsi was a very tough place, but on the other hand people were straight shooters," recalls Peter Lycurgus, a Pepsi marketing executive who followed Sculley out west to work in Apple's marketing business.

"The mentality was 'Either you perform or you don't,' but they would tell you whether you made it or not. Whereas at Apple, it was more an ideal mission that was kind of vague and a little bit different for every individual."

Indeed, Apple was a whole different animal. This was a company inventing itself as it went along, where titles meant nothing and one's status was influenced more by intellect—and the ability to speak loudly. Titles were considered such a joke that managers made light of them on business cards that would state SOFTWARE WIZARD or CORPORATE MOUTHPIECE. Even the title "chief executive officer" held less clout in Silicon Valley than anywhere else. Sure, Sculley was the boss, but what counted most at Apple was brains, the ability to comprehend fast-changing technology—and money, as in the ability of someone like Mike Markkula, who had used his fortune from Intel stock to provide initial financial backing for Apple, to fund a start-up venture. "The most important titles in Silicon Valley were 'cofounder' and 'largest shareholder,' " Sculley says.

Like Jobs, Sculley was no technologist. But unlike Jobs, he came on board unable even to understand the language, a failing demonstrated at one of his first meetings with employees in Cupertino, when a business systems manager named Peter Kavanaugh stood up to ask what he was going to do about "connectivity," the technology that links desktop computers together. "He leaned to an aide and asked, 'What is connectivity?' " Kavanaugh says.

As with everything else in his life, though, Sculley was a perfectionist who worked to overcome his shortcomings, such as his speech impediment. An introvert who would literally recoil at being touched, he forced himself to maintain a public persona at Apple to the extent that he would go to the Apple cafeteria during lunch and eat his peanut-butter-and-jelly sandwich with the rest of the employees. Many times he sat there all by himself, the chief executive of the world's most dynamic computer company munching nervously on his little sandwich. Unsure of how to react to such a powerful person in their midst, most employees would just nod hesitantly and scurry past to their own tables.

"John was very shy in crowds," recalls Barbara Krause, the tall, efficient head of Apple's PR department at the time. "We would sit down with him so he didn't have to be alone." Privately, though, Sculley exhibited a warm and personable side to his staff, making sure to send flowers to Krause, for example, when she was pregnant and later taking the time to meet and hold her infant son. He also wasn't shy about imparting good advice. Once Krause confided to Sculley about how nervous she felt about having to make a speech later that day. Sculley's eyes narrowed as he snapped, "Don't *ever* let your limitations hold you back." He then delivered a lengthy recounting of how he had beaten the stuttering problem he had suffered as a teenager. "He would always say to us, 'Don't worry about the things you can't change. Just worry about the things you can change,' " Krause says.

Sculley was most self-conscious of all about his lack of technical expertise. Here he was, leading the greatest collection of engineering minds ever assembled, and he didn't know what words like "connectivity" meant. But in classic John Sculley fashion, he sought to overcome that by burying himself in product briefings and assigning aides to accompany him around the campus to serve as translators of engineering jargon. One of those was a young man named Mike Homer, who joined Apple in 1981 as a twenty-six-year-old programmer to help install Apple's internal computer network. "The first thing I did was interview Nanette Buckhout [Sculley's assistant at the time] and ask what she did," Homer recalls. "I made sure that Nanette and John started using their computers. John, before this, would only use his computer for [interoffice] mail." Sculley also read up on all the technical manuals and used his marketing expertise to find potential for the masses in the cool new technologies he was seeing in the labs. "More than anyone else I know, he could understand technology and its implications," says Al Eisenstat, who was then serving as Apple's general counsel.

Though he would become reasonably well versed on the subject over time, many other people associated with Apple remained convinced that Sculley "didn't get it," as Jobs used to say about anyone who would disagree with him. "I don't think John understood the industry," says John Warnock, the seasoned chief executive of Adobe Systems, Apple's longtime software ally. "He never had any deep penetration of what motivated people to use computers. He gravitated more to 'I have one of these things on my desk because it does magical things.'"

It didn't help Sculley's credibility any when he tried to portray himself as a techie by keeping on his desk an oscilloscope, a dusty relic of the cathode-ray era. Or when he would employ his sharp memory to parrot, in TV interviews, what someone else in Apple had told him. After the 1987 stock market crash, for instance, he was asked to appear live on NBC's *Today* show to explain the economic implications for Silicon Valley. "He called me to ask, 'What do you think will happen?'" recalls Bob Saltmarsh, the treasurer. "I told him, and he said, 'Thank you very much.' Thirty minutes later, he repeated on TV almost verbatim my thought process."

As skilled and capable as Sculley was as a manager, in the early days his lack of background in technology proved a handicap, no matter how hard he tried. Conversely, the man who ran Microsoft, Bill Gates, was an entrepreneur blessed with the rare combination of a keen business sense and a strong technological intellect. Gates, having been a programmer himself, could look over an engineer's shoulder one minute and point out sloppy code. The next, he could huddle with marketing managers and devise an advertising strategy. Being so remarkably adept at many disciplines, Gates became a highly effective leader and was able to impose a more hierarchical structure at Microsoft—so much so, in fact, that the Microsoft hierarchy was not that much different from the Pepsi-Cola Sculley had known.

"It was real simple," Sculley says. "Gates was the boss. He had a very clear idea of what he wanted to do." Apple, on the other hand, was always what Sculley calls "a consensus culture." It was a culture where a single manager could sandbag a whole project, because everyone had to agree for anything to proceed. Jobs had been a screamer and yeller, but he had tolerated dissent; in fact, he had encouraged it. The idea was that if an idea was good enough to survive the dissent phase, it was good enough. The difference was that Jobs had such tremendous force of personality that he could will things to happen, as he had done with the Macintosh. Sculley did not have that will, in large part because technology wasn't his forte in the first place.

"Apple always had the DNA of Steve Jobs, even after he was gone," Sculley says. "There was a culture at Apple that was almost cultlike. It was much more of a cult than a real company."

To his credit, Sculley had galvanized Apple when it needed a galvanizer. He had put the right people into the right jobs. He didn't know beans about technology, but, hey, Gassée's engineers did. And if he had left after five years, as he originally planned, he would have gone down in corporate history as a hero, the savior of an American icon. But a metamorphosis occurred that would preclude him from leaving on his own accord. It was a metamorphosis of ego, an ego that fed on all the glowing news accounts, that basked in the hot glare of television lights.

By 1987, the Apple turnaround had become the hottest news in the computer industry and one of the biggest stories of American business. While he remained painfully shy in small gatherings, Sculley honed his public speaking skills to the point that he began to rival Jobs's charisma in talks before large groups. All the years spent huddling with computer gearheads and trying to understand what they had to say were starting to pay off. He still was no engineer, but he did possess the knack of absorbing technogibberish and translating it into plain English. This was no mean feat, since Silicon Valley was filled with propeller heads who couldn't explain to their own grandmothers what they did for a living.

Suddenly, Sculley was the hot draw on the speaking circuit, a poster boy for the media crowd. *Playboy* magazine devoted nine pages of one issue to an interview with him, in what the title of the article describes as "A Candid Conversation with Apple Computer's Dynamic C.E.O." In a profile in *Inc.* magazine, a full-page color photo of him appeared on the cover next to the caption "Apple Chief John Sculley on Managing Company Founders, Crises, and Change."

Sculley embraced the publicity as it embraced him. At one point he was giving four speeches a week. He gave many, many interviews, never eschewing an opportunity to get himself and Apple mentioned in the press. "He would say so many times that momentum is so important," recalls Saltmarsh, who relates a telling anecdote of the Sculley management style. The year was 1987, and he and Sculley were in New York City, making the usual Wall Street and media rounds. They were in midtown Manhattan, stuck in traffic on Fifth Avenue while en route to a radio station where Sculley had an interview scheduled. It was a scene all too familiar in the Big Apple: car horns blaring, taxi drivers shouting insults at one another, exhaust fumes merging into a toxic cloud. "He's sitting there, checking his watch, and the traffic is not moving. So he jumps out of the limo and starts sprinting to make the interview."

Many people would have called it runaway ego. In Sculley's own view, garnering publicity was the best way he had found of managing Apple. "I was highly visible because it was easier to manage the company from the outside than from the inside," Sculley says. "To me, Apple was a product. So I would do whatever it took to build demand. It happened that Apple got a huge amount of free publicity."

Sculley had even gained the confidence, at this point, to pen a book outlining his business philosophies. In his 450-page autobiography, *Odyssey*, he characterized Apple as the model for new "third-wave" companies that relied more on consensus management than the top-down hierarchy of traditional "second-wave" companies such as Pepsi. At the second-wave company out of which he had come, all the executives wore dark, conservative suits, decisions were handed down from the top to the bottom, and workers clocked in at regular business hours, such as between 9 A.M. and 5 P.M. The third-wave company, on the other hand, was one in which knowledge was more important than rank. If a janitor had a great idea, it could be taken seriously. Dress codes and work hours were also totally at workers' discretion so long as the work got done. Sculley predicted that this collegial style of the third-wave company would supplant the old one and allowed that Apple was the brave pioneer. "I firmly believe that by the time we cross over to the 21st Century, we and smaller companies will be the source of management concepts," Sculley elaborated in his interview with *Playboy*.

That vision of a utopian corporate society was never, in fact, a reality at Apple, as almost all former managers will attest. The same empire building and backstabbing that is a mainstay at almost every large bureaucracy went on at Apple almost from the beginning, and they increased as the years progressed. Surprisingly, since he was not a techie, Sculley was dead on in some of his predictions for the evolution of technology. In *Odyssey*, he described an omnipresent device of the future that he called "Knowledge Navigator," which would let a person steer through reams of data all over the world.

A 1988 Apple video of five minutes, forty-five seconds captured the essence of the Navigator. It showed a university professor breezing into his living room and popping open a tablet-shaped computer to see the digitized image of a bow-tied butler on screen. "You have three messages," the butler stated in a pleasant voice. The electronic butler went on to announce incoming telephone calls and put them through. One of the calls was from an academic colleague in another city, whose face appeared on the screen as she informed him that she had important research information to share for his upcoming lecture on deforestation in Africa and Brazil. The professor instructed his butler to pull up some of his deforestation maps to compare with those being shown by the woman. When the conversation ended, the butler appeared again to announce that the professor's mother had called with a reminder: Pick up the birthday cake. The video ended with an image of the Apple logo with the slogan "The Power to Be Your Best."

A decade later, the Internet's World Wide Web would explode, providing the same ability to scan vast databases as the Navigator promised while communicating with other people through the computer at the same time. It would transform the personal computer from a productivity tool into one focused around the exchange and transfer of information, exactly as Sculley had envisioned. Sculley was also years ahead of his time in predicting the importance of big 1990s trends such as the computer's new ability to combine video and sound. For all his later failings as CEO, Sculley would go down in computer history as a great visionary and seer.

Even at the peak of his game, though, Sculley did not seem happy. Sure, he was famous, a celebrity in the same class as Jobs. But within the engineering corridors at Apple, he knew he still wasn't getting the respect he craved. One sunny afternoon in the middle of 1986, an Apple manager named Phil Dixon bumped into Sculley on a street in downtown Saratoga, a tony community of Silicon Valley millionaires cradled in the oak-and-redwood foothills of the Santa Cruz mountains down the road from Apple. "I asked him how he was doing, and he said, 'Fine.' Then I stopped and asked, 'Who gives you your performance review?' " Dixon remembers. "He looked puzzled and said, 'Nobody.' I said, 'Well, that's too bad. Because you are doing a great job.' He didn't know what to say. Tears brimmed in the corners of his eyes."

Sculley really had done a magnificent job to this point. He had overcome enormous personal obstacles. He had endured the gut-wrenching task of having to boot a real-life American hero out of the company he had founded. And he was putting Apple onto the map as never before. He was a self-appointed visionary, pointing the way for Apple and the rest of the world to follow. The only problem was that Apple needed not so much a visionary as someone to kick some butt. This may have been a consensus culture, but a new regime was about to take hold that would be able to agree on almost nothing. It was 1987, and the natives were growing restless. Once again, it was time for somebody to take charge.

3

The Licensing Debate

Steve Wozniak made a decision very early on at Apple that would prove one of the company's most fateful ever. When "Woz," a prank-loving twenty-six-year-old who loved to tinker with machines, designed the very first Apple computer, he decided to use a microprocessor called the MOS Technology 6502, based on the design of Motorola Inc.'s 6800, essentially because it was cheaper than anything else he could find. Intel's 8080 chip was selling for $179 at the time, and Motorola's 6800 fetched $175. The MOS Technology chip, made by a Costa Mesa, California, company, cost only $25.[1] The microprocessor itself looks insignificant. Also called a "microchip," it is a tiny little piece of equipment no larger than a silver dollar. But it is critically important to a personal computer. Containing thousands of microscopic circuits etched onto tiny silicon wafers, the microchip is the very "brain" of the personal computer, controlling everything from the machine's processing speed to its ability to display images on a screen. Without one, the PC would sit useless on the desk.

The decision to go with the Motorola technology was fateful, because Intel would gain the license from IBM to make the microchips that went into almost every IBM-compatible computer. Motorola was a big company in its own right, a giant in cellular phones and pagers. But Apple, which soon after that first design by Woz began using Motorola chips exclusively, became Motorola's only sizable customer for personal computer microprocessors. Intel's whole life, on the other hand, revolved around microchips. In fact, it had been a young Intel engineer named Marcian E. Hoff Jr. who had invented the microchip in 1971, making the PC revolution possible.

Intel didn't have just one customer, it had hundreds. Not only did it supply chips to IBM, it supplied them to all the manufacturers of IBM-compatibles. By doing so, Intel created what is known in the industry as a "standard." Since every company but Apple was using Intel chips, technical specifications for all new computers would have to be designed around the Intel standard. Intel eventually began churning out a line of microprocessors based on the 8086 design, or "x86," which competitors hoping to carve a slice out of the widening PC pie worked to imitate. The competitors, which included chip makers such as Advanced Micro Devices and Cyrix Corporation, were never able to catch up, though, because Intel controlled the standard. With so much money pouring in from the hundreds of PC makers buying its chips, Intel could funnel the profits right back into the labs to come up with even faster chips. Whenever there was the slightest hint that someone might catch up, the Intel engineers would find a whip lashed across their backs by a wiry, bug-eyed Hungarian immigrant named Andy Grove, who was CEO and commander of the ship. No one was going to overtake Intel, at least not as long as a pulse beat in Grove's body.

His equal in paranoia was Bill Gates, who controlled the other most important part of the personal computer: the operating system. Just like Intel, Microsoft had been handed the keys to a kingdom when IBM had granted it rights to supply IBM and all the IBM-compatibles with the operating system software that controls every other program. While the microchip is the "brain" of the computer, allowing it to think, the operating system is the rest of the body, moving into action. Each is dependent on the other. And without an operating system, the microchip just sits there, paralyzed.

Microsoft had started out making the BASIC programming language for personal computers. That was a decent business, but nothing like the one for operating systems. Programming languages were sold mainly to software developers. Every computer, however, had to have an operating system. If the majority of computers contained a company's operating system, it had one more advantage: with all the money pouring in from sales of the operating system, it had plenty to invest in the software programs such as word processing and spreadsheets that customers actually used.

The Microsoft empire, therefore, was built with the operating system called MS-DOS (Microsoft Disk Operating System) as its foundation and the programming languages and software programs on top. And just as had happened with Intel, MS-DOS became an industry standard that everyone in the world of IBM-compatibles had to use. Another operating system couldn't just be popped into the box, because Apple was really the only other game in town and it was already using Motorola chips. MS-DOS was not designed to run on Motorola chips. Apple's operating system, which was completely different from MS-DOS, was designed to run *only* on Motorola chips.

Fast forward, now, to 1985, when John Sculley was presiding over an Apple in disarray. With a screen interface that allowed users to "point and click" commands, the Mac was vastly superior to anything else on the PC front, which then consisted mainly of MS-DOS, which forced the user to type arcane commands to open a program. The main thing Sculley had to do to get Apple back on track was to fix the obvious problems such as the Mac's low memory capacity and scanty software. After that, the Mac could practically sell itself. But Sculley could also have gone another route that, if taken, would have dramatically transformed both it and the rest of the computer industry. That route was licensing Mac software so other manufacturers could make their own versions of the Apple computer. Licensing was the same route taken by both Microsoft and Intel, which had allowed their standard to proliferate so quickly.

From a 1990s hindsight, the merits of licensing a technology are obvious. Instead of funding all research and development itself, Apple could have reaped the benefits of having dozens, even hundreds of imitators all adding their own unique value to the Mac. Legions of suppliers would have sprung up all around the world to furnish the manufacturers with components such as disk drives and memory. And since the software was light-years ahead of everybody else's, the Mac's, not Windows, might have come to dominate the personal computer market. That dominant market position would have forced software developers to devote the bulk of their resources to Apple and its compatibles, ensuring a plethora of programs that would meet almost any user's needs.

It would all have become one big corporate ecosystem centered around the Mac. Put another way, Apple would have created an industry standard, a playing field that it controlled and everyone else would have to buy into. This standard was envisioned by Bill Gates and outlined in one of the most important documents in Silicon Valley history, a highly confidential three-page memorandum from Gates to Sculley and Gassée dated June 25, 1985. Entitled "Apple Licensing of Mac Technology," the document read:

Background:

Apple's stated position in personal computers is innovative technology leader. This position implies that Apple must create a standard on new, advanced technology. They must establish a "revolutionary" architecture, which necessarily implies new development incompatible with existing architectures.

Apple must make Macintosh a standard. But no personal computer company, not even IBM, can create a standard without independent support. Even though Apple realized this, they have not been able to gain the independent support required to be perceived as a standard.

The significant investment (especially independent support) in a "standard personal computer" results in an incredible momentum for its architecture. Specifically, the IBM PC architecture continues to receive huge investment and gains additional momentum. . . . The investment in the IBM architecture includes development of differentiated compatibles, software and peripherals; user and sales channel education; and most importantly, attitudes and perceptions that are not easily changed.

Any deficiences in the IBM architecture are quickly eliminated by independent support. . . . The closed architecture prevents similar independent investment in the Macintosh. The IBM architecture, when compared to the Macintosh, probably has more than 100 times the engineering resources applied to it when investment of compatible manufacturers is included. The ratio becomes even greater when the manufacturers of expansion cards are included.

Conclusion:

As the independent investment in a "standard" architecture grows, so does the momentum for that architecture. The industry has reached the point where it is now impossible for Apple to create a standard out of their innovative technology without support from, and the resulting credibility of, other personal computer manufacturers. Thus, Apple must open the Macintosh architecture to have the independent support required to gain momentum and establish a standard.

The Mac has not become a standard

The Macintosh has failed to attain the critical mass necessary for the technology to be considered a long term contender:
   a. Since there is no "competition" to Apple from Mac-compatible manufacturers, corporations consider it risky to be locked into the Mac, for reasons of price AND choice.
   b. Apple has reinforced the risky perception of the machine by being slow to come out with hardware and software improvements (e.g. hard disk, file server, bigger screen, better keyboard, larger memory . . .)
   c. Recent negative publicity about Apple hinders the credibility of the Macintosh as a long term contender in the personal computer market.
   d. Independent software and hardware manufacturers reinforced the risky perception of the machine by being slow to come out with key software and peripheral products.
   e. Apple's small corporate account sales force has prevented it from having the presence, training, support, etc. that large companies would recognize and require.
   f. Nationalistic pressures in European countries often force foreign consumers to choose local manufacturers. Europeans have local suppliers of the IBM architecture, but not Apple. Apple will lose ground in Europe as was recently exhibited in France.

Recommendation:

Apple should license Macintosh technology to 3–5 significant manufacturers for the development of "Mac Compatibles":

United States manufacturers and contacts:

ideal companies—in addition to credibility, they have large account sales forces that can establish the Mac architecture in larger companies:

- AT&T, James Edwards
- Wang, An Wang
- Digital Equipment Corporation, Ken Olsen
- Texas Instruments, Jerry Junkins
- Hewlett Packard, John Young

other companies (but perhaps more realistic candidates):

- Xerox, Elliott James or Bob Adams
- Motorola, Murray A. Goldman
- Harris/Lanier, Wes Cantrell
- NBI, Thomas S. Kavanagh
- Burroughs. W. Michael Blumenthal and Stephen Weisenfeld
- Kodak . . .

European manufacturers:

- Siemens
- Bull
- Olivetti
- Phillips [sic]

Apple should license the Macintosh technology to U.S. and European companies in a way that allows them to go to other companies for manufacturing. Sony, Kyocera . . . are good candidates for OEM manufacturing of Mac compatibles.

Microsoft is very willing to help Apple implement this strategy. We are familiar with the key manufacturers, their strategies and strengths. We also have a great deal of experience in OEMing system software.

Rationale:

1. The companies that license Mac technology would add credibility to the Macintosh architecture.
2. These companies would broaden the available product offerings through their "Mac-compatible" product lines:
   - they would each innovate and add features to the basic system: various memory configurations, video display, and keyboard alternatives, etc.
   - Apple would lever the key partners' abilities to produce a wide variety of peripherals, much faster than Apple could develop the peripherals themselves.

- customers would see competition and would have real price/performance choices.
3. Apple will benefit from the distribution channels of these companies.
4. The perception of a significantly increased potential installed base will bring the independent hardware, software, and marketing support that the Macintosh needs.
5. Apple will gain significant, additional marketing support. Everytime [*sic*] a Mac compatible manufacturer advertises, it is an advertisement for the Apple architecture.
6. Licensing Mac compatibles will enhance Apple's image as a technological innovator. Ironically, IBM is viewed as being a technological innovator. This is because compatible manufacturers are afraid to innovate too much and stray from the standard.[2]

This heretofore unpublished document essentially provided a blueprint for how Apple could save itself from long-term debilitation—a course that, had it been taken, would have put Apple into the driver's seat into the 1990s and possibly beyond.

What would possess Bill Gates to offer such a helping hand to a competitor? Surely, it couldn't be out of the goodness of his heart. And of course it wasn't. The idea for the memorandum actually originated with a young man named Jeff Raikes, who had joined Microsoft in late 1981 at the age of twenty-three to become one of the company's first product marketing managers. Raikes, a Nebraska farm boy with all-American good looks, had joined Apple out of Stanford in 1980 and eventually risen to engineering manager but jumped ship to Microsoft a year later after he decided—correctly, as it turned out—that software would become more important than the hardware business Apple was focused on. Steve Jobs, who had asked Raikes to join his new Macintosh team, was furious when Raikes announced he was leaving. "Jobs read to me from the riot act," remembers Raikes, who went on to become one of nine members of Microsoft's powerful Executive Committee. "He said, 'Microsoft will go out of business.' " Right, Steve.

At Microsoft, Gates, too, had GUI (graphical user interface) on the brain in the early 1980s. MS-DOS was becoming the workhorse of IBM-compatibles, but Gates knew that software applications would become much more compelling when they could be presented graphically, in a manner that users would intuitively understand. Most people, Gates had told attendees of the Rosen Research Personal Computer Forum at Lake Geneva, Wisconsin, in May 1981, "want things to be user-friendly. They want a way of understanding how information is represented in their terms. Drawers, files, folders—whatever terminology you pick, it's got to somehow tie into something the user had used before."[3]

In those days, in fact, it wasn't just Steve Jobs and Bill Gates thinking GUI, it was practically the whole industry. Digital Research was working on GUI-based software called GEM. Apple was relying on it for the ill-fated Lisa project, which evolved into the Macintosh. And another company called VisiCorp, which had soared to industry stardom on the success of its VisiCalc spreadsheet, shocked the computer world—and Bill Gates—when it demonstrated, at the fall 1982 Comdex show in Las Vegas, the VisiOn, a graphical user interface for powerful IBM-compatible PCs. Gates, after seeing the VisiOn demo in VisiCorp's booth, called a Microsoft technologist named Charles Simonyi, back in Bellevue, and told him to fly down to see the technology.[4]

Simonyi, a Hungarian refugee and computer programming whiz, was perhaps Gates's equal in energy and intensity. He had joined Microsoft in 1980, following years of work as one of the elite scientists developing futuristic computer products at Xerox PARC in Palo Alto, California. Simonyi knew all about GUIs. In fact, he had written a word processing program for one at Xerox. "The minute Charles came on, we said, 'OK, it's in our future to do the graphical interface. The question is when,' " recalls Gates in an interview for this book in his suite on the twenty-ninth floor of the Las Vegas Hilton during the fall 1996 Comdex show in that city.

In 1981, at Simonyi's insistence, Microsoft procured the latest in GUI technology: a Xerox Star computer, which was the first commercial product to use the new technology but failed because of its prohibitive cost of $100,000, including a printer, a data-storage server, and a network to hook all the gear together. "We wanted people at Microsoft to understand the future," recalls Simonyi, seated on an ergonomically correct black chair in a room adorned with modern art originals in his mansion overlooking Seattle's Lake Washington. "Bill knew from the outset that GUI was the future."

Until he saw the VisiOn in action, Gates had been preoccupied with building software applications to run on top of MS-DOS and the proliferation of smaller computer platforms on the market. Since it was not yet clear which of the platforms would survive, Gates—who had been an avid poker player during his days at Harvard—covered his bets by supporting everything he could. "Understand, you make a lot more money selling applications than you do operating systems," Gates says, sipping from a can of Coke as he reclines in a chair with his back to a panorama of Las Vegas sprawling below. "Operating systems, you get a couple percent of the price of the machine [or $40 for a $2,000 PC]. Applications, you can get hundreds of dollars."

"Remember, back then," Gates adds, "we weren't talking about Microsoft being an $8-billion-a-year company. We were hoping we would be a $200-million [per year] company. Well, if you could get a few million Macs to sell a year, we would have been triple the size we were then." Microsoft's revenues in 1982 totaled just $25 million.

Upon their return from the 1982 Comdex, Gates and Simonyi set to work on a graphically based operating system called "Interface Manager," which later was renamed "Windows" when the first version finally shipped in November 1985. Windows, as originally designed, was clearly inferior to the Macintosh system because it featured a "tiled" look as opposed to the Mac's use of overlapping windows. If you opened three word processing documents on Windows, for example, they would appear as "tiles" that occupied equal amounts of space on the screen, obscuring much of the text from view. On the Mac, however, those same three documents overlapped one another, just as if they were lying on a desk. Each could be maneuvered to another part of the screen so that more of the document could be seen. The Mac, in short, mimicked the way people really worked, which is why it was so attractive.

As impressive as VisiOn had looked in Las Vegas, the operating system proved so clunky and filled with bugs when it finally shipped a year later that it never gained any momentum and eventually died a quiet death. Gates, however, began spreading the word of Windows everywhere, even as he quietly moved to hedge his bets after taking a sneak peek at Steve Jobs's Macintosh in 1981. At the time, Microsoft's biggest-selling application was a spreadsheet called Multiplan, which competed against VisiCalc. With Multiplan selling like hotcakes, Gates saw no reason why Microsoft should not support this new machine called the Macintosh, too.

And oh, what a machine it was. Fueled by a Motorola 68000 chip that was far more powerful than Intel's chips, the graphical displays fairly danced across the Mac's screen. After seeing a demonstration of the Mac in Cupertino during October 1981, "Our view was that it was exactly what we were looking for," remembers Jeff Harbers, who at the time was a Multiplan manager. In January 1982, Microsoft signed an agreement to develop applications for the Mac. Initially, Gates committed to delivering three programs for the Mac's launch: a spreadsheet, a business graphics program, and a database.[5]

By the next year, though, Microsoft's Macintosh development effort evolved from a "cover our bets" strategy to one of "bet the farm." The change in emphasis came after a start-up company called Lotus Development Corporation in Massachusetts began shipping a new spreadsheet for IBM-compatibles called 1-2-3. It was faster and more powerful than either VisiCalc or Microsoft's Multiplan, and it went on to become the "killer" application that solidified the IBM-compatible as the world's preeminent desktop computing standard. Lotus 1-2-3 was also proving a killer to Microsoft's Multiplan, as Bill Gates recognized with horror as sales of his spreadsheet began to wither under the assault.

On October 25, 1983, Gates convened with his top lieutenants in a retreat at a Red Lion Inn near Bellevue to ponder what to do about 1-2-3. In that retreat, Gates and his strategists came up with the concept of a new spreadsheet that featured a GUI and would later be named "Excel." "In our euphoria over the Mac and in our awe at 1-2-3, we decided we needed to focus on GUI applications," Raikes recalls. Initially, the plan was to offer Excel first on IBM-compatible PCs. But as the Macintosh grabbed so much industry attention in its January 1984 launch, Gates shifted gears and decided to put Excel onto the Mac first. "We bet on the Macintosh, hoping Windows would come in sooner rather than later," Raikes remembers.

It was a big wager, indeed. Gates committed fully one third of Microsoft's programming resources to the Macintosh, putting Jeff Harbers in charge of the project. "We were complete Mac fanatics," remembers Harbers, who along with other engineers would joke, "I'm going to the beach" whenever they wanted to go into a locked, windowless room at Microsoft where a Mac prototype, or "S.A.N.D.," had been stowed. Adds Gates, "We were in it together. We bet a lot of the future on the Mac."

From the outset, though, the spirit of cooperation was not reciprocated by Apple. "Steve was convinced that Bill would take ideas from the Mac and incorporate them into Windows," recalls Mike Murray, who was then Apple's Macintosh marketing manager and later became Microsoft's vice president for human resources and administration. "Steve would call Bill and say, 'Get down here right now.' We would go into a room at Bandley 1 [on the Apple campus], and Bill would go to a whiteboard and sketch out everything Microsoft was doing. He'd say, 'I shouldn't tell you this, but I'm going to tell you everything I'm doing.' " Gates would sketch out his Windows path, hop onto a plane, and go home.

Jobs had good reason to be paranoid. After all, Gates was on his way to becoming king of the IBM PC and made no bones about the fact that he wanted to push Windows as the software standard in the Intel world. Yet, Harbers remembers, "We felt we owed it to Apple to keep the Mac secret. Only Gates, Simonyi, and the Mac development team knew about it." Murray, who was friends with Gates's top lieutenant and Harvard classmate, Steve Ballmer, remembers getting frantic calls from the Microsoft chieftain. "One day, Bill called me and said, 'Mike, what are we supposed to do? Steve keeps yelling at us. I don't know whether to work on the Mac or not,' " Murray recalls. "I'd say, 'Bill, just keep the pedal to the metal. We need you. I'll manage Steve.' "

Microsoft Excel for the Macintosh would not be ready to ship until September 1985, after it was announced the previous May at that New York City press conference at Tavern on the Green. After the Mac's launch in 1984, Gates watched with relief as computer enthusiasts gobbled up the new machines. But anxiety set in for himself and the others at Microsoft when the Mac's sales tapered off in late 1984 and into 1985. "I remember having a meeting with Ballmer and the [Microsoft] Mac team," Gates says. "We were all saying, 'Jesus, you know, Apple may not do this well.' And Ballmer said,

'Well, we can help them. But we have to assume they're staying awake at night worrying about these same things.' "

One day in the first quarter of 1985, one of Microsoft's product managers, Chris Larson, made an offhand comment to Jeff Raikes as they commiserated about the declining fortunes of the Macintosh. "He said they should license the Mac operating system," Raikes remembers. A lightbulb flashed in Raikes's head, and he hurried to his computer to put the idea down on paper. "So I wrote a letter to Bill saying I really think Apple should license its operating system," Raikes remembers. "I said, 'They are competing against all of the R and D on the IBM platform.' My conclusion was that Apple should license the Mac. I sent the memo to Bill in May 1985." Gates took the memo and expanded it to include a list of potential clone manufacturers Apple could call on for help. Gates was careful, in compiling this list, to include manufacturers that could broaden the Macintosh market, not just cannibalize sales from Apple. Canon, for instance, was strong in Japan, while Apple at that time was not.

Before sending the memo, Gates put in calls to the senior executives he knew at both AT&T and Hewlett-Packard. "We talked to them about 'Well, if Apple approached you, would you be interested?' And those were the top two on our list," Gates says. Those companies, in fact, were interested. "If Apple really thought licensing was a complicated thing somehow, we were glad, because we understood licensing, to help out," Gates adds. "But the letter was very clear that we're saying we're not trying to make money off of licensing. If it's necessary, we'll facilitate it by being a middleman."

The memo went out, and Gates and Raikes waited. And waited. But after several days, there was no response. "We didn't hear from John, so Bill called him," Raikes says. "And Sculley said, 'Well, how do you do this? Do we sell system boards to the OEMs [original equipment manufacturers]?' They just didn't understand." Gates and Raikes had not worked out details of how a Macintosh licensing plan would be carried out, given Apple's lack of interest. But it quite likely would have followed the usual Microsoft model of licensing software to manufacturers in return for royalties.

Nor did Apple want to. Apple was always a religious company, and the religion of Macintosh made the subject of licensing Apple's most contentious and divisive issue ever. Jean-Louis Gassée and his engineers rightfully believed the Mac represented a quantum leap in technology, a watershed product every bit as significant as Woz's Apple II and IBM's first PC. No way, no how would Gassée see his precious Mac turned over to a ragtag army of copycats. This was Apple's crown jewel, and Gassée meant to defend it with his life. He was the guardian of the castle, the keeper of the flame. Never mind that he tooled around town in a Mercedes with license plates that read OPEN MAC. By that, Gassée was only illustrating his support for opening the Mac to hard drives, plug-in circuit boards, and other useful accessories that Jobs had ordered kept out of the original Mac. The OPEN MAC license plates, however, should have read CLOSED MAC, because that is really how Gassée felt about licensing Mac technology to the clone market.

"Apple was so committed to being different from the rest," recalls Kevin Sullivan, whose arrival in 1987 as head of Apple's human resources department would signal a new era in the company's management. "There was a glee, almost. We were elegant. Jean-Louis called it 'the beautiful business we are in.' "

The furor of the licensing debate manifested itself early on, during a meeting of Sculley's executive staff one day in 1985 after Gates's memo had been received. A young man named Dan Eilers would present his case for why Apple should license the Mac, a scant three years after he had joined the company upon graduating from nearby Stanford University with a degree in economics. Eilers, Apple's director of investor relations and then aged thirty, might have been young and inexperienced, but he was a business pragmatist detached from the religious fervor of the engineers. He knew Apple was in bad financial shape and simply thought the licensing plan would help out. Sculley invited Eilers to brief the executive staff on his plan.

Eilers was about to run into a buzz saw.

Eilers was no wild-eyed radical, though from the reaction he would receive you would have thought he was. A slight, soft-spoken man who liked to fly private planes and take long walks in the woods, Eilers was understandably nervous about the meeting. Although he had a fancy title, he was really a peon in the organizational structure. And here he was, about to give his very first presentation to the big brass, the members of Sculley's inner circle, which besides Gassée, Campbell, Spindler, and Coleman included Jay Elliott, head of human resources; Al Eisenstat, general counsel; and Dave Barram, chief financial officer. The company was still in crisis mode, just weeks after Jobs had been forced out, and executive staff was meeting with Sculley every day at 7:30 A.M. sharp to keep tabs on cash and inventories.

Apple headquarters at the time was atop a four-story building called De Anza 4, an easy stroll from the De Anza 7 building, to which it would soon move. Eilers took the elevator to the fourth floor and walked into the 7:30 A.M. executive staff meeting commencing in a tiny conference room, appropriately called the "Small Room." Seated around a rectangular table about ten feet in length were Sculley, Gassée, Elliott, Eisenstat, Barram, and Campbell. Most were dressed casually, as usual, in khakis, slacks, or jeans. Gassée, who typically looked like a biker in his trademark black leather jackets and black leather pants, glowered as the young man stood up to begin a two-hour presentation.

"Apple should recognize as a distinct advantage that its operating system is superior to DOS," Eilers said, according to people familiar with the meeting. "And the best way to make that a standard would be to put it on the Intel platform."

As Eilers displayed slide after slide on an overhead projector to support his argument, Gassée's face reddened and his eyes bulged. He was upset and could contain himself no more. In his thick French accent, he began yelling and screaming that licensing could not be done, according to those familiar with the episode. The scheme was flawed for two reasons, Gassée asserted: One, he did not believe it was even technically feasible for the Mac to run on anything other than an Apple computer, because it was so closely intertwined with Motorola's microchip. Furthermore, Gassée argued, opening the Mac to the outside world would give competitors a license to steal sales away from Apple itself.

Gassée did have a point. Rejiggering the Mac to run on an Intel machine would have been a tall order. The basic problem was that the Mac had always been designed to tie together the software of a machine with its hardware innards. Microsoft's MS-DOS, on the other hand, was designed primarily to tie into the Intel chip. Practically everything else needed for the computer, such as keyboards and disk drives, could be found at the nearest components junk lot and then plugged in to support the MS-DOS/Intel standard. But the Mac's software and hardware were virtually inseparable. Take away the software, and the distinctive look and feel are lost as well. Take away the hardware, and the Mac doesn't run as smoothly. That's why the Mac not only was far easier to use than a Microsoft-run computer but ran much more smoothly as well.

One possibility would have been to get manufacturers to use the Macintosh technology as is, just as Bill Gates had recommended. Another would have been just to slap the top layer of the Mac's operating system on top of, say, MS-DOS, and let users get a taste of the Mac. The machine would not run as seamlessly as a Mac, because the hardware was not tied in to the software as closely. But it would at least offer users the appealing look of the Mac, with its graphical icons. That was not only a possibility; it was already being done by Digital Research.

Digital Research had been founded by a software entrepreneur named Gary Kildall, whose operating system, CP/M (Control Program for Microcomputers), had been an early rival of MS-DOS. The success of MS-DOS eventually killed off CP/M. By 1985, another former Xerox PARCer named Lee Lorenzen had successfully copied the look of the Macintosh so that it could run on top of MS-DOS with Digital Research's GEM software. GEM was essentially designed to run a graphical user interface of any kind, no matter which. If Windows was taking off, Lorenzen could retool GEM to look like Windows. Since the Macintosh was the best of the GUI bunch, he designed it to look like the Mac—actually, to "look and feel" like a Mac. It looked like a Mac, down to containing the same trash can icon for discarding unwanted files. And it felt like a Mac, with the same ability to use the mouse to move objects around on the screen. Those three words, "look and feel," would become the focus of an industrywide debate over software copyright protection.

At the time, Lorenzen remembers, IBM was negotiating with Digital Research to license GEM for use on all its MS-DOS-based machines. That's when the Apple lawyers showed up at Digital's door in Pacific Grove, a village set in an idyllic setting of pine trees and crashing ocean waves on California's Monterey Peninsula. They pointed out, in no uncertain terms, that Digital was illegally copying Apple's technology. Digital had thought it was in the clear by borrowing just the Mac's look, not the actual technology. But software copyright law was still a very murky area, and IBM, for one, wanted no part of any litigation. "IBM was ready to acquire GEM, but Apple showed up and threatened suit," recalls Lorenzen, who is now CEO of a small software developer, Altura Software Inc. "IBM chickened out." And that was the end of GEM. Apple stopped this particular threat in its tracks, but it missed another opportunity. It could just as easily have acquired the GEM technology itself, to proliferate the Mac's look all over the place.

Years later, Apple would attempt what Digital had done, and the results would hold the potential for breathtaking implications across the whole industry.

Gassée was also correct in worrying that Apple would cannibalize its sales by opening itself to voracious competition from cloners, many of whom would consist of two guys and a screwdriver in a garage, who could seriously undercut the mother ship on price. Indeed, an all-out licensing plan would have required a fundamental change in Apple's whole business model. Gassée's biggest fear was that the company would have to undergo wrenching layoffs, perhaps on the order of half the workforce. And he had good reason to be afraid.

Apple was pulling in about $2 billion a year in revenues by selling roughly 700,000 computers at $3,000 each. If Apple were to license its Mac software to all 4 million of the Intel computers being sold per year at a premium rate of about $100 each, that would bring in about $400 million in sales. Assuming that sales of Apple computers would fall by half, as Gassée feared, Apple would shrink to a $1.4 billion company almost overnight. Bill Gates believes, however, that Apple could have structured its licensing in such a way as to protect itself. "They wouldn't have had to open it wide open," Gates says. "Let's just say they licensed H-P, or just AT&T or somebody in Europe, you know, like Olivetti, or somebody in Japan, like Sony or whoever. It would have made all the difference. Momentum creates momentum. If you have volume, then people write apps [applications]. If people write apps, you get momentum."

In any case, no one ever said it would be easy. The end reward, as Eilers,

Gates, and the other licensing advocates all argued, was the creation of a standard that, in the end, would provide more profit to Apple than to anybody else because it held the keys to a kingdom. Both Microsoft and Intel proved that theory true. With combined revenues only slightly higher than Apple's by the mid-1990s, Microsoft and Intel became so profitable that together they would account for fully half the entire PC industry's profits—an amazing feat in a $100 billion industry with thousands of competitors.

The great minds in the Small Room, however, were lost in small thought that day, far more concerned with the here and now than anything that *might* happen down the road. Gassée had done most of the arguing against Eilers's plan while the other executives sat and listened. It was clear Eilers had little support, because no one in the room, not even Sculley, rose to defend him. So when his presentation was over, Eilers simply scooped up his slides and papers and saw himself out. The licensing plan had died by lack of an endorsement. But this was not the end of the debate, not by a long shot.

It wasn't that Sculley didn't recognize the merits of licensing. After all, it was he who had put Eilers in charge of strategic investments to explore the possibilities of Apple forming various alliances. At Pepsi, he had learned the importance of forming strategic partnerships with outside companies, such as the legion of Pepsi bottlers. And he could certainly appreciate the significance of market share, since careers at Pepsi had been made or broken on as little as a tenth of a percentage point fluctuation between it and Coca-Cola. In point of fact, Sculley came to realize, the hostility directed at Eilers was really aimed at him.

"Dan was incredibly unpopular in engineering because they knew he was my agent," Sculley says. "Every time Dan would come in with an outside idea, not only would the idea be shot down, but he would be lucky to get out alive."

Sculley was having Eilers play around with some other wild ideas, such as Apple buying another company. Sculley had a gleam in his eye, especially, for Silicon Graphics and Sun Microsystems, small but thriving makers of big computer workstations, as well as Novell, a small company that was then pioneering a new form of software to link networks of computers together. Sculley saw great strategic opportunities in each of these companies, since all were focused on the big corporate market he wanted to crack. "But the engineers felt Apple didn't need anyone else," Sculley says. "Just because you had the title of anything did not mean they would do what you asked."

This attitude, which had originated in the Steve Jobs days, came to be known in Silicon Valley circles as "N.I.H.," or "Not Invented Here." If it wasn't invented at Apple, the smartest place in the universe, Apple's engineers wanted no part of it.

Unbeknown to many people in the company at the time, Sculley had also set up a strategic sales group to study, among other things, the possibility of putting the Mac's look and feel—the top layer of the software, which the user sees—on top of other computers, just as Digital Research had done. This was a less radical step than Eilers's plan to license the Mac technology with all its bells and whistles to clone manufacturers. Allowing others to use just the "look and feel" was more like an outpatient alternative to open-heart surgery on the Mac. It would not be necessary to ditch Motorola altogether. Using the Trojan Horse approach, the Mac interface could be sneaked into corporations on another company's computer. Once the workers saw for themselves how great it was, they would refuse to use anything else. Named to head that venture was Chuck Berger, an outdoorsman who loved to water-ski on northern California lakes. He and Eilers were kindred spirits and would become equally despised at Apple.

Berger, vice president of Apple's new strategic sales group, had been given the green light by Sculley to talk to as many manufacturers as he could about this particular scheme. Over a twelve-month period beginning in 1985, Berger and Sculley's former technical aide, Mike Homer, who was named to assist Berger, crisscrossed the United States, drumming up outside interest in the plan. There was more than enough to keep them hopping. Dr. An Wang, the founder of Wang Laboratories outside Boston, wanted to put the Mac software on top of his company's word processing machines. Digital Equipment, Wang's neighbor down the Massachusetts Turnpike in Maynard, planned to incorporate the Mac's look into a line of new desktop computers. AT&T was so interested in putting the Mac onto the company's Unix workstations that approvals had been made all the way up to Bob Allen, then AT&T's CEO. Silicon Graphics, which would go on to fame as creator of the digital special effects in 1990s movie blockbusters such as *Jurassic Park*, was also profoundly interested.

"All of these had either a handshake agreement or letters of intent," says an industry executive intimately familiar with the discussions. "John and Chuck flew to AT&T twice and had them in the bag."

Sculley, however, would go on to reject all deals on the table. Gassée was yelling and screaming again, and Sculley just could not bear to hear it. Like Eilers, Berger was left to fall on his own sword. As of late 1985, Sculley was on track with a plan that would inflate Apple's profit margins above 50 percent on forthcoming sales of the souped-up Mac Plus. In a series of executive staff meetings at which Berger presented his case for licensing, Gassée railed against going through with anything that would rob those profits.

"He made a strong stand that it was stupid to give up fifty-five percent margins for what would be, at best, forty-five percent margins," says an executive close to all the discussions. "Jean-Louis said there would not be enough money left to fund the 'insanely great' technology and that the engineers would probably leave." Berger argued that it was clear that closed, or "proprietary," standards did not work. The best example of that, he said, was Sony's failure in the early eighties to set a standard in the videocassette recording industry with its Betamax machine. While Betamax was widely regarded as technically superior to the rival VHS machines, VHS was an open standard that other manufacturers could copy. Since Betamax was not, VHS went on to take over the VCR market.

Berger, in one of the meetings, also said, "Eventually someone will catch up with the [Mac's] GUI." Rolling his eyes in disgust, Gassée snapped back, "No one will *ever* catch up to the GUI." Gassée could not have been more blind if he had had a blindfold on.

Gassée may have been the most outspoken person at Apple against licensing, but he was certainly not alone. Indeed, when looking back on it all, Sculley says he is not so sure the board itself would have backed any kind of licensing scheme, even if he had pursued it full tilt. "Remember, at the time the board was interested in one thing: gross margin," he said to me in our first of several discussions for this book, sipping from a cup of black coffee as he mused on the situation a decade later in his lawyer's office in Palo Alto, California. By gross margin, Sculley was referring to the gross profit margin, measured as a percentage of sales, which serves as a key barometer of a manufacturer's profitability. "The engineers wanted innovation. You had to fuel the innovation and manage the profits. So you had to stay within this envelope."

Others in the industry empathize with Sculley's situation, given the time and circumstances. "There was no question they should have licensed the software. It was leadership technology in the marketplace," says retired IBM president Jack Kuehler. "[But] it would have required an unusual person to do that early on. And you would never know if it was the right thing to do, because detractors would shoot you down. If it had not worked out according to plan, it probably would have cost Sculley his job."

Even Gassée, shockingly enough, now admits he was flat-out wrong. "I am aware that I am known as the Great Satan on licensing," he says. "My mistake was, I got into a debate that I should not have gotten into. I thought, financially, it didn't make sense. I was never for or against licensing. I just did not see how it would make sense. But my approach was stupid. We were just fat cats living off a business that had no competition."

Just as Gassée was vowing to Berger that no one would overtake Apple's lead, Gates was hard at work on Windows 1.0, the prototype of a successor to MS-DOS that would grow to envelop the planet. Gates badly wanted it to have the same look as the Mac and already planned to include some Mac-like features in the graphics, including Mac-like control panels and Mac-like pull-down menus. Actually, Gates was also influenced in this approach by the graphical user interface work at Xerox PARC, as well as other early implementations of the technology such as VisiOn. But it was the Mac that became the first commercially successful version of this concept and the one he most wanted to emulate.

This incensed Sculley, who began contemplating a lawsuit. One day in the fall of 1985, an Apple lawyer named Jack Brown showed up on Microsoft's doorstep. It was a scene reminiscent of the one at Digital Research a few months earlier. Only this time Apple was not dealing with a pushover. "He [Brown] came in and made incredible threats about patents, copyrights, and trade secrets," Gates remembers, indignation still rising in his voice years later. "And he said he is a lawyer who has never lost a trade secret lawsuit. And we said, 'But Apple's being very careful not to give us any of their trade secrets.' Everything Apple gave us, Apple was being very careful about because Apple knew exactly what we were doing. We didn't need a license at all, in any way, and that is very clear."

Gates was hopping mad. He had not stolen anything from Apple, he insisted then and continues to insist now. The whole idea of GUIs had originated not with Apple, he points out, but with Xerox. "The father of the Mac is Xerox. The father of Windows is Xerox," Gates says. Charles Simonyi, Microsoft's in-house GUI maestro, compares the similarities between Windows and the Macintosh to those found in different automobile models. "When you decide to build an automobile, you're not going to change the steering wheel," Simonyi says. "They all have common ancestry. This was such a silly and pointless argument that they were falling into."

After Jack Brown's threats, Gates and Bill Neukom, Microsoft's chief counsel, arranged to fly down to Cupertino to meet with Sculley and his top legal gun, Al Eisenstat. In a phone conversation beforehand, Gates, according to Sculley, put a gun to his head. "If we're on a collision course, I want to know it because we'll stop all development on Mac products," Gates told Sculley. "I hope we can find a way to settle this thing. The Mac is important to us and to our sales."[6] Gates denies ever making that threat, calling Sculley's statement "the most unfair characterization of anything I've ever heard."

Physically, Gates was hardly an imposing figure. Tall and thin, his hair was often tousled in those days, and, with his big glasses, he appeared to be little more than a teenager. But when it came to business, Gates was a Muhammad Ali, the dude you didn't want to mess with. And he most certainly would have had the gumption to carry out his threat, if in fact he made it. It was true that he needed Apple, but Apple needed him a lot more. At that time, Gates was rolling out Microsoft Excel, the spreadsheet program that would significantly increase the appeal of the Mac to business customers. The original Mac had no numeric keys to run a spreadsheet, much less the memory to do so. The forthcoming Mac Plus would. Along with other programs, including BASIC and Multiplan, Gates controlled roughly two thirds of all the software then available on the Mac. This was no guy to shove around.

Before Gates arrived for the meeting in the De Anza 4 boardroom on October 24, 1985, Sculley's executive staff pleaded with him not to cave in. But, mindful of Gates's power, Sculley was convinced that a war between Apple and Microsoft would seriously disrupt the company's resurgent momentum, stripping the Mac of its most important software ally at a critical juncture. In their meeting in Apple's boardroom, where Gates remembers enough sushi being brought in "for fifty people," he and Sculley haggled.

"I went to Sculley, and I said, 'We don't need a license. Steve [Jobs] and I talked explicitly about us doing graphical applications. You've seen Windows every step of the way,'" Gates remembers. "Sculley said, 'I understand what you're saying, but isn't there some concession you can make to us?' I said, 'OK, we'll do Excel first on the Mac and have a period of exclusivity.' And Sculley said, 'Well, what's going to happen if you don't perform on that?' And I said, 'Why don't you give us a license so this dispute doesn't come up again?'"

So Sculley instructed Eisenstat's legal team to draw up a contract allowing Microsoft to license the look and feel of the Mac — or "visual displays," as they were referred to in legal terms — but only in Windows 1.0. Gates and Neukom, however, refused to sign that agreement, believing Microsoft had the right to use those visual displays in its Macintosh applications as well as other present and future products. Neukom drafted a revised three-page contract and sent it to Eisenstat on November 14. Eisenstat shrugged and made a few minor changes, sending it on to Gates and Sculley, who signed it on November 22. With this contract, Apple thus agreed that Gates was free to come up with his own take on the graphical technology that had originated with Xerox, from which Microsoft had already obtained a license to certain GUI technology. "We were buying peace with Microsoft," Eisenstat recalls.

But Gates got an unexpected bonanza, after he successfully pushed Eisenstat to modify that agreement, in a way that would grant Microsoft a de facto license to copy the Mac at will. A phrase in the three-page contract, written by Microsoft, granted to Microsoft "a non-exclusive, worldwide, royalty-free, perpetual, nontransferable license to use these derivative works in present and future software programs, and to license them to and through third parties for use in their software programs." By agreeing to include the phrase "in present and future software programs," Apple had unwittingly given Gates carte blanche to use virtually any visual features borrowed from the Mac in Windows 1.0 and all future versions. The courts, in fact, in a case that would carry mammoth implications for the entire computer industry, would later interpret the phrase "in present and future software programs" to mean all Windows versions deriving from the one at issue in this agreement.

Sculley and Eisenstat had just given away the store. "If I knew then what I know now," says Eisenstat, sighing deeply as he recounts the blunder a decade later, "I would have said, 'Don't do it.' " Gassée and the other members of the executive staff had not wanted Sculley to give in to Gates in any way, much less by granting a license.

Gates himself downplays the significance of the licensing agreement, saying he had the right to pursue Windows anyway. What could have derailed Windows, Gates believes, is if Apple had followed the advice from him and Jeff Raikes to license the Mac widely. If the Mac had become the standard, Gates says, "We would have sold less Windows. But the key thing is, we could have sold more applications."

The matter of Apple cloning its beloved Macintosh had been shelved for now. Sculley was too busy tending to details of the turnaround to pay the subject more than passing attention. And as the first few years went by, it appeared that keeping the Mac in-house wasn't so dumb, after all. The industry slump of 1985 had decimated many PC manufacturers and crimped IBM's performance as well. Gassée and his engineers would point merrily to IBM and say, "Thank God we didn't listen to Eilers and Berger." IBM, however, was not exactly a textbook case on how to license. It had given up control of its computer when it had turned over the operating system to Microsoft and the microprocessor to Intel. The fortunes of Apple, in any event, had never looked brighter. So the timing could hardly have been worse when Berger presented his next case for licensing in 1987.

This time, Berger, whose strategic sales group had been renamed "business development," steered away from using the "L" word. He rejoined with his old colleague Mike Homer to explore the possibility of putting the Mac's software onto just a workstation, a much bigger version of the PC that was used heavily in data-intensive jobs such as engineering. Sculley saw great merits in putting the Mac onto a workstation. One of Apple's problems in landing big corporate accounts was that its computers did not "scale," or run the spectrum from bare-bones secretaries' desktops all the way up to a high-performance workstation that a rocket scientist could use. A big reason IBM's computers had become so popular in corporate America was that its computers did scale: all needed equipment could be bought from the same company, simplifying employee training and technical support. Apple had the desktops covered, all right, but it didn't have diddly for anything more powerful.

That's where a Mac workstation would enter the picture: If Apple were to put its software onto workstations manufactured by other companies, it might not be an Apple computer these corporations would be buying, but it would walk and talk like a Mac. That would make it a lot easier for a chief technology officer to recommend outfitting the whole corporation with Macintoshes, since the workers could all be trained the same. "John thought it would be a great marriage between us and a low-end workstation," says an executive familiar with the situation. Unlike the previous broad-scale licensing effort, though, Sculley wanted this deal limited to just one outside company. Berger's natural inclination was to approach Sun Microsystems first, since that company was right around the corner in Mountain View, California, and in the past had negotiated with Apple in a buyout deal.

Sun, which specialized in workstations, was run by an amateur hockey player named Scott McNealy. With his boyish face and mouthful of large teeth, McNealy resembled a large chipmunk when he smiled. Like most Silicon Valley executives, he hardly ever wore a suit. Even at big meetings with industry analysts, he would trot onstage in a uniform of pullover shirt and faded jeans. But McNealy was a tough, voracious competitor like Gates, a veritable pit bull whose company was starting to give fits to big rivals in the workstation market such as Hewlett-Packard and Digital. Scott McNealy was an up-and-comer, and, sure, he wouldn't mind getting into bed with Apple if he could come out ahead.

But McNealy's ego got into the way. He was insistent, for one thing, that any Mac/Sun computer use his company's new chip, called SPARC. This was a major stumbling block, because Apple had already decided to remain joined at the hip with Motorola. Sculley and McNealy also discussed, again, the possibility of Apple buying Sun and combining Sun's workstation line with Apple's Macintosh line. McNealy, though, insisted he be named president and chief operating officer of the combined companies, according to an individual involved with those talks. That would necessitate the demotion of Del Yocam, however, and Sculley wasn't yet in a mood to emasculate the guy who had stood up with him in the confrontation with Jobs.

Things were getting nowhere, so Berger and Homer packed their bags and headed east in the spring of 1986 to Boston, where they found a friendlier audience in the executive suite of Apollo Computer, a rival workstation maker based in suburban Chelmsford that, in fact, was still leading the market for workstations at the time. One reason Apollo was receptive was that its business was heading south, even as Sun's was on the way up. Apollo's executives were also concerned about the potential threat of personal computers becoming powerful enough to encroach into the low end of the workstation market, and Sun was also moving into that market fast. Apollo had just introduced the low-end DN 3000 for $10,000 in a bid to shore up that part of the market from attack when Apple came calling.

"We wanted to go down to five thousand dollars, but to get that far down we needed a cheaper architecture and a cheaper operating system," recalls Cheryl Vedoe, who was then manager of Apollo's low-end marketing. And that was where Apple could help. The two companies actually had a lot in common. Apollo, with its Domain operating system, was considered technically superior to its competition, just as Apple was with its Mac. And both Apollo and Apple maintained proprietary, or closed, systems that were not licensed to others.

Sun, however, had an open system that it licensed to others. In fact, Sun's very openness was the secret of its success. Founded in 1982 by Stanford graduate students McNealy, Andy Bechtolsheim, and Vinod Khosal, along with a man named Bill Joy from the University of California at Berkeley, Sun virtually gave away its software while letting other companies help manufacture its SPARC chip.[7] This unleashed a licensing fury that overwhelmed workstation competitors such as Apollo, with their closed systems. McNealy, who ran Sun, gained a reputation as a butt kicker, because he kicked the butt not only of the competition but of employees to keep costs down while producing more.

So, in April 1986, Apple and Apollo sat down to talk. There were Chuck Berger and Mike Homer on one side of the table, representing Apple. On the other side were Cheryl Vedoe and Ed Zander, Apollo's vice president of marketing. At the time, Apple was developing the Macintosh II, which was going to be twice as fast as and far more powerful than the Macintosh Plus. At a retail price of up to $5,500, it was a high-end machine for Apple but ideal, Vedoe and Zander thought, to put onto the low end of the Apollo line. The idea, according to Vedoe and Homer, was for Apollo to buy the Macintosh II and repackage it as an Apollo workstation, with minor adjustments such as melding it with Apollo's Domain operating system. Over the next ten months, Apple and Apollo worked together to make prototypes of Apollo Macs. In all, remembers Homer, Apollo planned to buy forty thousand Macintosh IIs over a two-year period for the initial stage of the cloning project.

All was going well, or so thought nearly everyone associated with the project, which was kept hush-hush. Near the end, the Apple bigwigs got in on the act as Chief Operating Officer Del Yocam accompanied Sculley on a trip to Apollo. "When we were in Boston, we toured the facility and went into the lab to see the Mac OS running on Apollo boxes," Yocam recalls. "I remember leaving there thinking, 'Everything is positive.' "

In January 1987, Apollo's chief financial officer, Roland Pampel, signed an agreement to license the Mac IIs from Apple. Back in Cupertino, Berger and Homer put together a presentation for the executive staff at which they fully expected Sculley to give the deal the thumbs-up. "Apollo was there. It had licensed the Mac," recalls Homer, who is now senior vice president of marketing for Netscape Communications, the early leader in the Internet software market that erupted in the mid-1990s. "That would have been the first of many such deals."

The contract was in Sculley's hands. Excited about the new opportunity that lay ahead, Vedoe and an Apollo attorney went to Boston's Logan International Airport to catch a flight out west to finalize the deal. It would be a glorious day, or so they thought. That same morning, in Cupertino, Sculley was presiding over his regular executive staff meeting. With the contract in front of him and Berger and Homer waiting anxiously for a signature, Sculley pushed it to one side and shook his head. "He said he had decided not to do the deal because Apollo was a declining star and Sun was a rising star," says an executive intimately familiar with the meeting. When they got over their shock, Berger and Homer looked at each other and dashed out of the conference room to the phones. They had Vedoe paged at the Boston airport and stopped her and the attorney from boarding just as their plane was about to take off.

"We were in the boarding area when Mike Homer paged us," Vedoe recalls. "He said, 'Don't get on the airplane. We need to talk about it.' It did come as a shock." Actually, there was nothing to talk about, except that the whole deal was *finis*.

The ironic thing was Gassée, the Great Satan of licensing, had nothing to do with killing this deal. This was just Sculley, acting on a whim. He ended up like the dog that lost its bone by trying to snatch the reflection it saw in the water. After that, Sun expressed no more interest than before, quashing any hope of a deal there. Apple was again alone, just as it had always been. For poor Apollo, meanwhile, this was the beginning of the end. Having devoted much of its time and resources to getting out the new Apollo Mac, the company was left so far behind in the development of its own Apollo systems that it could not catch up when Sun moved in with its new low-end workstations. Apollo hemorrhaged more market share and was soon acquired by Hewlett-Packard. Both Vedoe and Zander packed up and joined Sun.

Okay, forget licensing, Berger thought. With IBM-compatible computers proliferating like rabbits throughout the corporate world, could Apple at least do something to make the Mac fit in with all the others? As early as 1985, in the Macintosh office, the Macs had been rigged so that they could communicate with one another over the AppleTalk phone lines. But if you were a Mac person in an IBM office, you were on your own. "Everyplace we went, people were telling us, 'We love the Mac, but we can't even consider them unless you can hook into the networks of IBM computers,' " Berger later confided to a colleague. So Berger came up with a plan to help remedy that: put some extra software into the Mac so it could act like MS-DOS software and tap into the whole IBM network.

It was now almost 1988, and there was a clear trend in corporations to decentralize away from the huge, $1 million mainframe computers that had dominated the workplace in the past. In their place, corporations were deploying fleets of cheaper, sub-$5,000 desktop computers that could all be interconnected via smaller in-house networks. These new networks gave much more flexibility to employees and their managers, allowing files to be swapped and changed at will. The network was the way of the future, and it was time for Apple to get on board.

With Sculley's blessing, Berger got outside contractors to design and make these so-called IBM emulators. When an operating system emulates something, it looks and acts like another system. It doesn't run as fast as the system it is emulating, though, because it has to take extra time to translate that system's code. Companies such as Du Pont and Aetna expressed great interest in the Apple equipment and even started putting in large orders. The corporate appeal: office employees would be able to work on an easier-to-use Mac while still being hooked in to the rest of the IBM network. Gassée, however, didn't like this plan one bit. Just as he had dismissed the importance of licensing, Gassée never saw the need for Apple's computers to communicate with anything except other Apple computers. This philosophy had been demonstrated early on, in 1985, when he had addressed an Apple sales meeting in Hawaii and someone had had the audacity to ask what Apple's strategy would be in communicating with IBM-compatibles.

"Gassée stood up in front of the audience and held up a cutoff piece of a telephone wire and said, 'This is our communications strategy,' " recalls John Ziel, a sales manager in the Portland district who was in the auditorium. In other words, if you need to communicate with your IBM coworker, dial him or her through your computer modem. This was a terrible strategy, of course, because it did not seamlessly link Macintoshes with IBM-compatibles. "We looked at Gassée and said, 'Who is this guy?' "

Gassée elaborated on this novel concept in an encounter that same year with Peter Hirshberg, who was in charge of a fledgling program to develop networking and communications products. Hirshberg's group had already committed to a bunch of so-called connectivity products for corporate customers when Gassée sent word down that he was canceling them. Stunned, Hirshberg requested an explanation, and Gassée invited him to meet for lunch at Vivi's, a popular falafel eatery in Cupertino.

Over their falafels, Gassée repeated his telephone strategy. "He said, 'You must convince your customers that all they need is a simple telephone line,' " Hirshberg recalls. When asked, pray tell, how do you do that?, Gassée smiled slyly and leaned forward to say, "Public relations. You must use public relations, not advertising." Whenever Gassée wanted to drive home a point, he would slip into a French accent even more pronounced than usual. This is when he explained to Hirshberg the difference between public relations and advertising.

"With advertising, I, Jean-Louis, say, 'I am the most wonderful lover in the world.' Of course, this would not work in attracting the woman." By now, Hirshberg had momentarily forgotten the networking argument and listened in fascination. "But if two of the most beautiful women in the world say they spent the evening with Jean-Louis, this would work. *This* is the difference between advertising and public relations."

Three years later, though, Gassée was in no mood to use sexual analogies in attacking Berger's latest scheme. Headquarters had by now moved to De Anza 7, and he was still telling Sculley and everyone else who would listen that putting Mac/IBM machines into corporations would be tantamount to "another Vietnam War." "He said Apple could never win in this battle because IBM would keep changing the rules," says an executive who heard the discussions. Berger would counter by saying, "We can never sell a computer in big business unless we can hook into a business computer."

The tensions boiled over at a third-floor conference room in De Anza 7 during early 1988. Before approximately one hundred people in the room, including Sculley and the entire executive staff, Gassée and Berger almost came to blows. "Jean-Louis was trying to make everyone believe we should return the engineers to engineering," recalls an executive in that meeting. "Chuck began screaming and yelling at Gassée. At one point, he jumped up out of his chair and slammed his notebook on the table so hard it broke the back of it." As usual, Gassée prevailed. The IBM emulators were tossed out. By this point, Berger had had his fill of Gassée and Apple. He quit soon after to sign up with Sun and the McNealy butt kickers. Maybe there, he could get something done.

Jean-Louis Gassée had won nearly every fight. He was the undisputed master of engineering, the person who had almost always gotten his way. Now he would put another indelible stamp on Apple, one that would have repercussions as grave as the decision not to license. He wanted to keep those profit margins up—way up—and if that meant sacrificing market share, so be it. Sculley and the board could hardly have cared less at this point, since profits, revenues, and the stock price were all soaring to new heights. The gravy train was still chugging happily along, and John Sculley was still the apple of everyone's eye.

4

A "Noble Village"

When Apple was riding high in 1987, John Sculley was inundated with so many interview requests from the media that his staff could barely keep up with them all. Almost anything he did was big news, carrying a portent for the rest of the computer industry and, by implication, the whole world. But two of his personnel actions that year received scant attention in the press, even though they were the harbingers of a troubling new era.

One press release, issued in April, concerned the appointment of a man named Kevin Sullivan as Apple's new vice president for human resources. Sullivan, then forty-six years old, had worked the prior seven years in a variety of capacities at Digital Equipment Corporation, including most recently as that company's corporate personnel manager. The hiring, nevertheless, was considered so mundane that *The Wall Street Journal* didn't even mention it. The other, issued in June, revealed that one Allan Loren had been named an Apple vice president in charge of information systems and technology. Loren, then forty-nine years old, had previously served as president of Cigna Systems, the computer arm of insurance giant Cigna Corporation, for sixteen years. That news merited a passing, three-sentence mention in the *Journal*'s "Who's News" column.

Through the whole turnaround led by Sculley between 1985 and 1987, Apple had been so busy pulling itself back from the brink of financial catastrophe that the top executives had had little time to squabble with one another, aside from the intermittent screaming matches over licensing. It really was one team, with most of the managers pulling together and watching with almost parental pride as their hard-laboring employees yielded spectacular results. And though they all had their failings, most of the executives shared the common ground of having been on the Sculley express from the start. It was a family, almost—if a dysfunctional one.

In describing the Apple he viewed in those days, Sculley wrote in his book *Odyssey:* "We are, as Thoreau so eloquently said, not noblemen, but a noble village of men and women. We're trying to build a model corporation for the future. Not a company for the rational world I left—a world too consumed with power and competition, a world that rewarded people for building corporate empires, not beauty."[1]

If only Sculley could have left well enough alone. Granted, his managers had proven themselves when he had needed them most. But by now Sculley was living more and more in the future, and he foresaw, five years down the road, an Apple selling more than $5 billion worth of computers per year. In fact, he startled securities analysts when he made that bold proclamation at a meeting with them in early 1987. They thought he was out of his mind, since Apple was only then on the verge of topping $2 billion in annual sales for the first time. "I'm used to living out on the limb," Sculley said at the time.[2] Sculley was prescient on a lot of things, and he would prove himself correct on this score as well. Sculley was counting on the growing popularity of the Macintosh line to fuel that growth, allowing Apple to pump more money into research and development so it could keep spewing out new products. To handle that much growth, though, Sculley decided that Apple needed to start recruiting the kind of talent he thought was needed to run a company that big.

In other words, it was time to bring in the "suits."

To this point, Apple had been a fairly informal place. Sculley maintained an open-door policy that encouraged just about anybody to waltz into his office and drop a suggestion or two. Sculley's staff also made sure to pencil in "walking-around" time for the boss, so he could spend an hour or two each day just roaming the campus and chatting with the grunts. Things were about to change.

That year, Sculley reshuffled the executive ranks in sweeping fashion. Some of the changes were not a great surprise. Jean-Louis Gassée, for example, saw his engineering empire expanded to include all control over product marketing as well. Debi Coleman, Apple's highest-ranking woman, was promoted from head of worldwide manufacturing to chief financial officer as a reward for her good work in holding manufacturing operations together during the sales boom. The previous CFO, Dave Barram, was named Apple's vice president of corporate affairs.

Coleman, who held a master's degree from Stanford, had started her climb up the Apple ladder as controller of Steve Jobs's Macintosh division. When Jobs promoted her to run a new factory for the Macintoshes, she was ecstatic: she had grown up watching her father work in his machine-tool shop in Rhode Island and had gone on in adulthood to become a production supervisor at Texas Instruments and a member of the manufacturing manager's staff at Hewlett-Packard, before joining Apple in 1981.[3] Blessed with a booming voice that could carry above the clatter of an assembly line, she had manufacturing in her blood, as she demonstrated by skillfully overseeing Apple's global production after her promotion by Sculley in 1985.

Then came the suits. Among the first to arrive was Chuck Boesenberg, a sales and marketing veteran from Data General and IBM. He was named senior vice president in charge of Apple's U.S. sales division, replacing Bill "Coach" Campbell, who, despite his strong competence and popularity with customers and employees, was shunted aside to run a new software arm of Apple called Claris. "Bill was so charismatic he would get up and cry before his salesmen," recalls Peter Hirshberg, a manager then.

Campbell, who was thirty-eight years old at the time, had been wooed relentlessly to join Apple in 1983 because he possessed a broad background in the kind of consumer marketing that Sculley wanted to start using to sell computers. Campbell finally acquiesced, leaving his position as Eastman Kodak's vice president for marketing to lend his consumer marketing skills to Apple. It had been Campbell who had pushed for Apple to air the "1984" ad during Super Bowl XVIII after members of the Apple board had expressed misgivings about it. But Campbell's downfall, many people at Apple believed, was his keen orientation on sales to consumers at a time when Sculley had become obsessed with the business market. It was also attributable, they felt, to what Apple workers called Sculley's fickle, "all-star" mentality. One minute, you were a star like Campbell. The next, you were out, replaced by the next rising star.

A short time later, Sculley brought in Sullivan to fill a vacancy in human relations. Like Sculley, he was a dyed-in-the-wool easterner, a graduate of prestigious universities in New York and Connecticut. As Sculley would soon learn, Sullivan was also a corporate political operator of the first order whose power at Apple would far surpass that of his actual job. But in *Odyssey*, which was published in 1987, Sculley described Sullivan glowingly, saying he had been brought in "to help nurture our genetic code."

Sullivan was not outwardly impressive. A dour, bespectacled man who almost always wore the same outfit of khaki pants and baby-blue shirt, he was so visibly insecure that he gave colleagues the impression of a cornered rabbit. "Kevin always looked like a little boy with his lunch box," says one former executive aide. "He never looked like he had control of anything. Whenever he got nervous, he'd start coughing. Then he would sneak a cigarette from one of the girls. If his wife knew he was smoking, she'd have a fit."

For a person charged with fostering human relations, Sullivan went out of his way to hinder them. "To employees, he was short and brief," says a former aide, who did not want to be named. "I would tell him why someone was coming in to see him. And I'd say, 'Be nice, Kevin. This person is nervous.' He'd snap, 'Well, then, they shouldn't come in.'" That lack of personal warmth extended to his own staff. Executive aides who tried to engage in idle chitchat with the man say they invariably ended up listening to a monologue about himself. His own secretary does not recall him once mentioning the names of her children in the seven years she worked for him at Apple.

During one later episode, during the 1990s, Sullivan was traveling in Paris when an aide called from Cupertino to inform him that one of his top managers, Lee Kern, had lost a son in a plane crash in the Himalayas, according to an employee with firsthand knowledge of the encounter. All aboard had perished, and the wreckage lay strewn across a remote mountainside. "The aide said, 'Can the company pick up his airfare? He wants to look for his son's remains,' " the employee says. "I cannot believe to this day that Kevin said no."

Sullivan calls that account "a lie. It never happened." He agrees he was in Europe upon being notified of the tragedy but says he went out of his way to express condolences for Kern's loss, such as in a thirty-minute phone call to him and a follow-up letter. "I really took care of a lot of people," Sullivan says, also disputing that he was cold to anyone. "I basically told the truth. That's what people basically were pissed off at me about."

Sullivan's brusque style was felt throughout the corporation. In most companies, the primary role of the HR department is to ensure that salaries and benefits are equitable and that the hiring process is fair. Under Sullivan, however, Apple's HR gained control over virtually all matters related to compensation, including the old system of managers being able to use extra money out of their own budgets to reward an outstanding employee. It had been an informal system and one that did need more management control as Apple grew into a big corporation. A big-business guy from his years at Digital, Kevin Sullivan was quick to take charge of the purse strings.

"In the old days, I could take people to dinner or give them a thousand-dollar boat out of my own budget as a reward for performance," says Kirby Coryell, then a manager in service and engineering. "When Kevin came in, he made it incredibly bureaucratic. The reward system was shut off. It became 'working for a big company.' " Coryell soon encountered more evidence of the Sullivan bureaucracy, which included what former managers describe as "touchy-feely" meetings on management style and philosophy. In fact, not to attend one of these meetings was considered grounds for reprimand, as Coryell found when he was roundly scolded by one of Sullivan's underlings after failing to show for an HR meeting in Ireland. The reason: Coryell had had to be in Japan that same day, closing a $175 million computer deal with Xerox. "You didn't get rewarded for taking risks," he says. "You got punished."

Sullivan says the bonus system was so lax before he arrived that Apple "was on the verge of IRS problems" because managers were giving out petty cash without proper accounting for it. And Sullivan says he did not act alone in tightening the grip on the way bonuses were doled out. "I was directed by the board," he maintains.

Morale would take another drubbing with the recruitment of Allan Loren to the position of vice president for information systems and technology. That group was essentially in charge of Apple's in-house network of computers. A native New Yorker, Loren had been running the information services business of Cigna, the Philadelphia-based insurance company. This was a guy who decided what kind of computers big corporate customers would buy. And since Sculley had made landing these corporate accounts his highest priority, Loren was precisely the kind of person he wanted in his corner. In naming Loren to run Apple's information services business, his charter, as Sculley wrote in *Odyssey*, was to "make us a model company for personal productivity with computers."

Loren was a big man, with big ambitions. Standing at about six feet and tipping the scales at more than 200 pounds, the curly haired Loren was an imposing figure with an imposing personality. An ardent sports fan, favoring teams such as hockey's Philadelphia Flyers and basketball's Chicago Bulls, Loren used sports analogies to drive home a point and even punctuated his sentences with some of the same profanity so often used by coaches. "It's a forty-eight-minute game, and every single possession counts," Loren would say in comparing Apple's corporate strategy to that of a basketball game. Loren initially occupied a small-sized cubicle but soon commandeered a large vacant office on the fourth floor of De Anza 7 right next to Sculley's. The physical positioning of himself next to the CEO was seen by some colleagues as a calculated move by Loren to ingratiate himself with Sculley, although Loren himself remembers it as sheer coincidence. "That took a lot of balls," says Del Yocam, who was chief operating officer at the time.

An aide remembers suspecting that Loren would be a different breed of Apple executive when he made an unusual request as she arranged for him and his wife to fly out to California on a house-hunting trip. "He had this big black poodle that he wanted to bring out, and he insisted we get the airline to let him get out on a layover and check on the poodle," says the aide, who didn't want her name used. "He wanted to go out on the tarmac, go into the baggage area, and check on the poodle. I asked the airline and they said, 'No way.'" Loren, who now serves as chief information officer for American Express Company, recalls expressing that concern over his poodle, Denné (a French name pronounced "Den-*nay*") but does not consider his request so unusual.

"I was concerned because I was booked on a Philadelphia–to–San Francisco flight, with a layover in Saint Louis," recalls Loren in an interview for this book at an upscale restaurant in lower Manhattan. Upon being informed that he could not check up on Denné in Saint Louis, Loren says he had his flight rebooked on the nonstop route between New York and San Francisco.

Loren stood out in another way. When he landed in Cupertino, the management style at Apple was still fairly collegial. There were lively debates, to be sure, but people generally maintained a modicum of civility. Even Gassée, between tirades, was personable enough that he would stop at a secretary's desk and compliment her on her perfume. Coming from him, the secretaries did not consider that sexual harassment. Jean-Louis was just, well, Jean-Louis. Loren, on the other hand, had the gruff demeanor of a big-city beat cop. "When I first met him in a meeting, he had been there less than three weeks," recalls Bob Saltmarsh, the treasurer then. "Within thirty seconds of meeting the man, I said to a couple of other people, 'That is the most obnoxious, nastiest person I have ever met. This one is an asshole, a pushy New Yorker.' "

At Cigna, Loren had been known to rip up a subordinate's presentation — from top to bottom, before his or her eyes — if he did not like it. At Apple, he did the same thing in one meeting. Loren readily admits doing this but insists that ripping a presentation apart was his way of complimenting the presenter. "I don't keep files," Loren says. "Whenever they [files] were thrown away, that was good." In another meeting, Loren decided he had heard enough as manager Mike Homer plodded through a presentation. "He said, 'This was not the topic I wanted to hear discussed,' " recalls George Everhart, a former manager in the room that day. "He got up and walked out." Loren disputes that he ever did that.

There were other idiosyncrasies, too, such as Loren's insistence that his name be stated correctly. He made it clear, on more than one occasion, that he was not to be called "Al." It was Allan. And he also insisted that his surname be pronounced as *Lau*-ren," *not* "Lor-*en*." Consequently, Loren's managers learned to step so gingerly around the big guy that there were occasional awkward moments, such as the time he dozed off in front of his entire staff. "We had a huge staff meeting of his at which we had to make decisions for the next year," recalls Peter Hirshberg, a manager under Loren. "I presented the first two or three slides, and he was snoring. I went to the next slide and put my arm on his shoulder. I said, 'Only you can make this decision. It's either 'A' or 'B.' He looks up and says, 'B.' "

Al Eisenstat, a heavyset man with curly, graying hair and glasses, who in November 1985 was promoted to senior vice president as well as to the Apple board of directors from vice president, general counsel, and company secretary, shared the same habit of falling asleep on the job. Several former Apple managers say they were in meeting rooms when Eisenstat would just nod off. One former employee says he even fell asleep in the middle of giving dictation to a secretary.

So here was the new Apple lineup, as orchestrated by Sculley in 1987. And it made for a lively executive suite. There was Loren, lording it over underlings in his corner. To Sculley's admiration, Loren hung on his wall a shopping bag from the London department store Harrods, which was famous for the quality of its merchandise and its attentive customer service. Loren wanted everybody to know he thought Apple's customer service should be just as great. He was running computer systems, but he had his eye on a greater prize. And there was Sullivan in his own corner, eyes darting and nervously coughing in his office as he solidified a power base through his human resources domain.

Directly next door was Michael Spindler, presiding over Apple's burgeoning empire abroad. Known for a towering intellect but an inability to articulate well, he occasionally paused to spew his theories on global strategy at whichever poor sap happened to be breezing by. A large whiteboard near his desk was covered with nearly illegible scribbling. There was Gassée, the strutting cock of the walk, a half smile always on his thin lips as he raced between technical meetings to keep up with his engineering division. Eisenstat took notes at board meetings and managed the legal department, as well as rounding up tickets for San Francisco 49ers games and performing other errands for Sculley and the board. Some people in the executive suite suspected that Eisenstat was a spy for the board, since he was a member, so they kept their distance.

Debi Coleman sat in her office, punching the numbers to keep tabs on finance as she battled an ongoing weight problem, one that would contribute to her decision to leave the job to try to get it under control. In 1987, her power had reached its peak. At age thirty-four, she was the youngest CFO in the *Fortune* 200. But this accomplishment was overshadowed by her own admission that she weighed close to two hundred pounds at a height of five feet, six and one half inches.[4]

Keeping close track of them all, just under Sculley, was Del Yocam. A short, bespectacled man with salt-and-pepper hair and meticulously groomed beard, Yocam had been Apple's first professional manager when he signed on in 1979, leaving behind a job as a materials manager at Fairchild Camera and Instrument Corporation. Yocam was a southern California boy, with the love of water and sun that naturally resulted in his spending much of his free time tooling around on lakes in a speedboat. He was also a compulsive neat freak who would frown if he saw his office binders out of sync in their neat row, all with matching labels.

"If you moved a pencil on his desk, he would notice it," recalls one aide on his floor. On evenings when he had an armload of work to carry home, Yocam would ask one of the secretaries to accompany him downstairs with his expensive Hartmann briefcase. "He did not want it to sit on the garage floor, so I had to hold it until he could open up his car," says one who helped out. Another day, Yocam returned to the office, visibly distraught, after having walked the property of a new home in the mountains above the beachfront town of Santa

Cruz. "He had scuffed his shoes, and he wanted me to find a cobbler to take them and bring them back the same day," says the same secretary.

The son of highly disciplined Methodists, Del Yocam was just as fastidious in his work overseeing Apple's increasingly far-flung operations. Everywhere he went at Apple, he toted under his arm a big maroon engineer's notebook with green-lined pages, in which he jotted reminders to himself on anything and everything other managers had promised. "Del would say, 'Okay, Barbara. You're telling me you will do this by Thursday. Let me write that down,'" says Barbara Krause, who was then director of public relations.

Yocam's meticulous style made a lot of people nervous, but it was exactly what a company as frenetic as Apple needed. When he first arrived in Cupertino during 1979, Yocam recalls, Apple was in such a state of disarray that raw materials such as keyboards and monitors were heaped in big piles all over the place. Jobs's own office was a study in chaos, with disassembled computers strewn all over the floor. Yocam hired some temporary help to get the mess cleaned up and brought a giant whiteboard into his office to keep a running flowchart on the mechanics of the operation. On one side, he would jot down the sales forecast as estimated by the marketing group. On the other, he would track Apple's manufacturing response. If one side of the chart did not jibe with the other, Yocam would pick up the phone and start asking questions.

"I had to kick ass sometimes," Yocam says.

For about the first year after Sculley took Apple over from Jobs, Yocam and Gassée were left on equal footing. As executive vice president in charge of operations, Yocam ran the nuts and bolts of actually getting computers out to customers, while Gassée, then vice president for product development, oversaw the design and creation of new products. Their two personalities were so far apart, however, that they were like oil and water. Gassée was the flamboyant visionary, the new Steve Jobs. Yocam, on the other hand, didn't possess a strategic bone in his body. He was just a stickler for the boring but essential details. He was, in short, the classic operating guy. Which is why, in 1986, Sculley elevated him to chief operating officer, in charge of all company divisions. Not only had Gassée been bypassed, he was now reporting to his former equal. "That bent Gassée's nose quite a bit," recalls Bill Curley, than a midlevel manager in the information systems group.

Gassée was so busy pushing new Macs out the door that he didn't do much about this new turn in events until 1987, when he found new company in his distaste for Yocam's imperious style. By this time, Spindler, who was senior vice president for international sales and marketing, was spending more time in Cupertino, shuttling between the home office and his European base of operations in Paris. As chief operating officer, Yocam had nearly all the top executives, including Gassée and Spindler, reporting directly to him. Spindler made no secret of his contempt for the man, with whom he had to meet at least once a month. "Spindler said he hated coming over," recalls another former executive aide. "He would say, 'That Del doesn't have a brain in his head, and *I'm* coming over here.' "

According to this aide, Yocam further antagonized Spindler, Gassée, and some of the other top executives by the way he treated them. Bear in mind, these were no small egos. Both Gassée and Spindler saw themselves as among the great minds of the twentieth century. Yet, here was Del Yocam, standing out in the hall and clapping his hands to tell them when it was time to return to a meeting. It was almost as though they were back in grade school and Yocam was the sinister schoolmarm. "It got to the point that Spindler and Gassée would deliberately come in late just to upset him," says the former aide.

Kevin Sullivan kept his opinions pretty much to himself, but it soon became clear that he didn't care for Yocam either. Sullivan didn't make many close friends at Apple, but one was Spindler. Maybe it was because Sullivan was one of the few people who had the patience to endure Spindler's rambling monologues. Spindler, no doubt, also did not view Sullivan as a threat, since he was just the HR guy. Spindler did, however, harbor deep suspicions about his rivals in the executive suite. The Spindler-Sullivan relationship would only deepen over time, with enormous implications for Apple's future.

By late 1987, with Allan Loren now on board and on his own power trip, the knives were out and sharpened for Yocam. "Probably at an earlier time, you needed someone like that [Yocam] going around," Loren says. "But later on, when we had more professional management . . . I didn't think I needed someone to come around with a notebook." During the spring of 1988, Sullivan, Spindler, Gassée, and Loren attempted a mutiny. They pulled Sculley aside at a meeting in France, to which they had all traveled to visit Apple's bustling European operation and review the company's budget plan for the upcoming fiscal year 1989, beginning that October.

As Sullivan remembers, Yocam was bucking to become Apple's president, a title then held by Sculley in addition to his position as chairman and CEO, and was insisting in Paris that he drive the 1989 plan. "Del wanted to be president and had been promised by John that he would be president," Sullivan recalls in an interview for this book in a restaurant in San Francisco's Chinatown district. "Remember, there were big egos in that place at that time. Debi, Bill Campbell, Spindler, Sculley, Gassée, Yocam, Boesenberg. It was like a rock concert where everybody was scrambling for the microphone. They all wanted to run the place."

The tensions reached a boiling point in Paris when, according to Sullivan, Yocam unveiled a 1989 plan in which the projected revenues, expenses, and gross profit margins "didn't add up." Speaking for the others, Sullivan cornered Sculley. "I went to John and said, 'You've got a management team who won't work with this guy. You have to be more in control,'" Sullivan recalls. After that meeting, Sullivan brought Gassée, Spindler, and Loren in to vent their feelings to Sculley, at a hotel restaurant in Paris. Sullivan spoke for the group. "They wanted Del removed as COO. John turned them down," remembers a former top executive who witnessed the proceedings.

Sculley told Yocam about the meetings, chilling relations in the executive suite even more. "I required performance. That's what they hated," Yocam says. "They couldn't stand the fact that I would be right back at them." Several months later, in the summer of 1988, the Fearsome Foursome met with Sculley again. This time, they were insistent. Sculley was tanned and rested, having just returned from a nine-week vacation and sabbatical at a home in Maine, his first long break in the five years since he had moved out west. He had also designed a new barn for the sprawling horse ranch where he and his wife, Leezy, lived in the foothills near Cupertino. He had tooled around on a scooter, ridden out on the water in his Boston Whaler, and in general kicked back for a change.[5] Back in the office, seeing Sullivan and crew headed his way jolted him back to reality. "They came back and said, 'We won't work with him,' and they threatened to leave," says the former top executive. "So John decided he had no choice but to move Del out."

Yocam was stunned by the decision in August 1988, especially coming from Sculley. After all, hadn't he always demonstrated unwavering loyalty to him? He had proven his allegiance way back when, in the confrontation with Jobs. And hadn't he done a good job? On Yocam's watch, Apple's product inventories had always stayed in neat balance with customer orders. There was no reason, he thought, to make a change when things were going so great. Employees were perplexed, too. Yocam was a popular guy around the campus, a sort of father figure whose Apple lineage traced back to the earliest days. In their view, he was Mr. Apple.

Years later, Yocam can only surmise that Sculley somehow felt that he was becoming too powerful. "I had been running day-to-day operations for three years," says Yocam, speaking in the tranquillity of his 6,500-square-foot home beside an Oregon lake lined with fir trees. "John had written his book and had spent a lot of time on book tours and such. While he was gone, I gained in power. He may have felt I had gotten too powerful. Plus, Spindler, Gassée, and Loren all wanted the top job."

Sculley himself won't talk about the episode. But in later years he confided to a friend, "I'm really, really sorry we did that." Apple was a dysfunctional family, but Yocam was the glue that had held it together. Now there was no one to mind the store.

Since Sullivan was the key person behind Yocam's ouster, it was only fitting that he be the one to redraw the organizational chart, doling out equal parcels of turf to his coconspirators. They were fiefdoms, really, and each person could rule like a king. There was King Gassée, president of a new division called Apple Products, which now included not only product development and product marketing but product manufacturing. There was King Spindler, president of a new division called Apple Europe. And there was King Loren, promoted to president of the new Apple USA division, which was responsible for all sales and marketing in the world's biggest computer market.

With the COO's position eliminated in the new chart, they all now reported directly to Sculley. It was an organization model that Sullivan, to this day, remains proud of, despite the problems it would cause. "The organization chart I drew up was perfect," Sullivan says. "John needed to take control of running the company. We were getting too big, and those folks were getting unruly."

Poor Yocam was handed a crumb: he was named president of a new division combining Apple's big sales to schools with those in the tiny Pacific region. Don't even try to figure out why education should fit with the Pacific. The PR managers couldn't figure it out either, when Sculley left it to them to explain Yocam's new role. It didn't matter. Yocam was on his way out the door, anyway. Indeed, Sullivan and Company weren't content simply not to have Yocam as their boss. A short time later, they went back to Sculley and said they couldn't work *with* Yocam, either. Thus, six weeks after losing his job as COO, Yocam announced he would be quitting Apple entirely the following year, on his tenth anniversary at Apple. Yocam says he was not pushed out of Apple Pacific, but chose to leave after his demotion from COO.

To the outside world, the 1988 reshuffling didn't make much sense, coming so soon after the one in 1987. "It's really hard to keep up with all the reorganizations at Apple," Stewart Alsop, an influential consultant to the industry, mused at the time.[6] In his 1990 book, *The Macintosh Way*, Guy Kawasaki wrote that reorganizations had become so commonplace at Apple that employees had come to accept them. "The saying around Cupertino is, 'If you don't like this reorg, don't worry. There'll be another in 90 days,' " Kawasaki wrote after he left Apple to start his own business.

Kawasaki, as you remember, was Apple's outspoken crusader in popularizing the Macintosh among software developers. His was a clear, powerful voice, and one that the developers, in particular, found credible on most matters pertaining to Apple over the years. Kawasaki was, therefore, expressing sentiments widely shared among Apple people when he offered two explanations for why there were so many reorgs. One, Apple was growing so fast it had to make a lot of changes.

"Secondly," he wrote, "Apple is a very political place. Often decisions are made on the basis of what's politically acceptable, not what's right. Thus, organizations are thrown together so everyone can have their own sandbox. This is very different from the Jobs days, when he had the biggest sandbox with the most toys, and you were either allowed to play in it or watch from the classroom."[7]

But Sculley had a pat explanation for every reorganization, a knack for making sense out of what was really nonsense. In the 1988 annual report, he informed shareholders that Apple had undergone this reorganization to take advantage of its great momentum. "Our plan is a flatter organization—one with few layers of management—that will allow a larger Apple to become even more innovative, flexible, and locally responsive than we are today," he wrote.[8] That was pure garbage, of course. What had really happened was that he had once again buckled under a threat from underlings. He couldn't put that into an annual report.

You surely wouldn't have suspected any skulduggery from looking at the big photo of Sculley and his executive staff in that report. Sculley stood front and center as always, looking every inch the *Fortune* 500 CEO in his pin-striped suit and pocket handkerchief. Poised directly behind, almost like vultures, were Gassée, Loren, and Spindler, smiling wolfishly and looking resplendent in their dark, conservative suits. Befitting his status as a behind-the-scenes operator, Sullivan stood at the very rear of the eight-member group, which also included Coleman, Eisenstat, and Yocam. Yocam smiled bravely from a corner. If he had stood much further away, his image would have been cropped out.

Yet the ambience in which this picture was taken crackled with naked ambition. With Yocam out of the way, Gassée, Spindler, and Loren began to eye one another warily. All thought they could one day be CEO, so even Sculley was vulnerable. This was a far cry from the "noble village of men and women" that Sculley had so idealistically envisioned in *Odyssey*. This was a bona fide Machiavellian court. "At Apple, the team focused on the weakest," says Aaron Goldberg, a longtime industry consultant who is now executive vice president of Computer Intelligence, a market research firm based in La Jolla, California.

In the press accounts of the period, Loren and Gassée were described as the chief rivals for Sculley's job. If Loren played his cards right, the accounts suggested, he could push his way past Gassée. "He has neither Gassée's power nor his technical genius," wrote the *San Jose Mercury News*. "What he does have, however, is the status of a rising star." The September 21, 1988, article about Loren, entitled "Apple's Magician," was accompanied by a photo of him in his office, leaning back in a swivel chair under the backdrop of a wall poster that read "Satisfaction Is Your Right."

Loren may have looked good from the outside, but not to most folks in Cupertino. He had poor people skills and almost nothing in common with anyone else at Apple, even in his personal life. While the blue-jean set would explore the surrounding mountains in their environmentally correct boots

and backpacks, riding mountain bikes, Loren would spend his weekends foul-
ing the air with a huge recreational vehicle. Loren insists that he, in fact, has
long been an outdoorsman and enjoys a good hike, too. But it was clear he did
not fit into the Apple cult at all. "He was a square peg in a round hole," says
George Everhart, one of Loren's former sales managers.

Like Sullivan, Loren loved to surround himself with rigid bureaucracy,
the thing Apple people hated more than anything else in the world. After all,
these were the California free spirits, out to change the world. During employee orientations, in fact, Apple managers would poke fun at the traditional
establishment. "We would have a guy come in a suit with four suitcases and
make a spectacle of himself," recalls Peter Kavanaugh, who led orientations.
"The suitcases would say, 'Corporate Policies,' 'Business Plan,' and 'Procedure
Manual.' I would say, 'We don't do that here. We're a different company.' "

Imagine the reaction in Cupertino, then, when Loren roared in from
Philadelphia and in short order helped to convince Sculley to launch a mon-
ster called "New Enterprise." This involved a nearly two-year project that included everything from consultants' studies on how to redesign Apple's
in-house computer network to a "cultural initiative" on how to "think global
and act global," recall managers from that time. It was to be a five-year blueprint for Apple's corporate structure, and it reeked to high heaven of old-world
red tape.

"Loren said, 'Why don't we decide what kind of company we are going to
be and build systems to support this?' " Sullivan remembers. "So we all went
off and did an 'Apple in the nineties' projection. Some great ideas came out
of this, and it turned into New Enterprise." New Enterprise started in vintage
Apple fashion. At a kickoff conference at a resort in Palm Springs, Apple
brought in the late Gene Roddenberry, the creator of the *Star Trek* series, to
deliver the keynote speech. Roddenberry had long been an Apple fan and was
only too happy to make a loose comparison between the voyages of his starship
Enterprise with those of Apple's New Enterprise. As Gassée prepared to give
his talk, Patrick Stewart, the actor who played Captain Jean-Luc Picard in *Star
Trek: The Next Generation*, appeared on video to make the introduction.

New Enterprise went downhill from there. Before it was over, managers
from all over Apple were called in to participate in task force teams and
touchy-feely sessions. "We would have large management meetings, with up
to a hundred people present," says a middle manager from the time. "It was
generally thought of as a waste of time." And money. All told, New Enterprise
burned up roughly $100 million—with almost nothing to show for it in the
end.

Sullivan argues, however, that New Enterprise failed because the executives could not come to agreement on a basic strategic direction. "We could
not agree on whether to pursue a market share strategy or a premium-pricing

strategy," Sullivan says. Gassée was the proponent of following Apple's current premium-pricing strategy of keeping Macintosh prices high to feed gross profit margins, while other executives, including Bill Campbell and Sculley, favored the market share strategy of lowering prices to widen sales and share of the PC market. Indeed, Loren now believes that Sculley's failure to come up with a consistent strategy hobbled both New Enterprise and Apple as it entered the 1990s.

"The reason companies can be successful is to have good execution with a vision, a strategy, something that aligns the whole team so that their behavior, day in and day out, is consistent with winning," Loren says. "We were never able to come up with that at Apple, like Bill Gates has at Microsoft." Loren maintains that the only strategy that Sculley articulated to the executive staff was that he wanted Apple to grow to first a company of $5 billion in annual revenues and then to one with $10 billion. "But there are a million ways to do that," Loren says. Through New Enterprise, he adds, "we would have created that shared vision and a culture in which you will tell customers when they're going to get their products. [But] John did not have the courage to push it ahead."

Sculley expresses incredulity when asked whether he, in fact, lacked a strategy back then. "I had a very consistent strategy with Apple that never changed," Sculley remembers. "Using my marketing experience, I wanted to build a great brand, through advertising and public relations. . . . Secondly, because Apple was a feudal society and had been led by this mesmerizing cult leader [Steve Jobs], I did not know how to lead Apple from inside the company. My way of doing it was to lead outside the company [through speeches and external meetings], following distinct themes: education and multimedia."

John Sculley may indeed have had a strategy, but he clearly failed to articulate it in a manner forceful enough to get his executives to follow along. In going after business accounts, for instance, Sculley's idea was primarily to infiltrate key departments such as engineering and marketing, where the Macintosh's graphical capabilities were far superior to those of IBM-compatibles. Sculley remembers both Loren and Spindler, however, pushing the Mac as an all-purpose business machine, with little emphasis on the desktop publishing market. A disconnect was building between John Sculley and his executive team, and the chasm would only widen over time.

In any event, Sculley had decided, in his spirit of cooperative management, to give his executives as much free rein as possible. And few were less qualified to handle all that responsibility than Allan Loren. He had been on the job barely a year when Sculley elevated him out of information services to run Apple's sales and marketing for the United States. One might well ask, How does one go from information services to sales and marketing? That was a mystery to many people at Apple, too, as evidenced by the stunned reaction of the two thousand employees who assembled in the Flint Center auditorium at De Anza College to hear Sculley unveil details of the latest reorganization in August 1988.

"I'd like you to meet the person who will be running Apple USA," Sculley announced, as all heads turned to see who the big man was who was lumbering out to join him on stage. It was Allan Loren! "There was a stunned silence in the room and then a smattering of applause," says Bob Saltmarsh. "It was like, 'How could you?' "

One question on everyone's mind: What was so wrong with Chuck Boesenberg, the guy already running U.S. sales? Boesenberg may have come from corporate America, like Sullivan and Loren, but he was far more personable. He was well liked by just about everyone and, as far as all could tell, had performed well in the job. Boesenberg wasn't part of the in crowd, though, and did not have his office right next to Sculley's, as Loren did. "I thought Chuck Boesenberg was doing fine, but John didn't like his style," Yocam says. Boesenberg ended up having to report to Loren and, not surprisingly, left the company not long after.

Though Apple was a worldwide company, the United States was always the biggest and most important market for it and every other computer manufacturer. It was in the United States where most of the industry's innovation was taking place. So it was in the United States where new products were introduced first, thus setting trends for the rest of the world. This wasn't a market you wanted to screw up, though to many people at Apple it appeared that Loren surely tried hard to. It started almost from day one, when he canceled the annual sales conference.

Salespeople, as a whole, are an insecure lot who need to be coddled and flattered. Every major company knows it needs to hold a big sales meeting at least once a year to pat everybody on the back and dole out goodies to the top producers. It's basically "pump up the ego" time. At Apple, the annual sales conferences were also an excuse for a big shindig. The salespeople would shout and dance and have a grand old time, as when they had partied the nights away the previous year on the sun-kissed beaches of Maui.

In September 1988, when Loren took over the U.S. operation, everyone was really excited about the forthcoming sales conference at the Disney World resort in Orlando. Plane tickets had been booked well in advance. Hotel rooms were reserved. It had been a hard year, and now it was time to have some fun. Or so they thought. "When Al took over, he became nervous that he wouldn't have anything to say," says Peter Hirshberg. "So he canceled the sales conference with two weeks to go."

The decision to cancel the meeting was made in the Gigi restaurant in the Sofitel hotel in nearby Redwood City, California. There, Loren was meeting with Jean-Louis Gassée and Kevin Sullivan. Also in attendance was a man named Steve Scheier, a former chief of staff in the California legislature who was Loren's assistant at the time. As Loren remembers, "The senior guys were saying, 'Allan, what strategy are you going to lay out [at the conference]?' I said, 'I don't know.' Everybody said, 'Well, we shouldn't have this meeting.' I said, 'Well, if you guys are not ready to give speeches, I'll have to cancel the sales meeting.' In hindsight, I shouldn't have done that." Afterward, Scheier pulled his boss aside and warned, "You're gonna catch it big time," according to a former Apple executive who heard the exchange. "Allan said, 'I don't care. I think we'd be disingenuous if we did go.' "

Ironically, the theme for that show was supposed to have been: "Don't Worry, Be Happy." Apple would have plenty more to worry about soon.

It was bad enough that Loren was gruff with employees. But sometimes he could not restrain himself even with the customers he had vowed to please. Salespeople loved to take along one of Apple's top executives on a call, to impress the client. Bill Campbell and Chuck Boesenberg, who gave customers a sense of caring and partnership, were charismatic guys who made a favorable impression not only on employees but on customers. But, please, not Allan Loren. On one sales call to a large corporate customer in Chicago, for instance, one former Apple executive remembers Loren dozing off in the middle of a pitch. When he and Loren visited another customer, Motorola, he adds, Loren lectured the company's chief information officer on how to do his job. Motorola was a huge Apple customer, with legions of Macs. "After that meeting, the Motorola CIO called me back into his office without Loren and said, 'I'll have every Apple out of my building if you bring that guy back with you.' "

Loren denies ever insulting customers. Some other executives offer a different view of his customer relations. "When Allan was approached about an opportunity to meet with a customer, he would drop everything to do that," recalls Jim Buckley, a former subordinate of Loren who later became president of Apple USA. "I was not embarrassed to bring Allan on a sales call."

Loren's trips to meet his field people were equally memorable. John Ziel, then Apple's manager of northwest sales, remembers telephoning his counterpart in Denver as Loren was leaving there to fly to meet with him in the Portland regional office. "I asked the Denver guy how it went, and he said, 'You have to keep this guy fed or he becomes unglued,' " Ziel says. "So when Loren arrived here, we did everything around food." When asked about that, Loren looked up from his meal at Manhattan's elegant Hudson River Club, stared at me and snapped, "Do you like food? Is that un-American? I admit, I like to eat."

Complaints about Loren started pouring in from all over the organization. Phil Dixon, a pleasant, dark-haired man with an accent from his native Britain, was running a program called "Leadership Experience," as part of an on-campus think tank called the Apple University. Up to two hundred managers would spend about four days analyzing what changes the company would face in the future, as well as any barriers they could see toward continued success. "On one occasion, I had interviewed thirty to forty people, and the message we were getting loud and clear was that Allan Loren was an accident waiting to happen," Dixon recalls. Sculley would always give a pep talk at these sessions. Two days before he was to appear before the group, Dixon dutifully relayed to him what the managers were saying.

"When Sculley came to the workshop," Dixon recounts, "he said, 'I hear from a number of you that you have a problem with some of our key executives. I'm here to tell you that Allan is one of the best executives I have ever worked with.' " Sculley went even further to defend Loren telling *Fortune* in a May 8, 1989, article: "Allan scared the hell out of people and I'm thrilled. I knew a tough guy from the East Coast demanding implementation would be unpopular."

Sculley would later admit to friends, though, that one of his chief failings as an executive was placing his trust in the wrong people. Years later, it would become abundantly clear to him that hiring Loren had been a disastrous mistake, as practically everyone except Sculley could see at the time. "My naïveté was, I thought you should speak with one voice," Sculley says.

But the problem was certainly not just with Loren. As of late 1988, after Del Yocam's wings had been clipped, Jean-Louis Gassée had become every bit as powerful as Sculley by virtue of his dominion over the all-important engineering community. As described earlier, Gassée was a hero to the engineers. He let them do essentially whatever they wanted. They, in turn, would follow him to the ends of the earth. Sculley, on the other hand, was viewed with such scorn and disdain by many engineers that, according to Sullivan, "he was not allowed access into the technology community" through much of the 1980s.

In the executive suite, then, Gassée had the power to throw his weight around. He was an in-your-face antagonist, gleeful, almost, at the opportunity to wage verbal fisticuffs with anyone who got into his way. Sculley loathed confrontation, so much that he almost always backed down when faced with another fight with Gassée. "In terms of a business strategy, there were two points of view in the company: what John wanted it to be and what Jean-Louis wanted it to be," remembers Sullivan.

Gassée had won the battle over licensing, and he was about to win another of almost equal import to Apple's fortunes. In 1988, Apple was starting to make some serious inroads into corporate accounts, giving IBM a run for its money. That year, Big Blue came out with a souped-up new machine called Personal System/2 (PS/2), which was supposed to blow Apple and everybody else out of the water. The PS/2, though, proved too confusing and complex for many users, and IBM's momentum slowed. Characteristic of his genteel manner, Sculley avoided the temptation to mock a wounded enemy. "John told us, 'Don't be gleeful. It could happen to us,' " remembers Public Relations Director Barbara Krause.

Yet here was a window of opportunity, a chance to gobble up more market share by simply dropping prices across Apple's whole line. The Macintosh, which cost upward of $5,000, was as much as a third higher in price than the IBM-compatibles. Corporations were willing to pay the premium for the Mac because it was so much easier to use and had vastly superior ability to display graphics on-screen. It was a great tool for such tasks as page layout and design and engineering.

Executives such as Campbell, who was off running the new Claris subsidiary, pressed Sculley to go all out for market share. Debi Coleman, before she began a five-month leave of absence on February 1, 1989, to tackle her weight problem, even had prototypes assembled of a machine she called the "secretary's Mac": a leaner, cheaper version that could be marketed to administrative assistants and employees who used the machine primarily for word processing, low-level accounting, or file management. She requested a demotion to a less stressful job upon her return but left Apple soon after. It was time, Coleman and Campbell thought, to strike while the iron was hot. According to executives involved in the discussions, Sculley himself favored the idea of lowering prices to gain share. Of course, this would have resulted in the level of gross margins falling back in tandem. But wasn't it worth it to carve some territory out of your competitor's hide? He surely would have thought so at Pepsi.

Gassée didn't agree. Just as he had argued in the licensing debates, Gassée insisted that the Mac was so technically superior to anything else that it didn't need to have a huge share of the market. The machine would always sell for a premium price, he argued, and Apple would always have a comfortable market position. In fact, he would compare Apple's situation to that of Honda, the Japanese carmaker that during the eighties could charge more for its automobiles because they were better built than American cars. Honda hadn't dominated the U.S. market, but it had a nice, profitable business.

So, Gassée got Coleman's "secretary's Mac" shot out of the sky, while convincing Sculley to hew the line on margins. Indeed, for him, the 51 percent profit margin of 1988 was not enough, even though it was almost one third higher than that of rivals such as Compaq. "The slogan became 'Fifty-five or Die,' " says a former executive, referring to Gassée's quest for 55 percent margins. It became known as the "high right" strategy, marketing jargon for the position of Apple's high-priced products on the right-hand side of a price/performance chart. The farther to the right on the chart, the higher the price and performance of the machine; the farther to the left, the lower the price and performance.

Gassée had enlisted in his camp Allan Loren, none other than Mr. Rising Star himself. He and Gassée would grow to dislike each other, but they formed an uneasy truce. In fact, Loren went Gassée one better. His pitch: Why don't we just raise the prices? In the computer industry, there is a cardinal rule that is never, ever to be broken: *You do not raise prices.* Why? A new computer is based on the latest technology, and technology changes every six months or so. Once the new models hit the shelf, the old ones plunge in value. And the cycle keeps repeating itself ad infinitum. It's a lot like an automobile: prices on new models start out high but depreciate fast when the next batch is rolled out.

Now Loren had a method to his madness. Earlier in 1988, Apple had become alarmed at a run-up in the prices of dynamic random access memory chips, or DRAMs, caused by an industrywide shortage of the component. Since Apple had few sources of key components like this, as compared to the IBM-compatible world, it had stockpiled like mad to make sure it would have enough of the chips to meet the demand for the approaching fall and winter season. But the chip prices were so high that Loren did not want Apple to take the hit. There was another problem, too. No one in the executive suite was willing to cut the company's spiraling expenses. As of 1988, R-and-D expenses had surged to a record $273 million, up 42 percent from the year before, while general and administrative expenses were up 23 percent. Simple solution, Loren thought: pass the costs on to the customers—the same customers that Loren had told everybody he wanted to please, à la Harrods. Gassée clapped his hands in glee and seconded the motion.

Soon after, Loren called his sales managers into a big meeting at an Apple building in San Jose that had been nicknamed the "Paper Clip Building" because it looked like a giant paper clip. That's where Loren—on the job for only a few weeks—told the gathering of about two dozen that Apple would be raising Mac prices by up to 29 percent. "Many sales managers did not share that opinion, but they didn't protest much because Loren brooked no dissent," recalls George Everhart, at the time manager of national resale operations. A former Apple executive who worked with Loren bristles when asked about the episode, insisting that Loren welcomed input. "He appreciated it when people were honest with him. He never made excuses," this executive says. "His mantra was 'I can do better. I can do better.' "

Nevertheless, it was the stupid move to end all stupid moves. Customers howled in protest. They boycotted the fully loaded Macs that contained the expensive DRAMs—used to store video images—and moved in lockstep to snap up the stripped-down ones that came without the chips. They then bought their own DRAMs from cheaper suppliers. Alarmed, Sculley rolled prices back three months later. But the damage was done. The beloved profit margin dipped below 50 percent in the big Christmas quarter. Then overall profit plunged 29 percent in the next quarter, the first hiccup in a dozen quarters of consecutive increases in profits. Apple was stuck with its pile of expensive DRAMs and had left a bitter taste in the mouths of loyal customers.

Apple had bitten the hand that fed it.

"We took a business that was humming and sent it into a nosedive," Sculley concedes now, shaking his head. Gassée, too, today sees the error of his ways. "I thought we had a better product than anyone else and we should charge more for it," he says. "That is not always a good idea, as we found out." Loren also admits this was a mistake but adds, "We were all a part of raising prices."

Apple would rebound from this mess, but it marked a major turning point. A bruise had appeared on Apple's smooth skin. It would only get bigger.

5

An Engineering Morass

As Apple's top executives debated strategy and carved up turf, the engineers who made up the heart and soul of the company were essentially left alone to do as they pleased. These were an elite bunch, representing some of the greatest minds in computer science. They had converged on Apple from places such as Stanford, Harvard, Dartmouth, and California State Polytechnic, all with the common purpose of wanting to change the world.

"The analogy used by us was that there might be these storms raging at the top of the ocean, but at our level we were like plankton that don't move," recalls Lonnie Millett, an engineer who joined Apple in 1989, when the company was battling back from its price-rise mistake.

Sculley didn't understand the nitty-gritty of technology, but he had recognized the importance of Apple's engineering talent early on. Indeed, the whole point of his "high-right" strategy was to pump those fat profits into the labs as fast as he could so the engineers could come up with more cool products, like the Macintosh, that would once again revolutionize the young industry Apple was leading. Not only would this reinforce Apple's status as the premier innovator in the computer industry, it would keep the company so far out in front of the rest of the pack that customers would gladly continue to pay a hefty premium. This would keep Apple's profits and stock value pumped way up, making everybody happy.

Research and development, therefore, was considered so critically important by Sculley that between 1986 and 1987 he ordered its annual spending boosted by 50 percent to nearly $200 million. By 1989, it would more than double, to $421 million.

But what would happen if the R and D, heaven forbid, did not come through under this scenario? What if the geniuses in engineering could not come up with the next breakthrough? It wouldn't be pretty, as Apple was about to find out.

*   *   *

Jean-Louis Gassée may have been a fierce combatant in the executive suite, the guy who would take on the CEO himself in a verbal fight. And he may have wreaked terror in other parts of the organization, such as marketing. "Never go above him or around him," the former Apple marketer Guy Kawasaki warned in his book *The Macintosh Way*. "If he says no, back down, regroup, then approach him again. Telling him that you'll 'go to Sculley' will sink you."[1] Gassée could scream and shout in the faces of sales and marketing types because he was one of them. After all, almost all his background had been in sales and marketing.

But Gassée, while trained in math and physics, was no engineer. Consequently, he treated the engineers with respect, almost deference. And they got to do practically anything they wanted. "He was very cool, very classy, and he gave engineers room to do stuff," recalls Paul Mercer, one of the engineers at Apple at the time. "But he wasn't really adult management."

Gassée now concedes he could not control the engineers, but he blames Sculley and the Apple culture of unfettered freedom. "I tried to rein in some of the engineering projects, but Sculley did not want a scandal," he says. "I remember one project that I asked an engineer about, and I wanted to know what was going on with it. He said, 'Oh, I'm going on to something else.' I tried to force him to stay on it, but he went to HR [human resources] and they wouldn't back me up. Apple was making a ton of money, and so they didn't give a shit."

So consider the Apple power structure once again. There was the board, of course, but it was controlled by venture capitalists who for the most part were not intimately familiar with the dynamics of the PC industry. As of the late 1980s, the board's outside directors included Peter Crisp, Sally Ride, Arthur Rock, and John Rollwagen. Shrewd and reclusive, Rock was a legendary venture capitalist in Silicon Valley, having participated in the initial backing of both Intel and Apple. Crisp was general partner with a man named Henry Smith in the New York venture capital firm of Venrock Associates. Smith had served on the Apple board briefly, before being succeeded by Crisp. Crisp, too, was reclusive and shunned media interviews. Rollwagen was chairman and CEO of Cray Research Inc., a maker of supercomputers. And Sally Ride was on the board largely due to her name recognition as America's first female astronaut.

What seemed to be of primary concern to most of these board members, in the view of top Apple executives who dealt with them, was that the value of their Apple shares had gone through the roof. If it ain't broke, don't fix it. That was their view. There was also, of course, cofounder Mike Markkula, but he was content to sit back on his millions and enjoy a life of leisure. He had done his turn in managing Apple with Jobs but had retreated from the limelight when Sculley consolidated power in 1985. Sculley was technically the CEO, but he admittedly deferred to Gassée and just about anyone else in the executive suite who raised a stink. And Gassée was the engineering king, but he really answered to the engineers.

So, who did that really leave in charge? The engineers, of course. The patients were running the asylum.

As of the late 1980s, there were approximately five thousand Apple engineers, accounting for roughly half of the company's total workforce. They designed everything from the software that operated the computer to the appearance of the machine on a desk. The engineers, then, were the heart and soul of Apple Computer, and to be one during this period was to possess one of the most prestigious jobs on earth.

There was no place in Silicon Valley that rivaled the mystique and aura of Apple during this time and nowhere else that engineers wanted to work more. Steve Jobs was no longer around to guide and inspire personally, but his spirit of fierce individuality was still alive and well. And there was a definite financial incentive, too. Engineers were being given automatic pay raises of about 10 percent every six months, from a base annual pay range of $50,000 to $90,000 that was already 20 percent higher than in the rest of the industry. On top of that, they received profit-sharing contributions from Apple each year equivalent to 15 percent of their annual salary. It was the perfect combination: you worked for a great company, doing what you loved, and made a bundle at the same time.

So many engineers were having so much fun, they almost felt guilty for taking a paycheck. And many thousands more were clamoring at the door to join the party. So many, in fact, that the engineering managers held "résumé parties" to sort through all the applicants. "We would get a pizza and go through our stacks of résumés," recalls Gifford Calenda, a software manager then. "You would circle keywords that appealed to you and pass it on to the next guy. If it got past three managers, the applicant would be called in for an interview."

Apple worked hard to nurture an environment in which engineers would be free to think great thoughts. There were no set hours for work. If you wanted, you could show up at the office in the middle of the night and clock out at noon. Need a little break? There were basketball courts and volleyball nets outside where an engineer could usually scare up a game to clear the head. Indeed, Apple's official "corporate culture" codified the laissez-faire mentality: "We build an exciting environment. The company wants to make working at Apple a fun, rewarding and exciting experience. Openness, shared vision and a freedom to learn characterize the environment."[2]

Too much freedom, as it would turn out. Oh, there was an organizational structure that was supposed to channel all the great intellectual energy into making something Apple could actually sell. At the very top of R and D, of course, was Jean-Louis Gassée, but he admittedly could not get engineers to do his bidding, nor was he even a techie in the first place. Just below him were the parallel divisions of hardware and software research. Heading hardware at the time was a vice president named Eric Harslem. Heading software was another vice president named Ed Birss.

Off in its own world, apart from hardware and software, was Apple's Advanced Technology Group, or ATG, which had been started in 1986 as an in-house think tank by a brilliant computer scientist named Larry Tesler. The ATG was filled with some five hundred engineers whose charge was to explore future technologies, write technical papers, and generally behave like the highly educated scholars they were. Appropriately, since the engineers were living at the edge of technology research, the ATG's headquarters was situated in the late 1980s at one edge of the Apple campus, taking up the full floor of a building at the corner of Mariani Avenue and De Anza Boulevard. It was headed from 1986 to 1990 by Tesler, who had gained fame in the industry for being one of the scientists at Xerox PARC who had demonstrated Xerox's graphical user interface technology on that fateful visit to the PARC labs by Steve Jobs in 1979. A slender, intense man with a penchant for starting new research projects, he joined Apple a year later.

Although all product development for hardware and software had been put under one roof under Sculley's regime, the engineers warred incessantly with one another. Sculley had centralized the company after Jobs's ouster, in the hopes that the kinds of rivalries that had fractured Apple during the days of separate Apple II and Macintosh divisions would disappear. They did for a while, as Apple pulled together to emerge from its crisis of 1985. But by the late 1980s, when everyone in research was darting off in different directions, two distinct and often feuding camps arose, literally on opposite sides of the street.

This had to do with the design of the Macintosh, in which the operating system was intertwined so closely with the hardware that the two were almost inseparable. Every time Apple would make a new Mac, therefore, its engineers had to make adjustments from both the software side and the hardware side. There were the hardware engineers. And there were the software engineers. It was not intentionally planned that way, but the hardware designers ended up working on one side of De Anza Boulevard while their software counterparts clustered on the other. The setup was not only divisive but downright dangerous. Two programmers were struck by cars (though not seriously injured) while dashing across De Anza to meet with some hardware designers.

Hardware or software? Was Apple a hardware company like Compaq, in the business of selling mainly boxes? Or was it a software company like Microsoft, in the business of selling software? Arguments could be made for both, really. Almost all of Apple's revenues by the end of the 1980s came from the sale of Macintosh boxes. But those boxes would never have been popular in the first place had it not been for the software that made the Mac so unique. There were many people, however—including Sculley—who believed that Apple was really in the business of hardware. When Sculley made that statement to a gathering of employees one time, a new round of T-shirts sprang up the next day reflecting the software engineers' hurt feelings. They said APPLE IS A HARDWARE COMPANY and went on to list every software project Apple had ever done. "One of the fundamental problems we had at Apple was that we didn't understand whether we were a hardware company or a software company," says Konstantin Othmer, a software engineer then.

With no one to mediate disputes and loose supervision overall, the engineers were pretty much left on their own to do anything they wanted. It was really more like a college campus than a working corporation. You graduated with your master's in engineering, and you went to Apple to work on your doctoral thesis. "For me, personally, it was wonderful," says Steve Roskowski, an engineer of the era. "But for the company, it was terrible."

Roskowski's experience was typical for an Apple engineer. He signed up to work on one dead-end project. When that imploded, he moved on to something else. That went down the tubes, and he joined yet another project. In the entire five years he worked at Apple, beginning in 1987, he never worked on a project that resulted in a finished product, something that could actually be sold to customers. But he had a hell of a good time, anyway. "The compelling attraction of Apple was that everyone believed they were fundamentally doing the best thing they could," Roskowski says. "Engineers were gods."

Roskowski uses an analogy that neatly sums up senior management's approach to research and development at the time. "Apple was like a pond with a lot of bubbles [R-and-D projects] coming up from the scum. And the executives all stood on the sidelines. They would shoot down the little bubbles when they got too scary." Apple would spend approximately $1.5 billion between 1987 and 1997 on hardware and software development projects that mostly became mired in political intrigue and mismanagement and would either fail in the market or never see the light of day. Here is a tale of how a great R-and-D engine ran amok.

There would be plenty of projects to get scared about. Like Aquarius.

Computer engineering is so numbingly complex that R-and-D projects at any technology company tend to get simple code names, mainly so everybody involved can have a single reference point for the techie mumbo jumbo they are all speaking. Sometimes a code name is so well liked by the engineers, it ends up becoming the official name of a product. That was the case with the Macintosh, which was also the code name for that project. Aquarius was the code name of a grandiose endeavor started by an Advanced Technology Group engineer named Sam Holland, who in 1986 convinced Gassée that

Apple should design its own microprocessor chips. Its name would live on only in infamy.

To understand why this project—which engineers say was named after a New Age bookstore in nearby Los Gatos called the Aquarian—was so ridiculous, consider again Apple's strengths. First and foremost, Apple was the undisputed world leader in making innovative computers. Its software was ahead of everyone else's in the industry. And the machines themselves were a delight to behold, featuring the rounded sleekness of television sets and stereo systems instead of the jarringly angular look of the IBM-compatibles. Now remember the importance of the microprocessor. Along with the software operating system, the microprocessor is the most important component in the personal computer. It is the "brain" that allows the body to perform tasks.

Microprocessor technology was so complex that the two leaders in the field, Intel and Motorola, had spent billions to build laboratories and fabrication plants. They needed the investment. Under an axiom in the industry known as "Moore's law," named after Intel cofounder Gordon Moore, who formulated it in 1965, the number of transistors that could be built onto the same chip would double every eighteen months. As a result, chips would become ever more efficient and ever cheaper. If a company got into this game, then, it would be in an endless footrace against its competition. And this would take lots more bucks. Motorola, a multibillion-dollar conglomerate, could well afford the investment. Besides microprocessors, Motorola was involved in many other technology lines, including the pagers and cellular phones for which it was best known. Unlike Motorola, Intel's primary business was the microprocessor. Since it didn't have to worry about much else, Intel devoted almost all of its considerable energy to making faster and better microprocessors.

Apple had a lot of money to invest, but not billions. What's more, it was already receiving all the chips it needed from Motorola. But what the heck. Wasn't Apple the best at everything? If it wanted to design its own microprocessor, by God it was going to. The attitude was "Damn the torpedoes, full steam ahead." When Sam Holland presented the concept, Gassée was so gung ho that he ignored warnings from two of his managers, software's Ed Birss and a hardware manager named Steve Sakoman, not to go through with it. "Ed and I said to Gassée, 'Don't do this. This is silly,'" recalls Sakoman, who was director of Apple's hardware research between 1985 and 1987, when he turned the reins over to Eric Harslem so he could undertake a secret project. "I think Jean-Louis just liked the idea of doing something far-out and hoped something would come of it."

Believing that Gassée and the engineers knew best, Sculley gave Aquarius his unequivocal support, to the extent that he even bought the engineers a $15 million Cray supercomputer they could use to perform their design work on.

This was no ordinary computer. Measuring roughly ten feet in diameter and circular in shape, the Cray was so powerful that it required its own electrical substation to provide power. Bathed in eerie blue light in an antiseptic room, the Cray was something that looked as though it could have come out of a NASA lab. This was a really cool toy, and one that the fifty engineers on Aquarius spent much time tinkering on.

The underlying motivation behind the Aquarius project was Apple's fear that the Motorola line of microprocessors that it was dependent on would soon run out of steam and be surpassed by the rival line from Intel. Called the 68000 series, the Motorola chips had proven vastly superior to Intel's 8086 line in running the graphics that were so fundamental to the success of the Macintosh. But by 1986, Motorola's pace of chip development had slowed, resulting in a delay in replacing the 68030 chip with a newer 68040. "This was where Sam Holland came to the fore," recalls Terry Fowler, an Apple engineer between 1986 and 1989 who was in charge of making a hardware prototype of Aquarius. "We were tied in with the performance levels we could get from Motorola. The reason to go to an alternative was to see if we could find a way to [design a chip] to offer significantly more performance."

Holland's idea was as ambitious as anything ever undertaken at Apple. In a nutshell, Holland proposed that Apple design not only a new chip but one that would incorporate *four* microprocessors onto a single piece of silicon. The concept was known as parallel processing, and it was by means of this technique that supercomputers such as the Cray had gained their tremendous power. Instead of having one microprocessor responsible for the whole computer, the four could divvy up tasks and make the machine run much faster. Hence, Apple's computers "would have the power of a Cray on a desktop," says Al Alcorn, then an Apple Fellow who would briefly head Aquarius.

The only problem was that this had never been attempted before in a computer as small as a desktop, and there were all kinds of technical problems to overcome. For instance, certain components, such as the compiler, which translates software code to the microprocessor, did not exist then—nor do they now, Alcorn says. Indeed, the project's goal was so grandiose that Aquarius's own engineers now say that more experienced people would never have tried it. "Aquarius was an example of the willingness of the top management of Apple to embark on grand projects that skilled technical management would have known was unfeasible," Alcorn says.

Aquarius had been given the green light nevertheless, and Sam Holland was placed in charge of a team that grew to about fifty engineers from the hardware and software sides of Apple. The project was not just secret, it was super secret—so much so that when Holland left the project in 1989, when it was gasping for more funding after three years of work, the rest of the team was forced to publicize Aquarius throughout Apple so they could find a new champion to take it on. "The big thing at Apple was to get everyone else [in engineering] to buy into everything," Fowler remembers.

But so few managers wanted anything to do with Aquarius, given its difficult technical odds, that Sam Holland nonchalantly predicted that the project would be killed after he had gone. "He said to me that we would need to get another strong leader in here to carry the project forward, but that 'politically, I don't think anyone will take it on,' " Fowler recalls. Fowler thought about this for a moment and then told Holland, "How about Al Alcorn? He's an Apple Fellow and has nothing to lose." Indeed, he hadn't. Al Alcorn was a legendary figure in Silicon Valley, having gained renown for designing Pong, the world's first video game. It had also been Alcorn who, as chief engineer at the video-game maker Atari, had hired Steve Jobs in 1974 as a $5-per-hour technician. In recognition of his achievements, Apple had hired Alcorn in 1986 to serve as an Apple Fellow, an honor accorded only a handful of people over the years for their work in changing the course of an industry. So when the Aquarius team came calling, Alcorn agreed to be its new leader.

At about the same time as this was going on, a chip expert named Hugh Martin (Huge Martian, some engineers called him jokingly after an Apple receptionist mistakenly wrote his name down that way) was recruited from a smaller computer company called Ridge Computers to help plot Apple's future strategy on microprocessors. He, too, was charged with studying what to do about the problem of the Motorola chips losing steam. Besides Motorola's being late in getting out one new generation after another, Martin could see an even more profound problem with the 68000 chips: they were based on an older technology called "CISC," or "complex instruction set computing," that had a finite life. A tall, trim, dark-haired man, Martin was brought in by Sculley to spearhead efforts to design a Mac around another chip based on a newer technology called "RISC," or "reduced instruction set computing," which had a much longer life span.

CISC and RISC: a gargantuan industry battle would erupt in only a few more years over these acronyms, which were numbingly arcane to anyone not associated with the computer world. CISC is used to describe the earlier computer architectures for mainframes and minicomputers that use numerous instructions to execute a task. RISC executes the same task in less time because it relies on fewer instructions. As author Robert X. Cringely wrote in his 1992 book, *Accidental Empires*, "Where a . . . CISC . . . might have a special 'walk across the room but don't step on the dog' instruction, RISC processors can usually get faster performance by using several simpler instructions: walk–walk–step over–walk–walk."[3]

Two weeks after he started, Sculley called Martin up to his office in De Anza 7. "He said, 'What do you think about Aquarius?' " Martin recalls. "I said, 'John, that's ridiculous. Apple has no fab or chip experience. How do you compete with Intel and Motorola?' " But Sculley must have gotten the message. Within six months, in 1989, Aquarius was ordered shot through the heart. By then, though, the project's demise was academic. When Al Alcorn had convened a meeting of the Aquarius engineers sometime earlier, he had asked them all how they felt about the project. "My biggest surprise was that the guys doing the chip design weren't interested in finishing this thing," Fowler remembers. "Al said, 'Well, let's go in another direction.' But they just lost interest." Fowler quit Apple in disgust, while Alcorn learned a bitter lesson. "Developing advanced technology in a research group is easy," says Alcorn, who is now executive vice president and chief technology officer of Silicon Gaming Inc., a company he founded in 1994 after leaving Apple. "Getting it transferred to production is very hard."

All told, about $20 million in R-and-D costs had been flushed down the drain on the Aquarius project alone between 1986 and 1989. One bubble had been popped, but there were many more to come. The secret project that Steve Sakoman went off to start was one, and that bubble should have been popped but never was. This was the ill-fated Newton project, which, unfortunately would see the light of day.

Newton started out innocently enough, when Steve Sakoman approached Jean-Louis Gassée in the summer of 1987 to pitch an ambitious new research endeavor. Sakoman was something of a resident authority on the nascent class of portable computers, having been plucked away from Hewlett-Packard by Steve Jobs in 1984 for his role in developing the HP Portable, the industry's first laptop computer. While at Hewlett-Packard, Sakoman, a soft-spoken engineer from Ohio, had worked with calculators, personal computers, and minicomputers so much that he had often wondered whether a new type of device could be made that was easier for people to use. With all those machines, the user had to use a keypad to punch in numbers or words. What if, Sakoman remembers thinking, "you [could] just scribble this on the screen and have the computer recognize your handwriting?"

The idea in itself wasn't new. The concept of a portable computer that could recognize a user's handwriting and communicate with other computers wirelessly had been articulated many years before, in 1968, by a computer scientist named Alan Kay, who had envisioned a notebook-sized computer he called the "Dynabook." Kay was another of the Xerox PARC researchers who had done pioneering work on graphically oriented computers, and he, too, had joined Apple as an Apple Fellow.[4] Alan Kay exerted a strong influence over John Sculley, who borrowed many of his ideas for the Knowledge Navigator from Kay's futuristic research.

What was new, however, was that Sakoman proposed to actually start making such a computer rather than just theorizing about one. As he envisioned it, this computer would be the size of a stenographer's pad, and it would be revolutionary in every way. Instead of the user having to type into a keypad, he or she would use an electronic pen. Instead of using a mouse and cursor arrow to navigate around the screen, the same pen could be used to "drag" documents from one side of the screen to another. And instead of having to open different programs to embed charts, drawings, and pictures into a document, that would all be done automatically, without the user ever having to think about which programs did what. "We wanted to make it very easy to use," Sakoman remembers.

Sakoman was not, by nature, a pie-in-the-sky researcher. His career had revolved around hardware and meeting the unending deadlines of shipping a hardware product out the door. But he did want to try something new after presiding over back-to-back launches of the Mac Plus, Mac SE, and Mac II. And for a time he contemplated taking his handheld computer and working on it in a new company. That notion actually came about after a visit to Sakoman from an old friend named Mitch Kapor, a famous software pioneer. Kapor was a multimillionaire then, having designed the best-selling Lotus 1-2-3 spreadsheet that had given Bill Gates fits. Sakoman had gotten to know Kapor well while designing Hewlett-Packard's portable computer, into which he had installed Lotus 1-2-3.

Kapor resigned as Lotus's chairman in 1986 to pursue new technology ventures, and in 1987 he listened to Sakoman's new idea while on a business trip to California from his home in Boston. Afterward, Kapor was so enthused that he jetted back east to tell it to a colleague, Jerry Kaplan, who had also recently left Lotus, where he had been the company's principal technologist. "They all got excited and said, 'Why don't we start a company and do this?' " Sakoman remembers. "Jean-Louis had a similar reaction. Jean-Louis wanted himself, Mitch, Jerry, and me to all start a company." The four men discussed the prospect informally, but Sakoman finally demurred. "I didn't have a good feeling about it," Sakoman says. "There were a lot of people who wanted to be CEO of their own company, and I didn't think it would work." Given what would happen to Apple under Gassée's technical leadership, it's too bad it didn't.

After Sakoman decided not to pursue his research outside Apple, Gassée proposed setting it up as a special project inside the company. Actually, it was a "skunk works" project, so known for research that is kept secret. "Jean-Louis talked to John Sculley about it, and John nodded his head without knowing what it was," Sakoman remembers. Sakoman then set to work. First he needed a project name. Remembering Apple's original corporate logo, depicting the seventeenth-century scientist Sir Isaac Newton sitting beneath an apple tree, Sakoman decided to call it "Newton." "Part of the idea was to go back to Apple's roots of doing innovative, human-centered things," he says.

Sakoman worked briefly by himself, laying the groundwork for a product he expected to deliver to the market within three years. Then he assembled a small team, numbering no more than thirty members, whose technical core included Apple engineers Glenn Adler, Ernie Beernink, Sue Booker, Steve Capps, Eric Gruenberg, and Pete Foley. Both Adler and Gruenberg had worked with Sakoman at Hewlett-Packard. Capps was a member of Steve Jobs's legendary Macintosh team, who had just returned to Apple after a sojourn abroad. They worked mainly out of an abandoned warehouse on Cupertino's nearby Bubb Road, in which the windows were still broken out as they prepared to move in.

Coincidentally, as Newton was starting up, Apple had sponsored a contest among U.S. universities to see which could come up with the best design of a personal computer as it might appear in the year 2000. Universities from all across the country had sent in their submissions, out of which Apple had winnowed down the list to what it considered the five best. Among those was an entry from students at Princeton University, and it mirrored the research that Steve Sakoman was doing on handheld computers. Calling their device a "Personal Information Environment," or PIE, five students had written a twenty-page report describing a portable device that would incorporate the functions of a computer, telephone, television, and radio. Depicted in a crude illustration, the PIE looked like a radio "boom box," with carrying handle and giant speakers. "Done correctly," the report suggested, "the result will have an impact more far reaching than did joining the steam engine to the horse drawn railroad car."

Apple's engineers were intrigued. In a visit to Cupertino paid for by Apple, the Princeton team was interviewed by some of the Apple engineers. One of the students was named Mary Lynn Werlwas. Like her schoolmates, she had no background in technology; she was majoring in political science. "They asked Mary, 'What are your views on AI?' " remembers Howard Jay Strauss, Princeton's manager of advanced applications and the staff adviser on the project. "She started talking about Amnesty International and how much she admired its work. But by AI, they had meant 'artificial intelligence.' " These were rank amateurs, to be sure. But their ideas were good enough that the name of their PIE device eventually found its way into Apple Computer. Within five years, an entire Apple division dedicated to the design and production of handheld devices would also be named "PIE," only this time for "Personal Interactive Electronics."

The Newton research, meanwhile, was proving every bit as technically different as Steve Sakoman had first imagined. By the end of three years, he could see that his original completion goal had been wildly ambitious, since the team was nowhere near ready with a finished product. One big hurdle was the handwriting recognition. The group had obtained some of its handwriting recognition technology through a small Oregon software company that Apple had acquired named Arus. Adding to that body of knowledge, later on, was the work of some Russian programmers working in secret during the waning days of the former Soviet Union. And it fell into Apple's hands in cloak-and-dagger fashion.

Al Eisenstat, Apple's senior vice president of board and legal matters, remembers being awakened in his Moscow hotel room by a frantic knock on the door one night during a business trip there in about 1987. Weary after having spent the evening at a performance of the Moscow Ballet, Eisenstat opened the door to see a Russian programmer standing there with a copy of a disk containing his handwriting recognition code. "He was looking both ways down the hall to make sure he hadn't been followed," Eisenstat remembers. He handed the disk to the puzzled Eisenstat and disappeared again into the night. Eisenstat flew back to Cupertino and turned the disk over to the Newton engineers, who incorporated the technology into their research.

Despite the Newton's high promise, by the end of 1989, Jean-Louis Gassée was growing disenchanted with the project. As the research dragged on, he now says, "it became clear to me that the technology wasn't ready." If only he could have convinced John Sculley of that. Sculley himself would soon fall head over heels in love with the Newton. It married the notion of himself as an industry seer with his deep-burning desire to come up with something as startling and revolutionary as the Macintosh. The Mac had been Steve Jobs's baby. Sculley wanted one of his own. And when Sculley finally got his hands on Newton, it would look nothing like the small research endeavor begun by Steve Sakoman.

"Sculley fancied himself as a technologist," says Mansoor Zakaria, president of Agora Digital Corporation, a computer publishing firm in San Francisco. "It was almost like he had to prove his manhood," adds Zakaria, whose firm performed joint publishing with Apple between 1991 and 1994 for such projects as a directory of services for Macintosh developers.

It was not that the engineers were deliberately working on projects they knew would not pan out. Since they didn't have any direction from on high, they really worked in a vacuum, dreaming up things they thought would be great. And some of them really were. The problem was, though, that the senior managers were so technically out of touch that they couldn't tell the difference between the technologies that were worth pursuing and those that were not. Steve Perlman's experience epitomized this problem.

Joining Apple straight out of college in 1985, Perlman went to work as an engineer in the elite ATG and was soon named a technical manager. Widely recognized at Apple as one of the premier whiz kids of the company, Perlman was one of the main engineers whom Sculley would call upon to give advanced technology demonstrations at trade shows. Young and handsome, with flowing brown hair, Perlman resembled a Beatle when he trotted out onstage. After one demonstration, he really brought them out of their seats, and the reaction had nothing to do with the way he looked.

In his research at ATG, Perlman helped design new graphics chips in a technology called QuickScan. This video technology, developed in collaboration with other Apple engineers in his group, was designed to give 1980s Macintoshes the capability to run three-dimensional video clips, such as scenes from an action movie. This was truly awesome technology, years ahead of its time and the kind that would draw gasps of awe from people seeing it for the first time. In fact, Sculley brought Perlman out onstage at one conference to show off a QuickScan video of running horses. Perlman put his horses through their paces, using QuickScan to make them gallop from the screen of one Mac set up onstage to a bank of several others flickering alongside. The audience reacted with stunned silence, then wild applause.

"It knocked people's socks off," Perlman remembers. QuickScan was inexplicably canceled, though. Years later, it would serve as a foundation of QuickTime, a two-dimensional graphics technology that set the standard in video graphics when it appeared on the market in 1992. QuickTime would be based on software technology, unlike QuickScan, which was based on hardware technology. But QuickScan was just about ready in 1987, although it would have required fine tuning for a year or two before an actual release.

Engineers such as Perlman had some other tremendous ideas that, if implemented, could have strengthened Apple to withstand the storms to come. He was among a cadre of engineers who believed Apple should leverage its tremendously strong brand name into other consumer products, as Sony had done. The famous "1984" commercial, in which the Macintosh had been previewed to millions of Super Bowl viewers, had put Apple onto the map beyond its wildest dreams. By the late 1980s, Apple had become one of the most recognized brand names in the world. Why not capitalize on that great name, Perlman thought, and sell all kinds of things under the Apple name, such as portable CD players? That way, all the eggs would not be in one basket, as with the Mac. But the consumer strategy ran directly counter to Sculley's philosophy, which was to focus the Mac almost entirely on corporations and their big bucks. Well, make that Gassée's strategy, which Sculley followed. Sculley might have been a consumer marketing guy at Pepsi, but that could as well have been a lifetime ago. Now he was Mr. Technology.

Perlman therefore didn't get very far with his other ideas, which included plugging a mini-Mac into a TV so people could browse their favorite software programs from the comfort of their living room. That technology was shelved, even though it later served as the foundation for Apple's "Pippin" set-top box of the 1990s. (The Pippin, when initially introduced in 1996 for nearly $1,000, proved too expensive to gain mass-market acceptance.) He also came up with a little circuit card called the MacGS. By plugging it into one of the old Apple II models, it would make the computer look like a Mac for about $300. Senior management was buying none of this, though. The mantra was "bigger, more powerful." There was no room for anything else.

"I must have screamed myself blue in the face that mass market means products for under three hundred dollars," Perlman says.

By 1990, after five years of beating his head against the wall, Perlman was disgusted with the place. Not only was he getting no support from the top, he was being attacked by fellow engineers who thought his projects would detract from theirs. In one of the many episodes of infighting between engineers, it got so bad that there were actually cases of sabotage. One day, for example, Perlman flicked on the light in his cubicle to find important documents shredded and some disks destroyed. This kind of petty squabbling was not confined to engineers; it also extended to outside departments, such as marketing. During one memorable sales meeting in 1988, for example, some people in the Apple marketing department had prepared a video of a Mac running the graphic of a car, fitted with a helicopter propeller, whirling across the screen. Some engineers got hold of the tape and spliced in some footage from the Tom Cruise movie *Top Gun*, and when the video was played before the sales meeting, it showed the poor little helo car being blown to smithereens. Juvenile, but true.

In any event, Perlman wanted to quit, but Sculley talked him into staying. This time, he could work from home and report directly to Sculley. Perlman's final project involved another consumer product that would turn a TV into a giant computer. He was dead certain, though, that the project would be killed like everything else he had worked on at Apple—so much so, in fact, that his private code name for the project was "Tucker," after the fifty-one Tucker Torpedo cars that had been built in 1948 by Michigan entrepreneur Preston Thomas Tucker before his company tanked under criticism that the automobile—featuring a radical design including seat belts, a pop-out windshield, and a third headlight that could be shined into corners—was a hoax. Officially, Perlman's "Tucker" was known as "Gibson."

Sure enough, Tucker ended up being deep-sixed. As the decade ended, Perlman finally got out of Apple. This time, though, he planned ahead. He convinced Apple to agree to give him rights to some ingredients of the Tucker technology. Using those, he would start his own company called WebTV Networks Inc. to sell sub-$500 boxes that, in 1996, would allow people to browse the Internet from their television sets. In the Christmas season of 1996, WebTV became a household name after Perlman saturated the U.S. airwaves with advertisements for his new product, which was also being closely watched by the industry as a pioneer in a whole new computer category for devices appealing to "non-computer" people such as senior citizens.

Perlman's final vindication from Apple came in early 1997, when Microsoft bought his WebTV for $420 million. Perlman, who owned WebTV with some partners, became an overnight multimillionaire.

As of 1988, the Mac had been on the street for four years, and most of the original members of the team that had built it under Jobs had dispersed. Several, including programming wizard Andy Hertzfeld, had gone off to work on different ventures at other companies. Others, such as programmer Bill Atkinson, who had designed the QuickDraw software that enabled a user to draw and paint on the Mac's screen, buried themselves in work that had nothing to do with the Mac itself. Although the Mac had set a new standard for personal computing, it still wasn't the be-all and end-all of computer operating systems. There were still bugs to be worked out, such as the problem of frequent system crashes. If a user tried to do too many things at once, such as hitting the Print button on one document and then trying to open another file, a tiny bomb icon would appear, proclaiming a "system error": the Mac had crashed and would have to be restarted. Whatever a user had been working on and had forgotten to save was lost. The Mac, therefore, badly needed a feature called "memory protection."

Like everything else at Apple the stench of bureaucracy had begun to infiltrate even into engineering. Middle managers, often drawn from the lowest engineering ranks and with little skill in actually programming computers, were placed in charge of software development. Two of the managers, Sheila Brady and Gifford Calenda, were put in charge of overseeing evolutionary improvements to the Mac operating system. Like a spoiled brat who insists on picking his own baby-sitter, engineers who disliked a manager simply went off to work on something else, and they did not want to work for Brady or Calenda. Thus, five of Apple's finest software engineers persuaded their managers to let them break off and start work on a whole new operating system for the Mac. They came to be known as the "Gang of Five," and this is how a debacle called "Pink" started.

Erich Ringewald, who had started at Apple in 1985 and worked on a team that made badly needed memory improvements to the original Mac, was the group's project leader. A short, articulate young man who preferred sushi to cheeseburgers, Ringewald and his cohorts, including David Goldsmith, Bayles Holt, Gene Pope, and Gerard Schutten, all adjourned in March 1988 to the luxurious comfort of the Sonoma Mission Inn and Spa, a four-star resort located an hour's drive north of San Francisco in the heart of the California wine country, to "discuss doing something different." Joining the young men in this meeting were software managers Gifford Calenda, Sheila Brady, and Mike Potel. "We said, 'Look, there needs to be a group to look at new technical advancements for the OS,' " Ringewald recalls.

The engineers took out some index cards colored red, blue, and pink. On the pink ones, they jotted down their key priorities for the next-generation operating system. This would be a project called "Pink," after the color of the index cards, and it would contain memory protection as well as "preemptive multitasking." "Multitasking" is computer jargon for a feature that allows the user to run several different programs at once, such as word processing and a spreadsheet. For example, an accountant could type a word processing report and insert a chart into the same document without having to leave the word processing program. Under the way the Mac and every other desktop computer were set up at the time, one program had to be opened to write a report. Then the user had to close that and open another to create a chart. Multitasking was a feature customers would just love.

Some other advanced features were also discussed. It would be great, they all thought, to someday have a computer that could respond to the voice commands of its owner, just like in *Star Trek*. There would be a lot of technical hurdles to overcome before getting to that point, however, so they decided to roll the superadvanced features such as speech recognition into a project called "Red," after the index cards bearing that color. "We picked Red because it would be pinker than Pink," Ringewald says. With that settled, there was the matter of what to do with the current Mac system. It needed to be rejiggered to run faster, and it needed more memory. The engineers decided to call that one the "Blue" project, and they wrote down on the blue index cards the features it would include.

Sheila Brady and Gifford Calenda would run Blue. Ringewald took it upon himself to run Pink, as the technical lead. At first, Pink showed great promise. Ringewald and his gang initially arranged to set up shop in the third floor of an Apple building called De Anza 3, which was one floor down from the headquarters for all software development. This being a supersecret project, though, they soon relocated to a nondescript building about a mile away off Bubb Road, in the same warehouse where Newton was brewing.

As their ideas began to crystallize over the ensuing weeks, they realized that Pink was going to be even more radical than they had thought. It would be based on "object-oriented technology." This basically meant that Pink would be designed in such a way that it could be assembled with bits and pieces, or "objects," of software code. This would make it a lot easier to make future upgrades to the operating system, since only the necessary pieces to be changed would have to be plugged in. What's more, this object-oriented technology would make it simpler for software developers to write programs for the Mac, as well as for customers to use them. Instead of having to come up with an entire word processing program with spell checker, length counter, and so on, for example, a developer could write just a spell checker program or just a length counter program and attach those codes to a larger word processing program. That way, more little guys could get involved in the action, not just behemoths such as Microsoft or Lotus. As for customers, they could insert charts and drawings into a word processing document without having to open a new program. In fact, this was what Steve Sakoman proposed to do with the Newton, whose operating system would also be based on object-oriented technology.

The objects were sure to ignite the interest of the software community because they enabled programmers to mix and match code, although the concept really was not new. As with so many of the other PC technologies, the one for objects had also originated in the fabled labs of Xerox PARC. In fact, Steve Jobs had seen a brief demonstration of the objects technology in the visit to PARC that had inspired both the Lisa and the Macintosh. But, as he has said in public forums, he became so enamored of the graphical user interface that he forgot just about everything else. It was only later, after he quit Apple to start NeXT, that he remembered objects. In fact, he used a Mach operating system, which included objects technology, in his NeXT machine, which was introduced in 1989. The machine was sleek and ahead of its time but failed to attain any sales success because it was priced at $10,000 and lacked a floppy drive.

Even though the engineers wielded a lot of power at Apple, they were not united on much of anything. Ringewald, for example, had a clear notion that in order for Pink to be effective the project would have to be limited to a small group, just as Steve Sakoman had believed was necessary for the Newton project. The reason: small groups of engineers are almost always more effective than large ones, because there is more focus and intensity. (As proof of that, these engineers remembered what the original Mac development team had done with a core team of about twenty members.) The five-member Pink team doubled almost immediately when it recruited into the circle a separate, six-member team that specialized in the making of a crucial piece of software called the "microkernel." A kernel is a piece of software that gives an operating system the power of memory protection, which prevents system crashes, and preemptive multitasking. The original Mac operating system had been built without a kernel, as had Microsoft's DOS, and that is why neither could perform those two key tasks.

"We needed a kernel and there was a kernel team in ATG, and so we said, 'OK, you guys come on over,' " Ringewald says. Within another month or so, Pink doubled again to about twenty-five people. Pink was mutating rapidly, and Ringewald found himself losing control. As it happened, another of the original gang, David Goldsmith, decided that Pink should tackle even loftier goals than being the next successor to the original Mac system. He wanted everything plus the kitchen sink for extensive changes in the project. Ringewald argued for the team just to stick to its original goals so something could be finished in two years, as originally planned. "David was saying, 'Hey, there's a lot we have to fix, and we might as well redesign the whole Mac,' " Ringewald says. "I was saying, 'We're going to have enough trouble just reimplementing the Mac.' "

This was classic Apple management. Here was Ringewald, the project's boss, unable to get a subordinate on his team to follow the game plan. "It was hard to resist him because of the Apple culture of consensus," Ringewald admits.

By October 1988, Pink had been underway for about six months, and Ringewald and two of the other founding members, Gene Pope and Gerard Schutten, decided to bail out. "I had grave doubts about whether we could accomplish our goals," Ringewald says. Elsewhere in Apple, though, Pink was seen as having so much potential to change the company and the industry that engineers clamored to sign up. Indeed, in three more years Pink would gain attention as a focal point of a wide-ranging technology alliance between Apple and IBM.

One of the Apple engineers enamored of Pink in 1988 was a man named Dave Burnard, a tall, slim, bearded man with the aura of a scholar. The holder of a Ph.D. in astrophysics and an expert on powerful supercomputers, Burnard had joined Apple after seeing the Macintosh and falling in love with its technology. Burnard's job on Pink was to come up with the tools that software developers would need to make programs for the new operating system. From that vantage point, he was like a customer looking in. At first, he remembers, Pink was going great guns. "I don't think anybody had any serious doubts about what we were doing at that point," Burnard recalls. "We were progressing in all the right directions."

But by April 1989, the Pink staff was up to nearly a hundred people and already a joke was beginning to circulate in Cupertino: "When is Pink going to ship? Two years." The joke persisted into the 1990s, as the two years passed. "To me," Ringewald says, "it was clear the thing was out of control. It was this living, breathing, money-consuming thing." It wasn't yet clear to Burnard, though, or the other Pink engineers at the time. In late 1989, they had assembled a crude prototype, showing off new features such as Pink's ability to automatically switch a word processing program from, say, English text to Cyrillic. The graphics had also been improved demonstrably. Gassée came over one day to view the prototype at Pink's new headquarters in a two-story building in Sunnyvale, California, five miles from Cupertino, and he was impressed. "We had a real OS that could demonstrate the core [or fundamental] technology," Burnard remembers. "It would have been technically a lot deeper than the Mac."

That moment in time, however, was as close as Pink would ever get to shipping as a real operating system. When 1990 rolled around, the Pink development group was so big that it had its own, fancy organization chart. Ed Birss was at the top, as senior vice president over a new group called "object-based systems." Below him were 150 engineers, managers, marketing people, secretaries, even a three-member team from human resources. It was then that the decision was made for Pink to become *the* replacement of the Mac OS, not just a dramatic improvement, as Ringewald had wanted. As a result, it had become a multiheaded beast that had developed a powerful lore. Indeed, there was a great deal of press attention to the emerging field of object-oriented technology in general.

Following his work in setting up Pink, Ringewald drifted off to Paris to work in Apple's R-and-D operations there. He returned a year later, in 1989, to find himself heading up the software portion of a new beast called "Jaguar." Hugh Martin had convinced the executive staff to let him assemble a team to design a new computer based on the RISC chips that he had argued were the way of the future because they were faster and cheaper to make than CISC chips. "They said, 'Great, but we want it to cost eight thousand dollars and to sell to professionals,'" Martin recalls. When Ringewald landed back in Cupertino, still recovering from jet lag, Martin told him that the new RISC computer would have to have a whole new operating system, because it would be incompatible with all Macintosh programs. Martin suggested using Pink.

By now, Pink, was the hottest R-and-D project going at Apple. Almost everybody wanted to work on it, including the engineers who had been heading up the work on Blue, which would become a product that actually shipped called "System 7." Jaguar, since it entailed all new technology, was pretty hot, too. A rivalry developed between the two project teams to the point that the Pink engineers refused to let the ones from Jaguar even look at the computer programming code they had written for Pink. The Jaguar team ended up going all the way to Sculley to get permission to view the code, so they could determine whether it would fit their new machine. A compromise was struck, but it wasn't a good one. A Jaguar engineer named Phil Goldman, who had joined Apple straight out of college in 1986, went over to the Pink building to see the code, as Sculley had permitted. It was like walking into the Pentagon. "We were only allowed to come in the building and sit at a special Mac to see code, with no connection to any network and no floppy disk," Goldman recalls. "We had to have someone observing us at all times." And these guys all worked for the same company?

When Ringewald was asked about using Pink in Jaguar, he was aghast. "I said to Hugh, 'Pink won't ship for at least two more years. Let's put a small team of about ten people together and do a simple OS for your RISC box. It will be great.'" Ringewald prevailed and got his small team together. Once again the team expanded, eventually to include about eighty people. They actually came up with a working prototype, and it was a beaut. At the suggestion of Apple Fellow Al Alcorn, among others, the Jaguar team incorporated into their machine an advanced operating system called Mach, which had recently been developed at Carnegie-Mellon University and was based on Unix, an operating system used in powerful workstation computers.

Mach had a microkernel and therefore could enable memory protection and multitasking. The code name for the software part of the project was "Beaujolais," after the French wine. When the prototype was done, the machine included 3-D graphics, stereo speakers, even a camera for videoconferencing. Making it all hum under the hood was a new RISC chip called the 88110 that Motorola had been working on. "This was really the multimedia machine, years ahead of its time," Martin says.

The Jaguar bubble was starting to float up from the pond, and this time the shots to fell it began ringing out from below. Senior engineers in the mainstay Mac line, the one based on Motorola's aging 68000 chips, screamed bloody murder. They were incensed that Martin's group would come up with a computer that was intended, essentially, to put them out of business. "Leaders of the engineering teams on both sides went to Sculley and complained about each other," Ringewald says.

Jaguar, to be sure, had its issues. One was that the 88110 chip was still unfinished, which would have meant that Jaguar would have needed a brand-new microprocessor had it not worked out. This was not an insurmountable hurdle, but it would have proven daunting. Jaguar would also have presented a thorny marketing challenge for Apple, since it would have required customers to essentially throw away all their old Mac software and start from scratch. "The Jaguar thing needed to be rationalized a little bit," recalls a former senior executive. "The biggest problem was, you couldn't just go, 'Here is a new product from Apple and it has no installed base.'"

There was little doubt, however, that these problems could have been resolved if Sculley had rallied the company around Jaguar. Sculley, in fact, was a Jaguar supporter. But when in question, kill the project. That was the motto at Apple. Sculley took out his long gun and blew Jaguar out of the sky. Like Perlman, Ringewald and Goldman had had enough. They left Apple in disgust. Goldman would go on to join Perlman at WebTV as senior vice president of engineering, while Ringewald would reunite with Gassée as director of engineering of a new venture called Be Inc. The remnants of Jaguar were folded into a new hardware project called "Hurricane," which would mark the beginning of Apple Computer's storied march to a microprocessor called PowerPC.

On another front, a separate engineering feud helped doom a project called "QuickDraw GX," which, like all the other projects, started with great promise. The original QuickDraw had been a key feature of the original Macintosh, allowing the user to create special graphics with electronic paintbrushes, pencils, and other on-screen tools. This was what really set the Mac apart. You sure couldn't do *that* on your IBM clunker.

QuickDraw GX was going to be an ambitious update of that great software. It would still allow Mac users to paint and draw, but it would run even faster and be even more dazzling than before. As usual, the idea for a new and improved QuickDraw came from an in-the-trenches engineer, Cary Clark, not from the nontechies running the company. Clark, a graphics engineer who had joined Apple in 1981 and had worked on Jobs's Mac team, proposed in 1987 that QuickDraw be updated. Beginning in August that year, Clark remembers, he worked the next six to eight months alone, aided only by a student intern. After that, in early 1988, he says, engineers in the Mac's printing groups latched onto the idea of designing QuickDraw GX so that it could better reproduce graphical designs from the monitor screen onto a computer printout.

Thus, QuickDraw GX splintered into two parallel projects. There was Clark's group, which numbered just a half dozen or so engineers, in a project called "Skia" on the graphics side. ("Skia" is a Greek word for "shadow painting," an ancient form of drawing.) And there were a dozen software printing engineers in a project called "Tsunami." Tsunami was an appropriate name, because the GX project would end up wiped out in a tidal wave of engineering bureaucracy. More and more engineering groups got involved in GX. There was a team called "Peripherals," which specialized in the hardware side of printing. There were also teams specializing in color and international text. Just like Pink, QuickDraw GX grew and grew.

At one point, there were as many as a hundred engineers working on the project, often in conflict with one another. Because there were separate hardware and software teams, who communicated as little as possible and reported only to their respective managers, they would work in duplication of each other's efforts. Here was Tsunami, writing its own printer code for GX. And there was Peripherals, a hop, skip, and a jump away, doing the exact same thing. Even worse, there were graphics projects going on just about everywhere else at Apple. Konstantin Othmer, who then was a member of a team making enhancements to the original QuickDraw, counted them one day and came up with seven different teams all working on graphics. They included teams from Newton, ATG, Blue, Pink, GX's Skia, a multimedia project called Kaleida, and a computer acceleration project called GC.

"They were all working on the same thing. They never combined, never talked," recalls Othmer, who worked at Apple full-time from 1988 until quitting in 1994 to join a new video-game company called Catapult Entertainment Inc., which later merged with Mpath Interactive Inc., another game company. "At Apple, the problem was engineers worked in small groups like start-up companies. As an engineer, there was no technical direction."

Unlike so many other fiascoes, QuickDraw GX would actually ship as a real product. But so few customers wanted it that it would end up on only a tiny fraction of new Macintoshes when it was finally completed in 1994. The key problem: the final program had so many new features that it proved too cumbersome to bundle into the Mac's operating system, forcing users to have to install it separately. Adding further insult to injury, in a quest for perfection by the Tsunami team, GX was designed so it would not support any of the old Macintosh software programs. This required users to run out and buy new ones. Of course, very few people were willing to do that, especially since the new printing feature was not demonstrably better than the old one. With a total cost of about $100 million to develop GX, more good money went down the drain.

"GX was a debacle," confesses Clark, who quit Apple in 1994. (He later joined Steve Perlman and Phil Goldman as a software engineer at WebTV.) "It was much, much too late. It should have shipped earlier with less features."

With the boys in the labs spinning their wheels, Gassée concentrated on what he did know: getting out ever-bigger computers. Say what you will about Jean-Louis, he was a perfectionist when it came to product quality. Jean-Louis was such a stickler on quality that he would insist, for example, that all plastic molding lines be located in the corners of the computer's exterior box, or "chassis," as it is known in the industry, so that customers would not be offended by having to look at them. This was certainly a noble goal, but it also added greatly to the manufacturing cost. By custom molding in this fashion, Apple was having to pay about $100 for every chassis, compared to just $35 for the standard chassis that everyone else in the industry was using. "Gassée was not going to compromise on anything," says a product manager from the era.

This perfectionism proved both a blessing and a curse for Apple.

As 1989 rolled around, Gassée oversaw the launch of a souped-up version of the Mac SE. The new machine, called the Macintosh SE/30, could perform spreadsheet calculations and graphical renderings at a rate four times as fast as the previous SE model. Aimed at desktop publishing houses as well as corporations, the Mac SE/30 would sell for between $4,500 and $6,700, depending on configuration such as for extra memory and bigger hard drive, and, according to press reviews of the time, help "fill out" a product line that had become heavily tilted toward high-end machines. It says a lot that Apple considered a $4,500-to-$6,700 computer "midrange." For just about everybody else in the PC industry, the threshold for that would have been between $2,000 and $3,000. Apple did have a couple of low-end products—the Mac Plus for about $2,000 and the Apple IIGS for $1,000—but they were aimed at consumers and schools. Besides, the Apple II line was being discontinued, so Sculley was of a mind to practically give them away.

He, like Gassée, was in love with machines like the new Mac IIx, the screamers in power and performance that corporations were buying for up to $10,000 a pop. This was the cash cow, and Gassée had convinced Sculley not to mess with a sure thing. Sculley, for his part, had vowed early on to rid Apple of its toy image so it would be taken seriously by corporate buyers. By listening to Gassée, though, he would go too far in the other direction. Consider the saga of the "Luggable."

By 1989, Apple had been so busy cranking out bigger and better Macs that it had essentially ignored a groundswell of demand by customers for a laptop computer. The office had become so automated by the personal computer that professional people out on the road found it increasingly necessary to take computers with them, so they could knock out reports in their hotel room or on the plane rather than having to wait until they returned home.

Following Hewlett-Packard's lead, some of the Japanese manufacturers, such as Toshiba Corporation, had begun selling portables by the middle of the 1980s, as had their American counterparts such as Compaq. Apple had had its own portable incubating in the labs since about 1985, but Gassée refused to put it on the market until it was absolutely perfect. As Sculley told *The New York Times* in 1989, Apple's goals were to "preserve the unique character of the Macintosh" without making any compromises on performance.[5] He could have taken the words out of Gassée's mouth.

By fall of 1989, the long-awaited Macintosh Portable was finally ready to ship. And boy, was it loaded. It was every bit as powerful as a desktop Mac and contained revolutionary features such as a high-resolution, active-matrix screen that was the biggest of any portable around, and a lead-acid battery that was significantly more powerful and reliable than others then available. According to the six-page backgrounder Apple put out for the press, the Portable "offers complete Macintosh functionality in a portable design. It runs virtually all current versions of Macintosh software and provides full compatibility with other Macintosh hardware." And all for a cost of only $7,000.

There was just one problem. The Portable weighed a titanic sixteen pounds, compared to the standard of about ten pounds for all the other portables. That made it almost as heavy as a full-blown Mac desktop and mighty hard to carry around. Indeed, a *New York Times* review of the product on September 24, 1989, carried the headline: THE PORTABLE MAC: SHARP, BUT HEAVY and depicted a cartoon of a man hoisting the bulky contraption onto a dolly. Within Cupertino, the Portable was so widely ridiculed that it came to be known as the "Luggable," because it had to be lugged. A telling moment came at an employee gathering in the Flint Center auditorium of De Anza College, when a woman came up onstage to claim the Luggable she had won in a company raffle.

"She almost dropped it because it was too heavy," recalls Paul Mercer, an engineer in the audience that day.

It was funny, but not really. Not only was it heavy, but, unlike the machines put out by Apple's competitors, the Luggable could not be used on the planes where so many executives have downtime to catch up on paperwork. The first portable Macintosh would not fit onto a tray table and could be stowed under a seat only with great difficulty.

Gassée had blown it big this time. The Luggable landed on the market with a great thud and would never sell in great numbers. Sitting at a Silicon Valley coffee shop years later, Gassée shakes his head over the fiasco and sheepishly admits to me: "We knew the Luggable was a dud. But it was a first product." Then he leans forward with his wolfish smile and makes a joking reference to his company, Be Inc., which he started after leaving Apple: "I offered to give a two-hundred-dollar trade-in for anybody who brought in a Luggable in exchange for a Be box. I wanted to destroy all evidence."

Gassée wasn't laughing back in 1989, though. News accounts at the time were pitting him against Allan Loren in a battle for control to succeed Sculley as CEO one day. Just a few months before the Luggable came out, an unidentified former executive was quoted in Fortune as saying "On an unprecedented scale, a grab for power is under way; one of them [Gassée and Loren] will be gone or in a different position in six months."[6] The truth was, though, that both men's stars were starting to fade. It was Loren who had pushed Apple into raising prices at the worst of all possible times, causing a tremendous slowdown in sales and consequently a crash in profits. And it was Gassée who had given that pricing strategy a ringing endorsement, followed by the Luggable.

It was almost 1990, and both men were skating on thin ice. As was Apple.

6

The Fall of
Jean-Louis Gassée

One evening in about 1989, a secretary on the executive fourth floor of De Anza 7 got up from her desk to check on the status of her boss, Michael Spindler, who seemed to have disappeared into thin air after another marathon day at the office.

She walked into his office and was startled at what she found. Spindler, a large and excitable manager, was hiding underneath his desk of bleached-blond wood against one wall. When he ignored her nervous question if he was all right, she called for help from another executive secretary, who could not believe her eyes when she peered into the office through the window glass. "I remember being kind of nervous and laughing," recalls that latter secretary, who no longer works at Apple. "He was crouched on all fours, with his hands behind his head." They called for help from another person on the floor. The person, an unidentified executive, spoke softly to talk Spindler out. "We didn't say anything about it for years, and we all knew it."

Michael Spindler, at that time, was dividing his time between Apple's world headquarters and the company's base of operations in Paris as president of the fast-growing Apple Europe division. He was a man under intense pressure who was known by a few at Apple to succumb to apparent stress attacks, as well as to complain of chronic health ailments such as a bad back and weak heart. He would be under much more stress in the months and years to come. Change was once again in the wind at Apple Computer, and it would catapult this strange workaholic known as "the Diesel" past his peers in the executive suite to exhilarating corporate heights.

In 1989, the Apple world still belonged to the charismatic Frenchman Jean-Louis Gassée. And the two most loathsome words in his vocabulary were still "market share." Apple's computers, he would rail, were elegant, beautiful, in a class all by themselves. Apple, he argued, did not want or need market share. It just needed to keep making state-of-the-art Macintoshes that customers would willingly shell out big bucks for, stoking profits and that enormous R-and-D engine over which he had presided like an emperor.

That "high-right" strategy served Apple well during the late 1980s, at least on the balance sheet. By the 1989 fiscal year, which ended in September, Apple's revenue soared to an all-time high of $5.3 billion, while profits would surge to a record $454 million and the gross profit margin, as a percentage of sales, would hover at a fat and sassy 49 percent. There was another statistic, however, that boded serious trouble for Apple and Gassée's premium-pricing strategy. It concerned those two words you were not supposed to repeat in Gassée's presence: market share.

Apple had billed its first machines as "the computer for the rest of us," but by decade's end the product line had tilted so far to the high end of the spectrum that it was really "the computer for the elite of us." Apple therefore began losing share of the overall PC market at an alarming rate. In 1987, Apple's worldwide share of PC shipments had stood at 9.1 percent.[1] That was a level considerably shriveled from 1980, when Apple had had less competition and commanded nearly one fifth of all PC sales in the world. But it was healthy enough to sustain a business of ever-increasing profits and revenues. Apple kept making bigger and faster machines, and corporations kept buying them. But by 1989, over the span of just two short years, Apple's market share plunged to 7.6 percent.[2]

What had happened in those two short years was that the world had passed Apple Computer by. During this period, between 1987 and 1989, customers were increasingly looking for cheaper alternatives to the $5,000-plus computers that Sculley and Gassée had been pushing so ardently. The number of personal computers sold worldwide had mushroomed to about 60 million, or more than a sixfold increase from just four years prior. With so many companies making IBM-compatibles, price wars broke out, making PCs more affordable to general consumers. And with this increase in PC sales came a new era of "telecommuting," in which employees could buy their own computer and do more work from home.

The high-right strategy, in short, was proving to be an Achilles' heel. With precious few computers available for under $5,000, Apple was like a cruise ship with all its passengers at one side, listing dangerously because no one was on the other side. "High right would have been fine, if they had also had a low-left strategy," observes Roger McNamee, principal of Integral Capital Partners, a venture capital firm in Menlo Park, California.

It wasn't as though Apple was not getting a lot of good advice. Industry analysts practically begged Sculley to pay more attention to the lower end of the market. While applauding Sculley's success in getting the Mac taken seriously in corporations, industry consultant Richard Shaffer urged, in his "Technologic Computer Letter," that Sculley reread the early chapters of

Odyssey, which outlined the importance of market share in the Cola Wars. "Just as Pepsi found and exploited numerous chinks in Coke's armor, Apple is now beautifully positioned to make major inroads into the dominance of IBM-compatible personal computers," Shaffer, principal of the New York consulting firm of Technologic Partners, wrote in 1989.[3] "It seems obvious to casual observers, such as us, that the time has come to strike again for market share."

Jean-Louis Gassée had managed to isolate Apple in other ways, too. The Apple arrogance that he epitomized had by this point become legendary in Silicon Valley. Apple had alienated its own customers when Allan Loren had initiated the disastrous pricing increase the year before, after Gassée's enthusiastic endorsement. Now Gassée was starting to offend Apple's own software developers, the guys who had helped build the Macintosh into a rousing success story and whom the Apple evangelist Guy Kawasaki had coddled. But Kawasaki left Apple in 1987 to start a software company called ACIUS Inc., and no one of his caliber had stepped in to fill the void left in the relations between Apple and the developers.

Those important relations took a nosedive on September 12, 1988, when Apple made its price-hike announcement. Shortly thereafter, Gassée presided over a stormy meeting of the company's independent software developers. The developers were howling mad, because sales of their software programs had tanked along with those of the Macintosh. "It just killed us all," recalls Dave Johnson, who was among the Mac's first developers with his SpellSwell spell-check program. Rock musician Todd Rundgren, who at the time was also developing music programs for the Mac, stood up to complain that he and the other developers were not making any money. "Gassée replied, 'If you develop for the Mac, you should be an artist. You should not worry about money,' " recalls Johnson, who was at that meeting.

Gassée was an equal opportunity antagonist. He mixed it up with the big boys just as much as he did with the little ones. And they did not get much bigger than Bill Gates.

Remember when Sculley had agreed to license the Mac's visual look to Bill Gates back in 1985? Through a terrible oversight by both Sculley and his lawyers, Apple had permitted Microsoft, in writing, to use the Mac's technology not only in the primitive version of Windows that was in development but in "present and future" versions. Even though Gates has always downplayed the import of that document, it nevertheless opened the legal floodgates for him. He was legally free to incorporate the Mac's distinctive look—all the way down to the little trash can icon on the screen—in everything he did from that day forward.

Bill Gates was not the kind of guy you wanted to give an opportunity like this. Give him an inch, and he'll take a mile. That is just Bill Gates. Being a religious culture, though, Apple had always been more an emotional company than a pragmatic one. And it took Windows as a personal affront. Never mind that it had been Sculley's own blunder that had handed Gates the rights to make his knockoff of the Mac. By 1988, when it had become clear Gates was going to take that mile through a new version called Windows 2.03, Gassée pushed for Apple to teach the nerd from Seattle a lesson. Mike Markkula, cofounder of Apple and at the time its most powerful board member, also wanted action. This would evolve into what Bill Gates remembers as "the silliest lawsuit ever filed."

At the time, however, the legal problems between Apple and Gates's Microsoft were no laughing matter. While the conflict was brewing between the giants, Hewlett-Packard, just up the road from Cupertino in Palo Alto, had also come up with user interface software called NewWave, for use in IBM-compatibles in conjunction with Windows. It, too, looked a lot like some features of the Mac. Wanting to set an example, Apple filed suit in U.S. District Court in San Jose, California, on March 17, 1988, accusing both Microsoft and H-P of violating its copyrights for the Mac's distinctive screen look and eventually seeking $5.5 billion in damages. Apple had declared war on its longtime ally and pulled H-P along for the bumpy ride.

Copyright law, as it pertains to high technology, has always been a murky legal area. So much of technology is based on someone else's earlier research that just about everybody in the industry has borrowed ideas to produce some new breakthrough. The Mac itself was a great example of this, since it had been Jobs who borrowed ideas from the Xerox PARC, the premier research institute that gave birth to the graphical user interface, to create first the Lisa and then the Mac. Averse to confrontation, Sculley himself certainly was not a litigious fellow. But Gassée was a tussler extraordinaire. He had even told Bill Gates to "fuck off" in 1985, after Gates threatened to withhold development of the Mac when Apple complained about Windows 1.0.[4] Apple had been to court many times during the 1980s, taking just about anybody to the mat for copyright infringements, real or perceived. And usually it had won. So when Apple filed suit against Microsoft and H-P, alleging copyright infringement, it did so with a little swagger in its step.

"Apple's board was absolutely convinced we would win the suit," Sculley remembers. "Apple had an incredible record of setting precedent law."

The suit did something besides royally ticking off its most important developer. It forestalled, once again, the intermittent talk within the company of whether Apple should open up the Mac to all comers. The minority opinion within Apple, as articulated by Dan Eilers and others, was that the company should just license the thing and see what happens. "The sense on the board was that Apple could not do anything to show a doubt that we would win [in the courts], and so that impacted licensing," Sculley says. In other words, if

Apple were to license the Mac, its argument that the technology was so valuable that it needed to be kept out of the hands of the competition might be undermined.

Gates's position was always that Apple should have attacked it in the marketplace, not in the courts. So what if he was treading on some of Apple's precious ground? Windows was still light-years behind the Mac. If Apple wanted to keep its technology lead, it would just have to keep on innovating—in other words, compete. That was his attitude. And as it would turn out, it should have been Sculley's and Gassée's, as well.

The following year, on July 25, 1989, U.S. District Judge William W. Schwarzer in San Francisco ruled that 179 of 189 allegedly infringing visual displays in Windows 2.03 were covered by the 1985 licensing agreement. The words "present and future software programs" played a key role in the decision. "Had it been the parties' intent to limit the license to the Windows 1.0 interface, they would have known how to say so," Judge Schwarzer wrote in his seventeen-page decision. "Instead, the 'derivative works' covered by the license are identified as the 'visual displays' in the Windows 1.0 interface, not the interface itself. And there is nothing in the 1985 Agreement that indicates that it was intended as a product license restricting Microsoft and its licensees to the use of Windows 1.0 interface as a whole."[5] This ruling was a heavy blow to Apple's case, because it meant that most of Apple's visual displays at issue in this suit were not protected.

Bill Gates has said he never needed that licensing agreement. But on that day in court, it surely helped that he had it in hand. For Apple, the case went downhill from there. Nearly three years later, on April 14, 1992, U.S. District Judge Vaughn R. Walker issued a four-minute oral ruling that dismissed the bulk of Apple's remaining claims against both Microsoft and H-P, thus gutting Apple's case. The suit was really all over for Apple then, but Apple would appeal all the way to the U.S. Supreme Court before it was finally thrown out for good. Since Apple had not had a leg to stand on in the first place, the more than $10 million it wasted in attorney's fees would have been better spent helping it come up with new innovations over this tumultous four-year period of litigation.

Even though Apple lost all its claims against Microsoft and H-P, one could understand Gassée's hostility toward Microsoft, his direct competitor in the operating system market. Microsoft was granted full permission to use Apple's innovations in a market competition of unforeseen magnitude for years to come. But it was a lot tougher to comprehend why he would go after one of Apple's most loyal supporters with all the tenacity of a rabid pit bull—and by teaming up with his new enemy, Bill Gates, to boot. It was enough to make a grown man cry.

Gassée's next brawl was against a scholarly man named John Warnock, so gentle he would not hurt a fly. Warnock and Chuck Geschke were computer scientists at the Xerox PARC who started a little software company in 1982 to peddle a new kind of page description language Warnock had come up with, called PostScript. They called their firm Adobe Systems, after the Adobe Creek that gurgled past Warnock's home in the Silicon Valley burg of Los Altos.

What PostScript did, in a nutshell, was revolutionize the way computer documents looked on a printed page. Until then, when PC documents unfurled from the printer, they looked as though they had been hammered out on an old typewriter. PostScript, however, used a new formula to describe computer-generated characters. It also used a piece of software called an "outline font," which stored the computerized description of each letter so it could be printed. The outline font was particularly neat, because it was "scalable," which meant the letter would contain the same high resolution no matter how big or small it was reproduced on paper.

The end result of all this was that a document would come out looking as if it had been sent to a professional typesetter. Users were suddenly able to experiment with type sizes and styles and produce documents that looked as if they had been professionally designed. In a stunning leap for emerging desktop publishers, PostScript enabled the printed page to look almost identical to what appeared on the computer screen. This parity between the screen and actual pages gave users an incredibly flexible new tool for document design and presentation. There was just no comparison—the quality was that good.

Always one to recognize a great technology, Steve Jobs had taken one look at PostScript and realized it would fit in beautifully with the Mac and his new Apple LaserWriter. He got Apple to invest $2.5 million in a 15 percent stake in Adobe and embraced PostScript with open arms. Warnock, who ran Adobe, was so grateful that he dedicated himself to making the Mac a success. Without him, Apple's huge desktop publishing business undoubtedly would not have taken off the way it did. Indeed, the Mac became the de facto standard in the graphics industry. "He's the man who saved the Macintosh," Robert X. Cringely wrote in his book *Accidental Empires*. Or, one of them, anyway.

By 1989, Adobe had grown to a minibehemoth selling hundreds of millions of dollars worth of PostScript and related programs per year. Adobe licensed PostScript for use on Apple's Macintosh, with Adobe receiving royalty payments as well as money for the use of PostScript's related Type 1 fonts. Adobe also sold graphics programs such as its highly popular Adobe Illustrator to desktop publishers and other computer users. It had mushroomed in size in tandem with Apple's growth and had as much at stake in the Mac's success as anybody. Jean-Louis Gassée certainly appreciated all of Warnock's work, or so he said. That did not stop him from putting the knife into Warnock's back.

It all started with a dinner that year at the Good Earth Restaurant and Bakery in Cupertino, situated just in front of Apple's very first building off Stevens Creek Boulevard. Gassée, who had arranged to meet with Warnock there, told him over drinks that Apple was tired of paying so much money for the Post-Script technology. Apple paid Adobe royalties on PostScript sold in Laser-Writers, as well as an extra $300 for each Type 1 font needed to print characters. Gassée wanted a cheaper alternative for some new, low-end Macs he had percolating in the labs. Apple would abandon Adobe in a deal Warnock would deride as "with the Devil."

Warnock was a pleasant, bearded fellow who could have passed for a professor on the nearby Stanford campus. His eyes normally twinkled with delight, but at the Good Earth they were flashing in rage. "It was stupid," he says, his face reddening with anger years later. "They wanted to bring something out just to be different. Both Apple and Microsoft did a huge disservice to the industry." Apple did have a strategy to address the bottom of the market, but it had been given low priority at that point. When Warnock told Gassée that Adobe would keep making just the one PostScript, Gassée thanked him for the meeting and gave fair warning: Apple would come up with its own printing software. Not only that, it would team up with Microsoft, the same company it was dragging through the courts, to do so.

Microsoft was in the middle of practically every technology scrape in the PC industry, and this one was no different. As of mid-1989, while Apple was jumping up and down over Windows 2.03, Bill Gates and crew were putting the finishing touches to a new version of that software called Windows 3.0 that would debut in 1990. As far as Microsoft was concerned, this was the big kahuna, the graphical operating system that Microsoft's customers would embrace. It was neater, slicker, and far easier to use than all the previous versions of Windows, which had served as technical tune-ups. At this time, Microsoft also wanted the font technology for the company's collaborative work with IBM on another operating system called Operating System/2, or OS/2. That OS/2 pact would soon break down, however, as outlined here later.

Since Microsoft was about to enter the graphical market big time, it began foraging around for a scalable font technology that would give the IBM-compatible side of the world the same high quality in printouts as the Mac had. In June 1989, Dennis Adler, Microsoft's resident font expert, was instructed by his superiors to start working on fonts, which provide a full assortment of styles and sizes of printing types. "At the time, only PostScript printers could reproduce to the printer exactly what was on the screen," remembers Adler, who is now Microsoft's group program manager of advanced technology and research. "We saw this as a strategic technology that we could not afford to have controlled by someone else. So the mission was to come up with something as good [as] or better than PostScript's Type 1 fonts."

Microsoft did have discussions with Adobe about the rights to use Type 1 fonts in Windows, but the terms were unacceptable to Bill Gates, in part because Adobe would not agree to publish its font specifications. Microsoft wanted the fonts to be open to the rest of the industry, in order to make them a standard. To compete with Adobe, Microsoft followed its long practice of rarely inventing something new. Bill Gates had always relied on watching technology trends closely and picking up on those he believed would result in more profits for his company. That had been the case with MS-DOS, which was based on technology Microsoft had originally acquired in 1980 from a tiny company called Seattle Computer Products. If he did not have to reinvent the wheel, he was not going to. Gassée and his Apple engineers, of course, possessed the exact opposite mentality: if it was not invented at Apple, it was not worth a hill of beans anyhow.

Accordingly, Apple had started work on a font technology it called "Royal." (The code name for the project was "Bass.") In the summer of 1989, Microsoft acquired a company named Bauer Enterprises, located in Berkeley, California, which had developed a PostScript-compatible technology later called TrueImage. The head of Bauer Enterprises, Cal Bauer, approached Dennis Adler one day soon after and said, "Apple is dying to work with you," Adler remembers. Apple usually insisted on reinventing the wheel. An exception was made in this case, however, because Gassée had to come up with an alternative to PostScript for his new low-end machines, and fast.

So Microsoft licensed its new True Image technology to Apple, in exchange for a license to Apple's Royal. The two companies came up with a new name for their combined technologies: TrueType for the fonts and True Image for the printer language. "We had black T-shirts that said TRUETYPE with the fossilized imprint of a bass [from the Apple code name]," Adler recalls.

Warnock had received fair warning, but that didn't lessen the sting for him when the technologies were actually announced. It happened at the annual Seybold Desktop Publishing Conference in San Francisco on September 20, 1989. This was—and still is—a highly influential affair, put on by the respected industry analyst Jonathan Seybold and generally attended by the leaders of the PC industry. A day before the conference, on September 19, a woman from Apple's public relations department got a phone call at about 5 P.M. to drop everything and go to Gassée's office. She arrived to find Gassée and a young man named Jim Gable, TrueType's new product manager from Apple, prepared to fill her in on details for a press release. She then cornered Sculley to brief him on what to say at a press conference by Apple and Microsoft scheduled in just two hours.

Sculley, who was almost exclusively focused on long-range strategy, had delegated much of the company's decision making on day-to-day product strategies to Gassée and the other top lieutenants. Not surprisingly, then, Sculley did not know what on earth she was talking about. "Sculley was asking me,

'What is this? Why are we doing this? Why is Bill Gates here?' " says a person familiar with the conversation.

The following day, the mild-mannered John Warnock blew his cool. The lights went down in a theater at San Francisco's downtown Moscone Center as a Microsoft representative showed a "proof of concept" demonstration of the new printing technology to some one thousand people in the audience. "Proof of concept" meant that it was a demonstration of what the technology was intended to look like rather than the actual technology, which was not yet completed. Bill Gates stood up from a stool onstage to assure the throng that "two standards are better than one." PostScript, for lack of an alternative, was the standard on the Macintosh. Gates looks more his age today. But when he spoke in the early days, you had to rub your eyes and blink to make sure the mop-haired youngster with huge glasses really was the power behind the Microsoft empire. Gates looked like a lost boy, but his words would often drip with venom. You could almost see him smirk as he twisted the knife in an opponent, as he did to Warnock that day.

"Two is a good number," Gates repeated, as a few boos erupted from this hostile crowd of mostly Macintosh devotees. Sitting on a stool behind Gates was none other than the great Steve Jobs, who was attending Seybold to pitch the crowd on his new NeXT computer, which had just begun shipping only two days before. As Gates spoke of those two standards, Jobs could be seen on his stool, smiling slyly as he held up three fingers. Jobs wasn't referring to printing standards, though; he hoped his NeXT would become the third PC standard, along with the IBM-compatible and the Macintosh.

Now it was poor Warnock's turn to speak. He was clad in a gray suit, and onlookers could see his hand shaking as he took a gulp of water before standing up from his stool alongside Gates and Jobs. With the bright lights in his face, they could also see that his eyes were brimming with tears. Adobe's stock price had plunged by about half in the preceding days on rumors of the Apple-Microsoft alliance. He had the look of a man who had been betrayed by his best friend, and in fact he had. "That's the biggest bunch of garbage and mumbo jumbo," Warnock told the audience in a trembling voice. "What those people are selling you is snake oil!"

Relations between Apple and Adobe were so imperiled that Apple went out and unloaded all of its shares in Adobe, for a gain of $79 million. That was a great return on its original investment of $2.5 million. But deep emotional damage had been inflicted on a key ally. Ironically, for all the ill will this generated, TrueType ended up so inferior to PostScript on the Macintosh that it never ended up shipping on many printers. The reason for that, according to Duane Schulz, who joined Apple in 1990 to help run a new imaging business, was "because of lack of follow-through. Apple had a 'launch-and-ditch' syndrome." Microsoft, however, pushed TrueType into a rousing success on Windows.

To this day, Gassée still defends the decision to go with TrueType. "I know there is a perception of our arrogance, and I am more than ready to admit some mistakes," he says. "But in this case, it was about money. We were being charged a lot of money for PostScript fonts. So I don't think TrueType was a bad decision. Sometimes you just do the better thing." It is true that Adobe was charging a lot for its fonts. And in fact, the TrueType caper did force Adobe to lower its font prices. Still, the episode sent out a chilling message to all of Apple's developers: if Apple could do this to Adobe, it could do it to anybody. "There were obviously better ways to handle it [Adobe's high prices] than that," Sculley now agrees.

The developers would have their payback time in the years to come.

The deteriorating relations between Apple and the outside world in this period coincided with a plunge in morale inside the company. Engineers were seeing their projects get killed right and left. Marketing people were undergoing a re-organization every six months. Loren's U.S. organization was particularly hard hit, having undergone a half-dozen reorganizations since he had taken over. "There was this feeling that senior management was untouchable and that there was a lot of fighting at the top," recalls Elaine Fellenbaum, a project manager in Apple's creative services department. "It was like a macho, cutting-out-your-territory kind of place. I hated working at Apple by that point."

Some of the brightest engineers, such as Erich Ringewald and Steve Perl-man, were leaving, over their disenchantment with the lack of direction, as were marketing stars such as John Scull, who had been so instrumental in the desktop publishing business. "They were putting bozos in charge of every-thing," Scull recalls bitterly. "By the time I left in 1989, they were hiring con-sultants to come in and study everything. It was pretty clear the suits were taking over." Scull went on to become managing director of PF.Magic, a small software company in San Francisco.

Sculley himself seemed increasingly out of touch with the mood of the company. When Loren had taken over in sales and marketing, he had seen to it that just about everyone in his giant organization would have to go through him before getting an audience with the CEO. This effectively ended Scul-ley's open-door policy. Sculley became so immersed in giving speeches and press interviews that the lower echelons rarely saw him on the Apple campus. He did emerge from seclusion to survey the moderate damage inflicted on some of the company's buildings following the 7.1 Richter scale earthquake that rocked the San Francisco Bay area on October 17, 1989. But to many employees his visits were surreal.

"He came into our building followed by an entourage," says Fellenbaum, recalling Sculley's postearthquake tour of her creative services building just behind the De Anza 7 headquarters. "You had this feeling that Sculley was like a mayor. There was an ivory tower, even though there was not one."

Sculley was so out of the loop that he seemed genuinely shocked when, at a two-day managerial meeting at the Fairmont Hotel in downtown San Jose about the same time, results were released of an attitudinal survey that documented a precipitous fall in employee morale. "People were very unhappy and frustrated," recalls Apple Fellow Al Alcorn, who attended that retreat. "Middle management was angry, because it felt disempowered." After that, Sculley and Sullivan proposed that an employee council be formed to stay in better touch. But that idea never went far, and the morale problem continued to fester.

Sculley says he was indeed shocked by the fall in morale. "I was getting a lot of my information about employee morale from Sullivan, who was saying things were great," he remembers.

It was at that same retreat that the mounting tensions between Gassée and Loren came bubbling to the surface. The two men had started out as allies but increasingly came to resent and distrust each other in what other Apple people viewed as a classic power struggle. Each of the men was supposed to give a talk basically summarizing what his operations were up to. Gassée was more than up to the challenge. A silver-tongued devil, he would interlace his commentary with the kind of jokes and sexual double entendres that enlivened otherwise numbing discussions of technology's bits and bytes. Loren, on the other hand, was far less adept at public speaking and proved to be ill prepared for this speech. It was his bad fortune to follow a typically brilliant presentation by Gassée, in front of Sculley, the entire executive staff, and some four hundred of Apple's top managers in a Fairmont ballroom. It was an awful thing to watch.

"When Loren got up, he was unprepared and rambled and stuttered," recalls Alcorn, who was sitting in the audience. Gassée took it all in from his vantage point in a front row, a half smile on his lips. "Jean-Louis appeared delighted that Loren had fallen apart," Alcorn says.

The whole company, in point of fact, seemed to be falling apart. Apple was falling hopelessly behind in the burgeoning market for cheap computers. It had alienated both its customers and its own developers. Once a place where everybody in the Valley wanted to work, the best and brightest were leaving in droves. Fittingly, it seemed, even an earthquake had shaken up the place. And it was about to get worse.

As the big Christmas season of 1989 swung into high gear, sales of computers to consumers dipped in an industrywide slump. Having nothing demonstrably new to offer consumers on the low end it had essentially ignored, Apple saw that growth stall out. As noted earlier, Apple had built a stronghold in sales of computers to schools. Through another stroke of brilliance, Steve Jobs had recognized early on that schools would be a great place to stockpile his first Apple IIs. Besides being profitable, since Apple was selling to schools without the big dealer markups, the benefits would be twofold: many machines would be shipped, increasing market share, and Apple would start converting potential future customers at an impressionable age. But with precious few new low-end computers for the schools to buy, even this bastion was slipping. Finally, the Luggable's poor showing contributed to the mess.

The final results told the grim story. Sales in the Christmas 1989 quarter grew just 6 percent in that period from the same time a year earlier, compared to annual growth rates of 18 percent to 40 percent in each quarter of the preceding twelve months. Profits fell 11 percent, the first decrease since the one precipitated at the beginning of the year by the pricing fiasco of 1988. In one week in December, the stock price plunged 20 percent—a fall equivalent to $1.1 billion of Apple's market value then—after the company warned Wall Street of a poor showing in the quarter ending December 29.

During all this, Sculley was looking more and more despondent. When he had first arrived at Apple, he had vowed to stay just five years and return home. His wife, Leezy, hated California, believing the laid-back Golden State lacked the sophistication and charm of the East. She couldn't wait to get out. But Sculley had been on the job for seven years and couldn't just up and leave with the ship going down. On the Learjet he used to shuttle around the world, a former aide remembers returning from a trip to the restroom during a flight back to California from London and seeing Sculley slumped in his seat, looking haggard and tired. To some aides, he was known fondly as just "J.S."

"I said, 'J.S., what's wrong?' " says the aide, who spoke on condition of anonymity. "He looked up and said, 'You know, what I really want to do is start this think tank with bright people and bright ideas. I'm so tired of all these headaches.' Every year he would say, 'Next year, I'm going to leave.' But he wanted to leave Apple in good shape, and he wasn't going to leave until that happened. He was getting burned out."

On Saturday night, January 13, 1990, Ella Fitzgerald entertained six thousand Apple employees at a belated Christmas party. The gala was reminiscent of the good old days, but it was really more like a sad farewell to them. The new decade had begun, and it wasn't nearly as full of hope and promise in Cupertino as had been 1980, when Steve Jobs and his band of long-haired hippies had begun a revolution. The following week, Apple announced its disastrous quarterly results and Sculley called the troops together to warn them that he planned to cut costs significantly, including through layoffs to be announced. "We've succeeded in times of rapid growth. Now, we must prove we can succeed in times of slower growth," Sculley wrote in an internal memorandum.[6] A shudder rippled through the company; no one could feel safe.

About this same time, Sculley invited Gassée to dinner at an upscale French-Italian eatery in downtown Palo Alto called Maddalena's, which offers escargot as an appetizer. Sculley had backed down before Gassée's tantrums before but had now decided he wasn't going to take it anymore. At least this John Sculley wouldn't. There were really two John Sculleys at Apple. There was the John Sculley who excelled in crisis, the guy who would stand up on the deck of a ship buffeted by hurricane-force winds and take command of the rudder, just as he had done in 1985, when he had steered Apple from the precipice of collapse to a four-year run of unparalleled growth. And there was the wimpy John Sculley, the man who preferred to pontificate, philosophize, and avoid a fight at all costs. It was almost as though there were a John Sculley who was Clark Kent and another who was Superman.

It was Superman who was about to meet with Gassée. In the previous months, Sculley had been advised by aides that Gassée was criticizing him behind his back. "John would go in and tell Gassée that he was not going to tolerate it anymore," recalls one former Sculley aide. Sculley was actually goaded into the meeting at Maddalena's by none other than Kevin Sullivan, the wily HR chief who had also orchestrated the removal of Chief Operating Officer Del Yocam. With the company's momentum stalling out on the lack of a market share strategy, Sullivan remembers Sculley fretting one day over how he could get Gassée to finally accept the fact that Apple would have to pump up the volume and ship out large numbers of low-end Macs.

"Do you think I can run this company?" Sculley asked him, as Sullivan remembers. "I said, 'You can. But you have to be the leader. You either have to order Gassée to do it or get rid of him.' " And as another former senior executive remembers, Sullivan advised Sculley to schedule "a showdown dinner" with Gassée, the one that was about to get under way at Maddalena's.

Maddalena's is tucked into a discreet corner off downtown Palo Alto's busy University Avenue, just east of the Stanford campus. With its impressive concentration of chic restaurants and trendy boutiques along a half-mile strip, University has long served as the meeting ground of Silicon Valley. Inside these restaurants, in places like the tony Il Fornaio, deals are made that determine the fortunes of entire companies. Don't let the laid-back attire fool you. That twenty-four-year-old kid sitting at the next table in T-shirt and jeans might very well be a multimillionaire CEO of one of the myriad tech start-up companies in the Valley. University Avenue, in many ways, is Silicon Valley's version of Hollywood's Rodeo Drive. It has long been a stomping ground of the rich, the powerful, and the ambitious.

At Maddalena's, Sculley was accompanied by Kevin Sullivan. This was a bad sign, Gassée knew, for Sullivan had been instrumental in the coup that had resulted in Del Yocam losing his job. For good reason, Sullivan was becoming known around Apple as a henchman. Seated in a private dining room upstairs, Sculley looked across the table at Gassée and figuratively handed him the rope with which to hang himself.

"Sculley asked me what I thought of him," Gassée says. "Being a frank guy, I gave him pluses as well as minuses." That is putting it mildly. Interrupted only when waiters in black tuxedos would deliver plateloads of sumptuous entrees, five years of building tension between the two men all came pouring out at once. "Gassée basically told me that I was the wrong person to be at Apple," Sculley remembers. "He said, 'Apple is about the Macintosh. You do not know enough about the Mac and its technology. The customers know and the engineers know that you are an outsider. The engineers don't respect you. I don't respect you.' " Gassée paused to let that sink in and fired one last zinger—one that would prove most prophetic.

"Contrary to what you might think," Gassée remembers telling Sculley, "a lot of people want to stab you in the back"—namely, Sculley's own executive staff, whom Gassée remembers as feeling "fairly malcontent" with Sculley's leadership.

When Gassée had finally finished, Sculley was brutally frank, too. "I was telling him, 'We can't keep taking three years to bring out new products. We have to go for market share.' Gassée said, 'To hell with the market. That is not what this is about. You, John Sculley, don't know enough about the products for me to respect working for you.' "

Sullivan, who was taking it all in without saying a word, fairly quivered with delight. Gassée had said exactly what Sullivan had wanted him to. "From that moment," Sullivan remembers, "it was clear John and Gassée could not work together." Gassée figured that out for himself afterward, as the three men stood on the curb outside waiting for valets to bring their cars around. "Sullivan put his arm around my shoulders and said, 'I'm very proud of you,' " Gassée recalls. That's when Gassée realized that he had hung himself on his own words. It was, as Gassée says, "the Last Supper." Sullivan, indeed, was proud. "I said I was proud because he told the truth," Sullivan says.

Gassée was now all but washed up at Apple Computer, as was his old rival, Allan Loren. The innumerable personality conflicts aside, Loren's stewardship of Apple's U.S. business had been an abject failure. Sales in North America were the slowest of Apple's worldwide markets, so the layoffs were expected by most pundits to hit Loren's group the hardest. By the end of 1989, Loren was as disenchanted with Apple as many in the company were with him. At a board meeting that year, he remembers, a director chastised him for not growing the U.S. business as fast as the rest of the industry. But a big reason for that, Loren contends, was that Apple had delayed so long in getting a laptop computer out to the market, and laptops, in 1989, were a fast-growing part of the market. "In the markets in which we had products, we were growing faster than anyone else," Loren recalls. "But the laptop we didn't have." Loren, in effect, was pointing the finger at Gassée.

More fundamentally, Loren had grown alarmed at what he considered Sculley's constant waffling on strategic initiatives. During Apple's annual sales meeting in September 1989, held on the Big Island of Hawaii, Sculley stood at the lectern to tell his salespeople that "This is the year of education," Loren remembers. "But we had no new education products. It was like being a lineman on the San Francisco 49ers and having a new game book for all sixteen NFL regular-season games. You think that lineman is going to execute very well?" Loren, who was sitting with Gassée in the audience, leaned over to whisper, "What are we going to do?" Loren recalls. "He said, 'I don't know. We're already committed for six months.'" Sculley, however, points out that Apple USA, at that time, derived fully 55 percent of its revenue from sales to the education market. With what he remembers as "a very disproportionate number" of Apple's education salespeople in the room that day, Sculley says, "Not to have had a major education message from the CEO would have been pretty weird."

By this point, Sculley had distanced himself so much from the drudgery of actually running a business that it is not surprising to hear him espouse views totally different from those of his former staff. Indeed, Joe Graziano was shocked to find a management team in almost complete disarray after he was lured by Sculley to return to Apple in June 1989, taking Debi Coleman's place as chief financial officer. Graziano, who is known by the nickname "the Graz," had been away from Apple for four years, having departed in that tumultuous year of 1985 to join Sun Microsystems. Back then, Sculley had proven himself to be a take-charge, no-nonsense manager. There was a different John Sculley at the helm when the Graz returned.

"When Joe came in to help finance, he found out that, guess what? Every time John would have a meeting, Sullivan, Spindler, Loren, and Gassée would get together afterwards and say, 'OK, what part of what Sculley said will we implement?'" recalls a former senior executive who witnessed these meetings. "Joe confronted John and told him what was happening [shortly before Christmas 1989]. John called Joe at five-thirty A.M. the next day to ask him more about the management team. See, John wasn't in control. They had neutered him. Joe told John, 'The people heading up your team are fighting you.'" Graziano's advice: Get rid of both Gassée and Loren.

Sculley was thus ready to jettison the two most powerful members of his executive staff and try to turn the boat around without them. It had become clear to him that having four Apple presidents with equal power was not working. He needed to bring in a strong number two again, to manage the day-to-day business.

Someone like Del Yocam.

Yocam had taken his heave-ho like a man. There had been no running to the media, no threats of lawsuits. He may have been intensely disliked by the other members of the executive staff, who lusted after his job, but just about everyone else at Apple liked him. Sculley had always felt guilty about what he had done to Yocam — so much so that he arranged a huge going-away party when Yocam's "retirement" became official in November 1989. No one at Apple had ever been given such a rousing send-off, nor has anyone since. The party was held under the canopy of a big tent erected on the campus. There were speeches, songs, even funny videos. Yocam still keeps a nine-minute video of the highlights and is almost moved to tears when he views them again in a downstairs office of his home filled with Apple mementos.

"Del will be greatly missed," Sculley wrote in his annual message to shareholders for that year. Life had been good for Sculley when Yocam was his right-hand man. It was not so smooth without him.

Sculley planned to announce details of a new reorganization on January 29, 1990, a Monday. He had decided to put somebody back in as chief operating officer, and he wanted Del Yocam. The previous day was Super Bowl Sunday. Joe Montana and the San Francisco 49ers were in New Orleans, trouncing the hapless Denver Broncos, 55–10. A fanatical 49ers fan, Yocam was there for the game with his family. That same morning, as he bustled about his hotel room in preparation to leave for his skybox seat at the Superdome, Yocam picked up the ringing phone and was surprised to hear Sculley's voice on the other end. Yocam had been out of the company for only two months.

"It was out of the blue," Yocam recalls. "He talked about how his new organization was not working out. He said, 'I need to go back to having a president and COO, and I'd like you to come back and do that for me.'" Actually, Yocam had never been president and COO, just COO. He just could not do it, though. The decade he had spent at Apple had been like a whole career at just about anyplace else. Having earned millions on his stock options while at Apple, he was enjoying time off with his wife, Janet, and their children — going to Disney World, taking leisurely drives in his car across the country — and was in no hurry to jump back into anything as stressful as running a big computer company. In 1992, he would go on to become CEO of Tektronix Inc., a Wilsonville, Oregon, maker of computer printers. And in December 1996, he would become chairman and CEO of Borland International Inc., a software maker in Scotts Valley, California.

He had lived Apple. He had loved Apple. But he had moved on past Apple.

"I told John I wasn't ready to come back," Yocam says. "And I told him that on the spot. After I turned him down, he got Spindler."

Michael Spindler. Now, that would be a name that would go down in infamy in the history of Apple Computer. As of early 1990, Spindler had already come a long way. It had all started in 1942, when he was born in Nazi Germany as Adolf Hitler's stormtroopers waged terrible war on all sides. His father worked in a German munitions factory and during World War II was separated from his wife and infant son. With the war's end in 1945, the Spindlers reunited and young Michael busied himself in academia, going on to graduate in 1966 with a master of science degree in engineering from West Germany's Rheinische Sachhochschule.

Fascinated with electronics, Spindler worked his way through various engineering positions at technology companies including Digital Equipment Corporation, Schlumberger Ltd., and Siemens AG, before becoming European marketing manager for Intel. Along the way, Spindler impressed his coworkers so much with his tireless energy that they began calling him "the Diesel." One of Spindler's Intel counterparts on the other side of the Atlantic was a wiry, hyperactive young man named Mike Markkula. The two Mikes had a lot in common, despite their geographic differences. Both were equally interested in engineering and marketing. Indeed, Markkula had once designed an electronic slide rule and at Intel was product manager for the 8088, the chip embraced by IBM that would ignite the PC industry into a global force.

"To Markkula, Spindler was one of the smartest men he'd ever met," Yocam says. This relationship, forged in the 1970s, would stand Spindler in good stead later on. But it would also bring Apple serious trouble.

In 1980, an opening came up for someone to manage the European marketing activities of a flashy new computer company called Apple. As with every other company in the computer industry, the story of Apple's meteoric rise out of a California garage was well known by Spindler. He signed on in September of that year, working temporarily out of a cramped, one-hundred-square-foot office in Brussels. He must have been dedicated, because he worked the first six months for Apple without receiving a paycheck. "Spindler told me Apple could not figure out how to get the money over," says one of his former secretaries.

By early 1981, Spindler helped to found Apple's European headquarters in Paris, a city he absolutely adored. His wife was French, and, like many Europeans, he spoke the language fluently. English was his third language, behind German and French. In 1984, he was promoted to general manager of marketing and sales for the European region, which included such countries as France, Germany, and the United Kingdom. In the big 1985 reorganization, Sculley named him the vice president for international sales and marketing. Then, following the 1988 coup against Yocam, he was elevated to president of the new Apple Europe division, responsible for Apple's thirteen European subsidiaries as well as the company's distribution throughout Africa and the Middle East.

Sculley was impressed with Spindler from the very beginning. Even Spindler's many detractors speak admiringly of his keen mind when it came to product-selling strategy. Because he had roots in two European countries, oversaw sales and distribution in more than a dozen others, and commuted regularly to California, Spindler possessed a global view of how a business should be run. In his book *Odyssey*, Sculley gushed over the "multi-local approach" that Spindler began championing as head of international sales and marketing.

"For far too long, most American multi-nationals simply cloned their U.S. operations overseas, selling exactly the same product around the world that was successful in the United States," Sculley wrote. Then, quoting from Spindler himself, the passage in *Odyssey* continued, "The multi-national format has two drawbacks. It means too much jurisdictional influence from corporate headquarters and too much of a nationalist approach. Multi-local means you have a network model that adapts to local markets. You behave and act like a local company, yet you are within the network of the mother company back home. The whole world can thus become one big shopping cart for ideas and capital."[7]

It was a brilliant idea and one that, when implemented, would contribute to an explosion of sales overseas. In Japan, for example, Apple had had little success selling computers until Spindler helped see to it in 1986 that Macs sold there contained KanjiTalk, an operating system that let the Japanese work in their traditional alphabets. As president of Apple Europe, Spindler found that the strategy could apply in reverse for some situations. When he took over, Apple's prices varied as much as 40 percent across Europe, due to different dealer discounts in each country. Spindler seized control of all pricing, making prices the same for the whole continent. The end result of his actions was that Apple's sales in Europe tripled to $1.2 billion between 1988 and 1990, accounting for nearly one fourth of the company's entire revenues.

If the Diesel could do that in Europe, Sculley thought, just imagine what he could do for worldwide sales as chief operating officer. "The reports from Europe were that he had done a good job," Sculley remembers. "He also had strong support from Sullivan." The whole world would soon find, however, that Spindler's skills as a strategist would not translate into effectiveness as a hands-on operating manager.

Spindler had another compelling draw: passion. This is probably a difficult concept for people to believe if they have only seen Spindler making speeches to non-Apple groups. In public, he often spoke in a monotone, barely looking up as he laboriously outlined the most arcane of technical details. There was very little smiling and certainly no appearance of relaxation. He was nothing at all like Sculley, who seemed to glow onstage, breaking complex subjects into plain words that anyone could understand. But the Michael Spindler that Apple employees knew was something else entirely. He would stalk the stage, wave his arms, punch his fist into the air. The tight-fitting silk shirts he often wore would become soaked in sweat. His usually unruly black hair would become even wilder. Saliva would fly out of his mouth.

"We used to have a joke that you don't sit in the first ten rows at a Spindler speech," recalls John Ziel, a former Apple sales manager. "Because you might drown from all the sweat and spit." The object of Spindler's passion at these events was always Apple, but he might as well have been in a tent spreading the Word. "If you could take away his German accent and put him in the South, he could have been a religious preacher," recalls one senior executive who did not want his name used. He was a preacher who sounded like Arnold Schwarzenegger.

Unlike Sculley, Spindler also gave the appearance of being decisive. Part of that reputation came from his physical appearance. In the late 1980s, he didn't look overweight, but he stood a good six feet tall and weighed well over two hundred pounds. His burning eyes would bore into you from a meaty face that looked as though it had taken a punch or two. "One time at a meeting at the Fairmont in San Jose, when he still headed Europe, Spindler gave his opinion in front of two hundred Apple people, and his whole body language challenged anyone who disagreed with him," recalls George Everhart, a marketing manager at the time.

But appearances can be deceiving, as they were in Spindler's case. He suffered from many notable drawbacks, not the least of which was the fact that he wasn't an operating guy at all. Sure, international sales had soared on his watch. But it helped an awful lot that he had strong lieutenants under him who were adept at operations. "I always felt Mike was an exceptional marketing strategist when he worked for me," recalls Del Yocam. "But boy, did we have to shore him up in operations. I never felt there was an operating bone in his body."

An "operating guy," in the mode of a Del Yocam, is one who painstakingly watches over every aspect of a company's operation, from making sure the people in production are manufacturing enough machines to meet an order to cracking the whip on the salespeople out in the field to ensure those products are getting into customers' hands. It is by nature a dirty, unglamorous job but one vitally important to any manufacturer such as Apple.

Now, here is the antithesis of the operating guy. Say you are the head of marketing for somebody, and you have these great ideas for increasing sales.

You call all your managers into a conference room, sit them down around the table, and start prattling on about your strategy, all the while standing at a whiteboard and scribbling as fast as you can. Sweat is flying off your head, you are so worked up. Your eyes bulge, and you talk even faster. Since you're the boss, all heads bob approvingly. No one dares to ask a question. Then the meeting is over, and everybody rushes back out. There's just one problem: nobody has understood a word you said. What's more, you don't check back to see that they had. This was Michael Spindler.

"Many times we would walk out of a room and not know what he said," recalls Bob Saltmarsh, the treasurer at that time. "You'd feel like this fire hose had been aimed at you with this huge amount of information."

What Spindler really needed was a translator, someone who could put his ramblings into plain English. Or plain French, German, or whatever language he happened to be using. That is what he had in Europe in a man named Stefan Winsnes, Apple's director of human relations there. "Mike would hold product strategy meetings in Europe, and most of the people would look at Stefan and ask, 'What did he say?'" says Phil Dixon, who worked under Spindler in Apple's Europe business. "And he would say, 'OK, you do this. You do that. And you do that.' So he had a translator."

Whenever he traveled to Cupertino, Spindler left his translator behind. And he frequently ran into trouble similar to the fiasco involving *PC Week* magazine, the most influential trade magazine in the computer industry. On the IBM-compatible side of the business, *PC Week* was the big kahuna, *The Wall Street Journal* of computer trade publications. On the Apple side, there was *MacWEEK*, a trade magazine exclusively devoted to tracking Apple's Macintosh technology. Getting publicity in *MacWEEK* was great, but it was like preaching to the choir. Spindler wanted to reach out to the unwashed masses still toiling away on their dreadful IBM-compatibles. So when Spindler was running Europe, he suggested that Apple start trying to get more ink in the non-Mac trade publications. It was a great idea, and the people in public relations worked to make it happen.

In an effort to gain that increased visibility, they set up a one-on-one interview between Spindler and a reporter for *PC Week* named John Dodge. This was a real coup. Not only would Spindler's comments be included in a magazine for IBM-compatible users, it was going to be the *cover* story. Spindler met, as promised, and delivered his usual unintelligible monologue. Dodge thanked him at the end of the one-hour session and went on his way. "But he called later and said, 'Look, I can't understand what he was saying. I even taped it, and still can't understand it,'" says a former Apple employee familiar with the episode. "So PR set up a second interview, and Dodge still could not understand him. They never ran the story."

Spindler was so plodding that he had trouble even telling a joke. "When I was in John's office, Michael would come in and tell us a joke," recalls one former aide to Sculley. "He'd tell the joke, and I'd say, 'I don't get it.' He got all upset and started talking faster, and John didn't get it either. Finally, I told John, 'Let's just laugh whenever he tells a joke.' Two days later, John and I started laughing so hard we were slapping our knees. Michael walked away smiling. But since he thought only John and I understood him, he started coming in every day with his jokes."

That was funny, but Spindler's notoriously poor health was no joke. For years, he had complained of stress attacks and heart problems. In later years, as he battled a weight problem, he also complained of back pain. He complained so much that many people around Apple came to believe Spindler was a hypochondriac. But those closest to him knew he was not. One day in the late 1980s, when Yocam was still COO and Spindler was reporting to him, Yocam walked into Spindler's office in Cupertino to find the Diesel lying unconscious on a sofa. "It was almost like an epileptic fit," says one person who witnessed the episode but did not want his name used. Paramedics were called to haul him to the hospital.

Through the years, Spindler would make repeated trips to the hospital at Stanford University, some on his own and some in an ambulance. Another time, when he was found passed out in his office, the secretaries called 911 but asked for the paramedics not to pull in with sirens blaring. They didn't want anyone else at Apple to know what was happening. They also requested that the paramedics climb up to the fourth floor of De Anza 7 by way of the back steps. Spindler complained to friends that he suffered from a heart problem, but neither he nor his doctors would verify that.

What was clear was that Michael Spindler had a notoriously poor ability to handle stress. One former executive remembers seeing him "just start shaking," he would become so upset about something. And there had been the 1989 episode of him being talked out from under his desk. There had been a similar incident in 1987, when Allan Loren was hired. Loren was being introduced around De Anza 7 by another top executive, when they came to Spindler's office and could see no one inside. "He told Allan, 'Maybe you ought to wait outside,' " recalls a former executive who witnessed this incident and would not reveal the name of the man escorting Loren. "A few minutes later, he comes out with Spindler, and he and Allan met. Outside, later, Allan asked, 'What was that all about?' He [the executive escort] said, 'He doesn't like pressure.' " Spindler, no doubt, was under his desk, since the only other place that he could have been in the office that was obscured from view was in a cramped closet with the door closed.

With Spindler, finally, there was the issue of trust. Spindler's involvement in the Yocam coup convinced many aides in the executive suite that Spindler ultimately wanted to run Sculley out, too. Indeed, Gassée says Spindler had told him that. When asked to elaborate on that statement, Gassée declined. But Sculley's aides were concerned enough about Spindler's rumored ambitions that they approached the boss. "I never trusted him from day one," says one of Sculley's former aides. "I told John, but he said, 'He's all right.' " Another of Sculley's assistants remembers imparting the same warning at one of the morning staff meetings Sculley held every day with his aides. "I said to John, 'You cannot trust Spindler. He does not like you,' " this second aide remembers.

Having come from the corporate culture of Pepsi, where there were known rules and a defined hierarchy, Sculley was a naturally trusting person whose inclination when told someone was criticizing him behind his back to others was to go up to the individual and ask if it was true. When that person invariably said no, that was good enough for Sculley. In his world—and he admits now that it was a naïve one—people didn't lie. "John once confronted Spindler about bad-mouthing behind his back, and Michael said, 'Never, never, never. That's not true,' " says a former secretary who overheard the exchange.

At one point, shortly after the Del Yocam coup in 1988, Sculley had heard a rumor that both Spindler and Sullivan were plotting to dethrone him. That Spindler and Sullivan would be collaborating on something would not have been surprising.

Of all the personal relationships in the executive suite over the years, the bond between these two men was among the closest—and strangest. There are many theories on why this came to be. Many people who were at Apple then say they believe that Kevin Sullivan was the one person in the executive suite who did not pose a political threat to Spindler, and therefore the Diesel turned to him as a confidant. Jean-Louis Gassée, Allan Loren, Del Yocam— all had aspirations of one day being CEO. Sullivan, as far as anyone could tell, aspired only to keep his job secure. Others believe that Sullivan latched onto Spindler as a rising executive whom he could influence. As Michael Spindler climbed the corporate ladder, Sullivan would climb with him. Together, the two men would emerge to run the whole corporation by 1993, leaving John Sculley to wonder what had hit him.

Whatever their motivations, only those two men know for sure. All Sullivan will say about that friendship now is that "I liked Michael Spindler and I like Michael Spindler." In any event, Spindler and Sullivan had become almost inseparable by the end of the decade. They were like Siamese twins. The relationship went pretty much like this: Spindler would march into Sullivan's office, right next door, and talk almost without interruption, while Sullivan listened and offered sympathy and support. "Spindler would go into tantrums in Sullivan's office," recalls a former secretary to Sullivan. "He would pace, and Kevin would pace, too. Michael also told Kevin everything. Everything. I would say, 'Michael is going to take up your whole day.' "

Sullivan, for all his failings in the human compassion department, was inordinately gifted at corporate self-preservation. One evening after Yocam had been ousted as COO, he and Spindler were invited by Gassée and Loren to attend a dinner with them in the affluent San Francisco suburb of Atherton, a wooded enclave of breathtaking mansions where Spindler also lived. The subject of the dinner was to "talk about taking some load off John," as Sullivan remembers. Neither Sculley nor Yocam was invited. "So I went and invited Al Eisenstat [the corporate secretary]," Sullivan says. "I invited Al because he was a board member and Al was John's guy."

This tact proved to be an effective insurance policy. Afterward, someone tipped Sculley that Sullivan and Spindler had plotted to get him at that dinner. Sculley decided to confront Sullivan. Sullivan, of course, denied it vigorously. "I said, 'John, I invited Al,' " Sullivan remembers. "Under no circumstances was I going to allow those guys to do anything against John. I didn't trust those guys. . . . It would always piss Gassée off that I would never trash Sculley." Sculley had said nothing to Spindler then. But that same night, at about ten, the doorbell rang at Sculley's Tudor mansion in Woodside, a verdant enclave of million-dollar estates on the slopes of the Santa Cruz Mountains. Sculley, who normally turned in early because he arose each day before dawn, groggily opened the door to find both Sullivan and Spindler standing there. "They showed up at the house and were overly apologetic," says a person who knew of the encounter.

Sculley accepted the apologies and paid the rumors no more mind. Later on, though, that night on the porch would make vivid sense to him.

Not only had Sculley dismissed the notion that Spindler could be after him, he was ready to entrust him with even more power. The decision was made at, of all places, a run-down hotel near John F. Kennedy International Airport in New York City. It was a halfway point of sorts for Sculley, who was flying in from California, to meet with Spindler, who was flying in from Paris, where he was running Apple Europe. Accompanying Sculley on the trip back east were Eisenstat, Joe Graziano, and Sullivan. The meeting was hurriedly arranged for Monday, January 29, 1990, for Yocam had turned the COO's job down on Super Bowl Sunday, the day before. Sculley wanted to make his reorganization announcement that same day.

The Graz didn't like the idea of Spindler as COO one bit, and he told Sculley. It had been Graziano, in fact, who had urged Sculley to go back to having a chief operating officer so he could regain control over Apple. "Joe told John to bring in an outside guy," recalls a former executive who heard the discussions. "John said, 'No, I don't want an outside guy. I want Spindler.' Joe said, 'That's a big mistake, because Michael is not an operating guy.' But John insisted."

How prophetic those words from Graziano would turn out to be.

After the meeting in New York, Sculley put the announcement out: Spindler had been named the new chief operating officer, his right-hand man. At the same time, Allan Loren had resigned, while Gassée's control over products had been cut in half.

By this point, Loren's departure was no surprise to anyone at Apple. He had actually made the decision to leave a few weeks before, while on a camping trip with his two teenage sons in California's Yosemite National Park. Huddled around a campfire one night in the snow-covered wilderness, one of his sons observed his father staring into the flames and asked what he was thinking. "I said, 'Well, I'm not having any fun,'" Loren recalls. "He said, 'Well, Dad, why are you doing it? If it's not fun, then why do it?' That crystallized it for me. I went back to John and said, 'I'm not happy. I don't like it here anymore.' John said, 'Well, I'm thinking of making some changes. Let me think about things.'"

It was clear, though, that the feeling was mutual. Sculley accepted the resignation without trying to change Loren's mind. Loren retreated to the familiarity of the East, another star whose bright luster had quickly faded. He rebounded from his experience at Apple, though. Loren went on to the American Express Company, where he rose to his current lofty position of executive vice president and chief information officer.

As for Gassée, Spindler would include Gassée's former duties vis-à-vis manufacturing and product marketing in his own tent. Gassée was still left with R and D, but it was clear to everyone at Apple that he was now Jean-Louis Passée. It had been a long, wild ride for Gassée. And he knew it was finally over. In a meeting in Gassée's office a few days later, Sculley sat down and offered to let him return to Europe. "I told John, 'If you don't think I'm implementing your agenda, you should fire me.'" As it happened, both Spindler and Joe Graziano were recommending that very action. "Spindler told John, 'No way I want Gassée in Europe. I don't trust him,'" recalls a then senior executive who heard the conversation.

Sculley, then, was going to bow to Gassée's advice one more time. Just a week after he had been stripped of most of his power, Gassée—one of the more flamboyant and colorful characters in Apple's storied history—offered his resignation.

The reaction among the engineers was one of shock and outrage. About 150 of them marched outside De Anza 7, carrying placards of protest, including one that read JLG 4 CEO. A wreath of black flowers with a large black bow was delivered to Gassée's office. Gassée, strangely enough, was neither angry nor embittered. The overwhelming emotion he remembers was one of relief. "The five years I spent in Cupertino were among the most miserable of my life," Gassée now says. "I felt I was part of something corrupt, and I was as much a part of that as anyone. But now I'm happy. I have three kids, a new business. It was the best thing that ever happened to me."

Gassée was, no doubt, consoled by another factor: under the terms of his severance agreement with Apple, he would walk off with a cool $1.7 million. He would invest some of his money in a new venture that became Be Inc., which would work in secrecy until unveiling a product in 1995 that would thrust him, front and center, back into the unending drama of Apple Computer.

Several months later, near the time when Gassée's resignation would go into effect, Sculley and Gassée sat down for what would be one of their final encounters as Apple executives. They had just returned from Apple's Macworld trade show extravaganza in Boston and were nursing drinks at a party hosted by the company's Claris software subsidiary. Gassée had some parting advice. "I said, 'John, I need to get something off my chest,' " Gassée recalls. "He looked puzzled, and I said, 'It's about Pink. You should cancel Pink and blame it on me.' I was trying to help, because I thought the thing would be a disaster. The project was just too big and wimpy."

This time, Sculley thanked his old nemesis but did not heed the advice. It was too bad he did not. Pink was becoming an albatross around Apple's neck. In fact, Michael Spindler had just placed a fateful phone call to IBM's headquarters in Armonk, New York, to seek help in lightening the burden.

Apple was ready to get into bed with Big Brother himself.

7

Crossing a Canyon

Apple Computer's astonishing rise during the 1980s had been an American success story of epic proportions, a feat that epitomized the country's newfound economic vitality during the two terms of President Ronald Reagan. Under Reagan, the United States enjoyed unprecedented growth, fueling white-hot markets in real estate and on Wall Street. Personal incomes soared. Consumer buying went through the roof. The new term "yuppie" was coined to categorize all those young go-getters cashing in on the limitless riches. And there seemed to be no end in sight, just as it had seemed at Apple during much of the same time.

Apple and the country were on such parallel paths that Steve Jobs, in his heyday, was even invited by the White House to meet with the president. A snapshot captured the moment as Jobs, long hair flowing, shook hands with the ever-smiling Gipper as he was presented with the National Technology Medal in February 1985. They might have come from opposite sides of the planet, politically—Jobs was a certified member of the counterculture generation, while the archconservative Reagan represented the mainstream of Middle American values—but this was still the best of times for both men, and they shared that much.

The party had finally ended for the United States—and Apple—in almost the same year. The stock market crash on Black Friday in October 1987 revealed how fragile the country's economic underpinnings really were. Shortly thereafter, a recession would begin that would ripple across the country for nearly five years. Apple's own fragility surfaced again in 1988, beginning a decline of fits and starts without end.

Now, as 1990 and a fresh decade rolled around, a new empire was taking center stage in the personal computer industry: "Wintel," represented by the twin-headed beast of Microsoft and Intel. Despite an industry slump the prior Christmas, the PC boom, which had grown the industry to thirteen times its size in 1981, was really still alive and well. In fact, it was still just beginning. And the two companies driving that boom were Microsoft and Intel: Microsoft, with its software; Intel, with its microprocessors. Almost every IBM-compatible had to have the combination of the Microsoft operating system and the Intel microprocessor chip, or they simply would not run.

By 1990, computers containing the Wintel technology accounted for roughly nine out every ten of the 24 million computers sold that year throughout the world, although Apple's technology was still believed to be far superior by many users and industry experts. All told, 144 million PCs had been shipped since 1979, and the lion's share of the machines followed the Wintel standard.[1] Apple's shriveled domain consisted of much of the rest, leaving the Cupertino company surrounded on all sides and in danger of being squashed out of existence by the very industry it had created. *This* is why Dan Eilers and those other voices in the wilderness, way back when, had argued so passionately for Apple to license its superior technology while it still could. Apple had an indisputable lead over everybody else in its computers, but the competition was catching up fast. And leading the pack were Microsoft and Intel.

As soon as he had seen his first prototypes of graphical user interfaces back in the early 1980s, Bill Gates had decided GUI was the future of personal computing. And he had determined the Macintosh to be the best commercial adaptation of the technology on the market. "I mean, the Mac was a very exciting machine," Gates recalls. "And you sat somebody down and let them use MacWrite, MacPaint, and they could see something different there. We can say that was just graphical interface, but the Mac was *the* graphical interface machine." Ever since, he had been snapping the whip on his engineers to come up with an operating system that looked and acted the same way. The first versions of Windows were duds; everyone could see that. They were not easy to use, and their performance was hopelessly outmatched by the Mac's, primarily because of the limitations of the Intel microprocessor in processing graphical calculations as compared to the Motorola chips Apple was using.

But while Steve Jobs's whole business philosophy had been one of revolution, Bill Gates's was always one of evolution. He might not get it right the first time, or even the second, but he would keep trying until he did. The man was a ruthless entrepreneur, but he was also obsessively persistent. Bill Gates was like the Terminator. He would get you, no matter what. And when Gates unveiled Windows 3.0 on an exhilarating spring day at New York City's City Center Theater on May 22, 1990, Sculley suddenly had the Terminator in his rearview mirror.

From a giant video screen above the stage at his launch, the new Windows program Gates showed the world that day looked almost like a Mac. There were the familiar file menus that could be pulled down with the mouse. And there were the colorful little icons, which, like the Mac, contained the various programs a person would use.

But in order for Windows 3.0 to work, it needed a lot of horsepower under the hood. That is where Intel came in. Intel had just recently begun shipping large quantities of its newest 80386 processor, a real screamer compared to its 80286 predecessor. The 386 more than doubled the speed and performance of the personal computer and had all the horses necessary to give the mammoth new Windows program the oomph it needed to run. Intel was doing this not so much to help Microsoft. Andy Grove, Intel's CEO, was not believed to trust many people and particularly not Bill Gates. A naturally paranoid person, Grove saw his chief job as keeping Intel a few steps ahead of the competition. The competition, in this case, as led by Advanced Micro Devices, a small but fast-growing maker of chips that were patterned after the ones made by Intel.

If Apple was worried about this new threat, it did not show among the engineers and many managers. Their ace in the hole—or so they thought—was an upgraded version of the aging Macintosh software that was called System 7. This was the old Blue project, the one the really good engineers did not want to work on. The project was running into all kinds of delays and was already a year behind schedule. But the nerds were convinced it would blow Microsoft out of the water.

In fact, demonstrations of the dueling technologies in the weeks before Microsoft's official launch were set up all over the place to reassure the Apple cult that the Mac was still vastly superior. Apple's favorite technique over the years has been to place two computers side by side onstage—one a Mac, the other an IBM-compatible—and run the same software programs at the same time to show the Mac blowing the competition away. The matches would begin at the command of "Ready, set, go!" Inside a cavernous auditorium at the Santa Clara Convention Center, a hulking low-rise building situated just down the street from the roller coasters of Paramount's Great America amusement park in Silicon Valley, six hundred Apple engineers, marketing people, and other assorted nerd types assembled in early 1990 to watch a company-sponsored demo of the Mac's System 7 slugging it out against Windows 3.0. It was no contest, at least to their geek eyes.

"The engineers onstage proceeded to run programs side by side on two computers, and Windows had a lot of inconsistencies," recalls Duane Schulz, a manager in Apple's imaging business who attended that day. "Everybody would crack up. It was an attitude of 'We're better.' " If you were an Apple engineer, there was plenty to scoff at in Windows 3.0. The new software, for one thing, required about twice the memory as the Mac's did. The program also contained the usual plethora of "bugs," or software defects, that could cause the computer to stall out and crash. Bugs are commonplace in any new software and are fixed as they are discovered over time, but the first ones in Windows 3.0 were especially annoying because so many people adopted the new software and became, in effect, guinea pigs for Microsoft.

In the glass-enclosed cubicles on the fourth floor of De Anza 7, however, there was little of the macho chest beating that was going on down in engineering. John Sculley had been a marketing guy first and foremost, and he understood that, to Microsoft's legions of MS-DOS users, who were still forced to type in long commands to get anything done with their computer, Windows 3.0 would be seen as good enough. "When I saw it, I thought it was pretty damn impressive," Sculley says.

Suddenly, a cold chill ran up Sculley's spine. Apple, he now realized after seeing what Windows and the new Intel microprocessors could do together, was fighting the wrong battle. For so many years, it had been Apple against IBM, David versus Goliath. It had been a noble cause, the Apple people all thought, to try and rescue the masses of corporate workers from the tyranny of the faceless, shapeless blob known as Big Blue. And there had been battalions of IBM clones to try to ward off. But now, with Microsoft and Intel joining forces, the real battle was against this duopoly known as Wintel.

"In 1990, for really the first time, Microsoft and Intel started to work together," Sculley says. "Before, people in the industry thought the computer was the box. But Intel said, 'No, it's the processor.' And Microsoft said, 'It's the software.' Together, they could run the industry. Meanwhile, we, IBM, Compaq, and the other hardware manufacturers thought *we* were the industry."

With Microsoft and Intel in cahoots, Sculley figured it would be only a matter of time before they caught up to Apple's technological lead, which had underpinned the company's strategy of charging premium prices for the Macintosh. The old strategy of churning out bigger, faster Macs simply would not do. Apple was already getting killed on the low end by following this shortsighted scheme. It could get murdered on the high end, as well, if it didn't do something soon to outmuscle Intel on power and outmaneuver Microsoft by coming up with radically new software.

The first and most pressing order of business was to shore up the faltering balance sheet. One obvious thing to do was to take out the meat-ax and start chopping out the fat that Apple had accumulated over the years. As of 1990, Apple's sales and general administrative expenses had swollen to 30 percent of revenues, compared to 24 percent at the tightly controlled Sun. The hypocrisy of this new belt-tightening mentality was not lost on Apple's employees, who numbered about twelve thousand at the time. Sculley himself was already one of the nation's top-paid chief executives, with salary and bonuses totaling $2.3 million a year. He did not live modestly, either. At the time, he owned three homes in Silicon Valley, including the Tudor mansion in Woodside, where he had also built three state-of-the-art barns to house his wife's dozen show horses. He also owned a million-dollar vacation home in Maine, to which he shuttled in his private Learjet.

Sculley had been equally extravagant in rewarding his senior executives. In just the past year, for example, he had lured Joe Graziano back to Apple as CFO with a signing bonus of $1.5 million and a severance package worth $2.4 million. The Graz had run finance between 1980 and 1985 before quitting the company to join Sun. In his book *Accidental Empires*, which chronicled the rise of the personal computer industry, author Robert X. Cringely jokingly referred to the signing bonus as a new unit of Apple currency. "A million and a half dollars is now known as '1 Graz'—a large unit of currency in Applespeak."

Sculley knew, then, that the austerity campaign would have to start at the top. He shut down Apple's longtime practice of giving expensive cars such as Mercedeses and Jaguars to its one hundred top executives. As for everybody else, annual raise reviews were ordered to be conducted every twelve months instead of every six. Profit-sharing contributions by Apple to every employee were drastically curtailed. Layoffs were ordered, the first in nearly five years, sending four hundred workers out onto the street. Even the water coolers were not spared. In a hugely unpopular move, Graziano, the new CFO, ordered the coolers taken out to save on their expense. If people wanted water, they could bring in their own. An outcry from employees prompted the Graz to bring the coolers back.

In paring costs, Sculley hoped to get Apple into a position to take a serious run at regaining the share of the PC market it had lost since 1988. Indeed, CFO Joe Graziano had pushed for this approach since rejoining Apple in 1989. This was a 180-degree turn from his strategy of just one year earlier, when Gassée and his high-right approach to the business had still prevailed. Sculley devised a new strategy with two core elements: One, he would have to get cheaper Macs to market. This would be the low-left approach. And, two, Apple would have to deploy "hit products" every six months or so, to keep extending Apple's technology lead in front of Microsoft.

All of this would hurt profit margins, but so be it. The unofficial goal, within the executive suite, was to raise Apple's share of the PC market by 3 percentage points, to 10.5 percent from 7.5 percent, over the next year. The key to this rested on three new products: the Mac Classic, aimed at first-time buyers; the Mac LC, which stood for "low-cost color"; and the Mac IISI, Apple's first high-powered computer at a relatively low price. The products would start rolling out in mid-October 1990, in time for the big Christmas rush.

Michael Spindler, newly appointed as chief operating officer, was put in charge of the product strategy. Relocating permanently to Cupertino from Paris in March 1990, Spindler stormed onto the laid-back campus and delivered an impassioned speech to the employees, declaring, "There will be no more prima donnas at Apple."[2] Never mind that he was one himself. This was a deliberate jab at fallen stars, including Jean-Louis Gassée and Allan Loren, as well as a warning to everyone else that the old way of no discipline would not be tolerated anymore. "The idea was that Spindler would be a kick-ass drill sergeant," says one marketing manager at the time, who asked not to be identified.

With Spindler in place to run operations, John Sculley was giving careful thought to his own role within the company. For the past three years, he had focused primarily on promoting Apple outside the company, leaving Jean-Louis Gassée in charge of the crucial technology machine. But with Gassée stripped of power and on his way out as of early 1990, the engineers were on a rudderless ship. Actually, even with Gassée at the helm, they had really not had clear direction and purpose. But they had at least liked working for Gassée and considered him a charismatic leader. And they needed a new leader, a dynamo to guide them into the stormy new decade. Someone, Sculley decided, exactly like himself.

Sculley had been fascinated by electronics ever since childhood, but he was not a technologist, nor was he ever accepted as one by Apple's engineering community. Still, Sculley was reading a report by the McKinsey & Company consulting firm one day in early 1990 that, he concluded, applied squarely to him. "It said that the chief technology officer of a corporation is the person who has to deal with the consequences of technology from a business standpoint, not the best technologist," Sculley remembers. In other words, you did not have to be a rocket scientist to understand why people bought computers. Most users were not techies, either; they cared only about whether the machine was big enough, fast enough, and versatile enough to perform their tasks.

A lightbulb went off in Sculley's mind. Who, he thought, could possess a greater understanding of the consequences of technology than the CEO in charge of implementing it? He understood product marketing well enough, and his flair for translating computer jargon into something readily understood by the masses had become legendary in the industry. He therefore determined to name himself Apple's chief technical officer, adding to his duties as president, chairman, and CEO. When the decision was announced in March 1990, the engineers were outraged. "Every engineer should have walked out when he did that," fumes Konstantin Othmer, at the time an engineer who was working on the Macintosh QuickDraw graphics technology. "You're taking an executive from the soda industry and making him CTO of one of the best technology companies in the world."

Sculley, however, remembers the CTO decision as one of his best ever.

He convened meetings with Apple's technical managers every day at 7 A.M. The sense of urgency made it feel almost like 1985 all over again. Except that now Sculley was devoting almost all of his energy to the labs, presiding over development of the new products that would underpin his market share strategy. "Ironically, the times when I had the most power [were] when Apple was in trouble," Sculley says.

With Sculley immersed in the labs, Spindler took charge of nearly everything else. One of his big tasks was to restore some momentum to Apple's sagging U.S. business, the one that had been decimated by Loren's decision to raise product prices and Gassée's failure to deliver a marketable laptop computer. Spindler knew he needed a top-notch person with plenty of experience in the computer industry. He turned to Apple's neighbor Hewlett-Packard and snagged an executive named Bob Puette, general manager of H-P's Personal Computer Group, to take Loren's place as president of Apple USA. Although Puette would achieve dramatic sales results, it would come at the expense of employee morale and relations with Apple's important dealer channel.

Puette was a stocky fireplug of a man who had played football as a running back for Northwestern University. In his twenty-four years at H-P, Puette had become firmly indoctrinated in a monolithic corporate culture known in the Valley as "the H-P Way." Under the H-P Way, you spent most of your career at H-P. You rose up through the ranks at H-P. You held the same conservative values as H-P's legendary founders, William Hewlett and David Packard. And you wore a suit and tie to work. H-P, in short, was a carefully managed business renowned for its stability — quite the opposite of Apple, in fact, with all its free spirits. Puette would stand out at Apple in another way. A lifetime member of the NRA, Puette loved to go big-game hunting, sometimes as far away as Asia. This didn't sit well with the Apple yuppie crowd, many of whom didn't eat meat, much less kill animals for it.

So, as Allan Loren had been, Puette was a square peg in a round hole.

One of Puette's top priorities as head of Apple USA was to restore Apple's deteriorated relations with its army of dealers, through which roughly one half of all the company's sales were made. Apple dealers had felt like second-class citizens, even though they were the main point of contact between Apple and the general public. They tried to emulate their heroes in Cupertino, wearing their hair stylishly long and even cavorting around on the sales floor in the Apple T-shirts they had picked up at the latest trade show. They were "wannabe" Steve Jobses. But Apple, from the days of Jobs himself, had gone out of its way to antagonize this faithful bunch by selling more and more directly to large customers, by failing to support them in promotional campaigns, and by ignoring years of faithful service.

One example of a situation that happened frequently was a travesty visited on a dealer named Tony Stramiello in the small town of Astoria, Oregon, located on the windswept Pacific Coast about a hundred miles northwest of Portland. Stramiello was a fanatical Apple supporter, having spent $150,000 to remodel a store in downtown Astoria and devote it exclusively to selling Apple products shortly after the Macintosh first came out in 1984. He paid to send two employees down to Cupertino for Macintosh training. Every quarter, he flew down to Portland in his Piper Comanche 250 to attend Apple's regional dealer meetings. And he evangelized Apple so heavily around Astoria that he converted many of the schools and businesses to the Macintosh. He even set up a classroom upstairs in his shop to teach people how to use the Mac. Within his first year of business, he sold some $300,000 in Apple computers.

"I was very excited," recalls Stramiello. "Apple would tell me, 'We are partners in business.' "

Then one day, after about eighteen months in operation, Tony Stramiello got a letter in the mail. It said that Apple was "reviewing" his dealership and that, if he wanted, he should consider selling other computers besides those made by Apple. Soon thereafter, he started getting calls from his customers, asking whether it was true that he had been dropped as an Apple dealer. They had been told this by other dealers based in the Portland area, pushing for their business. "I didn't know anything," Stramiello says. "Then we got a letter saying we were canceled." Incredibly, Stramiello's competitors had been notified of his dealership's demise before he had. Stramiello was in a state of shock. Here he was, selling as many Macintoshes as he could get his hands on, evangelizing Apple to practically everyone with whom he came into contact. Sales were going through the roof. Wasn't he an ideal guy to be out peddling Apple products?

John Ziel certainly thought so. Ziel was Apple's regional sales manager, based in Portland, and he was appalled when Stramiello's dealership was closed along with hundreds of other small mom-and-pop dealerships across the United States in 1986. That happened after Apple's sales managers in Cupertino decided they no longer wanted to do business with any dealer selling less than $500,000 per year in products. When Ziel learned that the brass had pulled the plug on Stramiello, too, he rose to defend him. "They said, 'Sorry, no exceptions,' " remembers Ziel, who left Apple in 1994 after eleven years with the company. Insult was added to injury for Stramiello, who ended up having to threaten a lawsuit against Apple before the company would reimburse him for $30,000 in unsold computers left in his inventory at the end.

"They were great engineers at Apple, but they didn't have a clue about business," says Stramiello, who still lives in Astoria, managing rental properties with his wife.

Apple's dealer relations, then, had been abysmal for years. And under Puette they were about to enter an even stormier period. A sign of what was to come occurred at a meeting of about five hundred dealers in a hotel ballroom near Cupertino, shortly after Puette had taken over. He stood up on the stage and pointed to a chart filled with bullet points that concluded that 20 percent of the dealers were doing 80 percent of the business. He would "streamline" the dealers to just the ones doing the biggest volume or providing the best value. The dealers who did not go to one of these corners would not survive, he told them. The talk, then, became known as the "Go to Your Corners" speech.

"That scared us to death," recalls one California dealer, who asked not to be named, "because we weren't high volume. He was implicitly announcing to his channel of dealers that he believed most of them would go out of business." Puette does not remember that specific meeting, but he agrees that he had to deemphasize the smaller dealers so Apple could concentrate on landing bigger distribution accounts. This strategy, he adds, resulted in Apple signing deals to expand into mass-market outlets such as CompUSA, Montgomery Ward, and Wal-Mart. "We dramatically expanded distribution so you could find an Apple computer no matter where you liked to shop," recalls Puette, who resigned from Apple in 1993. "Anytime you affect one channel of distribution, I can imagine some of the dealers at some point in time being upset with me."

Puette, having joined Apple amid John Sculley's new strategy to gain share of the PC market, was under a mandate, along with other marketing managers around the world, to increase sales while also lowering expenses. And as Puette remembers, the pressure to cut expenses mounted almost every month he was at Apple, as profit margins kept going down. In his nearly three-year tenure, he had to undergo layoffs every six months in his big Apple USA organization, resulting in a workforce of some 3,500 people being cut to about half that size by 1994.

Working under Puette, in charge of Apple's sales to the big K–12 (kindergarten through twelfth-grade) market, was a woman named Cheryl Vedoe. This was the same Cheryl Vedoe who had worked at Apollo during the Macintosh licensing episode that had ended so badly in 1987. Vedoe had moved on to Sun after Apollo, joining Apple in February 1992. When she began running K–12 that year, she and Puette came up with a plan to help curb those expenses by reducing from two hundred to "seventeen to nineteen" the number of dealers in the United States specializing in sales to education. "We had to reduce dealer compensation for us to be profitable, so we decided to take it down," remembers Vedoe, who left Apple in 1994.

This move was akin to the arbitrary way in which Apple had closed down Tony Stramiello and a multitude of little dealers back in the mid-1980s. Instead of using a surgical knife to remove the dealers who were not doing a good job, Apple was using a blunt ax to thin the ranks. John Vito, who had been an Apple dealer in the farming community of Corvallis, Oregon, since

1978, complained to his Apple representative that this was going to force out a lot of good education dealers, ones who had acted as Apple enthusiasts in their communities. Vito got little sympathy.

"He said, 'Well, when you pull your hand out of a bucket of water, how long does it take to replace the hole?' " Vito recalls, demonstrating how the Apple representative had reached his hand into an imaginary bucket and pulled it out to illustrate his point. "I thought, 'So we're just a hole.' " The relations with this resale channel got so bad that one dealer in Anchorage took to placing a jar of Vaseline on his desk whenever the Apple people were scheduled to drop by. Use your imagination as to what that signified. "Apple had utter contempt for the channel," Vito says. "We were pond scum."

Puette acknowledges that many dealers were irritated by that move in education, but he shrugs off the criticism. "Anytime you change anything with a reseller, it is a highly controversial move," Puette says. In later years, as the company became more and more isolated in the market, Apple would sorely miss the dealers it had killed off. As of 1990, however, Apple's arrogance was still alive and well, even if its business strategy had changed to one embracing a larger share of the PC market.

If Bob Puette was exactly wrong for Apple's dealer relations, a man named Ian Diery was just what the doctor ordered for Apple Pacific—and eventually the entire company. A native of Australia, Diery had been recruited by Kevin Sullivan, Apple's head of human relations, in September 1989 to take Del Yocam's place as head of Apple's sales in the Pacific. Diery had most recently worked at Wang Laboratories Inc., running worldwide sales as that company slid precipitously. Diery, in fact, had just quit Wang after the Lowell, Massachusetts, company reported a record $424.3 million loss for the year.

As Bill Campbell had been, Diery was an infectiously charming back-slapper who called everyone "mate" in his pronounced Aussie accent. "A good day makes a good week, a good week makes a good month, and a good month makes a good year," was the motto he cheerily repeated to all his salespeople. But Diery was also a demon on accountability, the captain of an amateur rugby team who would excoriate managers who fell below their sales quotas with the same intensity he used for teammates who dropped the ball at his weekend matches.

Diery, in short, was the quintessential operating guy. And it was largely due to his influence that Spindler and Apple would remain powerful forces in the industry for as long as they did. The first critical juncture came just days before the October 15, 1990, launch of the Mac Classic, the low-priced computer that was to serve as the cornerstone of Apple's strategy to win back a greater share of the PC market. Puette and his executives in Apple USA wanted to price it at $1,999. Working with Diery in Asia was a young, bearded marketing executive named Satjiv Chahil, a native of India who bundled his hair into the turbans worn by members of his Sikh religion. Chahil told Diery that if Apple really wanted to ignite a sales explosion, the thing should be priced at $999. Diery tested that theory out by selling a few at that price in Asia, and the demand was overwhelming. He stuck his head in Sculley's office and advised him to stay with that price for the whole rollout.

"Sculley told Ian, 'You're right. I agree with you. Go to Spindler,' " says one senior executive from the time, who spoke on condition of anonymity. "But when Ian went to Spindler, he didn't really want to discuss it. Then in a staff meeting, Sculley said, 'Nine hundred ninety-nine dollars.' " Apple desperately needed a home-run product, and at $999, this was it. The market response was so huge that Apple could not keep up with all the orders. Sales also roared for the Mac LC, a machine with color monitor priced at $3,098 (color Macs had started at about $6,300 until then), and the Mac IISI, at $3,769.

With strong follow-on products priced below $4,000, Apple's revenues resumed double-digit growth for the first time in two years. Profits decreased because the computers were selling for lower prices, but the stock started soaring again, peaking at $73 a share in 1991 compared to a low of $24 just a year earlier.

Apple had dodged the bullet yet again. But it was still no time to break out the party balloons. For one thing, the low-left strategy of placing inexpensive machines in the consumer market had worked too well: Apple's profits were falling faster than Sculley had realized. In May 1991, he fired 10 percent of the company's workers, or about 1,500 people, in the most sweeping layoffs since 1985. This time, he took a 15 percent cut in his own salary and ordered cutbacks of between 5 and 10 percent in his senior executives' pay. The knife also cut into some perks that had always been considered sacrosanct. This included taking away Apple's subsidy of its campus cafeteria, resulting in a hefty price rise for meals, as well as charging $2 a week to anyone using an Apple fitness center, which had been free before.

"This was not a drive to lower expense rates in response to temporary market conditions" but rather to reduce operating costs permanently, Kevin Sullivan explained in a statement published in a 1992 case study on Apple conducted by the Harvard Business School. "We were building a new Apple that had to be leaner and swifter."

Even all this was not enough, with the forces of Wintel bearing down. Poring over the financials, Sculley and Spindler shook their heads as they worked the numbers and concluded that Apple could not continue its present course for much longer. Gross profit margins were headed inexorably down, since Apple was no longer relying solely on the high-right strategy of selling expensive machines to big businesses. R-and-D expenses, on the other hand, were rising ever higher as the technology battlefield kept expanding to include new fronts, such as the boom in computer networking. As of 1991, annual R-and-D expenses had surged to nearly $600 million.

Apple could no longer go it completely alone, Sculley realized. It needed to enlist help from the outside. It was time to call in Big Blue.

In 1990, IBM was a corporate powerhouse of almost unrivaled proportions. Its $70 billion in annual revenues were almost seven times the size of those of Apple, Microsoft, and Intel combined. IBM's $6 billion of net income for that year alone matched the combined annual revenues *and* profits of Microsoft and Intel. It was no wonder, then, that it was called Big Blue. It was big, bigger than you could imagine, like an octopus with tentacles of influence that spread all over the globe from a corporate headquarters building of industrial gray concrete in the New York suburb of Armonk.

But IBM's size was also its disadvantage. For decades, IBM had controlled the computer industry by dominating the market for huge mainframe computers that would fill an entire room, and it was also a dominant player in the newer market for smaller but extremely powerful minicomputers. IBM was big, its computers were big, and they were sold to the biggest corporations in the world. IBM could have gone on getting ever bigger and selling ever-increasing numbers of big computers, except that one thing happened: a new, tiny computer came along. It was called the "personal computer."

Likely nearly everyone else in the computer industry, the executives at IBM were intrigued by the PC, which was actually known then as the "microcomputer." But sales of the machines were so small, amounting to little more than $1 billion as of 1980, that IBM viewed the microcomputer as a niche device of primary interest to small businesses. Since Big Blue wanted a presence in every computer market, IBM's powerful Corporate Management Committee gave the green light to a proposal by members of an IBM lab in Boca Raton, Florida, to build one of the computers. The product that would emerge from this effort would be named the IBM Personal Computer, but internally it was known as "Acorn" and the research to design and build it was called "Project Chess."[3]

The person who had made the IBM PC proposal was a man named Bill Lowe, director of the lab in Boca Raton. While the PC market at the time was tiny, it was growing very fast: up 50 percent in unit shipments just between 1979 and 1980. The PC caught a lot of the old-guard computer giants like IBM flat-footed. It had been seen as an interesting toy back in the days when it was mainly geared toward computer hobbyists, but the birth of the Apple II had changed all that. The spreadsheet in the first Apple IIs alone was enough to justify their purchase by companies wanting to make accountants, finance managers, and anyone else who dealt with numbers a lot more productive.

Decisions usually do not come quickly at IBM, with its labyrinth of departments, divisions, and business units. But this little microcomputer category was taking off so fast that in the summer of 1980 Lowe convinced the Corporate Management Committee to give him just one year to get one out for IBM. This was practically an unprecedented delivery schedule, since IBM research projects had typically taken years to result in finished products. Lowe had his green light, but he knew twelve months was not nearly enough time to come up with a brand-new machine—at least not if IBM did the work all by itself.

So he decided the only thing he could do was cobble a machine together with parts from other suppliers and put the IBM name on it. The two key aspects of the machine were the operating system and the microprocessor. Intel's 8088 chip was slow and clunky but readily available off the shelf. So that choice was easy. The premier operating system then was CP/M, made by a small firm in Pacific Grove, California, named Digital Research. But IBM ultimately selected MS-DOS from Microsoft after failing to secure rights to CP/M in a now-legendary visit to Pacific Grove. In that visit, in 1980, the IBMers flew to Pacific Grove to meet with Gary Kidall, founder of Digital Research, but were unable to do so because he was off flying his private plane. Thus rebuffed, the IBM team flew up to Seattle to sign an operating system deal with Bill Gates's Microsoft. The rest is history.

Now, remember: back then, the PC industry was a tiny, tiny business. No one—not even Bill Gates—could have foreseen just how huge it would become. IBM just wanted to play a part in a new and growing market, and it wanted to get to market as quickly as possible. Lowe and his cronies therefore saw no harm in relying on Intel and Microsoft for the two most important parts of the computer, since there was no way IBM could replicate them in the time allotted to get the IBM PC to market. The strategy meant that the IBM PC would represent an "open architecture," one that other manufacturers could copy. And boy, would they ever.

The Apple II had kick-started the PC industry, but it took the IBM PC to transform it into a big-time business. The IBM name carried such weight in the corporate world that businesses everywhere rushed to embrace the PC. In just the first year after the IBM PC came out in 1981, worldwide PC shipments nearly quadrupled, to 5.2 million. As much as Steve Jobs had derided IBM's entry into the market with his company's "Welcome IBM. Seriously" ad, the IBM PC was no laughing matter for Apple Computer. In 1982, Apple's share of the global PC market plunged to 6.2 percent from 11.4 percent the year before, even though Apple's sales were still growing by leaps and bounds.[4] But the newfound gains and profits were not all going to IBM; they were being spread among legions of new "clone" manufacturers, such as Compaq

Computer, which were rolling out their own "IBM-compatible" machines. And to Microsoft and Intel, which, by virtue of having been in the right place at the right time, held the keys to a new kingdom.

Having inadvertently ceded control of the PC to Microsoft and Intel, IBM therefore robbed itself of the ability to control the future direction of what would soon become the world's most important technology market. It would have to rely on those two companies, gnats in size compared to Big Blue, to set the industry's technological pace. And it would have to follow along like an elephant being led by its trainer. By 1990, Microsoft and Intel had taken such command of the computer industry that it was almost a mockery to keep hearing personal computers referred to as "IBM-compatibles." When Microsoft's Windows became the standard in PC operating systems during the 1990s, the computers would be referred to just as Wintel compatibles.

IBM still had a fearsome arsenal at its disposal. Its R-and-D budget alone amounted to nearly $7 billion, fueling advances across a broad technological front. During the late 1980s, Big Blue tried to regain its independence by developing a new operating system called Operating System/2, or OS/2 for short. OS/2, which had a graphical user interface called Presentation Manager, would feature easy-to-use graphical capabilities like the Macintosh's, as well as additional technological improvements. IBM developed it in collaboration with Microsoft but really should have known better than to trust Bill Gates. Unhappy with IBM's technical direction on the project, Gates decided to pour his energy into his own Windows, leaving Big Blue alone to push OS/2. He picked up his marbles and went home.

So on one front, IBM was taking on Microsoft to reduce its dependency on PC software. On the other, it was pursuing a new technology for making microprocessors in an effort to loosen Intel's choke hold on that part of the industry. The technology was based on reduced instruction set computing—the same RISC initiative that Apple had been exploring in its Jaguar project back in 1988. It would be this arcane technology that would soon bring together Apple and IBM, two of the biggest names in the computer industry.

As detailed earlier, reduced instruction set computing, or RISC, held the advantage of speed and simplicity over the complex instruction set computing, or CISC, microprocessors that had been the mainstay of Intel and the rest of the computer industry. The RISC design was invented in 1975 at IBM's Thomas J. Watson Research Center in Yorktown Heights, New York, and the first experimental RISC machine, called the 801, was produced by Big Blue in 1976. By 1985, Sun Microsystems became the first company to deliver a commercially successful version of a RISC processor with its chip called SPARC. And the first IBM product that could use the new RISC technology was a family of speedy workstations, or souped-up PCs, and servers, which store huge amounts of data, called the RS 6000. This was announced in 1990.

The RISC development was being undertaken at IBM's big microprocessor research center in Austin, Texas, a picturesque college town of lakes and cedar trees nestled at the very edge of the Lone Star State's sprawling and rugged Hill Country. One day in 1990, the technical leader of the RISC project, Phil Hester, picked up the phone and put in a call to Jack Kuehler, IBM's president back in Armonk.

Kuehler (pronounced "Keeler") didn't fit the mold of the stereotypical IBM executive who spoke in a dull monotone and sang the company anthem with a zombielike expression. He did wear the blue suits, like everybody else. But Kuehler was a plain-talking westerner of wiry stature and modest manner who was more at home astride a saddle high in the Colorado Rockies than he was in a *Fortune* 500 swivel chair on the East Coast, of all places. In fact, he would go on to retire in his beloved Colorado. In another time, he might have been a cowboy, but at this time, in 1990, Kuehler had taken over responsibility for IBM's PC business when Hester's call triggered an epic bicoastal saga with Apple. "Phil called and said, 'Jack, we're going to have to get into the OEM business'" with the new RISC machines, recalls a former IBM executive familiar with the conversation.

"OEM" stands for "original equipment manufacturer," and it is industry jargon for a company that uses another company's technology in its products and sells it under its own name. When Compaq uses an Intel chip, for example, Compaq is an Intel OEM. When Compaq uses Microsoft's software, it is also a Microsoft OEM. In fact, both Microsoft and Intel had built their businesses on OEM relationships, originally by licensing the operating system and microprocessor to as many IBM-compatible manufacturers as they could. Hester wanted more manufacturers to use his RISC chips, mainly to bring about enough volume to offset the huge expense of R and D and construction of the fabrication plants that make them.

Kuehler decided to convene a meeting in Austin shortly thereafter. He invited other top IBM executives, including Jim Cannavino, who was running the PC business under Kuehler. Called "Jimmy" by his friends, Cannavino was a tough-as-nails businessman who didn't bat an eye at issuing threats to people who got into his way. "I'm going to get you!" Cannavino, stabbing a finger in the air, once hissed to an Apple executive who had badgered IBM into a lowball price on some components.

In Austin, Kuehler, Cannavino, and the others all agreed they needed to find some OEMs. They sat down in a nondescript conference room, in their nondescript suits, and started going down the list of possible candidates. Digital Equipment was out, they concluded, because it was already at work on a RISC chip called Alpha. Hewlett-Packard was also out, because it, too, was working on its own RISC technology. Leaning back in his chair, thinking, Kuehler remembered a strange call he had received months earlier.

Kuehler had never met Michael Spindler and knew Sculley only vaguely. Out of the blue six months earlier, according to a person familiar with the episode, Kuehler's phone had rung and Spindler had begun speaking from the other end to pitch an idea. "Mike said, 'Jack, I'd like to talk to you about the possibility of working with us on an alliance,' " says the person recounting the conversation. "He said, 'It would be with a very creative sort of software we've got.' Then Spindler described a project called Pink." Taken aback, Kuehler promised to get right back to Spindler. He walked over to Cannavino's office and talked about it, but the two soon concluded that IBM was already too far down the road on OS/2 to get involved with something else.

Polite as ever, Kuehler had called Spindler to thank him for Apple's interest, saying Big Blue just was not interested at this time. Remembering the call, though, Kuehler looked up from the table in Austin and asked, "What about Apple?" To Apple, IBM might have been the faceless behemoth it had ridiculed so many years before as Big Brother. But the people at IBM harbored little ill will toward the nerds out in Cupertino. In fact, they admired and respected Apple. Cannavino did not, however, admire and respect Bill Gates. He loathed him, in fact, with a passion unusual for IBM's above-the-fray mentality. That ill will stemmed from the fact that Gates had bailed out of OS/2. Yeah, Cannavino seconded, Apple would be a great choice. Everyone else agreed heartily.

Since he had already spoken with Spindler, Kuehler took it upon himself to call him back. "Jack called Spindler and said, 'Sorry we didn't make it in software. We'd like to get together and see if you could use our microprocessor technology called RISC,' " says the person familiar with all these proceedings. "Spindler was very amendable to a meeting and said he would bring up Pink. They agreed to meet at a neutral location in a hotel near Dallas. Spindler said, 'Is it okay to bring Sculley?' " Of course it was.

John Sculley had come a long way in just one year. The high-right baby had been thrown out with the bathwater, along with Jean-Louis Gassée, and he had finally admitted that Apple did not have all the answers. The big question was who to hook up with. He asked Hugh Martin, aka "Huge Martian" and the head of Apple's RISC engineering research, CFO Graziano, and a couple of other engineering executives to explore the possibilities. Graziano headed the team.

In their Jaguar work, when Martin and his engineers had tried to design a whole new computer to replace the aging Mac, they had seen how much more efficient a RISC chip was than the ones by Intel and Motorola based on the old CISC. A RISC chip was capable of performing calculations twice as fast as a comparable CISC and at one half the production price, and its speed and flexibility in displaying computer graphics were particularly dazzling. Motorola had always been Apple's faithful ally, supplying microprocessors beginning with the first Apple II. But Motorola did not have a RISC technology up and running, and its line of chips was starting to run out of gas. With Intel pushing out ever-faster chips at shorter and shorter intervals, Sculley knew it would not be too long before the Wintel machines would start running circles around the Mac, providing customers with one less incentive to buy it.

The first choice as a RISC partner, for both Graziano and Martin, was Sun Microsystems, located a hop, skip, and a jump away in the Silicon Valley town of Mountain View. Sun's CEO, Scott McNealy, had built a humming business of big workstations, or souped-up PCs, running on his SPARC chip, as well as an operating system based on a software technology called Unix that was in wide use among workstation makers. Apple could put the Mac's software on top of Sun's Unix machines and for the microprocessor use a new RISC chip developed by a Silicon Valley company called MIPS Computer Systems. MIPS was later acquired by Silicon Graphics Inc., which would become known for its digital effects in Hollywood movies. Martin remembers that Apple's engineers preferred the MIPS chip to Sun's SPARC, because it appeared technically superior.

Under an Apple/Sun partnership, Graziano and Martin thought, corporate customers could have Macs that ranged from the little ones used by secretaries to the industrial-strength workstations used by architects and engineers. It sounded an awful lot like Chuck Berger's old strategy from the 1980s, when he had tried to get Sculley to link up with either Sun or Apollo to accomplish the very same thing. And in fact it was. This time, though, there was no longer a Jean-Louis Gassée to quash the idea. And by now Apple was dealing from a position of weakness rather than strength.

On the Sun side, Bill Joy, a Sun cofounder and an influential member of that company's board, was supportive of a collaboration with Apple as were Scott McNealy and other top executives, according to the Apple executives who negotiated with them. Sun was a workstation company, but Joy worried that Microsoft would eventually build an operating system that would replace Unix. Indeed, Microsoft had already begun development of an advanced operating system called Windows NT, designed for network servers and low-end workstations. NT would not debut until 1993, but it was shaping up to be a potential Sun killer. Talks between Apple and Sun became so serious that Martin and Graziano urged Sculley and the board just to buy Sun, as they had wanted to do years before.

"It would have been a marriage made in heaven," Martin says. And in fact it almost was.

In the fall of 1990, Joe Graziano was sitting in his office on the fourth floor of De Anza 7, proofreading a draft version of a press release announcing that Apple had agreed to acquire Sun. Scott McNealy would become the chief operating officer of the combined companies, and Apple and Sun would meld their technologies. Other terms, such as the price of the acquisition, were yet to be finalized. "We had the deal almost negotiated, almost totally."[5] Then, out of nowhere, the phone rang in COO Michael Spindler's office. It was IBM President Jack Kuehler on the line, calling back to ask if Apple would be interested in joining forces on RISC. Spindler must have been beside himself with delight, because he faced an almost certain demotion if Scott McNealy came aboard.

"When IBM called back, we put Sun on hold," recalls a former Apple executive involved in the merger negotiations with Sun.

Hugh Martin was aghast. Big Blue's RISC chips were too complex and expensive, he argued. What's more, IBM was always so big and bureaucratic that he seriously doubted anything of consequence could get done.

Sculley, though, was not so sure. One of his main concerns was that it was going to take on the order of $1 billion for someone to manufacture RISC chips in the huge volumes Apple needed. Apple was shipping 2 million computers a year by this point and had to have a reliable source of supply. "Sun did not have a billion dollars to spend," Sculley says. IBM did. The other factor tipping IBM in Sculley's favor was a less tangible one: Sculley simply hit it off with Kuehler and Cannavino. Like him, they were old-school executives whose word was generally as good as their bond. Scott McNealy, on the other hand, was an incredibly aggressive young man with a more confrontational style. Indeed, a former Apple executive says that one big question in an Apple-Sun merger would have been whether McNealy or Sculley would have run the combined companies.

So the IBM deal sounded like the safer bet all the way around, and after a series of meetings with the folks from Big Blue, Sculley picked up the phone to break the news to Martin, on a Saturday. "I was in my bedroom with a portable phone, and Sculley called me to tell me he was not going to do the deal with Sun," Martin says. "That was the beginning of my leaving Apple." Martin would resign from Apple in 1992 to join former Apple marketing executive Trip Hawkins in a new software firm called 3DO Company. Martin went on to become president of the Redwood City, California, company, with Hawkins as its CEO. As for Scott McNealy, he went on to great success, building Sun into a dominant workstation company as well as a leading force in the Internet industry of the late 1990s.

At their first meeting in Dallas, in early 1991, Kuehler and Cannavino sat down with Sculley and Spindler to hash out the rough framework of an alliance. Speaking out of the presence of aides, the executives discussed IBM's chips and some IBM workstations that might be able to use the Mac software, along with Apple's Pink operating system project and advances Apple was making in the new multimedia technology. "We soon realized that we had more things to do than time to work on, so we prioritized the areas and agreed to keep meeting," says a former IBM executive close to the talks.

There was just one issue of concern raised in that meeting by Sculley and Spindler: they told Kuehler and Cannavino that they didn't want to put Apple into the position of becoming totally dependent upon IBM, a competitor, for all its microprocessors. They suggested IBM call Motorola into the deal. "That's a good choice," Kuehler replied in his easy drawl. Almost immediately afterward, Kuehler called Motorola's worldwide headquarters in the Chicago suburb of Schaumburg, Illinois, and confided to Motorola CEO George Fisher (who went on to become CEO of Eastman Kodak) what IBM and Apple were planning. "Jack said, 'I would welcome Motorola to become a major partner to IBM in RISC,'" says the IBM executive close to the discussions. "Fisher lined up his people, and Kuehler lined up his."

Over the next few weeks, the Apple and IBM people held meetings all over the country. IBM hosted tours of its chip-manufacturing plants in Burlington, Vermont, and Austin. The two sides tried to surmount their cultural differences, sometimes in amusing ways. When the Apple delegation arrived in Austin, for example, they were all wearing suits to try and look as buttoned down as their counterparts from Big Blue. The IBMers, however, were attired in T-shirts, shorts, and sneakers, hoping to impress the Appleites with their California casual look.

There was never much of a cultural divide, though, when it came to the business at hand. For one thing, Sculley was as much of an easterner as the executives from IBM, and certainly more so than the cowboy Kuehler. Although it had been Spindler who had initiated the talks between Apple and IBM, Sculley quickly took them over from him. He viewed Kuehler and Cannavino as straight shooters, and the feeling was mutual. "I found Sculley to be very honest, gracious, and trustworthy," Kuehler told me at his retirement cabin in an aspen grove above Telluride, Colorado. "In front of a microphone, he is unreal. He comes alive and captures his audience." Kuehler would not comment, however, on specifics of the negotiations.

Personalities aside, both companies realized they had a lot to offer each other. IBM needed Apple's software expertise, as well as a company that would be a big customer for its new chips. Apple needed the new chips, as well as another company with which to split the cost of developing new products. "Alliances don't work unless both sides need each other," Kuehler says. "We needed Apple, and Apple needed us."

Kuehler had something else in mind that would have enormous implications for Apple down the road. The two companies complemented each other so well, he thought, why couldn't IBM just buy Apple outright? "We brought to the table technology, money, and a major customer base," Kuehler says. "Apple brought world-class products and software creativity. But we first needed to make these alliances successful to see if we could, in fact, work together. Cannavino and I discussed this, and I obliquely discussed this with

Sculley. He did not object. I really had in mind this resulting in a fantastic opportunity to create a major PC company of the future."

For now, though, Kuehler was preoccupied with the alliance at hand. A rough framework was drawn up in which IBM and Apple would collaborate on three major areas. The first was IBM's RISC technology, which would be used in a new microprocessor called "PowerPC." The PowerPC research would be spearheaded by engineers from IBM and Motorola, with input from their counterparts at Apple. The second was an Apple multimedia technology called "Script/X," which was aimed at being able to use the same program for incorporating sound, graphics, video, text, and animation into a variety of different computers and consumer electronics devices. It would be a portable multimedia program, and the research effort would be undertaken by a separate company called Kaleida, to be jointly run and funded by Apple and IBM.

The third major area of collaboration would center on Apple's long-festering Pink operating system technology, the same one that Jean-Louis Gassée had suggested to John Sculley only a year earlier be taken out and shot. In 1991, Pink was little closer to shipping as a product than when its original specifications had been jotted down on those pink index cards at the Sonoma Mission Inn in 1987. The object-oriented technology it entailed, though, still held great potential to the software industry. As described earlier, object-oriented programming and its use of interchangeable "objects" of software code represented a radical departure from the industry's reliance on huge, monolithic operating systems.

The objects in object-oriented programming are analogous to standard parts, designed to fit and work together. "This allows programmers to 'assemble' applications in much the same way that assembly lines use standard parts to build a car," explained an Apple press backgrounder on the technology. "Just as today's car makers can incorporate dozens of options into their cars, or even mix models on some assembly lines, object-oriented programming allows for a great deal of flexibility—enough that a business can build a tailored application uniquely suited to its own needs by combining standard, pre-written objects with their own business-specific objects." Software developers, as a result, would be able to write programs faster than ever. And users would see the benefit by not having to close one program and reopen another one simply to insert a chart into a report.

Simpler. Faster. And therefore cheaper. This was the mantra of object-oriented programming, as it was with RISC. Pink, like Script/X, would be jettisoned from Apple into a new company called Taligent, also to be jointly run and financed by Apple and IBM.

One day in early June 1991, Hugh Martin had just returned home with his wife and their newborn baby, the happy couple's first. The phone jingled, and Martin found himself speaking with Al Eisenstat, Apple's senior vice president. Martin had been thoroughly disillusioned over the collapse of the Sun deal and now just wanted to spend time with his family. But Sculley was calling him into action again. "Al said we had to go to Austin," Martin remembers. "He said, 'We're going to stay in a building until we get a deal.' " The deal, of course, was with IBM. Martin begged for a delay of one day so he could at least spend one night at home with the baby. The next day, he was on a plane headed east.

Barbara Krause, who was running Apple's public relations, got the same call. She and another PR woman from Apple accompanied Sculley on the three-hour flight to the Texas capital aboard his Learjet. Sculley's face had been drawn with almost constant worry in recent years, but on this day he was as animated as a little boy. "He was particularly excited about Taligent," says one person familiar with the conversations aboard that jet. "He got stars in his eyes saying that object-oriented programming would change computing."

Once they had touched down in Austin, Sculley was more like a lost boy. A limousine whisked them to the site of the negotiations, a one-story, industrial affair used by IBM on the city's hilly outskirts that had no windows—and no apparent entrance. "The limo driver could not find the entrance," says the person familiar with Sculley's travels that day. "So he went to a service entrance manned by a security guard. John jumped out of the limo and banged on the door, but the security guard would not let him in. Barbara finally jumped out and started shouting, 'He's John Sculley! He's CEO of Apple!' "

The Sculley entourage gained their admission, and were handed IBM badges to wear. Over the next two weeks, Sculley and his two dozen underlings huddled in the little building with Kuehler, Cannavino, and their two dozen aides to hammer out the last details of a memorandum of understanding that would presage a formal alliance. A small delegation from Motorola was also on hand. Most people dressed casually, or tried to. Some of the IBMers wore shorts and jeans, like the Apple people, but with black socks and dress shirts. Some of the Motorola people wore suits. They just could not help themselves. No matter: everybody was working together, and they all wanted to make a deal.

Finally, after about fourteen days of having barely left the building and having eaten countless pizzas and take-out barbecue, the two sides emerged from seclusion to make their announcement. There was a slight logistical problem to overcome first, though. It was the week of the July Fourth holiday, when IBM normally shut down its headquarters in Armonk, New York. The PR people from IBM had to get the place unlocked and have the air conditioning turned on so they could deal with the expected media deluge when the press release would go out on Wednesday, July 3.

Word of the talks, which had been kept hush-hush, had already started leaking out. And the press response was largely positive. In its "Top of the

News" column, *Business Week* ran a big article under the headline AN ALLIANCE MADE IN PC HEAVEN, with a photo of Sculley carrying his captioned quote: "There are no sacred cows." On the cover of its "Money" section, *USA Today* ran the headline IBM, APPLE FACE "REALITIES," with smiling photos of Sculley and IBM CEO John Akers. Depicted in another photo, just below, was Bill Gates. "Odd Man Out?" the *USA Today* caption for Gates questioned.

The train was on the tracks now and picking up steam. There were just some final touches needed before the final agreement could be announced. The July 3 announcement had contained only preliminary details. More meetings were held. One week, in Armonk. Another week, in San Jose. Finally, on Tuesday, October 1, 1991, it was the eve of the Big Day. The announcement would be made the next morning at the Fairmont Hotel on San Francisco's exclusive Nob Hill. This was an opulent palace that towered above the endless procession of stretch limos pulling up in the drive to deposit their precious cargoes of corporate titans, visiting royalty, and even presidents.

Sculley and Kuehler were almost giddy with anticipation. But there would be one last hitch. Motorola was the lesser partner in this triumvirate, brought in only at Apple's request. People always talked about how buttoned-down IBM was, but Motorola was perhaps even more so. The Motorola people were also a conservative, homogeneous bunch, guarded of talk and deliberate of action in a manner emblematic of the H-P Way. Indeed, many people in the industry referred to them as "the Motorolans," they were so much alike. It was now well into the night, with the big press conference scheduled for only hours away, and the Motorolans were quibbling over some tiny details in a contract that had already been cleared by Apple and IBM.

"Mote [Motorola is called that in the industry, for short] wanted one more total pass at the contract to make sure they hadn't missed anything," says one IBM executive familiar with the incident. "We couldn't get them to sign the agreement, so we wrote two press releases: one with just IBM and Apple and the other with all three. We rehearsed both and told Mote, 'We'll use one or the other. It's your choice.' They didn't fold until two A.M. on the day of the announcement."

That day, October 2, 1991, was a glorious one for John Sculley. Apple was on a sales roll again, marking his second successful turnaround of the company. He had consolidated power over Apple, jettisoning the troublesome Gassée. And here he was, with his new friends from IBM, facing an audience of some two hundred press and analysts under great chandeliers in a ballroom of the Fairmont Hotel. "These agreements are the foundation for a renaissance," Sculley said in announcing the technology alliance.

The comments were beamed to Apple employees and customers worldwide via a satellite television linkup provided by Apple's own television studio,

AppleTV, which had strung big cables from the ballroom to portable trailers set up outside to broadcast the signal. The high point came when Kuehler, standing beside Sculley onstage, clasped Sculley's hand and raised their arms in victory. "This is like winning at the U.S. Open," Kuehler, a tennis nut, mumbled to Sculley as they stood with arms held aloft.

Michael Spindler was also onstage for the announcement, but from his body language, it was he who looked like the odd man out. "Spindler was sitting with his back to his boss, arms folded and glaring," recalls Peter Kavanaugh, who was running AppleTV then. "He looked totally uncommitted to his boss." Just how much would soon become vividly apparent.

The IBM-Apple alliance held such great promise. Here were the top two manufacturers in the PC industry joining forces. *Business Week* said it could be a "fearsome" combination. Indeed, it both could and should have been.

If only the alliance had worked as envisioned.

8

Looking for Another Way Out

One of the big problems with competing in the personal computer industry has always been that all your rivals are moving targets. Just when you come out with a super-duper computer that is the fastest and sexiest on the block, someone down the street announces one that is even faster and sexier.

So even as Apple and IBM were inking their deal to apply pressure to Microsoft and Intel, the Wintel Express was kicking into even higher gear. In just the first twelve months after its 1990 launch, Windows 3.0 sold 4 million copies around the world. Nobody had seen anything like it in the industry. Those ever-paranoid boys over at Intel, meanwhile, were readying the deployment of an 80486 microprocessor, the industry's most powerful yet.

John Sculley had finally done the right thing by attacking the low end of the market dead on, and this had halted and slightly reversed Apple's steady erosion in market share. By 1991, it had crept back up to 8 percent from 7.5 percent the year before.[1] And he had crafted a shrewd alliance with IBM that held great potential for eventually pulling both companies out of the fire. But it would take at least two or three years to see any tangible results from the alliance, since all the joint research was yet to get under way. Two or three years is an eternity in this business, as dictated by Intel cofounder Gordon Moore in his Moore's Law, which holds that the number of transistors that can be built on a chip will double every eighteen months. Already, as of 1991, there were nearly 100 million computers banded around the Microsoft-Intel standard.

The big danger that Sculley faced as he awaited help from Big Blue, then, was of losing so much ground to Wintel that the software developers (whose programs were mandatory to the survival of the Mac) would desert Apple and focus instead on Microsoft's operating system. Remember how Apple had treated Adobe, one of its most important developers, back in 1989, when it had teamed with Microsoft to topple Adobe's PostScript printing standard? Through mediation by Michael Spindler, that feud had been largely patched up by 1991. But the lingering sentiment in the software community was that Apple was difficult to deal with, that it went out of its way to be uncooperative.

Making matters worse, the Mac had never been a developer-friendly computer to begin with. Those brilliant programmers in their pirate's patches had worked so feverishly to make the Mac an easy device for customers to use that there was virtually no energy left over to do the same for developers making programs for the machine. As a result, developers had to wrestle with complexities that were not present in the Wintel standard. For example, almost every type of Mac contained its own, specially designed board containing the major circuitry, or motherboard. A single Intel motherboard, by contrast, could run on a wide variety of IBM-compatibles, making it simpler for some developers because they could write programs for just that motherboard that would work on any manufacturer's machine containing that piece.

"Every time Apple put out a new model, we had to check it out with our application software," says Bob Dusseault, former vice president of a company called Howtek Inc., based in Hudson, New Hampshire, that has made printing software for Apple since its early days. "This put a tremendous onus on the developer."

Microsoft, on the other hand, wooed and courted developers to its camp. Bill Gates, for example, made it a practice to give away advance copies of new operating systems before their release to the general market for the developers to start working on. Apple, however, has charged for the privilege. At Microsoft, too, there was always extensive hand-holding of the developers. Microsoft programmers were available to help with any problem the software developers might encounter. With Apple's persistent reorganizations, many developers didn't know who to go to with questions or problems. In short, Microsoft followed a clear, detailed plan to help its developers. Apple, however, never had a clear plan and hindered more than it helped.

Until Windows 3.0 came along, none of this really mattered. The Mac was so leading edge that many developers such as Adobe and Aldus wanted to write their programs on it first and just deal with the headaches. With the lack of a suitable alternative to the Mac's graphical user interface, the PC market for graphics-oriented programs was held captive by Apple. As a result, all the really cool programs, such as Adobe's PageMaker, the desktop publishing program, came out on the Mac first. But with Windows 3.0, things changed almost overnight. Granted, it was still nowhere as good as the Mac. For instance, long descriptive file names could not be used, as with the Mac, and documents were easily lost in the system, unlike in the Mac's easy filing system. But it was a working alternative. Better yet, a program written for Windows could be seen—and purchased—by nearly ten times as many customers. Although many developers resented Bill Gates's growing power over the industry, they figured if he could make money they could too.

Market share. That was what most developers really cared about. A developer spent $5 million or $10 million coming up with a new program, and it wanted that program to be in the hands of as many customers as possible. What *would* change a developer's mind about Apple was any indication that the pioneer in Cupertino was pioneering a way of radically increasing its market share—a way so radical that nobody could afford to ignore it. This kind of radical strategy was embodied in an Apple document entitled "Assessing the Need for a Discontinuous Jump in Macintosh OS Penetration."

This 112-page tome, dated August 30, 1990, and labeled "Confidential," laid out, in frightening detail, why it was urgently necessary to take steps to dramatically increase the Macintosh's presence in the market. The report was prepared over a six-week period that summer by a ten-member Apple team assembled by Dan Eilers, who by then had been promoted to vice president in charge of strategy and development. This was the same Dan Eilers who had been shouted down by Jean-Louis Gassée when he had first pitched a Mac licensing plan exactly five years earlier. Since that time in 1985, Eilers had been overseeing Apple's strategic activities in such areas as investing in small companies.

Dan Eilers would not have dared attempt another licensing gambit in Apple with Gassée still around. But as of the summer of 1990, Gassée was a lame duck, biding his time until his resignation became official in a few more weeks, and John Sculley was surrounded by a new administration that seemed more savvy to market realities. There was the CFO, Joe Graziano, who understood the need to increase market share and had, in fact, pushed Sculley in that direction when he rejoined Apple in 1989 from a stint at Sun. And there was Michael Spindler, the new COO, who had trebled Apple's business in Europe and wanted to increase Apple's business in the United States, as well. In a show of how highly he regarded Spindler, in November 1990 Sculley relinquished his title of Apple president and added that to Spindler's domain over operations. Sculley remained chairman and CEO.

Eilers was still widely distrusted in the engineering organization for having been a leading proponent of opening the Mac's "crown jewels" to the outside world. So he decided to buttress his argument by enlisting the services of the McKinsey & Company consulting firm to analyze Apple's competitive position. In its study, McKinsey confirmed Eilers's fears that the Mac was being locked into a niche of the market that would prove unsustainable over time.

When the report was completed at the end of August 1990, Eilers arranged a presentation for John Sculley and his executive staff. Eilers and his team, which had been working out of the third floor of De Anza 7, took the elevator one floor up to the executive headquarters suite, and laid their charts out on the long table of the boardroom called "Synergy." Hoping to keep the attention off himself, this time, Eilers did little talking. Instead, he sat and listened as members of his team, including Russ Irwin and Robert Lauridsen, outlined for Sculley, Spindler, Graziano, and the other members of the executive staff why Apple was looking down the barrel of a gun. Both Irwin and Lauridsen were pragmatic business executives who favored suits to the more casual dress of the Apple culture.

As their report showed, the fundamental problem was simple economics. As of 1990, the annual R-and-D investment by Microsoft, Intel, and all their hardware and software customers totaled about $3.5 billion, or five times as much as the $675 million spent by Apple and its comparatively puny cadre of customers and suppliers. The amount of investment by software developers in making spreadsheets and other key business productivity programs around the Microsoft/Intel standard totaled another $550 million between 1987 and 1989, or nearly eight times as much as the $70 million spent by Apple's developers in that period, while the money developers spent on selling and marketing their Microsoft programs was $1.1 billion during that time, compared to just $145 million for Apple's developers.[2] Apple, in short, was being grossly outspent on every front.

Then there was the matter of an issue known as "differentiation." The Macintosh had always been differentiated from IBM-compatible computers because it featured the easier-to-use graphical user interface (GUI). Microsoft's MS-DOS software, with its arcane commands, could not even come close. Through Windows 3.0, though, Microsoft was catching up. At the time, Eilers's group also worried about the potential high growth of IBM's fledgling Operating System/2, or OS/2, but that software would prove a market failure in the years to come. In their report, the team predicted that by 1994, Windows and OS/2 would account for 87 percent of the market for GUI operating systems, compared to a virtually nonexistent presence before. Sales of computers banded around the Wintel standard would continue to grow so fast that Apple would have to increase its Mac shipments by 17 percent each and every year—just to hold on to its 1990 share.[3]

Unless Apple took drastic steps to increase its market share, Eilers's report warned, the company's very financial underpinnings would deteriorate. Less differentiation would mean that Apple could no longer justify charging more for its machines than comparable IBM-compatible models. The fall in prices would lead to a fall in gross profit margins, which in turn would undermine Apple's ability to finance the in-depth research needed to keep pushing its technology ahead of everyone else's. It was a vicious circle, and if no action were taken, Eilers predicted, "Apple will become a living dead company." Living in terms of still existing as a company. But dead from the standpoint that it would no longer be relevant to the rest of the industry.

Apple's only hope in averting this, Eilers's team concluded, was to significantly increase the Macintosh's share of the PC market. The report suggested a level of 25 percent of the market, or three times Apple's own share as of 1990. To make this "discontinuous jump," over a period of the next three years, the report recommended four radical options:

1. "License Mac OS." Manufacturers could use the Macintosh's software but would have to come up with their own hardware designs.
2. "OEM to others." This would allow other manufacturers to sell "clone" versions of the entire Macintosh computer, not only the software.
3. "Make Mac OS processor independent." The Macintosh's operating system would be redesigned so it could run on other microprocessors, such as those of Intel, not just the Motorola chips to which Apple had always been tethered.
4. "Create second brand." This would amount to Apple starting up a whole new line of Mac-compatibles itself, to be sold under a different brand name. Even though the line would be controlled by Apple, it would force the Macintosh to be more competitive and would provide customers with an alternative to the Mac.

That was it. It had taken the better part of a day, but Dan Eilers and his crew had made their case. Now the ball was in John Sculley's court. And Michael Spindler's. It was decided to adjourn for the day and reconvene the next morning to brainstorm some more. When they had all gathered again, Sculley broke the meeting into two groups: one headed by Spindler, in the Synergy room, and the other headed by Sculley, in the "Imagination" room next door.

Sitting on red leather chairs in the Imagination room, Sculley seemed animated as he tossed out his own idea: Why not, he suggested, make a deal with the Japanese? The Japanese, he told his group, possessed a strong technology in laptop computers, but they had virtually no presence in the U.S. market for desktop computers. "Sculley said, 'Why don't we trade 'em?' " recalls Russ Irwin, who was in that meeting. "He said, 'We'll give them the Mac OS, and they can make desktops in the U.S. and Japan. And they'll help us make notebooks.' "

Actually, it was a terrific idea. And one that once again illustrated how John Sculley possessed the talent to articulate major business trends before they even started. At the time, in 1990, the Japanese had been drawing fear and resentment in America for their buying frenzy of choice U.S. properties and were being roundly condemned by American business leaders for unfair competitive practices in the automobile industry. But Sculley was recommending that an American company actually work *with* a rival in Japan, and that notion of U.S.-Japanese business synergy would come into vogue in the years ahead.

The suggestion showed that John Sculley's heart was in the right place. And he did follow up on it. Some months later, he dispatched Russ Irwin to pitch the proposal to NEC Corporation, the computer giant in Tokyo. But NEC declined because by then it had already committed to joining forces with Microsoft. Sculley's inaction afterward on the key proposals in the report, however, showed that he still didn't get it. Dan Eilers had intended the report to scare the dickens out of Apple's top brass, in the hope that it would get them off their butts and they would finally do something to break the company out of its box. Yet the two-day session ended with no conclusion or sense of urgency on the part of either Sculley or Spindler. "There was not a decision to pursue aggressively any kind of licensing or opening of the OS," recalls one former executive who helped prepare Eilers's report. "We came away with disappointment."

So the "discontinuous jump" proposal was shelved as another was introduced just days later. This time, it was Hugh Martin stepping to the plate with another radical plan. Martin, who was heading Apple's efforts to switch its computers to the new technology for RISC-based microprocessors, drafted a fourteen-page report entitled simply "NewCo." NewCo is a common moniker assigned a new company before it actually gets a name, and Martin's idea was for Apple to spin off a whole new company to make a new version of the Mac's operating system. This new version would be designed to run on any microprocessor, including Intel's, and would be based on System 7, the long-delayed Blue project that was supposed to significantly update the Mac. Martin, like Dan Eilers, pleaded for urgent action by Sculley and his executive staff.

"The primary objective for Apple and NewCo is to dramatically increase the installed base of personal computers running the Macintosh OS as quickly as possible," Martin wrote in his September 16, 1990, report. "By increasing the market share of 'Mac style' personal computers, Apple is again on the offensive, both in the developer's mind, and in the minds of customers." The NewCo software would not be a full-blown system in itself. It would be what is called in the industry a "shell," a layer of software that would sit on top of an operating system called Mach—the one developed at Carnegie-Mellon University—which in turn would sit on top of MS-DOS. The computer would boot up like a Mac. The screen would look like a Mac's. To the casual user, the machine would *be* a Mac.

In essence, Martin was resurrecting the plan pushed by Dan Eilers and Chuck Berger five years earlier to license the "look and feel" of the Macintosh to different hardware manufacturers. Berger, as detailed before, had roamed the United States, drumming up interest from a multitude of manufacturers in this plan, and in fact had had agreements with several. Sculley, however, had rejected all the deals after Gassée protested. With Gassée no longer in the way and Microsoft's MS-DOS customers facing a transition to Windows, Martin figured the timing was right to attack Bill Gates in his own backyard. "Most personal computer users prefer the Mac environment," Martin wrote. "With equal application availability, they would run Macintosh on their PC. 'Windows' is an attempt to emulate our GUI [grapical user interface] on top of DOS and it only partially succeeds." In other words, NewCo would out-Windows Windows.

Had it gone through, the NewCo initiative would have amounted to a Trojan horse attack on Microsoft. Sneak the Mac onto an IBM-compatible, and once customers see how great it is, they go on to buy Macintoshes or Mac-style computers from that day forth. Of all times to employ such a strategy, this was the one. Bill Gates was now a billionaire and a seemingly unstoppable force. But this was a rare moment for striking against Microsoft. Bill Gates had a whole world of MS-DOS users whom he would have to talk into following him into the wonderful new world of Windows. And in the beginning, Windows wasn't so wonderful, after all. It was filled with bugs, the kind that would sometimes make a whole computer crash and leave the poor user swearing to high heaven. While Gates was rushing to clean up the customer upgrade mess, Apple could have swooped in to steal his customers. And, oh, what a prize! As of early 1990, when Windows 3.0 first came out, there were about 70 million MS-DOS users in the world.

"The difference between Apple and Microsoft was that Apple did not have a plan to turn DOS users into Mac users while Microsoft had a plan for turning DOS users into Window users," says Marty Hess, a former programmer for Symantec Corporation, a leading maker of software utilities based in Cupertino, California. "The DOS user base was up for grabs."

Actually, Apple did have a plan. Or at least, Dan Eilers and Hugh Martin did—if anyone had listened. Martin presented his NewCo proposal to several of the engineering executives. They looked on with mild interest, thanking him for his time before proceeding on to more pressing matters. NewCo had died by lack of action.

After Sculley failed to act on his "discontinuous jump" report, Eilers was convinced the Macintosh was on its way to becoming an irrelevant computer platform and wanted to try something different. He was talking with companies outside Apple about the possibility of jumping ship, when an opportunity came up almost next door—at Apple's own software subsidiary, Claris Corporation. Since 1987, Claris had been run by Bill Campbell, the charismatic football coach who had been elbowed aside as head of Apple's U.S. business in one of Sculley's innumerable managerial shake-ups and replaced by Chuck Boesenberg.

Earlier in 1990, Sculley had given the green light for Campbell to oversee Claris's spin-off as an independent public company but torpedoed the deal at the last minute out of concern Apple would lose control over a critical base of software. Claris made word processing, spreadsheet, the leading database management software called FileMaker, and other programs for the Mac. The word processing and spreadsheet programs were not as popular as Microsoft's, but at least they were coming from a source that Apple could control. Campbell was not at all happy with the turnabout, since he was to preside over the Claris spin-off. So in January 1991, Campbell announced his resignation from Claris to become CEO of Go Corporation, a Silicon Valley software firm, which was established to develop a pen-based operating system for new handheld computers. He is now CEO of Intuit Inc. When he heard about the opening for a CEO at Claris, Eilers jumped at the opportunity. Eilers, after all, had a passion for Claris, having helped start the subsidiary in 1986 during his work on Apple's strategic investments.

Eilers was out of the power loop at Apple, but licensing the Mac was still close to his heart. One day in early 1992, he sat down with Sculley and Spindler to discuss strategies to help improve Claris's sales. Why not, he asked, let Claris become more of a "solutions provider"—a company that provided not only software but hardware in one neat package for the customer? And, while he was at it, why not let Claris manufacture and sell Mac look-alikes?

There it was again. Eilers was out of Apple, yet he wasn't out of Apple. He had been pushing licensing so long, he just couldn't help himself. Actually, this Claris proposal sounded a lot like the "second brand" proposal he had recommended in his "discontinuous jump" report of 1990. This seemed to be the safest way of all to start a licensing program. Sure, Claris would undercut Apple on prices, but Apple's consequent loss of revenues would just be funneled over to its subsidiary, whose money ultimately went onto the parent company's books. And by licensing in such a controlled manner, it would be like a laboratory: Apple could watch through the glass walls to see how a licensing program would really work, and make adjustments as necessary.

The idea was very appealing to Sculley, too. By this time, he had been watching with a mixture of awe and dread the meteoric ascendance of a firm called Dell Computer, after its young founder, Michael Dell. Dell, a University of Texas student who had started the company while in school, had adopted a whole different model for selling PCs. Instead of selling them through dealers and other resale channels, he would sell directly to customers via mail. He figured that the disadvantage of customers' not being able to get their hands on the box to take a look under the hood would be more than offset by the savings in not having to pay the extra cost of buying through a middleman. Was he ever right. Dell started his company in his college dorm room in 1984 and by 1987 had built the business up to $70 million in annual sales. By 1992, Dell's sales had exploded to nearly $1 billion. Needless to say, Michael Dell did not complete his undergraduate studies at the University of

Texas on schedule. Instead, he became one of America's youngest technology multimillionaires.

Since Apple was already higher-priced to begin with, compared to the competition, Michael Dell's mail-order model made the price gap even wider. Generally, Dell's computers were priced about 20 percent below other IBM-compatibles in the dealer market. Apple's, with the exception of the Mac Classic, were still priced about 25 percent above everyone else's. The Mac's premium was not as steep as it had been, but there was still a big difference. So Sculley saw in the Claris plan an opportunity to fight Dell on its own terms. He picked up the phone and dialed a number across the Valley. Guess who picked up on the other end? None other than Chuck Berger.

Berger, as you remember, had bolted Apple in disgust after the Apollo fiasco to join up with the storm troopers at Sun. Sun's business was rocking and rolling as CEO Scott McNealy ramrodded his way to the top of the market for big, expensive workstation computers, which were targeted for use in scientific and engineering environments. Berger was a Sun division president when Sculley called and couldn't have been more surprised when his old boss asked him to attend a secret Apple meeting in February 1992 at the Sofitel Hotel in Redwood City, just ten miles up the 101 freeway from Sun's offices in Mountain View. Actually, Eilers had suggested to Sculley that he make the call, since Berger had been his old ally in the licensing debates. "Sculley and some Apple managers met at the Sofitel to discuss what to do about Dell, which was just taking off," says a former Apple executive intimately familiar with the meeting. "Also, the price collapse had just started on the PC side and Windows was out. They wanted to build a Dell within Apple."

The Claris headquarters building was located several miles away from Apple, near Paramount's Great America amusement park in Santa Clara. It was a stone's throw, also, from mighty Intel. Seeing at long last a real opportunity for him to make a difference at Apple and significantly increase the Mac's market share—as well as take advantage of a lucrative employment package offered by Sculley—Berger agreed to sign on to run the endeavor and gave his notice at Sun. He did so with utter confidence that support for the project extended all the way to the top of Apple. Indeed, Sculley had assured him, "Absolutely, we will go through with this," according to an executive who heard that statement. Berger assembled a team of a half-dozen Apple people and set up shop in a building across the street from Claris's administrative headquarters. Within sixty days, they were to come up with a prototype of a Mac clone. Eilers suggested the code name for the project: "Drama," under a scheme used by Claris to assign code names to various projects in alphabetical order after college classes. Chemistry had already been used, so it was Drama's turn.

There are few places as beautiful and inspiring as northern California in the spring. The winter rains have subsided, and the brown hillsides erupt in a panorama of lush green grass and stunning wildflowers, as overflowing streams gurgle past. It was against this breathtaking backdrop that Berger and his team worked, with enthusiasm and hope, to get their prototypes finished. They put together a business plan and contracted with Nissan Design International, the San Diego–based arm of Japan's Nissan Motor Company Ltd., to design the exterior of the machines. Taiwan's Acer Inc. was contracted to perform the manufacturing. And Arthur Andersen & Company, the Chicago-based accounting and consulting firm whose name has since been changed to Arthur Andersen LLP, was retained to help set up an in-house computer network for the new cloning business.[4]

By July 1992, two months after they had started, they were all done, with three working prototypes. The models looked just like an IBM-compatible PC, with the large, boxy shape made of standard industry parts, but they contained the Macintosh's friendly software. The prototypes were crude, to be sure. After all, they had been slapped together in just eight weeks. But they were good enough to take before a meeting that month of the Apple executive staff to get the stamp of approval to kick off a real business.

Or so Chuck Berger thought.

Just a few weeks before, an earthquake, of sorts, had rocked the computer industry. Compaq Computer, based in Houston, Texas, had been taking a beating from, among other IBM clone makers, its cross-state rival, Dell, which was based in Austin. Compaq's sales had soared to an annual rate of $3.6 billion in 1990 but had been undercut by Dell's discounted pricing so much that those revenues had fallen back to $3.3 billion in 1991 — the first drop in Compaq's brief history. Mighty Compaq was in crisis and ready to launch a bold move. The Compaq board fired its CEO, cofounder Rod Canion, and replaced him with an energetic German national named Eckhard Pfeiffer. In the early summer of 1992, Compaq chopped its PC prices by about 20 percent, precipitating one of the most vicious price wars ever seen in the personal computer industry. It would go down in PC history as "the Compaq Shock."

The gambit worked: within two years, Compaq would go on to steal massive amounts of market share and dethrone IBM as the world's top PC maker. It wasn't just low pricing that vaulted Compaq to the top of the heap: the company was also inordinately aggressive in rolling out a hot-selling line of laptop computers, as well as data-storage servers for big business.

Faced with the prospect of having to compete against even cheaper Wintel computers, Apple's salespeople, in particular, did not relish the prospect of also having to compete against a Mac clone, even if it was one from Apple itself. Bob Puette, the president of Apple USA and former college football player, was highly concerned about Drama's likely impact on sales in his division. "Here we were, trying to balance everything on a delicate knife, and in comes another group who wants to slam in more products on this whole thing," Puette says. Those sentiments were shared by Ian Diery. Diery had done a bang-up job running Apple's Pacific business, cutting costs while sharply boosting sales volume in markets such as Japan. Just days before the executive staff meeting to decide the fate of Drama, Sculley had elevated Diery to the new post of executive vice president over worldwide sales and marketing.

The other key person opposing the idea of Drama was a man named Fred Forsyth, who had recently joined the executive staff as head of manufacturing and hardware engineering. Debi Coleman had run manufacturing for a time in the 1980s, before temporarily becoming CFO. After having taken off nearly half a year to tackle her weight problem, Coleman had returned to Apple only briefly before quitting to work at a smaller company. Forsyth, hired in 1989 by Sculley from Sullivan's old alma mater, Digital Equipment Corporation, was competent enough at his core discipline of manufacturing but, like so many of Apple's executives, displayed a disturbing tendency to intefere in matters outside his area of expertise, as he demonstrated with Drama and would do so on other strategic endeavors. Forsyth was not a passionate table pounder like Spindler, nor was he an in-your-face antagonist. Like Diery. Calm and soft-spoken, Forsyth was highly influential nevertheless, because of his tendency to talk issues out in a reasonable, convincing manner.

It all seemed like déjà vu to Dan Eilers, as he once again trudged up an elevator to press the case for licensing. The elevator stopped at the fourth floor of De Anza 7, and Eilers strolled toward the Synergy boardroom, where he and Berger were scheduled to deliver a lengthy presentation, followed by a demonstration of the Drama prototypes in the adjoining Imagination room. Seated around an oblong table were top executives, who besides Sculley included Diery, Eisenstat, Graziano, Forsyth, Spindler, Sullivan, and a new star, Dave Nagel, who had just been named a senior vice president of the Advanced Technology Group, where he had been vice president.

Nagel was a pleasant, bearded fellow with a faraway look in his eyes, as though he were boring into the mysteries of the universe. A holder of two degrees in engineering and a doctorate in experimental psychology, Nagel was a true intellectual, a deep thinker. From 1973 to 1988, he had worked as a scientist for the National Aeronautics and Space Administration, rising to become chief of NASA's Aerospace Human Factors Research Division. Nagel had joined Apple in June 1988 as manager of applications technology within the ATG. He had quickly risen through the ranks, becoming vice president of ATG in May 1990 before being promoted to his current job in November 1991.

Yes, Dave Nagel was a mighty smart guy. His only problem was that he didn't understand products. And as it turned out, that would be a very big problem for Apple.

Eilers and Berger stood up and launched into their spiel. Everyone paid close attention. Even the reclusive Mike Markkula had come in to listen. For the next two and one-half hours, they outlined, detail by detail, the projected benefits of cloning Macs through Claris. The imitation Macs would be sold directly to customers via mail, in the same way Dell sold computers and peripherals, and they would be priced 35 percent below comparable models from Apple. In the first year of operations, Eilers and Berger estimated, Claris would sell $600 million of the clones; the following year, $1 billion. According to people at the meeting, Markkula and Graziano expressed their support for the idea. Spindler, however, conveyed his skepticism through that Spindleresque body language.

"Through the whole meeting, Michael was physically distraught," says a person who was there. "He was perspiring, pacing, slumped in his chair. Finally, he blurted out, 'What Michael Dell has done has not created market share but rearranged market share.' Eilers and Berger produced data to refute that, but Spindler would not believe it. And he said, 'Besides, we're living through the worst of the price-cutting, and it won't get any worse.'" These proved to be famous last words. Diery also chimed in. "You picked the wrong way to do it. You picked a software company to do a hardware machine," he said. "It's not a bad idea. But make sure you put it on the right side."[5]

Diery contends he was not overly worried about Drama's impact on his sales, although three other people in that meeting insist he was. "Ian comes in and says, 'How the hell can I maintain my margins with my Mac product if we have someone out there selling the same technology at a lower price?'" recalls one former executive present. "Graziano said, 'At least we can be our own guinea pig.'" Another person at the meeting remembers Diery also specifically objecting to Drama's intention to strip away features such as a drive to automatically eject floppy disks to save on manufacturing costs. Diery feared that would make Apple's products look overpriced by comparison. "Ian said, 'Well, if you do that, maybe the customers won't buy our Macs,'" this person recalls. "Dan and Chuck said, 'Well, gee, maybe we want to do what the customer wants.'"

Forsyth expressed his reservations, too. Besides agreeing with Diery that Claris was ill equipped to manufacture computers, Forsyth warned the group that Drama's expenses would undermine the whole Macintosh operation. "The Drama group was presenting profit-and-loss numbers for Drama that were not right," recalled Forsyth, a tall, fit man with straight black hair, as he discussed the episode with me over coffee at a restaurant near his home in the well-heeled Silicon Valley community of Los Gatos. "I said, 'If Apple is going to do this, then we are going to tube the whole business.'"

Sculley had not said much to this point, but he interrupted to suggest a compromise. "John said, 'Well, how about if we let Claris pay a cannibalization tax over to Ian Diery's organization? But the key is, let's let Claris do this. Price the products appropriately. Let's just get it done,'" recalls a former executive who was at the meeting. By this time in 1992, Sculley had delegated much of the business of running Apple to Spindler, his trusted lieutenant. Sculley, then, deferred the final decision to Spindler. Big mistake. The Diesel effectively terminated the deal when he directed that Berger's Drama project report directly to Ian Diery—the man who had wanted it killed from the outset.

Afterward, Eilers and Berger wrote long letters to Sculley, pleading for him to resurrect the project. But nothing happened. Eilers returned, tail between his legs, to continue running Claris as its CEO. Berger and his team of six were out on the street. Chuck Berger had been to bat for licensing now four times. He resigned to become CEO of Radius Inc., a current maker of Macintosh equipment in San Jose, California.

As the Drama saga drew to an unceremonious close, another drama was unfolding behind the cloistered walls of R and D that had even greater potential for Apple's future. This one borrowed from another proposal in that "discontinuous jump" report: making the Mac's operating system "portable" so it could run on other microprocessors.

By now the engineers had actually shipped a completed product. Two significant ones, that is. The old Blue project, renamed System 7, finally limped to the finish line in early 1991, nearly two years behind schedule. With System 7, there was little of the marketing hype that Microsoft had promulgated around its Windows 3.0 launch. That was because System 7 was not really that great a leap from the original Mac. To be sure, it contained some nifty features, such as snazzier icons and "virtual memory" to free up unused space on the hard drive and create more memory. The engineers also added a menu item to invoke a little Help balloon over the various desktop icons, as well as a greater ability to switch between programs. But Blue really was just the old Mac, with bells and whistles thrown in. The major reason for that, former engineers attest, was an almost complete lack of focus in what the new software was intended to do.

"System 7 was just a complete fiasco in terms of planning, because the engineers were just throwing in everything but the kitchen sink," says Phil Goldman, the engineer who worked on the unsuccessful Jaguar project to create a brand-new computer.

To help get System 7 out the door, Sculley in early 1990 imported yet another executive from Digital, a tall, lanky man named Roger Heinen who had strong skills in business and leading software development. Heinen was soon placed in charge of software engineering as a vice president, filling a vacancy left when Ed Birss went off first to run Pink and then to help oversee the Apple/IBM venture called Taligent. When Heinen arrived, he found the software division in complete disarray and, in May 1991, recruited another software manager from Digital named Rick Spitz to help clean the place up. Spitz could not believe his eyes when he stepped into the job.

"I had six hundred people where half the people would not talk to the other half," remembers Spitz, who left Apple in 1996. "When I got there, I handed out budgets and my managers said, 'What are these?' " The major reason for the chaos in Apple's system software was the fact that Apple had bet all its marbles on Pink becoming the company's successor to the Macintosh. But when Pink had mutated into Taligent and then left the company altogether, about one hundred of the Pink engineers—representing Apple's best and brightest—had jumped ship to follow along.

That exodus, in 1991, had left Apple with younger and less experienced software programmers, many of whom were already tired and burned out after spending so many years getting System 7 out. As of early 1992, fears were growing in the engineering community that Taligent would never deliver, given the fact that the Pink project had begun in 1987 and had yet to ship an operating system. Meanwhile, Apple had committed itself to converting its entire Macintosh line to the new PowerPC microprocessors being developed as part of the 1991 accord among Apple, IBM, and Motorola. This was an absolutely essential project, because the Motorola 68000 chips that Apple was still relying upon were losing ground to ever-faster generations of microprocessors being produced by Intel. And to convert to PowerPC, the Mac's operating system would have to be retooled to run on a different chip.

So Rick Spitz, in his first few months on the job, was faced with a multitude of dilemmas. There was the need to come up with a PowerPC version of the Mac's operating system. There was the need to keep updating System 7 every few months as part of so-called maintenance releases to clear out bugs. And there was the distinct possibility that Taligent was not going to materialize after all, leaving in the hands of a group of burned-out, second-string programmers the awesome task of building a brand-new operating system from scratch.

It was against this ominous backdrop that Gifford Calenda, the project manager for the System 7 Blue team, walked into Roger Heinen's office one day in early February 1992 and dropped an idea. Calenda, too, was exhausted after the drive to produce System 7 and wanted to move on to something new. "I told Roger, 'You know, system software seems trapped in the Mac. It needs to work on other computers,' " Calenda remembers. "I was saying, 'Bill Gates is going to kill us because we are sitting at maybe 8 percent market share.' "

This was not a new idea. Heinen and Spitz, in fact, had discussed opening the Mac to other computers on a number of occasions. But the timing of Calenda's pitch could hardly have been more fortuitous. Barely a week later, on Valentine's Day 1992, Roger Heinen and Rick Spitz welcomed a visitor into their offices from Utah. His name was Darrell Miller, and he was vice president of strategic marketing for Novell, Inc., the Provo, Utah–based supplier of the NetWare operating system, which had grown to dominate the booming market for software that links fleets of personal computers together. This man was really an emissary from Ray Noorda, the hard-nosed chairman, president, and CEO of Novell who had driven the company's meteoric rise. His suggestion to Heinen and Spitz was a breathtaking one: Would Apple be interested in working with Novell to make the Mac's operating system run on Intel-based computers?

"Our first question was 'Are you going to sue us if we go ahead without you and implement a Mac-like OS on the Intel-based PCs?' " recalls Tom Rolander, then director of Novell's PC research and development. "Roger Heinen said, 'Well, maybe we can do things together.' "

Essentially, Novell wanted to provide an alternative to Windows in the so-called client-server market, which refers to personal computer "clients" that are connected together through a data-storage computer called a "server." This would put the Macintosh's operating system at the heart of work groups in major companies. "Microsoft was moving into the server area with Windows NT, so we thought that having GUI on the desktop and having NetWare on the server would squeeze Microsoft out of the networking business," recalls Rolander, who left Novell in December 1993 to cofound PGSoft Inc., a software company in Pacific Grove, California, where he currently serves as chief technology officer.

Talk about manna from heaven. At that time, in early 1992, Novell was connecting an average of a million new NetWare customers per month, or 12 million a year. If Apple could distribute a retooled Mac operating system to just 10 percent of those customers, that would translate into 1.2 million additional Mac users every year. This was a golden opportunity to achieve that "discontinuous jump" in market share that Dan Eilers had talked about. And yes, Roger Heinen and Rick Spitz were interested in pursuing this further. With Sculley's blessing, the two men flew to Utah to meet with Ray Noorda at Novell's campus sprawled in the shadow of the snowcapped Wasatch Range. In the meeting, Noorda expressed great interest in cooperating with Apple on a project to put the Mac on Intel-based computers.

Heinen and Spitz called in Gifford Calenda, who had just proposed basically the same idea, and put him in charge of assembling a small team to work with Novell's engineers to develop a working prototype of a portable Mac operating system. The goal was to put the Mac's "Finder," which provides the distinctive look and feel of the Macintosh on the screen, onto an Intel-based computer. The finder, in essence, looked like the top of a typical office desk, with files arranged to look like folders. Calenda designated a former System 7 manager, Chris Derossi, to head up Apple's side of the project. In a meeting with their colleagues from Novell, someone suggested the endeavor be called "Star Trek." "The idea being 'Boldly going where no Macintosh had gone before,'" Rolander recalls.

When Dan Eilers had suggested doing this very thing so many years earlier, Jean-Louis Gassée had sworn up and down that it would be technically impossible. Of course, Digital Research had proven him wrong when it came up with a Mac-like layer to MS-DOS called GEM in the mid-1980s. In fact, Tom Rolander knew all about GEM, having worked as Digital Research's vice president for engineering. Novell had later acquired Digital Research and with it Tom Rolander. Still, "porting," or moving the Mac OS to another microprocessor, was not going to be a walk in the park. The operating system contained literally millions of lines of code, intertwined in a chaotic mess not unlike a bowl of spaghetti.

Luckily for Star Trek, an Apple engineer named Fred Huxham was already down in the labs laying the groundwork. Fred Huxham, a quiet and intense man whose eyes would bore into you with the same intensity he used in glaring at a computer screen for hours on end, was one of Apple's best and brightest. At the time, he was a member of an engineering team called the "Blue Meanies," a part of the overall System 7 development group. As System 7 underwent its final testing prior to the launch, Huxham's job was to sit at a computer terminal and tweak some of the code to see if he could free up more memory. He was also on the watch for any big mistakes made by others in the software code. Then he had another idea.

"Some of the code was really old, like from 1983, so my suggestion was, 'Hey, why don't I just rewrite a huge mess of this code [from the original Macintosh operating system] from scratch?'" Huxham recalls. "I thought my supervisors would say no, but to my surprise they said, 'Go ahead.'"

As he was getting under way on this during the spring of 1992, Huxham was called into Gifford Calenda's office. The headquarters of the Mac software research was then on the third floor of a building called Mariani 1, located on Mariani Drive behind the main Apple campus. Calenda shut the door, turned to Huxham, and swore him to secrecy. "He said, 'This is more secret than any of the secret projects,'" Huxham says. "I was not allowed to even tell my own boss."

Then Calenda outlined the gist of the project. Huxham was being assigned to an elite group of programmers called Star Trek. This would be a joint development effort with Novell to make a version of the Macintosh operating system that could run on an Intel microprocessor. The Trekkies would be moved off campus, and they would stay in seclusion until a working prototype of the new software was finished. "We were just going to disappear," Huxham says, sipping a cup of black coffee at a San Francisco café as he recounts the affair. "I told Gifford, 'We need to come up with some reason why we are going.' But my boss, Jeff Miller, ended up working on the project, so it wasn't an issue with him on the disappearance." Miller, who had also been a manager on System 7, was named to help manage Star Trek with Derossi.

Calenda went all over the Valley to scout possible buildings for the Star Trek team to use, shooting reams of footage on a video camera he toted along. He ended up settling on a Novell marketing office in a thirteen-story building called Regency One, a triangular high-rise with windows of mirrored glass. It was situated in Santa Clara, about five miles from the Apple campus. The setting was apropos. Directly across the street and plainly visible through the windows of Star Trek's digs in Suite 400 on the fourth floor of Regency One, was Intel's worldwide headquarters. If you squinted hard enough, you might even see the dynamic Hungarian, Intel CEO Andy Grove, hurrying around at his usual run. Huxham went to check out the place, and his heart started beating faster. "I was pretty excited about it right off the bat," Huxham says. "We all thought, technically, it would be a fun project to work on."

In a separate corner of Apple, a young product marketing executive named Mark Gonzales was just beginning his eight-week paid sabbatical as Calenda briefed Huxham on the top-secret project. An Apple tradition that has survived all the other cutbacks in perquisites, employees are entitled to take a sabbatical after five years on the job. The sabbatical has always been highly popular at Apple, because it gives workers a chance to just "veg out" after all those ninety-hour weeks. It acts as a brain recharge more than anything else, and it has been good for the company as well as the employees. Gonzales sorely needed a break. He had been immersed, in a product marketing role, in an Apple project to design a camera that fed digitized images directly into the computer. With the so-called digital camera, it would never be necessary to go to the photo store again to have film developed: just pop it into the computer, pull the photo up on-screen, and punch the printer button for as many copies as wanted.

That had been a fun endeavor, although a frustrating one. Apple shipped one of the cameras but did not quickly follow up with more. Within four years, the digital camera market would begin taking off, and as usual, Apple would largely sit on the sidelines of a category of product it had helped popularize. So when Gonzales returned from sabbatical in midsummer of 1992, he was ready to do something different. He did not have to look far. "The first week I got back," he says, "a guy was sent to talk to me about a crazy idea of moving the Mac to Intel."

Gonzales was suddenly a Trekkie. His job was to run the product-marketing end of things. He joined Calenda, Huxham, Miller, and Derossi, along with seven other Apple engineers specially selected for the team. They included John Fitzgerald, Charles Haynes, Kelly King, Alan Mimms, Fred Monroe, Dave Owens, and Dean Yu. Wendy Santos, an Apple administrative

assistant, and Jane McMurray, an assistant to Calenda, were also members of
Star Trek. There were also four team members from Novell assigned to the
project, and they included Rolander, as well as Dave Brown, Susanne Slider,
and Russ Weiser. After weeks of planning meetings, the work finally began on
July 17, 1992. The Trekkies were given three months—until Halloween—
to come up with a working prototype of a Mac that could run on top of an
Intel microprocessor. As incentive, Roger Heinen dangled the promise of fat
bonuses of between $16,000 and $25,000 for each Apple Trekkie, if they completed the job on time. The engineers practically salivated, because the usual
bonus for a big R-and-D job was more like a few thousand dollars.

"In the case of the bonuses, it was Gifford and Derossi who suggested the
idea," Spitz says. "I agreed and asked Roger's opinion, and he agreed. My rationale was that this was a very-high-risk venture and that they would have to
work extremely hard to make the milestones we set down."

Although the Star Trek project was so secret that only a handful of people
at Apple knew it was going on, Intel CEO Andy Grove knew about it almost
from day one. In fact, he pledged his full cooperation. Intel's involvement in
Star Trek began after a series of conversations during 1991 and early 1992 between John Sculley and a Harvard Business School professor named David
Yoffie, who was also on Intel's board of directors. Yoffie was preparing a case
study on Apple for his Harvard classes and had spent time questioning Sculley
at length about his strategy and Apple's business model.

After one such encounter in about February 1992, Yoffie looked at Sculley
and remembers saying, "I don't think you have a prayer." Yoffie went on to
outline why. "The argument I made was that problem number one was, the
strategy was still premised on maintaining differentiation for a premium price
for Apple, at a time when Windows was getting better. And problem number
two was that the Intel platform was beginning to grow much faster than Apple
was willing to admit."

To prove the latter point, Yoffie arranged a meeting between Sculley and
Andy Grove in Sculley's office on the fourth floor of De Anza 7. "Andy presented to John some numbers of Intel's CPU [central processing unit, or
microprocessor] shipments and Intel's forecast on what would be the price of
Intel CPUs going forward," recalls Yoffie, who attended the meeting. The
forecast was far more aggressive than Apple's own estimate of Intel's growth.
"The reaction first by John and then the people below him was disbelief. I
went to dinner with Roger Heinen a week after that, and he was asking
whether these CPUs were going into toasters, because he couldn't believe
they were going into computers."

John Sculley should have been alarmed. No other company in the world
possesses more insight into the actual demand of personal computer sales
than Intel Corporation, not even Microsoft. That is because Intel is the

world's preeminent supplier of the microprocessors that power the personal computer and as such takes orders every day of the year from hundreds of manufacturers that rely on the Intel chip. Since operating systems do not change as quickly as microprocessors, Microsoft is not in the same position as Intel to see all the fluctuations in demand.

After presenting that shockingly high forecast to Sculley in their meeting, Andy Grove leaned forward and warned in his thick Hungarian accent, "John, you're going to get killed by Microsoft. You have to put your technology on Intel." Sculley nodded and replied, "I think you're right."[6]

Since Star Trek was going to use an Intel microprocessor, Sculley decided to solicit Intel's technical help in the project. Andy Grove was delighted to oblige. He was most interested, particularly because he had been very impressed by a new Apple technology called QuickTime and wanted to see it running on Intel computers. QuickTime, introduced in 1991, gave personal computers the multimedia capability to incorporate moving video, sound, and text. QuickTime was years ahead of its time and Apple's biggest technical innovation since the Mac. The reason QuickTime succeeded, when so many other projects failed, will be explored a little later.

Grove, in any event, viewed QuickTime as one more way of keeping Intel's microprocessors out in front of the competition, which, though small, was always trying to catch up. As other people associated with Star Trek believe, too, Grove was uneasy over Intel's reliance on Microsoft for the operating systems that ran the PC in tandem with Intel's microprocessors. They believe he wanted an alternative to his old comrade in arms Bill Gates. (Grove declined to be interviewed for this book.)

So, in that summer of 1992, a secret alliance among Apple, Novell, and Intel was set into motion, carrying a potentially even greater portent for the computer industry than the famous one announced a year before of Apple, IBM, and Motorola. This could be so, because the prospect of the Macintosh running on Intel-based computers would provide direct competition against Microsoft on its own platform, not a separate one.

The technical success of this grand mission rested squarely on the shoulders of the Trekkies settling into their new home across the street from Intel. The Regency One was stiffly corporate, filled with marketing and legal types with suits and briefcases. The Trekkies definitely stood out from the pack, with their T-shirts and shorts. The irreverence extended further, to the sign they put on the door of Suite 400: WE ARE ARROGANT BASTARDS & ASSOCIATES. "One of the Novell guys got concerned and had that taken down," Huxham says. "All the suites in the building had signs on the door identifying the company or group inside," Huxham adds. "We didn't have one and weren't going to get one, so we would put a new one up every week or so. It was an election year, so one week we were election headquarters." The door was kept locked, with card-key access only. Only team members and executives overseeing the project were allowed in.

The project became an engineer's fondest dream. Management was leaving them all alone. The team was kept small, as they found it most efficient. Roger Heinen came around every couple of weeks or so to ask just one question: What more do you need? "Heinen had told us, 'If you need anything, just go buy it,' " Huxham says. "So we all went to Fry's [a computer superstore] and got keyboards, monitors, and all the other hardware and software we needed. To do that, you usually had to go through a lot of red tape." There was one other rather odd request. The Trekkies were putting in unholy hours, like from 7 A.M. to well past midnight, and had taken to adjourning for sanity breaks at a local video arcade. Engineer Fred Monroe, the youngest of the group in his early twenties, was particularly fond of a race car game there.

"So we asked if we could have a race-driving game, so we wouldn't have to go to the arcade," Huxham says. "We were trying to embarrass Fred more than anything else. We didn't expect to get video games. But Roger said, 'Okay, you need video games. Tell us what you want.' Within a week, a pinball machine arrived, as well as a sit-down driving simulation game. We all became world-class drivers." Suddenly, the Trekkies had little reason to leave Suite 400. The kitchen was stocked with candy, and the fridge was filled with Sierra Nevada Pale Ale, the engineers' favorite beer. And Fred Monroe did not leave when everybody else went home.

"Fred had set up housekeeping in there at one point," recalls Gonzales. Monroe, at the time, had been house-sitting for Calenda while Calenda was away on vacation in Africa. He moved into Suite 400 after construction crews turned off the water and power to the house to do structural work. "When Heinen and some of the executives walked in one day, Fred walked right out of a room in his boxer shorts," Gonzales adds.

This was the fun-and-games part of Star Trek, but most of the time it was plenty serious business. Each Trekkie had two computers, sitting side by side: one a high-end Macintosh Quadra, the other an IBM-compatible running on a powerful Intel 80486 chip. Intel supplied the PCs and made its engineers available to answer technical questions. "We wrote all our code and tested it on the Macs," Huxham says. "Once we did that, we would put it on a PC two feet away." The engineers had their own private offices, all with windows facing Intel, stretching along a corridor with blue-and-pink carpeting. When they needed to talk, there was a large meeting room with a whiteboard and a reception lounge furnished with large, comfortable sofas.

Almost every week, the Trekkies hit a big technical roadblock that had to be overcome. "The first really big one was how to draw to the screen,"

Huxham says. "Macs and PCs did this very differently, and for a day or two, we thought we had failed before we even started. Tom Rolander and Alan Mimms, however, came up with a solution."

When the Trekkies weren't hitting roadblocks, they were crunching code—tons of it. "It was very slow going," Huxham recalls. "It was like each engineer was building a piece of a giant puzzle. However, until all the pieces were done, you couldn't really see that the puzzle was coming together. It wasn't until we were in the last month of the project that we began to see that we were going to succeed."

By Halloween, the Trekkies had met their deadline. It was time to show off their handiwork. Although the original goal of the project had been just to put the Mac's finder (the look and feel of the Macintosh on-screen) onto an Intel-based computer, Huxham and the crew had thrown in some other goodies, including the Mac's QuickDraw GX's graphical capability to paint and draw. They had even rigged Star Trek to make the same sound as a Mac when it boots up, as well as to display the familiar "happy face" logo that appears whenever a Macintosh is turned on. "We wanted to make it look, feel, sound, and smell like a Macintosh," Rolander recalls with some pride.

When some executives from Apple and Novell came over to see a demonstration, the engineers put the Mac/Intel boxes through their paces. A forty-five minute video summary of the Star Trek project, narrated by Tom Rolander shortly after it was all over, captured what those executives witnessed. The computer used was a garden-variety IBM-compatible running on an Intel 80486 microprocessor. But the similarities with the rest of the IBM-compatible world ended there. As soon as the screen flickered on, it was all Mac. There was the cutesy trash can in the lower-right-hand corner. There were the familiar Mac icons. And to show off the Mac's unique graphical capabilities, a "slide show" presentation of Apple's new QuickDraw GX technology was shown. In it, three-dimensional dice rotated on the screen, digitized marbles bounced around, and the letters "A-P-P-L-E" flew effortlessly through cyberspace. The grand finale was a QuickTime movie showing a rocket blastoff. "Liftoff. We have liftoff," a voice intoned from the computerized movie.

No IBM-compatible machine could do any of *that*, at least not with the Microsoft Windows operating system, which was still too crudely designed to perform the same kind of graphical calculations. "One executive from Novell was laughing and giggling and saying, 'I just can't believe it. I just can't believe it,' " Huxham says.

So, as of November and after three months of intense work, the project was over, or at least the first phase of it. The Trekkies were thoroughly wrung out by now and needed a good break. Fred Monroe, the video-game demon who had camped out in his cubicle, smiled slyly and suggested to his friends that he ask Heinen to send them all to some place outrageously exotic and then negotiate to a more reasonable locale, such as maybe San Diego. "So at our last meeting, Fred suggested that our next off-site be held in Mexico," Huxham says. "Roger just immediately said, 'That's a great idea. You need a rest after all this work.' We were all just stunned. We thought Roger was joking, but his office called later and got us all tickets. In November, we all went to Cancún for a week, paid for by Apple."

Apple had frittered away a lot of money in its time, but these were dollars well spent. After all, the Trekkies had accomplished in just three months what many people at Apple had long considered impossible. And think of the possibilities now. With tens of millions of MS-DOS users in the position of having to switch to Windows, what better way of stealing market share than by suddenly making the Macintosh available — on any Intel box? With Star Trek in the market, Apple could at least have slowed Microsoft's inexorable roll. Indeed, the plans were to have Star Trek out and shipping within two years. Although it had taken only three months to assemble a prototype, it would have taken much longer to fine-tune the portable operating system so it would be ready for the general market. Had that happened, it would surely have stolen the thunder from Bill Gates, who in 1995 would seal his control over the industry by launching Windows 95, a version of Windows that almost matched the Mac's quality.

"Star Trek would have certainly thrown a big curveball at the computer industry," Gonzales says, shaking his head years later over the project's sad fate.

Corporate politics, being what they are, often dictate that someone inside an organization champion a particular cause, lest it be carved to pieces by jealous factions. This is true in just about any business, and this is how Star Trek would bite the dust. Things started off well enough after the Trekkies returned tanned and relaxed from their sojourn in Mexico. The biggest champion of Star Trek had been Roger Heinen, the vice president for software engineering. He wielded tremendous clout with Sculley and gained a most favorable audience when he, Spitz, Gonzales, and Jeff Miller presented their case for Apple to design and launch a Macintosh operating system for Intel-based machines at a meeting with Sculley and the executive staff just before Christmas 1992.

The meeting was held on December 4 in the Synergy boardroom of De Anza 7, the same one where project Drama had died the past summer. Sitting around the same oblong table was the usual cast of characters: Sculley, Spindler, Eisenstat, Sullivan, Graziano, Forsyth, and the others. With the lights turned down and the curtains drawn, Heinen, Spitz, and Gonzales outlined the case for how Star Trek could help Apple, and Derossi gave Quick-Draw GX and QuickTime multimedia demonstrations on the new machine.

When he wasn't talking, Gonzales had a chance to peer curiously around this citadel of power. There was Sculley, smiling like a little boy. Being naturally somber, Sculley didn't smile often, so this was a good sign. Graziano was so excited, he paced constantly. "It looked pretty good to me," Graziano recalls. "I would have been in favor of pursuing that." And there were the others, chiming in with questions and commentary that repeated what someone else had just said.

"What amazed me was how out of control the executive staff was," Gonzales says. "I remember thinking, 'This is the group that makes decisions for Apple?' "

Another former Apple manager who was at that meeting remembers experiencing a sinking feeling when he glanced over at the foot of the table, where Fred Forsyth, head of Apple's manufacturing business and hardware engineering, sat with his hands clasped to his head as though in pain. Eric Harslem was the executive directly responsible for hardware engineering, reporting to Forsyth. "Fred said, 'This will mean a whole new business model,' " this former manager recalls. "I knew then it was going to die." Rick Spitz, who also attended the meeting, says Fred Forsyth was simply looking at the world through his manufacturing eyes, just as Ian Diery, who was a salesman, had resisted Drama because it might cut into his Mac sales. "Fred's view was that Apple was a big manufacturing concern, and he wanted to keep his factories running," Spitz says.

Forsyth recalls that he objected to Star Trek because he believed the project, if undertaken on a large scale, would attract Apple's best engineers at a time when the company was focused on converting its entire Macintosh line to the PowerPC microprocessors. "My concern was, we were always starting one strategy and then doing another," Forsyth says. "I didn't think we could pull off both PowerPC and Star Trek."

But Star Trek was not dead yet. When the one-hour presentation was over, the executive staff gave Heinen the green light to recruit a team for the next phase of the project, which was to begin work on a detailed development plan. It was full steam ahead, or so the Trekkies thought. Like most Apple people, they had become so inured to projects being killed that they thought if they could only get the executive staff to go along, they would have it made. There was one thing they did not consider: What would happen if Roger Heinen, the champion of Star Trek, were to suddenly quit? They were about to find out.

Keep in mind that Apple's engineering community was still split into often warring camps. Hardware resented Software. Software resented Hardware. And there were hotshots within both factions that sniped at each other. The feuds had raged since the geek brawls between the Apple II and Macintosh teams. It should come as no surprise to learn, then, that there were quite a few folks not involved in Star Trek who did not like the idea one bit. The Trekkies' fellow engineers in software, for example, were mighty ticked off when they heard each of the team members had been awarded five-figure bonuses, far higher than anyone else. The hardware side, led by Eric Harslem, was also working itself into a tizzy. Those engineers were busily engaged trying to re-design the Mac so it could run on the new PowerPC microprocessors that Apple, IBM, and Motorola were collaborating on. And they fretted loudly that both IBM and Motorola might get cold feet if they saw Apple devoting less than 110 percent interest to PowerPC.

"The big concern within Apple was what would happen to PowerPC if we went with Star Trek," Sculley remembers. "We thought we could tell the story of selling Mac/Intel and Mac/PowerPC."

Every year at Christmas, Apple closes down until the first of the year. There is really not much to do then, anyway, because all the big customer or-ders for the holidays are filled. When the Trekkies returned back to work at the Regency One after New Year's Day 1993, there was a nasty surprise wait-ing. Roger Heinen had resigned. And guess where he was going? *Microsoft.* The Evil Empire itself. "We were dumbstruck," Gonzales recalls. "We knew it couldn't be good."

That was surely an understatement. Heinen had not been at Apple long, less than three years. But he had proven an inordinately competent software manager and had rallied the troops around a common foe. It was particularly incongruous that he should go to work for Microsoft, because at Apple he had been one of the most outspoken people against the increasing power and in-fluence of Bill Gates. "In fact, he had given us T-shirts that said BREAK WIN-DOWS," Huxham recalls. But Heinen was gone, in fact out the door the very day he tendered his resignation. Star Trek was officially championless, like a dinghy bobbing in rough seas after its lifeline has snapped off from the mother ship. (Heinen, who has since retired to live in Maine, declined to be inter-viewed for this book.)

Project Star Trek really died the moment Heinen walked out the door. But it would remain on life supports for many months. The Trekkies at Regency One barely had time to pull their jaws up off the floor when the phone rang from headquarters, calling them back into the Cupertino campus. This was an ominous sign, because it meant they were being folded back into the R-and-D bureaucracy, with all its feuding camps. In February 1993, Michael Spindler named Dave Nagel, who was heading the Advanced Technology Group, to take Heinen's place over system software development, which was officially known as the Macintosh Software Architecture division. "The quick succession means that Macintosh software development efforts should

continue without the hitch normally associated with a top management position's vacancy," trumpeted the March 1993 issue of "Apple Direct," an Apple
newsletter put out for Apple's developers.

Nothing could have been further from the truth. Universally regarded
within Apple as an exceedingly nice guy and a brilliant intellectual, Nagel was
considered by his engineers to be a plodding researcher, lacking the sense of
urgency needed to get products shipped out quickly. This mentality would
bode ill for Apple in the years to come.

Once Star Trek was reeled back into the R-and-D campus, it seemed as
though a thousand different hands were reaching out for it. "We had a sexy
new project, and everybody wanted to work on it," recalls Jeff Miller, who had
cosupervised the actual engineering of Star Trek with Chris Derossi when it
was still in the prototype phase. The project had started with eighteen people.
Now that it was back on the Apple campus, Rick Spitz procured space for a
joint Apple-Novell Star Trek team in a building called Bandley 5, named after
Bandley Drive, which ran in front of it. In short order, Star Trek ballooned to
about fifty people. "The objective was to build a detailed plan to actually do
the full thing," Spitz recalls.

But Star Trek's days were numbered. By late spring of 1993, money was
getting tighter at Apple, and Michael Spindler decreed that all the company's
business units be self-supporting, as profit and loss, or "P-and-L" centers.
Since research projects do not make any money until they result in a finished
product, Dave Nagel's software division was given a budget based on the royalty value of the operating system contained in each Macintosh sold. The
royalty of $22 per machine represented what Nagel's group would have re-
ceived had it been selling the operating systems to an outside manufacturer.

With budget limits set on software research for the first time, Nagel
parceled out money for the meat-and-potatoes projects such as a revised operating system for PowerPC and System 7 "maintenance" releases. After all was
said and done, there was none left over for Star Trek. Rick Spitz figured he
would need $20 million for Star Trek to produce a marketable version of the
Mac/Intel operating system in what he estimated would take eighteen
months. "Nagel flew out with me to meet with Ray Noorda to see if we could
work out a licensing deal," which would help defray Apple's costs in Star Trek,
Spitz recalls. "But Novell wasn't interested in committing the money." Actually, according to Novell's Tom Rolander, Novell was interested, but not at the
high price Apple demanded. "The pricing from Apple was too high to market
it," Rolander remembers. "It was difficult to make a business case for competing with Windows."

Dave Nagel, who with his graying beard, pleated slacks, and long-sleeved
shirt looks more like a professor than an executive, remembers having his
hands tied on the matter of Star Trek. "I was a proponent of Star Trek, but I

was given a finite budget and told to do PowerPC," says Nagel, who left Apple in 1996 to become president of AT&T's prestigious AT&T Labs. "It had to be either Star Trek or PowerPC, not both." Nagel adds that the expense problem for Star Trek was compounded by the fact that he would have to commit as many as one thousand engineers to spend at least a year writing special pieces of software called "device drivers" so the Mac's operating system could support the thousands of companies providing peripherals such as printers for Intel-based PCs.

As Star Trek gasped for funding, Spitz arrived at the inevitable conclusion: it would have to be merged with another project. At about that time, in May 1993, a software manager under Spitz named Jean Proulx (pronounced "Proo") was starting a research project to explore the possibility of creating a brand-new operating system for the Macintosh, because Pink had failed to accomplish this and its successor, Taligent, was moving slowly. The project came to be known as "Raptor," after the dinosaur featured in the blockbuster movie *Jurassic Park*, and was intended as an alternative to Taligent, the sluggish Apple/IBM project to create a new Mac operating system based on object-oriented technology.

Jean Proulx had also been recruited from Digital, in August 1992, to help better manage Apple's software engineering teams, and she tried to find a way to meld pieces of Star Trek into the Raptor project. This would be an impossible task, though, because by this point the original Star Trek engineers were thoroughly disillusioned and just wanted to move on to something else. Fred Huxham knew it was over when he heard the Raptor managers talk about broadening Star Trek's mission to make a Mac that could run on *anything*, not just Intel.

"A lot of us from the original team were shaking our heads like, 'What in the hell do you think you're doing?' " Huxham recalls. "The managers told us it was the most important thing Apple had ever done and that if we don't succeed, it's over for Apple." Huxham, however, found himself shackled to a desk filling out paperwork most of the time. The Raptor managers insisted the engineers write down all the technical specifications instead of crunching real code. Huxham argued passionately that time was running out, that the new Mac software had to get out before Microsoft's Windows 95, which then was known by the code name "Chicago." The pleas fell on deaf ears. After Sculley promised to announce Raptor at Apple's annual developers' conference in May 1993 but reneged, Gonzales became so frustrated that he resigned from Apple altogether. Huxham wanted to resign from Raptor to work on something else at Apple but was told by his supervisors to stay on.

Finally, in June 1993, Dave Nagel folded Star Trek altogether as Raptor continued on. Raptor would set the stage for yet another operating system project called Copland, which would emerge at the center of an Apple crisis in 1996. There would be one last insult for the Trekkies, though. "They wanted us to do a postmortem," Huxham says. "They sent us a questionnaire with a hundred questions on what we did right and what we did wrong. I refused to fill them out."

In killing Star Trek, Dave Nagel's argument was that his was a dilemma of "either–or": either he committed to Star Trek, or he committed to the PowerPC project. He did not have funding approval from Sculley and Spindler for both. It was true that Apple had to pursue PowerPC, lest its Macintoshes fall hopelessly behind Intel-based PCs in speed and performance. But Apple faced an even greater long-term threat of being squeezed out of business altogether by the sheer volume of Wintel machines competing against the Macintosh on all sides. Star Trek could have vastly expanded Apple's business opportunity by letting it compete on both Intel- and PowerPC-based machines. Given the high stakes involved—Apple's very survival in the computer business—surely money and resources could have been found to bring this project to fruition.

It really is unbelievable, when you think about it, how many opportunities like this Apple squandered over the years. Time after time, somebody would step forward with a great idea to break Apple out of its hole. And time after time, Apple would shoot it down. John Sculley was, in many ways, a figurehead CEO who lacked the respect and support of his own executive staff, much less the engineers down in the trenches. But he *was* the CEO, and his day of reckoning was drawing near. In fact, it would be in June 1993, the same month Star Trek died.

9

Sculley's Waterloo

The collapse of the Drama and Star Trek projects meant that Apple Computer would be deprived of important strategic weapons against the onslaught of Microsoft and Intel in the years to come. Yet, even as these momentous undertakings were unfolding behind closed doors in 1992 and other problems were building, John Sculley was steering Apple to one of its greatest years ever.

During that year, Apple outwardly seemed to be firing on all cylinders again. Sculley had clinched the deal with IBM. His hardware managers had rolled out a sleek new laptop computer called the PowerBook that flew off the store shelves, contributing to the company's record $7.1 billion in revenues for the year and increase in global market share to 8.5 percent from 8 percent a year before—the highest in four years.[1] At the end of 1992, Apple had amassed a hefty war chest of $2 billion in cash reserves, its largest ever. Over on the software side, a band of engineers had just come up with a breakthrough technology called QuickTime, which for the first time enabled personal computers to run video clips complete with sound. It was an innovation that helped kick off the PC industry's rush to the multimedia revolution that Sculley had predicted in 1988.

Once again, Apple was at the leading edge of the technology wave. And with the Diesel, Michael Spindler, at his side running the nuts and bolts of the business, Sculley figured he had the ship back on course, freeing him to focus on long-term strategic moves. How wrong he would prove to be.

In my interviews with him for this book, Sculley took considerable pride in the technical innovations that were occurring at Apple at the end of his tenure, despite the company's management turmoil. But as was the case with so many of Apple's triumphs, the ones with PowerBook and QuickTime took place only after some renegades in the trenches usurped the company's Byzantine organization and charted their own paths. It was this very entrepreneurial spirit, indeed, that had fostered the creation of Steve Jobs's Macintosh.

Just like the Macintosh project, which was completed by a core team of fewer than twenty engineers, Apple's few successful technologies were almost always achieved by small groups of engineers. Star Trek was an example of this. Although that project was shot down in flames, the eighteen Trekkies had accomplished what many inside Apple had long denigrated as impossible: putting Macintosh software onto an Intel-powered machine. The QuickTime team was even smaller, with six core engineers. Yet the technology they produced in just eighteen months with $1 million of research money overshadowed the work of 160 engineers who spent four years and $100 million to spiff up the Mac's original software in a product called System 7, which had begun as the old Blue project.

QuickTime epitomized the best of Apple. System 7 was Apple at its worst. Unfortunately for Apple, there would not be enough QuickTime-style breakthroughs to offset the myriad flawed projects.

In contrast to QuickTime, Blue was doomed to mediocrity almost from the very start. Step back a moment in time to that fateful meeting of Apple's top engineers at the Sonoma Mission Inn during 1987. That was when a line was drawn in the sand: the "A" team would go off to work on the project called Pink to revolutionize the Mac's software, while the "B" team would handle the drudgery of Blue, updating the Macintosh's aging operating system. With few top guns wanting anything to do with Blue, that project's managers were forced to rely on green recruits fresh out of engineering school. Indeed, Gifford Calenda, who cosupervised Blue with a fellow software manager named Sheila Brady, remembers them hiring "practically the entire" class of computer science graduates from Dartmouth College in Hanover, New Hampshire, during the spring of 1990.

The other problem with Blue was that it simply tried to do too much. During 1988, when he pitched System 7 to Sculley and the executive staff, Calenda says he and Brady envisioned the project including a full twenty-two new technological features. The vast majority were so arcane, however, that Calenda and Brady ended up shelving half of them by the time the product was ready to ship in 1991. At that 1988 meeting, and others with Sculley involving the Mac's core operating system over the years, engineers in attendance say they rarely heard Sculley provide any meaningful input.

"He would nod his head at the appropriate time, but he really didn't know what was going on," says Cary Clark, an Apple software engineer between 1981 and 1994.

With Jean-Louis Gassée primarily focused on the hardware features of computers before Sculley took charge of all R and D, the software engineers were left pretty much on their own. In the case of Blue, at least the managers were solid leaders. Brady, for example, was likable as well as tough, an aging flower child whose idea of fun was to disappear for months into the mountains and jungles of South America. "She was born with a sense of how to keep a project forging ahead," says one engineer. "Sheila was a natural leader, and most of the engineers adored her." Brady would be instrumental in a later project to make the Mac's software work on a new generation of PowerPC machines, as part of a transition that would be vital to the company's survival.

Calenda was also a maverick, having knocked about on shrimp boats before signing on with Apple in 1986 as a software engineer. A veteran programmer with beard and shaggy brown hair, Calenda was also an ardent westerner who even adorned his home with accoutrements such as a lamp shaped like a cowboy boot. Well liked by just about everybody in engineering, Calenda was also a no-nonsense taskmaster.

He would have to be. By 1990, it was clear that the revolutionary Pink operating system was no closer to completion than when the engineers had first started work on it in 1987. This meant the pressure was on Calenda and Brady to get something out, and fast, to show the world that Apple wasn't just sitting on its laurels in the new world of Microsoft Windows. It was pedal-to-the-metal time. In the closing months of Blue (which by now had been internally renamed "Big Bang"), the engineers toiled seven days a week, twelve hours a day. A few members of the group buckled under the pressure, suffering nervous breakdowns and divorces.

"Maybe that's a tragedy, but if you are going to be a great composer, you dedicate your whole life to that," says Calenda, who would quit Apple in 1993 to help design software at video-game maker Electronic Arts Inc. The pressure cooker was so intense that Calenda and Brady arranged for everyone to take flying lessons to blow off steam, on Thursday nights. "It was a techie thing to do," Calenda says.

One of the technologies the Blue engineers were playing with involved John Sculley's favorite buzzword: multimedia. In 1990, one of the engineers in the Advanced Technology Group—the Apple think tank dedicated to futuristic ideas—wrote a technology paper for internal distribution on how personal computers would some day have multimedia capability. As per usual with ATG, the paper suggested all kinds of uses for the technology, ranging from animated screen icons (such as a moving, talking Bugs Bunny) to running videocassette recorders and laser discs off the computer.

Engineers in the Advanced Technology Group had in fact conducted extensive research into multimedia technology during the late 1980s. One engineer, Steve Perlman, had developed a hardware-based technology for multimedia called QuickScan, but that project was scrapped. Other engineers conducted research into a multimedia user interface, which would incorporate sound and moving video into graphical objects such as an on-screen postcard.

One day in early 1990, Dave Nagel, who was running the ATG before taking over software engineering in 1993, approached Sculley with two other managers to press the case for Apple to make multimedia development a top Apple priority. "We said, 'Look, this is important and we could get years ahead of Microsoft,' " Nagel remembers. The managers had a sympathetic ear in Sculley, who had just named himself CTO and had preached the vision of multimedia technology for several years. Since Sculley still lacked clout among the engineers to set technological direction on his own, Nagel encouraged the titular boss to preemptively announce that a new multimedia technology, called QuickTime, was coming—without telling the engineers first. Sculley took the hint and stood up onstage at Apple's Worldwide Developers Conference in May 1990 to announce that QuickTime was coming in a year.

This, of course, came as a shock to the rest of R and D, and most engineers paid the announcement little mind. After all, they were still pressing ahead with the long-delayed Blue project and were working on changes in the Mac's hardware architecture to incorporate a faster microprocessor. Nagel assigned some Advanced Technology Group engineers to the project in concert with some engineers from the system software side.

One of those system software engineers, a wiry, hyperactive man named Bruce Leak, was the person who made QuickTime happen. In 1990, most of the multimedia research in the PC industry was concentrated on the hardware side of the machine. Microprocessors were too slow and weak to handle much more than the rudimentary tasks of the computer. To get the needed oomph for running moving pictures and sound, the PC would have to be souped up with extra circuitry that would add to the computer's final cost.

Bruce Leak had a different idea—and a revolutionary one, as it turned out. Why not tackle the multimedia problem from the software side? Just fine-tune the code in a software program so that it alone could shoulder the load. With QuickTime still an informal research project with little support in R and D, Leak took the idea to his boss, Tom Ryan. Both men were part of the team trying to get Blue out the door. Ryan, who had joined Apple in 1988 as a database engineer, worked his way up to manager over small software groups. Ryan was intrigued by Leak's notion and took it to his boss, Calenda, who in turn told him to assemble a formal team and go for it.

Following the 1989 earthquake that ravaged the San Francisco Bay area, the headquarters for Apple's operating system software division had been relocated from the damaged building, De Anza 3, to another nearby, Mariani 1. Eventually, as De Anza 3 was restored, Ryan gave Leak the go-ahead to lead a core team of six other engineers, who included Jim Batson, Peter Hoddie, Mark Krueger, Sean Callahan, Kip Olson, and David Van Brink, and set up shop away from everybody else in a corner of De Anza 3. Following the Apple tradition of secrecy in special projects, known in the Valley as "skunk works," few besides Calenda were supposed to know what they were doing.

"We kept them hidden," says Ryan, who left Apple in 1996 to become vice president of engineering for MediaTel, a San Francisco firm that specializes in sending mass fax messages for customers. "I was their shield."

The team needed a shield in any case, because the inevitable rivalries between one group of engineers and another flared again as some engineers in the Advanced Technology Group saw Bruce Leak's work as pilfering from them, even though ATG and system software were collaborating on the project. "There was a lot of tension between ATG and QuickTime," Ryan says.

There would also soon be tension between QuickTime and Blue, as soon as the full Blue team could see what Bruce Leak and company had been up to. It all came out in May 1991 during the Worldwide Developers Conference (WWDC). This is a high-profile event that Apple has hosted for its software developers every year in the San Jose Convention Center, which sprawls across two city blocks at the western edge of downtown San Jose. Inside the convention center's cavernous theater, the three thousand developers in attendance were expectant. Seven years after Steve Jobs had unveiled the first Mac, Apple was finally going to show them the first major upgrade to the Mac's core software. This was a moment not to be missed.

It is a tradition in the PC industry to launch a new computer product with all the excitement of a rock concert. The lights go down. A recorded track from a trendy band such as Pearl Jam blares out of giant speakers flanking the stage. Instead of Mick Jagger, a nerd jogs out, bathed in spotlight, to introduce the real star of the show: the must-have new product of the day. If all goes well, the nerd or nerds on stage will have the audience of nerds jumping out of their seats, screaming for more. Just as Steve Jobs did in 1984.

Well, 1991 was not 1984, at least not for Gifford Calenda and his Blue gang. The rollout of System 7 was theatrical enough. Golf carts laden with cardboard boxes containing the first release of the software puttered out through the aisles for the developers to grab their copies. That was the high point. Then the demos began. There was an improved "MultiFinder," a collection of colorful icons atop the screen that looked snappier than the ones on the old Mac. There was a new feature called "Balloons," which permitted the technically impaired to click on an icon that affixed little Help balloons above every task button on a tool bar that runs above the programs. And System 7 was a lot faster than before, both in running programs like a word processor and in switching from, say, the word processor to an appointment calendar.

But that was about it in terms of new features that an average customer would notice or remember. System 7 was by no means a stunning new release. The developers applauded politely enough, and the product would go on to help shore up Apple's Mac sales. But for so much work—160 engineers, three years, and $100 million—even System 7's managers called the Blue project a major disappointment. "I created a monster in that System 7 had so much in it the market could barely digest it," Calenda says. "It was a huge mistake to do one big release. The user only saw ten percent of the work we put into System 7."

What the developers had hoped for was some sort of technology breakthrough, the kind that would once again give Apple a distinctive software lead over Microsoft. When he ambled out onto the stage at the same developers' conference, following the System 7 launch, Bruce Leak showed what a real breakthrough looks like. Working from a Mac facing the audience on stage, Leak clicked the mouse button a few times, and, presto, the machine began playing Apple's famous "1984" commercial, sound and all. Watching the demo on a giant overhead screen above Leak and his Mac, the developers went wild, cheering and applauding. *This* was something new and different.

"Bruce Leak, Mark Krueger, and the rest of the team made it so you wouldn't have to buy [as much] extra hardware to get multimedia," Ryan says. "This was multimedia for the masses."

Apple's new multimedia technology would not have gotten to the masses quickly had it not been for the brash Aussie, Ian Diery. Diery, remember, had been recruited by Apple from Wang in 1989 to infuse Apple with his aggressiveness in selling computers. Diery was more than just a salesman, though. He was also Mr. Nuts and Bolts, in the mold of Del Yocam himself. He was interested not only in making a sale but in seeing to it that enough inventory was in the pipeline to fill orders.

So while Michael Spindler held the title of chief operating officer, it was really Diery who acted the part of COO. In 1992, after QuickTime had come out, the forty-two-year-old Diery was busy in Apple's Pacific region laying the groundwork for a stunning turnaround in the company's then-moribund business in Japan. Aided by Satjiv Chahil, the beturbaned Sikh who had championed the $999 Mac Classic and was serving as Apple Pacific's head of marketing, Diery built Apple into a household name in Japan. In so doing, he tripled the company's sales revenues there between 1989 and 1992, in part through promotional gimmicks such as staging Apple-sponsored rock concerts by the likes of singer Janet Jackson.

As 1992 wore on and Apple continued to make little advance into the ever-rising Wintel tide, Diery, while still overseeing Asia Pacific, picked up the telephone in his office in Tokyo and called John Sculley at his office in Cupertino. Diery began touting the virtues of QuickTime and multimedia. "John, we have lost the battle with the GUI," Diery said. "We need to get something easy and identifiable to distinguish us from Microsoft. It's multimedia. DOS can't do this. We can."[2]

Diery went on to suggest that Apple incorporate multimedia technology into all its new machines. To do so, Apple would have to outfit each new Macintosh with a drive for a new input device, the CD-ROM (compact disc, read-only memory), which is designed to hold all the video and sound data that multimedia programs require. A CD-ROM can hold about 600 million characters of text information, compared to only about 1 million on the typical floppy disk that had been the standard in personal computers until then.

Diery had been asked to promote this idea by Chahil and a man named Paul Wollaston, who worked under Chahil as an executive in Asia Pacific marketing. As Chahil remembers, they became intrigued with multimedia technology after using it, in a primitive form, by putting ad presentations in the many different languages of the Asian region onto a big laser disc that could hold them all. "We couldn't access marketing materials [from Apple's headquarters] because they were all in English," Chahil recalls. "After putting our materials on laser discs, I discovered that multimedia was very cost-effective."

When Bruce Leak's QuickTime was unveiled in 1991, Chahil went to Diery and suggested that this was the technology that could drive multimedia in the computer. To further ignite demand, Chahil organized an event during July 1992 called the Hakone Forum, so called because it was held in the city of Hakone, Japan, at the base of Mount Fuji. The Hakone Forum lasted two days and was used to demonstrate Apple's multimedia technology to executives from recording labels and "new media" companies, such as those in desktop publishing. It was a watershed event that rallied wide business interest in the concept of multimedia.

Sculley, listening to Diery's pitch from Japan, quite naturally loved the idea. After all, he had been the great multimedia prophet. When Diery later took his idea to Spindler, however, the Diesel was initially unimpressed. "Spindler said, 'No,'" according to an executive with knowledge of the situation. "He wasn't interested." Spindler did schedule a meeting of the senior executives to debate the CD-ROM issue. In the Synergy room on the fourth floor of De Anza 7, Diery gave his pitch to the assemblage of forty executives, including Spindler. Chahil was also on hand to back Diery up, as was Paul Wollaston. Almost as one, the executives listening to the appeal voted thumbs-down, insisting Apple had enough problems on its hands without having to worry about something called a CD-ROM.

"Dammit," Diery spat in his thick Aussie accent, "I'm going to do this in Apple Pacific." And so he did, including QuickTime and CD-ROMs in 47,000 Macintoshes for the Japanese market that sold out almost immediately.

On July 14, 1992, Sculley rewarded Diery's work in Apple Pacific by promoting him to the newly created post of executive vice president for worldwide sales and marketing, answerable only to Spindler and Sculley. From that position of power, Diery again began beating the drum for multimedia, egged on by his old subordinates, Chahil and Wollaston. "We went to Ian and said, 'If we ship one million CD-ROMs, we will own the market,'" Chahil says.

Diery then announced at Apple's Macworld Tokyo conference in February 1993 that Apple would ship 1 million Macs equipped with CD-ROMs in the same calendar year, worldwide. It was a bold move and one that could have easily backfired had consumers not rushed to embrace the new technology. The gamble paid off, though. Thirty-five thousand of the CD-ROM machines were sold in the first quarter after that Macworld, and 900,000 more by the end of December.

Once again, Apple had kick-started a new technology. By Christmas 1994, the multimedia revolution would be in full swing. Unfortunately, by then Apple was in no position to capitalize on its lead.

In breaking new ground on the multimedia front, Apple had opened the new decade by once again extending its status as the computer industry's foremost innovator. The company, however, remained a laggard in one key technology area: the laptop computer. The story of PowerBook illustrated how Apple, when it fixated on a goal, was able to muster its resources and soar to great heights. This would prove an incredible accomplishment, made even more so by the fact that PowerBook was handicapped by a miniscule marketing budget and the inevitable resentment from competing hardware factions within the company.

Unlike QuickTime, PowerBook entered the picture carrying a lot of baggage. Remember Gassée's Luggable, the monstrously huge "portable" that could not even fit onto an airline table? The Luggable had been a wonder in engineering, perfect in every detail—save for its size and the fact that it had taken nearly four years to get to market, or three years longer than it should have. When Gassée left, the requirement for engineering perfection went out the window, too. The new decree from Sculley: Do something new, and do it fast.

Indeed, one reason Sculley in 1990 made the unpopular move to personally oversee all product development was to make sure Apple quickly delivered new computers to the market. The industry was moving too fast, he realized, for Apple to continue on its 1980s cycle of waiting two or more years to ship a new product. When he finally forced Gassée out that same year, he adopted the "market share" mantra pushed by his new CFO, Joe Graziano, and set out on a three-pronged strategy to increase it: lower prices; faster time to market; more "hit" products.

The Macintosh Classic, released in the fall of 1990, was one such hit product. The Macintosh LC, released at the same time, was another. Power-Book, when it shipped in October 1991, would prove one of Apple's biggest hits of all. "My focus was on," Sculley says.

When the PowerBook project started in 1990, the product had no name. Sculley just wanted a portable, and he wanted it fast—like within a year. Fortunately for him, the team responsible for carrying out this directive was headed up by a trio of savvy managers named John Medica, Randy Battat, and Neil Selvin, who pretended they were working for a small, start-up venture, not a multinational conglomerate. "One of the things that made us successful was that we looked at ourselves as 'The Portables Company,' not Apple Computer," says Selvin, who went on to become chief executive of Global Village Communication, a software firm in Sunnyvale, California.

Randy Battat, at the time, was vice president for product marketing. He had served as product manager for the ill-fated Lisa computer, which, of course, had failed in the market but had helped provide a technical road map for the Macintosh. Battat's was a prestigious title in name only, because of Sculley's organizational structure, which continued to lump groups together by function rather than product. Under the functional setup, Battat, for example, had no real power over any products because they were under the realm of a separate R-and-D organization. Marketing was kept to one side, product development to the other.

At well-run companies such as Hewlett-Packard and Motorola, by contrast, entire divisions are organized around a particular product line. At H-P, for instance, everyone having anything to do with printers is put into the same division; the same with personal computers, minicomputers, and every other product line. The beauty of this system is that it places responsibility for the profit or loss of a product squarely on the shoulders of each and every person working in that division. If it sells like hotcakes, the team is rewarded with handsome bonuses; if it fails, little or no bonus. Maybe they are even fired. In short, the division is forced to focus on a common goal: getting something out there to beat the heck out of the competition.

The functional structure at Apple, however, often discouraged groups from working together. There was a separate product engineering group. And there was a separate marketing group to push those products on the street. This resulted in an ongoing feud between the marketing people and the engineers, preventing each side from having much input into what the other was doing. The enmity was exacerbated by the fact that Apple's layoffs, to this point, had generally hit hardest in the sales and marketing groups. Engineers were rarely touched. "It was rare to hear the word 'marketing' without hearing the word 'weenie,' " recalls Adam Grosser, a hardware engineer at Apple between 1984 and 1990. Conversely, the term often used by marketing people to describe an engineer was "prima donna."

What the PowerBook team succeeded in doing was eliminating those artificial boundaries, if for just one shining moment in time. John Medica was the hardware guy in charge of engineering the new laptop. He and Battat decided to declare a truce and work together on the product, along with Neil Selvin, a marketing manager named by Battat to head the marketing effort. As happens so often in business, good personal chemistry between the men enabled this project to flourish, just as the chemistry between Sculley and the bigwigs at IBM had helped usher in that historic alliance. They were a nerdy version of the Three Musketeers, and even the naming of the product was a triumph in cooperative management.

"One day, I sat down and said, 'Let's come up with something memorable,'" Selvin recalls. "We had a number of names that started with 'Power' and others that ended in 'Book.' Somebody at one meeting said, 'How about PowerBook?' and the name stuck."

At the time, in 1991, the two leaders in the laptop computer industry were Toshiba and Compaq, and both had introduced snappy new models weighing as little as eight pounds. So Medica, Battat, and Selvin decided to put some heat on the competition for a change. Their laptop would weigh less than eight pounds. Not only that, but it would offer some eye-popping new features that customers were sure to love.

One was a little button called the "trackball," centered in the middle of the keyboard for users to move the cursor arrow around on screen at the touch of a fingertip. This was a breakthrough in design, since the mice on all other laptops had to be connected to the computer with an awkward attachment. The PowerBook also contained little palm rests just below the keyboard, allowing customers to rest their hands more comfortably while typing. This, too, was an industry first. Finally, the PowerBook featured an advanced liquid crystal display, or LCD, screen, that displayed graphics and characters on the screen faster than any other laptop could using older technology. The LCD screen was borrowed from the Luggable, in one of the few good uses that failed machine was put to.

The PowerBook looked elegant enough, but could it do everything a customer wanted? Not yet. In customer focus groups, the Three Musketeers learned that what hard-charging executives on the go really wanted was some way of hooking into their desktop computers back at the office to swap files and check their e-mail. Coincidentally, Apple's software engineers were cranking out a remote version of the company's AppleTalk networking technology that would do just that. AppleTalk had long been used to connect Macintoshes with one another in an office, using a simple telephone wire. Remote AppleTalk would do the same thing, except over hundreds and thousands of miles instead of just a few feet.

Medica, Battat, and Selvin browbeat the software team to ship remote AppleTalk in time for the PowerBook's launch, timed for the giant Comdex computer show in Las Vegas scheduled for November 1991. The software side got the work done just in time, setting the stage for one of the most successful product launches in the history of the computer industry. This happened despite some gross miscalculations at the top of Apple.

Burned by the Luggable fiasco, Sculley initially held cautious expectations for how well the PowerBook would do. Moreover, executives from the big desktop side of the Macintosh business, which accounted for almost all Apple's revenues, pooh-poohed PowerBook's importance to the extent that it was given less than $1 million in initial marketing money. By contrast, Apple had devoted $25 million to kick off the Mac Classic—Apple's sensationally popular low-end computer for $999—and two other new Mac models the previous year.

The Three Musketeers had a hefty challenge on their hands: How to tout the wonders of the new PowerBook with almost no money for advertising? They devised an ingenious solution: they would pour almost all their marketing money into a single TV commercial that people would remember. So they filmed retired Los Angeles Lakers basketball star Kareem Abdul-Jabbar, scrunched up in an airline coach seat with his seven-foot, two-inch frame, yet still managing to type on his PowerBook. A caption to the ad said it all: "At least his hands are comfortable."

The ad was a runaway hit, as was the product. Mac users were so starved for a Mac laptop that they swamped Apple with orders. But here again, Sculley and his executive staff miscalculated. The PowerBook actually came out in three models. There was the PowerBook 100, a stripped-down version priced at $2,300 on the low end, a midrange PowerBook 140, containing more features and priced at about $3,000, and the fully loaded PowerBook 170 for $4,300. Anticipating that customers would flock to the cheapest model, Apple stocked up heavily on the PowerBook 100s while scrimping on supplies of the PowerBook 170s. Apple also had an easier time procuring the 100s, because it had contracted with Japan's Sony Corporation to manufacture those models. Apple itself manufactured the rest.

Apple's customers, however, preferred to pay extra to buy the latest in Macintosh technology. They therefore flocked to the PowerBook 170s—not the 100s—and a product backlog swelled that persisted for six months. "We were dead wrong" in estimating demand for the high-end PowerBook, Sculley admitted then.[3]

Apple quickly resolved the supply problem, however, and PowerBook sales went on to balloon to $1 billion in the very first year after the launch. Apple correspondingly soared to dethrone Toshiba and Compaq as the industry leader in worldwide share of portable computer shipments. Apple had gone from dead last to first place in a product category for which it had once been maligned. When he took the stage to address a forum of industry consultant Richard Shaffer's Personal Computing Outlook on December 9, just weeks after the Comdex launch, Sculley was pleased as punch.

"The product which I feel best about is the PowerBook series, because that really, I think, will tell you a little bit about where Apple's heading in the future," Sculley said in response to a question from Shaffer, a former *Wall Street*

Journal reporter whose forums have attracted the industry's top executives over the years. "The PowerBook was conceived—recognizing we're a late starter getting into the laptop business successfully—it was conceived not so much as a computation device, but we reconceptualized it as a communications product. And that's been its real strength, and it's off to a great start."

That was the high point of PowerBook, but it would not be attained again. By early 1993, Medica and Selvin got job offers they could not refuse. Medica was called upon to run the fledgling laptop business of mail-order giant Dell Computer. Under Medica, Dell would go on to make major inroads in the market. Selvin, meanwhile, was recruited to run Global Village, which made communications software for PowerBooks and other portables. That company was doing well until it began to be pulled under by Apple's collapse years later. And Battat, the third musketeer, quit Apple a year later to head the wireless communications efforts of Motorola.

Without those champions, PowerBook would be cast adrift, resurfacing in news media reports years later in a humiliating incident that would serve as a metaphor for the administration of Michael Spindler as Apple CEO. And another, more serious miscalculation concerning the PowerBook would prove to be the final nail in Sculley's coffin.

As enamored as Sculley became with both QuickTime and the Power-Book, those innovations were still just enhancements of a Macintosh line that he had increasingly come to view as a low-profit commodity. What Apple really needed, he thought, was a brand-new type of computer, one that would create a whole new industry, just as the Apple II by Steve Jobs and Steve Wozniak had done—something, he concluded, like the Newton.

"This was going to be John's signature on technology, not just having inherited the Mac," says Bob Saltmarsh, the former Apple treasurer.

Sculley envisioned a type of computer that would be small enough to fit into the palm of the hand, yet so powerful it could handle rudimentary functions such as taking notes and scheduling appointments, while also enabling the user to communicate with anyone, anywhere in the world. Sculley had been influenced in this concept by Apple Fellow Alan Kay, who had articulated his idea for a "Dynabook" portable computer in 1968. Sculley saw in Newton many aspects of the "Knowledge Navigator" technology vision that he had written about in his 1987 book, *Odyssey*—the one of a portable information computer—and believed Newton would prove that many of the concepts in Knowledge Navigator weren't as far-fetched as they had seemed at the time he wrote about them.

Apple's research for a handheld Newton computer had been begun in 1987, by the engineer Steve Sakoman. Under Sakoman, the Newton project had remained mainly a small research endeavor, aimed at one day producing a product that would initially be targeted to the so-called technophile market—the one consisting of fellow computer nerds who would buy almost any new technology. Later—much later—the Newton would evolve into a consumer product.

But that modest goal changed the day after Sakoman walked out the door of Apple in March 1990, in protest over how his boss, Jean-Louis Gassée, had been pushed out of the company. Sakoman went off to cofound the secretive Be Inc. venture with Gassée. By this time, a number of other companies, including Hewlett-Packard and Japan's Sharp Corporation, had handheld computers in development or release that served primarily as personal organizers, with crude spreadsheet and word processing functions. Another category of handheld devices based on handwriting recognition was under development by Apple and an Alameda, California–based firm called Geoworks.

After Sakoman left Apple in 1990, Sculley initially planned to direct Newton himself but agreed to the request of Apple scientist Larry Tesler to take over the project. Tesler was another of the elite scientists who had worked on so many futuristic technologies at the Xerox Palo Alto Research Center (PARC) labs in the 1970s. In fact, it had been Tesler who had first demonstrated the technology of the graphical user interface on Steve Jobs's fateful visit there in 1979. Tesler joined Apple in 1980 as section manager of applications software for the Lisa computer. He went on to become founder and vice president of the Advanced Technology Group (ATG) between 1986 and 1990, before being named vice president of the Newton Group in 1990.

A brilliant mathematician trained at Stanford University, Tesler was a very smart guy, in the mold of his fellow deep thinker at ATG, Dave Nagel. But, like Nagel, Tesler suffered a fatal flaw: he had virtually nil experience in shipping an actual product. And this would show in his stewardship of Newton.

Tesler started off well enough. The first thing he did was arrange a meeting with the thirty Newton engineers at their offices in a nondescript white building off Cupertino's Bubb Road. "I asked, 'What are the great things about this product?' and they rattled off a bunch of stuff," recalls Tesler, who was Apple's chief scientist when he spoke with me in the spring of 1997. "I then asked, 'What are the problems?' and they said, 'None.' Finally, I asked the price they were suggesting for the product, and they said, '$7,000 to $8,000.' " When Tesler expressed incredulity at the high price, he remembers one of the engineers saying, "Yeah, well, our motto is 'No compromises.' "

Indeed, there were no compromises in a state-of-the-art prototype the Newton engineers had assembled. The batteries were so heavy-duty they could run for two weeks of continuous use, compared to a few hours on most laptop computers. A wireless computer network had also been built in, as well as three microprocessors instead of one—and the whole thing weighed eight pounds, or the same as a laptop. This machine was designed to be a "pen" computer, meaning that no keyboard would be required because an electronic pen would enable the user to navigate around the screen and input words at the touch of a pen to the screen. The product was beautifully engineered but, like Jean-Louis Gassée's Luggable computer, was way too big and expensive to be practical for anyone except the technophiles that Steve Sakoman had wanted to target.

Tesler knew another Luggable would not fly past Sculley, so he told the engineers to cut as many features as they could out of the Newton to reduce the price for which it could be sold. They came back a few days later, having trimmed it by half, to $3,000 to $4,000. Tesler told them to get it down more, to under $2,000. Finally, the engineers scaled back the product to a suggested selling price of $1,500 to $2,000 by such moves as cutting from three to one the number of microprocessors, shrinking the size of the screen, and including a weaker battery. The Newton was then reduced to the more manageable size of a school tablet.

Or so Larry Tesler thought.

It took a young, fast-talking marketing manager named Michael Tchao to help compress the Newton into a sub-$1,000, handheld computer—one with a much better chance of attaining sales volume than the bulkier and still expensive tablet Newton. This did not happen without a fight, though. Tchao, who had previously worked in marketing on Apple's emerging multimedia technology, joined the Newton team in late 1990 after Tesler asked Sculley for a marketing person to start the work of promoting and positioning the product. And Tchao was not shy about expressing his rather strong opinions to Tesler.

"When I hired Michael, he said, 'I would really love to do a handheld machine,'" Tesler recalls. "I said, 'Well, I believe in that, too. As soon as we can do little ones, we will. But this [tablet-sized Newton] is the best we can do right now."

Tchao agreed, but he still had handheld computers on the brain. He soon found company in this opinion with two other men: Michael Culbert, who had just been recruited by Apple from his studies at Cornell University, and a legendary Apple engineer named Steve Capps, who had gained fame within Silicon Valley for having coauthored the software that had given the original Mac its distinctive look and feel. Capps, in fact, was one of the last remaining members of Steve Jobs's Macintosh team still employed at Apple, and he had joined the Newton team under Steve Sakoman.

The three men—Tchao, Capps, and Culbert—took a look around the Newton project and decided to design a Newton that they believed could actually ship. That project, formed as an adjunct to the main Newton effort, came to be known as "Junior" because it would cost under $1,000. The tablet-sized product became known as "Senior." Not surprisingly, given Apple's stormy engineering history, a feud developed between the two camps. "A lot of the original Newton engineers became upset at seeing so many of their features included in Junior, so they would say, 'I'm not backing it,' " recalls Tchao, who resigned from Apple in 1994, a year in which many engineers would leave in disillusionment with Apple's plodding R-and-D pace. "So we had rival Junior and Senior teams."

Joining the Junior team in 1991 was another product-oriented engineer named Andy Stadler, who had spent much of his time since joining Apple in 1986 writing software code for the aging line of Apple IIs. Stadler was horrified at seeing a prototype of what the Senior team was working on. Although this Newton was drastically reduced from the old $7,000-to-$8,000 version being tested, Stadler considered that its cost of up to $2,000 was still prohibitively expensive. He also thought the engineers were wasting time pursuing arcane technologies such as an infrared system that would allow five Newtons in the same room to swap files by aiming beams at one another. That technology was really cool, except for one problem: the overhead lights in any meeting room could "blind" the infrared beams. Oops.

"It soon became clear to me that Newton was very much driven by its technology," Stadler recalls. And since Larry Tesler was foremost a technologist, he was a staunch backer of Senior.

In late 1990, yet another initiative for a handheld computer popped up on a wholly unexpected front. A software engineer named Paul Mercer was nearing completion of his work on System 7 when he sat through a lunch one day in December 1990 and heard two of his friends from Newton, Capps and Tchao, complain about "the dismal shape of Newton." Mercer says they encouraged him to "do something small" with the Mac. Mercer had been thinking along that line, anyway, after having recently seen a prototype for a tiny computer called the Sony PalmTop.

The key, though, was that Mercer believed it made far better business sense to develop a handheld computer based on the Macintosh's technology than a brand-new one as was being done with Newton. "I felt that a good product could be built using existing technology alone, without the shoot-for-the-moon risks that Newton was taking, even in Junior," Mercer says. So Mercer set to work on a project initially dubbed "Rolex," which officially was intended to design a PowerBook-sized portable computer that would feature the ability to operate by electronic pen. Mercer's real goal, though, was a computer he would call "Swatch," after the brand of affordable watches popular at the time.

The Swatch would be affordable, too, priced to consumers at about $400, or almost $600 cheaper than even the stripped-down Junior. For that lower price, Swatch would also contain some elements of the Newton's vaunted ability to recognize the user's handwriting. For such a low price—and given the huge Macintosh market already out there—Mercer figured there would be hot demand for a superportable computer that literally fit into a back pocket.

Two other engineers working with Mercer on the project were Steve Horowitz and Eric Knight. They all reported to an engineering manager named Phac LeTuan. The team was assisted by a freelance graphic designer named Bruce Browne, as well as Apple hardware engineers Ray DuFlon and Jay Meschter. Mercer and his team, beginning in early 1991, spent a full twelve months designing a handheld computer that would plug into a Macintosh. By the end of 1991, the Swatchers had their first working prototype. A few weeks later, in early 1992, they had ten, in colors including yellow, purple, and gray.

Just as ATG engineer Steve Perlman had tried to convince senior management that Apple needed to leverage its strong brand name into other consumer products, Mercer picked up the theme when he approached Randy Battat, the vice president for product marketing, with a working version of a Swatch. Battat was so impressed that he invited Mercer and his engineers to demonstrate the device before a meeting of the executive staff in De Anza 7's Synergy room.

"We pulled a working Swatch out of our back pockets," Mercer recalls. Larry Tesler, who was at the meeting, was furious. A working version of the Newton would not be ready for another six months. But Sculley was so intrigued that Mercer says he called him into his office one day soon after and said, "Paul, *Business Week* is going to be in next Thursday. Bring the Swatch over." Before that interview session, however, Sculley canceled the Swatch project. The reason: Mercer had elicited interest from the Japanese manufacturer Sony to make the computers. A major Sony competitor, Sharp, was already on board to manufacture the Newtons.

"Sculley said we cannot do two consumer electronics products with the Japanese," Mercer recalls. "He said, 'Go work with Newton.'" In the same manner in which Chuck Berger would soon be left holding the bag on Drama, when Michael Spindler effectively ordered that project killed, Mercer was left with a batch of unused prototypes that would never see the light of day. Mercer finally quit Apple in frustration in 1994.

By the time Sculley met with Mercer again, he had already reached the point of no return on Newton. A few weeks earlier, on January 7, 1992, Sculley had delivered one of the more stirring—and controversial—speeches of his career. It would later be derided by his critics as the "Trillion Dollar" speech, the one that set Newton up for its great fall the following year.

Flash back a moment to that day in October 1991 when Sculley had stood with IBM President Jack Kuehler on the stage at San Francisco's Fairmont Hotel to announce the alliance among Apple, IBM, and Motorola. The news was so breathtaking that Sculley was in hot demand again on the speaking circuit. The following month, in November, Sculley's public relations staff got a call from the nonprofit trade group Electronic Industries Association, which puts on the winter Consumer Electronics Show every January in Las Vegas. The group's scheduled keynote speaker at the forthcoming show had just canceled, and they asked if John Sculley might care to fill in.

When told about the offer, Sculley was initially uninterested, worrying aloud that he didn't know what to talk about. Then a young woman working on his PR staff asked him to wait before turning the gig down. "I said, 'Let's talk to the Newton people and see what they have to say,' " says the woman, who spoke on condition of anonymity. "The Newton people thought it would be a great idea."

Sculley was limited in how much he could say about Newton, because details of the technology had not been announced yet. He decided to talk about the general concept of a handheld computer that would represent the convergence of the consumer electronics, telecommunications, and computer industries. The concept came to be known as "digital convergence," and Sculley rewrote his speech the day before his address to coin the term "personal digital assistant," or PDA, for this new kind of computer. A staff member who looked at the revised speech pondered a moment and joked, "PDA? Oh, it's like a public display of affection." Sculley could also have called it "Knowledge Navigator," because the speech borrowed heavily from the Navigator's theme of seamless access to electronic information anytime and anywhere.

For consumers, this PDA would be a device that could connect them anytime, anywhere, to any other computer in the world. They could send and receive faxes, e-mail messages, and retrieve files from the computer back home, as well as use the PDA to compose reports, balance checkbooks, and track appointments. It was a powerful concept, and one that International Data Corporation, an industry research firm in Framingham, Massachusetts, predicted would fuel a nearly $4 billion market annually by 1998.

Sculley's keynote speech was one of the most highly anticipated ever for a trade show. The ballroom of the Las Vegas Hilton could hold only about 1,200 people, so the seats filled quickly as hundreds more show attendees were turned away. The lights lowered as Sculley, looking relaxed in his Apple attire of khakis and a casual shirt, ambled onstage, gripped the podium, and began drawing a word picture of his PDA as the center of a new digital universe, so immense that he predicted it would attain $3.5 trillion in annual revenues within a decade.

Since everyone in the computer industry is watchful for the next new wave, lest they be left behind, word of a brand-new, multitrillion-dollar industry rocketed out of the cramped ballroom into news reports all over the world. Although other companies had handheld computers in the works, none contained the promised flair of the Newton. And until this day, no one in the industry had as clearly articulated the grand potential of the PDA—nor set the nascent product category onto a pedestal of such grand hype.

Sculley would come to rue his words in Las Vegas, as would Apple. Months later, as it became clear that Newton sales would start out slow, he would try to backpedal on his $3.5 trillion prediction. But it would be too late. In a November 30, 1992, article in *Business Week*, which ran under the headline "The Great Digital Hope Could Be a Heartbreaker," Silicon Valley pundits were quoted as joking that "PDA" stood for "probably disappointed again." By then it was becoming increasingly clear that the market for PDAs would start off much more slowly than Sculley had first thought, judging from customer surveys.

Sculley at least had the right idea to lessen Apple's dependence on the Macintosh. During the previous year, 1991, Microsoft and Intel had spent $853 million on R and D to advance the Wintel standard, compared to $581 million spent by Apple on its plethora of technologies. And the Microsoft-Intel spending did not even take into account the amounts invested by the hundreds of Wintel makers such as Compaq Computer and Dell Computer to make their own enhancements to the technology.

And Windows itself was advancing fast. Microsoft's introduction of Windows 3.1, at the Windows World conference in Chicago in April 1992 provided customers with a version that was eminently more free of pesky bugs than the 3.0 version. It also came with a disturbing new message; disturbing, that is, if you were Apple. Windows would now feature "scalability," meaning it would be designed not just for personal computers but for any computing device ranging from a PDA all the way up to a minicomputer.[4] One company, one solution. The concept would hold powerful appeal for corporate information managers intent on keeping their myriad of computer systems as simple as possible.

It was precisely this scalability that the Macintosh did not have. Paul Mercer's idea for a Swatch would have extended the Mac to the lowest end. A combination of Apple and IBM technology would extend the Mac to workstations and minicomputers on the high end, but any products from that deal were still years away. In short, Apple not only was being outgunned in its core market of personal computers but was in danger of being snuffed out of existence altogether in a Microsoft pincer movement. It was, strategically, not dissimilar to when the Western Allies thrust into Nazi Germany from one end while Russian troops attacked from the other, squeezing the Third Reich into oblivion.

Just days after the Windows 3.1 launch, on April 14, 1992, Apple was dealt another body blow on the Microsoft front; this time in the courtroom of U.S. District Judge Vaughn R. Walker in San Francisco. This was when the judge issued his four-minute oral ruling tossing out the bulk of Apple's claims that the GUI software from Microsoft and H-P had infringed on the "look and feel" of the Macintosh. The judge's ruling gutted Apple's claims, rendering the lawsuit effectively brain-dead until the plug was officially pulled two years later, when Apple's appeals were exhausted. Gates had always expected to win this case, but he breathed a sigh of relief, anyway. After all, Apple had asked the court to inflict damages of $5.5 billion against Microsoft and H-P. For Sculley, it was just one more bitter pill to swallow, especially since Apple had to cough up more than $10 million in legal bills.

By now, John Sculley was feeling punch-drunk and bone-tired of the fray. He looked it, too. When he had joined Apple in 1983, he had looked buoyant and youthful and could have passed for a decade younger than his forty-four years. By 1992, though, his brown hair was streaked with gray and his lined face looked every day his age of fifty-three. His original plan had been to stay on at Apple for just five years, turning the reins over to a more mature Steve Jobs. That plan had obviously not worked out. Still, since the late 1980s, he had been constantly telling aides: one more year, and he was out. Just one more. By 1992, he really meant it. His wife, Leezy, had recently moved back east, into a new home the Sculleys had bought in Greenwich, Connecticut. The Sculleys had moved out west from Greenwich, and now John Sculley, too, was ready to go home.

At an Apple board meeting in May 1992, Sculley sat down with the directors to convey his wish in person. "I want to go back to the East Coast," Sculley told Mike Markkula and the four other board members present, according to a person in the room. "I want to leave." Sculley explained that he would be coming up on his tenth anniversary at Apple in April 1993 and wanted to leave by then to rejoin his wife in Connecticut.

The board members reacted with shock and dismay. "You can't leave us now," one said. The board members pondered the surprise disclosure by their longtime CEO and turned to Sculley again, asking him what they should do. "I think we should merge the company with someone else," Sculley replied in his calm, matter-of-fact tone. "I do not see how we can be sustainable as a stand-alone company."[5] And he really didn't, Apple's strong financial results that year notwithstanding. The Wintel standard was just too big, growing too fast. Sculley didn't think Apple could keep up, at least not by itself. That was why he had teamed up with IBM and Motorola. But Apple, he had finally concluded, needed more than an alliance. It needed a strong parent.

So he found himself nodding as Markkula and the other directors implored him to stay on just long enough to sell Apple to a larger company, one with the deep pockets necessary to fuel Apple's immense R-and-D engine as it attempted to bridge the gap between the declining profits of the Macintosh business with the new industry of PDAs, or personal digital assistants. Sculley said, fine, just so it doesn't take too long.

If only he had followed his first instinct.

The Apple name still carried such sex appeal in the public's eye that Sculley didn't have to look too far to find potential suitors. The first thing he did was to offload all of his responsibilities in R and D onto Michael Spindler, who was already in charge of just about everything else as president and chief operating officer. Then, accompanied by Robert Lauridsen, Apple's vice president of corporate development, Sculley packed his suitcase and headed hither and yon in his private Learjet, which he had leased to Apple. One day, they were in London, chatting it up with the big shots at British Telecommunications PLC, who expressed a passing interest in acquiring Apple; the next, in Eindhoven, the Netherlands, conversing with the Dutch electronics giant Philips Electronics NV.

The merger solicitations continued into the fall, when they expanded to include the German electronics conglomerate Siemens AG. Indeed, Apple's board had scheduled a meeting in Munich, where Siemens had its headquarters, during the week of the annual German festival called Oktoberfest. Once a year, the board held a meeting somewhere outside the United States, and this year it happened to be in Munich. Sculley and some of the board members met with the executives at Siemens, who professed interest in acquiring Apple's hardware business, according to a former Apple executive familiar with those talks.

None of these encounters went very far, though. But the ones with Kodak and AT&T did.

The notion of digital convergence, as articulated so clearly by Sculley at the Consumer Electronics Show earlier in 1992, had garnered much interest in the business world. AT&T Corporation, for example, was profoundly interested in technologies, such as Newton, that could leverage the company's dominance over long-distance telephone markets. The telecommunications giant in Basking Ridge, New Jersey, was also interested in branching out into the fast-growing personal computer market. In fact, it had acquired a struggling computer maker named NCR Corporation to launch that foray in 1991, but NCR was a dog that not even AT&T's big bucks could revive. Apple, on the other hand, was an attractive prospect because it possessed one of the most recognizable names in the PC industry.

Another notable that became intrigued by the idea of digital convergence—and acquiring Apple—was Eastman Kodak Company, the photography giant in Rochester, New York. In early 1992, Kodak had come up with technology for an affordable digital camera that could display photographic images on a computer screen that could then be printed out without ever having to go to a photo studio, recalls Don Strickland, who headed Kodak's digital camera effort before joining Apple in 1993 to run a similar endeavor there. The so-called imaging technology was already in use on expensive workstation computers, but the cameras cost upward of $15,000. To attain a mass market for a line of cameras that Kodak envisioned for under $1,000, Strickland says, Kodak knew it had to get into the PC market. And with what better bedfellow than Apple Computer?

The Kodak-Apple talks initially began in the late spring of 1992 as a technology alliance. Strickland talked Apple into buying a digital camera Kodak had under development and then coming up with its own technical design. Duane Schulz, who spearheaded Apple's side of the imaging effort, put a team of engineers together with Kodak to codevelop a black-and-white digital camera for $200. The end result of that work was a camera called the Apple QuickTake, which launched the whole category of PC digital cameras — aimed at the consumer market—when it shipped in early 1994. At $600, though, the camera was priced too high to attain much sales volume. And Apple, as was its custom, dropped the whole imaging effort to move onto something else, abandoning a lead to others in what Schulz estimates could have become a $300-million-per-year business for Apple alone, just as it had done, for example, with the laser printer. Apple had pioneered laser printers in the personal computer market, but had failed to extend that technology beyond the Macintosh. As a result, Hewlett-Packard went on to dominate the market for laser printers on the PC platform of Microsoft and Intel.

As they were exchanging technologies at the engineering level, Kodak's CEO, Kay Whitemore, and Sculley began to realize that Kodak and Apple had so much in common, a takeover of Apple might make good sense. Kodak was the industry leader in photography and photo publishing. Apple was the leader in computer desktop publishing. "It would be one-stop shopping," says a former Kodak executive involved in the talks.

The courting took place during the summer of 1992 and lasted into the fall. The two CEOs and their executives met with each other in Cupertino and Rochester. Al Eisenstat, Apple's senior vice president and corporate secretary, accepted an invitation by the Kodak people to spend a week aboard the Kodak yacht, anchored in the Mediterranean during the Summer Olympic Games in Barcelona. "I stayed on the Kodak cruise ship because there were no hotel rooms in Barcelona," Eisenstat says, adding that this courtesy had been extended before the two companies entered into serious merger negotiations.

By early fall, however, the deal crumbled before it could be put together. The biggest obstacle, according to people involved with the talks, were cultural differences that had become apparent between Apple's senior management and that of Kodak. Kodak, in short, was hesitant to proceed, while Apple was skeptical that Kodak understood the need to move quickly in the PC industry.

"Kodak's view was that 'Does it really make sense to get into the computer business?' " remembers a former Kodak executive. "Kodak had not made a commitment to digital because it feared it would cannibalize their film business. And Apple feared Kodak would move too slowly." Indeed, another top Apple executive from that time remembers some of the Kodak executives actually dozing off during presentations by Apple. "It was clear to me that Kodak would never have worked with that management," he says. Like lovers who remain friends after their affair does not work out, Apple and Kodak undertook an amicable parting of the ways, agreeing to continue sharing imaging technology. While Kodak still feared the cannibalization, it wanted to continue investing in imaging to hedge its bets.

Sculley was disappointed, but not for long. An even bigger prize—AT&T—was waiting in the wings.

Just as it had been with Kodak, the relationship between Apple and AT&T began as a discussion on how to share technologies. At the time, in late 1992, AT&T's top technology officer, Bob Kavner, had been meeting with Microsoft, Apple, and other computer companies about the possibility of working together on multimedia. "Somewhere along the way, Bob and John agreed to have some high-level discussions on the possibility of merging the two companies," says a former Apple executive intimately familiar with those talks.

Sculley and Robert Lauridsen flew back to Basking Ridge, New Jersey, outside New York City, on a cold and blustery day in January 1993. A powerful nor'easter was set to blow through that same night, so big that local weather forecasters were dubbing it "the storm of the century." As the skies darkened, Sculley and Lauridsen walked into the brightly lit lobby of the AT&T headquarters building and were ushered into a conference room to meet with Kavner, Dick Bodman, AT&T's head of corporate strategy, and AT&T Chief Financial Officer Alex Mansoor. For the next two hours, the five men talked almost nonstop about what they could do together and even laid the groundwork for a joint on-line service that would later become Apple's eWorld. It was a rosy picture, quite unlike that of the weather outside.

"It was like we were kindred spirits," recalls the former Apple executive familiar with the talks. "We saw the world exactly alike."

Sculley was dead set on selling Apple to AT&T, as were members of his board and executive team. For once, this was something everyone in Apple's management could agree on. "AT&T was a deal Apple wanted to make," says one former Apple executive. After that January meeting in Basking Ridge, AT&T Chairman and CEO Bob Allen got into the act, dispatching two plane loads of his executives out to the West Coast to review a merger deal in depth. Beginning in early February and continuing through April, Sculley and his teams of up to twenty executives at a time shuttled back and forth between Cupertino and Basking Ridge, generally as often as once a week and frequently over weekends. The meetings were conducted in complete secrecy.

Finally, at the end of April 1993, Bob Allen picked up the telephone in New Jersey and called Sculley in California to relay some bad news. "Boy, you have a phenomenal company. You have exactly what we need. But we bought the wrong computer company, John," Allen said, with a tone of regret in his voice, according to a former Apple executive with knowledge of the conversation. Allen went on to elaborate that he had become concerned that a merger with Apple would put a media spotlight on the problems of NCR, the lackluster PC maker that AT&T had acquired. Allen also told Sculley that AT&T was busy with plans to acquire McCaw Cellular Communications Inc., the cellular telephone giant based in Kirkland, Washington. AT&T was in discussions at the time to acquire McCaw, although that $11.5 billion merger was not completed until September 1994.

The long and the short of it was: all deals were off.

Sculley and the board were thunderstruck. They had thought, for sure, this deal was going to go through. And when it collapsed, after all those months of bicoastal negotiations, Apple was left more isolated than ever. "The board wasn't very happy," recalls a former Apple executive involved in the AT&T discussions, "because there was nobody out there to buy the company." Sculley, too, had a sick feeling in the pit of his stomach. Time was running out, he knew. Not only was he still stuck, a year later, trying to peddle a company that it seemed no one really wanted, but by this time he also realized he had incurred the enmity of the archconservative Apple board for his high-profile backing of Bill Clinton in the 1992 presidential campaign. Back up, just a minute, to the Clinton campaign.

In 1992, the young Arkansas governor faced the daunting task of unseating incumbent George Bush, who had ridden to a crest of popularity following his pummeling of Iraq's Saddam Hussein in the Persian Gulf War the prior year. Clinton knew he could not score points against Bush on foreign policy grounds, so he hammered hard on the more vulnerable domestic front, including the souring economy and a deplorable public education system.

As chief executive of the leading vendor of computers to schools, Sculley was constantly being called upon to address education forums and to serve on the boards of education think tanks, such as the National Center on Education and the Economy, based in Washington, D.C. In fact, Sculley was chairman of that think tank in 1992 and was joined on the board by David Barram, Apple's vice president of corporate affairs, and a bright, articulate woman by the name of Hillary Rodham Clinton, wife of the Democratic presidential candidate.

One day in the fall of 1992, Barram pulled Sculley aside and asked a fateful question: " 'Will you meet with Bill Clinton to talk about high tech and education?' " Sculley recalls. Sculley was a Republican, just like longtime Apple board members Arthur Rock and Mike Markkula, as well as the other

Apple directors. "But I got involved with the Clinton campaign because I thought it would help education and I thought it would help Silicon Valley," he says. "So I took a high-profile role, although the amount of actual time I spent on the campaign was small. Mainly, I did TV interviews from San Francisco."

Although Sculley now downplays his role with the Clintons, it was clear then that he relished the attention. Peter Kavanaugh, who ran the AppleTV studio across the street from De Anza 7, still remembers Sculley's boyish glee at recounting a ride to San Francisco from Los Angeles he had just taken with newly elected President Clinton aboard *Air Force One*, hours before this latest interview session at AppleTV. "He stopped in his tracks and went into a ten-minute monologue on what it was like to fly with the president," Kavanaugh recalls. "With John, his visit with the president was truly special. This was the first time I saw him really hyper about something."

Arthur Rock, however, did not see anything special about it. To Rock, according to people who knew him, Sculley was "hobnobbing" with the Clintons. The final straw for Rock, many people at Apple believe, was when Sculley appeared on worldwide television at Clinton's inaugural State of the Union address, sitting right beside Hillary. "That's the one that did me in," Sculley confesses. But there was more to that story than met the eye. Sculley says that Hillary had asked him to attend the State of the Union address, along with the usual multitude of campaign dignitaries. Sculley showed up in the Capitol Hill gallery well beforehand, when the seats were still mostly empty, and began chatting with an old friend, Federal Reserve Chairman Alan Greenspan.

"An aide came over and said, 'Mr. Sculley, you sit over here,' " Sculley recalls. "The next thing I knew, Hillary is sitting next to me, sandwiched between me and Greenspan." The juxtaposition was immensely symbolic, even if Sculley didn't realize it at the time. In one nationally televised moment, John Sculley and Apple Computer became synonymous with America's worldwide technological leadership.

Back in Cupertino, though, it was fuel for the growing fire against Sculley, not only on the board but on the executive staff. "After the State of the Union, everyone thought John didn't care about Apple anymore. There was also a lot of jealousy," says one of Sculley's closest aides. Spindler was publicly bad-mouthing his boss, as was Ed Stead, Apple's general counsel, according to people who heard the complaints.

"Spindler was irritated that John wasn't minding the shop," says George Everhart, the former vice president of Apple USA. "Spindler would make comments in meetings that 'It was a shame John wasn't here to make that point.' " Adds Kevin Sullivan, the human relations executive who had figured into so much intracompany warfare over the years, "Everyone complained about John. The last year, he wasn't around."

Yet the board knew full well why Sculley was not spending so much time in Cupertino. After all, the directors had been the ones who had asked him to stay on to sell the company when he had tried to leave in May 1992. One of the directors, Peter Crisp, the general partner of Venrock Associates in New York, even pleaded for Sculley not to go when he informed the board in March 1993 that he had been offered the job of chairman and CEO of IBM, to replace the retiring John Akers. It turned out he had not actually been offered the job — although he had been a finalist — but that was his impression at the time.

It may sound incredible that Sculley would tip his hand to his own board that he was under consideration to become CEO somewhere else. After all, in many companies that would convey a lack of commitment to the task at hand, undermining the board's confidence in him or her. In this case, however, it was not at all surprising. First of all, John Sculley was always known to be an honest, aboveboard guy. He therefore felt "obligated" to tell his directors, according to a person familiar with his thought process at the time. Second — and most important — he had already informed the board nearly a year earlier that he was planning to move on. It shouldn't have been a shock to anyone, then, that he might at least consider jumping ship to IBM, which, after all, was headquartered on the East Coast, where Sculley had already moved his family back home.

Sculley had long enjoyed good chemistry with the top executives at IBM. Two members of the IBM CEO search committee, Jim Burke and Tom Murphy, thought of Sculley when they started putting together a list of potential candidates to succeed Akers. They also knew Sculley as a superb marketing man who, they thought, could shore up a major weakness in marketing at Big Blue. According to a former IBM executive familiar with the search, Sculley's name was put down on an initial list of six people, which also included Lou Gerstner Jr., then the CEO of Procter & Gamble. This person declined to reveal the other names on that list, but they were believed to have included George Fisher, then chief executive of Motorola, and Larry Bossidy, chairman of AlliedSignal Inc. Burke and Murphy asked Don Kendall, Sculley's former father-in-law and the retired chairman and CEO of PepsiCo Inc., if he could set up a meeting between Sculley and IBM.

In the late winter of 1993, as Sculley was still holding secret merger talks with AT&T, Kendall asked his old subordinate to meet with the two IBMers at Kendall's Tudor-style mansion in Greenwich, Connecticut, nestled in deep woods some four hundred yards from the beginning of the driveway. Burke, Murphy, and Sculley subsequently met, with Kendall looking on, as Sculley spent the better part of the time explaining the trend toward digital convergence. "Kendall drove them back to the Westchester [County, New York] airport, and he later related to John that they thought it was a terrific meeting and did he think John could be persuaded to come to IBM if it later made an offer."[6]

Meanwhile, Sculley's old friend IBM President Jack Kuehler was telling him he hoped he would take the IBM job, as was former IBM Chairman and CEO Tom Watson, a neighbor to Sculley's vacation home in Maine. Even Akers telephoned Sculley to voice his support for him as the successor. A meeting was then arranged between Sculley and Akers at the Mayflower Hotel in New York City, to explore how Apple could be merged with IBM. Sculley, who had previously suggested that IBM separate into two companies—one for its core mainframe business and the other for desktop computers—suggested to Akers that Apple be merged into the desktop company, since both companies were committed to the PowerPC chip technology.

At that meeting, in February 1993, Akers told Sculley he should join IBM as CEO soon because the IBM board had already publicly promised to have a new chief executive by the time of the April 1993 shareholders' meeting. Akers said a merger with Apple could take place later.[7] Taking this to mean he had actually been offered the job, Sculley returned to his board and conveyed the news.

The Apple board's reaction was not good. The company's profits were under voracious assault, as protracted pricing wars in the PC industry would drive Apple's net income 18 percent lower in the fiscal second quarter ended on March 26, 1993, than it had been during the same period a year earlier. Sculley was also still in the midst of trying to sell the company. It was not so much that the board could not bear to see him go. The directors primarily wanted him to unload Apple before he did. "They were very unhappy [about Sculley's possible IBM job] and strongly urged John to try and persuade IBM to acquire Apple as a condition of his going to IBM," recalls a former Apple executive involved in the discussions then. Peter Crisp, in pleading for Sculley not to go, blurted out, "You can't leave us high and dry."[8]

First Kodak. Then AT&T. Now IBM. The Apple board was desperate for a buyer. Sculley indicated he would try, and in fact he told Jack Kuehler that it was unlikely he would accept any deal that did not include Apple. Since IBM was not yet ready to acquire Apple—in another year it would be a different story—Sculley took himself out of the running for the IBM job, as publicized on March 11, 1993. "I am not available or interested in being CEO of IBM," Sculley said in a statement quoted by *The Wall Street Journal* that day. "I believe Apple has a tremendous opportunity to be successful in the years ahead, and Apple will be the most important innovator and leader in the industry."

Although Sculley was never actually offered the position, he was definitely one of the top candidates. According to a former IBM executive intimately familiar with the search, Sculley was on the original list of six candidates, remained there as the list expanded to eighty, and was still in contention when it was finally narrowed to a final dozen or so. Louis Gerstner, who had always been at the top of the list, ended up getting the job. Had Sculley lobbied himself harder, though, he might well have beaten out Gerstner. As this former IBM executive remembers, "We weren't sure that he was all that interested."

The selection of Gerstner was not obvious, even after Sculley took himself out of the running. A few days later, IBM's Jim Burke telephoned Sculley to ask if he would be willing to call President Clinton and ask the leader of the free world to personally solicit one of the other hot prospects, AlliedSignal's Larry Bossidy, to consider taking over as head of IBM. "Intended message: that IBM is a national treasure and it was important to our country that this company attract an experienced, world-class CEO," recalls a former Apple executive who knew of that conversation between Burke and Sculley. Sculley was certainly well known to the president and in fact had authorized Apple to kick in $35,000 to help sponsor free public events at Clinton's 1993 inauguration. Given the president's propensity to rent out quarters in the White House to major donors in the years to come and extend other favors, Clinton might well have placed that phone call on Sculley's behalf.

But Sculley wasn't comfortable in exploiting his presidential connection in this way and agreed only to make the call to Bossidy himself. He did, and Bossidy wasn't interested.

Sculley's IBM saga had folded in March 1993. One month later, so did the one with AT&T. That same month, April 1993, it was time for the tenth anniversary at Apple that Sculley had not wanted to see. Indeed, a party to commemorate the event was markedly subdued for a man who had so come to personify Apple Computer. AppleTV, the company's television station, prepared a ten-minute video retrospective of Sculley's career at Apple, showing it to a small gathering of office and support staff who assembled with their leader in the balloon-festooned Synergy room in De Anza 7. Sculley smiled wanly as staffers munched cake and traded chitchat. Just one month later, in this same room, he would face a far less friendly audience.

After the collapse of the AT&T deal in April 1993, Sculley revived an idea he had been thinking about for some time but had never acted upon. It was a bold plan, more radical even than the strategic initiatives suggested in years past by Dan Eilers and his ilk. It was also one that would push his executive staff into full mutiny. Sculley's idea was to split the company into two pieces, just as he had recommended that IBM do. There would be the Macintosh Company, which would handle all the low-margin hardware side of the business. It could just as well have been called the Box Company, for it would primarily deal in the manufacture and sale of fully assembled computer boxes like a Compaq or Dell. And there would be the Apple Company, which would have all the sexy software projects like Newton and QuickTime. All the really cutting-edge and fun stuff would go there.[9]

This was not just an idle proposal, a "what-if" scenario, Sculley was contemplating. In early May 1993, according to two former executives familiar with this, Sculley gained the board's approval to proceed with the plan. He even retained the New York investment banking firm of Goldman Sachs & Company to begin preliminary work on the breakup, according to one of these executives. "The basic premise was that the company was more valuable split into two than as one," says a former Apple executive intimately familiar with the plan.

It wasn't such a bad notion. Apple's problem, all along, had been that it had to invest heavily in R and D to keep ahead of Microsoft on the software front, while also having to duke it out with every Compaq, Gateway, and Packard Bell in the increasingly bloody pricing wars going on down in the hardware box business. Since Apple derived fully 95 percent of its revenues from the boxes, it couldn't just dump that business. A brand-new software company, on the other hand, would be totally unfettered from the hardware, just like Microsoft, and free to license its technology with whomever it chose.

There was just one big problem with this plan: almost nobody on the Apple executive staff wanted to do it. Kevin Sullivan remembers the shock he felt when Sculley took him aside and confided that he wanted to split the company. "He said, 'You would be over here with Michael, and Michael could choose where he could be,'" Sullivan recalls. "I said, 'Why don't we talk about this?' It was not quite what I wanted to do." Sullivan adds that Sculley did have the right idea, but the timing was all wrong. "It would have just ripped the company apart at a time when we were having problems with orders," Sullivan says.

Indeed it was. While the rest of the industry was growing at a blistering rate of 20 percent more PC shipments in 1993 than in the year before, Apple was having to keep selling cheaper Macs to keep up. As a result, Apple's gross profit margins were sinking to a record low of 34 percent for that year, down 10 percentage points in just twelve months' time. And worsening the situation for Apple in the fiscal third quarter, which would end on June 25, was the fact that the orders that Kevin Sullivan referred to were slowing.

Indeed, the subject of Apple's financial health in this quarter was one of two key topics of discussion raised at Apple's regular board of directors meeting, held in the De Anza 7 Synergy room on May 21, 1993. Michael Spindler delivered that presentation, telling the board members that the quarter "will be tough, but we will make it," Sculley remembers. Securities analysts were predicting that Apple would earn $85.5 million, or 74 cents a share, in the period that would end June 25, 1993, compared to net income of $131.7 million, or $1.07 a share, in the year-earlier quarter.

The second topic of discussion centered on Sculley's plan to break up Apple. Sculley delivered this presentation, according to people in attendance that day, with investment bankers from Goldman Sachs invited into the room to look on. Afterward, the board instructed Sculley to return within a few weeks with a formal breakup plan that it could consider.[10]

Sculley set out to do just that. He went so far as to begin divvying up responsibilities for the two new companies among his executives. Sculley would run the Apple Company, taking "a large amount" of Apple's $2 billion cash hoard to help fund the new venture's costly R-and-D efforts for software development. Joining Sculley would be a team including Apple's CFO, Joe Graziano, and Dan Eilers, the CEO of the Claris Corporation unit. Heading up the Macintosh Company would be Michael Spindler, joined by his cohort, Kevin Sullivan, who would run that new company's human relations department. Spindler initially agreed to the plan but began to waffle soon thereafter.[11]

Soon after the May 21 board meeting, Spindler flew off to Australia to attend an annual gala called the "Golden Apple," which recognized the top sales producers in Apple's Pacific region. Kevin Sullivan walked into Sculley's office one day while Spindler was away to inform Sculley that Spindler was changing his mind about heading up the new Macintosh Company. With Sullivan still in his office, Sculley picked up the phone and placed a call to Spindler's hotel room in Australia, where it was the middle of the night. "John woke Michael up and asked if he wanted to do this," Sullivan says. "Michael said, 'No, but do whatever you want to do.' He gave Michael the choice of running the hardware company or being number two in the software company, under John." When Spindler continued to resist moving to the Macintosh Company, Sullivan says Sculley offered that job to Ian Diery, the executive vice president for worldwide sales.

Diery remembers that no one wanted to go to the Macintosh Company and that he would end up with it by default. Another senior executive from the period recalls Spindler storming back into the office, following the torturous fourteen-hour flight back from Australia, and "he just went ballistic." No way, no how, did he want to see the company split up. He relayed his misgivings to his old confidant, Sullivan, and the two found a sympathetic ear in the most unlikely of sources: Al Eisenstat, Sculley's faithful sidekick through the years, the Ed McMahon of Apple Computer. "Al went ballistic," Sullivan recalls. "He said, 'The guy [Sculley] is out of control.' "

Eisenstat had good cause for going ballistic: Sculley's breakup scheme pointedly excluded him. That was because Sculley and many other executives in the company considered Eisenstat, who by this point had been on the Apple payroll for thirteen years, a "hanger-on," who had no clear reason for continuing to work at Apple. Eisenstat, whose official title continued to be senior vice president and corporate secretary, had relinquished his general counsel duties to Ed Stead some time back, and by 1993, it had become unclear to many people in the executive suite what he really did. Still, Eisenstat was one of Apple's six board members and as such had the ears of the all-powerful. If Al Eisenstat could turn on Sculley, who was left to defend him?

As it would turn out, pitifully few. John Sculley never got a chance to implement his breakup plan.

With his number two man off in Australia waffling over Sculley's last-ditch effort to rescue Apple from its growing vulnerability in the market, the embattled CEO received some devastating news. It had been only a week since Spindler had assured Sculley and the board that Apple would "make" the fiscal third quarter, then winding into its final month. CFO Joe Graziano walked into Sculley's office with an ashen look on his face to announce, " 'We have a real problem. There's no way we're going to make these numbers,' " Sculley recalls. "I said, 'This is crazy. How could this be?' As soon as we learned this, we had to disclose it right away. In a matter of hours, we had to call board meetings and put out a press release."

The big problem, ironically, was the once-darling PowerBook. Apple had done a bang-up job of selling those laptops during 1992 and had planned for another big push through the first half of 1993. But Spindler, who was supposed to be overseeing operations, had grossly miscalculated. A big reason the PowerBook had been such a blazing success in the first place was that there had been a huge pent-up demand from the millions of Macintosh loyalists who had been waiting years for a usable Apple laptop. But most of those customers had already bought PowerBooks in 1992.

"We had saturated our installed base," Graziano remembers. "The sales didn't come."

When the final numbers for the quarter came in, they showed Apple earning just $4.6 million, or 4 cents a share, excluding charges, on a measly 6 percent increase in sales from the same quarter a year earlier. During the quarter immediately preceding, Apple's sales had increased a reasonably healthy 15 percent. This was not just bad news; it was disastrous. Spindler and Sullivan immediately charted plans to lop expenses out of the company, mostly by lopping heads. The planned layoffs of 16 percent of the workforce, or 2,500 workers, would not be announced until July, but Sullivan was already undertaking them when the Apple board decided it had had enough of John Sculley, too.

In June 1993, Apple's outside board members included Mike Markkula, Apple's cofounder; Arthur Rock, the venerable venture capitalist; Peter Crisp, general partner of Venrock Associates, a capital investment firm in New

York; and Bernard Goldstein, managing director of Broadview Associates, L.L.C., a venture capital firm in Fort Lee, New Jersey. The inside directors included just Sculley and Eisenstat. According to a person with intimate knowledge of the board's activities, the four outside directors, led by Rock, agreed in secret that Sculley had to go.

It was abundantly clear to all the board members that Sculley wanted to move back east, since he had told them that a year earlier. But according to the person familiar with the board, the directors had grown increasingly uncomfortable with the idea of their CEO dividing his time between the coasts. "That's when the board recognized that John had lost his stomach to be running the company," says the person. Eisenstat, too, now believed it was time for Sculley to go. "The Clinton situation was symptomatic that he was losing his grip on Apple," Eisenstat says. By that, Eisenstat was referring to the disenchantment in many quarters of Apple that Sculley seemed to be spending more time with politicians than tending to the affairs of his company. Sculley, as indicated earlier, insists the amount of time he spent on the Clinton campaign was actually insignificant.

It didn't matter. The decision had been made to oust Sculley as CEO. But the next question was: Who would be picked to replace him? The board did not have to look any further than the cubicle of a very intense German already residing on the fourth floor of De Anza 7, the old Diesel himself. That Michael Spindler would one day become CEO was no surprise to Sculley. After all, he had been grooming him for the part ever since promoting Spindler to chief operating officer. "It was clear Michael was the guy," Sullivan says. But the manner in which the transfer of power took place was hardly delicate or humane.

The board wanted Spindler, but it wasn't sure he wanted the job. Eisenstat was asked to feel him out. But even Eisenstat was unsure, since Spindler had long spoken of returning to Paris and in fact had never sold the home he had had there when he had been running Apple's European operations. There was another mitigating factor, as well. Spindler's wife, Maryse, was said by executives at the time to be seriously ill. She would go on to make a full recovery, but during this period Spindler was spending many of his days by her side at their mansion in Atherton, leaving Ian Diery in charge of operations.

Eisenstat figured the best person to consult with would be the man at Apple who knew Spindler best: Kevin Sullivan. "Al came to me one day, ranting and raving that 'I don't know what to do. Michael will never take this job,'" Sullivan remembers. "I said, 'Well, yeah, he would, provided three conditions are met. One, Michael would never do anything to leave his fingerprints on John's throat. Two, it depends on his wife, because she is not well. And, three, he would want a significant change in the composition of the board.'"

Spindler wanted new blood on the board—specifically, more people from the computer industry. The board's heavy makeup of venture capitalists had, in fact, long bothered Sculley himself. "He really wanted and needed a world-class board, like PepsiCo had," says Peter Lycurgus, Apple's director of corporate affairs as of early 1997 and the only executive Sculley brought with him to Apple from Pepsi. By this, Sculley wanted a more diverse board, including more women, who could expand Apple's influence into other parts of the business world, not just the close-knit venture capital community. In fact, Sculley had recruited onto the board astronaut Sally Ride in an effort to diversify beyond the white male makeup, but an executive close to the board says her input was never welcomed by the others and she ended up resigning her seat. Sculley's other efforts to expand the board were met by resistance from the panel's two main power brokers, Mike Markkula and Arthur Rock, according to a Sculley confidant.

On June 7, the board convened in the De Anza 7 Synergy room, where Sculley delivered the bad news about the surprise turnabout in the quarter's results. During a lunch break, Arthur Rock cornered Sullivan on the floor. "He said, 'You know, John has told us he wants to do something different. Michael keeps saying he wouldn't take the job of CEO, but Al says you think he would,'" Sullivan recollects from the conversation. "I told Art exactly what I had told Eisenstat. That was the only discussion I ever had with any board member in my entire career."

Actually, Spindler had not said he would never take the job of CEO. When Eisenstat finally approached him in early June, Spindler told him he wanted to think about it. He also wanted to know about the terms and conditions the board would offer him. Over a period of two days, Eisenstat and Spindler met constantly, sometimes in Spindler's office and sometimes in Eisenstat's, down the hall.[12] Sculley's office was situated right next to Spindler's, but he didn't seem to have a clue as to what they were talking about and didn't have reason to care. After all, the board knew full well he wanted to step down as CEO.

"Spindler said he wanted it clear that this would be a finite thing, like five to six years," says the executive familiar with those talks. "Then he made demands on compensation, and the board essentially gave him what he wanted." Eisenstat related a similar version of the events in a lawsuit he would later file against Apple that publicized the whole affair. The suit alleged that Eisenstat had been wrongfully terminated following an incident that would transpire within days.

The board called a special meeting for the morning of June 17, 1993, ostensibly to review the quarter's poor results. They gathered, as usual, in the Synergy room and discussed the results. Later that afternoon, the board decided to hold a closed session and asked Sculley and Eisenstat to leave. Ed

Stead, the general counsel attending the meeting, was also asked to step outside. That was when Sculley went into Graziano's office and asked the Graz, "Joe, what do you think they're doing in there?"[13] Sculley's office staff, too, had a strange feeling: the board rarely met without Sculley and Eisenstat.

The meeting became even stranger when Arthur Rock opened the door and said, "Al, can you come in for a second?" according to a person on the floor who witnessed the episode. The same person overheard, through the closed door, Markkula speaking in a loud voice: "Before we call John in, Al, we have one more question for you." A few moments later, Markkula called Sculley's executive assistant, Gerri Coleman, and asked her to send Sculley in. Eisenstat, looking nervous and fidgety, excused himself when Sculley strolled into the same boardroom he had been in so many times before. This time, there were no balloons awaiting him.

"John was only in for a few seconds when he came out," recalls an office aide who was present on the floor that day. "When he came out, he was visibly shaken. He was shocked. He said the board felt at this time that he had his interests elsewhere. They said they would have to have Spindler take over." Sculley confided to other people that none of the board members inside that room would make eye contact with him when the edict was delivered by Bernard Goldstein, who was designated to speak for the group. They all just sat in their chairs, looking away.

Boom. John Sculley had been shot through the heart. Ten years of work down the toilet. Sculley returned to his office, sitting down in his chair almost in a daze as the news spread like wildfire through Apple and then all over the globe.

Ian Diery and Kevin Sullivan were traveling together in Paris, when they were awakened by frantic phone calls from Cupertino at about 4 A.M. When he returned to Cupertino a couple of days later, Diery went into Sculley's office and spoke from the heart. "John, if you got fired for poor results, then we are all a part of that," he said, according to a person who heard the exchange. Then the blustery Aussie's voice lowered, and he added, "John, there are times when people show good character. Now you are showing good character." Upon Sullivan's return, he too, went in to pay his respects. "When he came in, Kevin had tears in his eyes, and tried to hug John," says a person who witnessed the encounter. "But John pushed him away."

In the months to come, Spindler would repeat over and over, to friends and Apple employees, that he had been given just fifteen minutes to make up his mind whether to take the job of CEO. That may have been true, from a technical viewpoint. But Spindler and Sullivan knew days in advance that Sculley was on his way out, and Spindler had spent hours with Eisenstat working out the terms of his promotion. It is also clear, by most accounts, that Spindler would not have been sorry to see Sculley go, nor would Sullivan, who was Spindler's right-hand man. For years, Spindler had complained openly of Apple having an absentee chief executive, and the two had been accused of plotting together against Sculley as long ago as 1988.

Yet Spindler had the gall to give Gerri Coleman a hug afterward and say, "I never, ever heard anything about it, and I'm shocked." He demonstrated even more gall in the way he treated Sculley afterward. After he was taken out as CEO, Sculley was left with the figurehead title of chairman. When he asked the board what he was supposed to do, Markkula told Sculley to "follow whatever Spindler says," according to a person who heard the exchange. "Spindler then told John he was not allowed to attend executive staff meetings. He was heard to say, 'The only thing you are allowed to do is talk about Newton,' " according to the same person.

Sugared water. Or a chance to change the world. That polite taunt from Steve Jobs on a Manhattan rooftop more than a decade before had convinced John Sculley to drastically change his own life. So much had happened since then. Sculley had booted out Apple's charismatic visionary. He had rescued the company from the precipice not once but twice. He had grown Apple from a company of $1 billion in annual revenues to nearly $10 billion, while at the same time establishing the Apple name as one of the premier brands on earth. But he had also set up a management structure that was doomed to fail and in the process had let Apple miss out on one of the biggest business opportunities of the century: the chance to take control of the dawning Information Age by unleashing an army of Macintosh clones, early on.

Now it had all come full circle. Just as he had stripped Jobs of power in order to save the company, Sculley had been similarly shorn. He was still chairman, but that was an empty title, and everybody at Apple knew it. Michael Spindler was the new captain of the ship, and on his watch the company that had brought the power of computing to the masses would founder and nearly sink in ever-stormier seas.

10

A New Sheriff in Town

For years, Michael Spindler had complained openly about his boss, John Sculley, even as Sculley had been boosting him ever higher on the corporate ladder. Now, at long last, the buck stopped with Spindler. He would soon find out for himself just how lonely life at the top of Apple Computer could be.

Spindler, as president and chief operating officer, had been overseeing Apple's daily operations since 1990 and had had a hand in every major decision that had affected the company during that time. As Ian Dicry had told a shattered Sculley after his ouster, if he had been fired for poor results, everyone on the executive team shared the blame for that. As other executives from the time believe, that went doubly so for Michael Spindler, since he had not only been running all operations, but had also been overseeing R and D in the year before Sculley was demoted.

Given Sculley's mixed record at Apple, no one could argue that it was not, in fact, time for him to move on. Indeed, he had been trying to do so on his own volition for more than a year. What shocked and outraged Sculley's many personal admirers within Apple was the demeaning and underhanded way in which it finally happened. After all, the man had devoted practically every waking moment to Apple Computer for a full decade and had worn himself to a frazzle in the process. And no one could question John Sculley's integrity. Indeed, it was his reputation as a "straight shooter" that had endeared him so much to the brass at IBM, helping that alliance to come together.

The Apple Computer of Michael Spindler, however, was considerably less straightforward, as evidenced the very first day of his new administration, when the company's PR department was ordered to craft a baldly untrue press release. The release, distributed over business wire services on Friday, June 18, 1993, announced that the board had elected Spindler as chief executive officer *and* that it had done so at Sculley's request. Sculley, Apple said, would remain as chairman but would devote his time to building alliances with other companies.

The Apple directors took the charade even further, with the reclusive Mike Markkula, of all people, going so far as to arrange an interview with *The Wall Street Journal* to report, among other things, that "we have to respect John's wishes." Markkula had long despised and mistrusted the press and has only rarely made himself available for media sessions in all the years of his involvement with Apple. Indeed, he was one of only a few longtime Apple executives who did not make himself available for this book. Adding insult to injury, the directors even trotted poor John Sculley out—only a day after his fall—to tell the world with a straight face that he really needed to be spending more time building the alliances. "These kinds of relationships have to be at a high level and are very time-consuming," Sculley said.[1]

Those testimonials notwithstanding, the always active rumor mill in Silicon Valley was abuzz with speculation that Sculley's departure had not been voluntary. Three months later, it would be longtime board member and Apple Senior Vice President Al Eisenstat who would spill the beans on what had actually happened. And the fate that befell him revealed much about what the new gang was really like.

Eisenstat had attended virtually every meeting of the Apple board since filling a vacant director's seat left by the departure of Steve Jobs in 1985. He prepared meeting agendas and acted as a liaison between the board and senior management, such as when Markkula and the other outside directors had asked him to approach Spindler about the CEO's job. On the day after Sculley was shown the door, the board convened again in the Synergy room atop De Anza 7. Spindler lumbered into the room, looking bleary-eyed from lack of sleep, and began passing around the table copies of a reorganized management chart that he, his confidant, Kevin Sullivan, and Apple's general counsel, Ed Stead, had been up all night putting together, according to a person who was in that room. Ed Stead had been named Apple's general counsel in June 1989, assuming Al Eisenstat's direct responsibilities over legal matters as Eisenstat continued serving on the board and as corporate secretary.

This reorganization would be Michael Spindler's first act in office as Apple's new CEO, and it called for sweeping changes. First of all, it ordered the firing of 2,500 people, or 16 percent of the workforce, in a move to cut expenses. Then it realigned divisions to put a tighter focus on the markets Apple served. For example, the engineers in charge of selling data-storage servers to big businesses would be lumped into their own division, not under the big, generic "product development" R-and-D group that had existed before.

Eisenstat picked up his copy and peered closely to find his name. He had to look hard, because his position had been eliminated and he was off in a corner doing something totally unrelated—and so trivial he cannot even remember exactly what it was. In fact, it was not really a job at all, and Eisenstat grabbed Sullivan at the first break in the meeting to demand, "What the hell is going on here?" Sullivan, looking noncommittal as always, replied coolly, "That's the way Michael wants it." When Eisenstat pulled Spindler aside after the meeting, the Diesel gave it to him straight. "There's no real role for you," Spindler told the man who had helped arrange his job.[2]

As Sullivan later explained, Spindler had been in the process of cutting out 16 percent of the workforce when he took over as CEO and was stunned to see from reading Apple's latest proxy filing with the Securities and Exchange Commission that Eisenstat was being paid an annual salary of $750,000, not including cash bonuses that had totaled another $760,000 between 1990 and 1992 and options to buy Apple shares valued at about $6.5 million. "We had a guy making $800,000 a year and didn't have a job," Sullivan says. "Al was supposed to be head of corporate development, but he wasn't doing anything. We had to cut back, so Michael said, 'We don't need this guy here.' "

Eisenstat's official job was board member and corporate secretary. He also then had control over Apple's corporate development activities, which included acquisition efforts, and he still nominally oversaw legal matters, as Ed Stead's boss.

But Eisenstat, it was true, really was not doing much. Eisenstat says that was because all the reorganizations directed under Sculley had left his role increasingly unclear. And he had wanted to retire soon, anyway, after having worked for Apple since those giddy days back in 1980. A decade at Apple was like twenty years anyplace else, the pace was so fast. And at age sixty-three, Eisenstat wasn't a young man anymore. He was mighty steamed but willing to go away quietly—if Spindler came through with a separation payment that would amount to more than Apple's standard payment to top executives of a full year's pay plus bonuses. "Al said, 'That's not enough. I want more,' " Sullivan recalls. "He said, 'I'll go to the board.' "

The board was in no mood to overrule its new CEO, so Eisenstat retained a lawyer. One day in September 1993, Eisenstat was seen hurrying from his office in De Anza 7, clutching a sheaf of legal papers and muttering, "I am suing Apple. They fired me." Sure enough, Eisenstat filed a lawsuit in California Superior Court in San Jose, California, on September 23, 1993, against Apple and Spindler, alleging wrongful termination and age discrimination, among other things.

It was that suit that first publicly unveiled the fact there had been a conspiracy to unseat Sculley. Eisenstat also alleged that Spindler had moved to eliminate him as a "voice of reason" within Apple's management on executive pay issues. Eisenstat asserted in the suit that he had always tried to get Apple to toe the line on holding down executive salaries, although he obviously hadn't done a good job of it, as his own hefty compensation proved.

Eisenstat further stated in the suit that he had realized, through their secret negotiations, that Spindler might make "significant financial demands on Apple" to assume Sculley's job. Eisenstat asserted that he had warned the board of that before they made Spindler the new CEO. Indeed, Eisenstat alleged in the suit, Spindler had told the board on June 18 that his reorganization would include a repricing of stock options "so as to create a substantial gain to specific individuals who would remain employed with Apple and that part of such plan was to force the removal of those officers and directors Spindler knew would oppose his plan"—namely, Al Eisenstat.

After the suit was filed, Apple issued two prepared statements saying that Eisenstat's position had been eliminated solely as part of the overall layoffs and that Eisenstat had rejected as "not sufficient" the standard executive severance package. One of the statements, quoted in *The Wall Street Journal*, added that Eisenstat "has been generously compensated by Apple for many years. For him to suggest he wasn't treated fairly is disingenuous." Apple also said it would defend itself "vigorously" and that all the allegations in the suit, which also included breach of contract, conspiracy, and intentional infliction of emotional distress, were without merit.

This time around, though, none of the board principals involved in the ouster would comment to the *Journal.* By then, Arthur Rock had resigned his board post, ostensibly because it represented a conflict with his dual service as a board member of Intel. Several Apple executives from the time, however, speculate that Rock may have suffered a pang of conscience over the Sculley episode, as have other senior managers since who turned their backs on him.

"I think the board, and myself included, failed in not having more compassion towards John in the way the decision had been made," Eisenstat now says. Kevin Sullivan, too, now admits he should have at least telephoned Sculley after the decision was made. Sullivan, as indicated before, was in Paris then with Ian Diery, the head of worldwide sales. Sullivan says he returned to California from Paris the weekend following Sculley's ouster and went into Sculley's office the next Monday. "I probably should have called John, and I didn't," Sullivan says, thumping his fist for emphasis on the table of a Chinese restaurant in San Francisco during an interview for this book. "But those were emotional times for everyone. Our layoffs would be announced two weeks later. The only regret I have in all the years is, I wish I had talked to John sooner."

Despite the sensational charges, the Eisenstat suit never came to trial. After a court-appointed mediator failed to resolve the dispute, Eisenstat reached an out-of-court settlement with Apple for an undisclosed sum that he will say only was not below the standard severance. The case was dismissed on November 19, 1993. Eisenstat rode off into the sunset without even a farewell party. By this time, John Sculley, too, was gone from Apple for good.

After the board removed him as CEO in June 1993, Sculley was left as a powerless figurehead. Although he continued to serve as Apple chairman, Spindler had told him he was not to have input into anything; he was only to talk about Newton. The loss of power was manifested within the first week of the ouster, as the number of people seeking daily counsel from Sculley's staff of three office assistants dwindled from the usual flood to none. "The first week, everyone was really sweet," recalls one of the assistants. "Then I just sat there for months. Spindler never cared enough to even take our files."

By late summer, Sculley returned from two months of sabbatical and vacation he took immediately following the coup to hear new rumors within Apple that Spindler was now planning to fire him as chairman that January.[3] Deciding to beat Spindler to the punch this time, Sculley tendered his resignation on October 15, 1993, leaving Mike Markkula, the vice chairman, to succeed him as chairman. There was no big good-bye party, virtually no trace of the man once he walked out of the storied corridors of Apple Computer for the last time.

"When John left," Sullivan remembers, "it was as though he never existed."

Sculley would not leave entirely empty-handed, though. Apple bestowed a handsome separation agreement giving him a windfall that amounted to $10 million, including a year's salary at $1 million; a $750,000 consulting fee (for services rendered after he would leave the Apple payroll); immediate vesting in unearned stock options valued at $2.4 million; and purchase of his $4 million home in Woodside as well as his $2 million Learjet. This was enough to help assuage the pain.

Almost immediately, Sculley shocked the computer industry by signing on as chairman of a tiny wireless firm in Manhasset, New York, called Spectrum Information Technologies, Inc., for a staggering $1 million annual salary and options to buy 18 million shares over five years for an expected profit of $72 million. The Spectrum deal imploded quickly, though. Sculley resigned just five months later, in February 1994, accusing Spectrum of misleading him about the company's financial condition and legal problems, including a Securities and Exchange Commission probe into alleged fraud. Spectrum filed for federal bankruptcy protection in January 1995. After a decade in the spotlight as one of America's most visible CEOs, Sculley would vanish almost completely from the public eye before reemerging three years later as an active investor in Silicon Valley start-ups, including Live Picture Inc., Seismic Entertainment, and Live World Productions. He is also cofounder of Sirius Thinking Ltd., a New York City children's educational entertainment company.

With Sculley and Eisenstat out of the way, Spindler consolidated power largely under a triumvirate that included himself and his two closest confidants, Kevin Sullivan and Ed Stead. They came to be known in Apple as "the Three Ss." Down the line, a fourth "S" would be added to the power structure, and it would not be someone one would expect.

Stead, forty-six years old in 1993, had been recruited by Eisenstat in June 1988 from Cullinet Software Inc., a developer and distributor of mainframe software programs. Before Cullinet, where Stead was senior vice president and general counsel, he had worked from 1973 to 1985 as a senior attorney for IBM. At Apple, Stead was initially named associate general counsel of the Apple USA division before taking Eisenstat's place as Apple's general counsel in 1989. Stead was a sharp-tongued, humorless man, described by even his friends as "anal." And he befriended Spindler early on, according to people who knew him, in part because he believed Sculley never liked him. "He used to love going out with Spindler to dinner, to talk and drink," says a former associate at Apple.

As for Kevin Sullivan, who had turned fifty-two in 1993, he wasted no time demonstrating loyalty to his old office pal. During a monthly meeting of the board shortly after Spindler had taken over, a person in the room remembers Sullivan jumping out of his chair to congratulate Spindler on his reorganization plans. "Boy, this is great," Sullivan said.[4] "It will make all the difference in the world."

Spindler's plan, in short, was to chop hard at expenses while also refocusing Apple to compete better against the Wintel market. In 1993, worldwide PC sales had ballooned to an annual rate of $75 billion, and Apple had accounted for just 9.4 percent of that.[5] But the PC had become such a commodity by then, with component prices being driven ever lower by spiraling volume, that profit margins on personal computers had eroded to only 15 to 22 percent from the 35 to 45 percent levels of just two years earlier.[6]

Accelerating the drop in profits had been that stunning move taken during the summer of 1992 by the wily Texans at Compaq Computer, who had slashed their PC prices by one fifth in an audacious bid to steal market share from their rivals. The strategy had worked: Compaq's sales had skyrocketed 73 percent to $7.1 billion in 1993 from $4.1 billion the year before. But Compaq had set off a price war the likes of which the young industry had never seen. The war ravaged profits for nearly everyone in the business, save for the Microsoft-Intel duopoly, which controlled the pace of technology innovation, and took an even bigger bite out of Apple.

This was precisely what Sculley had feared and why he had so desperately wanted to move Apple to a whole new technology, such as the Newton, that would be immune to the price wars. But the Newton was still so much pie in the sky, in terms of generating any meaningful revenues for Apple any time soon. What Spindler knew he had to do was increase sales volume and reduce expenses, to stave off the rising tide. Missing the mark on the PowerBook during that 1993 fiscal third quarter had caused Apple's sales to slow so much that profit margins had plunged to 33 percent from 44 percent in the same period only a year before. That was a steep drop, but Apple's profit margins were still at least 10 percentage points higher than the industry average at that time.

Drastic problems required drastic measures. Taking aim first at the expense front, Spindler put the order out throughout Apple: 16 percent staff cuts, across the board, with cuts of varying degrees in every department. To cover the costs of firing the 2,500 workers, he imposed a restructuring charge that amounted to $198.9 million, after tax, resulting in a net quarterly loss of $188.3 million, or $1.63 a share. It was an alarming decline from the same quarter in 1992, when Apple had earned $131.7 million, or $1.07 a share.

Apple had been through many reorganizations before this, but nothing on this order. In the past, for example, the engineering organization had been considered so untouchable by senior management that it had never had to bear the pain of a mass layoff. Not this time. "All of a sudden, we were sitting around a table figuring out who to lay off," remembers Jean Proulx, a manager of 130 of Apple's engineers in operating system development. "I was given a number, and we sat around my dining room table doing that."

That number was 10 percent, at least in the system software part of engineering, and the uncertainty over who would lose their jobs generated such anxiety that Apple began receiving bomb threats, presumably from disgruntled workers. During one afternoon in June 1993, in fact, all the software engineers were ordered to evacuate their building when company security officers discovered a package in an underground parking garage. "It was a box containing a timing device and explosives," recalls Rick Spitz, who was vice president for operating system software then. "We now had a serious safety problem on our hands. I demanded that Apple bring increased security to the building, or I would shut software engineering down. I also had the underground parking garage closed after business hours, as there was plenty of outside parking."

Other Appleites attempted to cope with gallows humor. At one point, a computer screen saver circulated called "JurApple Park," as a reference to director Steven Spielberg's hit movie *Jurassic Park*; in it, Apple executives—not dinosaurs—were eating the employees. There was another screen saver called "Spindler's List," which was modeled after another Spielberg movie, *Schindler's List*, about a benevolent Austrian during World War II. In this case, however, the screen saver represented an evil German named Spindler preparing a list of Apple employees to gun down.

For those who were able to keep their jobs, this was becoming an Apple almost unrecognizable from its 1980s heyday of high morale. Other aspects of

Spindler's cuts made life even more bleak. The belt had begun to tighten in 1990, with cutbacks in profit sharing and pay raises and even the temporary shutdown of the water coolers. It cinched even further in 1991, when the Apple cafeteria lost its company subsidy and employees were forced to pay $2 a week to attend an Apple fitness center that had been free before. Over that time, there had been another, less tangible measure of the decline in morale that had to do with the increasing bureaucracy of the place. By 1992, working for Apple had become working for a "big company" not so unlike the IBM in the "1984" ad, which had depicted a roomful of workers listening zombielike to an ominous Big Brother figure.

But somehow the money and perks still remained relatively attractive, compared to those at leaner companies such as Microsoft, which was known to work employees around the clock for comparatively little pay. Microsoft, however, compensated by offering its employees more stock options, providing a valuable incentive for everyone to band together to drive the company's stock value ever higher. A junior Apple engineer could expect to start at about $50,000 a year, with an annual raise of 10 percent. Cash bonuses of as much as $5,000 were still routinely doled out to participants of big engineering projects.

Then Spindler—and Sullivan—rained on that parade, too. With Spindler's blessing, Sullivan instituted a companywide salary freeze in 1993 that would last eighteen months. The effect was chilling. "That was a stupid idea because it was no way to motivate people," recalls one high-level manager who left the company shortly afterward. "We laid off all the bad people, but we couldn't give our good people a raise. And after it was all over, we had to raise salaries even more to keep people from leaving."

Just as stinging, if only on principle, was Spindler's decision to raise the price of using the fitness center again, to $5 a week from $2. "This was the major turning point for me," recalls Andy Stadler, the engineer who had worked on the Newton project before resigning from Apple in 1994. "This was like, 'Screw you. You're another employee.' After that, it was like, the magic is gone." The combination of layoffs, salary freezes, and the other belt-tightening actions precipitated an exodus of talent from Apple's engineering corps. "At the time, the rest of the Valley was hiring like crazy and the headhunters were having a field day recruiting from Apple R and D," Rick Spitz remembers.

There was another casualty that summer, and it was humor. For many years until then, there had been a tradition at Apple of conveying company messages in irreverent videos that came to resemble outtakes from *Saturday Night Live*. At the Apple sales conference in October 1992, for instance, a video promoting a new strategy to capture more office accounts networked into an "enterprise" opened with a sweeping camera shot of downtown

Nashville at night and a male announcer intoning, "It's Enterprise Live!" The theme of the show was for Apple to boost corporate sales by providing a bigger line of "servers," which are big PCs that act as a central repository for data in an office.

The skits were always organized by Peter Hirshberg, a senior marketing manager, and this one included employees of Apple's enterprise business — dressed in studded, black leather jackets — cavorting as their boss, Jerry Malec, belted out a ditty called "Own It," to the tune of pop singer Michael Jackson's smash hit "Beat It." Wearing Jackson's 1980s costume of red jacket, black hat, and wraparound shades, Malec, holding a microphone and strutting around a pool table, sang:

> We've got
> A golden market opportunity
> To build
> A franchise with mobility. . . .
> No one else has the Mac,
> We own it. We own it.

That number was followed by a skit called "Morris's World," based on the movie *Wayne's World*. Mimicking the aspiring rock stars from the campy flick, Morris Taradalsky, manager of Apple's server effort, and his lieutenant, Jim Groff, gamely donned long-haired wigs and sunglasses as Taradalsky strummed an air guitar and babbled, "Excellent. Excellent. Okay, party on. Okay." They invited on camera a special guest who turned out to be none other than Michael Spindler himself.

"The Spin Man! Michael Totally Awesome Spindler!" Taradalsky, playing Wayne from *Wayne's World*, gushed as the beefy Spindler hurried out in his yellow pullover shirt and beige slacks, an awkward grin slapped across his jowly face. Seating himself between the two men on a couch, Spindler stared straight at a TelePrompTer as he read aloud, "We have great confidence in the enterprise markets division to achieve what you might call awesome things this next year."

Somehow, the word "awesome" didn't sound right coming from the rigid Spindler. Nor, apparently, did Spindler really give a hoot about these video spoofs. When Peter Hirshberg quit Apple later that year, the videos he had conceived largely departed with him. (As for the much-ballyhooed server initiative, it never went anywhere under Spindler, even after he became CEO and made a renewed commitment to that product line.)

There was another facet of Sculley's Apple that Spindler absolutely detested, and that was the role of the CEO as the company's main cheerleader in public. Sculley himself never particularly liked public speaking and in fact had had to overcome a childhood stutter and chronic shyness to do it. But he had learned to excel, rivaling in charisma the great Steve Jobs himself.

As for Spindler, he didn't mind speaking in front of Apple employees, where he could work himself into a lathered passion, scribbling all over a whiteboard and walls. But he despised public appearances and appeared wooden and uninspired when he spoke at them. His speaking demeanor was very different outside the context of Apple's public events, however.

Apple employees will never forget, for example, how Spindler bared his soul in his first big company address as Apple's CEO at the annual sales conference in Las Vegas in October 1993. There was no pulsating rock music, no flashing strobe lights, as had presaged so many other Apple events. Instead, Spindler walked alone into the blackened theater of the Aladdin Hotel and paced the stage under a single spotlight as he ticked off his plans to revive the company and assured the audience of two thousand sales representatives that the worst for Apple was over. "This is not a lame-duck company!" he shouted.[7]

In concluding his speech, Spindler warned that he was about to get "very personal" as he described why he had decided to replace John Sculley as CEO. Just as he had told Kevin Sullivan, he related to the throng how he had been given fifteen minutes to make up his mind. Spindler said it would have been easier to say no. "I could see myself being a grandfather sitting with a grandchild on my lap in a tomato field saying, 'I didn't have to be CEO.'" Then, tears welling in his eyes and his voice wavering, the Diesel stabbed his fist in the air and added, "The reason why I made this fifteen-minute decision is: We can win this!"[8] The Apple faithful sat momentarily stunned. Then they erupted in wild applause.

"We were in tears. We were on out feet. It was his moment at Apple," recalls Barbara Krause, vice president for Apple's worldwide corporate communications then. Adds Jim Buckley, then vice president for Apple's higher education marketing in the United States, "That was one of the most unbelievable speeches I had ever seen. He was magical."

The emotion that Spindler exhibited before his subordinates that day was no doubt sincere. Spindler did love Apple. His entire life, in fact, revolved around Apple, to the extent that many people close to him were convinced it was harming his health. But in positioning himself as a hapless executive given just minutes to decide, Spindler was perpetuating an untruth that had begun with the very first press release about Sculley's supposedly voluntary step-down. There had been nothing voluntary about it at all, and Michael Spindler well knew it.

Yet Spindler could never muster that same passion when speaking to groups outside Apple. Part of the reason, no doubt, was that Spindler was far more at ease mixing with Apple people, who mostly shared his passion. After all, one could not work at Apple Computer without some driving desire to change the world. That had been the creed from the very beginning. But away from Apple, he was constantly being confronted with settings he could not control, where people could ask whatever they wanted. As a result, he was about as visibly comfortable in these public appearances as a little boy being sent to the principal's office.

Even more, Spindler loathed having to deal with the aggressive media and all the attention it devoted to Apple. That animosity no doubt sprang from his having worked for most of his adult life in Europe, where the business press tends to treat its executives like royalty. The role of the media, Spindler thought, was to listen as he lectured, as reporters in Europe did. The "in-your-face" style of the American press was such an affront to Spindler that during his entire reign as Apple's CEO, his only known favorite in the Silicon Valley press corps was a British-born journalist named Louise Kehoe from the *Financial Times*, whom he would tell, "You're from Europe. You understand."

Not surprisingly, then, one of Spindler's first acts in office was to shut down John Sculley's TV station across the street from De Anza 7. As mentioned before, AppleTV was a state-of-the-art facility that Sculley had used at least twice a month for interviews, satellite meetings with remote Apple managers, and such since it had opened in 1988. Under Sculley, "Spindler appeared on AppleTV 'as required,' " recalls Peter Kavanaugh, Apple's manager of video communications at the time. "When he was forced to appear, he appeared, but he seemed to do it under duress. He was not a volunteer, and his TV style was not the best."

During the first week of July 1993, Kavanaugh was instructed to fire his entire staff of fifteen people. Then, in October, Kavanaugh got his walking papers, too. As for AppleTV, in which Apple had invested $5 million since 1988, it was sold to an industry marketing firm in Cupertino called CKS Group for $250,000. Yet another less-than-stellar return for Apple on its money.

Apple was thus suddenly deprived of a critically important public relations tool: having a CEO who could spread awareness of the company's product by constantly appearing in the press. It had been precisely John Sculley's strategy, in fact, to conduct as many speeches and media interviews as he could to build awareness of the Apple brand. He had failed miserably as a technology manager but had proven brilliant at flogging the Apple name, to the extent that he would deliberately keep talking even when he knew his time was running out in a broadcast interview, to squeeze in as much airtime as he could. It was better than advertising—and free. And it had worked. By virtue of Sculley's innumerable public appearances as CEO, Apple had been highly visible and glamorous during his years, as epitomized in Sculley's fateful juxtaposition with the First Lady during the 1993 State of the Union address.

Public relations are all the more important when a company is in trouble.

This is when somebody—preferably the CEO—needs to get out there and re-assure customers, investors, and the press in a calm, soothing voice that the place is not about to go up in flames, everything is under control. The world of Macintosh suppliers and enthusiasts certainly became increasingly nervous not only because of the sudden change at the helm when Sculley was moved out but also because of the massive restructuring and reported losses. There were other uncertainties, too, concerning the slow pace of Apple's technology development, as well as how well the much-hyped Newton would really do when it came out in the late summer.

CEO Michael Spindler, however, would not appear in public for four months from the time he was made CEO, and when he did he assiduously avoided any mention of Apple's ongoing problems. His public coming-out speech was at industry consultant Jonathan Seybold's annual conference on desktop publishing in San Francisco on October 20, 1993, the same forum in which Adobe's John Warnock had nearly burst into tears over his fight with Apple and Microsoft. The theater at the Moscone Center in downtown San Francisco was packed to the rafters with approximately three thousand Mac developers, many of them from the publishing market. This would be a golden opportunity for Spindler to get up onstage and provide some clear di-rection as to Apple's future to a critically important audience of people who were actually in a position to influence the Mac's success in the marketplace with new and improved software.

But Michael Spindler did not like facing the outside world, not one bit. And it showed. The burly CEO stepped to the podium in his dark suit, stared at a TelePrompTer, and began reciting from a nine-page speech devoted en-tirely to his renewed commitment to the important desktop publishing market. The talk was stultifyingly dull, filled with jargon such as "color management," "workflow," and "idea capture, editing and manipulation." And how about this for a knock-your-socks-off statement:

> The computer has been, in large part, responsible for the division of re-sponsibilities in the workflow of the open systems world. As the tools have per-mitted us to tighten the process from "rough" to mechanical, the time frame for the front end has frequently been reduced. By and large, however, the approval process has been largely unaffected by these tools and shortcuts. If anything, it has become more complex as more people have gotten involved.

If you didn't understand much of that, don't feel too bad. Not many peo-ple at Moscone that day did, either. At the end of the talk, Spindler opened the floor to questions. In these forums, the questioners queue up behind stand-up microphones positioned in aisles around the hall. As Spindler's bad luck would have it, the first person he called upon at one of the mikes was a *San Francisco Chronicle* reporter named Laura Evenson, who asked in front of the whole crowd whether he could comment on the status of the Power-Book problem that had so ravaged the balance sheet during the year.

Business reporters almost never address such questions during an actual forum. They wait until a media question-and-answer session, usually scheduled right afterward in a meeting room nearby. But Evenson, like every other member of the Apple press corps, had been trying to snag an interview with Spindler ever since he had assumed command the previous June, without success, and no press session with him had been set up here. So the gutsy Evenson braced the big guy for all to see. Momentarily stunned by her affront, Spindler replied that this was not the proper forum to be discussing such matters and advised Evenson to arrange an interview through Apple's public relations department.

Moments later, when he had dispensed with more mundane technical questions from the audience, Spindler beat a hasty retreat out of the building—or tried to. This was where I entered the Apple story. As a reporter for the San Francisco bureau of *The Wall Street Journal*, I had just been assigned to cover Apple by my editor, Greg Hill. I attended the conference, therefore, to gain some insight into my new beat. As the attendees filed out of the theater, I and a reporter for *PC Week* magazine spotted the Diesel walking swiftly down a side hall and scurried after him to try and ask some questions. Spindler, following an aide named David Seda, mumbled for us, too, to go through the proper channels as they walked ever faster, frantically looking for the exit.

This was really a ridiculous scene, when you think about it: a reporter for *The Wall Street Journal*, the most influential business publication in America, and another for *PC Week*, the most influential trade magazine in the PC industry, having to chase after the chief executive of probably the most-watched computer company in the world, just to ask a question or two on where the company was headed. Yet for Spindler, it was as though he were Michael Jackson fleeing the paparazzi.

Keeping a watchful eye on the boss, Seda quickly found an open door through which they could disappear into a waiting limousine. Seda did a lot of watching over Spindler in the years to come, to the extent that his de facto power grew so much that this little-known man, whose official job was executive assistant, would become known at Apple as the fourth "S" on the Apple throne.

For all his idiosyncrasies, Spindler really was a clearheaded strategist as CEO, even as he had been in the old days in Europe. He knew Apple no longer had the resources to compete in practically every PC market in the world, under the scattershot approach it had used to compete in an increasingly diversified marketplace. So the second part of his strategy, after getting expenses down, was to realign Apple to focus the company more sharply on markets in which it could win.

Under Sculley, the engineering side and the one for sales and marketing had invariably worked apart from each other because they were set up in different divisions. Marketing was further fragmented by the strong sales role of geographical divisions such as Apple USA and Apple Europe. This was fine when Apple was still relatively small and a strong COO such as Del Yocam could keep track of who was responsible for what and how all the teams would work together to get a product out the door and to the customer. But by the early 1990s, when Apple was approaching $10 billion in annual sales, it resulted in conflicting activities going on under the same tent and little commitment to a product throughout the entire organization.

A good example of this was Apple's failed endeavor in digital cameras, when the people on the marketing side told their counterparts on the engineering side that the product would have to be introduced at $200 or less. The engineers basically ignored this directive, producing a QuickTake camera that sold for three times that price. The exception to this disconnect between engineering and marketing was the way the PowerBook engineers and salespeople had agreed to drop the walls and work in unison, resulting in that product roaring to spectacular success.

Spindler took Sculley's organizational structure—which essentially consisted of product development and all other R and D in one group, and product sales and marketing in the other, with the separate geographical divisions—and reshuffled this into four main pieces during that summer of 1993. They included a new PC division, which would include all Macintosh sales and related hardware development; a new R-and-D division called AppleSoft, under which the company's operating system development would be consolidated; another software division called PIE, or Personal Interactive Electronics, which would envelop all the Newton technology's research and sales; and finally, a new division called Apple Business Systems, dedicated to development and sales of data-storage servers for the business market.

By far the largest of the four was the PC division, which was to focus on selling Macintoshes and gaining more share of the personal computer market so that Apple could remain healthy and profitable enough to fund its other new ventures, such as Newton. The Macintosh line was the company's cash cow, the beast that would pull everyone else ahead, just as the Apple II had done for the original Macintosh. And this time all the Mac's sales and development were put under the same umbrella, headed by Ian Diery, the executive vice president who had been in charge of all sales and marketing.

To maximize the efficiency of the mainstream Mac business, Spindler devised a strategy for Apple to home in on its biggest markets of sales to schools, home users, and, most important, desktop publishers. As of 1993 Apple held 80 percent of the market for computer sales to professional publishers. On July 29, 1993, Spindler appeared before an intimate gathering of fewer than twenty low-ranking employees and managers from throughout the organization in an Apple conference room and spelled out the strategy step by step with the aid of a giant flip chart perched on an easel. An internal Apple videotape of the meeting captured the moment.

"This," he said, pointing to the desktop publishing part of the chart showing Apple's key customer groups, "is our most important business, which makes most of the profit in the PC business of Apple. It is this thing." Behind closed doors here, Spindler was impassioned, as usual. Wearing a faded yellow shirt with sleeves rolled up and unbuttoned to the middle of his chest, Spindler's voice rose and fell, his arms waved, his eyes flashed. The captive audience sat spellbound, slowly nodding. "It is extremely important that we get back and hound that marketplace."

This was Spindler at his best, and for a change he was speaking clearly and coherently, although his English did fail him at one point. At one moment, when pointing out how invaluable it was for Apple to possess such a strong market in schools, Spindler said, "Other people would kill if they had that," instead of "to have that." No one dared to laugh. Nevertheless, the strategy he was laying out for the Mac business represented a dramatic departure from the past, when Apple had sold computers, willy-nilly, wherever it could. Although John Sculley had repeatedly harped in public on Apple's strategy to target core markets such as education and desktop publishing, and growing ones such as in big business, he had exerted so little control over his various sales managers that they had pushed computers into practically any market they could. "In the PC business," as Spindler told the group that day, "we need a better alignment between customer segments, channels, and product on technologies that people will buy."

In other words, Apple could not be all things to all people; it should pick the battles where it could win and concentrate on them. It was sound reasoning but unfortunately one that Spindler would have great difficulty in getting the troops to carry out.

Another pressing task was how to rein in Apple's runaway train down in software development. To try to harness that energy better, Spindler took the software organization and split it into two divisions. AppleSoft was charged with developing "a leading edge operating system" that eventually could be licensed and moved to other computer platforms, such as Intel's. Put in charge of this effort was Dave Nagel, the former NASA scientist whom Spindler had called up from the labs of the Advanced Technology Group during February 1993 to take Roger Heinen's place over operating system software.

The other software division was PIE, or Personal Interactive Electronics, under which all the Newton research and sales would be conducted. (The name appears to have been influenced by the 1980s report for Apple by students at Princeton University, in which they had predicted the dawning of a Personal Information Environment.) Lumped into PIE was another new technology effort, for an on-line network called eWorld, designed to compete against the big established information and chat services—America Online, CompuServe, and Prodigy—which had already gained millions of customers. Like those networks, eWorld would also enable the subscriber to peruse an electronic catalog of services ranging from cybershopping to airline and hotel reservations. This was another Apple undertaking doomed to fail, however, because eWorld was very late in coming and would be confined to the closed world of Macintosh users.

The PIE division was headed by a newcomer to Apple named Gaston Bastiaens, a native Belgian whom Sculley had recruited from the Dutch computer giant Philips Electronics NV to take over the Newton project. His new title was vice president and general manager of PIE. Finally, Spindler formed a small division called Apple Business Systems to begin building a "profitable and growing server business going forward" for the market of small, medium, and large corporate customers, according to an internal memo outlining the plan. Named as general manager over that was Morris Taradalsky, the "excellent, excellent" Morris Taradalsky from *Morris's World* who had been in charge of Apple's server development.

The new organization seemed good enough—if it had worked according to plan. Spindler had the right idea, but then he handicapped the organization by insisting on another aspect. In addition to the new divisions, Spindler set up committees to micromanage each one. He named himself to head the new technical committee. "The first thing Spindler wanted to do was list every project in the company and see duplications and then remove them," recalls an executive who sat on that committee with Spindler. "That is not the way to do it. You decentralize the company and make each division accountable."

Actually, Spindler was decentralizing Apple, but he wasn't. That was the problem. On the one hand, all these new, tightly focused divisions had been created to bring greater direction and accountability to the company's various activities. But with the exception of Ian Diery's PC division, they were run by executives who would prove too weak for the job. Spindler had set up committees of managers from each division to oversee them. And, as might be expected, management by committee did not work. "When you have a large committee, you can only agree on the lowest common denominator, and you also get very slow reaction time," says one veteran Apple executive.

Slow reaction time is exactly what Apple did not need as it faced the accelerating Wintel juggernaut.

Spindler's other big problem in implementing this strategy was that he proved remarkably indecisive as a CEO, despite his "Diesel" moniker. This was a management flaw vividly exemplified in his handling of Newton. To understand this, let us pick up the Newton story again from when it was reaching full-development mode in mid-1992. There were the Junior and Senior teams, competing to see which product would win. And there was Larry Tesler, former colleague of Dave Nagel in the ATG, presiding over a project that to many within the company appeared to be spinning out of control.

Sculley had ignited such an industry fire in his big PDA speech at the Consumer Electronics Show in January 1992 that the Newton team was under tremendous pressure to get a product out fast. The Newton project had started out to create a small computer that could communicate wirelessly anywhere in the world, sending and retrieving e-mail, pager, and fax messages, as well as data, to and from the main computer back home. But Newton's hundred engineers and marketing people were splintered into one faction, led by Michael Tchao and Steve Capps, to develop the sub-$1,000, handheld Junior and the other, led by Tesler, to make the $1,500-plus, tablet-sized Senior. The big problem, for Tesler, was that he had already gotten Japan's Sharp Corporation to agree to manufacture the Senior. Sharp was also producing its handheld Wizard, a note-taking and spreadsheet device that Tesler feared would pose direct competition to Apple's Junior.

Tchao, however, convinced Tesler to ask Sharp if it could also manufacture the Junior, since that product was likely to be finished first. "So we went to Sharp and asked, 'Could you do the little one [Junior] sooner?' " Tesler recalls. "They said there was no way it would ever fit in such a small package" with all the advanced technological features such as handwriting recognition that were lacking in the more stripped-down Wizard. The Junior team, then, set out to design the Junior box themselves. Working tirelessly, a core team of Tchao, Capps, Michael Culbert, and an Apple industrial design engineer named Eric Gruenberg came up with a design that Sharp could use.

By this time, in early 1992, a new Newton marketing manager named Hugh Hempel had joined the team. Hempel suggested that the Newton group concentrate on shipping Junior first, as manufactured by Sharp, with Senior to follow. Tesler did not like the idea because he thought that Newton's efforts would become too fragmented, but he nevertheless sold the plan to Sharp. As 1992 dragged on, though, the Senior engineers gradually lost interest in that project and began migrating to Junior. "The Junior team created the image they were the hip group and that the Senior team was filled with old fuddy-duddies," Tesler says. "Suddenly, nobody wanted to work on Senior anymore."

This was a classic case of Apple's engineers, not the engineering executives, running the show. Tesler was the executive in charge of Newton, but in the Apple culture of consensus thinking—where everyone gets to have an equal say in decisions—he felt powerless to impose his will over the project. Tesler faced a thorny political problem, too: Tchao and Sculley were friends, and Tchao had convinced Sculley that Junior was the way to go. Not surprisingly, then, Tesler was moved out of control of Newton in the summer of 1992, after his Senior project imploded as a result of the defection of engineers to Junior. The episode refueled criticism of Tesler within Apple that he lacked the skill to ship a real product.

"Tesler was very much in love with technology but not in touch with the product," says Newton engineer Andy Stadler. By that he means that Tesler expressed far more interest in the neat technological features of Newton than in how that technology could be translated into an affordable product that many customers would want to use. "Somewhere early in my time at Apple, I got a reputation as not being a product guy," Tesler says, in a tone of resignation. "It got to the point where I considered it a joke. I'm a starter type of person. I start divisions and research projects and set things going in the right direction. And since I always start new things, somebody else comes in to clean up."

In July 1992, Spindler and Sculley designated as the new head of Newton a Philips executive named Gaston Bastiaens, who had been heavily involved in the launch of a Philips video-game and entertainment machine called CD-I (Compact Disk Interactive). Bastiaens, as it turned out, would also be the wrong person for the job. It was not for a lack of verve. Apple had had a long string of eccentric personalities going all the way back to cofounder Steve Jobs himself, and Bastiaens fit perfectly into that mold. Bastiaens, age forty-five when he joined Apple, had just spent twenty-one years with Philips, most recently as director of that company's Consumer Electronics division and general manager of its Interactive Media Systems group. In those capacities, he had overseen the worldwide rollout of Philips's CD-I player, which was technically impressive but failed to gain significant sales because it was initially priced at about $1,000.

When he started his job at Apple in September 1992, reporting directly to Spindler, Bastiaens was a sight to behold. Ruggedly featured with thick black hair piled high in an impressive perm, he wore silk jackets of so many different colors that some engineers put a "colorimeter" in the lobby each morning, with a little arrow pointing to the particular outlandish color (such as purple) they predicted he would wear that day. Bastiaens even exuded the same arrogance as Gassée. He didn't walk, he strutted, head held high. And like Gassée, the man worked incessantly, calling 7 A.M. and 7 P.M. staff meetings.

But Bastiaens was moving fast—too fast. "One night at seven, Gaston came into my office and said he needed a five-year Newton plan ready by the next morning," recalls Bob Saltmarsh, who had been transferred from his duties as Apple's treasurer to serve as vice president for finance of the PIE division. "I did it off the top of my head. Gaston ran off and showed it to Sculley. They were all giddy. The next thing you know, it was in AT&T's office. It had taken me only four hours. Gaston was like a kid in a candy store with unlimited resources." In other words, Bastiaens had been given carte blanche by Spindler and Sculley to do essentially whatever he wanted to get Newton out, and he spent money as lavishly as Gassée ever had.

Initially, Bastiaens provided sorely needed direction and leadership for the Newton team, which under Tesler had been fractured. He moved quickly, for example, to kill off the $1,500 Senior tablet to focus Apple's resources around the more marketable Newton Junior prototype for under $1,000. Then, seeing that Junior lacked any communications features that would make it more appealing, he ordered a scheduled January 1993 launch of the product postponed until the following August so it could be redesigned to include one-way paging capability.

"The first guy who said Newton wasn't ready was me," Bastiaens says. "The ultimate goal for us was to bring out a two-way wireless communications product, but that was going to take a couple of more years." Bastiaens insisted on emphasizing the communications ability of the Newton, because it was clear to him that the handwriting recognition that had drawn so much industry attention was nowhere close to perfection. By so doing, he hoped to lessen the hype that Sculley had built around Newton.

Bastiaens was decisive on other fronts, too. The business plan for the Newton, for example, called for Apple to license the technology to other vendors for manufacture. However, licensing had been such a controversial issue in the Macintosh's whole history that the manager in charge of Newton licensing, Subrah Iyar, remembers getting little support to pursue deals until Bastiaens entered the picture.

"When I got onto the Newton team under Tesler in 1992, no one had done analysis on licensing Newton," recalls Iyar, who left Apple in 1995 to become CEO of Stellar Computing Inc., a software maker based in Sunnyvale, California. "I would say, 'Should I go after Motorola?' and they would pooh-pooh it. But Gaston is a doer, and he supported the hell out of it." With Bastiaens's unequivocal support, Iyar went out to sign up about ten licensees to manufacture the devices, including Japan's Matsushita Electric Industrial Company and Germany's Siemens AG.

Sculley had originally recruited Bastiaens to Apple for the Belgian's experience at Philips in consumer electronics and getting products to market quickly. With that consumer-centric view of the world, Bastiaens also set into motion a plan by Apple to follow up the launch of the first Newton product with another, improved one only a few months later. This strategy was challenged by some members of the Newton team, who were accustomed to the Apple tradition of launching a great product and then waiting years to follow up. Bastiaens ignored the naysayers, though, and gave Phil Baker, manager of Newton's hardware engineering, the green light to develop a second Newton.

"Gaston gave me authority to just do my plan," recalls Baker, who left Apple in 1995 to become an industry consultant based in San Diego. "He certainly motivated me, and I felt very good working for him."

The Bastiaens fan club was not very big within the Newton team, however. Newton managers and engineers grew to loathe him for what they considered his unwillingness to deviate from a course, no matter how ill advised it appeared to be. An example of this was Bastiaens's refusal to heed warnings that the Newton was being directed to the wrong market. The warnings came from outside Apple as well as inside. Outside consultants had been retained by Apple to gauge just how much customer demand for this new kind of computer really was out there. One was Mark Macgillivray, an independent consultant based in Sunnyvale, California, in the heart of Silicon Valley. Macgillivray had conducted hundreds of interviews with people in Europe, Japan, and the United States on their interest in a handheld computer.

"They all said, 'Great idea. We will use it in selected markets,'" Macgillivray remembers. A selected market meant a so-called "vertical" market, such as a hospital, where all the nurses and doctors tote around PDAs as they check up on patients, or a shipping company, whose delivery drivers can send updates into the home office via a PDA. What it did *not* mean was the mass consumer market, and this was a point that Macgillivray tried to drive home to Apple. "We told middle managers, but there was a lot of aversion to telling Sculley that this ubiquitous device would not work as planned," Macgillivray says. "It was almost like telling the emperor he is not wearing clothes."

Bastiaens denies he was single-mindedly focused on the consumer market, as evidenced, he says, by the fact that the Newton technology had gained some fifty software applications for more narrowly targeted corporate markets such as hospitals and trucking fleets. In any event, it was Sculley, not Bastiaens, who first targeted Newton at the consumer market. Bastiaens, however, was unwilling to modify the plan even when it became clear to others it was wrong.

Another warning came from Newton's own product manager. In the late spring of 1993, Junior had evolved into a sleek little black box called the Newton MessagePad, and a big launch was scheduled for August 2 that year at the

Macworld Expo trade show in steamy Boston. Macworld Boston, like Macworld San Francisco in January, is a major conference held every year for Apple's customers, suppliers, and developers. The Boston event is targeted more toward Apple's East Coast following, whereas the one in San Francisco is aimed for the one on the West Coast. Michael Tchao, the Newton product manager, was worried. The handwriting recognition feature was not working at all well. You could write in, say, "Meet me for lunch today," and Newton would translate that into something like "Meat me far launch toenail." Sometimes it worked. But many times it did not.

Just to confirm his fears, Tchao ordered an in-house audit—an internal test of a new product—to review whether all of the Newton MessagePad's functions worked well enough for the machine to ship. A dozen people from marketing and engineering put the computer through its paces, and they, too, uncovered serious problems with the handwriting system, as well as with other features. "But Gaston came in at the end of the day and said, 'So, do we have a product that is ready to ship?' " Tchao remembers. "I said, 'If we ship this product now, we will have a lot of quality problems,' to which Gaston replied, 'If you don't think we can ship this product, I will find a marketing person who will say we can.' He was very upset."

Bastiaens angrily denies this exchange ever took place, calling Tchao a "brilliant young kid" and his story "total bullshit." Bastiaens says there was no need to call a special audit, because the product was being evaluated on a weekly basis and was the subject of daily meetings between engineers. If anything, Bastiaens counters, he toned down a product launch plan that he considered overly aggressive. Whereas that plan called for Newton to be rolled out in several countries around the world, with an ambitious production schedule, Bastiaens says he curtailed it to just computer retail stores in the United States and limited production.

Tchao maintains, though, that he and other members of the Newton marketing team argued, to no avail, that Apple limit the rollout even more, to a few selected cities in foreign countries such as Australia and Canada, so the bugs could be worked out before the Newton hit the United States. "But the entire corporation was under a lot of pressure to say, 'This is the future,' " Tchao says. "Mac sales were declining in growth, and the hype around Newton was destined to jump-start an industry." And besides, Apple had spent approximately $500 million on Newton since the project was begun in 1987. It was time to get some return on the investment.

There was no turning back now, yet even some members of top management were feeling dread. Before he got the boot, Al Eisenstat warned Sculley and Spindler to hold off on the launch. Ironically, it had been Eisenstat who had spirited the handwriting recognition software from a Russian programmer he had met in the middle of the night in Moscow to help the Apple engineers in Cupertino. "I went on record as saying I had my reservations with the product," Eisenstat says. "I had real doubts the handwriting recognition was going to be functionally useful."

Bastiaens, too, knew the handwriting was not up to snuff, and he fully expected some criticism of the Newton's crude features. But, he adds, Apple's aim was to help create an entire new industry over time. "You have to do a step-by-step development like the Japanese do," he says. "It's like Sony and the camcorder market. It took them four years to build a market. The people in Apple didn't have a clue about consumer marketing. You need to build a presence."

All the warnings had been duly registered and ignored. Apple's PR department worked overtime, burying the business press with Newton packets the size of a phone book. The launch was all set for the Boston Macworld show. The usual laundry list of software developers supporting the technology, such as Aldus Corporation, Oracle Corporation, and Apple's own Claris Corporation, was trotted out, along with canned quotes from some big-name corporate customers expressing their excitement about the new technology. And the launch proceeded, on schedule, with thousands of the devices sold from the booths of Apple distributors at Macworld.

This early, enthusiastic showing was no indication of how the Newton would do in the real world, however, because Macworld is attended by gadget fanatics who will snap up anything with Apple's familiar rainbow-hued logo. When the intended customer audience started actually using the Newton MessagePad days later, the PR nightmare began. Sure enough, customers were complaining like crazy about the handwriting system. "How could a company with smart people, nifty technology and born-again followers in the marketplace make such a mess of things?" *The Economist* wondered in its August 28, 1993, issue, in lamenting Newton and Apple's overall decline.

Newton was so bad it was even lampooned by cartoonist Garry Trudeau in a week-long series of his *Doonesbury* strips, beginning on August 23, 1993. In one, a woman tells her husband holding what appears to be a MessagePad, "Mike, we can't afford another expensive toy." Mike replies, "It's not a toy, J.J. It's a digital assistant, an indispensable desktop tool of the future. In addition to keeping addresses, dates, etc., it also can read handwriting. Watch this." Then Mike uses his electronic pen to write the message "Hello, J.J., how are you?" The screen, however, displays this gibberish: "Hell jars, howard yoyo?" J.J., with arms folded, then asks, "First generation, is it?" as Mike replies sheepishly, "Hold it. Let me check the manual."

Press reviews were equally savage, and not only on the handwriting. "It's increasingly clear that the rollout of the MessagePad was several months premature," opined a September 13, 1993, editorial in the trade magazine

MacWEEK. "Most important, the MessagePad was released without being subjected to the kind of shakedown that only customer testing can provide. Even a minimal beta-test program would have averted such embarrassments as a Getting Started card that wouldn't start and an alarm clock that couldn't tell time." And in his "Computer Letter," published on October 4, 1993, industry consultant Richard Shaffer added, "As a digital assistant, the MessagePad is sometimes more like a jester than a butler. It does offer hints of the help that mobile machine intelligence might one day provide, but for now, Newton's IQ is low."

Michael Tchao and Al Eisenstat had been dead right. Mark Macgillivray's warning that the consumer market was all wrong for Newton was also about to be proven true.

Selling for a base price of $700, the MessagePad was far too expensive to sell to many people other than computer enthusiasts, the so-called early adopters who will buy any new circuitry. Even at that price, the device was woefully lacking in the features that could have made it compelling, especially communications. When it shipped, the MessagePad could receive only pager messages and otherwise was able to communicate only when it was hooked into a standard telephone line—just like a laptop computer.

Still, Bastiaens could not see the handwriting on the wall. In the weeks after the launch, he called his staff together and asked each one to go out to a retail store in the San Francisco area and assist the clerks in demonstrating MessagePads. Over the next two nights, Bob Saltmarsh camped out at the Good Guys! store in San Francisco's Stonestown Galleria. What he witnessed did not bode well for Newton or Apple.

"The Newton was hidden away in the calculator section, and the sales staff had no interest in promoting it, because it took too long to explain what it did," Saltmarsh recalls. "So I went back and told Gaston and his team that we were going after entirely the wrong market. I said, 'This is a vertical, niche market product that would sell well to insurance adjusters.' Gaston said, 'No, no, no. You're wrong. You have to work harder.' "

Bastiaens says he does not remember such an exchange.

On January 5, 1994, Saltmarsh was attending Apple's rollout of its new on-line service, eWorld, at the Hotel Nikko in San Francisco's Union Square shopping district. Michael Spindler was also on hand, and, during a break in the speeches and product demos, he pulled Saltmarsh aside and asked him how things were going in PIE. Saltmarsh took a deep breath and told his CEO the truth. "I told him that we were unfocused and that the Newton was aimed at the wrong market. I also said, 'Michael, Gaston is driving us crazy,' " Saltmarsh says. "Michael's eyes narrowed, and he listened. When he listened, you knew he believed you."

One week later, at an executive staff meeting back at De Anza 7, Bastiaens was standing up touting the Newton sales when Spindler broke in to repeat the criticism he had heard from Saltmarsh. "Gaston barked back at him that he was wrong," recalls Saltmarsh, who was in the room along with twenty-five other top executives. Another executive present confirmed the exchange: "Michael backed down." Bastiaens denies upbraiding the boss in such a manner, saying, "I'm too polite. I do remember many times in which we debated strategy."

Bastiaens's fate was sealed, however, when the sales numbers came in for the Christmas season, and they, in fact, proved horrible. In the five and a half months since the MessagePad had been launched, Bastiaens announced in mid-January, Apple had sold only about 80,000 of the little computers. Worse still was the fact that Apple had sold only 30,000 of the MessagePads since mid-September 1993, when the company had last provided a sales total of 50,000. That meant Newton had gone from 50,000 sales in just over one month, mostly to early adopters, to an average of 7,500 per month during the Christmas season. And since industry analysts had set a target of several hundred thousand initial sales to ensure a hit, the results confirmed that Newton had flopped badly.

"It dropped with a thud on the market," said John J. Girton, vice president of research for the securities firm of Van Kasper & Company.[1] In an interview session at the San Francisco offices of *The Wall Street Journal* later that year, Microsoft's Bill Gates summed up the Newton saga succinctly: "Newton has set the whole category of PDAs back by two years."

By April 1994, with Sculley no longer around to support him and Spindler intent on slashing Apple's financial support for Newton, Bastiaens left the company to "set up his own business activities," according to a company press release. "For me, it was clear I had to go," recalls Bastiaens, who is now president of Lernout Hauspie Speech Products, a software maker based in Boston and Wemmel, Belgium. "Nobody had to tell me." There were many on the Newton team who exulted in his departure, but also a few who mourned. "To some extent, you could say Gaston was reckless," recalls Iyar. "But he really, really wanted to make Newton succeed. He gave his heart and soul to the project."

Newton would drift on for one more year, eventually being pulled out of the consumer market and targeted at the corporate, "vertical" markets where it had belonged all along. Later versions of the MessagePad corrected the initial flaws. Indeed, as of mid-1997, the MessagePad had evolved into a useful, reliable device that was beginning to attain acceptance in the market, although not to the extent that John Sculley had once envisioned.

With the Newton fiasco, the Sculley ouster, and the financial beating Apple was taking in 1993, 1994 was shaping up to be a make-or-break year for the company. It would be up to Commander Ian Diery and his PC battalion to lead the company through a perilous transition to a new line of Macintoshes running on the new PowerPC chips being developed as part of the 1991 alliance among Apple, IBM, and Motorola. In a much-publicized period of transition, Spindler was literally betting the company that sales of the new Power Mac would take off fast enough to carry Apple over the bridge between the past and the future. It would turn out to be one rickety bridge indeed.

11

The March to PowerPC

The date was December 7, 1993, the forty-second anniversary of the bombing of Pearl Harbor. A Silicon Valley crowd wearing everything from suits and wing tips to jeans and sneakers had filed into a ballroom of the Hyatt Regency hotel in the San Francisco suburb of Burlingame to hear a debate called "Can Apple Computer Survive as an Independent Company?" Worried that Apple was slipping into irrelevancy, Richard Shaffer, principal of the well-respected industry consulting firm Technologic Partners, had staged the event at his annual Personal Computer Outlook forum. Moderating the debate, he took the podium to explain the rules.

Two-person teams from opposing coasts would represent the affirmative and negative sides in four seven-minute sessions, followed by rebuttals, in the classic Oxford style of debate. Since each team had been asked to prepare for both sides of the debate, neither knew which would defend Apple until Shaffer flipped a coin to determine that it would be the West Coast pair of venture capitalists Roger McNamee and John Doerr. Arguing against Apple would be the East Coast team of industry consultants Andrew Rappaport and Charles Ferguson. The four men bounded onstage to take seats at their respective tables, as Shaffer, looking distinguished in his silver hair and dark suit, ripped off his jacket and donned a striped referee's shirt to cheers of approval from the audience of some four hundred high-level industry executives.

Starting first was McNamee, general partner of Integral Capital Partners in Menlo Park, California, who drew loud applause when he held up a large cardboard poster with a giant "thumbs-up" symbol drawn on it. The "thumbs-up" and "thumbs-down" signs had also been given by Shaffer to a panel of seven judges, seated together nearby onstage, consisting of analysts, stock investors, and one technologist. Pointing out Apple's enormous base of 11 million Macintosh customers as well as the company's cash on hand of $800 million and almost no debt, McNamee assured the audience, "Not only can it survive, it *will* survive. It will prosper."

Then McNamee called attention to one of the most-watched events in the computer industry at that time: the coming of PowerPC, the ace in the hole for Apple's new CEO, Michael Spindler. Apple's launch date for its first Power Macintoshes was set for March 14, 1994. "Within a hundred and twenty days," he said, "Apple will be shipping PowerPC. PowerPC is faster than Intel at one third the price."

During their turn, Rappaport and Ferguson ticked off a litany of Apple's woes: tiny market share, limited R and D with which to compete against so many rivals, a diminished lead in the Mac's software and performance, and a monstrous challenge in getting its developers to follow it to PowerPC. "In conclusion," said Ferguson, leaning into the microphone for emphasis, "I think that we have to say we are looking at a company which is living on its past and has a very desperate and difficult future ahead of it."

When the votes of the judges were tallied, the result was close. Four had held up "thumbs-up" signs, while three had turned thumbs-down. The results matched the sentiment of the overall industry almost perfectly: Apple still had a chance, but the clock was ticking.

Just two years earlier, Apple's John Scullcy and IBM's Jack Kuehler had stood on stage at the Fairmont Hotel in San Francisco, hands clasped together in a victory salute over an alliance between the world's two biggest PC companies. Together, they could be invincible, many analysts at the time had thought. And together, along with their third partner, Motorola, they had spent many months since then incubating the new microprocessor chip called PowerPC in the hope of turning the computer industry—and Bill Gates—on its head. But now Sculley was gone, and Kuehler had retired. It would be up to Michael Spindler to lead the PowerPC charge.

The importance of PowerPC to Apple at this time cannot be understated, nor the risk the company faced as it embarked on switching its entire line of Macintoshes over to this new technology. To understand what a gamble this was for Apple, consider again very briefly the disaster of the Newton.

In the computer industry, new technologies are usually trotted out with the full expectation that it may take years for them to catch on in the mass market. Indeed, that had been Apple engineer Steve Sakoman's original goal with the Newton computer, to test-market it to the nerdy types who will buy anything and do not mind dealing with the inevitable glitches of a new product. After these "early adopters," the machine would be fine-tuned enough to target the business market. And after manufacturing volume had built up sufficiently with these new customers, prices could be lowered enough to finally reach the mass consumer audience. Of course, Sakoman's plan had gone out the window when he had left Apple in 1990 and Sculley had aimed Newton dead-on at the consumer market.

Now consider PowerPC. Unlike Newton, the PowerPC chip was not an entirely unproven technology. The concept of a microprocessor that could perform functions at blazing speed, while using far fewer transistors than conventional microprocessors, had been successfully pioneered by Sun Microsystems in its fast-selling line of computer workstations. But PowerPC was a brand-new chip based on this technology, and as such there was no guarantee it would work as well as advertised. Complicating the problem further was the fact that Apple faced having to redesign its computer hardware and software so the new Power Macintoshes could run not only new software programs but all the old ones used by the millions of loyal Apple customers.

Apple was walking a tightrope. And there was almost no room for error.

But Michael Spindler, and John Sculley before him, had concluded that Apple really had no choice but to set out on this path. As indicated before, Microsoft's Windows operating system was fast erasing the Macintosh's lead in operating software. That was the battle of the operating system. Down in the guts of the computer, though, another battle was brewing on a piece of electronics circuitry about the size of a silver dollar. This was the microprocessor, and it was a battle that Apple was losing. The Macintosh, to this point in 1993, had been fueled by Motorola's family of chips called the 68000. But the 68000 was an old chip dating to the early 1980s that was running out of steam. Intel, on the other hand, was churning out faster and faster chips based on its 8086 technology, which dominated the PC industry.

If Apple didn't do something, and fast, the Intel-based PCs would so far outpace the Macintosh in performance that even Apple's most loyal customers would have to consider jumping ship to the Intel side. So, while the Power Mac was a huge gamble for Apple, the company really had no choice, especially since it had closed off the option of rewriting the Mac operating system so it could run on Intel computers, as embodied in the doomed Star Trek project. In so doing, Apple had drawn a line in the sand: Apple and PowerPC on one side, Microsoft and Intel on the other. No compromise. No surrender. It was admirable bravery, but on the other hand Apple's position was not strategically so unlike the hopelessly outnumbered Texans at the Battle of the Alamo. They surely would have embraced PowerPC, too, had it enhanced their firepower against the Mexican army.

And in strategic terms, the Power Mac promised to be a formidable weapon indeed. Although Microsoft was encroaching on the Mac's superior software technology, Apple's computers still remained far easier to use than the ones based around the Wintel standard. If Apple could cling to that lead, the PowerPC microprocessor would make the Mac even faster than the competition. Apple would therefore have two powerful marketing arguments: superior ease of use *and* greater power. Not only could the Power Mac keep Apple's loyal customers from abandoning the Macintosh platform, it also held the potential of attracting new converts from the ranks of undecided computer users known in the industry as "fence-sitters." These were the people who had never used a computer before and were considered fair game by both the Apple and Microsoft camps.

In technical terms, this battle was pitched as a war between RISC and CISC. RISC was PowerPC's reduced instruction set computing technology, which enables a microprocessor to be more efficient by carrying only those instructions that are most commonly used. CISC was the complex instruction set computing technology, which required engineers to keep adding more and more transistors to make each new generation of chip faster. This was the technology used by industry leader Intel, as well as in Motorola's 68000 line, and was the basis for the chips that ran Microsoft Windows. Theoretically, then, RISC could go on forever, while CISC would soon topple under its own weight. Intel argued vehemently that it could pack a lot more punch into its CISC chips, and was by no means sitting on its market lead. A high-tech war of words was on.

The heart and soul of the PowerPC project was a three-story office building with large, tinted windows called Somerset, nestled in the hills above Austin, Texas, where the fragrant scent of abundant cedar trees fills the air. Both IBM and its chip partner, Motorola, had long based much of their microprocessor research work in Austin, a laid-back college town known in Texas for being so liberal, by the standards of the conservative Lone Star State, that nude sunbathing was permitted in a section of nearby Lake Travis. Austin had also become a hotbed of technical activity, with computer companies moving manufacturing, service, and some research operations there during the 1980s and early 1990s to take advantage of the low cost of labor and a plethora of young engineering talent being spawned in the corridors of the University of Texas.

It was into this intellectually fertile environment that IBM, Motorola, and Apple decided to situate PowerPC on the neutral turf of Somerset, which the companies converted into a research lab from its former use as offices of a hospital management company. To further blur all corporate barriers, dress codes were thrown out and working hours would be whenever an engineer wanted, day or night. Impromptu volleyball games could be played on a sand court built right outside the front entrance. The vast majority of the 340 employees were from IBM and Motorola, since those companies were bringing to the table their world-class prowess in microprocessor research.

"We have badges that show a logo of the state of Texas, with the IBM and Motorola insignias, so you can't tell who you work for," Russell Stanphill, a Motorola engineering manager who directed Somerset, said then.[1] Although Apple had contributed six engineers to the project, its primary role in this endeavor was to act as PowerPC's first big customer.

Somerset began operation during March of 1992, and it did not have a moment to lose. In announcing the big alliance the previous September, John Sculley had told the press he wanted the PowerPC chips to be running on a new line of Apple computers by the first half of 1994. Much of the formative work had already been done by IBM, since PowerPC was based on Big Blue's Power technology for larger computers. Here at Somerset, the engineers had to make that technology scale down to work on personal computers, and they needed to provide a pathway to ever-faster microprocessors.

So the engineers split into teams. The first and most important was for the development of the PowerPC 601 chip. This would be the first PowerPC out of the gate and the one that Apple would rely upon as it underwent its first year of transition from older Macintoshes. The other engineers were divided into teams for the successive generations of chips that would be rolled out over an eighteen-month period following Apple's 1994 launch. There was the PowerPC 603, a lower-powered chip designed for laptops and other portable computers; the PowerPC 604, which would feature far more power than the 601; and the PowerPC 620, aimed at PC servers, workstations, and super-computers. This approach would enable Apple, and its PowerPC allies, to appeal to the entire spectrum of computing platforms—from individual laptop and desktop PCs to interlinked work groups in large companies.

With corporate rivalries between the team members largely tamed, the Somerset engineers stoked their competitive juices by taking dead aim at Intel, the chip behemoth in Santa Clara, California, 1,800 miles to the west. Just like Microsoft's, Intel's domination over the PC market was growing stronger year after year. By 1993, when Somerset kicked into high gear, Intel's share of global microprocessor revenues stood at a staggering 74 percent, up from 69 percent the year before. Motorola was a distant second, with 8 percent, and IBM's microprocessor sales were a miniscule 1 percent.[2]

The David-versus-Goliath nature of the battle did not deter the high spirits at Somerset, nor the swagger. One evening during the project, Russell Stanphill took the PowerPC 604 team out to celebrate the completion of one technical milestone at a popular night spot called Esther's Follies, located in Austin's Sixth Street club district. The engineers performed an amusing skit onstage, pitting a mock PowerPC battleship against the good ship *Intel*. "Our battleship sank their battleship in one shot," Stanphill recalled some months afterward. "The entire room applauded." Asked about that skit later, Paul Otellini, an Intel senior vice president, shot back with a smile, "They forgot about our submarines."[3]

Back in Cupertino, there was another David-versus-Goliath battle raging. Only it was between two tiny engineering teams that would provide the technological breakthroughs needed to make the PowerPC work on a Mac and giant engineering groups that mostly spun their wheels. The results would demonstrate, again, how Apple's biggest successes were accomplished by small groups and its biggest failure by grandiose ones.

Shortly after the PowerPC alliance was announced in 1991, top executives of Apple's engineering organization convened to set work schedules for getting the new Macintoshes developed. During one such meeting on Apple's R-and-D campus, in early 1992, Fred Forsyth, the head of manufacturing and hardware engineering, told a group of software engineers that his hardware team was shooting for a launch date of January 24, 1994, to mark the tenth anniversary of the launch of the original Macintosh. He asked when they could be ready. "They said, 'October 1994,' " Forsyth remembers.

That, of course, was unacceptable, so Forsyth pressed for more urgency. The software engineers performed some quick calculations and told him they could be finished by July 1994. Working with Roger Heinen, the head of Apple's software engineering, Forsyth got the engineers to adhere to a more aggressive schedule than that. In fact, he convinced them to work toward two schedules: an aggressive internal one, of January 24, 1994, and a more realistic external one—publicized outside the company—of March 14, 1994. That way, Apple could let the first goal slip to March without the rest of the world finding out. With the two schedules in place, it was then left to the engineers in the trenches to come up with a working Power Macintosh. Luckily for Apple, the work had already started.

Apple's movement to a RISC chip from Motorola's aging 68000 series of microprocessors had begun in 1989, with the ill-fated Jaguar project that was intended to completely replace the Macintosh. After Jaguar was killed under heavy criticism from engineers working on Apple's mainstream 68000 line of Macs, a new RISC effort began under the code name Hurricane, which, unlike Jaguar, would be compatible with the Mac. HURRICANE: PREPARE TO BE BLOWN AWAY, read T-shirts circulated among the Hurricane engineers. By 1991, Hurricane had evolved into a new project called "Tesseract."

That was a code name only an engineer could love, for a tesseract, according to Funk and Wagnalls Dictionary, is "a construct intended to illustrate graphically or in the form of a model the general appearance of a four-dimensional figure." The Apple engineers indeed had great fun with their code names, but they occasionally ran into trouble with them. During the PowerPC effort, for example, some engineers in 1993 code-named one of the new computers "Carl Sagan"—and butted heads with the famous astronomer Carl Sagan, a Cornell University professor who has since died.

After Sagan learned of this through the trade magazine MacWEEK in November 1993, his attorneys warned Apple that this was an illegal use of his name for commercial purposes. The engineers obligingly changed the code name to "BHA," which Sagan took to stand for "Butt-head Astronomer."

Apple insisted that the letters were random. Sagan filed a defamation suit in U.S. District Court in Los Angeles against Apple, lost at trial, and then appealed. The two sides ended up settling the dispute out of court, with terms undisclosed. Instructed by Apple's legal department after this to change the code name to something inoffensive, the ever-mischievous engineers settled on LAW, which might be interpreted as Lawyers Are Wimps.

Tesseract's basic mission was to build a new Mac, running on a RISC chip, which would sell for about $4,500 to Apple's high-end customers. With John Sculley's new emphasis on low-end machines as of 1990, some engineers took it upon themselves to start a project aimed at the same kind of machine at the bottom of the market. The idea for this actually came one cold night in March 1990 at the Northstar-at-Tahoe ski resort in California's Sierra Nevada mountains, as a group of Apple engineers huddled inside a lodge around a roaring fire after a day of skiing. The engineers had just completed development of the 40-megahertz Macintosh IIFX, which was then touted as the fastest personal computer in existence. Sales never took off for that machine, though, because it was priced at $10,000.

"We were sitting around that night trying to figure out what to do next," recalls one of the engineers, Jon Fitch, who resembles Robert Redford with his wavy, light brown hair. As Fitch remembers, he and the other engineers wanted to try the RISC approach, but on an inexpensive machine of under $2,000 that they hoped would sell better than the IIFX. Product volume, they believed, would be the true key to the success of Apple's impending transition to Macs powered by the RISC microprocessors.

Upon returning to Cupertino, those engineers started a project they called "PDM," after the notorious Piltdown man hoax of 1912 in which amateur naturalist Charles Dawson claimed to have discovered the fossilized bones and tools "of the long-sought missing link between the apes and humans in the evolutionary chain."[4] Piltdown, named for the supposed discovery at Piltdown in southern England, was proven a hoax forty years later upon closer examination of the fossilized remains, but for Apple's purposes PDM signified the "missing link" between the existing Mac and future ones. But PDM was assigned much lower emphasis in R and D, resulting in a core group of engineers that eventually numbered just eight—Keith Cox, Gary Davidian, Fitch, Carl Hewitt, Bob Hollyer, Jack McHenry, Steve Smith, and Jimmy Wong—compared to a hundred at the peak of Tesseract. They were the "B" team, the backups who were not expected even to start the game—but who would come in to lead it.

Much of this work was happening on the hardware side of Apple. Equally critical to PowerPC's success was redesigning the Mac's finicky software so it would be able to support the new microprocessor. After the IBM alliance was signed in 1991, Apple recruited a part-time computer science professor named Philip Koch to assemble a team of software engineers to make that happen. A personable and highly articulate engineer, Koch was working at Dartmouth at the time and confided to friends that he had grown bored with the esoteric routine of academia. He wanted to get back out into the real world and practice what he was preaching. The world he encountered in Cupertino was, if anything, more surreal.

At the time Koch joined Apple, in December 1991, software development was already a full-blown mess. There was Blue, with its 160 engineers plodding toward a System 7 upgrade that would hardly be worth the four years of effort. And there was Pink, the intended replacement for the whole Macintosh operating system, which had become such an albatross that Apple was in the process of jettisoning it into the joint Taligent venture with IBM. Taligent's goal, too, was to produce a brand-new operating system, but for the Mac as well as IBM's PowerPC computers. Koch, in fact, vowed to use Pink as a lesson in how *not* to approach the PowerPC project.

There were basically two ways of tackling the issue of software. The first was to redesign the Mac's operating system from the ground up, so that it would correct all the shortcomings of System 7 and run entirely "native," or completely intertwined with the PowerPC chip. The advantage to the user from this approach would be that every single piece of software code would be designed specifically for PowerPC, resulting in a dramatic increase in the speed and performance of software programs. But rewriting an operating system is quite a mean feat, as the Pink team had found, and Koch certainly did not think his team could get it done in time for Apple's PowerPC launch in 1994. The other problem in doing a total rewrite, he figured, was that it would make it really hard for the new Macs to be able to run all the old Mac programs. In techie parlance, this is called "backward compatibility," and without it a company runs the risk of customers opting not to make the switch and junk all their old files.

So in consultations with Sheila Brady, who was helping to oversee system software, and Jack McHenry, who was project manager of PDM, Koch settled on a safer—but surer—way out. Why not, he thought, just tweak the Mac's operating system so enough of it could run "native" on PowerPC for the user to see performance gains, while also making sure it could still run all the old programs? The approach was essentially designed to "fool" the Mac into thinking it was still running on the old 68000 chips when, in fact, it wasn't. This strategy relied on what software engineers called the "90/10" rule: in most programs, 90 percent of the computer's time is spent executing just 10 percent of the code. The vast bulk of the program is rarely executed, and thus speed is not critical for that part. The idea was to identify and recode for PowerPC only the critical 10 percent of the system. The other 90 percent would remain in the old 68000 code.

With the strategy decided, the next thing to do was put a team together. The one criterion Koch wanted to adhere to, above all else, was that it be kept small. He ended up in a building called Mariani 1, with a group of twenty handpicked engineers ready to start work on a project that began life under the code name "Cherokee" but evolved to adopt the names "Rock-and-Roll" and finally "Psychic TV," after a rock group by that name. Rock-and-Roll became the code name for the entire Power Macintosh project, including the hardware and software parts of it.

Psychic TV had a lot in common with PDM. Both were tiny teams by Apple standards, and both were accorded second-class status within the engineering hierarchy. "It was widely believed among the engineers that PowerPC would be a death march that would be doomed to fail," recalls one engineer closely involved with Psychic TV. "Many engineers believed it impossible to port [move] Macintosh to PowerPC." While this may have been the case down in the trenches, that sentiment certainly was not shared by engineering management. "Our number one priority was to be there for PowerPC with system software," says Rick Spitz, then vice president for system software.

Few software engineers wanted anything to do with PowerPC, and that was just fine by the Psychic TV bunch. "Initially, Apple just left us alone," says the engineer, who spoke on condition of anonymity because he still worked at Apple when interviewed. "We knew we were going to save Apple, so we worked our butts off."

Any doubts about PowerPC would be erased, however, when a bearded man in T-shirt and jeans named Gary Davidian accomplished the seemingly impossible. Davidian, a brilliant software engineer, was working on both the software and hardware elements of PowerPC. As much as anyone else, he epitomized the Apple culture of renegade "cowboy" engineers such as Macintosh programming wizard Andy Hertzfeld and QuickTime guru Bruce Leak, who would work all night to single-handedly produce the kind of technical breakthroughs for which Apple had become famous. The cowboy ethos did not work on huge projects, because there were too many cowboys. But it did on small ones, such as Psychic TV and PDM.

Before he could achieve his breakthrough, Davidian collaborated with several other Psychic TV engineers—Bruce Jones, Allan Lillich, Jean-Charles Mourey, and Eric Traut—in developing a crucial piece of software that allowed the 10 percent of the operating system that needed to be rewritten for PowerPC to be altered without affecting the rest of the system. This was, essentially, a layer of glue called "mixed mode," because it allowed the seamless mix of code written in the two modes: "native," or rewritten for PowerPC, and "emulated," or the process of making software written for one microprocessor operate on another microprocessor with little visible degradation in performance. Without mixed mode, the operating system would never achieve the performance potential of PowerPC.

The next hurdle was the biggest, though, because it involved that little matter of "backward compatibility." Here is where the parallel courses of Psychic TV and PDM intersected at a crucial juncture. PDM, remember, was that little team assigned the grunt work of designing a dirt-cheap PowerPC machine that almost nobody else in engineering cared one whit about. The team's morale was not helped any by an October 1991 visit to their small lab — called "The Lab" — by Michael Spindler, still Apple's president and chief operating officer at that time. Bob Hollyer remembers the group showing the big boss a RISC demo and trying to explain to him just what they were up to.

"Spindler was listening with his eyes glazed over," Hollyer recalls. "And then he would start talking about enterprise computing. It became painfully obvious that Spindler didn't have a clue. He said, 'This is it? This is RISC?' We were continuously attempting to translate the key technical details into a format understandable by Spindler." John Sculley, for all his faults, would later demonstrate that he did have a clue, at least in this regard.

One day just before Christmas of 1991, the phone rang in "The Lab." The call was from an engineer down in Somerset, advising the PDMers that Big Blue planned to deliver its first working PowerPC chip to them on September 6, 1992. The PDMers did not take that delivery schedule seriously, at first. "Based on our prior experience with Motorola chip schedules [which were often delayed], we were skeptical that IBM could deliver a fully functional microprocessor by that date," recalls Hollyer, a tall, thin, bearded man. Over the course of the ensuing months, however, the engineers at Somerset kept calling with updates on their PowerPC development. To the surprise — and increasing anxiety — of the PDMers, IBM was hitting every milestone right on target. That meant the PDMers were going to have to kick their work into even higher gear.

By the summer of 1992, the Mixed Mode Manager was done on the software side and the PDM crew was closing in on the design of its little machine. Tesseract was lumbering along, pretty much oblivious to PDM. One day in July, Spindler came over to PDM for another demo. "Through the whole meeting, Spindler looked like he was going to fall asleep," recalls Carl Hewitt, a blond-haired young man with glasses and a mirthful personality. "At the end of the meeting, Spindler got up and started rambling about enterprise computing. He still had no idea what we were doing."

Meanwhile, Davidian had borrowed another RISC chip from IBM to play around with in trying to get the PDM Mac to run all older Macintosh programs in the mode called "emulation," which allowed the 90 percent of system software code not rewritten for PowerPC to continue running as it had on the Motorola 68000 microprocessor. Apple had to have emulation to achieve the backward-compatibility features that Philip Koch had decided the Power Mac must include. "By August 31 [1992], I had the Mac up and running in emulation, but it was very unstable," Davidian recalls.

Six days later, on September 6, a package arrived in the mail, and lo and behold, it was IBM's first working PowerPC chip, exactly on time, as promised—to the amazement of the PDMers. With Tesseract running three months behind PDM in its schedule, it was up to the "B" team to run with the ball. Suddenly, senior management sat up and took notice. If the team could show a working version of a Mac with PowerPC by October, Eric Harslem, the vice president in charge of hardware R and D, promised they could all fly out to Hawaii during that month to demonstrate it before a scheduled sales meeting of Apple's Pacific region.

Working night and day for three weeks, Davidian and his colleagues finally got the job done at 5 A.M. on a Sunday. It was a watershed moment in the history of Apple Computer, for here at long last was a working computer that could take the Macintosh into the promised bright future of the PowerPC's RISC technology. A few days later, John Sculley walked into "The Lab" as part of his frequent visits to the engineering groups as chief technology officer following Jean-Louis Gassée's departure in 1990. "He says, 'So this is Tesseract?'" Hewitt recalls. "We said, 'No, this is PDM.' He said, 'What?'" The engineers, as dubious of Sculley's technical ability as anyone else at Apple, had jokingly prepared a list of questions on a whiteboard for Sculley that they did not really dare ask of their CTO. They included this doozy: "What is the exact sequence of bus activity leading up to a spurious instruction fetch from I/O space?"

Sculley impressed them all, however, with his decisiveness on this day. "Sculley says, 'So how many of these do you think you can have at intro?'" Hewitt recalls. "So we said, 'Thirty to forty thousand.' Sculley said, 'No, we'll need at least a hundred thousand.'"

Suddenly, PDM was in the background no more. It was thrust onto center stage, literally, at the beachside Waikaloa Resort on the Big Island of Hawaii, before four hundred people at the Pacific sales meeting that Harslem had promised they could all attend with a working Power Mac. Even that trip proved to be an ordeal, however. On the five-hour plane ride over from California on October 24, the PDMers tapped furiously at the keys of a Power-Book to finish the code. On October 26, the night before the sales meeting, they set up the world's first Power Mac, ready to put it through its paces the following morning at 9:30 sharp.

"The next morning, at eight-fifteen, we turned on the machine and it was completely dead," Davidian recalls, wincing at the memory. "I called Keith

Cox in his room and said, 'It's dead. Bring everything.' Spindler, then president and COO, was addressing the conference by satellite as the frazzled engineers huddled backstage with their itsy-bitsy screwdrivers, replacing every component in the main circuit board. "It still did not work," Davidian says. "So we put it all back together, and it worked. We didn't know why, and we didn't know how long it would last. When I got there onstage, the first thing I did was wiggle my mouse to see if it worked. When it did, I looked out in relief at Carl and Bob in the audience." The crowd went wild, giving the PDMers a standing ovation.

Subsequently, PDM, not Tesseract, was put in charge of the whole Power Mac engineering effort. With a working Power Mac now in hand, the whole company rallied behind the new machine and the PDM engineering team. The Power Mac engineering team, including both hardware and software, would balloon to some eight hundred engineers. Even Spindler belatedly recognized PDM's importance. Gary Davidian was a hero, as were his friends. You would have thought Apple would have rolled out the red carpet to thank them. Think again.

Slap in the face number one was their treatment in Hawaii. "The people in Tesseract complained we were taking too much money by going to Hawaii, so Jack McHenry told us, 'OK, double up in rooms and stay in a cheaper hotel,'" Hollyer says. Slap in the face number two: each year, Apple gave out a bonus of up to $50,000 to engineers who received the company's prestigious Technical Achievement Award. "We got a message that congratulated us on winning this award," Davidian says. "But then I saw at the bottom of the message: 'Message Unsent.' It had been sent as a mistake." The PDMers were given bonuses of about $5,000 each—no less and no more than the four hundred people in Tesseract. And slap in the face number three: Carl Hewitt, the likable software manager for PDM who was responsible for such tasks as making sure the new computer would boot up, returned from a sabbatical after the project to find his office door bolted and the lock changed. He had been moved to another office, with no advance notice.

"It was a symbol," Hewitt says, "of how you were treated."

The PDMers did present themselves with a special memento: a T-shirt with a slogan that read I HELPED SAVE THE COMPANY, AND ALL I GOT WAS THIS LOUSY T-SHIRT. Not surprisingly, Davidian, Hollyer, Hewitt, and most of the other PDMers eventually quit Apple to take other jobs in Silicon Valley after the Power Mac was launched in March 1994. In fact, Hewitt, who resigned in October 1994, and Davidian and Hollyer, who both resigned in 1995, all went to work as engineers for Power Computing Corporation, which became the first manufacturer of Macintosh clones in 1995. "We all left because it got harder and harder to come out with a good idea," Hewitt says. "The corporate antibodies would kill any good idea."

Eric Harslem, now at Dell Computer Corporation, declined comment. But a Harslem confidant says Harslem saw few problems with the development efforts behind the Power Macintosh, nor did he recall the PDMers being slighted in any way. This person says that Harslem, in fact, has described that entire Power Mac project as "one of the good holy grails we actually pursued." Hewitt, however, says that senior executives were so out of the loop on what was really going on down in engineering that they probably really were not aware of any problems. "I guess I would say our treatment was not malicious, but just an example of how management was unaware of how products got done," Hewitt says.

By 1993, the Power Mac was almost ready for prime time. It had a Power-PC chip. The PDM crew had designed a machine that would run the new chip. Psychic TV had rejiggered the Mac's software so that it would take advantage of PowerPC's speedy performance, while also still running all the old programs. And it had the energetic and well-liked Sheila Brady bringing all the engineering activity together into a cohesive unit, now that the groundwork had been laid by PDM and Psychic TV. But the machine still lacked one thing, and that was actually the most important of all: a batch of software programs to show off Power Mac's speed and power. Without these programs, Power Mac would be little more than a bucket of bolts.

Remember how the original Macintosh had floundered until PageMaker had come along, turning the Mac into a miniature publishing house? Power Mac could well end up in the same predicament, and possibly fail altogether, if the developers did not come through. The story of how this actually almost happened reveals how dumb luck, sometimes as much as the company's engineering prowess, played a role in Apple's successes.

To understand what happened on this front, step back just a moment to review Apple's historic relationship with its developers. The word that best summed up Apple's attitude toward them was "arrogant." Apple had arrogantly stabbed Adobe's John Warnock in the back on the print font fiasco, even after Warnock's PostScript technology had made it possible for Page-Maker's beautiful graphics to be reproduced on the printed page. Apple had arrogantly launched an all-out legal war against Microsoft, even though Bill Gates had proven a loyal backer of the Mac from the outset and had explicitly urged John Sculley to license the technology as quickly as possible.

If this was how Apple treated its biggest developers, imagine how the little guys fared. Dave Johnson was one. Johnson ran a little company called Working Software in Santa Cruz, California, a beachfront community known for its great surfing. Like many of Apple's small developers, Johnson fell in love with the Mac at first sight, and he committed himself to making programs for it mainly because it was so much fun. "The Mac had features like the 'talking moose,' which would just pop up on the screen while you were working and say something stupid," he says.

Johnson created SpellSwell, the Mac's first spell-check program, and he went on to develop other little programs for printing and word processing. He had experienced Apple's high-handed attitude early on and recalls it being vividly demonstrated at that meeting of developers during the late 1980s, when Jean-Louis Gassée told rock musician Todd Rundgren: "If you develop for the Mac, you should be an artist. You should not worry about money."

In 1990, Apple told Johnson and some other developers it needed their support for a new technology it was planning to include in the System 7 operating system called AppleEvents, which was designed to help the different programs inside the computer communicate better with one another. AppleEvents, or AE, as it was called, would enhance the speed and efficiency of the computer.

Johnson spent the next eighteen months developing a method for how the programs would work together on this technology. He completed the product, wrote up a business plan, and went out to a venture capitalist for funding to proceed further. "The guy said, 'This looks real good,' and then he said, 'So you say Apple is behind this,' " Johnson recalls. "And he just laughed and said, 'Apple eats its young.' He then said he would back this only if I could get in writing from Apple that they did support this, and a budget from Apple for promoting the technology. But then Apple dropped AE. They got the small developers hyped up about it and just moved on to something else." Since he had tied up most of his resources in AE, the episode left Johnson nearly out of money—and with a sour taste in his mouth about Apple. (Apple eventually did include AppleEvents in System 7, but it was too late to help Johnson.)

With many other Mac developers having experienced similarly shabby treatment, it was not so hard for them to decide to start supporting Windows when Microsoft shipped the first usable version in 1990. After all, they figured, Microsoft held by far the larger customer base, by a ten-to-one margin. Bill Gates was also not nearly so cavalier as Apple, although you certainly would not want to turn your back on him if you developed a product he might be interested in competing against. But, hey, Bill was Bill. And he did, in fact, throw out the welcome mat to developers, providing them with reliable technical support as well as a world-class set of development tools to help make the programs run on Windows.

Tools. These are among the more arcane facets of software development, but they are vitally important. And Apple's failure to deliver tools for the PowerPC would jeopardize the whole Power Mac transition.

Development tools are to a software program what plumbing is to a house. No one notices the plumbing if it's working. But if it isn't, the house is unlivable. The same is true in software development. A software program begins with a sleep-deprived programmer hunched over a computer, punching in line after line of software code. These are the instructions that will tell the program what to do. But after the code is written, it has to go through a set of tools before the program can actually be used by anybody on a computer screen.

Two of the key tools are a piece of software known as a "compiler" and another called a "debugger." The compiler takes a programmer's instructions, written in a computer language such as C or C++, and converts them into a stream of instructions that the computer can understand. This is how software is "built," to use an industry word. After this is done, the debugger helps the programmer to weed out the inevitable bugs, or defects in the software, that can cause a program to freeze up, run the wrong calculation, or even crash the entire computer.

The people who specialize in the making of these tools occupy perhaps the most unglamorous job in software engineering. It is dirty, mundane work, but somebody has to do it. Microsoft had to have tools, or it would have a hard time getting all its developers to write programs for the Windows and DOS operating systems. Apple had to have tools so its developers could write programs for the Macintosh operating system.

Related to the tools was another piece of software called the "framework," which is also crucial to software development. Using the house analogy again, the framework is like a prefabricated wall in a home under construction. Instead of having to go to the lumber yard and build a wall from scratch with two-by-fours and nails, you can just go to a building contractor and buy a wall already assembled. That saves so much time that you can concentrate on adding your own features, such as chandeliers and a fancy staircase, to the house.

In software development, the framework contains prefabricated code to address some of the more mundane parts of writing a program for a specific operating system. This frees the programmer to concentrate on adding special features, such as the world's fastest spell checker, without having to waste time on the code already contained in the framework. Microsoft had a framework for Windows, and Apple had a framework for the Macintosh.

Apple failed miserably in getting a new framework out for the Power Mac, though, and this set up its ensuing debacle in tools. It all started with a nightmare called "Bedrock."

The impetus behind Bedrock was a rush of developers from the Macintosh camp to also support Windows in the early 1990s. This new trend worried the folks at Apple mightily, and for good cause. The Mac was still technically superior to Windows, but Microsoft had drawn nearer to closing the gap when it shipped Windows 3.1 in 1992. That latest version had corrected many of the bugs contained in Windows 3.0 and was easier to use. In other words, Windows had become more Mac-like.

As more Mac developers moved to support Windows, they faced a problem: having to write one version of an application for the Mac and then performing an almost total rewrite for the one on Windows. This not only wasted a lot of time, it was expensive as all get-out. But they could not ignore the economics that favored Windows. After all, Windows had mushroomed to a seemingly unstoppable force. During 1993, some 30 million computers containing Windows software would be shipped worldwide, or ten times more than the 3 million shipments of Apple's Macintosh.

This was not just a problem for the Mac developers, it was a potentially huge one for Apple, as well. As more and more of its developers supported Windows, they would devote less time to coming up with new programs to help sell the Mac. They might also, one day, decide to abandon the Mac altogether and focus just on Windows. Apple therefore needed to find a way to keep its developers from jumping ship.

Pondering this dilemma, Steve Wyle, director of Apple's tools group at the time, decided in early 1992 that the best solution would be for Apple to come up with some way that a developer could write a program just once and then have it automatically converted to both the Mac and Windows formats. The technology for this was actually already under development at three companies—Adobe (known for its PostScript printing technology and desktop publishing programs such as Illustrator), Aldus Corporation (known for its desktop publishing programs such as PageMaker), and Symantec Corporation (known for its desktop maintenance software such as Norton Utilities)—and it was called a "cross-platform framework." All of those companies' cross-platform framework projects had started as internal projects to simplify their development of programs for both the Mac and Windows.

A cross-platform framework was based on the original framework concept of having prefabricated "walls" of arcane code that the developer would not have to worry about writing from scratch. But the cross-platform technology went a gigantic step further: the developer would have one framework that would assign the prefabricated code for a Windows version of a new program and another for the Macintosh version. So on one day you could feed your raw code into the framework and tell it to spew out a Windows version. The next day, you could put in the exact same code and instruct it to churn out a Mac version. No rewriting of the original code would be necessary; the cross-platform framework would take care of that.

This was a powerful concept and one that stirred great interest in the computer industry as Windows continued to grow. Indeed, it served as the foundation of a great deal of debate among developers on other emerging trends in the industry, such as programs that could be made "portable" to run on any personal computer. The portable software idea did not really take off, though, until the Internet began exploding in 1995. Developers could then produce on-line versions of smaller programs that could run on most any computer, through a popular new programming language developed by Sun Microsystems called Java.

In evaluating the different cross-platform frameworks, Wyle concluded that Adobe's was not very good and Aldus's was too expensive, recalls Lonnie Millett, an Apple tools engineer at the time. Aldus, he says, wanted $1 million to sell its version, called Vamp, to Apple. Not wanting to pay that much, Millet says Wyle focused on the Bedrock cross-platform framework project that Symantec had started about a year before.

Symantec, a neighbor of Apple in Cupertino, was run by a chief executive named Gordon Eubanks, who is widely known in the PC industry as a "lapdog" of Bill Gates because of his longtime unabashed praise of the Microsoft kingpin. Eubanks's company specialized in making a type of software called "utilities," which handle behind-the-scenes drudgery such as backing up files, and also made development tools. And his allegiance to Microsoft was based on the simple fact that the lion's share of his company's business was in making programs that would run on Microsoft software. This is important to bear in mind when you hear what happened to Apple on Bedrock and later on a joint tools project called "Rainbow."

Eubanks was also a supporter of the Macintosh, as long as it didn't cost him too much. Seeking to defray his own Mac development costs, he got Symantec to acquire, in 1987, a small company in Bedford, Massachusetts, called Think Technologies, which specialized in making Think Pascal development tools for the Macintosh, according to David Neal, Symantec's former director of Macintosh development tools. (Pascal is a programming language that was widely used in Macintosh software development at the time.) Later, in 1991, Eubanks sought to hold down costs further by instructing his Think division to develop software that would convert one program into Windows and Mac versions. This was Bedrock.

One day in early 1992, Wyle arranged a visit with his engineering counterparts at Symantec's headquarters in Cupertino. He took a look at Bedrock, which Symantec described as nearly completed, and agreed to a joint development deal under which Symantec and Apple would work together to produce a cross-platform framework that would let developers write one program that could be automatically converted into Windows and Macintosh versions. Under the terms, Symantec would retain all rights to Bedrock, selling it to whomever it chose. If Apple wanted to use it too, Apple would have to pay Symantec royalties.

Apple's Lonnie Millett was deeply skeptical, and he told Wyle so. All Symantec had shown Apple, he told him, was the Windows piece of Bedrock that was up and running. The Macintosh side of it had not yet been developed. As Bedrock stood then, a developer would be able to convert a program to run on Windows but nothing else. It was like half a cross-platform framework, favoring the Microsoft half. Furthermore, Millett argued, the deal was structured to favor Symantec in almost every way. Symantec got to own Bedrock. Symantec would be paid every time Apple used it. It was a hell of a deal—for Symantec. "I said we were giving away too much," Millett recalls.

By the summer of 1992, a joint development team of thirty engineers—twenty-two from Symantec and eight from Apple—had been assembled to start work on the Macintosh version of Bedrock. As soon as work commenced at Symantec's labs in Cupertino, Millett's worst fears about the project were confirmed. Symantec, he recalls, had done little on the Mac part of the project. What's more, all the Symantec people whom Apple had dealt with before had quit or were forced out that very first week because of unrelated problems within Symantec. It was strangers meeting strangers, and as a result there was palpable tension between the Symantec and Apple engineers.

"Apple really resented being there," recalls Marty Hess, one of the Symantec engineers on Bedrock. "They thought, 'We should be doing that.' " That resentment was rooted in the apprehension expressed by Millett and members of his team that the Bedrock deal was a shaky one in the first place, as far as Apple was concerned.

But the two camps worked together in fits and starts, getting precious little accomplished as the weeks dragged into months. As Millett remembers, he and his Apple engineers spent about six months, until January 1993, helping the Symantec team members deal with problems in getting Bedrock to work on Symantec's Windows applications. The Macintosh work had barely even started. Seeing that little was left to be gained by working together, Millett convinced Symantec to let Apple take its part of the Bedrock code and build its own Bedrock. Symantec would be free to continue on its version. By May 1993, Apple's Bedrock had progressed to the point that Millett and his Apple team were able to show off some of the features at Apple's annual Worldwide Developers Conference. This whetted the Mac development community's appetite, and it wanted more.

But Apple still needed Symantec's help to finish Bedrock. The whole deal would soon fall apart over two things: money and pride. By the summer of 1993, after Apple had showed off its partly completed Bedrock version at the Worldwide Developers Conference, Symantec CEO Gordon Eubanks was pressing his troops more and more to deliver products that would make the company some money. After all, this was not a charitable enterprise. As former Symantec manager David Neal remembers, Symantec's executives concluded that summer that Bedrock would not make money unless it was designed to fully embrace Microsoft's technology.

At that very time, Microsoft was spreading the word among its developers about a new technology it had come up with called OLE. OLE (pronounced "Oh-lay") stood for Object Linking and Embedding, and it was a Microsoft tools technology aimed at making it easier for programs to communicate with one another. It also would support the use of "applets," or tiny programs such as dictionaries, that could be plugged into a big program such as Microsoft Word. As usual, Apple was working on its own rival tools technology. It was called OpenDoc, and it was intended to accomplish pretty much the same thing.

OpenDoc versus OLE. This was another of those deep, nerdy tech battlegrounds that carried enormous import for the power structure of the industry. Here was Microsoft, a monstrously big competitor on one side, with its technology for helping software developers make programs for Windows. And there was little Apple, outnumbered and outflanked by the Wintel standard, proudly raising the flag of its own development technology. Microsoft had actually approached Apple on several occasions during this period, to propose that the two join forces in integrating OLE into Macintosh, since it was much nearer completion than OpenDoc and—most important—represented a simplified approach for both Windows and Macintosh developers. More about this debate between OLE and OpenDoc will be presented in the next chapter, but suffice it to say that Apple would have none of OLE. In fact, it was Apple's intransigence on the subject of OLE that torpedoed Bedrock.

In seeking to embrace all Microsoft technologies, Symantec wrapped both arms around OLE for use in Bedrock. It was at that point, in the summer of 1993, that Apple "totally flipped," Marty Hess recalls. Adds David Neal, "Apple looked at OLE as a competing technology to OpenDoc. They wanted Symantec to go towards OpenDoc." As Millett remembers, Apple could not support both OLE and OpenDoc in Bedrock, so an impasse was declared and Apple and Symantec parted company.

The kicker, though: Symantec made Apple cough up $1 million to walk away with its part of the Bedrock code, or the same amount that Steve Wyle had decried as too high when he had rejected an offer to buy the same technology from Aldus, a loyal Mac developer. Aldus's Vamp technology for a cross-platform framework was primarily centered around that company's efforts to simplify converting its PageMaker program for Windows. But the technology existed for other Mac developers to do the same thing, using Vamp. Back at Apple, Bedrock eventually floundered and collapsed before being folded into OpenDoc, which would go on to an ignominious end in 1997.

After all this time and money, Mac developers were still left to do what they had always done: write the same program twice for Macintosh and Windows. At the same time, a golden opportunity had been missed to keep developers addicted to the Mac platform by making it easy for them to convert a separate version for Windows. This would bode ill for Apple in the years to come.

Bedrock was a disaster, and it led to Apple's subsequent fumbling of getting development tools ready in time for the Power Mac. As the Bedrock saga was still playing out, Apple, in early 1993, called Symantec in to see what development tools it was planning for the Power Mac. The tools needed to make a program run on a computer include the compiler, to translate the code into language the microprocessor can recognize, and the debugger, to help weed out those troublesome bugs.

Apple's "tool kit" for the Mac was called the Macintosh Programmer's Workshop, and it had not been significantly updated since it had first shipped in 1986. Symantec had its own tool kit for the Mac, called Think, and it was considered so much easier to use that many Mac developers had turned to that instead. Since Apple was already working with Symantec on Bedrock, Apple's tools group decided to contract Power Mac tools development to Gordon Eubanks. In a deal announced on May 12, 1993, Symantec would launch an effort to develop tools for the Power Mac under the code name "Rainbow."

Bedrock was the cross-platform framework effort aimed at addressing Apple's long-term strategic threat of losing its developers to Windows for good. Rainbow, with its Power Mac tools, was just as important, because it dealt with the here and now of getting programs ready for the Power Mac.

Very few people in Apple management saw the folly in placing in the hands of another company—a Microsoft devotee, no less—a development effort so crucial to the success of a new computer. That was because Apple was a place where glamour and excitement reigned and executives were too often preoccupied with potential breakthroughs such as Newton and Pink. Tools were considered so dull that only about two dozen engineers were assigned to the tools group in 1993. One was Greg Branche, who would lead a quixotic effort to save Apple from Symantec's conscious lapse.

By May 1993, with an anticipated ship date of January 1994, the launch of the Power Mac was not far around the corner. Apple knew it would have to have some killer applications lined up to wow the crowds at the launch with PowerPC's dazzling speed. It especially wanted the big programs, such as Microsoft's Excel and Aldus's PageMaker, which could show off the performance gains. Excel would run its spreadsheets way faster. PageMaker would display graphics quicker and more brilliantly.

But every developer, big or small, had to have tools to recompile, or rebuild, its programs to PowerPC. With none in hand in 1993 and a skeleton-force tools team, Apple's temporary solution was to make developers replicate those tools by using a high-powered operating system called Unix on IBM's RS 6000 workstation. This approach was taken because the RS 6000, with its Unix software, was already using Big Blue's Power technology for RISC computing that was the basis of PowerPC. It could therefore understand PowerPC. There were just two snags: an RS 6000 cost about $20,000, and the Unix software was so complex that many Mac developers couldn't understand it.

Developers then had a choice: go out and buy their own RS 6000, or wait for Rainbow.

The RS 6000 approach was no option if you were one of the legions of small Mac developers living hand to mouth in a fiercely competitive industry and did not happen to have one of those babies lying around. Apple did give away some RS 6000s to help out, but primarily to the biggest developers, such as Adobe and Aldus. The Rainbow option was also not palatable, since many people in the industry, and even some at Symantec, viewed putting Symantec in charge of something so important as the Power Mac tools as incredibly risky for Apple. Symantec's first allegiance, remember, was to Windows. "I was thinking, 'Why would Apple give away something so key to their business?' " recalls Marty Hess, the Symantec engineer on Bedrock.

By the time Symantec got around to staffing Rainbow in the fall of 1993, after months of legal wrangling with Apple over terms, the Windows snowball was continuing to pick up such speed that Symantec CEO Gordon Eubanks decreed that all his product groups try to grow revenues by 20 percent per year to keep up with the momentum. Since the Macintosh market had stagnated by this time, Symantec's tools group essentially shelved Rainbow to make tools for Windows. "There was no urgency to get products on PowerPC," recalls David Neal, who oversaw both Rainbow and Bedrock. "The urgency, instead, was Windows 3.1. So we basically sat there and drifted for months."

Within Apple's small tools group, some of the engineers also had grave misgivings about turning the PowerPC effort over to Symantec. On his own initiative, an engineer named Reggie Seagraves succeeded in porting a tools compiler used on Unix to Apple's Macintosh Programmer's Workshop, the old tool kit. Just a few weeks later, in July 1993, Seagraves, as well as one-half of the tools group, was laid off under Michael Spindler's big restructuring plan. A colleague left behind, Greg Branche, talked his manager into letting him continue the PowerPC tools work on his own.

"We were saying to ourselves, 'We should do this,' " Branche remembers. "We thought that forcing developers to spend all this money to buy Unix equipment would discourage them from going to PowerPC." Under the agreement with Symantec, Branche says, Apple could not improve its Macintosh Programmer's Workshop, although it could make changes to keep it current with changes in the Macintosh operating system. Interpreting this to mean that Apple could update it for PowerPC, Branche barricaded himself in his cubicle and spent the next eight months transforming the Macintosh Programmer's Workshop into a workable tool kit for the PowerPC. Since Apple had already contracted for Symantec to do the same work, Branche says he got almost no help on the project, resulting in its not becoming publicly available until the spring of 1994, weeks after the Power Mac launch. He resigned in July 1995, in general frustration with Apple's muddled R-and-D process.

As it would turn out, it did not matter that both the Symantec and Apple were dropping the ball completely on tools. A small company that nobody had heard of came racing out of the night on a white horse to save the day. Meet Metrowerks, one of the most important names behind the launch of the Power Mac.

Metrowerks, then based in Montreal, had been founded in 1986 by Greg Galanos to design Macintosh software compilers, primarily for the education market. Like everybody else in the Mac software community, Metrowerks's two partners, Galanos and Jean Bélanger, wondered why Apple was going to so little effort to make new development tools available in time for the Power Mac launch. Galanos remembered a similar situation developing when the Mac had first been introduced and the only tools for Mac development were on the Lisa.

The first tools on the Mac, then, were provided by a company named Lightspeed Technologies, which later became the Think Technologies that Symantec acquired. Seeing a huge market void, Galanos and Bélanger decided in late 1992 that they could take this market over if they could come up with their own set of PowerPC tools six months ahead of anyone else. "We were a grassroots team of Mac fanatics who saw an opportunity," remembers Galanos, who is now president and chief technology officer of Metrowerks, working out of the company's Silicon Valley office in Cupertino. Bélanger is the chairman and CEO, based at Metrowerks's headquarters, which has since relocated from Montreal to Austin, Texas.

One day about that same time, Galanos received a diskette in the mail from a computer programmer named Andreas Hommel in Hamburg, Germany. It contained a compiler that could work for PowerPC. Hommel sent diskettes of his compiler to Galanos, as well as to Apple and Symantec. Hommel never heard back from Apple or Symantec. He did almost immediately from Galanos, who summoned him to Montreal. John McEnerney, a former Symantec engineer, flew to Montreal to examine the compiler as a consultant to Metrowerks. "John looked at Andreas's compiler and said, 'This is a diamond in the rough,' " Galanos remembers.

Hommel and McEnerney were hired immediately and set to work on a project Galanos named "CodeWarrior." CodeWarrior would be a PowerPC tool kit, just like the one that Rainbow was supposed to provide. In February 1993, they flew out to Cupertino to try to solicit Apple's support for the project. Apple declined, saying it intended to rely on Symantec. So the Mac fanatics retreated to their labs. Galanos ran the engineering project out of Montreal and hired a core Metrowerks team around McEnerney and Hommel that included engineers Dan Podwall in Boston, Greg Dow in Berkeley, California, and Mark Anderson in Richmond, California, along with two programmers in Montreal, Marcel Achim and Berardino Baratta. Bélanger, a former venture capitalist, raised money for the venture.

The team worked out of Montreal, Boston, Hamburg, and Berkeley and began cranking out code, exchanging it over the Internet. "We worked nights, weekends, all the time," Galanos remembers. "It was absolutely nuts." A prototype of CodeWarrior was finished by the late summer, and that is when Metrowerks began shopping it around to big developers such as Adobe, which had no other alternative than to use the IBM RS 6000.

"Adobe officially was going to wait for Symantec, but privately they started using CodeWarrior," Galanos says. "In addition, engineers at both Apple and Apple's Claris unit were secretly using Metrowerks tools to convert [Claris's] Clarisworks and [Apple's] MacWrite Pro for the PowerPC."

The watershed moment for CodeWarrior—and the Power Mac—came in early September 1993, when Adobe used it to successfully rebuild its entire Macintosh Illustrator program for sophisticated graphics to a PowerPC computer from the Macs based on Motorola's 68000 chip. The time saving was the most impressive feature of CodeWarrior. Using the RS 6000 tools, it could take as long as twenty-four hours to convert a program so it would run optimally on the new PowerPC microprocessor. With CodeWarrior, that process of converting, or rebuilding, the old code to run on PowerPC took less than twenty minutes.

Galanos and the Metrowerks engineers showed off CodeWarrior's amazing speed in a demo to executives from Apple's developer relations group in Montreal on September 15, 1993. To underscore the point, Galanos started to build a program using a prototype of Symantec's PowerPC compiler at the same moment that he had instructed one of his engineers, Dan Podwall, to begin traveling from his home in Boston to the meeting in Montreal. Podwall took a train to the airport, flew to Montreal, grabbed a cab, and walked into the meeting exactly three hours and fifteen minutes later—as the build with Symantec's tools kept grinding away.

"Then we tried it with our tools," Galanos says. "It took one minute, fifty seconds. That absolutely blew everybody away. That was when the dam burst. Then it was like everybody jumped on the bandwagon."

CodeWarrior was such a hit that developers attending Apple's Macworld show four months later, in January 1994, were snapping up copies of the new tool kit off the convention floor and porting programs in their hotel rooms through the night. No one was bothering with the RS 6000 anymore, nor did they care one whit about Symantec's Rainbow. As a result, the Power Mac would have about a hundred software programs rewritten expressly for the new machine available to customers within the first three months of Power Mac's launch. With all these programs available, customers would have a compelling reason to buy a Power Mac.

"Metrowerks was like a godsend for Apple," says Symantec's David Neal.

Metrowerks had indeed saved Apple's butt, a fact that would not be publicly acknowledged by Apple until a year later, when Guy Kawasaki, the now-famous marketing whiz, would return to Apple to shore up developer relations and cite CodeWarrior's crucial role in a speech at the Macworld show in San Francisco. As for Michael Spindler, Galanos says the Diesel never once talked with him in all his time as Apple's CEO. "Our relationship with Apple management was disappointing, to say the least," Galanos says.

It had taken perseverance against great odds by a small number of Apple engineers and a breakthrough by a little company in Canada, but all pieces of the technical puzzle were finally in place for Power Mac to be a success. Now all that was needed was for senior management to fire on all cylinders on the marketing and manufacturing side. The accomplishment of this is a tale of one of the finest hours at Apple Computer—and perhaps the finest in the career of that hard-charging Aussie, Ian Diery.

Diery, remember, had been elevated from Apple's Pacific region to executive vice president for worldwide sales and marketing in 1992, and then was named to run Spindler's new PC division in the big shake-up of 1993. Diery had demonstrated strategic shortsightedness, as when he helped kill the Drama project of Mac clones that could have broken Apple out of its box. But when it came to focus and intensity, few in the business could surpass him. Ian Diery was Spindler's Del Yocam, with an Aussie accent.

To his salespeople, Diery was both a blessing and a curse. A blessing, in that he was one of them and knew that side of the business inside and out. But a curse, if they failed to meet quotas or slacked off on the job. "Ian ruled by intimidation and fear," recalls one senior executive from the time. "He would go into some country and ask the general manager in front of his staff for answers. If he did not have answers, Ian would rip them to shreds." Diery's habit of going straight to someone in the field to issue a directive, bypassing that person's boss, also proved annoying to Apple's sales managers.

"Ian was a little Napoleon," says Bob Puette, the Apple USA president, who was passed over for the worldwide sales chief job that Spindler and Sculley gave Diery in 1992. "It was 'Do it his way, period.' Ian would go to any of your people in the organization and contradict stuff you already had in place." Puette resigned in October 1993, a victim, some executives said at the time, of the organizational shake-up instituted by Spindler the prior July. Puette is now chairman, president, and CEO of NetFrame Systems Inc., a maker of big computer servers based in Milpitas, California.

Given Apple's long history of bad management, Diery's take-charge approach was not such a bad idea.

Yet on the fourth floor of De Anza 7, where he sat in Jean-Louis Gassée's old office, Diery displayed a softer side. Indeed, he was regarded as a real sweetheart by many of the secretaries, with a weak spot for the homemade chocolate truffles that one assistant in public relations would frequently present him. "I really liked Ian," recalls one secretary assigned to Spindler's office. "He would always come over and say, 'Bloody hell! It's too quiet over here.'" Diery also possessed the ability to defuse a tense situation, such as the day when John Sculley was still CEO that Diery showed up late for an executive staff meeting and the mild-mannered Sculley blew his cool.

"Sculley snaps, 'Where have you been?'" Diery remembers. "Thinking fast, I say, 'Oh, John, I'm sorry. There was an accident outside, and I was called as a witness.' 'Accident,' he says. He had a white Mercedes 500 SL parked outside. I said, 'Yeah, somebody wiped out a white 500 SL downstairs.' Sculley races out of the room. I had to run after him to tell him it was a joke."

Sculley didn't get mad, he got even. Some weeks later, at an off-site management meeting at the Claremont Resort and Spa in Oakland, Diery was sauntering inside after leaving his blue Mercedes 500 SL with the parking valet. "A bellboy came running up and said, 'Someone has just smashed a blue 500 SL outside,'" Diery recalls, laughing at the memory. "I see Sculley coming inside, and he asks if I'd like a beer, which was unusual because the guy never drank. I tell him I think my car has been smashed, and Sculley tags along with me to investigate. I take a few steps and look back to see a whole gang of Apple executives giggling. Sculley had a huge smile."

All joking aside, Diery's aggressiveness rankled some of his peers in the executive suite, and, according to several former executives, greatly threatened CEO Michael Spindler himself. Although Diery now insists he was "never disloyal" to Spindler, it was clear he did not care much for Spindler, either—especially after his boss likened PCs to commodities like washing machines and hamburgers in an address before Apple's annual shareholders' meeting in January 1994. Diery, standing at the back of the room, glowered. "Ian was furious," recalls a confidant in the executive suite. "Here was the CEO calling our main product line hamburgers."

Diery was determined to prove to Spindler that PCs were more than hamburgers, and he intended to demonstrate that through the launch of the Power Mac, which had by now been postponed from January to March 14, 1994, to give manufacturing enough time to meet the expected high customer demand. The machine was aimed both at existing Macintosh customers seeking an upgrade to the higher performance of PowerPC and the fence-sitters discussed before. In ramrodding Power Mac, Diery during the summer of 1993 assembled a "war room" on the fourth floor of De Anza 7 that included himself and senior product managers such as Jim Gable and Brodie Keast. Gable really got into the spirit, adorning his Porsche with a California license plate that read POWER MAC.

Together, in weekly meetings, they pored over manufacturing charts and stoked a fire under sales teams all around the world to spread the news of PowerPC to customers. They then orchestrated a series of sharp price cuts on the existing Mac line in a successful effort to keep customers from holding off on all Apple purchases until the new Power Macs had launched. On October 21, 1993, Diery instituted price drops of up to 35 percent on some Mac models, following five previous rounds of cuts since the previous April. This, of course, further hurt profit margins, but the name of the game at Apple since 1990 had been to rebuild market share, and the margins had been on a downward slide anyway. Customers who had just bought a Mac were not too happy at seeing the devaluation of their investment, but Apple had no choice but to drop the prices if it was going to compete.

Then Diery embarked Apple on one of its most aggressive marketing campaigns in years. It started in earnest at the fall Comdex show in Las Vegas that began on November 15, and it marked the beginning of an epic industry struggle that would come to be known as the "chip wars." The fall 1993 Comdex, with almost two hundred thousand attendees, had grown from its origin in 1979 as the Computer Dealers Exposition to become the largest computer trade show in the United States and the most important in the world. It was so important because it was the venue where the industry's major trends and innovations were first unveiled. Apple's PowerBook, for example, was publicly demonstrated for the first time at Comdex, marking a new era in sleeker laptop computers. Multimedia technology, after Apple pioneered it, got its first wide exposure at Comdex. The show was also the public starting point for some of the industry's most famous names, including Compaq Computer and Borland International, a software firm in Scotts Valley, California.

Fall Comdex was so big and unwieldy that practically everybody grumbled about it. It took two hours or more of standing in line to grab a cab. Hotel room prices were jacked up to more than $200 a night, as much as three times their normal rate. Restaurants were packed. The corridors of the convention hall were overflowing. It was a bruising, exhausting, and expensive ordeal. Yet almost everybody in the industry felt they had to be there. If you weren't, your competitor surely would be. So fall Comdex evolved into an annual ritual in Las Vegas, the only city in America with enough hotel and meeting facilities to host such a crowd, becoming the center of the universe for the computer industry for one week.

Comdex, in short, was the perfect place for Apple and its PowerPC allies to declare war on Intel, Microsoft's partner in the duopoly over the PC business.

You have heard the PowerPC side of the story up to now. Now consider what this meant to Intel. The key to Intel's success in the microprocessor industry was to continually churn out ever-faster chips. There was the 80286. Then the 80386. And then, by 1993, the 80486. Each time Intel came out with a new generation of chips based on its 8086 architecture, the company's two main clone rivals, Advanced Micro Devices Inc. (AMD) and Cyrix Corporation, fought like mad to catch up with their knockoffs of the Intel chip. That competition spurred Intel to move on to the next generation of microprocessors as fast as it could, so it could rake off as much profit as possible from a new line before prices started falling as AMD and Cyrix jumped onto the old one.

Intel executed brilliantly on this strategy, as demonstrated by its 74 percent share of microprocessor revenues in 1993. AMD held just 6 percent of that market in 1993, while Cyrix commanded just 1 percent.[5] The threat posed by PowerPC was potentially more formidable, though. For one thing, PowerPC was backed by three of the biggest companies in the computer industry— Apple, IBM, and Motorola. For another, PowerPC's backers extolled this microprocessor as having the capability to make Intel's technology obsolete. It was their RISC-versus-CISC argument again: RISC, or reduced instruction set computing, was the future; CISC, or complex instruction set computing, was the past.

As was the case with so many of the computer industry's battles, the one between Intel and PowerPC was noteworthy because as of 1993 the PowerPC chip had not even been shipped yet in the personal computer market. The real aim for the PowerPC alliance at this Comdex show, then, was of grabbing "mind share," or the attention—and allegiance—of the rest of the computer industry. Apple, IBM, and Motorola had PowerPC. Intel had the 80486 and a new weapon in its arsenal: a powerful successor to that chip called Pentium.

So there, at the cavernous Las Vegas Convention Center that served as the hub of Comdex, Ian Diery joined forces with IBM and Motorola to plaster the town with anything and everything related to PowerPC. There were PowerPC banners and billboards. PowerPC buttons and T-shirts. There was even a "PowerPC Pavilion," erected on the parking lot outside the arena to showcase PowerPC demos such as one pitting a prototype Power Mac against its counterpart from Intel to see which could run graphics programs faster. The Intel machine contained Intel's newest microprocessor, the Pentium. The Power Mac always won hands down, in a contest pitting graphics capabilities that Intel CEO Andy Grove did not find at all amusing as he sat through the demos.

Intel had also festooned the convention center with banners and memorabilia touting its Pentium and had even set up an elaborate exhibit inside with actors, giant models of the chip, and a video. Here, in the glitter of Las Vegas, it was PowerPC versus Pentium. There was just as much energy and enthusiasm as if it had been Tyson versus Holyfield.

Michael Spindler, who had appeared "clueless" to his engineers when reviewing the RISC technology only a year before, got in on the act, too. He delivered the prestigious keynote address at Comdex, taking the stage at the Aladdin Hotel on the famed Las Vegas Strip to talk up PowerPC. This was the same hotel where he had appeared, only a month before, stabbing his fist in the air as he shouted, "We can win this!" As he prepared to speak in the Aladdin Theater for Performing Arts, the place shook with excitement. Rock music blared from giant speakers flanking the stage. Strobe lights washed over the sea of faces. And facing the audience were the new Power Macintoshes, lined up in a neat row at the back of the stage, their screens glowing. Spindler, speaking in his usual monotone before a non-Apple gathering, told the audience of seven thousand computer nerds that Apple planned a swift transition to the Power Mac, with sales eventually exploding to "millions." He performed his own demonstration of a Power Mac knocking the socks off an Intel Pentium PC.

In a press conference afterward attended by more than one hundred journalists—facing the media for his first time as CEO—Spindler sat on a stage of a nearby small theater, flanked by his executives, and fielded questions on Apple's strategy. The Diesel had a pat reply to every query, save the final one from myself. Representing *The Wall Street Journal*, I asked Spindler if it were true that John Sculley had been pushed out against his will. Glaring into the audience at me, Spindler snapped, "I won't get into personnel matters."

After Comdex, Ian Diery turned up the heat on the advertising front. A particularly memorable Apple ad appeared as a full-page spread in *The Wall Street Journal* on Valentine's Day 1994. The headline: "How to Explain the Difference Between CISC-based Computing and the New RISC-based Macintosh to a Five Year Old." Below were two photos, one of a road ending at a brick wall and another of a road stretching unimpeded off into the horizon: CISC, the dead-end road; RISC, the open road. "The simplest explanation is that RISC-based computing gives you an open road [a future] and CISC-based computing faces, well, obstacles," the ad said.

Intel, of course, was not taking this lying down. The chip giant took the fight to Apple's own backyard, taking out a two-page ad in the Valentine's Day issue of the Apple trade magazine, *MacWEEK*, that showed two roads diverging in the woods. A PowerPC sign pointed to one road and a Pentium sign to the other. Under the title "It's Time to Stop and Ask Directions," Intel's ad read, "The PC is not what it used to be. Everything you want to do on a Macintosh, you can just as easily do on a PC."

It was no more Mr. Nice Guy on Andy Grove's part. He had helped Apple on the Star Trek project and had warned John Sculley that Apple faced insurmountable odds if it stayed outside the Wintel market. When Apple would not listen, Grove was ready to go for the jugular. During a February 1994 interview about PowerPC between myself, representing *The Wall Street Journal*, and two of Grove's top lieutenants in a windowless conference room atop Intel's six-story headquarters building in Santa Clara, California, the Grovester himself popped in, unannounced, to offer his two cents. "What is this all about? The second coming?" Grove asked sarcastically in his Hungarian accent, locking his blazing eyes on me and gesturing vigorously. "I don't see an influx of [Intel users] into the Apple world. I see a flux out."

The battle had just begun as far as Andy Grove was concerned, and Intel would have a lot more to say about the future of PowerPC — or lack thereof — in years to come.

For now, though, Apple Computer was center stage in the industry once more. The Power Mac launch would be its most important event since the rollout of the original Macintosh. At this point, Ian Diery and the others had done all they could do. Now it would be up to the customers. For a few glorious months, they would not let Apple down. Within just the first two weeks of the March 14, 1994, launch, Apple would ship 145,000 of the machines, a figure that analysts at the time called most impressive. By October 1994, Apple would ship approximately 600,000 Power Macs, keeping the company on track to meet its goal of shipping a total of 1 million within the first year of the launch.

12

From Power Mac to the Cliff

The morning of March 14, 1994, broke freezing cold and overcast in New York City, typically gloomy weather for that time of the year. A parade of yellow cabs and sleek black limousines pulled up curbside on Sixty-fifth Street, on Manhattan's bustling West Side, to unload their cargoes of men and women in dark business suits and overcoats at the Lincoln Center for the Performing Arts. Lincoln Center is America's premier performing arts center and the home of such bastions of old culture as the New York Philharmonic and the New York City Ballet. On this morning, however, the fabled hall was being taken over by a new culture: that of the change-the-world revolutionaries from Apple Computer.

It was not symphony music that filled a seven-hundred-seat theater inside that morning. Loud rock music pulsated from speakers on stage as a kaleidoscope of lights washed over the members of the personal computer industry, and the press, who had been invited to witness Apple's historic launch of its Power Macintosh. Apple CEO Michael Spindler took the stage to laud the event, then turned the show over to his top lieutenant, Ian Diery, the man who had galvanized Apple's far-flung forces to make this launch possible. When he took the stage, his balding head gleaming in the spotlight, Diery smiled with the look of a climber who had just conquered a mountain.

"Today," he announced as a hush fell over the audience, "we make a quantum leap forward." Behind him, three Power Macintosh models flickered with strength and vitality as the crowd roared its approval. Jim Gable, the Power Mac's product manager, was called out to demonstrate what was under the hood. Gable, a thin, wispy dynamo, was dressed in Apple's usual demo attire of casual dress, and he put the Power Mac through the same head-to-head competition with a Wintel machine as had been staged at Comdex four months earlier. Of course, the Power Mac won hands down.

Then came a procession of testimonials from industry luminaries, as is so common for a computer industry rollout. There were Adobe's CEO, John

Warnock, and Paul Brainerd, president of Aldus, which had created Page-Maker, the page layout application. There was Pete Higgins, head of Macintosh development for Microsoft. Even Bill Gates was there, although not in person. Unable to appear because of a previously planned business trip to Europe, Gates offered his commentary via a videoconferenced segment broadcast on an overhead screen at the Lincoln Center gathering. A few good-natured boos erupted from the crowd when his familiar boyish visage appeared.

All in all, it was a rousing performance by Apple and one that seemed to invigorate Spindler, who appeared uncharacteristically relaxed and outgoing when he agreed to sit down afterward for his first *Wall Street Journal* interview as CEO. Seated on a couch in a small meeting room nearby, flanked by his trusted aide, David Seda, and Christopher Escher, Apple's director of worldwide public relations, Spindler spent an hour with me reciting a laundry list of strategic moves he planned with this machine. That same day, in a statement broadcast by Apple over the PRNewswire, Spindler said, "This introduction marks a major milestone in personal computing. Just as Macintosh changed the course of computing ten years ago, today we are defining a new era in personal computing with Power Macintosh."

Speed! Power! Those were the battle cries of Power Macintosh. Microsoft might have erased much of the Mac's technical lead in operating systems. But Apple, and its PowerPC partners, were convinced that the Power Mac was so robust compared to Intel-based computers that even Wintel customers would sit up and take heed. Indeed, Brodie Keast, vice president of Apple's PC division, went so far as to predict in a briefing with me just before the launch that huge Power Mac sales to both Apple and Wintel customers would more than double the Macintosh's share of the PC market to 20 percent from its current 9.4 percent over the next two years.

This was bold talk coming from a company that had already squandered so many opportunities and was now virtually surrounded by its competitors in the computing world. But Apple had laid it all on the line before, with Steve Jobs's Macintosh exactly one decade earlier, and it was doing so again.

Just as Spindler and Diery had hoped, Power Mac shot out of the starting gate like a bat out of hell. On the strength of the fast rollout of more than 200,000 Power Macs in the ensuing fiscal third quarter, ending July 1, Apple's profits in the period soared to $138.1 million, or $1.16 a share, reversing the year-earlier loss of $188.3 million, or $1.63 a share. By the end of the fiscal year on September 30, the Power Mac contributed to record sales of $9.19 billion, up 15 percent from the year prior, as well as a nearly fourfold jump in profits to $310.2 million from $86.6 million.

The icing on the cake for Apple came in November, when the market research firms of Dataquest Inc. and International Data Corporation each released reports showing that Apple had shipped more personal computers in the United States during the third quarter than any other company had. With combined sales of the Macintosh, PowerBook, and now the Power Mac, Apple, which had been running at number two in the United States, had actually dethroned market leader Compaq Computer, which earlier that year had overtaken IBM as the world's leading PC vendor. Apple had ranked as the United States' top PC vendor in 1993 but had lost that position to Compaq earlier in 1994. Analysts at the time pointed out that Apple would not be able to sustain the lead, since the company typically comes on stronger than its rivals in back-to-school sales, which it had dominated during the third quarter. Still, given all its problems in the past and the great risk of this transition, the number one ranking was a major PR boost to Apple.

"The company is focusing on its core business and has got its act together," Philippe de Marcillac, Dataquest's principal PC analyst at the time, said.[1]

Morale in Cupertino was buoyed to the point that some of the old braggadocio began to resurface. Ian Diery, for instance, blustered to reporters of a coming "Wintel rupture," when Wintel customers would bolt to Apple's technology as Intel's microprocessors fell farther and farther behind that of the PowerPC. Joe Graziano, Apple's CFO, said in a letter to *The Wall Street Journal* that the Wintel platform "stands on the edge of a cliff." Indeed, Apple was counting on defections from Wintel to boost its market share to the 20 percent level that Brodie Keast had predicted before the Power Mac launch.

It all looked good, but really it wasn't. Apple was still fighting an uphill battle. By failing to license the Macintosh technology early on, Apple had remained trapped in a box as Microsoft's software went on to control almost every other PC in the world. Indeed, by 1994, the Microsoft-Intel standard controlled some 210 million PCs that had been sold in the world to that point, while Apple's computers accounted for a comparatively measly 25 million.

Apple's problem, in short, boiled down to the "M-word": momentum, or lack thereof. Bill Gates had spoken of momentum, when he had recommended to John Sculley back in 1985 that he license the Macintosh in order to make it a long-term success. Sculley had declined, and now the "M-word" was all on the side of Bill Gates and the Wintel empire. The Microsoft mantra, beginning in 1992, had been "Windows Everywhere." Windows 3.1 had all but taken over the desktop. Windows 3.1 had all but taken over the laptop. In 1993, Microsoft had introduced a new operating system called Windows NT, designed to run high-speed corporate networks. The Windows express was barreling down the track with nothing in its way.

Power Mac enabled Apple to keep its own customers by preventing them from jumping ship. Sales of Power Macs had soared in the months after the launch, but they had mainly been to existing Apple customers who wanted to follow along on the transition to a more powerful Macintosh machine. This was the case despite Apple's direct appeal to Wintel customers, as embodied in the company's CISC-versus-RISC advertising campaign and in a "stand out and fit in" strategy announced shortly before the Power Mac launch. Apple would "stand out" by making regular improvements to the Macintosh operating system, and it would "fit in" by making it easier for Wintel users to switch to Apple through special features such as new software that would allow them to run their PC files on a Mac machine.

By 1994, however, this strategy might better have been called "too little, too late." One problem was software. The other was hardware.

Even though the fortuitous intervention of little Metrowerks had saved Power Mac from having almost no updated programs at the launch, the software industry, in general, had tilted decidedly in support of Windows. As a result, Mac programs in 1994 accounted for only 14 percent of the PC software market, down from 17 percent five years before, according to a Dataquest report. Typical of the exodus was the decision by Electronic Arts Inc., one of the largest developers of game and education software, to ship only five CD-ROM programs for the Mac in late 1994 and early 1995, compared to twenty-five to thirty for Wintel PCs. "It's simple: we can't sell enough to make it a viable business," Lawrence Probst III, CEO of the San Mateo, California, firm, said.[2]

Another trend had begun that made the Power Mac launch an even greater challenge: new software programs were being developed first on Windows and later on the Macintosh platform. One reason for this, besides the simple economics of Windows being a vastly larger audience, was Apple's dearth of technical support for developers. In addition to getting rid of many of Apple's engineers in charge of developer tools during the 1993 layoffs, Spindler had decimated the company's corps of "evangelists," whose job was to evangelize developers to support Macintosh. This left almost no one at Apple with whom developers could consult, as Camilo Wilson found out. (The most famous Apple evangelist, after Steve Jobs, is Guy Kawasaki, who is still an avid Apple fan and spokesman today.)

Wilson is president of Cogix Corporation, a small developer in San Anselmo, California, located in tony Marin County just north of San Francisco. In early 1994, his company was finishing a crossword puzzle program called Cross Wizard for the Power Mac. "We worked fourteen hours a day, seven days a week, for three months to get it ready for PowerPC," Wilson recalls. "I tried to call Apple for technical help, and they never gave me any. I called half a dozen times, and they wouldn't even return calls. Their attitude seemed to be 'We are Apple. You need us more than we need you.'" Frustrated and angry, Wilson shelved the Power Mac effort and redirected Cross Wizard to Windows, where he found plenty of help. Cross Wizard went on to become a best-seller on Windows, with a Power Mac version following months later. Wilson, tired of Apple's lack of cooperation and the resulting difficulty in creating programs for the Mac, went on to focus most of his development efforts on Windows.

The situation was even grimmer in business applications, the kind a computer maker has to have in order to win any corporate accounts. Since Apple had not licensed the Macintosh operating system and had only belatedly endorsed the trend toward office networks, its share of PCs in businesses stood at just 6 percent in 1994. By contrast, Apple held an 80 percent share of the market for desktop publishing and 60 percent of the market for sales of computers in the big kindergarten-through-high-school market.

Consequently, Lotus Development Corporation decided not to rewrite its best-selling 1-2-3 spreadsheet for the Power Mac. Similarly, Allegro New Media, a Fairfield, New Jersey, maker of several popular business programs such as Multimedia Business 500, withdrew its support for Apple altogether. Microsoft had long dominated the market for business software on the Mac with its Word and Excel programs, and by the end of 1994 Microsoft was essentially the only big player left in that market. Apple's predicament could hardly have been more ironic. As much as the Apple executives disliked Bill Gates, they had to have his support. And for a frightening time, it looked as though Gates was not going to deliver.

As of 1994, William Gates III was the undisputed king of the computer industry. Microsoft's stock valuation had soared to $30 billion from $8.5 billion when the company had first gone public in 1988. Since Gates owned approximately 24 percent of the shares, his net worth had mushroomed as well, to about $7 billion in 1994 from a paltry $2 billion in 1988. Gates was so rich that he alone was worth almost twice as much as Apple, whose market valuation in 1994 had declined to $4 billion from a 1991 peak of $6.8 billion. The nerd genius who had solicited a relationship with Steve Jobs back in the 1980s was solicitous no more. Just about everyone in the industry groveled to him; everyone, that is, except for the nerds at Apple Computer.

The Apple-Microsoft relationship had been a topsy-turvy one almost from the outset. John Sculley personally liked and respected Gates, and vice versa. "During his time at Apple, he was always willing to meet," Gates writes in an e-mail follow-up to an interview for this book. "He [Sculley] understood that we didn't view Apple as a competitor even though they had to view Windows as a competitor, so he felt he could learn by talking to me about issues of mutual interest."

But almost no one else on Sculley's management team liked Gates, in part because of their growing fear of him. "They were afraid of Microsoft's success," says Ben Waldman, former group development manager of Microsoft Office, the suite of productivity applications including Word and Excel, and currently the head of Microsoft's Mac development team. That animosity and distrust had led to the big copyright infringement suit that Apple had filed against Microsoft and Hewlett-Packard in 1988. But the two companies' mutual need for each other had remained strong enough that they had continued working together. Microsoft needed Apple, because Macintosh applications generated more profit than anything else did. And Apple certainly needed Microsoft, because it was the primary source of business productivity programs on the Mac.

By 1994, though, the relationship had become decidedly tilted in Microsoft's favor. Windows' success lessened Microsoft's need for Apple, as Microsoft's total share of business applications revenue slid to just 20 percent for the Mac while Windows' business applications revenue grew to 80 percent. Until the early 1990s, Microsoft earned more money on each Mac program sold than on its programs sold on IBM-compatible PCs. That quickly changed with the success of Windows 3.0 and Windows 3.1. Apple, on the other hand, was so dependent on Microsoft that fully 90 percent of the Mac's spreadsheet market was dominated by Microsoft Excel, while Microsoft Word accounted for 75 percent of the Mac's word processing market.[3] Apple, therefore, was in a highly vulnerable condition: if Microsoft were suddenly to pull the plug on applications development for the Mac, Apple's hopes of building a sustainable franchise in business markets would likely be ruined.

Yet Apple kept tweaking its old rival at almost every turn. A major reason for this was that Michael Spindler "hated Gates," according to a senior executive from that administration. Ed Stead, Apple's pit bull general counsel, and Dave Nagel, the top technologist, were also vocal critics of Gates in Apple's executive suite. One episode involved the debate over Microsoft's OLE and Apple's OpenDoc. Apple's refusal to use OLE in Bedrock had ruined an opportunity to make life easier for Macintosh developers. That OpenDoc obsession would also lead to a further chilling of relations between Apple and its most important developer.

Both OpenDoc and OLE were created as tools to help developers make programs designed around the new "object-oriented technology"—the same one John Sculley had been so enamored of when he pitched Apple's Pink project as part of the big alliance with IBM in 1991. Under this technology, a developer would no longer have to build a huge, monolithic program, such as Microsoft Word, from scratch. By using reusable chunks of code, called "objects," that developer, or any other, could make a new spell checker or word counter without changing anything else. The process was analogous to the making of a tapestry. The old way was to weave a web of interconnecting threads, with each new stitch affecting the entire tapestry. The use of objects, however, was more like a patchwork quilt, which can be extended by simply adding new patches.

This new process presented an enormous opportunity for small developers, because it would open up software markets to them that had been dominated by big developers such as Microsoft and Lotus Development, which had the deep pockets to finance development of giant applications. By using objects, the big developers stood to gain, too, because they could update their big applications much faster. And computer users stood to benefit. Since object-oriented programs were designed to run independently from one another, they could be opened from another application so a user could perform several tasks at once. For example, one could simultaneously view a movie clip, conduct a meeting via two-way videoconferencing, and type a letter on a word processing document.

Object-oriented technology, in summary, was one of the holy grails of the computer industry in the early 1990s. It was then being pioneered by Steve Jobs's unsuccessful NeXT venture. Apple's Pink project, too, was aimed at creating an object-oriented operating system on which these new programs could run more easily. Pink had evolved into the joint Taligent venture between Apple and IBM, and it, too, was charged with developing an object-oriented operating system.

But as the failure of the Pink project and the impending collapse of Taligent demonstrated, object-oriented technology was no stroll in the park. This was highly complex stuff, and the making of object-oriented tools such as Apple's OpenDoc and Microsoft's OLE was just as much so. Indeed, Microsoft had approached Apple in 1988, when the two companies' object tools efforts had just been beginning, to suggest they coordinate their efforts on the Microsoft technology, known then as Direct Data Exchange, or DDE. (Apple pursued a rival effort that became OpenDoc.) Microsoft's goal: to make life easier for developers, such as Microsoft, which had to support both the Mac and Intel-based PCs by having just one set of these tools, not two.

"We met with Jean-Louis Gassée to propose that Apple incorporate DDE into their OS," recalls Jeff Harbers, who then was Microsoft's director of applications development. "We told them that Windows apps are supporting this and that we wanted better integration capability for the Mac. Apple was non-responsive—they were more interested in doing a more technically difficult approach."

In 1992, as both OpenDoc and OLE were under way, Microsoft began talking with Apple again about working together on OLE. "We were always of the point of view that there were many more things Apple and Microsoft could work together on, and then they could pick their battles where they could be different," says Pete Higgins, Microsoft's former senior vice president of desktop applications and now group vice president of the company's Interactive Media Group. Like most of the top executives at Microsoft, Higgins is boyish-looking and, wearing a preppie ski sweater in his interview for this book, looked ready to hit the slopes of the snow-covered Cascades visible out his third-floor corner office in Redmond, Washington. Higgins does not do it much, but several other managers at Microsoft rock as they talk, back and forth, just like Big Bill.

Apple maintained that OpenDoc was a superior technology, and one that would be open to the whole industry as opposed to the proprietary, or closed, one owned and controlled by Microsoft in OLE. A developer could thus use the OpenDoc tools to write an objects program and it would be able to run not only on the Mac but on Windows and other operating systems. Indeed, Apple did not own OpenDoc, although it had originated the technology. Apple, in conjunction with partners including IBM, Novell, Oracle, and Sun, had formed a consortium called the Component Integration Labs to create OpenDoc, with Apple in charge of the design.

OLE was a technology controlled by Microsoft for Windows and Macintosh programs. One might find it hypocritical for Apple to be touting itself as the "open" company when it had eschewed licensing for so long. Apple's motivation here, though, was one of paramount self-interest. Since the vast majority of the PC market belonged to Microsoft, Apple had to make a compelling case for developers to support Apple, too.

In any event, between 1992 and 1994 the two sides argued. At one point, Higgins remembers, he told Nagel and the other top executives at Apple that OpenDoc was going to force software developers to make a choice: support Windows or Macintosh, not both. "We would tell them it doesn't make a point to make your stand on plumbing, something the user would never see," Higgins says.

Dave Nagel remembers, however, that Apple was reluctant to embrace the technology because Microsoft was the company's foremost competitor. "I would agree to support a Microsoft technology if Microsoft were any other company," Nagel says. "But that would guarantee we would be late to market [with Microsoft's technology] because Windows would always have it first. I knew that if we adopted the OLE technology, we would have a time-to-market deficit we would have to live with the rest of our lives."

The OpenDoc and OLE debate was also uppermost on Bill Gates's mind when he sat down with Michael Spindler for an hour at the Comdex show in Las Vegas in 1993. It was the first of what would be exactly three meetings between the two men. Gates had requested the meeting but went away disappointed. "Our whole message to Apple at this time was to focus on areas of innovation that count to users—not object plumbing but user interface including voice, graphics, video and information sharing," Gates wrote in his e-mail response for this book. "Our position was that Apple should pick the things that count and make sure to focus their resources there. In particular, we were worried that by having different Object plumbing in OpenDoc and OLE that developers would be unable to share development work for the

Macintosh and Windows." Gates did most of the talking as Spindler listened. "I was disappointed that Mike seemed so uncertain and wary that he hardly said anything," Gates remembers.

The Apple-Microsoft talks were still under way in May 1994 when Apple pulled a fast one. At its annual Worldwide Developers Conference (WWDC) in San Jose, California, that month, Apple went ahead and announced Open-Doc. "They didn't even tell us about it," Higgins recalls, his face flushing in renewed anger as he recalls the episode. "And we had been talking with them about OLE for two years."

It had been at an earlier WWDC that a former Microsoft manager remembers Apple employees "stealing" invitations to a Microsoft-sponsored party in the sports bar of the Fairmont Hotel, a few blocks from the San Jose Convention Center, and then showing up to berate him. Microsoft had shelled out about $25,000 for the event and had included a video spoof of Microsoft. "Apple people were yelling at me even as they drank my beer," recalls the manager, who worked on Microsoft's Mac development and asked to remain anonymous.

Microsoft's road to Power Macintosh was similarly disenchanting. In January 1994, Jim Gable and some of the other Power Mac executives visited Microsoft's Mac development team in Redmond, Washington, to say, "We need you to be at the Power Mac launch," recalls the former manager. "They said we should support it because it was RISC." As Higgins and other Microsoft executives remember, Microsoft had fully planned to support the Power Mac all along. What Microsoft needed, though, was a simple business plan from Apple outlining how Microsoft, as a developer, stood to make money off the new machines. The religion at Microsoft was always about changing the balance sheet, not changing the world.

The next month, February 1994, a Microsoft marketing manager named Don Pickens and five other members of his Mac marketing team flew down to Silicon Valley to meet with Jim Gable and his entourage in a Microsoft office in Menlo Park. The meeting to review Apple's marketing strategy for Power Mac started at 5 P.M. and droned on past midnight. "They kept saying this machine would get them the fence-sitters [the new users who were undecided between Windows and the Mac], but we wanted to know who they were targeting and why they would buy," recalls the Microsoft manager, who was in the meeting. "Microsoft is all about focus. At Apple, they wanted to do everything, or 'random,' as Bill would say."

Under persistent questioning from the Microsoft side, the Apple team honed a strategy that essentially narrowed down the Power Mac's key selling points to its faster speed and upgrade for existing customers. Pickens got Gable to put all this into a purple folder, which Pickens took back to Redmond to show Gates. Gates was willing to support the Power Mac launch with a Microsoft presence at the New York rollout, but, as usual, he wanted some concessions. A key concern: that Apple discontinue its practice of bundling, or including for free, the ClarisWorks business productivity program made by Apple's Claris unit in any Power Macintosh for the first eighteen months after the launch. Gates insisted on this because he viewed the bundling as giving an unfair advantage to Claris.

"That became the basis of negotiations," says the Microsoft manager. "Ian Diery said he could give us no assurance they would not bundle ClarisWorks. We said, 'Either bundle us with Claris, or don't do a bundle at all.' Ian, who was under pressure from other Apple executives who hated us, said there would be no Microsoft bundle." Gates was so furious that both Pickens and Higgins were convinced the whole deal was about to go down the drain, as they discussed one night by telephone as Pickens sat in the hot tub of his Seattle home.

After all this, Gates told Pickens that Microsoft would participate in the Power Mac launch only if Apple put up $1 million against another $1 million by Microsoft to jointly advertise Power Mac and Microsoft's new Office suite for the machine. Gates also insisted that Apple include Microsoft's software in some kind of bundle. Apple agreed, but only to include the bundle in computer superstores where the Mac's business was very small. It was a bone, really, but better than nothing. Gates agreed to roll out Microsoft Office for Power Mac in June.

The Microsoft saga did not end here, though. At the New York launch, Higgins remembers Michael Spindler being "very friendly, very cordial, but he was also suspicious and unsure of how much to work with Microsoft." Back in Redmond, meanwhile, Ben Waldman and his Microsoft programmers were busy developing the new Power Mac Office suite. But they ran into a serious roadblock when Apple denied their request to supply software tools to help in the development process, forcing the Microsoft team to go another route that delayed completion of Office by several months. And Microsoft screwed up its end, too—royally.

The linchpin to Microsoft Office is Microsoft Word, because that is the program that office workers spend the majority of their time using. To maximize the speed and performance gains on PowerPC, Microsoft planned a complete rewrite of Word called Word 6.0 for Power Macintosh. Microsoft's head of Macintosh technology then was Ben Waldman, an affable engineer who had joined Microsoft in 1989 with the express desire of writing programs for the Mac that he had grown to love. Waldman also headed the development of Mac Excel 5.0, the Microsoft spreadsheet program being developed as part of the Office suite for Power Mac. "We wanted the [Power Mac] platform to succeed because we knew we would ship more products," Waldman says.

But Word 6.0 for Power Macintosh turned out to be a fiasco of unprecedented scale. When it finally shipped in October 1994, it took thirty seconds to "boot up" on the computer screen and ran so slowly that a simple count of words in a document took many seconds longer than the Word version on Windows. The problem, Bill Gates says now, boiled down to three things: The first release had a slow "boot" time, caused in part by Microsoft not spending enough time in testing it. The Mac's operating system could not handle the large memory of the program well (Apple later put some general fixes into the system that speeded up performance). And Word 6.0 required too much memory for the older Macintoshes being upgraded to PowerPC through add-in circuit cards.

Mac users were furious, and the press had a field day trashing the product. Apple's loyalists, and many people in Apple itself, were convinced that Microsoft was intent on sabotaging the Power Mac by delivering a poor software program. Privately, some Apple executives confided that they felt Microsoft had delayed shipping Microsoft Word and the whole Office suite to give its ally, Intel, time for Pentium to build up a wide lead in sales and momentum. They also felt the problems in Word 6.0 were illustrative of Microsoft's growing lack of commitment to the Macintosh platform.

This was hardly the case, however, for even Bill Gates was so upset that he fired off an e-mail message to Don Pickens calling Word 6.0 "our biggest embarrassment ever." He repeated that admission in his e-mail memo to me. "Overall I am embarrassed we didn't do better," Gates wrote. "If Apple had cooperated with us, we would have done a lot better but that is not an excuse for our mistakes." Microsoft did take the unusual step of running ads apologizing for the mistake and within a few weeks shipped free updates to customers that corrected the problems.

Microsoft's delay in hitting the market with a major productivity program for so long hindered Apple's ability to make any inroads into the corporate market and created considerable anxiety on Wall Street. Indeed, Salomon Brothers recommended a "hold" on Apple's stock in April 1994, largely because of Microsoft's initial absence from the Power Mac when it had been launched one month before, in March. The Microsoft business programs — Excel, PowerPoint, Word, and the Office suite — did not begin shipping until September and October of 1994. For the same reason, Power Mac sales began slowing in May at some business-oriented distributors, precipitating a 10 percent slide in the stock over a one-week period. Sales rebounded after that, as more programs became available and Apple's customers continued their heavy upgrade buying.

But the availability of Microsoft's business programs was not the answer to all of the Power Mac's problems. Indeed, by the end of 1994, Apple had still made no inroads into the Wintel market for a second reason: its hardware was priced too high.

In an interview with me before the Power Mac launch, Apple's Ian Diery had promised to position Power Mac so aggressively against the competition that Power Macs would be priced roughly $200 below comparable models from top rivals such as Compaq and IBM. The whole selling point of Power-PC, in fact, was that a user would get more bang for the buck. The PowerPC chip was cheaper to make than Intel's Pentium, and the cost savings would translate into Apple, for the first time, actually being priced below most other brands. In other words, Apple would have the advantage of a higher price-to-performance ratio.

"For the first time," Diery said in that February 22, 1994, interview for *The Wall Street Journal*, "we are invading the enemy's territory."

When Diery said this, in his De Anza 7 office with fresh snow dotting the peaks of the Diablo Range visible to the southeast, he really meant it. Diery, first and foremost, was a sales guy, and more than anything else he wanted to push as many boxes out the door as he humanly could. He knew he would never have a chance of gaining much market share if Apple kept pricing its machines higher than the competition's, so he devised a strategy of going after volume. There was one big problem with this plan, though: Spindler and the Apple board wouldn't let him do it.

Diery suffered the dilemma of running practically the only division in Apple making any money. The AppleSoft division was making no money, because its charter was research. The PIE division was making no money, because its Newton MessagePad product was off to a rocky start. And the Apple Business Systems division was not making much money, because its presence in the database-server market was small. Not only that, but Macintosh sales accounted for 95 percent of Apple's revenue, yet the division comprised just 60 percent of the company's head count. The remaining 40 percent of the employees were tucked away in various projects such as Newton, eWorld, and system software, which were consuming money like a drunken sailor.

Diery, in short, was shackled from head to toe, with the rest of the organization sucking money out of his PC division like so many leeches. With the Wintel manufacturers driving prices in the industry ever lower and talk resurfacing in Cupertino about opening up the Macintosh to its own clone market, Diery began pleading for Spindler to drastically chop Apple's expenses so it could compete. The Diesel had taken the meat-ax to the budget in 1993, when he had let 2,500 heads roll, but Apple's expense structure was still out of line with those of its hardware competitors. In 1994, for example, Apple spent 15 percent of its total revenues on sales, general, and administrative expenses, or SG and A, compared to Compaq, which spent about 11 percent. Apple's R-and-D expenses, moreover, amounted to 6 percent of that year's revenues, compared to 3 percent for Compaq.

"Ian went to Spindler and the board and said, 'You have to unleash me,' " recalls a former senior executive familiar with the episode. "He said, 'At the moment, I have to generate hundreds of millions of dollars to support all other divisions. But I have to drive down the cost of the Mac so I can compete.' They all got frightened."

Unleashing Diery so he could compete with the Packard Bells and Gateways of the world on price would require another round of layoffs, possibly even more massive than the big one of 1993. Diery wanted all departments to tighten their belts further, as well as for Apple to stop funding research endeavors that were losing money. "Ian spoke several times of exiting businesses we weren't making money on, like Newton," recalls Don Strickland, then vice president of Apple's imaging and publishing business. The Newton had consumed roughly $500 million of research money and was losing about $50 million a year in this period, according to Apple executives familiar with Newton's performance.

Despite Spindler's reputation as a tenacious cost-cutter, the Diesel had been at Apple too long to consider rocking the boat as much as Diery suggested. Other senior executives were not enamored of the notion, either. At one point when Diery was trimming expenses in his own division, recalls the same senior executive familiar with these matters, Dave Nagel, the general manager of AppleSoft, went up to Diery and complained, "I've got problems. If I cut expenses, my engineers will get all upset at me." Nagel's concern stemmed, no doubt, from the fact that morale had sunk to a precipitous low in engineering following the layoffs of 1993, when the R-and-D ranks had been thinned out along with all the others.

With the rest of the organization unwilling to go along, Diery was forced to maintain a premium-pricing strategy that kept the Power Mac priced as much as $1,000 higher than a comparable one based on the Wintel standard. According to an October 1994 survey by the market research firm InfoWorld, a Power Macintosh 7100, running at 60 megahertz of speed and with a 500-megabyte hard drive, was selling for $3,212, compared to $2,299 for a comparably configured Gateway 2000 P5-60 and $2,846 for an AST Bravo MT P/60. Apple officials tried to disguise the differentials by listing prices that did not include essentials such as keyboard, monitor, and modem. They then complained vociferously—in letters to the editor and even visits to the publisher—whenever I pointed this out in articles for The Wall Street Journal.

Customers were not fooled, though. As a result, Apple lost out on another golden opportunity to gain market share when Christmas 1994 hit and the multimedia technology that Apple had pioneered swept the industry. Christmas is the most important selling time of the year for computer manufacturers, accounting for as much as 40 percent of an entire year's sales. And that Christmas, multimedia was the buzzword not only in the industry but in living rooms across America. In 1993, Apple had been the first company to widely distribute computers equipped with CD-ROM drives, which allowed video clips, text, and sound to be played. By late 1994, with Intel's powerful new Pentium chip and a flood of new multimedia programs, the Wintel hordes followed suit.

Driven by the rush to multimedia by home consumers in the United States, PC sales shot to an all-time record, surging 32 percent higher in unit shipments than the Christmas period a year earlier. Almost everyone in the industry racked up huge sales gains, except for Apple, whose unit shipments were essentially the same as in the comparable quarter a year earlier. Apple's balance sheet was bolstered: profits more than quadrupled from the previous Christmas, to $188 million, or $1.55 a share. But its quest to regain market share was dealt a shattering blow: its share of the worldwide PC market fell to 8.3 percent in 1994 from 9.4 percent in 1993.[4]

It was abundantly clear that Power Mac, by itself, was not going to save Apple's bacon. But a separate initiative that was already under way could have. It involved that dreaded "L-word"—licensing—and before it was all over the big "L" would lead to one of the more intriguing mating dances in corporate history.

The renewed impetus for licensing the Macintosh had actually begun in mid-1993, when Sculley had been booted out as CEO and Spindler had put it high on his strategic agenda. Spindler had finally become convinced it was time to take the bold step, in part after hearing a shocking report from Randy Battat, vice president of portables and Mac desktops, about a trip Battat had taken to Taiwan in 1992 to see if Apple could get manufacturing and design help from the Taiwanese clone makers. At seeing dozens upon dozens of PC companies making everything from circuit boards to monitor boxes, Battat had returned to Cupertino ashen-faced.

"It dawned on Randy just how vast the computer industry was," recalls a former Apple executive who heard Battat's report. "He came to the conclusion that Apple was in deep shit. Apple was playing alone outside the computer industry and had to come up with everything itself." Apple not only manufactured almost all its computers itself, it also designed every circuit board and relied on a small circle of suppliers for parts. The circle was small, because the Macintosh market consisted of just Apple.

At the time, Robert Lauridsen was still Apple's vice president for corporate development. He had assisted Sculley in shopping the company to suitors such as AT&T and Kodak and, after Sculley had been bumped upstairs, had begun holding weekly meetings on how Apple could license and with whom, according to a person involved with them. These talks coincided with a short-lived initiative by Spindler to change the name of the Macintosh's operating system to Navigator OS, after Sculley's Knowledge Navigator, to make licensing more appealing to potential cloners.

Actually, Sculley had pitched the same idea to his executives in 1992, but nothing had ever come of it. Spindler's Navigator proposal did not pan out either, but he allowed Lauridsen's group to pay informal visits to PC manufacturers including IBM, Dell, and Compaq to gauge their interest in licensing the Mac. At this point, their interest was tepid; Compaq, for instance, was most interested in "whether PowerPC was a threat or not," recalls a former Apple executive who met with them.

Apple had almost fallen off the radar screen.

In the fall of 1993, Battat appeared before Spindler and the executive staff to make essentially the same pitch that young Dan Eilers had in 1985. "If we don't license quickly," Battat said, according to a person present in the meeting, "we will be out of business. Time is running out. If we are lucky, maybe we can encourage an industry of Mac components which we can feed off." Ian Diery was reluctant to push ahead, though, just as he had been in leading the opposition against the Drama project in 1992 to let Apple's own Claris unit sell Mac clones. At another executive staff meeting some months later, Diery had blown his cool when the subject was brought up again.

In that meeting, in the De Anza 7 Synergy room, Russ Irwin, an executive working under Robert Lauridsen in corporate development, had stood up to make his case for cloning the Mac to others when a shouting match erupted between Ian Diery, on one side of the table, and Dave Nagel, on the other. The argument broke out after Diery suggested that Apple sell Macintosh licenses only to manufacturers willing to include a PC-compatibility program called "SoftPC" that would add $500 to the cost of each clone box, recalls a person who was in the room. This, Diery figured, would ensure that the licensees would sell to people coming from the PC, because they would want this program to run their MS-DOS and Windows applications. "Diery says, 'Licensing is great. I'm all for licensing, so long as they sell to the other guys [or non-Macintosh customers],'" recalls the person in the room that day. "Then he says, 'But I don't want to be cannibalized.'"

Dave Nagel was no wild-eyed licensing fanatic. In fact, his support for it was remembered by colleagues as fairly lukewarm. But he found Diery's suggestion preposterous. "Nagel was basically arguing against this [adding the SoftPC program], saying that it was a totally arbitrary burden to place on a licensee and would make the overall proposition unattractive," says the person in the room. After arguing back and forth for about a half hour, Diery finally backed off his proposal. During the debate, Spindler watched mostly in silence. He may have been the Diesel to the outside world, but he was a pussycat around domineering types such as Diery. In that regard, curiously enough, Michael Spindler was not unlike John Sculley.

It was not just Ian Diery who feared licensing. The previous summer, in August 1993, Aaron Goldberg, executive vice president of the Computer Intelligence research firm in La Jolla, California, had flown to Cupertino to deliver a licensing presentation to a group of twenty Apple managers. Goldberg was one of a number of consultants called in by Apple to give advice on licensing and other strategies. He almost did not get out alive. Goldberg, a tough Massachusetts native who is built like a professional football player, warned the group that Apple had, at best, a nine-month window in which to license because Microsoft's newest operating system, code-named "Chicago," was coming hard and fast. (The product would ship in 1995 as Windows 95.) "Four guys were screaming, 'You're lying! That is wrong information!' " Goldberg remembers. "I told them they had no choice but to clone. I said, 'You guys are going to lose on cost to Wintel.' "

Goldberg was granted a more favorable audience with Spindler. In this meeting, Goldberg remembers, the CEO ambled over to his ever-present whiteboard and scribbled, in true Diesel style, "IBM," "Compaq," "Gateway," and "Dell." Spindler turned from the board and said, "We won't announce a licensing strategy until these guys sign up." Following the meeting with Battat and the others, Spindler impaneled a licensing task force, with Randy Battat as its head. Diery still did not relish the idea, but he, too, knew that some form of licensing was inevitable. Time was so short that Battat pressed for Spindler to make some kind of licensing announcement in the keynote address that the Diesel would deliver at the 1993 Comdex show in Las Vegas.

With the licensing strategy yet to be hammered out, Spindler waited until Apple's annual shareholders' meeting on January 26, 1994. There, he told the shareholders he wanted PC manufacturers to make Mac clones based on the PowerPC chip. Later, a spokesman for Spindler added that the company was in active talks and expected to sign at least one licensing agreement by the end of that year.[5] There. It was out. After nine years and untold agonizing, Apple Computer had finally bitten the bullet. And guess what? Not many people seemed to care anymore. "The situation was that everyone at Apple thought everyone wanted the Mac OS terribly," Irwin says. "So Apple was clinging to the Mac OS like its crown jewels. But the fact was, the world had passed on the Mac."

That same month, the licensing effort was dealt another setback when Randy Battat announced his resignation, effective January 31, to become vice president and general manager of Motorola's wireless data group. Battat, who would not comment for this book, told me then that he had been motivated to take the Motorola job because of the great career opportunity. Named by Spindler to take his place was Cheryl Vedoe, the same Cheryl Vedoe who had been told not to board the plane at the Boston airport in 1987 when John Sculley had decided at the eleventh hour to pull the plug on a licensing deal with her then-employer, Apollo.

After that, Vedoe had moved on to Sun and had joined Apple in February 1992 as vice president of marketing for Apple USA, under Bob Puette, president of the division. Two weeks later, her job was eliminated in one of the biannual reorganizations going on in Apple USA at the time, and she was asked to head marketing for Apple's big K–12 school division instead. After Puette resigned in 1993, Vedoe ended up on Battat's licensing task force. Ian Diery briefly took over Puette's responsibilities, before the presidency of Apple USA was turned over to a nine-year Apple marketing veteran named Jim Buckley in January 1994. Buckley would play a fateful role in the licensing drama further down the road.

When Vedoe took the licensing reins, she remembers Spindler being fully supportive. "My impression from Michael was that he was gung ho about licensing," Vedoe recalls. But before any serious licensing negotiations could begin with anybody, she says she first had to work out exactly how Apple would approach the new business. One of the big issues was that Apple would have to have enough technical support on hand to support both the software and hardware needs of any cloners. This was necessary because the Macintosh's operating system was so tightly integrated with the computer's hardware. There were also the strategic questions to wrestle with, such as: With what kind of companies did Apple want to license? What were the implications for the low end of Apple's Mac business, where price competition from cloners was likely to be most fierce?

After several months of studying these issues, Vedoe came to the conclusion that Apple should license all out or not at all. "We looked at a lot of options, but, quite honestly, if you look at anything short of aggressive licensing, it won't work," she says. "Our goal was to achieve significant market share through Mac licensing. But to shift a company's strategy, overnight, to competing against a cheap clone threatened Apple's core business." Vedoe would not have time to follow through on the licensing plan, though. She announced her resignation from Apple, effective on June 3, 1994, less than six months after being placed in her position. Like Battat, Vedoe left to pursue better opportunities. She became CEO of a small software concern named Media3 in the nearby coastal village of Half Moon Bay, California. The company's name has since been changed to Tenth Planet, and Vedoe still heads it.

Suddenly, it was a game of musical chairs all over again. That month, June 1994, Spindler called into the licensing job Don Strickland, Apple's vice president for imaging and publishing. Formerly an executive at Kodak, Strickland had joined Apple in 1993 to run its imaging business. Strickland was well suited to the job, because he was an analytical thinker with strong business depth. Just as important, he was such a newcomer to Apple that he did not have the baggage of being a participant in the long-simmering licensing debate.

Strickland's first task was to compile estimates on how much Apple's hardware business would be cannibalized by licensing. One option he considered was licensing to just one or two manufacturers, minimizing the cannibalization of Apple's sales. The other was to go all out, as both Vedoe and now Strickland recommended. This was a frightening scenario, though, because there were two diametrically opposed views on what this would do to Apple: one, held by Apple's sales corps, that the company's revenues would fall by one fifth; the other, favored by strategists such as Strickland, that revenues would actually increase as the Mac pond widened with new Wintel customers.

"There was no consensus on which would happen, so we had to make the call: 'Do you do it or not?'" Strickland says. One day in late June 1994, Spindler called Strickland up to his office atop De Anza 7 and, with a smile on his face, announced, "I've decided to do it. I know it won't be an easy job," Strickland recalls. By this, Spindler had decided to license to all comers, no restrictions. "He told me to put together a business plan to execute it, and do it quickly."

Strickland worked through the Fourth of July weekend, poring over all the pertinent research data. On September 19, 1994, he announced his plan to the world. Licensees, he said, would not be subject to any marketing restraints whatsoever. "They can offer any kind of Mac they want, at whatever price they want and in whatever market they want," Strickland told me for *The Wall Street Journal*. The initial number of licensees would be limited to six, he said, because Apple did not have resources to deal with any more just then. Getting even those six, however, would prove to be no picnic, despite the rosy view portrayed in an Apple video called "I Think We're a Clone Now."

The video, produced by Apple's competitive analysis group for internal consumption and marked "For Apple Eyes Only," represented a solitary return of the humorous videos that had been a staple at Apple during the Sculley years. It featured a licensing manager named Dave Garr singing "I Think We're a Clone Now" to the tune of "I Think We're Alone Now," the 1987 hit by pop star Tiffany. In the video, Garr, wearing shades, a purple T-shirt, and jeans, cavorted on the lawn outside Apple's R-and-D campus, flanked by two female Apple employees in black Apple T-shirts, as he began singing:

> *Isn't it strange*
> *We used to own the whole Mac market*
> *What would Sculley say*
> *if only he knew that we were*
> *Licensing as fast as we can . . .*

The song went on to describe how Apple was journeying to Taiwan and Japan to show manufacturers how to build a Mac clone and concluded with a snide reference to Jean-Louis Gassée no longer being around—apparently to stop licensing again.

As Garr belted out the lyrics, a female Apple employee wearing a Michael Spindler mask stood at a little table, handing out Mac cardboard boxes to "licensees" lined up behind a sign that read: "Mac Cloners Form a Line Here."

When he went out to beat the bushes for real licensees, however, Russ Irwin was encountering no lines at all. Over many months throughout 1994, Irwin had met with representatives of AST, Compaq, Dell, Gateway, IBM, Motorola, and Zenith Data Systems in the United States; Germany's Vobis Microcomputer AG and Italy's Ing. C. Olivetti & Compagnia SpA in Europe; and Taiwan's Acer Inc., Korea's Goldstar Company, and Japan's Toshiba Corporation in Asia. Irwin encountered skepticism at nearly every stop on whether Apple was really serious, having reneged on licensing so many times in the past.

"There was not a single major manufacturer who had the hots for it," Irwin recalls. "They wanted us to prove we were sincere, and to prove they could overcome the Apple brand and cost advantage." Apple would hold a cost advantage, the companies thought, because they would have to pay to license the Mac's operating system while Apple would not. Irwin pointed out, though, that those costs were actually much higher for Apple, which supported all the R and D that went into making the operating system. Still, Apple would possess the advantage of being the biggest Mac manufacturer and thus being able to procure components at cheaper volume prices.

The other concern, about Apple's brand advantage, was a more serious issue because Apple did have the advantage of being able to charge a premium based on loyal customers who would be willing to pay more for the Apple name. Internally, Apple figured the premium would amount to a price 10 to 15 percent higher than that of a clonc.

"Also," adds Don Strickland, "the hardware and software of the Mac were so tied together that it would be hard to differentiate from Apple. If you can't differentiate, you can't be much different from Apple. Plus, you also have a marketing problem: How do you keep from confusing your Wintel customers?" Dell's customers, for example, might become confused by seeing the maker of Wintel machines suddenly start selling Mac clones, as well. Dell, then, would face the challenge of marketing the two lines separately.

To demonstrate Apple's sincerity, Irwin provided the manufacturers with Apple's cost of goods figures, "to dissuade them from the fear that Apple would screw them on cost of goods." The prospective licensees learned that they did not have to actually buy much from Apple itself other than the Mac's operating system and a license to use the main circuit board. And those costs were not insurmountable. Apple was offering to license the circuit boards, for instance, for a onetime fee of $50,000 to $100,000.

The solution to the cost and differentiation problem was supposed to rest with a new initiative by Apple, IBM, and Motorola called CHRP (pronounced "chirp"), which stood for Common Hardware Reference Platform. Under CHRP, a new PowerPC machine would be designed over the next three years, using commonly available parts so prices could be driven down just as with the Wintel industry. The trail to CHRP was a tortuous one, though, and it very nearly culminated in one of the great business mergers of the twentieth century: a combination of Apple Computer, the PC industry's premier innovator, and IBM, the world's biggest computer company. Just as the relationship between Apple and Microsoft had been a strained one over the years, the one between Apple and IBM had been a stormy affair. In the early days, of course, Apple had chided and berated IBM, even as Big Blue and its legion of clones roared in to steal control of the market. The great truce had been declared in 1991, with John Sculley and IBM President Jack Kuehler raising hands in victory over their historic alliance to share technologies. But the close bonds between the two companies had dissipated with the ouster of Sculley in 1993 and Kuehler's retirement the same year. Apple and IBM, along with Motorola, had achieved great technical success with PowerPC, and the new microprocessor was helping keep Apple afloat as it tried to figure out a way out of its box.

But the other two key parts of the deal—Taligent, which would create a new operating system, and Kaleida, which would develop a new multimedia software language—were crashing in flames by 1994, to the tune of about $300 million in Apple and IBM money down the drain when it was all over at the end of 1995. Al Eisenstat, the Apple executive vice president booted by Spindler, could have said "I told you so." When Taligent and Kaleida had been formed as part of the 1991 alliance, Eisenstat had written a six-page letter to Sculley advising him not to participate in those projects. "It will cost the company a bloody fortune," Eisenstat had warned Sculley. Sculley's reply: "Thank you."[6]

Both projects relied on Apple technology, plus money and management from both Apple and IBM. Taligent, of course, had represented Apple's attempt to offload its amorphous Pink project, originally conceived as a replacement for the Macintosh's aging operating system, into a joint entity whose spiraling costs would be offset by IBM. But just as Pink had mutated out of control because it had never had any focus, that same disease afflicted the Taligent operating system effort.

Taligent began in late 1991, and its first CEO was an IBM veteran named Joe Guglielmi, better known in the industry as "Joe G." Named as his chief operating officer was Ed Birss, Apple's former senior vice president for software engineering. Staffed almost exclusively by Apple's former Pink engineers, the Taligent project was so Applecentric that it was headquartered in low-rise buildings right behind Apple's campus in Cupertino. And the Taligent engineers proved no better able to deliver a working product than they had been at Apple.

Dave Burnard saw the deterioration of Taligent firsthand. Having joined the Pink team as an engineer in 1988, Burnard had joined his colleagues in the exodus of some one hundred Apple engineers to Taligent. Almost immediately, Pink's old goals of becoming Apple's next operating system—based on that great holy grail, "objects"—had changed to Taligent's goal of creating an operating system that could run on any computer: a portable OS. "At this point, I didn't know what was going on," Burnard recalls.

Taligent had grown from about 120 engineers and marketing and support people in 1991 to about 350 by the end of 1992. Through it all, the goals had kept changing, and engineers had formed subteams to tackle esoteric problems such as how to get the computer to simulate dialing the telephone. It was precisely the kind of stuff that most customers could not give a hang about, yet Taligent had four engineers assigned to this technical challenge. When Taligent had finally gotten down to asking what customers did want, a year into the research, it had discovered that the world really did not want another operating system, after all. That was when Taligent's Joe G. had pulled the plug on the OS plan and instead focused the engineers on a less grandiose "layer" of object-based software that would lie on top of an existing operating system.

But Microsoft had already been marketing its object-based layer, called OLE, for two years, and Apple itself was pushing its OpenDoc. And Taligent was still "two years" to market, just as it had been since the first days of Pink. In short, Taligent did not have a prayer.

Kaleida was just as badly off. Originally, that venture had been supposed to produce a multimedia programming language code-named "ScriptX," with delivery by October 1992. But it had taken nearly that long—until July 1992—just to get Kaleida started. Apple and IBM had selected an industry venture capitalist named Nat Goldhaber to head the venture, officially called Kaleida Labs Inc. and based near Apple in Mountain View, California. Goldhaber, however, had begun running into problems almost immediately as an entrepreneur trying to manage a staff of about 125 Apple and IBM engineers accustomed to working for years in big companies where projects often went nowhere. "The culture of IBM and Apple is largely about getting more benefits, perks, larger offices, fancier computers, and more employees," Goldhaber told me in an interview for *The Wall Street Journal* in 1994.

Many of the engineers, conversely, saw Goldhaber as a penny-pincher lacking in management skills. One time, for example, he nixed their request for graphically embroidered business cards that would cost $1 apiece. Instead, Goldhaber requisitioned plain-vanilla ones for $20 per five-hundred-card box. "I can't tell you how many points I lost with the staff on that," Goldhaber said.

Unable to coordinate the Kaleida research effort, Goldhaber resigned a year later, in 1993. He was replaced by Mike Braun, formerly IBM's vice president for multimedia. At the time, Kaleida was bogged down in dead-end projects such as running the ScriptX language on a handheld CD-ROM player code-named "Sweet Pea." But that player, developed by Apple and Toshiba, proved so underpowered that it was eventually dropped after Kaleida had worked on it for eighteen months. Outside interference by both Apple and IBM also undermined the venture, such as when the two parent companies ordered a total of nine technology audits in one year when one or two would have been normal. The audits basically consisted of managerial reviews on how the work was going, and each one took an average of three grueling days of presentations.

Braun moved quickly to try to refocus Kaleida, slashing the staff by 40 percent, or 50 positions, and trimming Kaleida's goals back to just ScriptX. In the process, he jettisoned auxiliary projects such as Sweet Pea, an interactive operating system, and a special graphics chip. It was too late, though—for both Kaleida and Taligent. In November 1995, Apple and IBM pulled the plug on Kaleida, and a month later they dissolved Taligent. Half of Taligent's now-four-hundred-member staff was laid off and the rest were folded into IBM, along with the venture's software technology. Dave Burnard and his ill-starred colleagues at Taligent got the word on Thanksgiving Day.

"My office mate and I used to have this joke about 'Reality Man' and 'Fantasy Man,' " he recalls, sipping a latte in Seattle's Pioneer Square a few blocks from his new job as an engineer for Adobe's research arm there. "Fantasy Man was not worried about the project. Reality Man was worried from 1992."

The track record of cooperation between Apple and IBM was not exactly pretty, so it was little wonder that the CHRP effort also got off to a rocky start. CHRP's foundation was laid in August 1993, when IBM's chief technologist, a Japanese national named Nobuo Mii, hopped a shuttle flight from New York to Boston to meet with Apple's Dave Nagel at the Macworld Boston show. Lou Gerstner had replaced John Akers as IBM's chairman and CEO in February of that year and, together with Jim Cannavino, his top strategist, had conveyed to Spindler a desire to pursue either licensing the Mac's operating system or merging it with OS/2, according to an Apple executive familiar with those discussions. As Mii remembers, Nagel asked why IBM did not just license the Mac for its fleet of PowerPC machines, in which IBM intended to use its new OS/2.

OS/2 was the operating system effort that IBM had begun in the 1980s, initially with Microsoft's help. When Microsoft had bailed out of the project to concentrate on Windows, IBM had pressed ahead with OS/2, positioning it as an alternative to Windows. Since Windows was already the standard on Intel-based computers in the early 1990s, IBM hoped to push OS/2 on a new line of personal computers based on the PowerPC microprocessor, as well as on Intel's. While Apple had used PowerPC to replace its old Macintosh line, IBM planned to develop PowerPC-based computers that could run a variety of operating systems, including OS/2, Windows NT, IBM's Unix-based AIX system, and the Mac.

"They wanted us to do a straight clone, but we wouldn't benefit from that," says Mii, who is now chairman and chief executive of SegaSoft, a Redwood City, California–based software unit of Japan's Sega Enterprises Ltd. Nagel kept pressing, and finally Mii suggested a compromise: Why not collaborate on the design of a new PowerPC machine that could run not only the Mac's operating system but also OS/2, Windows NT, and Unix systems? (Unix is an operating system for minicomputers and workstations that is made in many different versions.) This would be called CHRP. When Nagel would not buy into the plan, Mii says he went back to IBM's headquarters in Armonk, New York, and launched work on a similar initiative called PReP, or the PowerPC Reference Platform. There was one big difference, though. PReP was initially designed to run all those operating systems—except the Mac's.

"I was ready to move forward with CHRP, but Apple pushed the Mac clone too hard," Mii says.

Nagel, however, denies he pushed IBM just to license a Mac clone. "That isn't true," Nagel says. "It must have been a language problem [on the part of the Japanese-born Mii]." Nagel adds that the real hindrance to negotiations then was IBM's insistence that Apple turn over its Mac OS source code, which contained the secrets of the Macintosh technology.

When IBM unveiled its PReP strategy at Fall Comdex 1993, Spindler was livid at the Mac being left out. He got on the horn to IBM and demanded a meeting, which was set up at a neutral spot in Dallas, Texas, in the late spring of 1994. Flying in from both coasts was an IBM team that included Jim Cannavino, Rick Thoman, then head of IBM's PC business, and Nobuo Mii, as well as an Apple team that included Spindler, Nagel, Joe Graziano, and Spindler's powerful aide, David Seda. Seated around a conference table at a hotel, the IBMers listened as Spindler agreed to license the Mac if Big Blue would renew its commitment to the CHRP initiative.

Spindler's concession was a 180-degree turnabout from that 1993 meeting between Dave Nagel and Nobuo Mii. But remember that in 1993, Apple was barely formulating its licensing strategy and there was still considerable resistance to the idea from many people within. The IBM side agreed, setting the stage for another round of meetings at Apple's R-and-D campus in Cupertino in the early summer.

During the interim, though, Apple started waffling again. At first, when Spindler agreed to license the Mac, "IBM thought this was a great thing," Mii remembers. But when IBM began insisting that the choice of which operating system to use on the new CHRP machines should be left up to the customer, Mii says, Apple balked. "Apple said, 'We need a licensing agreement with IBM.' Apple wanted to announce this to the world," Mii recalls. "But we did not think we needed a licensing agreement because we were going to leave it up to the customer."

As the two sides haggled—Nagel, representing the Apple viewpoint, and Lee Reiswig, head of IBM's OS/2 development, heading software talks for Big Blue—Mii and other top IBMers came to a conclusion. "I told Cannavino, 'We should just buy Apple,' " Mii recalls. "Frankly, we were tired of so many negotiations. We were almost out of patience." On the Apple side, Spindler and Company were reluctant to share much of the company's operating system technology without a formal commitment by IBM.

The two sides met again later that summer at Apple's sprawling R-and-D campus, where a giant, rainbow-colored Apple logo affixed to one of the four-story structures is plainly visible from nearby Interstate 280. Fittingly, considering the projects that seemed to go on endlessly inside the research corridors, the campus was encircled by a road called Infinite Loop. The small delegation of executives huddled inside a conference room in one of the buildings. As had been the case in the first negotiations between Apple and IBM on PowerPC, the Apple people wore suits while the ones from Big Blue did not.

At one point, Spindler pulled Cannavino out of the conference room to meet privately, in the company of their respective aides. Spindler asked him whether everybody would not be better off if the two companies just merged. It was the same idea broached by John Sculley in early 1993, when IBM had courted him about the possibility of succeeding Akers as IBM's chairman and CEO.

"Spindler thought we should go all the way, not part of the way," remembers an IBM executive who attended all these meetings. "He thought we would pull apart if we only went part of the way. That's why we couldn't agree on the CHRP platform or the Mac license." Indeed, the idea of IBM buying Apple was an attractive proposition, articulated as early as 1991, when Cannavino and then–IBM President Jack Kuehler had discussed the possibility among themselves, and obliquely with John Sculley, in the negotiations that led up to the technology alliance between the companies.

The synergies were obvious: IBM had great technology, a vast base of customers in the business market—and gobs of money. Apple possessed world-class computer products, a famous brand in the home and education market, and software leadership in the PC industry. With Apple, IBM would gain access to all that technology and a strong footing in markets such as the home and education, where it was relatively weak. And Apple would gain access to the business markets that for so long had eluded it, as well as Big Blue's seemingly unending financial resources to fund further development.

Cannavino flew back to Armonk, New York, and relayed Spindler's proposal to Louis Gerstner. Gerstner phoned Spindler and Mike Markkula, Apple's new chairman following Sculley's departure, to discuss the possibility of IBM buying Apple.[7] Afterward, Spindler walked up to Robert Lauridsen, Apple's vice president for corporate development, with a faraway look in his eyes. "I had a conversation," Spindler said coyly, according to a former Apple executive who heard the exchange. Then the Diesel outlined what had been discussed with Gerstner. Two days later, according to this same person, Spindler stopped Lauridsen over at the R-and-D campus and asked, "Does it make any sense for us to be talking more seriously with IBM?" Lauridsen didn't hesitate: "You're damned right."

A few days after that exchange, in early October 1994, a second Dallas meeting was arranged between an IBM entourage that included Cannavino, Thoman, Thompson, and Lee Reiswig and an Apple delegation that included Spindler and Ian Diery. This time there were no suits, only casual clothes. "We spent most of the time in that meeting talking about the software," recalls the IBM executive involved in the talks. "We talked about how to put the Mac OS and OS/2 together. Would we use QuickTime and QuickDraw? What to do with Taligent? Spindler wanted to segment the market." Using a whiteboard again in the conference room in Dallas, Spindler drew a chart showing the low end of the computer market, where Apple was strong. "We need this to be 'Forever Mac,'" Spindler told the group, according to the IBM executive. "Then he drew on the chart a converged space in corporations where we could merge OS/2 and the Mac for the high end."

Spindler was becoming more and more enthusiastic about the prospect of a merger, as was Ian Diery. Diery, after all, was a hardware guy through and through, and he practically salivated at the thought of two of the top PC makers in the world—holding 20 percent of the world market between them—joining forces. "I think it would have been a great idea," Diery said later, according to a former Apple executive who heard the conversation. "It was an opportunity for IBM to create a great franchise in the PC market. And Apple would have gotten a big boost in business. It was something that customers would have embraced."

When Cannavino reported back to Gerstner on the results of the second Dallas meeting, Gerstner decided to get serious. He appointed an in-house merger team, putting Rick Thoman in charge of the hardware side of an Apple acquisition and Cannavino on the software side, according to the IBM executive involved in the talks. Jerome York, IBM's chief financial officer, was asked to run the financials. "Lou asked Rick and Jim to put a game plan together," recalls the IBM executive.

While all this high-level intrigue was going on, not a word had leaked out to the press. Soon after the second Dallas meeting in early October, the two sides met again on neutral turf, this time in Chicago. Then, in mid-October, an IBM delegation winged back out to the West Coast, setting up camp on the second floor of the three-story Summerfield Suites Hotel, about a ten-minute drive from the San Francisco International Airport. With jets roaring directly overhead, shaking the walls of the ninety-two-room hotel, ten high-ranking engineers from IBM spent the rest of October working out technical details of an Apple/IBM merger with ten of their counterparts from Apple. Top honchos such as Cannavino and Thoman flew in and out to sit in on some of the meetings. Everyone, from both IBM and Apple, checked into rooms registered under IBM's name.

An Apple engineer who attended those meetings remembers the claustrophobic nature of a conference room where they gathered each day. It was designed to hold about ten people but was packed with twenty. The misery index was raised even higher by the fact that the hotel's air conditioning was not working. It was little wonder, then, that all business ceased promptly at 6 P.M. each day, when "someone would yell, 'Hey, it's popcorn and beer time,' " recalls an IBM person who sat in on the talks. The Summerfield served those refreshments for free to guests each day at that time in a room off the lobby called the "Guest House" equipped with tables, chairs, and a television set.

The two sides haggled over how to make OS/2 the foundation of a joint operating system, with the Mac's "look and feel" residing on the top for users to see. The advantage of OS/2 was that it had a modern "microkernel," a type of advanced software that keeps a computer from crashing and allows it to perform multiple functions at once. Apple's System 7 did not have such a kernel and was therefore prone to seizing up and crashing when more than one program was run at the same time.

During all of this, Spindler was complaining of his chronic poor health. For years, all the way back to the 1980s, colleagues and subordinates of Spindler had witnessed his occasional stress attacks, such as when he would start shaking visibly or retreat under his desk. At various times, they say, he had been treated at a hospital following a seizure or other ailment. At two of the high-level IBM-Apple meetings, Dave Nagel, Joe Graziano, and Ed Stead, Apple's general counsel, apologized for their CEO's absence, telling the IBMers that he was too sick to make it from the Valley to the Summerfield.[8] (Ed Stead, a former IBM lawyer, proved to be a big hindrance to the whole process, refusing steadfastly to let IBM have any access to the Mac's operating system technology until after a deal had been finalized, say IBM executives involved in the talks.)

IBM's big concern through all the talks was that it would take as long as a year for the merger to clear all the government regulatory approvals, including a Justice Department antitrust review. In the interim, IBM wanted Apple to grant it a limited Mac license so that Big Blue's team of PC engineers in Boca Raton, Florida, could start "gluing" together a new operating system combining OS/2 and the Macintosh so that it could be ready to hit the street once the merger was completed, recalls an IBM executive participating in the talks. "We even told Stead we were willing to put source code in escrow and have a limited development team work on this, and if the merger falls through, give back the source code and view the people working on it as 'contaminated' and not to work on OS development," says one executive involved in the talks.

Stead was insistent that this not happen, though, and he was supported in this view by Joe Graziano. Stead declined to be interviewed for this book, but a former colleague remembers his position. "Ed knew that if we gave technology to IBM to use while we were going through a Justice review, and it didn't go favorably, how do you keep IBM from utilizing what they learned?" this person says. "And he did position that as just a ploy for IBM to get out stuff without necessarily having to pay for it. And we weren't really going to have very much protection on the technology if the merger wasn't approved."

This intransigence on Apple's part was generating some great concern even among some of IBM's biggest backers of the merger, including Cannavino. By losing so much time in getting access to Apple's "crown jewels"— the core software code that made the Macintosh so unique—IBM was genuinely worried that the ensuing uncertainty among customers of both itself and Apple might result in a free fall in sales. That is why Lou Gerstner was visibly nervous when he boarded a jet the next month, November 1994, to fly to Chicago to try and hammer out a deal. This time, everyone was wearing a suit.

It was a crisp autumn morning in Rosemont, Illinois, as delegations of somber-faced executives in dark business suits from both Apple Computer and IBM boarded elevators to the Premier Gold Floor, twelve stories atop the 525-room Westin Hotel near Chicago's busy O'Hare International Airport. The IBM delegation had arrived from the East Coast that same morning and included Gerstner, Cannavino, Thoman, Jerome York, and John Thompson, an IBM senior vice president. Gerstner arrived in his leased Gulfstream jet. The Apple delegation, which had arrived the night before, included Spindler, Markkula, Stead, Diery, Nagel, Graziano, and Lauridsen.

This was potentially a historic moment of even greater consequence than when Apple and IBM had teamed up to share their technology in 1991. Here were the top executives from two of the biggest computer makers in the world, convening in secret to consummate what could have been one of the great technology mergers of all time. With IBM's $64 billion in revenues that year and Apple's $9 billion, this would have been a colossus of combined sales totaling $73 billion. The merger's impact on the PC industry would have been even more profound: with IBM's 8.7 percent share of the world's PC market and Apple's 8.3 percent, the combined companies would control 17 percent of all personal computer shipments in the world, far surpassing industry leader Compaq, with its 10 percent of the market.[9]

A merger between IBM and Apple would also have ended Apple's exhilarating ride as an independent company—and with a company that, only a few years before, Steve Jobs and his wild-eyed brethren had decried as the evil Big Brother. The Macintosh, in fact, had been billed as the machine that could liberate the masses from the tyranny of big computer conglomerates such as IBM. Yet, a decade later, Apple would be swallowed up into the belly of the beast. It would have been a bittersweet moment in the industry, indeed. But Apple had backed itself into a corner by pursuing the losing strategy of "playing outside the industry," keeping the Mac to itself. It needed to team up with a big company. And Big Blue was as big as they came.

On the flight from San Jose, in one of Markkula's private jets, there was palpable tension in the cabin. More and more, Spindler was expressing a reluctance to go forward. Graziano, however, very much wanted the deal to go through. Apple had been shopping itself since 1992 without success, and there were not any other takers in the wings just then. Leaning forward in his seat, according to a person with intimate knowledge of the conversation, the Graz told the wiry Markkula, "You better really think long and hard about whether it's worth it to try to bid the price up [with IBM] because we only have a limited amount of time. And you can benefit by just having IBM stock."

By this time, the merger talks had progressed so far that both Apple and IBM had notified their respective boards and had retained legal counsel and investment bankers. Representing Apple was the investment banking firm of Goldman Sachs & Company. Representing IBM was Morgan Stanley & Company. Merger task forces had also been assembled by the companies: Dave Nagel from Apple and Jim Cannavino from IBM coheaded a task force to address the operating system issues, while IBM's Rick Thoman was put in charge of a task force to address other issues related to integrating the companies.

Atop the Westin, with views of the daily traffic buildup on Interstates 90 and 294 snaking past below, the Apple and IBM executives filed into the hotel's boardroom and sat down across from each other in black, padded chairs on both sides of a twenty-four-foot-long mahogany conference table. The room, which fairly reeked of corporate power, was adorned with dark beige carpeting, curtains of a printed beige pattern, and, on one wall, an oil painting of an empty boat on a lake. The image was fitting for Apple. If it did not take this boat from IBM, another might not come along.

According to three executives inside the room that day, here is an account of what happened: At 8:30 A.M. sharp, with the roar of jets overhead, the meeting began. The IBM executives gave their presentation, essentially saying "This can work." There was discussion and more presentations by IBM and Apple. Finally, at 11:30 A.M., Gerstner turned to Spindler and Markkula and announced, "I'd like to have a small meeting." Gerstner escorted the two Apple executives into a side room and invited Cannavino and his CFO, Jerome York, to attend. The five men huddled for forty-five minutes as their colleagues sat and fidgeted in the boardroom, the long table bathed in light from three overhead lamps. Suddenly, the door to the side room opened and Gerstner walked quickly to the table to retrieve some papers he had left there. "We're going home," he told his subordinates as everyone around the table looked up in shock.

According to confidential accounts later related by participants in the private meeting to the executives who had been left out, Gerstner told Spindler and Markkula he was willing to buy Apple for $5 billion. Gerstner used only a market capitalization price for the transaction, but it amounted to $40 a share based on Apple's number of shares outstanding. Very little premium was affixed to the Apple stock, since it was then trading for about $37 a share. "Well, that isn't close," Markkula replied. "But I'm sure we can reach an agreement." When pressed to be more specific, Markkula suggested Apple would settle for about $60 a share, or $7.5 billion. Spindler chimed in with his own demands. He wanted a hefty golden parachute should things not work out for him in the merger, and he insisted he be able to report directly to Gerstner in the new organization.

Needless to say, Gerstner was appalled—and, according to an IBM executive who was in the Westin boardroom that day, relieved. After all, Apple's refusal to share the secrets of its Macintosh software technology had made just about everyone at Big Blue nervous, not the least of whom was Lou Gerstner himself. "I think that when Apple put the very high price up and Spindler demanded that he report directly to Gerstner, that was the perfect out," this person says.

That was that. The IBMers flew east. The Appleites flew west. They had come so close, only to have the whole deal go up in flames. It was partly due to greed and arrogance on the Apple side, the same kind of greed and arrogance that had cost Apple so much throughout its history. But just as big a factor was Apple's reluctance to part company with its Macintosh "crown jewels," if only for a Justice Department review. It was the same paranoia that had cost Apple so many opportunities to transform the Mac into a healthy industry standard.

Now Apple was truly alone, with 1994 drawing to a close and not even able to announce a single licensee, much less the merger of the century. The company's market share was dropping like a rock. The squeeze on profit margins was tighter than ever, as they fell to 26 percent from the previous year's 34 percent. Given Apple's increasingly precarious situation, Mike Markkula and Michael Spindler should have gotten down onto their knees at that meeting with IBM, begging Lou Gerstner to save Apple from destruction. Spindler would return to IBM, but with humiliating results, and the Mac licensing effort would finally begin, in equally humbling fashion. The year 1995 was fast approaching, and for Apple Computer it would be a year of reckoning.

13

The Wreck of
the Diesel

As winter settled over Cupertino and the rest of northern California at the beginning of 1995, the region was hammered with some of its fiercest Pacific storms in years. The Russian and Napa Rivers rushed out of their banks, flooding Guerneville, Napa, and other quaint communities in the California wine country just north of San Francisco. Mud slides swept across roads and into some homes, creating a gooey mess in the 3,000-foot Santa Cruz Mountains above Silicon Valley. Gale force winds knocked great trees over onto electrical lines, knocking out power to thousands and forcing the deployment of platoons of repair crews.

A storm cloud was also settling in over Apple Computer, but it was not the kind that would soon blow away. At the end of 1994, Apple's share of the worldwide personal computer market had fallen to 8.3 percent from 9.4 percent, its first drop since 1990 and its lowest level since 1991.[1] The company's gross profit margin, as a percentage of sales, had fallen to an all-time low of 26 percent from 34 percent in just the year prior. That was a far cry from Apple's heyday of the late 1980s, when the margins had ranged between 49 percent and 53 percent. Yet Apple was continuing to have to fund almost all its own R and D, at a cost in 1994 of $564 million, or 6 percent of its annual sales. Unbridled by such a leg iron, Compaq Computer, by comparison, was having to spend only 3 percent of its sales on R and D. That is because Compaq—and every other PC manufacturer—could depend on Microsoft and Intel to fund almost all the rest.

In short, Apple Computer was locked in a vise that was tightening with each passing month. Spindler had chopped expenses, but it was not enough to relieve the pressure of having to compete in a market battered by fierce pricing wars while trying to pump enough money into R and D to maintain a technological lead over Microsoft. And there was more bad news to come.

As 1995 began, Microsoft was finishing up an operating system that had been code-named "Chicago" but would be launched in August of that year under the official moniker "Windows 95." It was part of Bill Gates's strategy of "evolution, not revolution." He had evolved Windows from a crude prototype that had drawn mostly derision in the industry during the 1980s to a serviceable version with Windows 3.0 in 1990 to a very workable version called Windows 3.1. Windows 3.1 was by no means perfect. It still crashed, just like the Mac, and lacked the Mac's elegance and finesse. But it was good enough to be embraced by practically the entire industry, and its replacement, Windows 95, was almost a Mac—and superior in terms of reliability.

Bill Gates was turning the vise on Apple's head on one side. Turning it from the other was Intel's Andy Grove. Ever paranoid, Grove had become even more so after seeing the lightning-fast performance of the PowerPC in those demonstrations at the 1993 Comdex and hearing the doomsday predictions from the PowerPC coalition of Apple, IBM, and Motorola of Intel's CISC-based technology crashing into a brick wall. He had begun pumping up the volume, increasing Intel's R-and-D expenditures from $780 million in 1992 to $1.1 billion in 1994. Much of that expense had been aimed at making Intel's new Pentium chip ever faster and ever more powerful. So by 1995, Andy Grove's engineers had performed such designing wizardry that the Pentium had erased much of PowerPC's cost and performance advantages.

"We were quite sure we could outgun Intel, but Intel moved the CISC generation faster than we thought," IBM's retired president Jack Kuehler observed in his interview for this book.

At this time, Apple had basically two long-range strategic options in competing against such economies of scale. It could merge with a larger partner, such as IBM, which would have the deep pockets to wage a protracted technological battle. Or it could spawn a whole new industry of clones based on Macintosh. The first option had gone up in smoke during 1994, when Spindler and Apple Chairman Mike Markkula had unceremoniously chased IBM away. The second, embodied by licensing, had all but fizzled out amid Apple's insistence on signing the big-name cloners, which, by this late date, were not to be had so easily.

Following the collapse of their merger talks, Apple and IBM did go on to announce their CHRP accord. It would be nearly three more years, though, before any CHRP machines were likely to be ready for market. With its market share sliding and its software developers growing increasingly restless, Apple had to line up a company to kick off its licensing program well before then. Spindler had repeatedly insisted on an IBM, a Dell, a Compaq—a big company—as he had scribbled on the whiteboard on at least one occasion. In the end, though, Apple had no choice but to cast its lot with a no-name start-up firm headed by a Korean immigrant who had been instrumental in launching the IBM clones during the early 1980s. The success of this man would, ironically, set Apple's licensing efforts back even more.

His name was Steve Kahng (pronounced "kong"), and to his many admirers in the industry, he was fondly known as "King Kahng." Kahng was a king by deed only, though. Acting as a consultant to the Korean conglomerate Daewoo Corporation, Kahng, based in Silicon Valley, had been responsible for the design that had gone on to become the Leading Edge brand of IBM-compatible computers, one of the most successful of the early clones. Kahng, however, had not cashed in on this great achievement personally, because he had failed to cut himself a deal for royalties, which could have earned him as much as $50 million. It was a bittersweet contribution to the computer industry — one that had left Kahng with a great reputation but forced him to keep on eking out a living by hiring out as a consultant and doing other jobs in the industry.

So at age forty-four, when opportunity came knocking again in late 1993, Kahng was itching for a chance to strike another gusher, so he could follow his dream of building his own successful computer company from the ground up. Out of the blue, one day in September of that year, Kahng was sitting at his desk in the Silicon Valley manufacturing town of Milpitas when the phone rang and an industry friend named Carl Amdahl — son of Gene Amdahl, founder of the Amdahl Corporation, a maker of computer mainframes — asked him to meet him the next day for lunch at the Peppermill, a coffee shop and lounge located on De Anza Boulevard in Cupertino in the shadow of the sprawling Apple campus. Carl Amdahl was then chairman of NetFrame Systems Inc. in Milpitas, a position he has since resigned. "He said it was important, but he would not say what," Kahng recalls.

When Kahng showed up, Amdahl was sitting at a table with another man named Elsireno Piol, vice chairman of the Italian computer conglomerate Ing. C. Olivetti & Compagnia SpA, which manufactured personal computers primarily for the European market. Piol had heard of Kahng's work and thought it might fit in perfectly with Olivetti's plan to help finance a start-up computer maker specializing in machines based on the new microprocessor, PowerPC. "I had said to myself," Piol recalled in 1995, "the only alternative to Microsoft and Intel is PowerPC. I thought it would be a good idea to build a company to focus on a PowerPC design."[2] Piol had thus arranged this meeting through Carl Amdahl, a business associate of one of Piol's industry friends. And Piol was not disappointed when he finally met the legendary Kahng.

"He doesn't spend a lot of time to discuss or bullshit," Piol remembered. "He is a doer, and he is very careful about spending every dime." Piol's assessment was most astute. Kahng indeed wastes little time in superfluous conversation, asking short, direct questions and delivering equally crisp responses. A bespectacled man with an engineer's training and demeanor, Kahng is also, by his own admission, a cheapskate who at the time of this meeting was still tooling around in an eleven-year-old Mercedes with more than 200,000 miles on it and dined frequently on McDonald's value meals. Kahng did not have to be so cheap. After all, as a consultant he had been earning up to $3 million a year. But having lived in the rigidly thrifty culture of South Korea for the first seventeen years of his life, before emigrating to the United States with his family, he had learned not to waste.

At the Peppermill, Piol laid his cards on the table. He wanted someone to run an Olivetti-backed start-up to make PowerPC-compatibles, and he thought Steve Kahng was perfect for the job. Olivetti would put up $5 million in the new venture if Kahng would match him another $4 million. The company would be independent, but Olivetti would be able to buy the new computers. Thinking about the offer as he sipped his black coffee, Kahng made a snap decision. "I said, 'Fine. I always wanted to run a systems company,'" Kahng remembers. Thus was born Power Computing Corporation.

To create a PowerPC-compatible computer, Kahng would have to get access to Apple's Macintosh operating system, the only one with the kind of mass appeal that could drive sales quickly for Power Computing. In February 1994, when Power Computing still consisted largely of Steve Kahng, Elsireno Piol arranged a meeting with Michael Spindler to discuss the possibility of Olivetti licensing the Mac for just the European market. The meeting was inconclusive but led to a second in April 1994, between Kahng and Cheryl Vedoe, who was still heading Apple's fledgling licensing program. "I had to bring Olivetti people with me because Apple was not interested in meeting with very small people," Kahng remembers.

Apple's interest in Power Computing was still tepid, Kahng remembers. In the meantime, he had hired away some of Apple's top hardware engineers, including Gary Davidian, Carl Hewitt, and Bob Hollyer, the PDM guys who had contributed so much to the technical success of the Power Macintosh. Kahng still needed access to Apple's technology, to get a PowerPC prototype up and running, as he wanted, in time for the Comdex gala in Las Vegas in November 1994. Since Comdex had ballooned into the world's premier showcase for new computer products, Kahng considered it imperative to have something to show by then.

In June 1994, Kahng met with Russ Irwin, Apple's man in the field behind the effort to round up licensees. While Michael Spindler and the upper echelons of Apple Computer wanted to deal only with the big-name vendors, Irwin knew that industry interest in cloning the Mac was still so lukewarm that Apple needed any help it could get. So he turned over all the technical access Kahng needed to get his design going. Afterward, Kahng celebrated by going out to the Los Altos Golf and Country Club, of which he was a member, and treating himself to a bottle of cabernet sauvignon. The next morning, bright and early, he was back on the job.

By October, Kahng's prototype was nearly ready to go. It was a Mac, but it looked like a PC. To shave costs so he could compete against the Wintel world, Kahng had opened up the machine to use Wintel-standard components such as power supplies and monitors. He had also figured out a way of cutting the main circuit board in two, so it would fit into a standard PC box. He would save even further, by selling in the direct-mail market, where Apple did not compete since it relied heavily on dealers. Mail order is a lot cheaper than the dealer channel, because it cuts out the middleman with its markups and manufacturer incentives. This was the thrifty, efficient approach, exactly the kind that Apple had always feared if it opened itself to competition from guys such as Steve Kahng. Yet by November 1994, Steve Kahng was the only person who actually had a Mac clone in the works, as he successfully demonstrated at Comdex in the booths of IBM and Motorola.

Michael Spindler did not want to do it, but he had little choice but to grant Power Computing the world's first Mac cloning agreement in December 1994. After all, the Diesel had said, in his interview with me for *The Wall Street Journal* at the Power Mac launch on March 14, 1994, that he expected to announce a Mac licensing deal by the end of 1994. Well, 1994 was almost gone, and Spindler was under pressure to announce something—anything. "I was the guy who was ready," Kahng says.

That agreement almost did not come to pass, though, for some other Apple executives were having some serious second thoughts about Steve Kahng even as the license-signing date approached. On October 28, 1994, for instance, Don Strickland, the vice president for licensing, fired off an angry e-mail to Russ Irwin, demanding an explanation for why Power Computing suddenly needed more technical support than had been indicated in the past. Kahng had done well by his ex-Apple engineers and had initially indicated he needed little of Apple's help. But the job of making a Mac clone was proving more difficult than he had first thought. "Why do we want to continue talking to them?" Strickland asked Irwin. "There are bigger fish to fry if we get the converged platform [CHRP] done."[3]

But Irwin pointed out, in a testy e-mail response to Strickland dated October 30, 1994, that there were not exactly a lot of alternatives. "As far as I can tell," he wrote, "we're not getting any anxious phone calls from the 'big fish.' Are we getting calls from Compaq, AST, Dell, Acer, NEC, etc.? We've talked to all these companies and thus far they have no interest in helping us be successful. They see the share we gain coming at their expense. They're happy to line up behind Intel and Microsoft."[4]

Irwin, in his memo to Strickland, pointed out another reason for going ahead with Power Computing: "They are a perfect alpha test site. They are intelligent, local and tolerant. Nobody else is going to cut us as much slack while we're coming up the learning curve on everything from licensing terms to support issues and real world technical problems. If we want to see anyone shipping Mac clones in 1995, it's probably going to be based on something from PCC [Power Computing Corporation]."[5]

As it turned out, Strickland was echoing the concern of Michael Spindler, who, according to a former senior Apple executive, "did not want the first licensee to be a no-name guy. Spindler was saying, 'I want a big name.' " That sentiment was shared by Ed Stead, the general counsel who had done so much to block the IBM merger by his insistence that Big Blue get no access to the Mac before a merger with Apple was completed. "On the morning of the Power Computing signing, Ed Stead was calling Strickland and saying, 'Why are we doing this?' " recalls a former Apple executive.

It took several more weeks before all the paperwork was done so the Power Computing deal could be announced. In the interim, Steve Kahng learned that a rival, Radius Inc., maker of monitors and other Mac components, was also on the verge of getting a license to make Mac clones for the high-end engineering market. Radius, as it happened, was being run by none other than Chuck Berger, the veteran of so many unsuccessful licensing battles in his years at Apple. Berger was set to announce his agreement at the Macworld trade show, opening January 5, 1995. But Kahng beat him to the punch, announcing his license two days after Christmas, on December 27, 1994. With an agreement in hand at long last, Kahng put the pedal to the metal and would work himself and his thirty-person crew twelve-hour days, seven days a week, to roll out the first bona fide Mac clones—called "Power" machines—in May 1995.

By then, Russ Irwin would be gone from Apple, resigning in January 1995 to help Japan's NEC set up a new venture capital fund. He would go on to become general partner in Convergence Partners, a Menlo Park, California, firm charged with managing that fund.

The Power models flew off the assembly lines that Steve Kahng had borrowed, in a characteristic cost-saving move, from the unused part of a factory in Austin, Texas, operated by a declining maker of Wintel clones called CompuAdd Corporation. The joint was strictly no-frills: Power Computing's worldwide manufacturing headquarters consisted of twelve open cubicles, including one for Kahng, in a corner of the warehouse floor. Demand within the Apple market for an alternative Macintosh was indeed strong, just as Ian Diery and his ilk had dreaded. E-mail inquiries poured into Power Computing at the rate of 150 per day. All the trade magazines gave the Power models rave reviews. Power Computing's clone launch was so successful, in fact, that it contributed to the death of a licensing deal Apple was on the verge of making with Gateway 2000. That this would happen sounds incongruous, considering Spindler's emphasis on landing just such a big-name cloner.

To understand why Spindler suddenly changed his mind, consider what happened at Apple between January and May of 1995. It surely was not pretty. First, there was that little matter of having to merge with a deep-pocketed partner—and fast. A few days into the new year, CFO Joe Graziano walked into Michael Spindler's office atop De Anza 7 and asked him to call Lou Gerstner at IBM back. Since that meeting at the Westin Hotel in Chicago the prior November, Spindler had heard nothing from IBM. That had surprised him and the others in the executive suite, because they had expected Gerstner at least to come back with a counteroffer to that $60-per-share demand.

By January 1995, though, the Diesel had cooled to the notion of merging with IBM at any price, as a former top Apple executive remembers from his account of an exchange between the Graz and Spindler in Spindler's fourth-floor office atop De Anza 7 after Graziano asked him to call back: "Spindler told Joe, 'When I go to China as CEO of Apple Computer, I get to meet with the prime minister. You think that would happen to me if I was a vice president at IBM?'" recalls this executive, who heard the conversation. Graziano, his face red with anger, lost his temper and fired back, according to this person, "You know, Michael, I really don't give a fuck. If that's all you're worrying about, you're crazy. You gotta be worrying about something else, which is a year from now you're gonna be presiding over a company that's going down the tubes."

As Apple's top finance guy, the Graz-man was intimately familiar with the numbers, and he knew as well as anyone that they just were not going to keep adding up much longer if Apple remained an independent company. There was just no way, no how, he thought. Graziano kept pestering Spindler to renew merger talks with IBM or another company, until the Diesel caved in and brought the issue up before a regularly scheduled meeting of the board in March 1995. It was an evening meeting, and the main item on the agenda was a presentation by Spindler on Apple's strategic position. Guess what? The Diesel told the board that Apple could no longer go it alone and it would have to find a merger partner quickly. Three years earlier, John Sculley had made the exact same presentation to the board, when he had first alerted the directors that he wanted to step down soon as CEO.

"Michael did a magnificent job on this," recalls a person intimately familiar with the presentation. "He outlined the problems that Apple faces in the industry and the fact that we couldn't go it alone. Now this was the most amazing thing: the same Michael, who didn't want to have Apple be sold to IBM, saying to the board that the company probably can't make it on its own, and we need to partner with somebody." In that meeting, in the De Anza 7 Synergy room, the board members went around the table suggesting likely candidates: IBM, Hewlett-Packard, Japan's Sony Corporation. Spindler also suggested Japan's Toshiba Corporation and the Dutch giant Philips Electronics NV.

"Michael's priority was Toshiba first, if IBM didn't come back," recalls the person familiar with the presentation. "He asked for guidance from the board. They said, 'Go back to IBM. And talk to H-P.' "

Mike Markkula called Gerstner afterward to suggest that Apple was "more willing to look at something reasonable and wondered if the teams could get together again," recalls a former IBM executive familiar with the conversation. This was now the spring of 1995, though, and IBM had moved past Apple — to Lotus Development Corporation, its neighbor up the East Coast. The deal would not become public until June of that year, but Big Blue was in the process of formulating a hostile bid for Lotus, the Cambridge, Massachusetts, software maker whose hit 1-2-3 spreadsheet had been so instrumental in driving Bill Gates into the Mac market in the first place. The hostile bid would turn into a successful friendly offer of $3.52 billion for Lotus, which Gerstner saw as a good strategic fit in IBM's increasing emphasis on computer networks in corporations. (Lotus Notes software had been specially designed for network communications.)

According to the former IBM executive, Gerstner telephoned John Thompson, his senior vice president involved in the old Apple talks, and asked his opinion on Markkula's call. "Thompson said, 'I feel obligated to at least listen to Michael,' " according to the executive who heard the exchanges. Another meeting was set up for May 1995 at the Westin Hotel near Chicago's O'Hare International Airport. Even the meeting room was the same: the boardroom on the Westin's Premier Gold Floor. This was about all the two Westin meetings had in common with each other, though.

This time, IBM was represented, at the top, by only John Thompson and Lee Reiswig, the director of OS/2 development. Jim Cannavino had just retired after thirty-three years with IBM to spend time with his terminally ill son, who later died of cancer. Cannavino, who was only fifty then, went on to become president and COO of Perot Systems Corporation, a computer services company founded in 1988 by the Texas billionaire Ross Perot. On the Apple side, there were Spindler, Graziano, and Dave Nagel, Apple's software chief. This time, though, Markkula was not present, nor was Ed Stead. And instead of IBM doing most of the talking, as before, Spindler took the floor and held it for the first hour, "venting" about how disappointed he was at not hearing back from IBM before and insisting a deal could still work, according to an IBM person who attended the meeting. Spindler's body language, though, did not jibe with his words. "He just sat there, in the meeting room, with his head hunched between his shoulders," recalls an Apple executive familiar with the proceedings.

At one point, recalls the IBM participant in the meeting, Spindler excused himself to go to the restroom. "When he did that, both Graziano and Nagel said they were there on behalf of Markkula and that the board had given a green light for an acquisition with someone, and the first choice was IBM," this person recalls. "You could see Nagel and Graziano were cringing in the meeting." One of the IBM executives stood up to a whiteboard and drew a timeline on the wall to rehash the old stumbling block: IBM would have to wait as long as a year to get regulatory approval for a merger with Apple, and without Apple's willingness to license the Mac in advance, Big Blue was not interested in a deal. After two hours, the meeting concluded, each side flying in opposite directions again and agreeing to sleep on it. This was the end of the line, though.

"We all went back to the East Coast, and to be honest, we were so busy with Lotus we didn't have time to deal with it," says the IBM participant in the meeting. "John [Thompson] called Spindler back and said, 'This just won't work out.'"

Michael Spindler was back to square one. He followed the board's directive and got onto the horn to Hewlett-Packard. H-P, based in Palo Alto, just a fifteen-minute drive north from Apple on Interstate 280, was—and is—a finely tuned growth engine that, in 1995, was one of the fastest-growing big companies in the world. A powerhouse in workstations, minicomputers, and printers, H-P had set its sights on the PC market and by 1995 had blasted from the back of the pack to join the ranks of the top ten PC makers. Spindler arranged a dinner meeting with Lewis Platt, H-P's chief executive officer, and sounded him out on the possibility of a merger between the two companies, according to a former H-P executive who heard Platt speak of the encounter in a staff meeting.

"From H-P's point of view, there was no interest in acquiring Apple for the reason that there was little strategic confluence," this executive recalls. "We are in opposite camps in almost every single area. H-P is very heavily involved in the Intel architecture. H-P is also heavily in the Microsoft camp because of laser printers and inkjets, all linked to Microsoft personal computers. But Apple is in PowerPC and is not in the Microsoft camp."

So the very sensible H-P made the very sensible decision not to take this thing with Apple any farther. Spindler also talked with Toshiba and Philips, but these encounters did not get anywhere, either. Then, in late spring 1995, Apple started talking merger with the most unlikely of candidates—Compaq Computer, the company that had been responsible for igniting the industry price wars that had wrecked Apple's whole business model. The discussions were initiated by a call from Mike Markkula to Compaq Chairman Ben Rosen.[6] At the time, Compaq's hard-charging CEO, Eckhard Pfeiffer, had had a falling-out with Intel's Andy Grove. Grove had just decided that Intel would move heavily into the design and production of so-called mother-boards, which contain all the major circuitry of a computer, including the microprocessor. Before this, much of the motherboard work had been per-formed by the PC makers or their subcontractors, enabling each manufac-turer to add unique components. Compaq was furious, because this would mean one less area in which it could differentiate itself from the competition.

But Apple's talks with Compaq lasted only a few weeks. According to a for-mer Apple executive familiar with the discussions, Joe Graziano and Mike Markkula met with Compaq's Pfeiffer and Rosen at Markkula's sprawling wooded estate in the appropriately named community of Woodside. "We would merge the two companies," this executive recalls. "Compaq's goal at that time was to get away from Intel." Compaq, however, quickly kissed and made up with Intel, and the talks died on the vine.

After Compaq, there was a discussion with Sony, which was more inter-ested in buying a minority position in Apple than in a wholesale merger. But Graziano argued against this, because Sony was offering to do this without paying any money up front; there would instead be a delayed payout of some sort. After just two meetings, both sides went their separate ways. All the merger talks were collapsing, leaving Apple more and more isolated. Michael Spindler was displaying signs of mounting insecurity and paranoia, as evi-denced by his bizarre attempt to torpedo the Microsoft relationship once and for all. This is the story of the "Canyon" incident, and it was so ludicrous that Bill Gates still shakes his head in amazement over it.

Remember, the Diesel hated Bill Gates, just despised him. Gates did not exactly harbor the warmest feelings toward Spindler, either, but as a consum-mate professional he knew enough to set personalities aside in the interest of business. After his first meeting with Spindler at 1993 Comdex, Gates says he decided he should meet with a broader group of Apple executives to talk about mutual business opportunities. One idea he and other Microsoft execu-tives had been pushing was for the two companies to jointly sponsor a market-ing campaign to show how Macintosh and Windows computers could work well together. Apple had never warmed to that notion, though.

"Mike arranged for me to come speak at a staff meeting, and I did a lot of work getting ready for a two-hour presentation and discussion in Cupertino," Gates recalls. "Two days before the scheduled meeting [in November 1994], Mike decided to cancel it, giving no reason and saying he didn't want to reschedule it. This sent a very negative message to the Mac supporters at Microsoft. We pursued communication through every channel we could, but the paranoia about being able to do something with us seemed to block everything."

Spindler, as it turned out, was paranoid about something else: a ten-person firm called San Francisco Canyon Company and the work it was doing on behalf of Intel and, indirectly, Microsoft. Canyon, based in San Francisco, had been contracted by Apple in 1992 to develop software that would help enable Apple's QuickTime multimedia technology to play back video images on a Windows computer. QuickTime had originally been designed for the Macintosh, but Apple, hoping to elicit more interest in its technology from software developers, had also decided to make QuickTime available on Windows. In one of the rare cases of Apple actually opening up its technology to the outside world, QuickTime for Windows had subsequently been released in November 1992, using a rudimentary type of software from Canyon called "drivers," which helps tell a chip what the software wants it to do.[7]

At the same time as the Apple release, Microsoft had announced a rival multimedia technology called Video for Windows. Shortly after that, Intel—working without Microsoft's knowledge—had begun looking into ways of accelerating the performance of Video for Windows to make the images on the computer screen bigger and less jerky. So in July 1993, Intel had contracted with San Francisco Canyon to provide the drivers that could help accomplish that.[8] Several months later, in late 1993, Microsoft had discovered what Intel was doing and decided to merge their independent efforts in a joint technology venture called Display Control Interface (DCI), which was rolled into Video for Windows.

This was all really mundane, techie stuff of interest primarily to software developers, since both Video for Windows and QuickTime for Windows were "tool kits" designed to help the developers make their multimedia programs, such as the ones in the exploding CD-ROM category. The trouble started when Microsoft published the technical specifications for DCI to graphics chip makers and software developers in late 1994 and someone at Apple took a close look at the code and recognized the part from Canyon as being identical to Canyon's code in QuickTime for Windows.

Now, bear in mind: the offending software amounted to only several *hundred* lines of code out of the *millions* in Video for Windows version 1.1D, of which a few advance copies were sent out to developers in the fall of 1994. To remove it would take, at most, two weeks of work. To Microsoft—and Intel—it was no big deal. But to Apple, it was tantamount to World War III. Ian Diery, Spindler's top lieutenant, was sitting at his desk atop De Anza 7 one day in early December that year when Ed Stead ran in excitedly. "You have to help me!" Stead told Diery, according to a person who heard the exchange. "I want to put starch to somebody's bones."

The "starch" turned out to be a lawsuit that Apple filed on December 6, 1994, against San Francisco Canyon in the U.S. District Court of San Jose, California, alleging that it had infringed on a video copyright in the Video for Windows code developed by Microsoft with help from Intel. In so doing, Apple also obtained subpoenas to review code from both Microsoft and Intel to see if any contained any of the QuickTime for Windows code. When news of the suit broke, the software industry was abuzz. Here was Apple Computer, again, jabbing a finger into Bill Gates's eye.

The first that Microsoft knew about this was when it received a terse legal letter from Apple's attorneys seeking cooperation in Apple's investigation. Carl Stork, general manager of Microsoft's Windows platform group—and a dead ringer for John Denver in that singer's younger days—pressed for a meeting with Dave Nagel and some other Apple executives to talk about the problem. After six weeks, Apple finally agreed to a meeting, which was attended in Cupertino by Stork and a Microsoft attorney named Cory Van Arsdale. "I explained that none of the code was in any shipping product and that less than 1 percent of the offending code was in Video for Windows," Stork recalls, rocking softly in a windowless conference room on Microsoft's university-style campus. "I just said, 'Hey, we ought to be able to settle this.' " The meeting ended with no resolution, and Stork returned to Microsoft and unilaterally had the Canyon code yanked out. The 1.1D version was swapped out with Video for Windows version 1.1E, containing no Canyon code.

Gates, meanwhile, had wanted to meet with Spindler and his executives to discuss mutual strategic steps Apple and Microsoft could work on. That meeting was canceled with less than two days' notice, but Ian Diery convinced Spindler to set up another one for January 13, 1995.

One reason Diery wanted the meeting to take place was because Microsoft had been dragging its feet in giving Apple usable advance copies called "betas" (nearly completed test versions) of the Windows 95 operating system. Since Apple had introduced a Macintosh that could read Windows and DOS programs earlier that year, Diery wanted to make sure his so-called DOS-compatible Macs would also be compatible with Windows 95. To do so, he needed beta versions of Windows 95 so Apple's engineers could get a head start on design before the new operating system actually shipped the following year, in August 1995. Microsoft insisted it had already sent the betas, but Apple claimed the disks containing them were "defective and unreadable."

The meeting was so surreal that the fact it took place on Friday the thirteenth was most appropriate. That day, Bill Gates and Roger Heinen (the former Apple software executive whose departure to Microsoft had left the Star Trek project adrift) boarded the elevator at De Anza 7, getting off at the fourth floor to meet with Spindler, Dave Nagel, Diery, and some other Apple executives in the good old Synergy room. There, Gates remembers, Spindler opened the meeting by launching into a dissertation about new benchmark tests by an outfit called Ingram Laboratories that showed the Power Mac outperforming comparable Pentium machines by margins of 24 to 54 percent. Gates, according to a former Apple executive present in the meeting, finally interrupted to say, "Mike, I don't understand a word you are saying." (Gates was one of the few industry people who still called Spindler "Mike," as he had commonly been known in the early Apple days, as opposed to "Michael," as his power grew.)

Gates, in his interview for this book, remembers being more diplomatic. "I said I had never heard of the company [Ingram Laboratories] and wasn't sure why that was a key point for the meeting," Gates says. Gates could have been excused for saying "I don't understand a word you are saying" if, in fact, that is what he did say. Innumerable Apple people, through the years, had often thought the same thing whenever the Diesel launched into his frenzied whiteboard lectures.

In any event, the meeting went on as Gates renewed his old campaign that Apple and Microsoft work together on OpenDoc and OLE in the interest of making life easier for Mac developers. Gates also pushed again for some kind of a comarketing program between the companies, an idea that Diery endorsed. Unlike the other Apple executives, Diery harbored no outward animosity toward Microsoft. "I always thought Ian was a guy who just wanted the Power Mac to be successful," recalls Microsoft's Pete Higgins. After the meeting, Gates recalls Spindler inviting him into his office for about ten minutes to discuss "some of the horizons of innovation and how Apple and Microsoft were two of the companies who could really push them forward." All in all, Gates says, he and Heinen thought "it was a good meeting."

Well, that is Bill Gates's version. Apple would have an entirely different one. According to a sworn statement that Nagel would later provide a court looking into Microsoft's business practices, Gates was asked in the meeting why he had still not shipped a Windows 95 beta to Apple. "He responded that he had personally made the decision not to ship the beta release to Apple and that it was 'cause and effect': since Apple sued Canyon, Microsoft would not deliver the beta release." Nagel's statement went on to allege: "Microsoft's attempt to bully Apple into settling the Canyon lawsuit by withholding the Windows 95 beta release appeared to be defused when Mr. Gates advised Mr. Spindler that Microsoft would provide copies of the beta release and associated Microsoft developer support if Mr. Spindler would agree to contact him personally before filing a complaint against Microsoft in the Canyon case. Mr. Spindler assured Mr. Gates that he would telephone him before Apple filed suit against Microsoft."

Nagel also stated in his declaration that, in reopening the OpenDoc-versus-OLE debate, Gates issued "a thinly veiled threat to stop developing software for the Macintosh if Apple maintains its position." Gates, according to Nagel, cited the increased costs of developing a Mac program using OpenDoc as opposed to OLE, and he wanted Apple to drop OpenDoc altogether. Gates denies ever making threats to Apple, veiled or otherwise.

When the Windows 95 betas still had not shown up by January 31,

Spindler fired off a "Dear Bill" letter to Gates, saying, "I am disappointed to find out that we still do not have the Windows 95 beta for the Apple Cross Platform Development Group, despite your promise that you would not hold it up. Please follow through on this as soon as possible. As you know, this is important to Apple." Gates called Spindler back on February 6, saying he had expected "a business discussion" regarding Canyon to take place before those betas were sent.[9] Spindler agreed to follow up and reiterated his promise not to sue Microsoft before notifying Gates.[10]

On February 8, the betas finally arrived at Apple. The very next day, Apple filed suit against Microsoft and Intel, adding them to the pending case against Canyon—without notifying Microsoft first. When word of the suit reached *The Wall Street Journal*'s news bureau in downtown San Francisco, a reporter named Don Clark was on duty to handle the "spot," or breaking, business stories. That afternoon, someone in Apple's public relations called Clark and told him that Apple CEO Michael Spindler would be telephoning shortly to discuss the Canyon suit. Since Spindler had been a virtual recluse from most of the media, having granted just one interview to the *Journal* prior to that, Clark sat up and took notice. Soon the Diesel was on the line, railing against Microsoft. "This is a major area of investment and a technical lead that we have," Clark's ensuing article about the suit quoted Spindler as saying. "We have to protect it."

Within ten minutes of news of the suit being broadcast over the business wire services and by video, an agitated Bill Gates was on the phone to the fourth floor of De Anza 7 in Cupertino, roaring at the Diesel. He repeated his displeasure in a follow-up letter to Spindler dated February 23: "Based on the video press release and other orchestrated press activity, the suit had been in planning for some time. . . . I think it was inappropriate for you to promise to talk to me before filing a lawsuit and then not follow through on that commitment."

In his letter, addressed "Dear Mike," Gates added, "When we finally met you requested additional beta copies of Windows 95, and you also asked about the Canyon matter. Apple had already received a number of betas and wanted more. . . . I did not think we needed to give you additional betas, but I was willing to provide them to Apple as a courtesy. In return, I requested a simple courtesy from you. I said if Apple would have business people meet with us to discuss the Canyon issue and show us the basis for Apple's claims, and if you would at least talk with me before you sued Microsoft, I would have those betas sent. You committed to this, confirming it in your fax to me of Jan. 16."

After the phone exchange, Spindler paced nervously in his office, wringing his hands as Ian Diery tried to calm him down. "Michael, don't get upset," Diery told Spindler, according to a person who heard the exchange. "These are big boys playing the game." Spindler, though, had always taken conflicts like this personally, so he "stewed and stewed and stewed," according to this person.

Gates was peeved, too, but for reasons that were undoubtedly influenced by events beyond just the Apple-Microsoft relationship. Microsoft's power over the PC industry had grown so complete that Gates's competitors were increasingly complaining to the federal government of monopolistic practices by the behemoth in Redmond, Washington. Indeed, in 1990 the Federal Trade Commission had begun looking into possible antitrust violations by Microsoft in its near monopoly over PC operating systems. Microsoft had abused this strong position, various developers alleged, by leveraging its dominance over the operating system to provide its own applications programmers advance copies of new OS code. This practice, denied by Microsoft, allegedly gave Microsoft an unfair advantage over its competitors in the market for applications such as in business productivity.

In 1993, the FTC deadlocked on two votes to file a formal complaint against Microsoft. But as the FTC closed the books on its investigation, antitrust investigators in both the U.S. Justice Department and Europe launched their own inquiries into the same complaints. Microsoft settled these very public investigations in a consent decree signed July 16, 1994, to change its contracts with PC manufacturers and eliminate certain restrictions it had imposed on software developers. As the dust from those disputes was settling, the complaints of monopolistic practice resurfaced in October 1994, when Microsoft announced it planned to acquire Intuit Inc., a rival maker of PC finance software, in a stock deal that was initially valued at $1.5 billion but climbed to $2.1 billion as Microsoft's stock rose.

This would be the biggest software merger to date, and it sent another shudder of fear through the computer industry. Intuit, then based in Menlo Park, California, was one of the few developers beating Microsoft in a key market, this being the one for money management programs such as Intuit's Quicken, which assist computer users in keeping track of their household finances. Since the Intuit deal had to be approved by the Justice Department in a routine antitrust review, the last thing Bill Gates wanted or needed was a public flap with its old gadfly, Apple — over software "drivers," of all things.

Seeing that exposed flank, Apple's Ed Stead determined to put some more starch to Gates's bones. It had long been suspected in the industry, though not proven, that Apple was among a cadre of Gates haters who had anonymously egged on the federal investigation into Microsoft. On February 13, Stead dispatched a letter to U.S. District Judge Stanley Sporkin in Washington, D.C., alleging that Gates had threatened to withhold crucial software if Apple did not drop the Canyon suit and the OpenDoc initiative. Dave Nagel, and some others at Apple, issued their sworn declarations backing this allegation up. Judge Sporkin, as it so happened, was at that very moment reviewing the validity of the antitrust settlement between Microsoft and the Justice Department. And Stanley Sporkin was not the teeniest bit intimidated by Bill Gates and his Microsoft empire.

On Valentine's Day the judge threw out the settlement, charging that it had failed to take into consideration other issues, such as allegations that Microsoft had illegally announced products long before they were ready in order to hurt competitors. The judge did not mince words, either, charging in his ruling that Microsoft's practices represented "a potential threat to the nation's well-being," in terms of stymieing competitiveness in the software industry.

Bill Gates, then, was beside himself when he fired off his "Dear Mike" letter on February 23: "I am writing to make it clear how disappointed I am in the lack of candor and honesty Apple has shown in dealing with Microsoft during the last several months." As always, though, Gates closed the three-page letter by leaving the door open: "I still feel that a constructive dialog between you and me would be helpful to both of our companies and our mutual users. Microsoft is very committed to its Macintosh customers. I think the Macintosh has a bright future. I feel more straightforward communication from Apple to Microsoft is called for."

The Justice Department's consent decree with Microsoft was reinstated by a higher court on appeal of Judge Sporkin's decision by Microsoft and the Justice Department. Separately, Gates was compelled to withdraw his planned acquisition of Intuit after the Justice Department sued in April 1995 to block it from going forward on monopolistic grounds. The Canyon caper itself dissipated into the wind like a bad dream as all related litigation was settled out of court. Really, Canyon was a tempest in a teapot, all over a few hundred lines of arcane code. But the episode spoke volumes about how little Michael Spindler valued Apple's relationship with Microsoft, its biggest developer, and about how the Apple executive suite was a nasty place that was becoming even nastier.

Remember that "noble village of men and women" that John Sculley had written about in describing Apple in his book, *Odyssey*? It was not so noble in the late 1980s, when he wrote the book, and it was certainly not so in early 1995. Over in one corner of De Anza 7's fourth floor was the venerable Edward B. Stead, Esq., who just loved to "put starch to someone's bones." Off in another was the omniscient Kevin J. Sullivan, still running human relations and more powerful than ever now that his old buddy Michael Spindler was top dog. Seated in Jean-Louis Gassée's old office was Ian Diery, personable and charismatic but a fearless rugby player who made no secret of the fact he would one day love to be CEO of Apple Computer. There was David C. Nagel, a bearded, professorial chap described by many as just the nicest guy but totally incapable of instilling any discipline into the chaotic engineering organization.

And don't forget the fourth "S" in the Apple power structure at this time. There were Spindler, Stead, Sullivan—and David Seda. Seda's name did not appear on page 46 of Apple's 1995 annual report, which lists all the top officers in the company. It should have. By virtue of his Sullivan-like influence over Spindler, Seda emerged as one of the more powerful people in Apple Computer, even though his official title was "Executive Assistant to the President and Chief Executive Officer." Everywhere Spindler went, there was David Seda, right behind. Need an appointment with the big cheese? Go through David Seda. Have a speech for Spindler to read at the next powwow? David Seda would have to screen it first. David Seda, in short, wielded God-like power over access to Michael Spindler, and it was power that several people in the executive suite say he abused.

"Every person who wanted to get on Michael's calendar had to go through David," recalls a former executive secretary from that time. "People wanted to get on his calendar and couldn't." As this person, and others, describe the situation, Seda was not such a bad guy; he was just motivated, first and foremost, by his fierce protectiveness over Spindler, in a role tantamount to him being an attack Doberman with allegiance only to his master.

For his part, Seda says he "wishes it were true" that he had so much power but denies it was ever that great.

As far as anybody could tell, Seda did not have much of a life outside of Apple Computer. A single man originally from Kenya and one of the few African-American employees at Apple, he was described as "an incredible workaholic" who put in a numbing eighteen to twenty hours a day and often slept over in the office. Seda's chief preoccupation seemed to be anticipating Spindler's every wish and shielding him from any stress whatsoever. Since the Diesel stressed out easily, as over the Canyon fight with Bill Gates, Seda was one busy dude. "Seda would take what Spindler said literally, like, 'I don't want to talk to the press,'" recalls a former, high-level executive from that time. "David would say, 'Right,' and then he would cancel all appointments with the press."

The internal e-mail messages that Spindler perused every day, as early as 4 A.M., also gave the chief serious indigestion—especially those relaying complaints from disgruntled workers. Seda, the Doberman, raced in front of his master, baring his teeth as he contemplated actually removing Spindler's access to Apple's e-mail system, called AppleLink. "One day, David said, 'Call AppleLink and take off his AppleLink,'" recalls a former secretary. "Fortunately, David later decided not to do that." Seda denies that happened, calling it "totally ridiculous."

Seda even took it upon himself to edit speeches for Spindler that had already been carefully prepared by the public relations staff. In one such episode, Seda got his hands onto a speech written by Christopher Escher, one of Apple's top writers and a highly articulate spokesperson. "Chris had worked on it for days, and Seda took it and ripped it apart," recalls a former executive who witnessed this. "Spindler read it, and it sounded like gibberish." Seda agrees he "edited" speeches, but only to add phrasing that was more in "Michael's language." Since the Diesel was frequently incomprehensible, Seda performed the job well.

At times, this proximity to so much power deluded Seda into believing he was actually running the company. "I actually heard him say, 'How can I run a company when I can't get any good help?' " says a former secretary. And Seda threw his weight around even outside the company. In fact, his was one of those sworn declarations to Judge Sporkin regarding that infamous Friday the thirteenth meeting between Gates and Spindler. In it, Seda admitted to having "briefly debated" with Microsoft Vice President Pete Higgins the "openness and interoperability of OLE." Wait a minute. An executive *assistant* was debating one of the highest-ranking executives at Microsoft? That sounds incredible, but it is right there in black and white, with Seda's signature at the bottom.

As the spring of 1995 ushered in the usual color show of green hillsides and flower canopies across northern California, dark forces were at work in the executive suite of De Anza 7. There was, technically, one executive staff. But there might as well have been three. There were the four "S"s—Spindler, Stead, Sullivan, and Seda—a close-knit clique who seemed to communicate mainly among themselves. There were Graziano and Nagel, who were pretty much doing their own thing. By now, Graziano was increasingly on the outs with Spindler because he was so upset with what he considered the Diesel's mishandling of the IBM deal. A climactic showdown between Spindler and the Graz was fast approaching. Finally, there was the unflappable Ian Diery, the one-man show who was the executive really running the nuts and bolts of Apple's business while everybody else hemmed and hawed about strategy.

Diery certainly had his failings. He had proven shortsighted in fighting the licensing issue for so many years, and he was not regarded as a great strategist. He could also be a royal pain in the butt, especially if you were the Apple sales manager in some backwater country squirming like a toad as the rugby-playing Aussie dressed you down in front of your whole staff for missing a quota. "If he referred to me as 'mate,' I knew everything was OK. If he called me 'bloke,' I knew I was in trouble," recalls Jim Buckley, the Apple USA president under Diery. But Diery did have his hand on the rudder of the ship, performing the dreary but necessary duty of making sure computers were getting out the door to customers. He had been "Mr. Power Mac," executing the transition from the older Macs flawlessly in every way except one: market share was falling.

Diery, remember, had wanted to go for market share, dropping Power

Mac prices so Apple could really compete. To do that, though, Apple would have had to dramatically cut back its expenses, through such measures as jettisoning the Newton business, which was consuming so much of the cash brought in from Diery's PC division. Lacking support for this from either Spindler or the board, Diery pursued another strategy of keeping prices up while also purposely holding down volume. He did this to give Apple a chance to rebuild its profits so it could be in a stronger financial position to take another run at building market share. "It's much better to gamble on market share growth from a strong balance sheet than a weak one," he said then.[11]

What Diery did not say at the time but had conveyed in the executive suite was that he was desperate to reduce spending by the other groups in Apple. Every year, when a new forecast for growth was issued, the various divisions such as AppleSoft and PIE would plan budgets to match that forecast, whether it would turn out right or wrong. So if Diery predicted that Macintosh unit shipments would grow by 25 percent, the other divisions would commit to a budget increase of 25 percent—and spend it up front, at the beginning of the new year.

This was an extraordinarily dangerous practice and one that Diery wanted to curb when he proposed holding unit shipment growth down to 15 percent during fiscal 1995, which began in October 1994. "That way, Ian could brake the spending by the other divisions and any excess money could go to the bottom line to fund price drops," says a former Apple executive familiar with Diery's strategy. But the fall in market share during 1994 was continuing in 1995—dropping to 7.6 percent in the first quarter[12]—and Spindler was growing nervous. He was nervous about something else, too, according to many who were at Apple at the time: Ian Diery's power. "Michael was a very indecisive person who had a hard time telling people 'no,' such as with Ian," recalls another former top executive. "Ian was a street fighter, so Michael could never talk to Ian. As a result, Michael was under stress."

Spindler had such difficulty dealing with Diery, according to this person and others in the executive suite, because Diery would challenge him on points with which he did not agree. "Ian, being Ian, is an aggressive guy, and he stands on his own two feet," says a former executive. "You just don't walk over him, and that was the exact kind of guy Michael just couldn't deal with." Gaston Bastiaens, the colorful former head of Apple's PIE division, had been another in Diery's aggressive mold. Spindler had not been able to stand up to him, either, as evidenced when Bastiaens had barked back at his CEO when questioned about flaws in the Newton sales strategy.

Diery's strong position at Apple was undermined, however, when his strategy to bet conservatively on market share backfired, resulting in widespread shortages of Power Macs in the Christmas quarter of 1994 as sales of other

PCs exploded in the public's rush to multimedia. Diery was also weakened by political forces within. A hard taskmaster, Diery had alienated some of his top managers, as well as some fellow executives who chafed at his continual insistence that costs be brought down. The lack of cooperation at the top was so great that Kevin Sullivan organized a three-day executive retreat in March 1995 at the Inn at Spanish Bay, the posh lodge located in view of crashing waves on California's Pebble Beach Resort. The goal: to help Spindler set a vision for the company that everyone would follow.

As Sullivan recalls, he called the retreat because many people on the executive staff, including Graziano, were upset that Diery had countermanded the five-year-old strategy of trying to increase market share. "Ian set the gross margin that year to rebuild share value and bring the value of his stock up," Sullivan maintains in a charge that Diery adamantly denies. "Ian was pushing his agenda, even though we had a business plan under Joe Graziano's leadership to drive share and growth." Upon his return to Apple in 1989, Graziano had helped convince John Sculley to drive for higher market share.

As seagulls squawked outside and golf carts puttered nearby on Pebble Beach's magnificent links, Sullivan, Diery, Spindler, and the other top executives huddled behind the closed doors of a meeting room, along with representatives of the consulting firm McKinsey & Company, which Sullivan had retained to provide advice. Sullivan handed out a seventeen-page memo that he had prepared for the retreat. It read, in part, "Even though our revenue has increased significantly, our market share has eroded and the dominance of the major competitive platform has increased. We are again at a critical crossroad which requires us to make another quantum leap to remain competitive. Tick, tick, tick, tick . . ."[13]

The fundamental problem, as Sullivan argued, was that Apple's marketing efforts were fragmented and ineffective because they were not focused on the company's core markets of education, desktop publishing, and the home. "We were spending an enormous amount of marketing money, for example, on business markets that were generating only 6 percent of the revenues," Sullivan remembers. Michael Spindler, too, had recognized this problem early on, as when he had stood at the easel in 1993 and emphasized that Apple needed to concentrate on its strongest markets. But Spindler, as was typical of his management style, had never pushed the company to implement that plan.

After Spanish Bay, Spindler gave his blessing for Sullivan to huddle with Graziano and the McKinsey consultants to put together a reorganization plan. Sullivan had demonstrated his power many times in the past in reshaping the organization to suit his will. In so doing, he had effectively removed executives, including former COO Del Yocam and former R-and-D chief Jean-Louis Gassée, and had drawn up the chart that had ousted former corporate secretary Al Eisenstat. Sullivan insists he let his CEOs make their own decisions, but it is clear his handprint was on practically every high-level shake-up since he had joined Apple in 1987. And Ian Diery was about to become the latest casualty.

Sullivan's new plan sliced Apple into four new pies: research and development, which would include software and hardware, as it had been before 1993; worldwide marketing and "customer solutions," which would oversee all marketing efforts, with special focus on the key customer markets of the home, education, and desktop publishing; worldwide sales and support, which would pull Apple USA, Apple Europe, and Apple Pacific together under one umbrella; and manufacturing and distribution, which would be spun off from the old PC division.

The new organization, Sullivan believed, would better focus Apple in a sort of high-tech circling of the wagons against the Wintel marauders. Under the new organization, the new divisions would be shared out thus: Dave Nagel would run all of R and D, not just the software part. Dan Eilers, who had gone off to run Apple's Claris unit in 1991 after getting nowhere on licensing for so many years, would be pulled back in to head up the new marketing division. Worldwide sales would be run collectively by the existing regional presidents of Jim Buckley at Apple USA, Marco Landi in Europe, and John Floisand at Apple Pacific. And manufacturing would continue to be run by Fred Forsyth, the executive who had expressed such misgivings about changing Apple's business model when the ill-starred Star Trek project had been presented to executive staff in 1992.

In presenting the plan to Spindler, Sullivan and Graziano gave the Diesel two main options: one with a chief operating officer, one without. Since Diery was the obvious choice for COO, Spindler practically shuddered at the prospect as he picked the option without one. Sullivan admits to no ill intent regarding Diery, but given his long and close association with the Diesel — and knowing full well how he felt about Ian Diery — it is highly likely Sullivan knew which option he would pick.

Suddenly, Diery was out of a job. Spindler suggested that maybe Diery could oversee sales. That would amount to a huge demotion, since Diery's old turf was now being split into pieces. Diery was not happy, not one bit. But he was about to become even unhappier. After Spindler broached the idea of the sales job, Diery mulled it over on a two-day business trip he had previously scheduled to Europe. "When Ian walked back in from Europe, Michael said, 'I don't think the head of sales is a serious position. So I've asked Kevin to organize the separation package,' " recalls a former executive who witnessed the exchange. Diery was thunderstruck, but he did not show it. "Ian said, 'Fine, we need to close the books first on this quarter so it does not hurt sales,' " the same executive recalls.

The announcement of Diery's "resignation" was thus postponed until

April 4, after Apple's fiscal second quarter had come to a close on March 31, 1995. Ironically for Diery, the quarter had been a good one, with sales rebounding to a year-over-year pace of 20 percent, keeping Apple in line with the rest of the industry and temporarily halting its slide in market share. Publicly, Diery toed the official Apple line that he had essentially reorganized himself out of a job. "There wasn't really a position to suit my experience or aim," Diery told me in an interview then for *The Wall Street Journal.* "I decided I would just leave." Spindler, in a statement, also praised Diery's contributions to the company, saying the reorganization "did not provide a role that would meet his personal goals."

Behind closed doors, of course, the story was different. When Joe Graziano heard about what had happened, he was aghast. He had fully expected Spindler to agree to having a COO in the new plan. Graz hurried into Diery's office and told him, "I can't believe you're taking this so well," according to a former executive who heard the conversation. "Ian said, 'Joe, there's no way this organization is going to work. I'd rather leave than let the situation disintegrate.' " As much as the firing pained Diery, he was equally upset at the fact that not a single member of the board took him aside to ask what had happened, as he would complain to friends later.

The board's makeup of its outside directors had changed significantly under the Spindler administration, with the old guard consisting of just Markkula, Peter Crisp, and Bernard Goldstein following the departure in 1993 of Arthur Rock. Spindler expanded the board to include B. Jürgen Hintz, a private investor in London; Katherine M. Hudson, president and CEO of W. H. Brady Company in Milwaukee; Delano E. Lewis, president and CEO of National Public Radio in Washington, D.C.; and Gilbert F. Amelio, president and CEO of National Semiconductor Inc. in San Jose, California. (Amelio would play a pivotal role in Apple's later transformation.)

It may have been a new board, but inattention to Apple's management beset this body as much as it had through much of the company's history. After all, here was the number two executive of Apple Computer, the man who had been a hero for his stewardship of the Power Mac transition that was so vital to the company's very survival, being unceremoniously bounced out. Yet not one of the outside directors deemed the event curious enough to merit asking the simple question: Why? The board would have more to atone for in the ensuing months—much more.

Michael Spindler's new organization, which went into effect in May 1995, looked and sounded good. There was just one problem. All four of the new divisions had to report directly to Spindler. No longer was there an Ian Diery to run interference, to take care of the grunt work as the Diesel hobnobbed around talking to Chinese prime ministers and such. The Diesel was going to have to prove, in fact, that he was a take-charge, Diesel kind of guy.

That would be asking a lot of a man who, on one occasion, had been seen by a middle manager beating a meaty fist on an office table during a meeting, thundering, "We need more discipline!"—without ever following up.

Joe Graziano and most of the other members of the executive staff knew that the big boss would have trouble standing up to the strain of so much decision making. "We all told Michael this would not work," recalls a former executive. Adds another, "Michael told us, 'No, I'll be different. We've got to do this.'"

Spindler's first big test at decisiveness came all too quickly.

Back up just a few months, to January 1995 and the little flurry of licensing activity that had been dribbling into the news. First, there had been the news that "King Kahng" and his Power Computing had received the first Mac cloning license. A few days later, at Macworld in San Francisco, good old Chuck Berger had announced that his Radius Inc. was also entering the licensing game. Berger was another Dan Eilers—he just could not get enough of that "L-word." In the same month, Michael Spindler had received a phone call from a young man named Ted Waitt, who was the chairman, CEO, and cofounder of Gateway 2000 Inc., the powerhouse maker of mail-order PCs based in North Sioux City, South Dakota. He had wanted to know if Apple was still interested in signing up Mac cloners.

Gateway 2000: *this* was one of those big-name computer companies that Spindler had originally insisted Apple sign up as a Mac licensee, before ever getting the program off the ground. In fact, Gateway had been one of the names the Diesel had scrawled on a whiteboard as companies he most wanted to bag. Gateway was another rags-to-riches story in the computer industry, only that company had started in a barn instead of a garage. Like his archrival, Michael Dell, Ted Waitt had dropped out of college and with his brother Norm and a friend named Mike Hammond, had set up a shop to sell PCs in his father's barn in South Dakota.[14] Sales in 1987, the first year, when Ted Waitt was just twenty-three, had totaled $2 million. By 1990, they had mushroomed to $276 million. And at the beginning of 1995, when Waitt placed his call to Michael Spindler, Gateway had just logged $2.7 billion in annual sales and was one of the biggest PC makers in America.

Gateway was a big name, indeed.

After hanging up the phone, the Diesel ambled over to the office of Don Strickland, the vice president for licensing. "Gateway has some interest," Spindler told Strickland, according to a person who heard the conversation. "Follow up." Strickland would not comment about the Gateway matter. The meetings that ensued were like a miniversion of the grandiose ones involving the Apple-IBM merger talks. Strickland would get onto a plane, as would his midlevel counterpart at Gateway, and they would rendezvous at a halfway point in Denver, Colorado.

Spindler and Waitt, meanwhile, held a number of follow-up conversations over the phone. And Waitt was excited. Gateway, he said, was willing to commit a task force of two hundred people, solely dedicated to building a Mac clone business that would quickly balloon to $300 million a year in sales, according to a Gateway executive intimately familiar with the talks. Gateway ran the risk of royally ticking off Bill Gates and Andy Grove, but Waitt calculated that it was worth it because they would probably get over it. Gateway could then go on to land a huge slice of what he thought could still be a fairly sizable Mac clone industry. As the conversations progressed, though, it became clear to Waitt that Spindler did not sound very enthusiastic about the idea. He kept raising the concern, for example, that Gateway would steal a lot of market share from Apple, share the boys in Cupertino could ill afford to lose.

"Ted told Michael, 'You're going to lose market share anyway. At least lose it to me and keep the Mac OS strong,'" recalls the Gateway executive familiar with these talks, who spoke on condition of anonymity.

Don Strickland, on the other hand, was highly receptive to Gateway. Sure, it was a big company and could pose a formidable competitive challenge to Apple. But, he figured, Gateway's channel of distribution was through the mail, not in the stores and resale vendors where Apple was concentrated. Not only that, Gateway held a strong presence in corporate America and could open doors for the Mac in big business that had long been closed. By May 1995, the talks had progressed so far that drafts of licensing term sheets had been drawn up between Apple and Gateway, according to a former Apple executive involved in the negotiations. "It got down to where it was ready to go," this person says.

Okay, three guesses on what happened next, and the first two don't count. You have read enough about the endless litany of botched opportunities not to be surprised to see another one flushed down the toilet. That is exactly what happened. Poor Dan Eilers. The guy has to be given credit. He might have been beating a dead horse on licensing all those years, but at least he had kept beating it, as in 1985, 1990, 1992, and again at a meeting of Spindler's executive staff in May 1995. This time, though, Eilers had risen to the inner sanctum of Apple power and in fact was regarded around the company as the heir apparent to Spindler if he played his cards right.

In the meeting, in the now-infamous Synergy room, Eilers urged Spindler to go ahead and give Gateway its Mac license so it could get to work. In the past licensing fights, the chief obstructers had included Jean-Louis Gassée and Ian Diery, but their views had had a wide following in the company. The ironic thing in all this is that Ian Diery had actually changed his mind about licensing, just as Randy Battat had suddenly found religion when he had seen all those Wintel clone makers for himself on his trip to Taiwan. In fact, before he had been tossed out, Diery had deployed focus teams within the company to study more about how Apple could compete against clones. As a result, had Diery been in the Synergy room that day, there would likely have been synergy between Apple and Gateway, and the sagging Mac market would have gotten a major boost.

But Diery was gone. And in place to catch the baton was Apple USA President Jim Buckley, the latest self-appointed guardian of Apple's crown jewels, the pit bull *du jour* against licensing. Buckley was not really a bad guy. He had joined Apple in 1985 and worked his way up through the sales organization, becoming the president of Apple USA in 1993 after Bob Puette had resigned. A charismatic speaker with a trace of his native New York accent, Buckley had tried to restore Apple's damaged relations with the dealer channel that had been treated so miserably in the past. "I had phone numbers of the top ten U.S. dealers on a card in my back pocket," Buckley remembers. "I would call them each morning while I was going to work to see how we were doing." Buckley was also extraordinarily well liked by his salespeople.

Buckley, though, was under inordinate pressure to keep his numbers up following Apple's roller-coaster ride of the past few years and did not at all like the prospect of losing sales to a hard-nosed competitor such as Gateway's Ted Waitt.

It was not just Jim Buckley who opposed doing a deal with Gateway. Apple's very first cloner, Power Computing, had shot out of the gates to stunning success. With a Mac clone at a price one fifth lower than Apple's and a faster PowerPC chip, Power Computing would sell an estimated 50,000 machines—or $100 million worth—by the end of 1995.[15] And much of its gains were coming out of Apple's hide, since Power Computing appealed to both existing Macintosh users and new converts. Consequently, the old anti-licensing fears came bubbling to the surface again among salespeople and engineers. "Everybody was saying, 'What have we done?'" recalls Don Strickland, who left Apple in 1996 to become president and CEO of Picture-Works Technology Inc., a software firm in Danville, California. "Finally, the competition was there and Power Computing was aggressive. Now people wanted to reassess the impact." But it was Jim Buckley who voiced those sentiments that day in the Synergy room.

As Buckley recalls, he was not against Mac cloning in general. "My argument was that we didn't even have product of our own because of the shortages [related to Diery's erroneous forecast on Macintosh shipments]," says Buckley, a big, plain-talking man who clasped his hands behind his head while speaking with me for this book. Buckley's other concern was with doing a deal with Gateway itself. In selling directly to customers, both Gateway and Dell were able to offer discounts of as much as 20 percent off the price of comparable computers sold in stores and other distribution channel outlets, which had to add in local sales taxes and overhead costs. Consequently, the sales channel resented both mail-order manufacturers with a passion.

"I said [in the Synergy room], 'Look, if we give this thing to Gateway, there's no way I can go back to my channel and say we want a big order at the end of the quarter. And, oh, now you have new competition from Gateway,' " Buckley recalls. "So I said, 'If we are going to license, let's license to someone who will complement our strategy.' " Seated nearby, Fred Forsyth nodded in agreement. "Fred respected Jim's position that his business was going to get trashed," recalls an executive in the room that day.

Dave Nagel, who had been an advocate of licensing for some time, argued that Gateway was so big that it could only expand the Macintosh market. Eilers did the same. "Buckley's argument was the same old thing: cannibalization," recalls a former top Apple executive who was in that meeting. "He was a sales guy with one hundred percent of the Mac market today who thought he only stood to lose from competition. Dan said, 'Guys, you're viewing the Macintosh clone market as our primary competitor. Our primary competitor is Windows.' "

Eilers, as always, was on one side of the licensing fence. Buckley had his feet firmly planted on the other. But neither Dan Eilers nor Jim Buckley was running Apple Computer. Michael Spindler was, and it was up to the Diesel to make the final decision. Without offering much commentary, Spindler, in the same meeting, pulled the plug on the whole Gateway deal in a move that still leaves Ted Waitt shaking his head.

"Apple was so politically divided on the subject of licensing, they could never make up their frigging mind," says Waitt, who declined comment on the negotiations with Apple. "Either you license or you don't. But Apple never could reach a consensus. They knew they had to do something, but they were afraid to do it."

There it is again. That consensus culture. Only at Apple could a thousand people in a room agree on one course of direction, only to have that vote overturned by a lone naysayer raising his hand. There was not even consensus at Apple, in May 1995, that the company was in trouble. Joe Graziano was increasingly convinced that Apple did not have a prayer, unless it merged with another company soon. Dan Eilers, way back in 1990, had concluded that Apple would end up a "living dead company" if it did not move to license: living, as a still functioning company, but dead in terms of being relevant anymore to the computer industry. When Eilers returned to Cupertino from Claris in May 1995, he saw the look of the living dead on the faces of a roomful of Apple employees he called together for a brown-bag lunch in a conference room.

"Dan was standing in front of the room and said, 'You guys seem a little down here,'" recalls a former Apple executive who attended the meeting. "Then he said, 'So, if your best friend is out of work, how many of you would say, 'Give me your résumé. I'll try to get you on at Apple'? How many of you would do that?' Out of forty-five managers, not one raised a hand." For Eilers, who had spent his whole professional career at Apple, it was depressing. After all, when he had worked at Apple in the 1980s, there had not been another computer company on Earth that the hot young programmers wanted to join more. The résumés had come in by the thousands.

This was the Graziano and Eilers camp of pessimistic thinking. There was another camp of wild-eyed optimists. Jim Buckley, for example, thought that if he could just keep his nose to the grindstone and the whole Mac market to himself, everything would be fine. Dave Nagel thought Apple would very soon blow Microsoft and everybody else out of the water when his engineers completed the new operating system project, called "Copland." Michael Spindler himself was so enamored with Copland that, at one Apple meeting to demonstrate the technology before industry analysts in Cupertino, a consultant named Tim Bajarin remembers the Diesel pulling him aside to say, "Bill Gates would love to get his hands on this, but he will never get it." Nagel, on May 8, 1995, confidently announced at Apple's Worldwide Developers Conference that Copland would be ready to roll out by the middle of 1996.

By that time, though, not a single one of these executives would be around at Apple Computer. Not Eilers. Not Graziano, Buckley, or Nagel. Not even Michael Spindler. The storm clouds were darkening as the Apple Computer of Michael Spindler hurtled toward corporate Armageddon.

14

Spindler's Last Stand

"**W**indows 95!" That was the marketing cry heard round the world in the summer of 1995. Everywhere you looked, there was Windows 95. On billboards. On television. On radio. In newspapers and magazines. At computer trade shows. Windows 95 was coming, introduced by greater hype for the launch of a new computer product than had ever been seen before.

Microsoft would spend a staggering $150 million to promote the latest iteration of its PC operating system, pulling out so many stops that it licensed rights to the Rolling Stones' classic "Start Me Up" as the official Windows 95 theme song and hired NBC-TV's *Tonight Show* host, Jay Leno, to yuck it up with Bill Gates at a rollout party on the Microsoft campus in Redmond, Washington, on August 24. That same morning, at precisely 12:01 A.M., computer stores all across America opened their doors to lines of computer enthusiasts wanting to be first on their block with Windows 95. The scene at a CompUSA store in San Bruno, California, just outside San Francisco, was one repeated over and over from coast to coast: under the glare of a powerful searchlight sweeping the black sky, several hundred shoppers—mostly young and mostly male—poured in just after the stroke of midnight, attacking the piles of blue boxes containing Windows 95. The free pizza ordered for the event was gobbled up in the first few minutes.

Bill Gates was no longer just the most powerful person in the computer industry and among the very richest in the world; he was being transformed into a cultural icon, befitting the PC's evolution into a mainstream consumer appliance from its former status as a tool for primarily big business and techno geeks. Through the skillful work of his longtime public relations handler, Pam Edstrom, Gates was no longer appearing at interviews and other public events with mismatched socks, unkempt hair, and flecks of dandruff sprinkled over his shoulders. He was dressed up, cleaned up, and trained to smile at each interviewer's question, no matter how many times it had been asked, or how stupid he thought it was.

In the not-so-old days, Gates had been notoriously quick-tempered, having once stormed out of an interview with former CBS-TV anchor Connie Chung after she committed affronts such as mispronouncing "DOS" as "dose" instead of "doss." But he was pushing forty, and had just been married for the first time, to a Microsoft executive named Melinda French, in a private ceremony arranged by his billionaire buddy, real estate tycoon David Murdock, on the Murdock-controlled island of Lanai in Hawaii. A baby would soon be on the way, and Chairman Bill was looking more at peace with the world than ever.

The same could not be said for the boys down in Cupertino, who chafed at all the publicity Gates was getting. Apple Computer's PR department began working overtime, inundating *The Wall Street Journal* and other business publications with fax messages and overnight packets detailing why the Macintosh was so much superior to Windows 95. Apple even compiled an eighteen-page booklet containing testimonials of Mac users on "Why people think Macintosh computers are better than PCs running Windows 95, in their own words." A Mac user from Massachusetts named Ted Warren summed up the sentiments in this way: "Using the Macintosh is like a day of skiing on 10 inches of packed powder with good friends. Using Windows 95 is like a day of skiing on wind-swept, rocky, icy slopes with a really good looking instructor who doesn't care the least about your progress."

Apple seemed to make an effort to thumb its nose at Microsoft in a typically juvenile manner. As practically every other member of the computer industry sent dignitaries to pay homage to Chairman Bill at the August 24 launch, Apple ran newspaper ads that read: "C:ONGRTLNS.W95," a snide reference to MS-DOS's file-naming protocols in which users were limited to cryptic file names of no more than eight letters, such as "C:\MARKKULA.DOC." In a Macintosh file, by contrast, the user could label that same document "MIKE MARKKULA."

The Mac-versus-Windows debate had been raging for years, and doggedly Apple had beaten its chest on how much superior its software was compared to Macintosh. But with Windows 95, there was precious little left to boast about. With Windows 95, users could put in any file name they wished and could copy files, just as on the Mac, by simply "dragging" a document, represented by a picture of a manila file folder, to the desired location on the screen and "dropping" it. Under the old Windows, the task of copying a file consisted of laboriously typing in a series of arcane commands. Windows 95 was Mac-like, in almost every way and even superior in others. Microsoft had improved the system's "memory protection" to the point that Windows 95 would rarely suffer the problem of sporadic crashes, which had afflicted Windows 3.0 and Windows 3.1. By contrast, the Mac, running on creaky old code dating as far back as 1984, was prone to crashing several times a day.

The main advantage Apple retained was the tight integration between the Mac's software and hardware, which made installing peripheral devices, such as a printer or a removable hard driver, a breeze even compared to Windows 95. Wintel machines consisted of a hodgepodge of parts made by many different companies, making it difficult to get new things up and running on the computer. In fact, the tremendous retail sales of Windows 95 in the days after the launch began to sag as customers trying to load the new operating system into their older Wintel computers encountered all kinds of installation problems, such as insufficient memory and system conflicts. Still, Windows 95 would go on to become an unmitigated success, selling about 20 million copies in the first six months as more and more manufacturers such as Compaq preloaded the software into all their new machines.

With the eyes of the world on Microsoft that summer, Apple mostly stayed out of the limelight. It would roar back into the forefront of the news very soon, but not in a manner that anybody in Cupertino would have wanted. Licensing was not going anywhere. The on-again, off-again merger activity, which had begun in earnest with John Sculley in 1992, was moribund. With no long-term solution to its predicament, Apple's core business began to unravel. The first sign of crisis came in July 1995, when Apple released its quarterly results for the period ended June 30 of that year and disclosed that the backlog of unfilled orders had ballooned to a record $1 billion—more than double the amount in the spring of 1994. As a consequence of the shortfall, Apple's worldwide market share dipped again, to 7.4 percent from 7.6 percent in the first quarter of 1994 and 8.3 percent at the end of 1994.[1]

The problem boiled down to a gross miscalculation by Apple in forecasting demand, resulting in a shortage of some 500,000 Macintoshes. The timing could hardly have been worse. Here was Windows 95, barreling down the track, and Apple was jumping up and down like a little child, screaming, "I'm better! I'm better!" But it did not matter whether the Mac was better or not if customers could not get their hands on the machine. In the month before the Windows 95 launch, for example, Apple introduced a speedy new Mac for under $2,000 that Donald Ryerson and many other potential customers tried to snap up. Ryerson, a business development consultant typical of the Macintosh customer, called all the shops around his home in New York City and dialed catalog stores as far away as Salt Lake City. After four weeks, he had still been unable to locate one of the models. "It makes you wonder how this could happen," Ryerson, still seething, said to me in an interview for an August 11, 1995, article in *The Wall Street Journal*.

To understand how this did happen, let us take a brief walk down memory lane again.

Remember the mid-1980s, when Del Yocam would walk around with his engineer's notebook and jot down everything managers would promise him?

As chief operating officer, Yocam had maintained almost a fanatical diligence in making sure manufacturing kept in sync with forecasted demand. Yocam would gather in all the forecast reports from the field and deduct for the usual overoptimism on the part of regional sales managers. He was assisted in this process by a seven-member forecasting team, whose sole job was to make two hundred phone calls each and every week to Apple's dealers, suppliers, and distributors, asking such questions as which products were moving and which were not. They would also call thirty key Apple salespeople in the field and ask them the same questions. Their plus or minus margin of error in predicting demand was 5 percent, remembers Peter Lycurgus, a marketing executive who managed the forecasting team. At the end of the day, Del Yocam made the final call, issuing manufacturing orders that nearly always matched how many computers Apple could actually sell.

Now, fast-forward to the early 1990s, with Michael Spindler as chief operating officer and Bob Puette as president of Apple USA. During a 1991 reorganization of Apple USA, under which the forecasting team worked, Puette laid off five of the seven forecasters. In their place, Puette and Spindler called in Fred Forsyth, the head of manufacturing, to help out on the forecasts. "Those two forecasters left could only make fifty calls a week, with a margin of error of 50 percent, plus or minus," says Lycurgus, now an Apple manager of strategic alliances.

During this same time, in the early 1990s, Apple's number of product models exploded. Whereas the company had had only a handful of models to sell at any given period during the 1980s, that number soared to as many as forty by 1995, as Apple began manufacturing Macintoshes in different configurations of hard drives, microprocessor speed, and memory capacity in an attempt to keep up with a PC market that was growing by leaps and bounds. There was no way anyone could predict with any degree of certainty which models would perform well and which ones would not.

Consequently, Apple lost its feel for actual customer demand, resulting in a seesaw of product gluts and shortages in years thereafter. A good example of this was with PowerBook: when the new laptop was first introduced in 1991, Apple built way too few; two years later, it built way too many. This is not a problem unique to Apple, by any means. Product forecasting is an inexact science for most computer companies, but there is far greater latitude for error at a Wintel manufacturer such as Compaq, which can tap into hundreds of different supply sources if it undershoots too much on a forecast and needs to quickly procure more components. The same was not true for Apple, since it was the only manufacturer of Macintoshes in the world and therefore had far fewer suppliers.

When Ian Diery was given control over all PC operations in 1993, he did get a firmer grip on forecasts. Diery, for example, says he ordered his line sales managers to provide on his desk by 9:30 every morning the latest report on all company billings and revenue, by model number, in the United States and around the world. "I would spend fifteen to twenty minutes every morning going through these numbers, and then I would call people on it," Diery recalls. And each Thursday, Diery received reports from Apple's resellers indicating how much product had actually been sold the week before, so he could match those numbers against Apple's product backlog.

Diery's technique, while not as methodical and comprehensive as the one used under Yocam, was for the most part effective. The first time he really missed the mark on a forecast was in late 1994, when he predicted the 15 percent growth in Apple's unit shipments for the forthcoming fiscal year. Motivated by the desire to rebuild Apple's profits, Diery had chosen to bet conservatively, hewing close to analysts' pessimistic estimates for the PC industry to grow only about that much from the previous year. That number was also influenced by Diery's desire to constrain growth so he could rebuild enough profits for his PC division to keep funding all the money-losing ones at Apple.

Being as prone to error as anything else in this fast-paced industry, the analysts' predictions proved incredibly wrong. Following the PC boom of Christmas 1994, which had been fueled by consumers' rush to new multimedia-equipped computers, industrywide sales surged by 25 percent through the first half of 1995 compared to the same period the year before. The increase caught nearly everyone by surprise, resulting in shortages of key components such as CD-ROM drives and logic chips. The Wintel purveyors were able to catch up quickly, though, because they had so many alternate supply choices. Apple, however, had nowhere to turn. Hence, the $1 billion backlog in unfilled orders.

This was problem number one, in the summer of 1995. Problem number two was a blowup—literally—in Apple's new line of PowerBook laptop computers. Ever since the Three Musketeers—Randy Battat, John Medica, and Neil Selvin—had left Apple, the PowerBook line had languished. Management had rallied, instead, behind Power Mac. As a result, between 1991, when it was introduced, and 1995, the PowerBook underwent only one upgrade. In the meantime, competitors such as IBM and Toshiba surged ahead, becoming among the first manufacturers to include color screens and whopping (for that time) 500-megabyte hard drives. This resulted in a dramatic decline in Apple's leading 11 percent share of the global laptop market, as of 1992, to 6.7 percent by mid-1995.[2]

By late August 1995, a brand-new line of PowerBooks was ready to ship, with bigger screens, longer battery life, and other features to match the competition. But after only one thousand PowerBook 5300 models—intended for the high end of the market, such as business and graphics professionals—had shipped, Apple ordered a recall. The reason: two of the machines being used internally by Apple had burst into flames. The first episode occurred while an Apple programmer was testing the product at his home in Silicon Valley. Steve Andler, Apple's senior director of marketing for mobile products, and some other Apple executives, including Michael Spindler, learned of the problem upon boarding a jet in early September to attend a big launch of the new PowerBook at an Apple conference in Paris. By the time they landed in France, word was relayed to Andler from headquarters that the faulty Power-Book was a production model, not a shipping one.

"We thought maybe the problem was some defective components," recalls a former executive involved in the episode. Since the PowerBook had origi-nated at Apple's factory in Fountain, Colorado, outside Colorado Springs, a temporary shutdown of production was ordered there until the problem could be diagnosed. Apple's two other PowerBook factories, in Singapore and Ire-land, proceeded on, and the PowerBook launch in Paris went ahead as sched-uled, too. The very next day, however, Andler answered a call on his cellular phone from the home office in Cupertino: a second PowerBook had just burst into flames, and this time it had happened at the factory in Singapore.[3]

Steve Andler, who declined comment for this book, had been recruited just a few months prior to restore the vitality of the PowerBook line. Andler, a respected industry veteran, had formerly been a key mover behind Toshiba Corporation's great inroads into the laptop market. When he took over the PowerBook and Newton lines, Andler quickly moved to streamline to two from five the number of major Apple engineering projects under way on mo-bile computers. Then he set out to push the PowerBook 5300 to market. The Paris launch should thus have been cause for great rejoicing for both him and Apple, a milestone in PowerBook's resurgence. Instead, it was panic time.

After getting the bad news in Paris, Andler spent hours on his cell phone receiving updates and details from a man named Charlie Tritshler, Apple's product line manager for the 5300. It turned out that both PowerBook explo-sions had resulted from the same problems: a defective circuit in their lithium ion batteries. That had resulted in the batteries overheating and leaking corro-sive acid, which had set the PowerBook's plastic casing on fire. The batteries had been supplied by an outside vendor, which Apple never identified, but a former Apple executive says Apple shared the blame for failing to communi-cate the new PowerBook's specifications more clearly.

Although Apple determined that the probability of such a fire occurring with the battery defect was one in 350,000, Andler concluded he had no choice but to order a recall of the machines already sent out. As it happened, only one of the PowerBooks had actually landed in the hands of a customer; the other 999 were all still in the distribution channel. And Apple resumed shipments within days, replacing the lithium ion batteries with ones made from metal hydride. But immeasurable PR damage had been done. "There were stories of us bringing down an airplane, and covers of trade magazines showed an exploding PowerBook," says a former executive, sighing heavily. "It was an incredible press nightmare."

Over the years, Apple had lost a lot of things: its market share, its technological lead over Microsoft, and a good deal of its swaggering pride. But the one thing that could always be said about Apple Computer, through thick and thin, was that its computers were of the highest quality around. At least, that was true until its computers started exploding in flames.

Soon after this incident, some analysts and investors began the drumbeat for Michael Spindler's head. Apple's shares so far that year had peaked at $47 in June but just four months later, in September, were battered down as low as $35, an erosion of 25 percent, or $1.5 billion in market value. Apple's stock, in fact, had been drifting down since 1992, when it had stood as high as $60. The rest of the PC industry, meanwhile, had been going gangbusters. An industry stock index compiled by Standard & Poor's, the New York bond-rating firm, showed the market value of the eight firms it tracked nearly doubling in market value between January 4, 1993, and February 5, 1996. By the key measure of return to investors, Michael Spindler's reign as Apple CEO, from 1993 through 1995, had proven an abject failure.

"Apple's board of directors should seriously consider replacing CEO Michael Spindler," Eric Nee, then editor of the influential trade magazine *Upside*, for technology professionals, concluded in a blistering critique of Apple's performance in an October column entitled "A Rotten Apple."

Spindler's reaction to all the bad press was anger and denial. During July, in a rare interview to introduce a line of low-priced computers, the Diesel had startled a group of business reporters as he pounded the table of a conference room, demanding, "Don't count us out. Come on." Spindler went on to chide the media, Microsoft, and cut-rate PC makers such as Packard Bell Electronics Inc., which within three years had grown from a basic start-up to the number one position in sales of computers in retail stores. Spindler derided Packard Bell as "an el cheapo packeteer" and slapped the table with his palm to demand, "Who are we competing with on price? The guys who are dumping volume and getting 15 percent return rates? We're not going to ship stuff that doesn't work."[4] At least, until the PowerBooks started exploding.

Two months after that session, on September 20, Spindler granted an equally rare interview to myself and Greg Hill, then chief of *The Wall Street Journal*'s San Francisco bureau. Spindler had just moved the executive suite to another Apple building called City Center 3, an eight-story mass of concrete and steel connected to a coordinated tower by two glass-enclosed walkways overhead. From afar the complex, appropriately, resembled a fortress, although up close it was stylishly appointed with blond furniture, banana-colored carpeting, and palm trees in the atrium lobbies. Spindler, according to one former Apple manager, had made the move in part to get out of "John's building" at De Anza 7, where so much of Apple's current predicament had been shaped. Taking an elevator up to the top floor, Hill and I were escorted into a small conference room, where Spindler sat on one side of the table—his back to the wall—flanked by his aide, David Seda, and Barbara Krause, the vice president of corporate communications.

Spindler had assiduously dodged interviews with the *Journal* and many other publications in the past. The lone exception for the *Journal* was when he had made himself available to me to flog the Power Mac back at the New York City launch. The Diesel was making another exception this time because he was under attack. Apple's board was set to begin a two-day monthly meeting on October 2 in Austin, Texas, and rumors were building that he might be sacked. Throughout the hour-long interview, however, Spindler repeatedly sought to downplay Apple's problems, insisting they had been grossly exaggerated. "This is like the O.J. trial, everybody goes into orbit," he snapped. "These sirens about the death of Apple—there is no letup in the growth of Apple."

When asked about criticism from people outside Apple that he was cold, the Diesel's eyes narrowed menacingly as he shot back, while thumping the table, "I'm cold? I'm cold? In 1993, I gave a speech to twenty-five hundred Apple people [at the Las Vegas sales conference]. At the end, they cried. I had them right here," he added, cupping his hands. "Some people have said the reason they stick it out here was because of that speech." Reacting to general criticism of his management, the Diesel lost his cool again. "Gee, people say this guy is a turkey," Spindler said, his words dripping with sarcasm. "Let them come in and do it." After the interview, Barbara Krause led me to the office of Kevin Sullivan, who was ready to offer up a glowing profile of his boss. "He has probably the best understanding of this industry that I have experienced," Sullivan told me, clasping his hands behind his head as we sat at a table in his cubicle office.

If there was one other executive more media-shy than Michael Spindler during this period, it was Apple's cofounder Mike Markkula, the "kingpin behind the throne." Spindler and Markkula, you will remember, were close friends who loved to sit and talk for hours about global business strategy. Markkula was not nearly the hard worker that the Diesel was. By all accounts, he cherished his leisure time, slept in late, and left the dirty business of running Apple Computer to his CEOs. But while Markkula did not share the same work ethic—and did not have to, because of all his millions—he was as loyal to the Diesel as an old hound dog. Indeed, Markkula went so far to defend his man that he actually consented to a brief telephone interview with me in September 1995, offering staunch support for Spindler and hope that Apple would rebound soon.

"Demand is very strong for our products," Markkula said. "That gives me reason to believe we can gain market share and we can continue to grow." Neither Markkula nor Spindler would be interviewed for this book.

Spindler and Markkula were reading from the same prayer book, chapter and verse: Apple was not really in trouble, it was all typical exaggeration by the media. They may have sounded that tune in public, but behind the scenes both men had taken steps in the previous months to cushion themselves, personally, in the event of Apple's fall. Markkula, between July 25 and August 17, 1995, sold a million of his 5 million Apple shares at an average price of $47, for a gain of $42.7 million, according to Securities and Exchange Commission records. Markkula was the largest single individual investor in Apple at that time, and it was his largest annual sell-off of the 1990s.

As for Spindler, on July 27 of that year he sold 100,000 of his shares for an average of $46 each, for a gain of $4.6 million. That transaction was also his biggest annual sell-off of the decade. The Apple board had also, on June 9, 1995, adopted a severance plan and retention agreement with Spindler that provided the Diesel with a handsome "golden parachute" in the event he lost his job following a "change in control" at Apple, such as through a merger. That would include a cash payout equal to three times his annual combined salary and bonus of $1.4 million, or $4.2 million. Under previous agreements, Apple had also agreed to pay Spindler $2.9 million for his mansion in the exclusive enclave of Atherton, California, and $25,000 to move him and his family back to his old home in France, should they so desire following a termination. In all, Spindler could look forward to a windfall of more than $7 million.

Spindler became quite testy when asked about that golden parachute in his September 20, 1995, interview with myself and Greg Hill. "This is standard business practice," he spat. "We did it because of these constant goddamn rumors [of a merger] being planted. We have to react to these bloody rumors coming up. I did it as a precaution, so I would not have to tell my people every Monday" that Apple was not being sold.

Financially, at least, neither Markkula nor Spindler had anything to fret about, regardless of what happened to Apple Computer. The same certainly could not be said of the thousands of employees in Cupertino, whose mortgages, car payments, and other assorted responsibilities all hinged on their jobs at Apple. They were worried, and the events following the October board meeting would do nothing to allay their concern.

During the months of August and September 1995, Joe Graziano was taking his sabbatical, the eight-week leave accorded all Apple employees every five years. At his home in nearby Saratoga, which abuts the Santa Cruz Mountains, Graz pondered what Apple should do. Ever since Spindler and Markkula had torpedoed the IBM merger, he had become convinced that Apple was heading off the cliff. He was the chief numbers guy, and the numbers did not look good.

The parts shortages were crimping everything from market share to cash on hand. But it was the cash situation that had Graziano worried the most. By the end of Apple's fiscal year on September 29, 1995, cash and cash equivalents on hand had dwindled to $756 million from $1.2 billion a year earlier. Even that $756 million was a misleading figure, because much of it was tied up overseas and would be subject to heavy taxation in the United States if Apple pulled it back stateside. Given the unrelenting price pressure in the industry, Graziano thought, it would not take much to upset the Apple cart, especially if there were any more screwups.

That is another reason he was worried, along with his friend in the pessimists' camp, Dan Eilers. By the late spring of 1995, the executive suite was divided between Graziano and Eilers, on one side, and the optimists' camp, including Apple USA President Jim Buckley and Apple Pacific President John Floisand, on the other. Like Buckley, Floisand was an amiable but ambitious chap, with an accent from his native South Africa that made him all the more charming. And like Buckley, he was a salesman first and foremost. Graziano had already fallen out of favor with Spindler in their arguments over the failed merger deal with IBM. Since Eilers was Graziano's political ally, his power was on the wane, too. Spindler was most receptive, then, when Buckley and Floisand suggested, in May 1995, a plan to recapture market share—and Kevin Sullivan heartily endorsed it.

The plan essentially entailed flooding the market with Apple's low-end line of Macintosh Performas, which were aimed at customers in homes and small businesses. According to a former executive privy to these conversations, Buckley and Floisand argued that Apple would have to go all out for market share to compensate for having lost so much ground because of the shortages of Power Macs. They talked Spindler into a plan of increasing Mac shipments by 25 percent, year over year, in the upcoming Christmas quarter and 30 percent for the fiscal year beginning in October 1995. That would be heady growth, indeed, considering that Apple would post a record $11 billion in sales in the fiscal year ending on September 29, 1995. (The company's revenues kept increasing despite the fall in market share because Apple's sales were still growing, just not as fast as the industry's.)

Sullivan supported the plan because it dovetailed neatly with his insistence at the Spanish Bay retreat the previous March that Apple rebuild its market share by attacking its stronghold markets. Well, the home market was one of those markets, and it certainly would be attacked under this strategy. As the summer progressed, there was another cause for optimism, too. While profits were still under pressure, revenues in the fiscal third quarter, ending in September, were soaring on the huge pent-up demand for Macintoshes that could not be delivered before. Indeed, the 20 percent jump in revenues from the same period a year earlier would result in Apple's share of the PC market rebounding to 9 percent from 7.4 percent in the preceding quarter.[5] And the stock was climbing, to $45 in July 1995 from a low of $35 the prior March. "We felt then that we had come out of the storm," Sullivan says.

Fred Forsyth, who also endorsed the market share plan, remembers all the reports from Apple's salespeople in the field indicating that they could sell practically as many Macintoshes as the company could manufacture, demand was so high. "We did not want to miss out on that Christmas [1995] quarter," Forsyth says.

Had Ian Diery still been at Apple, it is highly likely he would have vetoed the Performa plan, as good as it might have looked on paper. Diery wanted market share, all right, but the reason he had held to conservative growth in the first place was because he knew that Apple's balance sheet was far too fragile to take the chance of making a big mistake in forecasting demand. Without Diery, in fact, there was nobody watching the numbers from on high. The formal forecasting process had been scrapped years before. Now it was just Buckley and Floisand, in collaboration with Apple Europe President Marco Landi and manufacturing chief Fred Forsyth, essentially holding a finger to the wind and saying, "We'll sell this many."

Buckley disagrees that the process was that arbitrary. Indeed, he says, he and those other three men met every Wednesday at 7 A.M. to review forecasts and hear manufacturing and sales updates via a videoconference link with Apple managers in Europe and Asia. They all felt, he says, that demand would be strong for Performas at Christmas, because the home market had proven so strong the Christmas before. "If I had been a wizard and could forecast the future and know of the problems we would have, I would never have put in that forecast," Buckley says in his frank style. "I'm not making an excuse for forecasting. We weren't perfect, and we could have done better."

Ian Diery was not there, but Dan Eilers was. And he warned Spindler that Apple would lose money in the Christmas quarter if he proceeded with the aggressive growth plan. The reason: Apple's profit margins were already so low— 21 percent by the July-to-September period—that focusing on the least profitable segment of the market made little sense. It made better sense, he and some other executives, including Don Strickland, believed, to focus on Apple's more profitable markets—desktop publishing and education—in addition to the home. Another executive, Satjiv Chahil, the beturbaned Diery protégé then running a new business targeting the Hollywood entertainment industry, suggested loading up on the profitable high end and aiming not only at Apple's stronghold markets but at the largely untapped one of music and movie artists.

Graziano, too, was convinced the plan would not work. And he planned to tell the board that himself, at the two-day meeting set to begin on October 2. Graziano had actually conveyed his concerns about Spindler's management to Mike Markkula and other board members before departing on sabbatical. Shortly after his return in mid-September, Graziano flew down to the meeting at Apple's technical support center in Austin, Texas, aboard Markkula's private jet. Gil Amelio, the president, chairman, and CEO of National Semiconductor, accompanied the two men on the flight from San Jose. Like Markkula, Amelio was a private pilot and aviation enthusiast who tooled around in his own small jet. Amelio was a plainspoken businessman who had gotten a reputation as a turnaround artist by pulling National Semiconductor from the brink. He was new to Apple, having been called onto the board only the previous year, but he was the only outside director who had any experience in actually running a major computer company.

The meeting commenced the next day, Monday, in the afternoon. The directors reviewed the operating results for the quarter just ended, asked Spindler and Graziano to leave, and met in executive session into the evening. Since Spindler and Graziano were inside directors, they were not allowed in these sessions unless they were invited or a special request was made to make a private presentation such as the one Graziano had in mind. They called Spindler in at one point and then adjourned for the night.[6]

With rumors flying that Spindler would not survive the meeting, members of the Austin news media gathered at a local hotel where the Apple board members were staying and confronted Graziano, Markkula, and the other directors as they got off a shuttle bus there at about 11 P.M. The directors ignored the questions and the phone messages from reporters. They resumed the meeting the next morning with Spindler being summoned in again, without Graziano. As soon as Spindler left the room, Graziano was invited into the large conference room to give his presentation. Sitting around the table were Markkula, Amelio, and the other outside directors, including Peter Crisp of Venrock Associates, Bernard Goldstein of Broadview Associates, private investor B. Jürgen Hintz, Katherine Hudson of W. H. Brady Company, and Delano Lewis of National Public Radio. They listened impassively as the Graz dropped his bomb.[7]

According to a former Apple executive with close knowledge of that meeting, here is what Graziano had to say: "The company has a fundamentally flawed and unsustainable business strategy. And we are on the verge of a crisis, the collapse of the business. The board should not be accepting the [Spindler] plan for 1996. There's no way this [30 percent increase in unit shipments] is going to happen." Graziano paused as the directors continued sitting in silence, then took dead aim at Spindler himself. "We need to look at other alternatives in getting the company sold, and somebody from the board should take over that activity. Spindler, in my view, is not willing to follow through on that."

In a normal business situation, such an attack on one's boss would be considered tantamount to corporate treason and grounds for dismissal. But Apple was not a normal company, and its financial situation at this time certainly appeared to Graziano to be on the verge of perhaps irreversible deterioration. True, revenues for the year ended September 29 had soared to an all-time high of $11 billion and year-over-year profits were up by 37 percent, but profits in the fourth quarter had plunged by 48 percent and the gross profit margin had sunk to a new low of 21 percent. And cash was running low. Apple had precious little room for error.

So on the one hand, Graziano had a duty, as Spindler's subordinate, to support the CEO. But as CFO and one of the two inside Apple board members, along with Spindler, he also had a duty to the board and shareholders to sound a financial alarm. It was that latter allegiance that compelled Graziano to deliver this warning to the board that fall day in Austin. The warning went over like a lead balloon.

According to a cover story in the May 1996 issue of CFO magazine entitled "Graziano's Last Stand," this is what happened when Graziano ended his presentation, as reported by one unidentified director: "As soon as he walked out of the room we all looked at each other and turned thumbs down." The same director added that some board colleagues actually trembled with anger. "The body language was incredible."

None of the board directors, except Amelio, would consent to be interviewed for this book. As Amelio remembers, he and the other directors believed that Graziano could well be right that Apple needed to find a strong partner. "But I felt that the way Joe went about doing it was not productive," Amelio recalled in his interview with me for this book. "It was a way of almost guaranteeing failure in terms of getting his point across. Instead of making it an appropriate intellectual inquiry as to what we were doing and getting everyone thinking together, he tried to make it confrontational. And I just didn't think that was going to succeed."

The board's anger certainly could not have stemmed from personal fears of what might happen to them if Graziano was right. Markkula had dumped a chunk of his Apple shares only a few months before. Three of the four new directors appointed by Spindler—Amelio, Hudson, and Hintz—collectively held just 7,018 shares of Apple stock, according to SEC filings at the time, while the fourth, Delano Lewis, owned not a single one. So the board members had little to lose, from the point of view of having a personal stake in the company, by taking another roll of the dice with Spindler. And that is exactly what they did. Graziano was called back in before the board later that same day and told by the directors that they intended to give their full support to Spindler. In a dramatic and empty moment, Graziano replied, "I will stay and work this if you want," according to the former Apple executive familiar with the conversations that day. "We don't see how, if you feel this strongly about the issues," snapped back one of the directors.

The board offered to let Graziano resign his position as CFO but remain on the board so long as he pledged support behind Spindler's plan. Since the whole point of his presentation had been to throw cold water all over that plan, Graziano had no choice but to resign from Apple altogether. He had served at Apple for eleven years: from 1980 to 1985 as CFO, and again from 1989 through 1995 in the same role. All that was left was for the board to work out the terms of Graziano's severance package.

Markkula, who had always been friendly with Graziano, worked out a deal that was acceptable to Graziano. The board, however, turned it down, giving him an unspecified smaller amount, according to the person familiar with the affair. This was a blow not only to Graziano, but to Markkula. Until now, Markkula had always been the kingpin behind the throne. But the new board members, led by the strong-willed Gil Amelio, had been at Apple such a short time that they felt far less compelled to automatically defer to Markkula by virtue of his status as the largest individual shareholder and last remaining co-founder of the company. Mike Markkula—the behind-the-scenes recluse who had helped force out Steve Jobs and John Sculley—would soon see his own wings clipped, as well.

Graziano, then aged fifty-two, joined the long list of other Apple executives who had walked the plank in Cupertino. To this day, however, he expresses no regret over his mutinous stand that day in the cedar hills of Texas. "I feel strongly that what I did was the right thing," says Graziano, who has spent much of his time since serving on boards of various other companies and investing in start-up ventures. "I firmly believed the company was going to take steps in the ensuing months that were going to lead to disaster. I couldn't believe, as a board member, that what I was telling them didn't get more consideration. I was willing to stay as long as the board got more involved and not let Spindler be the sole driver. That's a pretty big warning coming from the CFO. And this board did nothing. And for that, I think, figuratively, they should all be shot. Every last one of them."

In the span of just seven months, Apple's number two executive, Ian Diery, and its top finance executive, Joe Graziano, had been tossed out like so much garbage. Just as it had with the Diery ouster, Apple tried to describe Graziano's departure as "amicable." A press release, issued on October 4, also quoted Markkula as pledging to "continue working with Mr. Spindler to address the challenges and exciting opportunities we face in the dynamic personal computer industry." Another board member, speaking on condition of anonymity, told me at about the same time, "It is frustrating that the company is not doing better, but the board is overall happy."

The board may have been "overall happy," but hardly anybody else working at Apple was—especially the following month, when the other shoe dropped and Dan Eilers, head of Apple's worldwide marketing, was booted out. Eilers and Graziano were soul mates, in a sense. They both believed very deeply that Apple was in big trouble and that anything short of cataclysmic change would fail to avert a financial catastrophe. They had also, in their separate ways, beaten their head against the wall to no avail: Eilers, by pushing licensing so persistently for so many years; Graziano, by pushing for Apple to latch onto a stronger partner.

Since being pulled back into the Apple management fold in May 1995, Eilers had spent the intervening months assembling a team of managers to implement Spindler's new plan to coordinate all of Apple's worldwide marketing activity from Cupertino. This was supposed to focus Apple's sales efforts better, as opposed to the previous method of letting each region handle its own marketing. Eilers was all set to implement a plan by that October to focus all of Apple's marketing efforts on its stronghold markets: education, desktop publishing, and the home.

To attack the core markets, Eilers assembled a team of eight vice presidents, each of whom would help manage marketing and promotion for the plan. He also suggested that R and D help out by tweaking the Mac's operating system so there would be customized versions for each of the markets. "It was about making sure we were clearly differentiated from the competition in those spaces," recalls an executive involved in that plan. Eilers, though, believed even these steps were not enough to save Apple. So he also began formulating a plan to split the company in two.

This plan, which he began preparing with his staff, entailed breaking off the Macintosh operating system and putting it into one company. Under that business, Apple would attempt to forge an alliance with Sun Microsystems to use Sun's Solaris operating system, which was designed to run high-performance computer workstations. That way, the combination of the Mac's software on the low end and Solaris on the high end would meet all the needs of a corporate network. As for Apple's hardware business, Eilers wanted to make that a separate company producing both Macintoshes and computers based on the Wintel standard. Since this would be an enterprise dedicated solely to building unit volume, it did not matter which operating system was used.

It was a takeoff on John Sculley's grand split-up plan, the one that had died with his ouster as CEO. Eilers was all set to make his pitch to Spindler but never had the opportunity to do so.

After the board had bid Graziano a hearty farewell, Spindler returned to

Cupertino and told Eilers the worldwide marketing approach was not such a hot idea, after all. The Diesel wanted to go back to letting each region handle its own turf. This was a stunning blow to Eilers, whose team had just completed its marketing plan and was getting ready to deploy it. As had happened so often at Apple, Eilers's plan died for lack of a consensus. "We told people [in the executive suite], 'Here's what we need to do,' and people didn't want to buy into even the first level of we have a problem with how the resources are being aligned against these markets," a former executive recalls. In other words, the faction of "preserve the status quo," as supported by Buckley, Floisand, and their ilk, had prevailed.

Consequently, Spindler enlisted Eilers to redelegate all marketing responsibilities back to Apple's main regions in North America, Europe, and Asia. In so doing, Eilers found himself—and his eight vice presidents—without a seat at the table. Funny, but the same thing had happened to Ian Diery back in the spring. Only it wasn't funny at all. It meant that Eilers—at age forty—was left without a job and forced to resign, as announced on November 2. There was no shouting. No melodrama. After giving his heart and soul for thirteen and a half years to a company that would never listen to his ideas for change, Eilers's services were simply no longer required. Eilers went away quietly and, like so many fallen executives before, put on a brave face for the press. "I love Apple, but at the same time there isn't a position at the level of responsibility I hold today," Eilers told me for a *Wall Street Journal* article published on November 3, 1995.

Eilers went on to become "CEO in waiting" for a computer venture backed by the powerful venture capital firm of Kleiner Perkins Caufield & Byers in Menlo Park, California, before eventually settling in as president and CEO of CIDCO, Inc., a Morgan Hill, California, producer of smart phones and other telecommunications products. He declined to comment for this book.

Finally, at long last, Michael Spindler had purged Apple of all dissenters. No more John Sculley. No more Al Eisenstat, Ian Diery, Joe Graziano, or Dan Eilers, just the inner circle of the four "S"s—Michael Spindler, Kevin Sullivan, Ed Stead, and David Seda. Sullivan, Stead, and Seda remained fiercely loyal, as always. "Sullivan would go around and say, 'Michael is the smartest guy I know,'" recalls one former Apple executive. Apple's jaded workforce, however, knew their emperor was not wearing any clothing. "What really killed Spindler's credibility was when he undid the Dan Eilers reorganization only a few months later," one middle manager told me at the time. "There's a lot of, frankly, disgust and impatience to say, 'Come on, let's get our act together.' Decisions are being made by Spindler and his small circle, and that's it. Parts of the company, like R and D, are just running. Other parts that are confused, like corporate marketing, are sitting and waiting."

Sitting and waiting for the bullets that were about to hit. Eilers and Graziano had been dead right about Spindler's new market share plan being doomed to fail. Apple went ahead and manufactured quantities of the low-end Mac Performas, hoping to lure in some of those first-time computer buyers who had ignited such an industry selling frenzy in the Christmas season of 1994. These were "fence-sitters," novice users who could go either the way of Macintosh or Wintel. The Performa was actually a competitively priced machine that contained many of the same features and components as comparable models based on the Wintel standard. Apple still faced the disadvantage of having far less software support for the Macintosh than Windows did, but the Performa, like Macintosh models in general, was still easier to set up and use. It was a sleek little machine with everything, including the monitor and keyboard, coming in one neat package. All a user had to do was take it out of the box and plug it in.

It was an ideal computer for anyone who had never used one before. There were two big problems, though. One was that by this time the first-time buyers had largely dried up and blown away. The other was that an advanced Performa model featuring the vertical "tower" configuration that had recently been popularized by Wintel competitors was not available to ship to market because of a development delay that would last several months. The problem of product delays had afflicted Apple for years, and it also screwed up forecasts.

At the end of 1994, approximately one third of all U.S. households owned a personal computer, giving rise to hope in the industry that the remaining two thirds that did not would rush out to snap one up. But the numbers were misleading. Although the PC had become a mass-market product, it was still a big-ticket item that set the average buyer back a cool $2,500, when everything, such as monitor and printer, was included. With the vast majority of American households scraping by, it turned out that only that one third could actually afford to buy one. According to a survey of 1,500 American consumers of all demographic classes in mid-1994 by the San Francisco research firm of Odyssey L.P., 83 percent of the households without PCs indicated that "they [were] not at all likely" to buy one within the next six months.

What *had* fueled the Christmas 1994 sales so much was that there were still quite a few higher-income households that had not yet purchased a computer and wanted to get onto the bandwagon. But by 1995, these households were already equipped with a home PC. That resulted in a big shift in home PC sales, to people mainly interested in either buying a second computer or replacing their old one. Indeed, the research firm of Computer Intelligence found that, in 1995, more than half of consumer PC purchases were repeats. And the important thing to remember about repeat buyers is that they typically do not cut corners when it comes to a personal computer. They want the latest and greatest and are willing to shell out the bucks to get it.

But these were exactly the people Apple was not targeting that Christmas. And the trend meant that Apple was in big trouble, as was another manufacturer, Packard Bell Electronics Inc. Packard Bell was a privately held company in Sacramento, California, that had roared to the top of the retail PC heap by virtue of the single-minded determination of its cofounder and CEO, a reclusive Israeli immigrant named Beny Alagem, to capture as many first-time computer buyers as possible. Packard Bell failed miserably in getting its customers to make a second purchase because the company offered lousy technical support, which is a must for something as complex as a computer.

Like Apple, Packard Bell saturated the market at Christmas 1995 with low-end computers. While the Packard Bell models were powered by Intel's increasingly passé 75-megahertz Pentium chip, the repeat customers who dominated sales wanted Intel's more powerful and expensive chips, such as the 90-megahertz and 100-megahertz Pentiums. So Packard Bell's once-dizzying annual growth of as high as 50 percent crashed back to earth, rising only 5 percent that Christmas from the one prior. Having operated on razor-thin profit margins all along, Packard Bell had to borrow $400 million from Intel to cover its parts bills, and Alagem ended up, a few months later, ceding near financial control of the company to his biggest investor, Japan's NEC Corporation.

Michael Spindler was caught in the same squeeze. He could not count on those first-time fence-sitters trying to decide between the Mac or Wintel. He also could not count on existing Apple customers, since they traditionally were such a technologically dedicated bunch that they were willing to shell out extra for the best new Mac. What could have helped, had horrible timing not intervened, would have been the Japanese—but not in the manner that pulled Packard Bell's Alagem out of the fire.

Let us take a journey to the Land of the Rising Sun to learn about the final piece in the puzzle that would cement the fate of Michael Spindler and Apple Computer. Ian Diery and his right-hand marketing man, Satjiv Chahil, had engineered an amazing surge in Apple's business in Japan during the early 1990s. Part of that success had been due to slick marketing, such as sponsoring a Janet Jackson concert and a women's professional golf tournament and plastering Apple's famous multihued logo on billboards, TV ads, and subway trains all over Japan. "We were selling people on Apple's cool, hip image," John Floisand, president of Apple Pacific, explained to me when I visited Japan that fall for *The Wall Street Journal*.

Diery was also able to capitalize on the fact that NEC, with its text-based operating system, still dominated the emerging market for PCs in Japan. The Mac's graphical look meshed perfectly with the graphical nature of the Japanese language's Kanji alphabet. So after Apple introduced a Kanji-based Macintosh in the late 1980s, it held a clear appeal for the vast masses of middle-class Japanese who were coming to discover the power of a personal computer.

Apple therefore had the graphical market all to itself for a glorious while. Apple's share of Japan's PC market, in terms of computers shipped, shot up from 2 percent in 1990 to 5.4 percent in 1991 and up all the way to 15.4 percent in 1994, second only to NEC's according to estimates by Dataquest's Tokyo office. By 1995, the Japanese market accounted for fully one fifth of Apple's sales. And this was not all. Since the Wintel market had not yet caught up in Japan, where NEC and other domestic manufacturers kept slugging it out with their own arcane operating systems, Apple could continue charging the kinds of premium prices that would have made Jean-Louis Gassée's eyes tear up with joy. That kept Apple's gross profit margins in Japan inflated to nearly 50 percent through much of the early 1990s, even as its overall margins kept sinking lower under the pricing wars back home.

Apple Japan, in summary, was a cash cow that Michael Spindler could milk in times good and bad. "This was a gold mine," recalled Kenji Muto, an analyst at the Tokyo offices of International Data Corporation, the industry market research firm based in Framingham, Massachusetts.[8] That is, until Bill Gates and the gang caught up with Apple there. In late 1992, Microsoft introduced its Japanese-language version of Windows. That created a common platform for Japan's software developers to rally around, consolidating the market of diverse and competing operating systems into essentially two: Macintosh and Windows. Meanwhile, the industry price cuts that had been started in the summer of 1992 by the "Compaq shock" began to ripple their way five thousand miles across the Pacific by early 1994. Then, in early 1995, Japan's Fujitsu Ltd. out-Compaqed Compaq, unleashing a price war the likes of which the PC industry had never seen anywhere in the world. It would become known as the "Fujitsu shock," and it rocked the walls of Apple's executive suite in Cupertino.

To get an idea of how significant the Fujitsu shock was, bear in mind that PC price cuts heretofore had rarely exceeded 20 percent to 25 percent at any given time. Fujitsu, as is the case with many Japanese computer companies, is a multiheaded conglomerate that produces everything from memory chips to circuit boards. To make its manufacturing plants more efficient, Fujitsu needed to drastically increase its worldwide presence in the PC market. The Japanese manufacturers had long been unable to make serious inroads into the PC business against fleeter-footed American rivals such as Compaq and Dell, so Fujitsu decided in 1995 to fortify itself for a global assault by capturing a huge chunk of the market on its home turf. The goal, according to industry analysts in Japan at the time, was for Fujitsu to double—in just one year—its share of Japan's PC market from the 9 percent level it had attained in 1994. To accomplish that, Fujitsu chopped its PC prices by 37 percent, to $1,900 from $3,000.

The Fujitsu shock forced all the company's competitors to match the discounts, igniting a consumer buying frenzy that blasted Japan's PC shipments up 70 percent during 1995 from the previous year, the fastest growth for a big market in the world. You had to be there to believe it. And I was. It was the last week of November, and the streets and storefronts of bustling Tokyo were festooned with lights, trees, and other symbols of Christmas, which the Japanese celebrate, even though the predominant religion is Buddhism. The epicenter of the PC boom, in this earthquake-prone capital city, was in a shopping district called Akihabara, where consumer electronics stores soaring as high as ten stories are clustered so closely together along a quarter-mile strip that the effect, from the street, is akin to standing in a concrete canyon.

Yet this canyon was a riot of sound and color that overloaded the senses. Huge banners advertising computer names such as Epson, Canon, and Fujitsu were draped across the fronts of buildings. One store's banners unfurled a full seven stories, in yellow, green, blue, red, and purple. At street level, vendors hawked personal computers on the sidewalk like so much expensive candy. Queues of young men, puffing on cigarettes as honking cars and trucks incessantly streamed by, formed to play the video-game machines set up outside. And inside the stores, on level after level, shoppers were packed in to peruse the latest models featuring Windows 95, which had just arrived in Japan.

None of this boded well for Apple. In interview after interview for my article in *The Wall Street Journal,* Japanese businesspeople in their usual attire of suits and ties would shake their heads sadly about how much they liked the Mac but insisted they had little choice but to buy into Windows. The language they spoke was Japanese, but the words, as related by an interpreter, could have been spoken by just about any PC user in the United States.

"In the graphics world, Mac is very common, and for people using it themselves, Mac is very popular," observed a construction engineer named Nobuhiko Hatta, checking out Windows 95 models in the giant Laox store. "But in the business world, you can't do business if you don't learn Windows. You really have no choice." Hatta consequently had made the decision to buy no more Macs, even though he had two at home. Inside a neighboring Laox store, software designer Yoshiyuki Kawate was compelled to buy his first home computer for the same reason as so many other Japanese: so he could take work home and be more efficient. "It is not a question of the Mac being good or bad," Kawate explained as he inhaled on a cigarette. "It's a question of software availability. It's not as high on the Mac. The issue is, everything is on Windows."

To be sure, there were some Mac holdouts here in Akihabara, as there continued to be staunch loyalists throughout the world. But Apple was having to work harder and harder even to keep these people. Apple, for example, instituted such deep discounts that a Power Mac 5120 model that at the time sold for $2,800 in the United States was priced at $2,300 in Akihabara. Just two years earlier, Apple's computers had been selling for premiums of as much as 70 percent higher in Japan than in the United States. That Christmas, Apple also began giving rebates of up to $150 to people buying a Mac.

Apple also had to dig deeper to try to counter the Windows 95 advertising blitz that hit Japan in late 1995. The company increased its marketing budget by 50 percent from the year before for Mac ads on television and radio and in fifteen local Mac-user magazines as well as in the pristine subway cars that rocket through the tunnels that form a Byzantine honeycomb underneath Japan's capital city. And Apple tried to maintain its hip, trendy image, sponsoring its third annual "Mac 'n' Roll Night" in a smoke-filled nightclub in another section of Tokyo. At this year's "Mac 'n' Roll," held on November 28, rock bands with names such as "Peter, Paul, Wolf, and Mary" and "Oriental Rug" jammed before a packed house of four hundred, vying for the attention of a panel of judges in the back for the first-prize award of a free Macintosh. The winner: a punk band named "H.M.V.," whose music blared as the admonition "No Windows" appeared in giant letters on an overhead video screen and a female dancer stripped off her top to cavort bare-breasted.

This was all catchy, exciting stuff, but it was not enough to halt the slide in market share and profit margins. By the end of 1995, Apple's share of the Japanese PC market would slide to 14 percent, according to Dataquest, while its profit margins fell by more than half, to 20 percent.

In the United States, meanwhile, it became clear by early December that the Performas were not selling as planned. Hoping to spur demand, Jim Buckley, whose title had just been changed to president of Apple Americas, slashed Performa prices by up to 25 percent, dropping the Performa 640CD, for example, to $1,499 from $1,999. This helped move machines, but it drove Apple's already thin profit margins on sales even lower. In Japan, John Floisand was doing the same thing, chopping prices to drive volume. During all this, Michael Spindler was blissfully unaware of the looming disaster. According to a former executive, Spindler assured the Apple board in mid-December that sales were going well and that the quarter looked as though it would end up close to plan. The next day, however, Buckley and Floisand informed the Diesel that they expected to sell 100,000 *fewer* Macintoshes than Spindler had told his board. That was about $200 million that had just dropped off the revenue chart, not including the price drops that were obliterating profits.

"Spindler was fucked," says this executive.

Spindler, then, was in the position of having to return to the board to report that the quarter was not going to be so great after all; in fact, a loss was likely. For Spindler, it must have felt like déjà vu. After all, it had been he who had informed John Sculley and the board in May 1993 that Apple would probably "make" the quarter then, only to have it go up in smoke. Shaken to his core, the Diesel summoned Buckley and Floisand into an executive staff meeting and demanded to know what the hell had happened. The price drops by the two men had made a bad situation worse. "How could you sell these things for a loss?" Spindler demanded as he sat in an open-necked silk shirt glaring at his subordinates. Buckley and Floisand spoke quickly, assuring the boss they had simply been following his orders to move product. "I asked you to move the units, not to wrap money around them!" the Diesel snapped.[9]

But Buckley maintains that he and Floisand had to drop prices to move "old product" since the new tower line of Performas had failed to materialize. Buckley adds that he and Floisand could not come up with a revised forecast for the quarter in time for that board meeting, resulting in Spindler relying on outdated numbers. "We worked hard to scrub the numbers to make sure they were right," Buckley says. Forsyth maintains that no single executive should be singled out for blame in the forecasting error that resulted in these price drops. "Anybody who was part of that team has to take some responsibility," he said in his interview with me, looking relaxed in a long-sleeved shirt as he sipped decaffeinated coffee.

Michael Spindler did not handle stress well in the best of times, much less when he had a crisis on his hands. The strain of the job was acutely apparent. Phil Dixon, an Apple executive who had left in 1989, remembers bumping into Spindler in the lobby of one Apple building where Dixon was meeting a friend for lunch one day around that time in 1995. It had been years since Dixon had seen the Diesel, and they had not been kind. Spindler had gained weight, his skin appeared pale and unhealthy, and he was no longer cracking lame jokes. "He shook my hand and asked how I was doing," Dixon recalls. "He said, 'I bet you've having more fun than I am ' "

The first public signal of an impending disaster came on Friday, December 15, 1995, when Apple issued this ominous press release: "Apple Computer Inc. today said that while it expects quarterly units and revenue to increase over the year ago quarter, the current trend is below the company's internal projections. The continuation of this trend would lead to a loss in the first fiscal quarter," which would end on December 29. The release went on to blame the problem on pricing pressures in Japan and the United States, as well as the unexpectedly low revenues overall. "Our anticipated results for the first quarter are obviously disappointing," Spindler said in the release. "We are currently engaged in an intensive review of all aspects of our business, including the factors contributing to our first quarter results, and will take appropriate actions to address the challenges."

Securities analysts had been bracing for a poor quarter for earnings, but never in Apple's history had the company lost money during Christmas, the busiest quarter for both it and the rest of the industry. Before this announcement, their consensus estimate had been for Apple to earn $87 million, or 72 cents a share, compared to the net income of $188 million, or $1.55 a share, in the same quarter a year earlier. After the announcement, they revised those estimates to a predicted loss of $5 million, or 4 cents a share. Apple's shares fell $3 that day, to close at $35.25, and they plunged another $3 when the markets reopened the following Monday, to close at $32.25. Apple's stock value had shrunk by 15 percent, or $720 million, in just four days, and things were about to get uglier.

The new year of 1996 brought Apple little good cheer. When the smoke from the Christmas quarter had cleared and a full damage estimate could be tallied, the news was even worse than expected. The gross profit margins had imploded by almost one half, to just 15 percent, from 29 percent in the Christmas period of 1994. Only five years earlier, the profit margin had hovered above 50 percent. When Michael Spindler had assumed command in 1993, he had restructured Apple so it could operate on profit margins of between 20 and 30 percent. With 13,191 employees as of 1995, Apple was, once again, too fat. And once again, heads would have to roll.

That wasn't all. The Diesel was facing a crisis in his personal life. At 7:10 P.M. on Monday, January 8—the eve of the big Macworld Expo show in San Francisco—Spindler answered the door at his mansion in Atherton to find a process server slapping a copy of a lawsuit into his hands. He was being sued, along with his seventeen-year-old daughter, Laurie, for a traffic accident she had recently been involved in in the nearby community of Woodside that had left the driver of another car, a thirty-five-year-old woman, seriously injured.[10]

Laurie Spindler had been driving her father's 1985 white Chevrolet Blazer at 3:11 P.M. on October 11, 1995, when, according to a witness, she had run a red light on Woodside and collided broadside with a 1991 black Infiniti, which was turning left onto Woodside from an Interstate 280 off-ramp. Laurie Spindler had suffered only a small cut and minor bruises, but the other woman, Karen Finzi, had been rushed to the emergency room for treatment of multiple bone fractures and a serious head injury. The suit plopped in Michael Spindler's hands, then, was a petition from Finzi seeking compensation for medical bills, as well as for loss of wages from her job as a computer industry consultant.

Michael and Laurie Spindler would deny any responsibility for the accident, asserting in court papers filed with the California Superior Court that Finzi, in fact, had caused the accident. Laurie Spindler had told officers investigating the crash that her light was "full on green." A report by the San

Mateo County Sheriff's Department on the accident, however, concluded that "it appears" Laurie Spindler had been at fault, based on a witness's statement that she had run a red light. The Spindlers initially demanded a jury trial but ended up settling the case in December 1996, when their insurance company agreed to pay an undisclosed sum to cover Finzi's costs. (Finzi was still undergoing rehabilitation treatment more than a year after the accident.) Spindler's daughter, Laurie, enrolled in an out-of-state boarding school after the incident, according to court records.

But on the evening of January 8, 1996, it was all too much for Michael Spindler. According to a former Apple executive, the Diesel checked himself into the Stanford University Hospital for one night, following complaints of "heart palpitations." The next day, he showed up at his office in City Center 3 with a heart monitor strapped to his chest. Indeed, over the Christmas holiday Spindler had shown a friend a letter from his doctor warning that if he did not quit his job soon, he would be dead.[11] Spindler had no scheduled appearances at Macworld, beginning January 9—Jim Buckley had been designated to deliver the keynote address—but the mounting crisis coupled with his health problems prompted him not to attend the show at all.

The absence of an Apple CEO at the most important gathering of the Macintosh world seemed to accentuate the severity of Apple's problems, casting a pall over the Macworld show as it opened on the morning of January 9 at the Moscone Center on the southern fringes of San Francisco's financial district. As indicated before, there were two Macworlds held in the United States: one in Boston every August, the other in San Francisco each January. Macworld San Francisco was historically the larger and more prominent show because it was where Apple executives laid out their strategy for the upcoming year.

During his keynote at the Yerba Buena Ballroom at the nearby San Francisco Marriott, Buckley put on a brave face as he assured the faithful that all was not lost. He briefly turned the show over to an engineering manager, who ran a demo of cool features being included in Copland, Apple's project to replace the Mac operating system that was supposed to be out later that same year. It could open two files at the same time. It could summarize documents containing the same subject matter in seconds, neatly coalescing them into one file. The audience applauded, and Buckley returned to the microphone to say, "It's helpful to know we always seem to be moving forward."

Out in the vast expanse of the Moscone show floor, though, many of the 450 exhibitors whose livelihoods were tied to the success of the Macintosh platform were not so confident. "They can't continue to go on the way they have for several years," John Wilczak, chief executive of MetaTools Inc., a software developer in Carpinteria, California, complained to me as bag-toting showgoers swarmed through the aisles surrounding his company's booth.

"Either they get it together and remain an independent player, or someone is going to take them over and do it."

Funny that Wilczak should mention the "T-word." Takeover was very much a possibility for Apple at that precise moment, although that had not become public yet. On the second day of Macworld, January 10, Apple sent out a press release indicating that it expected the Christmas quarter's loss to total $68 million, far more than the analysts had predicted even after revising their estimates in December. Apple also said it was planning yet another restructuring, to entail "significant" layoffs. Exactly one week later, Apple released its official quarterly results, reporting a loss of $69 million instead of $68 million and announcing layoffs of 1,300 employees and contractors, or 8 percent of the workforce. More ominously, the company said the losses would continue for at least another quarter and that it expected to incur a restructuring charge of $125 million.

Whew. This ship was not just listing, it was on its way to capsizing altogether. The drama heightened on January 23, when *The Wall Street Journal* published an article that rocked the computer industry. Apple, it said, was on the verge of being acquired by Sun Microsystems for a stock swap estimated at about $4 billion, or $33 an Apple share. This would represent a slight premium over Apple's stock price, which had closed at $30.50 the day before. The article, written by me, appeared on the same day that Apple's fifteenth annual shareholders' meeting was convening in the Town Hall theater on the R-and-D campus, an enclave of eleven glass-enclosed buildings clustered in the shape of a horseshoe around a road called Infinite Loop. At this meeting, Spindler's heart monitor—which he was wearing regularly now, beneath his suit jacket—was doubtless working overtime.

So many shareholders poured into Town Hall that video monitors of the proceedings were placed in two different rooms set up to handle the overflow. The investors who turned out were in a foul mood, made all the worse, they complained, by Apple's lack of preparedness in providing enough food and seating for the attendees. Michael Spindler lumbered onstage, as did Mike Markkula. Standing at a podium, Markkula introduced Spindler, who spent the next forty-five minutes speaking. "Apple's management team considers the company situation as serious, and we are treating it as such. We have a sense of urgency and are fully committed to working through the challenges," Spindler intoned as all eyes remained glued on his bulky figure. He then outlined Apple's plans for capitalizing on the emerging Internet, which was rapidly evolving as a new and important industry. When he finished, the shareholders let the Diesel have it—right between the eyes.

Jumping up from his seat in the fifth row, a New York investor named Orin McCluskey could barely contain his rage as he spoke, staring at Spindler. "You have mismanaged assets. You have wasted a valuable franchise, and you have brought a great company to its knees," said McCluskey, owner of 10,000 withered Apple shares. "Mr. Spindler, it is time to go." Scattered applause broke out. There was broad applause when another shareholder, Richard Ash from Philadelphia, used his turn at a stand-up microphone in an aisle to demand, "We want new leadership." Through it all, Spindler just stood there, arms folded defensively, a pained expression on his face.

In spite of all this criticism, Mike Markkula continued to stand by his man. At a press conference after the shareholders' meeting, he addressed the question of his support for Spindler by patting the Diesel on the shoulder and telling reporters, "I like this guy. He's a very good person." When Spindler was asked if he took responsibility for Apple's current troubles, the Diesel blurted out, "Sure, I take responsibility. How can I not?" The two men had fielded questions from reporters and shareholders, and they responded in candor to all save the one that was uppermost on everybody's minds: Was Sun really about to buy Apple, as reported in *The Wall Street Journal* that morning?

Before the shareholder's meeting, Apple's PR staff had handed a written statement to journalists that read, "The company is not for sale, but certainly the company's board and management have been and remain aware of their obligations to maximize shareholder value." At the press conference, Markkula said he would not comment on any merger negotiations. But when a reporter asked him to repeat that Apple was not for sale, the board chairman smiled and said, "Apple is not for sale." The statement was true only in the strictest legal sense. Apple was not for sale, as in a public auction with the company available to the highest bidder. But Apple had in fact been very much for sale since 1992. In fact, Markkula, Spindler, and the board were set to meet that very afternoon with Sun executives to hear a serious bid.

The very fact that Sun would now be contemplating a run at Apple underscored Apple's ignominious turn of fortune in the 1990s. After all, John Sculley had snubbed his nose at Sun not once, but at least twice. The first time: in the late 1980s, when he had scuttled a plan to buy Sun, in part because Sun CEO Scott McNealy would have to replace Del Yocam as chief operating officer. The second time: in 1990, when Joe Graziano had prepared a draft copy of a press release announcing that Apple had acquired Sun as merger talks between the companies appeared to be heading toward fruition. But Sculley had pulled the plug when IBM called. Again, McNealy would have been COO of the combined companies.

Sculley was now long gone, and IBM was out of the picture, too. But Scott McNealy, the hard-charging guy with the chipmunk smile, was kicking butt faster than ever at Sun. Between 1991 and 1995, he had doubled Sun's revenues to $6 billion a year, and Sun's stock had soared from about $10 a share to almost $50. And on January 23—the same day as the Apple shareholders' meeting—Sun released a new network computing language called Java to drive the company's growth in the Internet. Java was the Internet's equivalent of the BASIC programming language that Bill Gates had written two decades earlier, which had allowed developers to make programs a PC could understand. By 1997, Java would explode to become the dominant programming standard on the Internet, cementing Sun's position as a leading innovator in the new market of cyberspace.

The Internet had actually been around since 1969, when it had been started by the U.S. Defense Department as a way of linking computers all around the world into an on-line network that would still function in case of catastrophe, such as a nuclear attack. The Internet had expanded in the 1980s, when it had been opened to academic researchers, whose heavy use of electronic mail between universities had caught the eye of businesses in the early 1990s as a way of saving time and money on communications that had previously had to be conducted by mail or telephone.

Prompting the Internet's explosion in 1995, though, was a service called the World Wide Web, which had been developed in 1990 at the European Organization for Nuclear Research.[12] This was a way for scientists to share documents by means of clicking onto a highlighted phrase, such as "Apple Computer," and having all the information available in electronic topic form and linked to the Internet appear on the computer screen after traversing a cyberhighway. In 1994, a small start-up company called Netscape Communications Corporation, based down the road from Sun in Mountain View, California, had launched a software product called the Netscape Navigator that could help users quickly browse through the millions of documents on the World Wide Web, thus making the Internet a font of inexhaustible information for businesses and consumers alike.

The Navigator was based on a browser called "Mosaic," developed in 1993 at the University of Illinois's National Center for Supercomputing Applications by an undergraduate student there named Marc Andreessen. Netscape had been born the following year when an executive named Jim Clark, founder and chairman of Silicon Graphics Inc., had resigned that job to back Andreessen in starting the browser venture. As the Netscape Navigator proliferated around the world, opening up vast databases to the masses, a new information and communications boom was on. And it was every bit as momentous as the PC revolution that had started in Steve Jobs's garage.

It was this Internet revolution that had helped convince Scott McNealy to turn the tables and go after Apple for a change. Sun's main business at the time was the sale of big workstation computers to businesses. But that business was under voracious attack, not only from workstation rivals such as Digital Equipment and Hewlett-Packard but from Wintel machines, which were becoming powerful enough to function as miniworkstations. McNealy badly needed to expand into something far less vulnerable—something like the Internet, on which Sun's Java language could become the dominant standard for how software would be written and used on the World Wide Web. And what better way to spread Java than through a company like Apple with its mass appeal worldwide? McNealy certainly did not want to rely upon Microsoft to do that, because Microsoft, to him, was a sworn enemy dedicated to eating into his workstation market through Windows NT.

By the same token, Apple was also increasingly looking at the Internet as a way of breaking out of its box and moving beyond the cutthroat business of selling PCs to a new one not dominated by Bill Gates. Apple's initial major foray into cyberspace was through its eWorld on-line service, launched in 1994, but the service had failed to gain many subscribers because it was confined to Macintosh customers and because giant rivals such as America On-line were already well established. Apple had also designed a VCR-style device called the Pippin that could peruse the World Wide Web on a simple television set. The Pippin, whose idea had first been conceived back in the 1980s by engineer Steve Perlman, would enable your everyday couch potato to "surf" the Net without ever leaving the comfort of the living room or having to fuss with a $2,000 PC. It could be a whole new product category.

But any such mass market was still years off, too far in the future to save Apple's bacon just now. Besides, Apple's R-and-D efforts were so chaotic by this point that the company was making very little headway into the Internet. In fact, Apple actually fell at least a year behind Microsoft and the rest of the industry in taking the steps necessary to align itself around the Internet. Microsoft had been late, too, since the explosion of the Web had taken nearly everybody by surprise. But in the fall of 1995, Bill Gates issued a directive that henceforth Microsoft would be an Internet company. Every product, every feature, would tie in with the Internet. Gates turned his nine-hundred-pound gorilla on a dime and set his sights on tiny Netscape, in a battle between Microsoft's Internet Explorer and Netscape's Navigator that would become known as "the browser wars."

Microsoft's lightning-fast decision to embrace the Internet perfectly exemplified the contrast between Bill Gates's crisp and efficient management style and Apple's chaotic one. Microsoft's story was one of management continuity, with Bill Gates and a trusted inner circle, including lieutenants such as Steve Ballmer, Jeff Harbers, Jeff Raikes, and Charles Simonyi, involved with running the company and setting its technical direction from the earliest days. Apple's story, however, was one of a continual revolving door in the executive suite as reorgs became almost an annual event. As new faces kept entering the Apple picture, the company's strategy was in a constant flux. And since the Apple culture required consensus from just about everyone down to the janitor, the company had great difficulty following any direction for long, much less turning on a dime, like Microsoft, to pursue a new opportunity such as that which the Internet offered.

This was the larger picture enveloping the Apple-Sun situation. The way the talks had gotten started was with a simple telephone call, back in the waning days of the summer of 1995, between a man named Regis McKenna, at his office in Palo Alto, California, and another named John Doerr, at his office in neighboring Menlo Park. Regis McKenna was a Silicon Valley marketing guru whose advertising agency had come up with Apple's distinctive logo of a multihued apple with a bite out of it. In the intervening years, McKenna had become a confidant to Apple's various CEOs and was particularly close to Michael Spindler. John Doerr was the same John Doerr who had teamed with fellow venture capitalist Roger McNamee to argue Apple's side in the 1993 debate called "Can Apple Computer Survive as an Independent Company?" Doerr is an influential venture capitalist in the VC firm of Kleiner Perkins Caufield & Byers—and a member of Sun's board of directors.

"I suggested Sun and Apple sit down and talk," McKenna told me in early 1996 in an interview for *The Wall Street Journal*. (He declined to be interviewed again for this book.) "I followed up with an e-mail." McKenna explained that Apple might be receptive to a merger bid by Sun, and Doerr obliged by arranging a meeting with Spindler. Spindler, indeed, was receptive, and thus began merger negotiations between Apple and Sun, as other former Apple executives confirm.

Through the fall, there were more meetings, back and forth. A code name was given the deal: Gatorade. The discussions centered not so much on price but on how Apple and Sun could meld their technologies. As for Michael Spindler, his chief concern seemed to be who would be top dog of the combined companies, recalls another former Apple executive. Spindler, of course, thought he should. "Michael saw himself as a very seasoned, broad senior executive kind of guy and Scott as kind of a young whippersnapper kid," this executive remembers. "I think Michael thought that would work."

The prospect of Spindler running the combined companies was a laughable prospect, of course, given all his troubles at Apple. By late fall, in any event, Spindler did not seem inclined even to want to run Apple anymore, much less a grander entity. He confided to a Silicon Valley friend one afternoon that he was burned out and "wanted out of the rat race."[13] Scott McNealy, conversely, was fairly bursting with energy and became so enamored of his quest for Apple that he flew to New York City in early December 1995 to make his case directly to Apple's board. The board was convening in the ultra-exclusive St. Regis hotel in midtown Manhattan, where the suites fetched up to $5,000 per night. An Apple participant in the meeting, held in a St. Regis conference room, remembers McNealy standing before the small assembled group and speaking passionately, and convincingly, about the need to unite forces against Bill Gates.

"Every once in a while, there is a sea change and an opportunity, and this [the Internet] is it," McNealy said, according to this person. "The giant is vulnerable. Microsoft has missed the Internet." While Gates had just refocused Microsoft around the Internet, it was true that the mighty empire had been caught napping. As this executive remembers, the Apple directors mostly seemed to favor the prospect of aligning with Sun, and the two sides suggested calling the combined companies Apple, since it was the better-known corporate name. By early January, however, executives close to the talks say that McNealy backed off temporarily after being appraised by Apple of its alarmingly bad Christmas results. Gatorade was shelved, for now.

Spindler was not concerned. He had an ace up his sleeve. It was called Philips.

Back in early 1995, Spindler had bowed to Graziano's insistence that he renew the effort to merge Apple with another company. In delivering his merger presentation to the board, the two candidates at the top of the Diesel's list had been Toshiba Corporation and Philips Electronics N.V. Talks had not proceeded very far with either of those companies at the time. But in early December, at about the same time that Scott McNealy was talking up Gatorade with the Apple board in New York, Spindler had gotten Philips to the bargaining table.

Philips, based in Eindhoven, the Netherlands, is one of the biggest electronics conglomerates in the world. With $40 billion in annual revenue, Philips operates a hundred businesses in 150 countries, manufacturing and distributing everything from lightbulbs and cellular phones to computer monitors and semiconductor chips. Philips, however, had one gaping hole in its product mix: it had little worldwide presence in the personal computer market. There was obvious synergy, then, between Philips and Apple.

Apple possessed a globally recognized Macintosh brand. Apple, moreover, was strong in the markets that Philips was especially interested in: education, desktop publishing, and the home. Philips had already committed itself to the emerging industry for interactive entertainment, such as through its small computer called CD-I, which allowed users to play movies and video games on a television set. And those Apple markets were prime targets for Philips's interactive technology. As for Apple, Philips would provide greater access to fast-growing markets such as China, where it held a strong presence. Philips also commanded a huge infrastructure of manufacturing and distribution that Apple could use. And it had tons of money to keep Apple's R-and-D labs stoked.

"We thought Philips would be an excellent opportunity," recalls a senior Apple executive involved in those talks. "Michael was very strong on it."

Spindler was undoubtedly drawn to Philips more than to Sun, because of his European heritage. Philips also represented a more traditional style of management that he favored, a big company being run by executives with many years of experience, not the wet-behind-the-ears kids tooling around Silicon Valley in their Porsches and Ferraris. Most of Philips's top managers, by contrast, were in their late fifties and sixties. The president and chairman of Philips's board of management, Cors Boonstra, was fifty-eight years old at this time.

So as it had been between John Sculley and his brethren at IBM, there was good chemistry for a deal.

The negotiations between Apple and Philips lasted about a month, beginning in early December. Michael Spindler flew to Eindhoven to meet with Philips. Philips's entire six-member board of management flew to California to hear a half day of formal presentations on what Apple had to offer by top Apple executives including the R-and-D chief, Dave Nagel, and Satjiv Chahil, the vice president for entertainment industry marketing. The Dutch-born Boonstra and his executives, including Philips CFO Dudley G. Eustace, a native of Britain, sat and listened in Apple's new boardroom atop the eight-story City Center 3 building. It was nicknamed the Synergy room, after the old one at De Anza 7.[14]

"Satjiv talked about multimedia and entertainment trends and where it was going. Nagel talked about all the technologies Apple had, including QuickTime," recalls a second Apple executive intimately familiar with these proceedings. And, as Nagel recalls, "As far as I could tell, the Philips guys were impressed with our presentation."

Cors Boonstra was indeed impressed, as were the others in the Philips delegation. They even discussed a possible price of $36 a share, or $4.3 billion, to acquire Apple, which would represent a 13 percent premium over Apple's stock value of about $32 per share in December 1995.[15] The Apple side was impressed with Philips, too. "They did the best job of anybody in understanding the multimedia market," remembers one former Apple executive who participated in the negotiations. "They showed us a detailed breakdown of how multimedia could be used all over the world. In the Middle East, for example, they calculated that a person could spend three or four hours a day using multimedia after taking time for sleep, prayers to Allah, and other activities."

Boonstra and his board returned to the Netherlands to deliberate whether to proceed further. Apple, meanwhile, had been told, in no uncertain terms, to keep its mouth shut. "They had said, 'If a word of this leaks out, the deal's over the same day,'" says one of the former Apple executives. And not a word did.

Spindler waited expectantly as Boonstra and his board convened in Eindhoven during early January 1996 to vote on the matter. At Philips, a unanimous vote was required for any such endeavor to move forward. The Apple merger fell short by one vote. Apple's executives were not told which board member dissented, but that Philips concluded that expanding into the PC business, with its cutthroat competition, was simply too risky at that time: thanks, but no thanks. Philips officials would not comment on this matter.

"The Philips people did not say this, but my feeling was that they were worried about the cultural differences between Philips and Apple," Nagel says. "Philips has fantastic basic research, but there would have been cultural differences between a company based in Europe and one in California." Those differences would include the more rigid European style of business, as contrasted with the more freewheeling one of California.

Spindler was crestfallen, for this left only Sun to bail his ship out of rapidly rising water. And Apple's stock was falling again, from $34.25 on January 5 to $29.88 on January 19. The stock decline meant that the price for acquiring Apple was becoming a better bargain for Sun's Scott McNealy. He reopened the negotiations and arranged to appear before the Apple board again to discuss an offer on the afternoon of January 23, the same day as the shareholders' meeting.

Apple's board members, before that January 23 meeting, had been left under the impression by McNealy that Sun would be willing to pay a slight premium over Apple's market value, which would have equated to the $33 per share figure quoted by anonymous sources in The Wall Street Journal. With price not appearing to be an issue, since the board was prepared to accept that, the Apple directors were also confident the two companies had enough in common that many of them, as well as top Apple executives involved in the talks, believed a deal was imminent. Perhaps that explains why Mike Markkula had been smiling when a reporter had asked earlier that day if Apple was for sale. It was not for sale, he might well have thought, because it was all but sold.

So when Mike Markkula opened the board meeting in the City Center 3 Synergy room, there was a sense of eager anticipation among the Apple directors, who mostly just wanted to unload the heavy burden that Apple Computer had become. Supporting the board in its desire to sell Apple to Sun were members of the executive staff, including Buckley, Forsyth, and Nagel, who were invited to come in and deliver a ten-minute presentation each. "We were all asked by the board if we believed Apple could make it on its own," recalls one of the executives who participated in the meeting. "We all said, 'No.'"

The anticipation of an impending sale dissipated, however, when Scott McNealy began talking. McNealy looked friendly enough with his boyish grin, but he was as shrewd as they come. McNealy, according to a person present in the room that day, said that Sun was still interested in acquiring Apple—but at the equivalent of about $23 a share, or about $2.8 billion. That specific figure was not used, but McNealy used a complex formula that boiled down to that. The formula, in essence, was based on an average of Apple's expected stock price if its financial reports came in on target for the next two quarters, according to another person involved in the talks.

Apple's board of directors was horrified. How, they wondered, could they sell Apple Computer—one of the greatest corporate names in all the world—for an amount that not only did not even match Apple's stock price that day, which had edged up to $31.63 on the publicity of the talks, but was nearly a third below that? "We were surprised," recalls one of the Apple board members. "I think they were just trying to get a bargain."

McNealy was playing hardball, but who could blame him? Buying into Apple would give him access to an incredible brand name and a Macintosh customer base that then numbered some 22 million worldwide. But he would also be inheriting Apple's myriad problems: shrinking market share and profits, an out-of-control R-and-D system, and a corporate culture that defied the kind of strict management discipline he had instilled into Sun. McNealy would be buying into a world of headaches in taking over Apple, and he knew he had better get a good price, or he could be facing a lynch mob of his own shareholders. Indeed, some of Sun's board members were concerned over how an Apple merger might dilute Sun's shares, although both Eric Schmidt, then Sun's chief technology officer, and Ed Zander, president of Sun's big Sun Microsystems Computer Company unit, were known to be high on the deal. (This was the same Ed Zander who had been spurned by Apple in the proposed Macintosh licensing deal with Apollo Computer, back in 1987.)

Apple's board told McNealy they wanted time to think about the offer, which had been presented so informally that Apple was not legally compelled to publicize it or even to acknowledge that talks were under way. By this time, the board had shrunk to eight members following the recent resignation of Joe Graziano. The board retreated into seclusion, holding talks in person and over the telephone over the next week.

The outside world, meanwhile, was abuzz over the affair. Business publications clambered to serve up the latest juicy tidbit from the negotiating front. *Business Week* prepared a cover story entitled "The Fall of an American Icon," while *Fortune* writer Brent Schlender opened a lengthy article about Apple's decline with "It's enough to break your heart." Radio talk-show hosts and trade magazine columnists tried to infuse humor into the situation, suggesting that the name of the combined Sun/Apple should be "Snapple," after the bottled drink. This was no fun and games for the Apple board, however, because Macintosh sales were taking a disturbing dip amid customer uncertainty over what was going to happen. At the six-outlet Computer Stores Northwest chain in the Pacific Northwest, for example, sales fell 15 percent that January from the company's internal expectations prior to the merger talks.

"Being able to make a commitment one way or another probably is more important than what commitment Apple makes," John Landforce, president of the chain, based in Corvallis, Oregon, told me then. "Apple just needs to get the news out, one way or another."

Inside Apple, the atmosphere among employees verged on panic as their leader appeared to spiral more out of control. While the rest of the board deliberated, Spindler retreated into his City Center 3 bunker, listening primarily to the other three "S"s, Kevin Sullivan, Ed Stead, and David Seda. One day, he issued an edict that anyone caught being quoted in the press would be summarily dismissed, according to a former executive who heard the threat. On January 29, Spindler dispatched an eight-page AppleLink memo to all employees that rambled on about strategy, reiterated his "sense of accountability that I feel personally for the situation we find ourselves in," and warned, "I urge you not to believe any media reports—no matter who they quote, even if they say 'sources close to the company' or 'an executive who refused to be named.' These are no friends of Apple and their intent is disruption. When there is anything new to report, we will communicate to you directly—that is our commitment to you."

"It was like the Nixon White House," recalls the former executive.

The eyes of the computer world were on Mike Markkula and his Apple board, and the board was feeling the heat. "You had a company that was clearly embattled, with directors nervous about their exposure," recalls the Apple board member who participated in the discussions. "Clearly, we were under a lot of pressure." Other people close to the talks said at the time that the option to continue with business as usual had disappeared after the January 23 shareholders' meeting, when so many investors had drawn their swords against Michael Spindler. It was clear, the board thought, that it really had two choices: take McNealy's deal or install a new CEO to fix the ship. Some of the directors, after they had gotten over their shock, continued to favor the Sun option, since that seemed to be the only way out of the company's mess. Gil Amelio, however, argued that the deal was not good for the company, because Sun's offer was way too low.

" 'You won't make good deals when one party is weak and the other is real strong,' " Amelio told his board colleagues, according to a person who heard the conversation. "So Gil said, 'Let's fix the company.' "

On January 30, exactly one week after receiving Scott McNealy's lowball offer, Apple's board of directors checked into the St. Regis in midtown Manhattan for a meeting the following day. The fact that they chose to stay at this particular hotel in the first place was telling in itself. Here was Apple

Computer, on the ropes and bleeding red ink after years of mismanagement. Yet the Apple board had selected as its respite the most exclusive hotel in New York City and one of the finest in all the world.

Built in 1904 with a Beaux Arts facade, the twenty-story St. Regis, towering above Fifth Avenue with its gilded ceilings, magnificent domes, and ornate paneling, was such a work of art that *Architectural Record* noted at the time, "It is intended for a class of people who want absolutely the best quality of hotel accommodation, and who do not mind paying for it." Nearly a century later, the same description was apt, after its new owner, ITT Sheraton Corporation, invested $100 million beginning in 1988 to renovate the aging beauty top to bottom. Reopening three years later, the St. Regis drew plaudits from architectural critics for such extravagances as the cherrywood-paneled King Cole Bar, the gilded cornices of the Cognac Room, and 313 rooms and suites adorned with everything from Louis XVI–style furniture to Oriental motifs and silk wall coverings. On top of all that, each guest was assigned his or her very own English-style butler, ready at any time of the day or night to adjust "sir's tie," fluff the terry-cloth robe in the bathroom, or snip the end off a cigar.

"It is a gathering of legends," the St. Regis gushes in a promotional brochure. "It is luxury defined."

Into this lap of luxury settled the custodians of Apple Computer. Michael Spindler checked into a room with his French-born wife, Maryse, as did Markkula and some of the others, including a small entourage that included Satjiv Chahil and David Seda. On January 31, the directors stepped outside the St. Regis to take the five-minute taxi ride to Rockefeller Center, where their meeting was to take place in a conference room of the fifty-fifth-floor offices of Venrock Associates, the venture capital firm where longtime Apple director Peter Crisp served as a managing general partner. There, overlooking the streets choked with yellow taxicabs below, Markkula broke the bad news to his old friend Michael Spindler. He was being canned, not only as CEO but from the board altogether.

It is fair to surmise that the Diesel's head must have been spinning, and not from the altitude of the room. According to a close associate, Spindler had no inkling that he would be ousted that day—just like John Sculley, the CEO he had replaced. "If he knew he was getting laid off, he would not have brought his wife with him," says the associate. Spindler knew he was in trouble, but he still figured he could pull Apple back together if given a little more time. "Give us one good quarter, and all this will go away," the Diesel had said in October, following the weak results of the September-ended quarter.[16] The board would give him none, though. The rest of the meeting, which lasted much of the day, was devoted to a discussion among the directors on who should take Spindler's place. Gil Amelio had the answer to that one: himself.

There are many people from those days at Apple who now believe Amelio had positioned himself for the Apple CEO's job ever since he had come onto the board in 1994. Amelio, however, insists that is not true. "I did it because, like so many people, I have a great love for the products of this company," Amelio recalls. "As a resident of Silicon Valley, I just could not bear to sit there and watch the unraveling of Apple if there was something I could possibly do to help."

Amelio, in any event, was not the only director who lobbied for the job. According to a person privy to the discussions, the choice boiled down to either Gil Amelio or Jürgen Hintz. Hintz, age fifty-two, had been a marketing executive at Procter & Gamble Corporation for twenty-seven years and was currently between jobs. After leaving Procter & Gamble in 1991, Hintz had served from 1991 to early 1995 as CEO of Carnaud Metalbox S.A. With his marketing experience and availability to start work, he was given consideration.

But Amelio's credentials were far stronger. Amelio, also age fifty-two, had restored a money-losing National Semiconductor to profitability after he had taken over as CEO in 1991, and he boasted impressive technical credentials, holding sixteen technology patents and a bachelor's, master's, and Ph.D. in physics. It really was no contest. Amelio was the overwhelming choice to become Apple's new CEO.

Amelio was not going to leave National Semi without insisting on a few concessions from Apple, though. Wanting total control of Apple, he got the board to name him to the additional position of board chairman, a move that demoted Markkula to vice chairman. Afterward, several board members toasted a new beginning in the Astor Court, a luxuriously appointed tearoom on the ground floor where a harpist plays under ceiling murals, before scattering to the four winds.

Almost everybody had checked out of the St. Regis that night, except for Spindler. With his wife and an unidentified woman friend, he ventured out into the 15 degree cold to walk two short blocks to Il Tinello, a ninety-seat northern Italian eatery described by reviewers as having excellent cuisine and service. There the Diesel sat glumly, chatting with the two women in French until a waiter interrupted him to take a phone call. Picking up the receiver, Spindler barked, "Hello?" and paused a moment when he heard a reporter from *The Wall Street Journal*—me, in fact—asking him to comment on his ouster from Apple. "I have no comment to make, mister!" he bellowed, slamming down the phone.

On the six-hour commercial flight back to the West Coast the next morning, February 1, Spindler beckoned Satjiv Chahil over to his seat and told him, "It's finished. Talk to Ed [Stead]." Chahil went to Stead and told him,

"We need to tell the press." At 35,000 feet, Chahil began coordinating for an announcement of the news of a change in leadership at Apple later that day. When Stead and Chahil returned to their desks in Cupertino, however, they learned that Gil Amelio's compensation package had not yet been finalized.[17] And as day progressed into night, it was still not done. "Ed Stead was going insane because Amelio kept upping his terms," recalls a former Apple executive who witnessed this. "Ed was saying, 'These terms are outrageous.'"

These were the conditions that the Apple board finally agreed to for Amelio: A minimum $2.5 million annually in pay and performance bonus. A $200,000 signing bonus. A $5 million loan. A $10 million cash payout if he lost his job for any reason other than "cause" following a change in control of Apple within the first year. Apple agreed to lease Amelio's private plane "on terms to be negotiated." And Amelio would be entitled to receive a minimum of 200,000 Apple shares each year, subject to shareholder approval. Apple Computer had seen some wretched excess in its time, but this took the cake. And all for a man who had no experience running a personal computer company, presiding over an Apple that was already bleeding red ink and having to lay off hundreds of workers.

Late into the night of February 1, Apple still had not prepared its release, even though the PR staff at National Semi had theirs all ready to go. Pestered by me, and reluctant to keep withholding information so material as the departure of its CEO, National Semi went ahead and issued its press release alone. The news, when it hit the next morning, Friday, February 2, struck Silicon Valley like a thunderbolt. Apple's beleaguered workforce was fairly beside itself with joy. "There will be a block party in Cupertino!" cried one. Apple, when it finally issued its statement that day, provided this quote from Amelio: "As an avid Apple user since the days of the Apple II, I am delighted to be joining the management team of Apple, a company with an outstanding reputation for superior technology and customer loyalty."

Down in the seventh paragraph of the eight-paragraph press release, Apple acknowledged Spindler's accomplishments in his sixteen years with the company but included none of the usual comments of public praise usually accorded a fallen executive by those wielding the ax. Spindler issued his own farewell message. Distributed to all Apple employees via AppleLink, the February 2 "Memo from Michael Spindler" began: "Dear Colleagues: The end of a long voyage. A page in my life has turned. Almost 16 years of professional and personal engagement to root for a cause which has made impact on society and has not ceased to exist and progress . . ."

Even with himself out of the picture, Spindler went on to express the conviction that the Apple "crusade" of providing the world with a unique "personal information environment" would continue. For several more paragraphs, Spindler sounded remarkably upbeat, describing emotional high points in his Apple career that, characteristic of his global view, revolved around his meetings with heads of state around the world to promote Apple products.

There was the late night meeting with the Indian prime minister to discuss how Apple could assist in that country's education reform. There was the stirring meeting with South African Vice President Tambo Mbeki, after the fall of apartheid, during which Mbeki spoke "with glowing eyes" of a bright new future for that country's young people to grow with the help of Apple's computers. Apple had resumed business with South Africa following what Spindler termed the company's "gut-wrenching decision" to abandon the market in 1985 as part of the worldwide protest against apartheid. And, Spindler reminisced, there was the unforgettable scene when he visited China's first computer publishing center, and "a proud official" showed him a newspaper produced entirely on Macintosh as a traditional lion dance cavorted by. It was old world meeting new.

As the fifteen-paragraph memo neared its conclusion, Spindler addressed the most recent events that had caused him to topple from power. While pointing out that it was Apple's board of directors who decided to replace him, he made no attempt to excuse himself from blame for the company's problems. "Mistakes or misjudgments made? Oh yes, — even plenty," he admitted. Acknowledging further that he bore responsibility "for things that didn't work and should have been worked," Spindler insisted that he had tried his hardest at the job — "both intellectually and physically in every corner of the world to carry this cause and its color."

The memo ended, finally, with a passage as complex as the man himself: "In fading away from the place which I loved and feared, I will become whole again — hopefully renew the father, husband and self I am."

It was a poignant, if strange, farewell, and one well received by Apple employees. As one said, "It was a messy process, but a pretty classy good-bye memo, in my opinion. I hope things work out for him." The memo that appeared on AppleLink, though, was a heavily edited version of the one the Diesel had originally planned to send out. "It was filled with bitterness, saying he had been stabbed in the back," recalls a former member of the PR department who saw the unedited version. "Before it went out, we went to Ed Stead and said, 'We have to get him to change this.' "

In any event, it was all over. Spindler cleaned his desk out that same morning and simply vanished without a good-bye. Deeply hurt, he retreated to the solitude of his mansion, where he took up business consulting and spent more time with his family. Friends who met with him months later reported that he had lost weight and seemed considerably more at peace. Out with the old, in with the new. It had been almost a mantra of Apple's management from the company's humble origins, and now it was time for Gilbert F. Amelio to take center stage in the stormy history that has been Apple Computer. Could he pull it off? Could he restore Apple to its former greatness? No one said it would be easy. In fact, Amelio would find the task even more daunting than he had thought.

15

Mission: Impossible

On Monday, February 5, 1996, the new Apple era of Gilbert F. Amelio started bright and early, with a meeting to greet his staff in the City Center 3 Synergy room. The new chairman and CEO wasted no time settling into his new digs. Shortly after 8 A.M., an executive on the floor passed Michael Spindler's hastily vacated office and noticed a sweater hanging inside. It was a stylish, expensive one, the kind not out of place in the ski lodges of Aspen or Telluride. And it belonged to Gil Amelio.

For this meeting, though, Amelio was wearing a conservative business suit, the kind befitting his former status as an upper-echelon member of Silicon Valley's semiconductor industry, an old-boys' club of multimillionaires. When he walked into the Synergy room at 9 A.M., taking his place at the head of the long conference table—where he could take in the panorama of the Santa Cruz Mountains rising out the window to the west—he faced a roomful of Spindler's old top staff, about twenty in all. There were no looks of nervousness on the faces, though; there were excitement and anticipation, and not over the prospect of having a new CEO.

The events of January that had culminated in the ouster of Michael Spindler had taken wild and unexpected turns, making observers in the computer industry dizzy with trying to keep up with it all. When Apple finally issued a press release on February 2, 1996, announcing Gil Amelio as its new chairman and CEO, it seemed to indicate that the company was going to pursue a turnaround on its own, with new leadership. At least, that was the conventional wisdom outside Apple. Inside, the story was far different.

Step back just a few days, to that terrible afternoon of Thursday, February 1, when Apple could not issue its press release on the change in its leadership because the contract terms with Amelio had not been finalized. Kevin Sullivan, the human relations chief, Jim Buckley, the Apple Americas president, and other top executives were sitting in their offices atop City Center 3 at about 4:30 P.M. when a man named Doug Solomon, Apple's new vice president for corporate development, poked his head into their offices and announced, "Gatorade is on. We have a meeting at five P.M. in the Synergy room." "What are you talking about?" Sullivan demanded. "Our CEO has been fired."[1] Solomon had recently taken over corporate development, following the departure of Robert Lauridsen to help run R. B. Webber & Company, a Palo Alto management consulting firm.

The senior executives filed into the Synergy room, blinking in confusion. There were Sullivan and Solomon. There were also Buckley, Apple Pacific President John Floisand, manufacturing head Fred Forsyth, and Jeanne Sealy, vice president for corporate finance. Also attending was an investment banker named Frank Quattrone, then of the firm Morgan Stanley & Company (Quattrone, a next-door neighbor to Gil Amelio in Los Altos Hills, has been a key player in Silicon Valley mergers and acquisitions). Ed Stead, the general counsel, presided over the session, with Mike Markkula, newly demoted to vice chairman, listening in via a speakerphone on the table. Markkula, according to a person involved in the talks, had renewed the merger negotiations with Sun after making a phone call to Sun's CEO, Scott McNealy.

"Ed told us the board wanted us to do two days of due diligence and to be ready to give presentations," recalls a participant in the meeting. "Due diligence" is the legal term used to describe the final part of a merger deal that includes the preparation of detailed reports on the implications of an acquisition on a company's balance sheet, corporate assets, and organizational structure. The executive team was surprised and angry. Here they were, being told to bust their butts and get ready for a merger with Sun, with no one from the board physically present to explain why Gil Amelio had been recruited as CEO if this was going to take place, after all. Amelio's appointment had yet to be announced.

"It was one angry meeting," recalls the participant. "No one would tell us whether Gil was the new CEO."

The meeting adjourned after two hours, and the executives set to work. They worked all day Friday and Saturday, reconvening at noon on Sunday, February 4, in the two-story offices of Wilson, Sonsini, Goodrich & Rosati, a law firm in Palo Alto where a Sun attorney named Larry Sonsini serves as a partner. There was a small army of Apple and Sun executives, as many as sixty in all, broken into a dozen committees of five members each to work out merger issues such as human relations, marketing, and corporate strategy. Sun's Scott McNealy had been playing at the Pebble Beach National Pro-Am golf tournament that weekend but flew back up to Silicon Valley to participate in the meetings, which lasted until about 6 P.M.[2]

Afterward, Mike Markkula stood before the Apple executives, as they continued to work until 10 P.M. back in Cupertino, and gave a pep talk to ready them for scheduled formal presentations before the Apple board the following night. "You have to put your best foot forward," Markkula said, according to a person who heard this. "This is it." One of the Apple executives was so convinced the merger was finally going to happen that he went home to tell his wife that Apple was being sold. "We wouldn't make a lot of money on this, but we felt a merger with Sun would create critical mass," recalls this executive. "The cultures were aligned with each other. And Scott would have been a dynamic leader. Of course, nobody knew what would happen to Gil."

Gil knew what was going to happen to Gil: he was not about to go anywhere. In his Monday-morning meeting with Apple's senior management, Markkula introduced Amelio and the new CEO spoke for a few moments "on how we're going to run this company more button-down," recalls a participant. After just ten minutes or so, he waved his hand to dismiss the group. Mystified as to why the subject of Gatorade had not been brought up, Buckley raised his hand and asked, " 'Gil, I'd be interested in your opinion on what you think will happen [with Sun],' " recalls the participant in the meeting. "Gil said, 'We don't need Sun. We're going to run this company on our own.' "

Then Amelio asked Buckley and everyone else in the room how they felt about Gatorade. "We all said we were for it," recalls a second participant in the meeting. "We said we thought there would be dynamic leadership with Sun. Buckley said it could help us in the commercial marketplace." The discussion went on for two hours. Seated next to Amelio was Mike Markkula, who only the night before had delivered a rousing pep talk in favor of a deal with Sun. But through the entire discussion, Markkula—the king behind the throne for so many years—sat there and said nothing. If there had been any question before about who really ran Apple Computer, there was none now. Finally, Amelio adjourned the meeting, promising to make a decision on Sun by 2:30 P.M. the next day.

That day, Tuesday, the executives reassembled in the Synergy room at noon and went over other business until a few minutes before 2:30, when Amelio excused himself from the room, accompanied by Ed Stead. Returning just ten minutes later, Amelio broke the news to his staff: "We made the decision to go it on our own," according to a person in that room. Gil Amelio, the king on the throne, had personally made sure to torpedo the Sun deal, once and for all. There would be no more presentations to the Apple board.

Buckley, Sullivan, and the others were crestfallen. Earlier in the negotiations, they had harbored reservations about whether an Apple-Sun combination could work. Yet the more they had looked at it, the more they had seen compatibility between the two corporations. Apple had the Macintosh for lower-end computers; Sun had the Solaris operating system for high-end computers. Apple had a huge presence in the mass consumer market; Sun had almost none but possessed the Java programming language for the Internet, which could have been used to spread Sun's technology rapidly while at the

same time bolstering Apple's low presence in the new medium. And cultur-
ally, the companies were closer than any of the other potential Apple merger
partners had been because they were both Silicon Valley, engineering-driven
organizations. Apple, of course, lacked Sun's discipline, but Apple's executives
believed that Scott McNealy could take care of that problem.

"I thought it would have been fantastic," says Dave Nagel. "Bill Joy [a Sun
cofounder and board member], Eric Schmidt [then the Sun CTO], and I all
liked each other. Scott McNealy wanted to do it, although he faced some opposition from his board. When Gil put an end to it, I was pretty glum."

As Amelio remembers these discussions with his staff, the Sun deal was already over when he took over as CEO. "I may have asked the staff's opinion of
this after I came aboard, but by then Sun was already history," he said, looking
fit in a green dress shirt and slacks as he spoke in a private conference room
outside his eighth-floor office atop City Center 3. The room is spartanly appointed with framed copies of his university diplomas and a glass case containing a century-old dagger from Malaysia given him by that country while he
was still at National Semiconductor. "The discussions with Sun terminated
before I took the job as CEO," he adds, seated ramrod straight at a rectangular
table of blond wood framed by six black reclining chairs. "Clearly, the primary
reason I was coming aboard was to try and fix something, because the board
didn't need me to sell the company."

Amelio, while insisting then that Apple could be "fixed" by itself, maintains that he was not against a merger if a deal had been good. "I think the
right kind of alliance could have made sense for the company," he says. "But
the position I took on the board was that the way you normally do these things
is, you articulate a strategy for the company that you believe in, and then you
go see the ways you can implement this strategy, including aligning yourself
with someone. You don't come at it the opposite way, which says, 'Gee, we're
in trouble, so we better go make a deal with somebody and back into a strategy
based on that.' You have to decide what kind of company you can become and
then make the steps. But at that time, I think Apple did not have a clear picture of how it was going to succeed."

The spurned suitor, Sun's Scott McNealy, retreated into his lair. He gave a
fitting epitaph to the whole saga: in the week after Amelio was named CEO,
McNealy took the stage at a private meeting with industry analysts in Laguna
Niguel, California, and opened his presentation by producing an apple and
taking a bite out of it. "That's all I'm going to say about that," he said, according to witnesses.

Meanwhile, Amelio kept a low public profile during his first two weeks in
office, holding scores of meetings with Apple executives and employees to assess how bad the damage he had inherited really was. He had already proven
that an Apple CEO could be decisive, as demonstrated when he overruled

every member of the executive staff to ensure an Apple merger with Sun did not go any farther. On February 19, 1996, he would also show that he could be open and candid with the press—a trait distinctly missing in the Spindler administration.

That morning, the asphalt parking lot outside an Apple building called R&D 4 began to fill with cars, trucks, and vans containing a platoon of journalists representing the print, radio, television, and Internet media. Cameras and tripods were carefully unloaded. Microphones and tape recorders were checked and double-checked. Even some of the print reporters armed only with pen and notebook made sure their pens were working, for nobody wanted to miss out on what was about to be said. Amelio was due to make his first public remarks since replacing Michael Spindler, and the computer industry was dying to hear from the latest victor in an Apple boardroom coup.

And now the fate of this American icon called Apple rested in the hands of a Ph.D. who, appropriately in this case, was being referred to in the press as "Dr. Amelio." On this day, the doctor was in, ready to hold court for the press inside R&D 4, which serves as the hub of Apple's horseshoe-shaped research campus because it contains the complex's library and cafeteria, as well as the offices of the Advanced Technology Group, a formidable think tank known for brewing up wild things in the lab. If climactic conditions were any indication, the day harbingered a promising beginning for Apple and its new CEO. Only the previous day, heavy winter rains had soaked Cupertino. This morning, Presidents' Day, the clouds parted, a blue sky unfurled into a brilliant canopy overhead, and the temperature stood at an idyllic 65 degrees. It would have been a great day for Amelio to take off and partake of his flying hobby or even sit out on the deck of his $2.3 million home overlooking Silicon Valley. It turned out to be an even better one for him to show the world that someone at Apple was finally in charge.

The throng of journalists, numbering about fifty, was ushered into a cafeteria called Café Macs, where bottles of California wine and fresh hors d'oeuvres were spread in a sumptuous buffet. Satjiv Chahil, Apple's multimedia guru, stood near the entryway, greeting reporters by name as they arrived. The bearded Chahil was bedecked in his usual turban—a blue one, this time—and he was grinning from ear to ear. "I feel more excited every time I hear him talk," Chahil gushed to me, representing *The Wall Street Journal*, about the new boss. Chahil, no doubt, was conducting the usual "spin control" that underlings perform for a big executive at such a big event. But he seemed sincere, as did other executives who had weathered the dark moods of Michael Spindler. Indeed, their relief was palpable. "The fighting spirit has resurrected itself in the last two weeks," John Floisand, the Apple Pacific chief, told me. His eyes twinkling, Floisand added, "We're going to fight like tigers."

With such a buildup, it was hard for even the most jaded Apple watcher not to feel a twinge of excitement, too. The business press had been increasingly critical of Apple in recent years, but as a whole the reporters who followed the company wanted it to succeed because Apple's had always been such a colorful and intriguing story to follow. Almost no one in the computer industry, in fact, wanted to see Apple go away because that would leave the PC world with only the standard of Microsoft and Intel, diminishing competition and giving customers few alternatives. And it was most refreshing, coming after the bunker mentality of the Spindler administration, to encounter a CEO like Gil Amelio, who appeared ready not only to take command but to talk frankly and at length about Apple's many problems.

The press conference was informal. Journalists huddled in cafeteria chairs or sat cross-legged on the carpet as Gil Amelio walked out in a conservative blue suit and stood in the hot glare of television lights. "After two weeks, I am hardly ready to make new announcements," Amelio told the throng. Then he offered an olive branch, saying, "We want you to come in the front door, and we want you to be welcome." Amelio quickly moved to the heart of the issue: Can Apple survive? "We have ourselves in a little trouble now," he said in his folksy manner. "The troubles are very fixable. I have been down this road before."

Indeed he had. Reared in New York City's Bronx, Amelio was the son of a World War II veteran named Anthony Amelio who had been awarded a Purple Heart while serving in General George Patton's Third Army during World War II. After obtaining his bachelor's, master's, and Ph.D. in physics from the Georgia Institute of Technology, he had signed on as a researcher at Bell Laboratories, where he had obtained sixteen patents, either alone or jointly with other colleagues. In 1971, he had become a researcher for the semiconductor division of Fairchild Camera and Instrument Corporation, eventually being promoted to general manager over two divisions. In 1983, Amelio had moved on to Rockwell International Corporation as president of the company's semiconductor division.[3] He had earned a reputation as a turnaround artist there by reviving that division's foundering businesses.

In 1991, Amelio was called upon to put those turnaround skills to an even bigger test when National Semiconductor—a then–$1.7 billion maker of semiconductor chips for everything from computer networks and telephones to automobiles and satellites—recruited him as president and CEO to rescue a company that had just suffered its worst loss in thirty years. Amelio applied a technique that would become known as the "chartreuse strategy": when faced with a struggling business, he was so willing to try anything to change attitudes that "it didn't matter if I had to paint the building chartreuse."[4] By 1995, the "chartreuse strategy" had succeeded in turning National Semiconductor from a downward spiral in 1991 to a record $264 million profit in 1995. National's board rewarded him by naming him the company's chairman, in addition to his other titles.

That success led Amelio to coauthor a book with a writer named William Simon, called *Profit from Experience: The National Semiconductor Story of Transformation Management.* The 312-page tome, aimed at CEOs and their managers, was well written but interspersed with such turgid jargon as "Setting the Initial Vector" and "Direction Setting and Visioning." The book emphasized that a corporate turnaround could be achieved only if the CEO maintained a clear focus and vision. Amelio, however, bristled at the term "turnaround manager," saying that the term implied a manager who comes in and slashes and burns to restore profitability, while cutting the soul—and innovation—out of a company. The description he applied to himself was a "transformation manager," or one who looks for long-term solutions.

Just how well Amelio actually had transformed National Semiconductor was a matter of considerable debate in the months after he jumped ship to Apple. Critics of the National turnaround point out that National's sales increased just 18 percent between 1993 and 1995, when the semiconductor industry was booming, as compared with Intel, whose sales almost doubled. "While we did well, our competition did better," grouses Peter Sprague, National's retired chairman and the man who had brought Amelio in from Rockwell.

Amelio did perform admirably when he first arrived at National, most everyone agrees. The company was suffering from excess manufacturing capacity, brought on by an industry slowdown and exacerbated by National's acquisition of Fairchild Semiconductor in 1987. With the company running at only half its manufacturing capacity in 1991, Amelio consolidated plants and cut jobs to bring expenses under control. As a result, National's head count fell from 29,800 to 22,400, or by 25 percent, between 1991 and 1995, mostly through attrition. "The company did not have its house in order when Gil first came in," recalls Charlie Carinalli, National's former chief financial officer and chief technical officer. "In terms of his performance in the early stage, I would give him an 'A.' "

The key measure of how well an executive actually turns a company around, though, is in how well that company is positioned to continue performing after he or she has moved on. And that is where Gil Amelio's turnaround fell short. One problem was that he did not move to kill off low-profit parts of the chip business, even after his CTO, Carinalli, advised him to do so. "Gil is a very optimistic guy," says Carinalli, who first pushed him to do that in 1991. "He would tend to err on the side of thinking things could be turned around." Amelio, too, failed to deliver new product categories that could have given National a richer profit stream, although he was attempting to do so when he left. And finally, he appointed an office of three chief operating officers with no guidance as to which one would be left in charge when he was gone.

As a result, National was ill prepared when Amelio served a solitary day's notice that he was resigning to, as he told his executive staff, "save one of America's great companies." Without so much as a personal good-bye to the rank and file—just an e-mail note—Amelio left behind a company with no clear leadership and an eroding market position. Indeed, National underwent a tumultuous period in the months thereafter as 600 jobs were cut, two of the chief operating officers resigned, and 14 of 56 vice presidents resigned or were fired amid a restructuring by the new CEO, Brian Halla, a former top executive at LSI Logic Corporation.[5] In the six-month period ended November 30, 1996, National posted a restructuring-related loss of $178.1 million, compared to a profit of $153.3 million in the same period a year earlier.

"I made a terrible mistake in hiring Gil," says Peter Sprague, who had clashed openly with Amelio. "If I had it to do over again, I would have used a search firm." Funny, but Mike Markkula and the Apple board had not used a search firm in selecting Amelio as their new CEO, either.

In any event, Amelio's challenge at Apple was far more daunting than anything he had attempted before. For one thing, he was a chip guy and this was a personal computer company, a whole different beast. One difference between the two is that semiconductor companies such as National Semiconductor typically spend a lot of money up front building chip-making plants that are not designed to bring a return until years down the road. A PC company such as Apple, however, depends on a high-velocity model of new computers going out the door at intervals of six and nine months and being sold quickly to keep the corporate engine fueled. Thus, in the PC business, it is difficult to plan financially far into the future.

Moreover, the legacies of Michael Spindler and John Sculley had left Apple in a shambles. Apple's worldwide share of the PC market had slipped again in 1995, to 7.9 percent from 8.3 percent in 1994.[6] As a consequence, software support for Apple was eroding at an alarming rate. Macintosh software sales during 1996, for example, would plunge by 29 percent below that of 1995, according to a survey by the Software Publishers Association, the largest software-industry trade group. Sales of Windows programs, meanwhile, would increase 16 percent in that same period.

The market share situation was a vicious circle for Apple. As its share went down, fewer software developers wrote programs for the Macintosh. Without the programs, customers had fewer reasons to buy the Mac. And as fewer customers bought the Mac, its market share was continuing to erode, prompting even fewer developers to support the Mac and even fewer customers to want to continue buying. A microcosm of this dilemma is illustrated by the story of a San Francisco periodontist named Kirk Pasquinelli.

Pasquinelli bought a Mac Plus in 1987 to start his business of treating people with gum disease. Enraptured by the Mac's ease of use, Pasquinelli went on to outfit his office with five Macs and his home with two more. "When I first got mine, the Mac was great," he remembers. "It was the only computer I had ever used." Pasquinelli was the ideal Apple customer. He replaced his old Macs with new models every eighteen months. He relied on Macintosh for nearly everything related to his office, from writing letters and maintaining forms to preparing slide-show presentations for lectures. But by 1995, when it was time for him to upgrade again to the new Power Mac, Pasquinelli discovered that an updated version of his favorite dental office program was not coming out anytime soon because the developer was concentrating on first bringing out a version for Windows.

"So I sent my staff to a dental convention in L.A. and told them to look at all the computer software and tell me which was the best one for our office," Pasquinelli recalls. "They came back and said the best was a Windows 95 program. So we bought six Windows 95 machines, and we'll buy six more in the next few months. I have donated the old Macs to a school."

In the blink of an eye, loyal Mac customer Kirk Pasquinelli abandoned the computer he had built his business with—*because he could not get software.*

By this time, there were Kirk Pasquinellis all over the world. And even the customers who had not yet abandoned the Macintosh platform were so shaken by all the Apple turbulence in January 1996 that many held off on new purchases. "We were getting the shit kicked out of us in the U.S.," remembers Jim Buckley, who was still heading sales there then. "I launched Operation Reboot, in which twelve of us in teams of two flew to thirty-five cities to have breakfast, lunch, and dinner meetings with our key accounts." That tactic did not work, though. On April 17, Apple would report a staggering loss of $740 million on an 18 percent fall in revenues for the fiscal second quarter ended March 29, prompted in large part by nearly $400 million of unsold inventory. That forced Amelio to widen the previously announced layoffs of 1,300 employees to total 2,800, or 20 percent of the workforce.

Yes, indeed, the doctor was going to have to administer some mighty powerful medicine to right this vessel. All he asked from the press and the public was a little breathing room as he spent the first hundred days of his administration in "sponge mode," diagnosing all the ills that afflicted Apple so that he could prescribe a cure. The shareholders who had been at Michael Spindler's throat were more than willing to give the new guy a chance. They were just relieved that Apple had not jumped at Sun's $23-per-share offer, an amount that would have caused a good many to incur steep losses.

"If they get the right management in there, the company is worth substantially more than that," Marian Kessler, portfolio manager of the Crabbe Huson Fund, a big investor in Apple based in Portland, Oregon, said then.[7] "They have the wherewithal and technology. They just haven't been managed right."

An even bigger cadre of support came from the faithful Macintosh customers, those cultish diehards who would as soon jump off a cliff as switch from their beloved Macs to "Windoze," as they derisively called Microsoft's linchpin software. Their high priest was Guy Kawasaki, Apple's former chief evangelist, whose early work in recruiting software developers to write programs had been crucial to the Mac's original success. Kawasaki had returned to Apple in June 1995, having been recruited by Dan Eilers to try to shore up the sagging relations with developers. After leaving Apple in 1987, Kawasaki had become a successful author and entrepreneur, running small software companies. He had agreed to return to Apple in exchange for being named to the prestigious position of "Apple Fellow," the honor accorded only a handful of scholars for extraordinary contributions to personal computing.

Kawasaki is a charming man with no small ego. "I am a warrior and a warrior needs a war," Kawasaki said in a press statement shortly after returning to Apple. "My war is to bring cool Macintosh software to fruition, create the finest developer program in the industry, and kick Microsoft's butt—in this order." Kick Microsoft's butt? Yeah, right. Kawasaki *was* living in the past. But his fervor would prove an important tool in the battle to keep the Mac stalwarts from jumping off that proverbial cliff. One of his first ideas upon returning was to start an Internet newsletter called "EvangeList." Therein, he posted anything and everything positive he could find about the Macintosh, such as the tidbit that Macs were being used by everyone from climbers on Mount Everest to Coptic monks in the Sahara.

"EvangeList" proved wildly popular, surging from a thousand Internet subscribers to about fifty thousand in 1997. With all the negative press about Apple, these Mac loyalists were starved to hear something good, and they followed "EvangeList" so fanatically that Kawasaki took to calling them his "Listas." When this author was preparing an article on Kawasaki for *The Wall Street Journal* in 1996, he discovered the power of "EvangeList" firsthand. Asked for comment about Kawasaki in an e-mail posting on "EvangeList," more than eight hundred people responded from all corners of the globe, even Tasmania. "I believe he has done for Apple Computer what Rush [Limbaugh] has done for middle-of-the-road conservatism," wrote Matthew Coombs from Hyde Park, Utah. "He identifies his purpose and enemies and he does whatever he thinks is necessary to win."

Amelio inherited another important tool. Her name was Heidi Roizen. The T/Maker Company she had cofounded to make consumer and business programs had been one of the first software developers for the Mac, and she had earned widespread industry acclaim for her work in such organizations as the Software Publishers Association, of which she had served as president from 1988 to 1990. A vivacious woman with the California look of blond hair and a tan, Roizen was also a confidant of Bill Gates and was well liked and respected by practically everyone in the software community. Just a week before Amelio became CEO, she had accepted a new job at Apple as vice president for developer relations. In this role, her job would be to build and maintain relationships between Apple and its developers and coordinate Apple's communications with the developers. Just getting her to take that position amounted to a rare victory for the Spindler administration or, more specifically, for Dave Nagel, the head of Apple's R&D.

Like many Mac developers of the time, Roizen was an outspoken critic of Apple, furious that the company was not working more closely with its developers. In October 1995, a headhunter called and asked if she would be interested in a new Apple job handling developer relations. "I said, 'No way. I have too many complaints about Apple,' " Roizen recalls. "The headhunter said, 'Could you talk to Dave Nagel?' " Roizen agreed, but only so she could give him a piece of her mind. " 'Well, I'm so happy to see you interviewing for this job,' " Nagel said, according to Roizen, as she walked into his office, then on the ground floor of an Apple building called R&D 3. "I said, 'I'm not interviewing for this job. I'm here to tell you what is wrong with Apple.' " With that she launched into a two-hour diatribe against Apple, explaining that she, like many of the old Mac developers, had been forced to shift much of their work to Windows. "After that, Dave said, 'Well, I want you to have this job,' " Roizen says.

Roizen left, still thinking, "No way." In December, though, she found herself in the same room with Dave Nagel again, at an annual conference of industry executives hosted by David Coursey, the editor of the influential "P. C. Letter," sitting around a roaring fire in a lodge at Lake Tahoe's Squaw Valley, snow heaped deep against the towering ponderosas outside, with luminaries such as Philippe Kahn, the firebrand founder of Borland International, and Bill Krause, former chief executive of 3Com Corporation. "They bashed Dave Nagel for an hour," Roizen remembers. "Bill Krause said, 'Dave, we're not bashing you because we hate Apple. We love Apple. We want you to fix it. There is not a company we want to succeed more than Apple Computer.' Suddenly, I could see there was this marvelous opportunity. Finally, in January, I decided to do it. I didn't need the paycheck. And after thirteen years in the same job, I could afford to take a chance."

The hiring of Heidi Roizen was about the only breath of fresh air that Apple enjoyed that January. One person alone, of course, could not fix the ailing Apple. But software support was crucial, and what better person to have in charge of rallying the developers than one of their own?

Gil Amelio also brought an important attribute that had been sorely lacking at Apple through practically its entire history: a willingness to listen. Apple executives had always lived in such an insular world that they had rarely asked or cared what the outside world wanted. The previous two CEOs, Spindler and Sculley, had rarely been seen wandering the floors of trade shows to see what the competition was up to, as Bill Gates and Intel's Andy Grove made a habit of doing. It was the old "N.I.H." syndrome: Not Invented Here.

Amelio would listen—to anybody. He had instituted the practice at National Semiconductor, for example, of holding a series of monthly "kaffeeklatsch" meetings with about a dozen employees, selected at random from throughout the organization, to hear what was really going on down in the trenches. Managers were not usually invited to these sessions. He also listened to customers—to their surprise. After five months at Apple, in July 1996, he invited the fourteen members of an advisory council for the North American User Group—an influential panel that represents some 500,000 members of Macintosh user groups on the continent—to sit down with him in Cupertino and air their gripes. "He was supposed to talk to us for twenty minutes," recalls Dan Sailers, a council member from Dallas, Texas. "He came in, took off his jacket, and stayed with us for forty-five minutes. One of our statements was 'Get advertising that works.' He said, 'Look, we have to do something about it.'" Spindler, by contrast, had never met with this group, although Sculley had.

Another time, in April 1996, an Apple reseller named James Bradley dispatched a lengthy letter to Amelio via regular mail, outlining some technical ways in which Apple could adjust the multimedia performance of its computers to appeal more to Hollywood's entertainment industry. The very next day—on a Saturday night, no less—Amelio sent this response back to Bradley by e-mail: "What a great letter! You raise some excellent points that I intend to follow up on. You may not know that among my patents is the pioneering work I did on CCD image sensors (been more than 20 yrs now . . .) so I understand the points you are raising reasonably well. This is clearly a very important field. Thanks for the heads-up." Bradley, when he received the response at his business in Los Angeles, was flabbergasted. "He reads his own mail and is clearly on top of it to reply to me so quickly," Bradley says. "Not only that, he took action." That was, indeed, quite a feat, since Amelio estimated that he received some one thousand letters from Apple well-wishers in his first two months on the job, or an average of nearly twenty per day.

Morale within Apple headed sharply up, too, during Amelio's one-hundred-day honeymoon as he sought to reassure employees through messages such as the "ReachOut" memos he posted on e-mail addresses companywide. In one, titled "Let's Make a Deal" and posted April 10, 1996, Amelio laid out his personal values to the workforce. The internal memo, obtained by me from an Apple employee, read:

HERE'S WHAT I WILL DO:

- I will respect Apple's history, Apple people, Apple talents and Apple values—and work to recapture the legendary Apple spirit as I set the goals to take us forward profitably towards the new century.
- I will walk the talk—I will continue to reach out to get your input, to really hear and consider what you are saying.
- I will consider YOUR interests always—measuring my success in terms of you—working to make Apple great for you, for the customer and the people we do business with.
- I will take the blame when things go wrong—and give you the credit when things go right.
- I will tell you how things are going, share news of our successes, be candid about the problems we are addressing, and be clear about what I want and how I measure success; I will help you to succeed.

AND, HERE'S WHAT I NEED YOU TO DO:

- Be an Apple evangelist. Be proud, talk with confidence, get back some of that old fire I've heard so much about—wear Apple pins, T-shirts, etc.
- Become people/customer-focused, putting the customer (the user) at the center of everything you do; keep continually in touch with what our customers want and need.
- Start to maintain schedules as an absolute, especially on critical products.
- Be a good partner—even when your ideas are not used, fully support all plans and decisions.
- Build on the strength of Apple's successes. Find out what's been done in the past—build on what the smart people have done before you got the assignment—respect experience and people who have been selected as consultants.

I wonder how many of you will download this list. Will I begin to see it posted alongside people's computers? I would like that—but only if you take a moment to re-read it often. It will help keep us on track.

Recently someone told me about the "One Apple" theme that supported Apple's culture. I would like to take it out of mothballs and extend the spirit of One Apple to include developers, customers, vendors, partners and the press. I hope you agree that they should all be treated as an intrinsic part of Apple.

The next ReachOut has already begun to be written in my mind. It will be about some strategic specifics that I'm sure you are waiting for. Check HotLinks in a couple of weeks for ReachOut #3.

Respectfully,

Gil

The memo was so well received that workers throughout Apple did, in fact, post a copy of it by their computer terminals. An incident several months later, however, would prompt them to reread a certain portion of the memo with considerably less enthusiasm.

On Apple's Web site, employees using only their first names began posting copies of testimonial letters to customers and relatives concerning their revived faith. In one addressed "Dear Dad," a Philadelphia account executive named Michael wrote, "We have many things to be proud of, and some mistakes to correct. But one thing is certain: We are not finished, and I would rather take this ride with Gil and see it through than do anything else!" In another, addressed simply to "Mom," a product-marketing employee named David wrote, "Armed with a formidable arsenal of facts, opinions and hopes, I now fight for the cause with more zeal than ever. I study every move of our competition in the Internet arena, and I assure you, the Battle is just beginning. . . . With incredible products and a new Admiral aboard, we will again return Apple to preeminence in the computer industry. I'll be home when the fight is won."

Given the turn of events to come, that could be a long time.

Gil Amelio had asked the world to give him one hundred days to devise a turnaround strategy, but he could not wait that long to attack Apple's worsening cash problem. When he took over, in fact, Apple was three months from running out of money altogether.

"The cash problem was so serious that it virtually consumed me until well into June," Amelio remembers. "Of all the problems I wanted to work on in the company, I didn't have the luxury to work on them because this one was so critical and urgent."

As confident as Amelio appeared to be that he could restore Apple to its former glory, he knew he could not do the job himself, nor with just the executive team he had inherited from Michael Spindler. Executives such as Jim Buckley, John Floisand, and Dave Nagel were all bright, energetic managers in their respective fields, but they had all been at Apple so long that Amelio believed he needed the fresh eye of an outsider—one whom he knew and could trust, such as his chief administrative officer at National, George Scalise.

Scalise, sixty-two years old at the time, had been so instrumental in helping implement the cost cuts that had rallied National that Amelio had looked on him there as his number two executive. Scalise is an unflappable businessman, trained as an engineer but with vast management experience at computer companies including Maxtor Corporation, where he once served as president and CEO, and Advanced Micro Devices and Fairchild, where he helped build chip-making plants. A wiry, short man with a receding hairline, bushy eyebrows, and an intense demeanor, Scalise is a veritable productivity machine, wasting little time on small talk as he hurries from meeting to meeting.

Scalise followed Amelio to Apple in late February 1996, becoming the company's first chief administrative officer responsible for areas including licensing and communications. Once again, he was Amelio's de facto number two, as Jim Buckley soon discovered. Amelio publicly reprimanded Buckley in one meeting for failing to first obtain Scalise's permission before agreeing to take back $7 million worth of unsold inventory from a dealer, even though Buckley had succeeded in negotiating that amount down from the dealer's initial demand to take back $28 million worth, according to a former executive familiar with the incident.

The second weapon Amelio employed in his campaign to balance the numbers was a tall, easygoing man named Fred D. Anderson, the highly regarded CFO of Automatic Data Processing Inc., a Roseland, New Jersey–based provider of computerized data transaction and other services that he had helped build from $1.9 billion in annual revenues when he joined in 1992 to $3.6 billion when he left in 1996. Anderson, fifty-one years of age, had actually been approached for the CFO's job by Michael Spindler in the waning days of that administration but had not taken the job because Spindler had been booted out. He was approached again by Gil Amelio a few weeks later and signed on with Apple on April Fool's Day 1996. Like Scalise, Anderson is a workaholic, but he emits the aura of a television evangelist by prefacing each utterance with an engaging smile.

When Scalise and Anderson walked through the corridors of Apple's City Center 3 headquarters, Apple's cash reserves had dwindled to just $400 million and the company had $400 million in loans coming due. "We had a liquidity crisis," Anderson recalls. Scalise and Anderson formulated a strategy to rectify this situation. Appropriately, they dubbed it the "Crossing the Canyon" plan.

The first step was to try to dissolve Apple's bloated inventory of $2 billion in unsold Macintoshes. The computers had been built in anticipation of Michael Spindler's grand market share plan but had ended up collecting dust when the big sales had failed to materialize. Scalise and Anderson got Apple to refocus its sales efforts to target these unsold computers at the company's key markets, rather than at the broad, general market as they had been before. The result was that models began moving into customers' hands and the inventory level dropped. Scalise also arranged for the sale of Apple's manufacturing plant in Fountain, Colorado, to SCI Systems Inc., and other functions such as data processing were contracted to outside companies.

Meanwhile, Anderson had to keep the creditors at bay. He convinced Apple's suppliers to extend their deadline for Apple to pay for components from 30 days to 45 days. And he hopped onto a jet with another Apple executive and headed across the Pacific to Tokyo, where he met with five Japanese banks holding the Apple loans that were coming due. "We had to pitch Apple's strengths and our business plan," Anderson says. "We got them to extend the loans."

Through these actions and a few others, Scalise and Anderson managed within a few months to rebuild Apple's money trove to a healthy $1.8 billion. The cash canyon had been crossed. Now there was the matter of Amelio formulating a long-term strategic plan.

While George Scalise and Fred Anderson were putting out fires, Gil Amelio, after just sixty days, had already devised the broad outlines of his transformation plan. He began laying it out to small groups of employees—and in a background interview with *The Wall Street Journal*—before presenting it for approval to the board. On the morning of March 29, 1996, I, accompanied by Charles McCoy, chief of *The Wall Street Journal*'s San Francisco bureau, and Paul Carroll, a *Journal* reporter, were ushered into the eighth-floor Synergy room of City Center 3 for our first one-on-one chat with the CEO. Within a few moments, Amelio appeared in the doorway, wearing a stylish light-colored sweater, and heartily shook hands all around. Seated at the head of the long conference table, he spoke for more than an hour on what he had learned. A man with the congenial manner of one's favorite uncle, he was considerably more at ease than Michael Spindler had ever been in such sessions.

"We will have to focus more. We will have to get back to our roots," Amelio said, ticking off a litany of strategic directions that essentially boiled down to delivering more value to customers so a higher price could be justified. "I drive a Cadillac STS, and my wife has a Mercedes," Amelio said. "We could find cheaper cars to buy, but we made a choice to buy something a little more expensive. There is value worth the extra cost. If you deliver the value, people will pay the cost."

Uh-oh. This was starting to sound like Jean-Louis Gassée and that premium-pricing fiasco all over again. But Amelio's seeming madness had a method. It hinged on Apple being able to deliver the new operating system called Copland, the one that was already running a year late, as well as entering new markets as fast as it could. If Copland could pack more punch into a Macintosh than a Wintel machine had, Apple's customers in high-end markets such as desktop publishing would not mind paying more. Apple's profit margins would creep back up to a healthy enough level to continue funding R and D, while Mac cloners such as Power Computing could continue to keep the Mac platform price competitive. At the low end of the market, Amelio said, Apple could also compete by helping to open up the new market for inexpensive, dedicated devices like Apple's Pippin for TV Web surfing.

At the end of the meeting, we went away with a strong positive impression of Amelio but remained skeptical that he could turn around Apple at this point.

Later, in one of his kaffeeklatsches, Amelio elaborated on the premium-pricing strategy, saying Apple could be the "Mag-Lite" of computers. The Mag-Lite, made by Mag Instrument Inc. of Ontario, California, is considered the Cadillac of flashlights, selling for nearly $20 compared with as little as $3 for a standard flashlight. Amelio kept one in his home and, according to an Apple employee who was in the klatsch that day, had taken Mag-Lite and an "el cheapo" flashlight into a recent board meeting "and noted that it was interesting that what he had in his home was the Mag-Lite, specifically for its dependability and durability." (The unidentified employee provided a recount of this on Guy Kawasaki's "EvangeList" under the subject heading "Meeting with the Doctor.")

In his first companywide speech to employees on April 19, Amelio broadened his plan further, telling a packed auditorium at De Anza College's Flint Center that Apple needed to emphasize more profitable products such as data servers, handheld computers such as the Newton, and Pippin. The talk was delivered from the same stage that John Sculley had used as a pulpit so many times. Amelio was not the polished speaker Sculley had been. He tended to ramble, clear his throat, and lean wearily on the podium. But what he lacked in style, he made up for in sincerity. Amelio was so frank about Apple's problems, and seemingly heartfelt about its ability to rebound, that the two thousand employees present jumped to their feet at the conclusion of the two-hour address and gave him a loud ovation. "What I liked about it was that it was kind of back-to-the-basics kind of stuff, not flash-in-the-pan visionary, hype kind of stuff," one attendee told me later.

This crowd was not too hard to please, though. After all, their livelihoods depended on Gil Amelio, and they had also cheered wildly when their previous boss, Michael Spindler, had delivered his impassioned oratory at the sales conference in Las Vegas back in 1993. Amelio would face a much tougher audience on May 13, when he was scheduled to appear before Apple's annual Worldwide Developers Conference to unveil the specifics of his turnaround strategy. These developers had been stung so many times before by Apple, and they were already putting one foot into the Wintel camp. They were primarily interested in one thing: When could they get their hands on Copland? The answer would not be what they wanted to hear.

In spite of all the support from employees, there were other storm clouds building around Amelio. One had to do with worsening problems on the quality front. On May 8, 1996, for example, Apple had to institute a repair and recall program on a wide line of its portables and desktops. The PowerBook 5300 and 190 models, for instance, suffered problems such as "The AC power connector on some systems can become loose or inoperative" and "The display bezel and housing on some systems can crack at the hinge," according to a special bulletin Apple sent its dealers. In addition, the bulletin said, extended repairs were being ordered for twelve Macintosh Performa models and two of the Power Macs, because of problems including "system freezes caused by specific, known component issues identified by Apple" and "sudden or intermittent changes in the monitor's color hue on some models, due to a particular cable."

Even Apple's vaunted technical support was breaking down. Jacquelen Shlens, from San Marino, California, wrote to Amelio on April 29, 1996, to complain of her hellish experiences in getting Apple's technicians to walk her through the installation of an Apple program onto her Power Mac. Four different technicians, she wrote, had told her four different things to do, none of which had worked. After dealing with a total of "10 to 20" tech support people over a seven-hour period, Shlens ended up having to reinstall all of her files, disconnecting her printer in the process. "I WANTED TO SCREAM," she wrote, noting that she had switched from Wintel PCs to the Mac for what she thought would be greater quality and support. "Sadly, not even one individual ever called me back after promising to do so. Apple Technical Support offers no better support than that which I have encountered in the PC world."

The PR snafus worsened when Apple began running television ads on May 6, 1996, touting the use of a PowerBook in the movie *Mission: Impossible*, a reprise of the 1960s television series, starring Tom Cruise. The Paramount Pictures movie was set to open in the United States on May 22, and Apple had planned an advertising campaign tied in with the movie, including a planned "Webcast" from the Hollywood premiere. Later that summer, Apple was also set to unveil an ad campaign centered around the use of the PowerBook in another movie, 20th Century Fox's *Independence Day*, in which actor Jeff Goldblum plays a scientist using the computer to save the world from invading aliens. That led to the Apple campaign slogan "The Power to Save the World." All this was both sexy and glamorous enough— costing Apple $8.5 million for both movie campaigns—except for one thing: The latest PowerBook fiasco had left dealers with no models in stock. Tons of advertising and massive exposure were being unleashed for a product that consumers could not even get.

The movie campaigns were actually a brilliant idea conceived by Satjiv Chahil. Chahil, in his role of spearheading a new marketing emphasis on the entertainment industry, had amassed numerous powerful contacts in Hollywood. Since both *Mission: Impossible* and *Independence Day* were going to feature PowerBooks anyway, Chahil suggested to the producers in late 1995 that Apple be allowed to promote both itself and the movies through a separate ad campaign. *Independence Day*'s Jeff Goldblum, a Mac enthusiast, readily agreed to the idea, as did *Mission: Impossible*'s Tom Cruise, a fellow Mac fan who gave Chahil that famous smile and a hearty thumbs-up when asked for permission. When Chahil approached Steve Andler, Apple's director of mobile products marketing, about the idea in January 1996, Andler initially fretted that the PowerBook's tie-in with films loaded with explosions and fires would remind customers about the real-life exploding PowerBooks of 1995. "Satjiv said, 'Well, if we can't make fun of ourselves, who can?' " recalls a former Apple executive familiar with that conversation.

It was not until a month before the movie promotions started, though, that Andler discovered the new problems with the PowerBook 5300 and the recall was ordered. It was too late to stop the promotions. "It was the total depths of despair for us then," recalls a person on the PowerBook team.

In addition, Amelio committed a public relations gaffe that focused press scrutiny on his lucrative pay package. Just a few weeks after taking the helm, Amelio closed on the purchase of a $4.7 million mansion at Lake Tahoe. The mansion, built of massive pine logs, stood amid a forest of pines and firs on 3.5 acres of property nearly obscured from view by a fence of pine logs and stone columns, on the shore of the emerald-green waters of one of the most breathtaking alpine lakes in the world. When news of the Tahoe deal broke, Amelio was criticized for appearing more interested in feathering his nest than in saving Apple.

"Most unseemly of all, however," opined a lengthy article on Apple's downfall in the April 18, 1996, issue of *Rolling Stone* magazine, "is that Amelio arrived open-mouthed at the trough. . . . Many looked on with disgust when, just a few weeks after Amelio's appointment was announced, while he was rumored to be focusing on a strategy for Apple's comeback, he found the time to shop for [an] estate at Lake Tahoe."

Amelio, asked about this criticism more than a year later, still bristles at how he felt the media reported this story out of context. "I made the decision to buy that home and, in fact, closed the deal before Apple was in the picture at all for me," Amelio insists, his face reddening with renewed outrage. "I actually signed the contract in November [1995], but the transaction didn't close until after the year. I was already using the house as of that Christmas. So it was just a total misfabrication of facts [to suggest he shopped for it while Apple's CEO]."

Feeding at the trough was not so unusual for Apple's executives, since they had been doing it for years. And as Guy Kawasaki points out, "If you want someone to leave another *Fortune* 500 company, that's what it takes." Amelio himself sought to downplay the money issue, telling one reporter who questioned his compensation that professional athletes earned just as much. To be sure, no one would care a whit about how much Amelio was making or if he blew it all at a blackjack table in Las Vegas, if he could restore Apple Computer to some semblance of its former glory. On the stage of a packed auditorium in the San Jose Convention Center, at the annual Worldwide Developers Conference, he laid out for a standing-room-only crowd of four thousand anxious and frustrated Apple software developers how he aimed to do so.

"I'm delighted to be here this morning for this cozy little chat," Amelio told the group, which with its abundance of long hair, jeans, and T-shirts would not have looked out of place at a rock concert, except that it was 8 A.M. Amelio, by contrast, was dressed in a conservative blue suit and a red power tie. He looked as though he would have been more comfortable addressing a Rotary Club meeting. With both hands gripping a gray-colored lectern, Amelio blinked into the lights of a swarm of TV cameras that bathed him in an incandescent glow and continued in a shaky voice, "Can you believe the press on this thing? You'd think I would part the Red Sea." That line drew polite chuckles as Amelio launched into his speech: "I approach this task with a degree of humility, a characteristic, I might add, I'd like to see more of in this company." Amen. "Apple has two roads," he continued. "One, to prosperity. The other, a long, slow decline into irrelevance."

Amelio, of course, pledged to lead Apple down the first road. To help bring costs back into line, he said, Apple would simplify its product lines by eliminating half of the Macintosh models over the next twelve months. This drew enthusiastic applause, since the Mac's product line had become so convoluted it consisted of some forty models. Apple would also reduce from five to two or three the number of motherboards, which contain the main circuitry, that the company made for the Macintosh. This would shave off still more in manufacturing costs.

Then he addressed Apple's problem of software support—the most critical issue facing Apple and the issue of paramount concern to this audience. Amelio pledged, among other things, that Apple would home in on the Internet; put Heidi Roizen in charge of dispensing $20 million to help promote developers' products; and deliver Copland as soon as possible. "The developers are what made the Mac great," Amelio said, as someone from the blue-jeaned audience yelled, "Take off the tie!" Amelio, looking painfully out of place in his suit, momentarily looked flustered. Later, he would explain to reporters that he had intentionally worn the suit because "this is a reminder to everyone that we have to be serious about our business."

But he pressed on, concluding his hour-long talk with an emotional appeal: "I have a dream that we fulfill our destiny to bring computing to the rest of us, the nontechies. And that we change the world again. This is Apple. Expect the impossible." With that the theme music to *Mission: Impossible* began pulsating out of giant speakers as the new TV ad ran on an overhead video screen, only with the words "Mission: Unstoppable. Amelio Takes Command."

For a speech that had had one of the biggest media buildups in corporate history, the consensus among developers was that Amelio had performed as best he could, given Apple's dire circumstances. They did not expect any miraculous overnight cure. But they *had* hoped to receive a beta copy of Copland, the long-awaited new operating system for the Mac. The fact that a Copland beta was not available at this conference stirred near panic among the hundreds of engineers working on the much-anticipated software project down in the bowels of Apple's R-and-D campus. The rest of the world did not know it yet, but Copland was on life support.

Though not as pressing as the "Crossing the Canyon" cash issue, improvement of the Mac's operating system was vital to Amelio's turnaround plan. Since Microsoft had nearly erased the Macintosh's technical superiority with Windows 95, Apple was in the tough marketing position of not being able to continue distinguishing its products from the competition's. Unless Apple could move the Macintosh out in front again, the company faced losing the allegiance of its remaining developers and customers.

The roots of Copland went all the way back to 1987, when a group of Apple's brightest software engineers had assembled at the Sonoma Mission Inn to propose building a brand-new Macintosh operating system. The problem with the original Mac, as detailed before, was that it had been cobbled together with little rhyme or reason and contained millions of lines of code that were jumbled together like spaghetti. The Mac's original programmers had done a wonderful job creating a graphical user interface that even a child could use. But they had neglected to provide a strong foundation for the operating system that would prevent it from crashing, as well as permit the user to work on several applications at once. These two features were called "memory protection" and "preemptive multitasking."

Originally, the answer to this problem was supposed to rest with the project called "Pink." But Pink had mutated into the joint Apple/IBM project Taligent, which had finally died in late 1995 without producing the vaunted new operating system. Apple's software engineers could see that Taligent was in trouble in 1993, when they had been in the process of modifying the Mac's software to run on the new PowerPC microprocessor. It was that year the Star Trek project had been canceled because Apple's senior management had refused to commit the money for it. (Star Trek was the project to create a "portable" version of the Mac's OS that could run on Intel microprocessors, providing Apple access to the huge industry infrastructure that surrounded the Intel architecture.)

In 1993, Dave Nagel had been placed in charge of Apple's system software, following the sudden departure of the former manager, Roger Heinen, to Microsoft. Directly under Nagel was Rick Spitz, a likable but intense vice president. And just below Spitz in that hierarchy was Jean Proulx, an Apple director who had been recruited from Digital Equipment Corporation in August 1992 to help manage the system software projects. Spitz and Heinen were both Digital veterans.

When Nagel disbanded Star Trek, he and Spitz turned over the Trekkie engineers to Jean Proulx, who was put in charge of the Raptor project, so named for the raptor dinosaurs featured in the movie hit *Jurassic Park*. Proulx, in turn, appointed another woman named Ruth Hennigar to act as Raptor's engineering manager, or DRI (directly responsible individual). Hennigar, too, had originally come from Digital. "We called it DUI [as in driving under the influence]," Hennigar remembers with a throaty laugh. Proulx asked her to look into what it would take to come up with a brand-new operating system for the Mac. This was essentially Pink, starting all over again. "Part of what we were trying to do was say, 'OK, what are we doing?' " Proulx remembers.

The impetus behind Raptor was Bill Gates and his Windows 95 operating system, known in 1993 under Microsoft's code name "Chicago." Not unlike in the scene in *Jurassic Park* when the footsteps of an approaching *Tyrannosaurus rex* are felt long before the creature is seen, the industry drumbeat announcing Windows 95 had already begun. And without Taligent to come to the rescue, the software engineers at Apple were quaking in their Birkenstocks. Ruth Hennigar figured that Apple had, at most, an eighteen-month window of opportunity in which to deliver a new operating system. Since that was not a lot of time, given the years of work that had gone into other research projects, she decided to focus her efforts on creating a new OS piecemeal, adding more pieces later.

The first and most important piece would be a microkernel. The "kernel," as it is also known, is essentially a small chunk of software that has complete control over the computer. Sitting at the very bottom of the operating system and providing the crucial link between the hardware part of the computer and the software, it tells all the other software what to do. Neither the Macintosh nor Microsoft's MS-DOS contained a kernel, and the resulting setup was akin to construction workers building a home with no supervision. As a result, programs tended to work independently of one another and could crash, or bring down the whole computer, if one bogged down.

The kernel provides another important feature called "preemptive multitasking," which allows programs to run independently of one another so that more than one can be used at the same time without freezing up. This function is analogous to traffic control at an intersection: with multitasking, a cop is at the corner directing traffic; without it, there is no cop and traffic runs fine until one motorist acts up and ties up every other car in the intersection. The Mac contained a rudimentary form of multitasking, but it was not sufficient to keep one program from affecting every other. As a result, you could, for example, be printing a document from a word processing program but be unable to close that application until the print job was completed.

Windows 95 would include a kernel, although not a great one, as some critics would say. Windows NT, on the other hand, featured a great kernel and was therefore considered state of the art. So any new Apple operating system would have to have a kernel. It just so happened that Apple had had a new kernel project, aptly called "NuKernel," that had been percolating down in the labs the past few years. "We would start with doing a new kernel, and then get developers in early," Hennigar recalls. "Then we'd sort of 'chunk' it along, doing one piece in eighteen months and another piece in eighteen more months, which is exactly what Bill Gates did." At Microsoft, this was the technique known as "evolution, not revolution," and it had, in fact, evolved Microsoft quite well.

Hennigar was the point person on the project, another of those wild, wacky Apple characters. She rode a Harley-Davidson, wore black tights and black leather boots, and had one side of her head shaved with the hair on the other side dyed in the Apple logo of six rainbow colors. Hennigar had also been one of those "cowboy" engineers from Gifford Calenda's System 7 "Blue" team and relished inviting coworkers over to her desk for a little nip of scotch that she poured into coffee cups. Hennigar played hard, but she also worked hard. And she was so hell bent on moving Raptor to a living, breathing product that she fired up the troops, and herself, by having her hairdresser sculpt an image of a raptor in her hair, dying it black so it would stand out.

Hennigar's first priority was to assemble a full-blown team that could figure out exactly what kind of operating system Raptor could come up with in time to head off Microsoft's "Chicago" system, soon to be called Windows 95. With 120 engineers working out of the system software headquarters in the R&D 3 building on the research campus, Hennigar concluded after a few weeks that the scope of the project would have to be limited because of the need to ship something before Windows 95 came out.

Hennigar and Proulx calculated that a working Raptor, under this plan, could be delivered with about a hundred engineers at a cost of about $20 million. They went to Rick Spitz and Dave Nagel for approval. Like Michael Spindler, Nagel was a great thinker, in addition to having a reputation as an inordinately nice guy. He had little experience in shipping a commercial product, although at NASA he had once brought to fruition a massive project involving more than three hundred researchers to develop a digital flight simulation facility. "To say I'm a researcher and cannot manage a project is nuts," says Nagel, who has a distinctly professorial look with his graying beard and hair and working attire of pleated slacks, long-sleeved shirt, and loafers. Nagel, moreover, was wrestling with Spindler's newly imposed budget restraints on engineering, which limited his resources for research.

"Dave wanted to know why we don't have 3-D," Hennigar remembers. "Some people at Apple were working on 3-D, but we didn't know when they would be done." Then Nagel started asking questions about why Apple even needed a new operating system. In fact, Proulx says, he held up the whole

Raptor project by insisting that the team prepare "white papers" to answer that question and other technical ones.

Proulx was so furious that, in November 1993, she stormed out of Apple altogether. Hennigar quit the same month. "In my exit interview with Dave Nagel, he asked what it would take for me to stay here," recalls Proulx, who returned to work on software projects at Digital. "I said, 'It will take a clear decision that you are moving forward and prepared to build this operating system.' He was not prepared to make a decision." Hennigar was frustrated, too, but she blamed Rick Spitz as much as Nagel for not taking more charge. By the accounts of many engineers from that time, Spitz was a pleasant, articulate fellow, known for keeping painstaking notes, but not an effective leader. "He couldn't spit without somebody telling him to do so," says Cary Clark, an Apple engineer between 1981 and 1994. As Hennigar adds, "I was a junior manager, and so it was hard for me to tell them, 'But wait, guys. But wait, guys.' "

Nagel says he never demanded white papers from Proulx, just a report "of two or three pages" defining in basic terms what Raptor would accomplish. "What I did not want to do was turn over a bunch of resources and time on a project that I wasn't even sure I was going to do," Nagel says. Rick Spitz adds that both he and Nagel were severely handicapped in committing to big projects at that time because of the budget limitations. This new emphasis on curbing the runaway R-and-D costs was laudable, except for the fact that it was being applied so arbitrarily that it had resulted in the death of Star Trek and was now endangering Raptor. In fact, shortly after Proulx and Hennigar left, Nagel and Spitz let Raptor die.

In the meantime, other software engineers were busy getting System 7 ready for the forthcoming Power Macintosh. That effort had begun as a small project called "Psychic TV." After Psychic TV, the Apple engineers' penchant for unusual project code names went into hyperdrive. First, Psychic TV was renamed "VO," or Version O. Next there was "VO.5," a new project to make even more of the old software code run enhanced, or "native," on the Power-PC microprocessor. That was a pretty esoteric code name, even for an engineer, so they renamed VO.5 "Capone," as in Chicago gangster Al Capone, because the engineers hoped this project would "kill" Microsoft's "Chicago" (Windows 95).

The problem with Capone, however, was that there was precious little code left from System 7 that could be rejiggered for PowerPC without unraveling the whole system. This was because the software code was so intertwined that if an engineer changed one piece of the operating system the rest of the pieces could suffer. Customers, moreover, were demanding more than a simple upgrade—they wanted memory protection and preemptive multitasking.

It was now a few days before Christmas 1993, and Dave Nagel was stewing over the operating system issue again. He told anyone who would listen, "Dammit, I need a kernel. I need memory protection." This was odd, many of the engineers thought, because Nagel had just killed Raptor, which would have given him both. But Raptor was, in Nagel's estimation, too big and unfocused. He needed something by the time Microsoft's "Chicago" was due to ship—within eighteen months, it was thought at the time. "Isn't there some way we can have something that we can say is memory protection, to get customers off our back?" Nagel asked his software engineers.[8]

Philip Koch, the quiet, intense man who had headed Psychic TV, and another senior engineer named Alan Mimms had an idea. Late one night, they camped out in front of Nagel's office, then located on the fourth floor of the R&D 1 building, waiting for him to leave. They cornered him as soon as he stepped out. "They said, 'We have to talk about Capone,' " according to a person who knew of the conversation. The trio went into a conference room—this one called "Finagle"—and closed the door. "They said, 'Maybe we can give you a little of what you want.' " Koch and Mimms recommended that Capone be scrapped in place of a new project, called "V1," in which essentially the only thing that would be done would be adding the new kernel, along with a new file system. It would take eighteen months to finish the project, and only twenty-seven engineers would be needed, they said. This was wildly optimistic, but it was what Nagel wanted to hear. Nagel looked at Koch, then at Mimms, and snapped, "Dammit, we're going to do that!"[9]

Thus was born Copland. It was not called that at first. After early 1994, when work began in earnest, the project went through several code names. The nerdy "V1" moniker was dropped for one called "Faraday," after Michael Faraday, the nineteenth-century English chemist and physicist who had discovered electromagnetic induction. That name soon gave way to "Maxwell," after the nineteenth-century Scottish physicist James Clerk Maxwell, known for illustrating the theory of kinetic gases, before finally becoming "Copland," after the late American composer Aaron Copland. (Apple's engineers liked to name some of their projects after scientists and artists, because they considered their work to be both scientific and artistic.) A composers' theme had begun during System 7, when the official code name for the project had been "Blue" but one used internally by the engineers for it had been "Mozart," after the eighteenth-century musical great Wolfgang Amadeus Mozart. (The name of another composer, the American George Gershwin, was used for the next operating system project that was planned replace to Copland, although no work would ever actually be done on that.)

Copland did, in fact, start out small. But it mutated almost as quickly as the code names did. At the core of the team, in early 1994, were just four people: Tim Dierks, a boyish-looking young man who served as the project's technical lead; Jeff Eliot, the project manager; Vito Salvaggio, in charge of product marketing; and Linda Lamar, the product manager. The team was headquartered out of R&D 2, on the research campus, and was overseen beginning in late 1994 by a new senior vice president of system software named Isaac "Ike" Nassi.

Short and rotund, Nassi was an engineer in the Dave Nagel mold, having been in charge of Apple's advanced research lab in Cambridge, Massachusetts, before being summoned by Nagel to take the place of Rick Spitz, whose responsibilities had shifted to vice president for education software development. Spitz finally left Apple in 1996, to become president of Meta Knowledge Interactive, a small software firm in Nashau, New Hampshire. Nassi was another "nice guy," according to the engineers who worked under him, but they described him as more of a research-oriented manager than one focused on quickly getting a finished product to market. Nassi, however, "categorically" rejects that description, saying he had successfully shipped computer products before joining Apple in 1989.

Nassi appointed as vice president, under him, another engineering manager named Mitch Allen, who would actually run the Copland project. Allen could have passed for one of Steve Jobs's old pirates because he actually looked like one, with his wedge-shaped face and shoulder-length hair. The other key member of the Copland team was an engineer named Wayne Meretsky, who became the technical leader of the core operating system portion of Copland. Meretsky was a domineering, volatile man who had a habit of losing his temper and disrupting meetings. He was a brilliant, legendary figure at Apple, though, and would often clash with Allen over the direction of the project.

Copland was first announced publicly in March 1994, when the Power Macs started rolling off the line. By the end of the year, the core Copland team had ballooned to about fifty engineers, while hundreds more worked full-time to support the project. These included fifty members of a team devoted to the project called "NuKernel," who were helping to supply the mandatory kernel. Other engineering groups throughout Apple were working on Copland versions of QuickDraw (the Mac's drawing and painting capability), sound managers, memory, and just about everything else except the kitchen sink. And this was Copland's downfall. Copland had essentially started with the goal of producing a new kernel. As the months wore on, though, it expanded to include everything from new graphical screens that could be configured to a user's taste (such as a child being able to add more color and sounds) to electronic "agents" that could automatically back up the hard drive and perform other mundane tasks.

Dave Nagel says that he tried to keep Copland focused as much as he could but the project was almost impossible to contain. For one thing, he says, the new operating system would have to be able to run Apple's QuickTime multimedia technology, because the company's strongest market was in the multimedia-oriented world of desktop publishing. Nagel says he was also besieged with demands by product-marketing managers throughout Apple to include additional features, such as enhanced graphical capabilities and networking access, to compete against Microsoft's "Chicago" project. Too, as Ike Nassi remembers, Apple was being bombarded with requests for even more features from software developers and other Apple supporters outside the company, in order to outmaneuver Microsoft. "They were saying, 'Apple, you are our only hope,' " Nassi remembers. "Dave was really looking for any way he could to help with that."

As a result, Copland morphed into another of those enormous projects, called "bloated pigdogs" by one engineer, that never see the light of day because they keep getting bigger and bigger in terms of product features. By 1996, fully five hundred Apple engineers were committed to various aspects of Copland, drawing some $250 million a year from the company's engineering resources.

"The question from management was 'How can we build the one, true, perfect operating system?' " recalls one of the Copland engineers, who quit the team in 1995 out of certainty it would never ship. "This whole move to a new kernel represented vast changes for the Mac OS. It was like pulling on a string. You pull and pull, and that implies changing more and more of your old code. As a result, we ended up like we were going to have to do a complete rewrite. From day one, I didn't think this was going to work." Putting in a new kernel was hard enough, and in fact that was mainly all that Philip Koch and Alan Mimms had proposed to do when they convinced Dave Nagel to sign off on a new operating system during Christmas of 1993. That might have worked, had Dave Nagel, Ike Nassi, and Mitch Allen adhered strictly to that plan. Because they did not, Copland's delivery schedule slipped from 1995 to 1996 to 1997, earning the regular top ranking on a monthly "VaporList" of long-simmering industry projects compiled by the influential industry newsletter "P. C. Letter."

There was actually considerable dissension within the Copland team as to the project's direction. The volatile Wayne Meretsky, for example, repeatedly warned Mitch Allen that Copland had become too big and would be doomed to fail, according to engineers who heard these discussions. Allen, a strong-willed manager in his own right, insisted on staying the course.

Ike Nassi was worried about Copland, too, but he hesitated to intervene because time was running short. "I could have done radical organizational surgery or let them continue down the path they wanted and fix things later as we went along," Nassi says, adding that he had chosen that latter path because it would be less disruptive. Dave Nagel adds that Copland was also hindered by unexpected pitfalls, such as when an engineer in charge of writing a new file system approached him to announce that it did not work—more than a year into the project. "And this person had been adamant all along that he was close to schedule," Nagel says, declining to reveal the engineer's name.

The episode underscored Copland's fundamental problem: Apple, by virtue of having failed or fallen short in its previous operating system projects Pink, Taligent, and System 7 (Blue), was in the position of having to compress four years of work into a two-year period. Even Microsoft, with its demonstrated prowess in shipping new operating system versions, would have been hard pressed to meet this schedule. "We always said this would be a risky project," Nagel says.

The beginning of the end for Copland came on May 13, 1996, when software developers had gathered to hear Gil Amelio's turnaround strategy and came away empty-handed without a Copland beta, which had been promised by Apple months earlier. "We missed that by a mile," recalls one of the Copland engineers, who, like others still working at Apple at the time of their interviews for this book, spoke on condition of anonymity. "It was, at that point, all over." Copland was over, many of these engineers thought, because Apple had missed this crucial deadline, putting the already-delayed project hopelessly beyond schedule.

After that crucial deadline was blown, morale was so low among Apple's engineers that the company's R and D came almost to a halt. "People were leaving early and coming in late," recalls the Copland engineer. "It was a fantasy land, and really eerie." As the summer of 1996 began, Amelio ordered an emergency evaluation of Copland to see if it could be revived. The senior engineers responsible for Copland—Wayne Meretsky and Winston Hendrickson, along with Koch and others—recommended that Copland be scrapped and replaced by the original V1 project for just a kernel and new file system— no bells and whistles this time. In fact, that is what Koch and Alan Mimms had originally recommended to Nagel. Ike Nassi offered another alternative. Fearing that Copland would not be able to deliver, he had secretly deployed a small team to develop another microkernel. Nassi proposed to Amelio that Copland simply be dropped on top of that technology, since it was nearly completed.

Amelio, however, did not believe he had the luxury of time to pursue only those options. "I had to scramble and decide what we needed to do," Amelio recalls. Shortly after the Worldwide Developers Conference, he had instituted a shake-up of the entire organization, surrounding himself with a five-member executive team that included George Scalise, the chief administrative officer; Fred Anderson, the CFO; Marco Landi, the chief operating officer and previously president of Apple's business in Europe, Africa, and the Middle East; John Floisand, executive vice president of worldwide sales, who had been head of Apple Pacific; and Satjiv Chahil, senior vice president of worldwide marketing, who had been running Apple's entertainment and new media business.

The new structure would prove every bit as convoluted as the ones orchestrated by Michael Spindler. In fact, Apple Americas President Jim Buckley resigned shortly afterward after going on record within the executive suite that he did not think Amelio's organization would work. Marketing functions, for one thing, were dispersed across twenty-two different organizations. After eleven years with Apple, Buckley went on to become president and CEO of CBT Group Plc, a fast-growing developer of interactive training software in Menlo Park, California. Nagel also resigned, to head up the AT&T Labs. By the end of the year, resignations would also be accepted from two of the three remaining "S"s from the Spindler era: Kevin Sullivan and Ed Stead.

Although Sullivan would later characterize his departure as amicable, saying he was ready to move on after so many years, a friend in whom he confided said he had complained that summer of "being moved to Molokai," a reference to the former leper colony on the Hawaiian island, after he and Stead were moved to offices off the City Center 3 executive floor. As for the last remaining "S," David Seda, he remained as an executive aide to Amelio but left the company in 1997. But he held none of the influence he had before, when he, Sullivan, and Stead had held such great sway over Michael Spindler. Amelio, indeed, seemed then not to be influenced by anybody. He was the boss, and that was that.

"Gil said his philosophy was to let people 'self-select' whether they will stay at the company or not," says one former member of the Amelio administration. "He said, 'People will show their colors over time.'"

There was actually supposed to be a sixth executive reporting directly to Amelio: the chief technical officer. Since he had not yet filled that post, Amelio appointed himself CTO for the interim. That delay, however, would prove a mistake in the eyes of some Apple executives, for time was running out faster than he expected. Copland was dead; it just had not been unplugged from life support yet. Indeed, a former Apple executive maintains that Amelio had been warned about the problems with Copland by then-CFO Joe Graziano in 1995, when Amelio was only an Apple board member.

Amelio, however, says he was so busy shoring up Apple's cash position those first few months that he did not have time to address Copland. "It wasn't until June that I got focused on the operating system," Amelio recalls. "After I studied Copland, I realized it wasn't a winner."

The doctor was going to have to come up with a solution to the software problem that was now paramount in determining Apple's survival. In a drama befitting Apple's storied history, it would bring him face to face with the ghosts of Apple's past.

16

NeXT: A Founder's Return

There are few places more uncomfortable than Boston, Massachusetts, in August. With the temperature in the nineties and the humidity level often that high, the misery index is so overwhelming that you can break into a soaking sweat just by walking from your car into a shopping mall. Ever since 1984, though, the faithful customers, developers, and vendors of Apple Computer had persevered through these stifling conditions to attend the annual Macworld Expo held there for East Coast Macintosh enthusiasts. The week of August 7, 1996, when Macworld descended on Boston again, the fifty thousand show-goers got welcome relief from the weather, which was unseasonably cool and dry, as well as from the state of affairs at Apple.

Gil Amelio had been awfully busy in his first six months on the job. He had reshuffled the executive ranks. He had chopped expenses and obtained new loans, shoring up Apple's cash position to $1.4 billion—$1 billion more than the coffers had held when he had taken over. And most important, he seemed to have arrested Apple's frightening downward spiral. Apple's financial results for the fiscal third quarter, ended on June 28, showed surprisingly strong revenues of $2.17 billion—flat from the prior quarter—and a lower-than-expected loss of $32 million.

Although Apple continued to lose market share in this period (its year-over-year revenues declined by 15 percent compared to an 18 percent increase in growth of the overall PC market), the fact that revenues had stabilized from the disastrous two quarters before was cause for measured jubilation in Boston. On the night before the show opened, Apple tried to whip up a festive atmosphere by hosting a rock 'n' roll shindig at the Roxy, a popular nightclub in downtown Boston frequented by many tourists. Inside, a six-member band called Eight to the Bar belted out numbers such as "Mustang Sally" and "Shake, Rattle, and Roll," as waiters and waitresses served guests potato wedges, fried shrimp, and other goodies; all as the images of Apple's famous

"1984" commercial played silently, over and over, on video monitors surrounding the dance floor.

During a break in the music, the Mac's great cheerleader, Guy Kawasaki, bounded onstage to crack a few lame jokes, one of which poked fun at Apple. "What's the difference between Apple and the Cub Scouts?" he asked, looking around the packed house in his black T-shirt and blue jeans. "The Cub Scouts have adult supervision." Then he introduced Marco Landi, the new COO. Landi was a relative newcomer to Apple, having taken over the company's European business in 1995 after serving for more than twenty years at Texas Instruments, the big semiconductor maker. Landi was a certified "suit" who looked out of place in this gathering of Mac enthusiasts in their T-shirts and jeans as he strode out in his blue, tieless shirt and dress pants. "I am convinced we have a bright future," Landi proclaimed in his singsong Italian accent.

That would not be so if Landi's taste in film were any indication. Asked on Apple's Internet page to provide certain personal preferences, he listed a most unfortunate choice as his favorite movie of all time: *The Alamo.* Kawasaki interjected more levity when he pointed out the distinctly Italian lineage of Apple's new management team: "We have Amelio. We have Scalise. We have Landi. You think I should change my name to Guido Kawasaki?" Loud laughter from the crowd. Pointing out that a grand total of 25 million Macintoshes had been made as of that date, Landi went on to say, "We want to celebrate not only the past but the future. We want to continue changing the world. Is that what you want to do?" The crowd: "Yes!" Landi then theatrically stripped off his dress shirt to reveal an Apple T-shirt underneath. Hey, I'm cool after all, he seemed to suggest.

The next morning, at 8:30, a line of 1,500 people snaked around the block to enter the John Hancock Center, waiting for the doors to open so they could hear Gil Amelio's keynote address for the show. This would be Amelio's first Macworld keynote, and it was highly anticipated by both the press and the Macintosh industry because he was expected to deliver a state-of-the-company report, six months into his new term. Inside the theater, when the throng of Mac supporters had taken their seats, rock music blared from speakers on the stage as a man was overheard grumbling to his seatmate, "It used to be you'd see people like Bill Atkinson [a member of the original Macintosh team] at these things. It's like Christopher Columbus. Now we have guys who say, 'I was on the boat with Chris.' " The lights went down, and Colin Crawford, president and CEO of the trade Macworld, which was helping to put the show on, stepped onstage, surveyed the sea of expectant faces, and proclaimed, "It sure doesn't feel like we're here for a wake." He then introduced the man of the hour, Gil Amelio.

When Amelio emerged to take the podium in his striped blue suit, he was greeted with a hero's welcome. The applause lasted for a full thirty seconds, and when it finally died down, Amelio, looking far more at ease than he had at the Worldwide Developers Conference three months before, started off, "I'm going to just relax and have some fun here with you." Then, pointing out the replenished cash in the bank, he added, "And so Apple's survival is no longer in question. That's not the issue. The issue now is, how exciting is it going to be? How exciting can we make it?"

To muster up some of that excitement, Amelio called out a young man named Frank Casanova, who seemed to embody the image of Apple hipness with his flowing, shoulder-length hair, green sport jacket, and black shirt. Casanova, Apple's director of advanced prototying research and longtime demo master, previewed software that could transform a digital photograph into liquefied images and watched as an eleven-year-old boy named Gregory Miller, son of an Apple engineer, used a forthcoming graphical program called "Cocoa" to create a simple video game for play on the Internet.

It was indeed cool stuff, and it drew the expected cheers and applause. The applause was even heartier at the end of the two-hour keynote, when a video clip was shown of the boy, a fifth-grader with short brown hair and rosy cheeks, being asked what he wanted to be when he grew up. Standing on a skateboard, Miller smiled impishly and said, "I want to be president of Apple Computer." Pause. And "Yes, I'm certain Apple will be around." The music from *Mission: Impossible* then cranked up. Afterward, attendees were revved up. "Gil doesn't talk that well, but I don't care. He rescued the company," said Demian Rosenblatt, whose business card read "New Media Guru" for an advertising agency. "I think Amelio and Apple are, like, a perfect fit. It's, like, karma."

At the show itself, the Apple community seemed to be more spirited than ever. Over at the downtown World Trade Center, overlooking Boston Harbor, Steve Kahng's Power Computing (the successful Macintosh clone maker) was grabbing all the attention with a 225-foot bungee crane it had erected to tout the company's newest lineup of 225-megahertz PowerTower Pro machines, the fastest Mac on Earth. By this time, Power had shot up to some $200 million in annual revenues and was so popular among Mac enthusiasts that crowds spilled into the aisles surrounding the sprawling Power Computing booth, which was festooned with placards reading "We're fighting back for the Mac!"

Nearby, almost lost in the Power Computing pandemonium, was a small booth showcasing a new arrival to the Mac licensing market, UMAX Technologies Inc. UMAX, a Fremont, California–based subsidiary of a Taiwanese company, UMAX Data Systems, had recently purchased its Mac license from Radius, the company run by Chuck Berger (formerly Apple's vice president of business development), after Radius's high-end clones had failed to attain many sales. In June, UMAX, targeting the low end of the market, had shipped its first Mac clone, called the SuperMac, and almost immediately had been inundated with a $19 million backlog of orders. This was a good sign for the Mac market, because it showed there was still demand, even if it was not going to Apple. Earlier in the year, Amelio had welcomed in another licensee, Motorola. Motorola was a giant in cellular phones, pagers, and semiconductors but had little experience in personal computers. Still, it was a big name.

Yes, the Mac world was breathing a deep sigh of relief. But Amelio secretly was not, despite his calm demeanor during the keynote. Halfway through his speech, he lobbed a subtle bombshell that took a while longer for some of the attendees to digest. It involved Copland and signaled for the first time that Copland could not be counted on to solve Apple's operating system crisis. Given the complexities involved in bringing a brand-new operating system to market, Amelio said, Copland would be released in dribs and drabs as regular biannual upgrades to the existing Mac system. "So the stuff has been sitting on the shelf and we're saying, 'It's not like wine; it doesn't age very well,' you know?" Amelio said. "Copland will appear, but it's going to appear over a series of releases. . . . We're just not going to have this big event; rather we're going to roll it out as we can."

It took a few days for those words to sink in, but what Amelio had actually done was pull the plug on Copland as an all-or-nothing software release. He had something else up his sleeve. Apple had missed the crucial deadline to get an early version of Copland into the hands of its developers back during the May 13 conference in San Jose. After that the engineers had pretty much given up hope on the project, as had Amelio. As with every other aspect of Apple, he knew he would have to take control of engineering. "Amelio told a manager he had never seen a company where the engineers take the CEO's direction as a suggestion," said one Copland engineer, to whom the comment was relayed by the manager. Amelio had named himself the chief technology officer, but he knew he needed a true technology manager if he was going to kick-start R and D again. So before the Macworld show, he turned again to a former colleague: Ellen Hancock, who had been one of his three chief operating officers at National Semiconductor. On the Fourth of July, he named her chief technology officer and executive vice president.

Hancock, a short woman with close-cropped silver hair and a penchant for conservative pantsuits, carried herself like an executive with a lot of business experience. Indeed, at fifty-three years of age, she was a seasoned twenty-eight year veteran of IBM who had overseen much of Big Blue's hardware and software work in computer networking. Having once worked with Amelio, when she was at IBM and Amelio was participating in a Big Blue project while still at Rockwell, Hancock had moved to National Semiconductor to assist Amelio in his turnaround there. She had resigned in May 1996 after being passed over for the CEO's job when the National board had recruited Brian Halla from LSI Logic Corporation.

The selection of Hancock was considered curious by some in the industry. IBM was considered a stark opposite of Apple in terms of corporate environment and philosophy. It was a company of lemmings, managers following blindly behind older, plodding executives in a predictable, unruffled bureaucracy. The last thing Apple needed was a plodding bureaucrat. It needed lightning-fast decisions. Hancock, though, would quickly demonstrate that she was in no mood for plodding around. Stern of expression and decisive, she came to be called "the Iron Grandmother" by some engineers. "I did, by the way, talk to the engineering teams and say, 'Give me a [shipping] date,' " Hancock recalls of her first days on the job at Apple.

One of the first groups Hancock met with at Apple was the one from Copland. Sitting in a conference room on Apple's sprawling R-and-D campus, she sat and listened for hours as Copland's top engineers and managers summarized the project's status. What she heard did not sound good. For one thing, she discovered that Copland had been engineered in such a way that the two biggest goals for its improvement over the Macintosh operating system — memory protection, to prevent computers from crashing, and preemptive multitasking, to allow the user to seamlessly use several programs at once — were being included only in the operating system. The software programs themselves would not benefit from these improvements until a later release. This was a huge problem, of course, because users spend almost all their time working on programs.

"I came away from that meeting, frankly, worried," Hancock told me, sipping a bottle of mineral water in her corner office on the ground floor of the R&D 3 building.

Following the debacle of the Worldwide Developers Conference in May, when the developer's release of Copland had failed to ship, Apple had planned to make up for the delay by giving it to developers at the Macworld Boston show in August. However, Hancock and Amelio had concluded that Copland was so bad that they ordered a stop to that rollout, as well. Without a full-blown Copland to show, Hancock and Amelio settled on the interim solution of incorporating certain features from Copland into the biannual upgrades to the existing Mac system that Amelio announced in Boston.

Upon returning from Macworld Boston, though, Amelio and Hancock were faced with the same dilemma: coming up with a replacement for the Macintosh operating system. And just as he had gone outside Apple to recruit its top technologist, Amelio started looking outside for a solution to the Copland problem. A methodical scientist, Amelio carefully pored over a checklist of possible options. There were essentially three: Start from scratch to develop a new operating system. License an operating system from someone else. Or buy an operating system.

"Developing internally would mean major reforming of Copland and would probably cause the schedule to slip another year to year and a half. That was unacceptable," Amelio recalls. "In licensing, there wasn't really anything compelling in terms of what I could do. I mean, how many other personal computer operating systems are out there? It's mainly [Microsoft's Windows] NT and Windows 95. But even if we were interested in those, there were technical barriers. So the only other thing that came back was, I had to buy something." In settling on this option, Amelio looked all the way to an inimitable Frenchman named Jean-Louis Gassée. That's right. *That* Jean-Louis Gassée.

After John Sculley had finally found the courage to fire him back in 1990, Gassée had remained uncharacteristically quiet. But that was only because he had immersed himself in one of those Silicon Valley "skunk works" projects that are carried out in absolute secrecy. Just days after walking out of Apple for the last time, Gassée had secretly formed a new company with former Apple engineer Steve Sakoman, who had started Apple's work on the Newton technology. Their idea was to build a brand-new desktop computer, with a new operating system. Before they could settle into work, though, the two men needed a name for their venture. "I came up with 'United Technoids Inc.,' " Gassée remembers, "but Steve thought that was a little sophomoric. So Steve said he would look through the dictionary for a name. One day, I asked how far he had gotten. He said, 'Oh, I'm tired. I stopped at "B." I said, 'Be is nice.' End of story."

Thus was born Be Inc. Gassée and Sakoman went on to recruit a team of former Apple engineers, including Erich Ringewald, one of the founding members of the old Pink team that had tried to design a new Macintosh operating system, and Bob Harold, one of the early members of the Newton team. Working largely from their homes the first years, the Be engineers assembled a machine called the BeBox. Unlike existing desktop computers, which were designed to run on a single microprocessor, these machines were designed to run on two or more, vastly increasing performance. And the Be operating system they designed contained a microkernel, which provides memory protection and multitasking—the two key features the Macintosh lacked.

By 1995, Be was a bona fide enterprise, with thirty employees and $14 million in backing from French and American investors. (Gassée had managed to round that money up after initially footing the tab for Be's expenses out of his own pocket. At one point, in fact, he had had to take out a mortgage on his home to meet the payroll.) Finally, in September 1995, Gassée took the wraps off Be at the Agenda conference, an exclusive meeting of the computer industry's top executives that is hosted each year by the influential industry consultant Stewart Alsop in Scottsdale, Arizona. When Gassée unveiled his secret BeBox, the Agenda audience was so impressed they gave him a standing ovation, a rare honor at this conference of product-jaded executives.

"Jean-Louis Gassée wants to make computing fun again," David Coursey wrote afterward in his "P. C. Letter," in a front-page column entitled "The Incredible Brightness of Be Inc." "If he's successful, the BeBox will be every computer geek's second (third, fourth, fifth . . .) machine. Gassée will also have succeeded in lighting a nice fire under Microsoft and Apple as they play catch up." In his demonstration at Agenda, Gassée made his BeBox play animated 3-D graphics, show a movie, download a Web page, and play multiple streams of audio—all at the *same* time. "I have a very simple marketing strategy, which is to expose the exciting to the excitable," Gassée told Coursey in an interview with him afterward.[1]

This appeared to be a truly revolutionary product, and it was one that Gassée went out of his way to design in a manner that would not repeat his critical mistakes at Apple. Foremost among those: the machine would not be priced out of the reach of the mass market. Indeed, Gassée told David Coursey in that interview in 1995 that his goal was to market the BeBox for $2,000 or less. Coursey was so enamored of the machine that, in February 1996, he wrote an open letter to Gil Amelio in "P. C. Letter" recommending that Apple adopt the BeBox as its next-generation Macintosh. "The great part about this arrangement is that since the Be team really is part of Apple, you can commercialize the BeBox without having to confront the not-invented-here syndrome that has paralyzed Apple over the past decade," Coursey wrote in his February 19 issue.

Coursey's argument made a lot of sense. The BeBox ran on PowerPC microprocessors, just as Apple's new Power Mac did. It was designed around the Common Hardware Reference Platform (CHRP) specifications set forth in 1994 by Apple, IBM, and Motorola for future PowerPC machines. And, of course its operating system, called the Be OS, contained the microkernel needed for memory protection and preemptive multitasking. There was one downside, however, and it was a biggie: the Be OS had not been designed to be "backward-compatible"; it could run none of the existing Macintosh programs. The reason for this, Coursey postulated, was that Gassée had recognized that the Be OS would have been too burdened down by adding in all the software code needed to run old programs. In fact, the Be OS had precious little software support at all. It was a diamond in the rough and one that Coursey and a growing number of people in the industry began to press Amelio to hone as Apple's own.

Back in his Apple days, Jean-Louis Gassée had been no shrinking violent when it came to self-promotion. Since leaving Apple in 1990, he had lain low. But with the announcement of the BeBox, he launched such a strong round of familiar self-promotion that some people in the industry suspected him of starting a campaign to inundate Amelio with e-mail testimonials about the Be technology. In June 1996, Amelio telephoned another Be supporter, an independent software entrepreneur named Peter Barrett, and invited Barrett to meet with him in Cupertino after reading Barrett's glowing praise of Be in an article in *Fortune.*

Barrett, a young, blond-haired Australian who had helped shape the technical direction of companies including the unsuccessful video-game maker Rocket Science Games Inc., decided to surprise Amelio. He spent a week developing a prototype of the Mac running on top of the Be OS. During his meeting with Amelio in Apple's eighth-floor Synergy room atop City Center 3, Barrett told Amelio there was no way, no how that Copland was going to solve any of the Mac's key problems of memory protection and multitasking, because it was simply too big to run well. Also sitting in on the meeting were the brilliant Larry Tesler, the former Xerox PARCer who had headed the early work on Newton and was now in charge of Apple's Internet strategy, as well as Ike Nassi, the research-oriented protégé of the scholarly Dave Nagel, who was heading system software.

"Apple needs to break from the past and build a modern operating system," Barrett told Amelio. "It's a new world, and Copland is outdated already. One way to do this is to buy Be. I think it could be a strategy to save Apple." Then Barrett demonstrated his Mac/Be prototype. "Ike Nassi seemed furious," reports Barrett. "He became very agitated." Nassi remembers that Be "was an interesting operating system, but that the most important things were missing—like backward compatibility."

Under Ellen Hancock, Nassi would become a lot more agitated. By the end of 1996, after seven tiring years at Apple, both he and Mitch Allen, the principal manager over Copland, would tender their resignations, or, in Amelio's parlance, "self-select." Nassi, who is now a visiting scholar at the University of California at Berkeley, says he resigned after Amelio and Hancock "locked" him out of any discussions concerning the Be OS. He blames the failure of Copland on the fact that it simply started too late, in 1994. "It should have started in 1991 or 1992," he says.

Suddenly, Jean-Louis Gassée was the Be-all and end-all. At about the same time that Peter Barrett and other industry luminaries were talking up Be, Gil Amelio was quietly putting a feeler out to Gassée about a possible Apple acquisition of the Be operating system. As Gassée remembers the chain of events, Apple first contacted him in early June, when Chief Administrative Officer George Scalise telephoned him to suggest a meeting. During the meeting in an Apple conference room a few days later, attended by Scalise and Doug Solomon, Apple's vice president for corporate development, Gassée gave a demonstration of the Be OS.

"Doug Solomon asked what our valuation of Be would be," Gassée says, looking stylish as always in a black vest, checkered shirt, and pressed jeans as he sipped coffee in the outdoor patio of a café one overcast morning across the street from Be's headquarters in Menlo Park. "I said, 'I don't know.' And I said I would not want to have discussions like this without talking to my board."

The next time Gassée met with an Apple executive to discuss Be was the following month, in July, when he attended a dinner hosted by Apple's new vice president of developer relations, Heidi Roizen, at her home in the ultra-exclusive community of Atherton. Atherton is a small town, really, with only about 7,000 residents, but it contains some of the highest-priced real estate in California, with gated mansions, tree-lined lanes, and private tennis courts and swimming pools—all sandwiched in the middle of Silicon Valley be-tween Interstate 280 and U.S. Highway 101. Standing at Roizen's kitchen counter, Gassée found himself chatting with Ellen Hancock, Apple's new CTO.

"Ellen said, 'You and I are going to be the deal makers on this one,' " Gassée recalls. "I said, 'If that's what you want.' " Hancock does not remember any substantive discussion about Be at that party. "He and I just chatted in the kitchen," she says. "He gave me some advice on how to manage engineers at Apple."

More and more, as the summer of 1996 progressed, Be was being touted by people in the industry as Apple's savior. At Macworld Boston, Be's tiny booth in a remote corner of the Bayside Exposition Center overflowed with admiring onlookers. Back at the World Trade Center, the sister convention hall for the Macworld show, more throngs gathered in the Power Computing booth to view the Be operating system running on one of Steve Kahng's Power computers. All this hoopla was an exceptionally ironic turn of events for Apple—and a humiliating one, too, since it had been this very same Jean-Louis Gassée who had devised the high-price, low-market-share strategy that had failed miserably and sealed Apple's current fate. Yet here was Jean-Louis again, back to save the day. To be sure, Gassée had learned much from his mistakes at Apple. He was humbler, for one thing, and had come to appreci-ate the value of software over hardware. Back in the Apple days, he had pri-marily been interested in bigger, faster machines.

Later in August, Gassée was invited to another dinner in Silicon Valley with Ellen Hancock, this time a formal business affair also attended by Apple's chief operating officer, Marco Landi, and a Be board member named David Marquardt, who also serves on the board of Microsoft. Over their meals at the Woodside Village Pub, which specializes in such hearty fare as lamb chops, pork chops, and steak, Gassée and Hancock started talking turkey. "Ellen said, 'If you can deliver [a combination Mac/Be OS] six months earlier to market than we can, then we can have a deal,' " Gassée recalls. (Hancock will not talk about the details of these negotiations.)

On August 29, 1996, *The Wall Street Journal* let the cat out of the bag. Quoting an unnamed source, a *Journal* article declared that Apple was in discussions for a possible acquisition of Be. Talks between Amelio and Gassée continued for weeks. In the interim, Apple's morale—and its stock price—got another shot in the arm when the company released its financial results for the fiscal fourth quarter, ended on September 27, showing a profit of $25 million, despite a continued slide in sales from the year before. The profit was not very great, considering that Apple had sold $2.32 billion worth of computers that quarter. But since Amelio had not been predicting a return to profitability for another six months, it was a pleasant surprise for Wall Street, which initially ratcheted the stock price up $3 a share to $28, the highest level in months.

The share price quickly subsided, though, when investors concluded that the profit had come mostly from cost cuts, not from any fundamental improvement in Apple's health. Indeed, fourth-quarter sales were actually *down* 23 percent from the same quarter a year earlier, accelerating the erosion in market share. Amelio was running into another roadblock, one that was partly his own doing. By the middle of October, the talks between Apple and Be had been under way for nearly five months, in one fashion or another. Initially, the discussions had centered on the Be OS's technical capability and how Be could be merged into Apple's research engine. Gassée favored his company becoming a separate research arm of Apple, called Modern OS, with Be engineer Erich Ringewald in charge. As for himself, Gassée insists that he wanted only a minor role at Apple—so minor that he told Amelio's executives, "I will work for a dollar a year."

Gassée had never been a charitable guy when it came to business, though, and he fully intended to cash in big off his alma mater. So while it was true that he never wanted much actual money from Apple, he did want a substantial stake in the company's future—like 10 percent of its outstanding shares in exchange for Be. With Apple's 120 million shares trading for about $23 apiece in the early fall of 1996, that would have translated into a windfall to Gassée and his investors—on paper—of nearly $300 million. Not bad for a company that he and the investors had built for less than $20 million without having shipped a product to market!

"Apple resisted that idea, because they thought their stock at the time was undervalued," Gassée says. "But we wanted everyone there to understand that we were willing to lash ourselves to the mast. If Apple does well, we do well; if Apple goes down, we go down."

Apple insisted that any deal be consummated in cash, since Gil Amelio believed the company's stock was too depressed in value to be doling out in such huge chunks. As Gassée haggled with Ellen Hancock on that and the postmerger organizational issues, which were still not resolved, he says, Amelio telephoned him one day in late October and asked him to fly to the Hawaiian island of Kauai immediately. for a private meeting. (Amelio was on Kauai then, to speak at Apple's Asia-Pacific sales conference.) Since Gassée lives only twenty minutes away from Amelio in Silicon Valley, he says he found it a bit odd that Amelio could not wait to talk until he returned from Hawaii. Nevertheless, Gassée boarded the next jet to Hawaii and found himself sitting in a conference room of the Marriott Kauai, facing Amelio and his executive assistant, David Seda.

This is Gassée's version of events. Amelio's is completely different. "That's a total bullshit story," Amelio says. "Jean-Louis wanted to see me. I said I would be delighted to see him. However, I was getting ready to leave for Hawaii, and [I said] that I would see him as soon as I got back. He didn't want to wait until I got back. So he came out there. I was only going to be there two or three days."

It was a typically glorious day in paradise. Sunbathers lounged by the pool outside. Palm trees swayed gently in the breeze as the waves of the blue Pacific crashed onto a nearby beach. For an hour and a half, Amelio and Gassée met. It was a pleasant meeting, for the most part. They discussed Amelio's strategy to revive Apple. They also talked about the technical issues facing the Macintosh operating system. Finally, near the end of the meeting, Amelio looked straight at Gassée and asked, "What will it take to do this deal?" Gassée recalls. "I told him, 'As soon as we get these organizational issues resolved, we can talk money.' "

Amelio did not say so in this meeting, but he had complained to David Marquardt, the Be board member, that he was convinced Gassée wanted to "wring the last penny out of the deal," Gassée says Marquardt told him. Amelio agrees that he was concerned about how much to pay Gassée but primarily about the fact that Apple would still have to spend as much as $100 million in extra research money to make the Be OS work on the Mac. It is probably not surprising that Gassée wanted so much. After all, he had always been a premium-price guy at heart. What disturbed many people outside Apple, however, was how naïvely they felt Amelio had negotiated the opportunity by tipping his hand at Macworld Boston, when he had all but pulled the plug on Copland. Gassée, for all practical purposes, had thereby become the only known game in town and felt he could name his price for an exciting operating system solution to Apple's tired technology.

Pressure was indeed mounting on Amelio to come up with an operating system strategy, one way or another. As popular *MacWEEK* writer Don Crabb wrote in his "Steamed Crabb" column on October 24, "Unfortunately, a number of Apple's key developers have no more patience to give. They have no more interest in a platform that they believe has used up its ninth life and more. They have no more development cycles to waste on software that may or may not have to be completely rewritten to work with a new OS . . . , a new strategic vision."

For most of the computer world, it did not really matter what Apple did or when it did it. By that point, the industry was so dominated by Microsoft Windows and Intel's Pentium chip technology that when the annual Comdex extravaganza opened in Las Vegas on November 18, it was almost a tribute to that duopoly. As always during Comdex week, Las Vegas was a logistical nightmare. The 1996 show drew a record 210,000 attendees at exhibit venues spread from the Las Vegas Convention Center to the Sands Expo and Convention Center. Workshops, demonstrations, and meetings were scheduled in practically every hotel conference room and suite in town. And participants spent much of their time waiting in two-hour taxi lines or queued up at restaurants and in check-in lines for exorbitantly priced hotels.

Inside the Las Vegas Convention Center, the joint was so packed you could hardly move, with sights and sounds launching an all-out assault on the senses. Off in one booth, a Mexican mariachis band was in full swing. At another, a parade of male and female fashion models strutted their stuff. And the most crowded place of all was the Microsoft Partner Pavilion, a massive booth featuring the latest products from Microsoft and its Windows developers. Intel had a high profile, too, since this Comdex was celebrating the twenty-fifth anniversary of Intel's introduction of the world's first microprocessor, which had made this whole phenomenal industry possible. Appropriately, two of the featured keynote speakers at this show were Bill Gates and Intel's Andy Grove.

And where was Apple Computer? Apple had a booth, but it was obscured in a remote corner of the convention hall, nearly devoid of foot traffic as showgoers scurried through the hundreds of Wintel-related exhibits. Even the once-bustling PowerPC Pavilion was as deserted as a ghost town, in contrast to the fabled Comdex in 1993, when the forces of PowerPC had vowed to wrench domination of the industry from Microsoft and Intel. Inside the PowerPC Pavilion tent, the only demonstration computers running on PowerPC were Macintoshes, made by Apple, Power Computing, UMAX, and Motorola. One Apple and three clones: four companies up against hundreds. There were strobe lights and a digital art gallery, creating the effect of a high-tech museum. At this rate, the Macintosh did, in fact seem destined for the Smithsonian.

Apple tried to raise its voice above the din, inviting journalists and analysts to a party one night atop the 1,194-foot Stratosphere, a hotel and casino that features the Let It Ride Roller Coaster and Big Shot thrill ride one hundred stories above the ground. But even this setting was curiously apropos to Apple's dilemma. The party rooms were small and crowded, made more claustrophobic by deafening rock music. Outside the windows glittered the neon lights of the Las Vegas Strip. But the Stratosphere was situated in a decrepit neighborhood, all by itself, blocks from the Strip—so near, yet so far from the real action of Las Vegas's grand casinos. Just like Apple. The Stratosphere was struggling financially, its isolation a hindrance to capturing enough business. Apple, too, was teetering—on the brink of irrelevance.

Ironically, the company that had started the whole PC revolution two decades earlier was in a poor position to influence a new revolution that was sweeping through the industry and was the theme of this Comdex show. The revolution was the Internet, and everywhere you looked there were products being introduced that sought to capitalize on the enormous potential of this new medium to enhance worldwide communications and information. Just as the PC, a tool that dramatically increased people's productivity both at work and at home had transformed society, the Internet, with its vast, interlinked libraries of cyberdata all over the world, held the potential for providing limitless information at the touch of a computer keyboard.

The personal computer was thus evolving from primarily a productivity tool to an information and communications resource. The Internet is so powerful that in the extensive research I did for this book, I obtained everything from back issues of newspapers and magazines to corporate profiles, SEC filings, and even home telephone numbers of prospective contacts—all without ever leaving my computer (a Macintosh, by the way). Just type in a keyword while on line, and the powerful search engines of the Internet guide you to practically any subject you could name. This provides a huge savings in time and energy and is the reason why practically everybody at Comdex was talking Internet.

Like practically every other company, Microsoft had been late to recognize the importance of the Internet. But Bill Gates had transformed his empire so completely that Microsoft was now at the leading edge of the wave. Microsoft had positioned itself there in part by jumping into the fast-growing market for a new kind of software called a "browser," which provides a graphical view of the Internet's World Wide Web. This enables the user to "browse" through reams of data by flipping "pages" at the click of a button. Microsoft had developed a browser called Microsoft Internet Explorer that was gobbling away at the lead of the Netscape Navigator browser, which had galvanized this new industry.

Gil Amelio, too, had vowed to transform Apple into an Internet company. But all that Apple had come up with in 1996, in any significant way, was a browserlike program called Cyberdog, based on the OpenDoc technology that was designed to make it easier for developers to create programs with the reusable chunks of software code under the object-oriented programming technology. But almost nobody else in the industry cared to support Open-

Doc. As of the end of 1996—three years after it was announced—only twelve developers had programs ready to ship. "Rather than trying to learn from the OpenDoc experience, Apple tried to vindicate itself with Cyberdog, which served two purposes: it was something Apple could point to as vindicating OpenDoc, and as demonstrating that they did have a clue about the Internet after all," says longtime Mac developer Amanda Walker, senior software engineer of InterCon Systems Corporation. "Unfortunately, this is a hard sell. Apple's never really 'gotten' the Internet and has a long history of ignoring or misunderstanding the entire Internet/networking arena."

Larry Tesler, Apple's chief scientist in 1997, defends Apple's work on the Internet, saying that Cyberdog "is the most reliable Internet access platform there is" and that it is a misconception to say Apple "doesn't get" the Internet. "Once a catchy phrase like that gets into the public, it's hard to shake," Tesler says. "I think the blame Apple takes is in our public relations effort of not being able to shake that moniker."

In fact, Apple's mistakes vis-à-vis the Internet go back years. In 1994, Apple had launched the on-line service called eWorld that only Macintosh customers could use. Amelio had pulled the plug on that, early on, after it had failed to attain more than a few hundred thousand subscribers against the millions already on board the established on-line services such as Prodigy. Tesler says he tried to convince management to preserve eWorld, as a more open Internet provider, but funding resources were spread too thin to support that. Mansoor Zakaria, president and CEO of a San Francisco Internet publishing house called Agora Digital Corporation, remembers pleading with some Apple managers in 1994 to let him help put an on-line service onto the Web, or even just for eWorld, dedicated to just Mac software developers. By so doing, Zakaria says, Apple could have brought people into Web development, setting the company up to become a leader in the Internet explosion instead of a distant follower.

"The Apple guys said, 'We want to do something, we want to do something,' but nothing really happened. So we disengaged from Apple."

As a result of Apple's lax effort on the Internet, even Internet programs for the Macintosh were arriving late, if at all. America Online, for instance, did not deliver a Macintosh version of its AOL 3.0 program, which featured far easier and faster Internet access, until some six months after one had been shipped to Windows customers. This was a death knell for anyone who wanted to compete in a fast-changing marketplace.

On the floor of Comdex, Internet developer after Internet developer told of concentrating, first and foremost, on Windows. One, called IFUSION-Com, was showcasing a nifty new program called Arrive that would continuously update on-line news broadcasts to a computer. Available only on Windows 95 and Windows NT, it had no plans for development on the Mac.

Another company, called Intermind Corporation, had shipped its Windows 95 version of software for enhancing e-mail access in the summer of 1996; the Mac version would not be out until January 1997. Still another, called Flat Connections, had just shipped its Windows 95 version of Internet security software called Sumba in October, with no plans for the Mac. "I have a Mac at home. I love the Mac. But as a developer, I hate the Mac," explained Kalyan Krishnan, vice president of software for the Fremont, California, firm, as mariachis crooned in his booth. "They were so full of themselves. That's the story."

For those who still cared about Apple, the question of what would happen with the Mac's operating system was the only one that mattered anymore. "If that can be solved, then everything will be all right," Frank C. Huang, chairman of UMAX, said in his company's Comdex booth. In the midst of pervasive doomsaying on the convention floor, Ellen Hancock, Apple's new chief technology officer, was scheduled to provide press and analysts with the latest update on the OS strategy at a lunch meeting inside a restaurant and lounge called the Beach, across the street from the Las Vegas Convention Center.

As it turned out, Hancock, standing before an audience of about 150 people munching on chicken breast and mashed potatoes, did not have much new to say. "We're engaged in a transformation to build a new Apple that's much more in tune with the industry today," said Hancock, looking distinguished in her blue dress and multicolored scarf. "And I believe it will lead to a breakout strategy for Apple technology. . . . A breakout means that from here on at Apple, 'N.I.H.'—not invented here—is dead. If we find the best answer outside the company, we'll bring it in."

That segued into the Apple/Be rumors, which she addressed indirectly. "There have been a lot of rumors in the media and the Net the last two months," she said. "We will make an announcement by early 1997." Then she paused, looked around the room, and added, "Not everyone we are talking about is talking to you." That prompted laughter but also some puzzled looks. What? Apple has something else in the works besides Be? No one else realized it at the time, but Hancock had dropped a hint on what would be one of the most incredible developments at Apple in its entire history. And the world would not have to wait long to hear it.

To understand what Hancock meant, back up to the summer of 1996. In pulling the plug on Copland, Amelio and Hancock hadn't discarded the technology altogether, just scrapped the idea of it all being included in a huge software release as Microsoft had done with Windows 95. After Macworld Boston, Hancock huddled with her engineers in a conference room adjoining her office, called "Eyes on the Prize." They jotted Apple's operating system alternatives on a giant whiteboard. One option was to rework Copland completely but preserve the basic technology. But since Copland was already late, that was the least desirable option. Another option was to license the Solaris operating system from Sun Microsystems, using that as a foundation for a new Mac operating system. A third was to license the Windows NT operating system from Microsoft, putting the Mac's system on top of that. The fourth option, of course, was the Be OS.

Just a few days before Comdex, a fifth option had landed in Hancock's lap. Two marketing managers from Steve Jobs's company, NeXT Software Inc., John Landwehr and Garrett Rice, called her out of the blue. "They said, 'You know, you might be interested in the NeXT operating system,' " Hancock recalls. "I hadn't even thought about that, so I sent a team over to check it out. They came back and said, 'Ellen, it looks better than we thought.' " The NeXT technology contained both memory protection and multitasking and, unlike Be, had already been tested in large corporations because it was used primarily in high-end business computers.

On December 2, the Monday after Thanksgiving, Hancock rode the elevator up to the eighth floor of City Center 3 to attend a meeting Steve Jobs had arranged with Gil Amelio to discuss the possibility of Apple using the NeXTStep operating system for the Mac. After Jobs finished his pitch, Hancock smiled and told him she had already done her homework.

The news leaked out on December 16, 1996, when *The Wall Street Journal* reported that Apple had been negotiating with its cofounder and former chairman, Steve Jobs, to possibly buy or license NeXTStep. First, Jean-Louis Gassée. Then, Steve Jobs. Who would Apple be talking with next, Steve Wozniak? Well . . .

Steve Jobs. Now, there was a man who could inspire excitement in the Macintosh community at the mere mention of his name. Jobs had been a busy bee since 1985, when his onetime friend and mentor John Sculley had won the epic battle of wills in Apple's executive suite. Selling all but one of his 6.5 million Apple shares for $135 million[2] in a move to sever his ties with the company he had loved, Jobs immediately started his next venture, aptly called NeXT. At NeXT, Jobs and his engineers created a sexy black cube-shaped computer that they launched in 1989 at the Davies Symphony Hall in San Francisco. The NeXT computer was powered by a cutting-edge operating system called NeXTStep, which relied on the object-oriented technology that Apple's Pink engineers were just starting to develop.

Object-oriented technology relied on reusable "chunks" of software code that could be used to build a more versatile and adaptable operating system. Instead of having to perform major surgery on the operating system each time it needed upgrading, the reusable chunks of code could be swapped out at will. This would make it far easier, faster, and cheaper to keep the operating system spiffy and new. This, too, was a technology pioneered at the famous

Xerox Palo Alto Research Center and a technology that Jobs had seen demonstrated during his legendary visit there in 1979. But he had been too enamored of the Xerox PARC's graphical user interface to bother with object-oriented technology—until he left Apple to start NeXT.

Jobs initially targeted his machine as a computer workstation for the academic market. He then attempted to make inroads into the corporate market. But there NeXT encountered entrenched competitors such as Hewlett-Packard and Sun Microsystems, which could roll out models faster and at a lower price. NeXT suffered also because the ever-stubborn Jobs refused to include a standard floppy drive in the machine. He insisted, instead, on an optical disk drive that developers refused to support because it was too new to the industry. As a result, they never wrote many applications for NeXT, resulting in Jobs being able to sell only about fifty thousand of the machines before pulling out of the hardware market in 1993 to concentrate on the NeXTStep software. But by then, NeXT had lost momentum. The company drifted on for years, subsisting on hundreds of millions of dollars in investment from companies such as Japan's Canon Inc. and Texas billionaire Ross Perot. Jobs, indeed, was known to have tried to take NeXT public but had never gotten enough support from Wall Street to get that effort off the ground.

"All this amounts to a steep fall from a very lofty perch," G. Pascal Zachary and Ken Yamada, reporters for *The Wall Street Journal*, wrote in a front-page piece on May 25, 1993, about Jobs's failure to attain success with NeXT. ". . . his NeXT workstation seems destined to become a high-tech museum relic. He himself is fighting to show he still matters in the computer industry."

Jobs still had the Midas touch, though. In 1986, he bought the computer division of Hollywood producer George Lucas's Lucasfilm Ltd., incorporating it as a company called Pixar to make computer-animated movies. Pixar's crowning moment came on November 22, 1995, when the company's animated film *Toy Story* was released by Walt Disney Pictures to rave reviews. The film would go on to gross a whopping $184 million at the U.S. box office, third highest of all time for an animated movie, behind Walt Disney's *The Lion King* and *Aladdin*. Just a week after the movie hit, Pixar launched an initial public offering of 6.9 million shares at $22 each, which almost immediately shot up in value to $42 a share. Over the next year, Pixar's stock would fall back to earth, settling at about $13 a share. But Steve Jobs had struck the jackpot again: owning 80 percent of Pixar's 40 million shares at the end of 1996, he was another $400 million richer.

All the money in the world, though, could not erase the pain Jobs still felt for having been deprived of his first love, Apple Computer. Del Yocam, the Apple chief operating officer who had also succumbed to a coup, remembers telephoning Jobs the week after *Toy Story* was released to congratulate him on Pixar's success. His old colleague waxed nostalgic on the other end of the line.

"We were commiserating about how sad it was at Apple," Yocam recalls. "Steve paused and said, 'Del, why don't we go back? We could do it again.' He said there were only two people who could turn it around—me and him. He said, 'Del, you can run the company and fund me, just like before [when Yocam had run the moneymaking Apple II division to support the money-losing Mac division].' We got to talking about that for ten minutes, and then he said, 'Jeez, I don't know if I have the energy to do it. And no one would want us.' "

Since then, the Silicon Valley rumor mill had been abuzz with speculation that Steve Jobs was in fact planning another run at Apple by joining with a good friend, software billionaire Larry Ellison, to take over the struggling computer maker in Cupertino. Ellison, president, chairman, and CEO of the database giant Oracle Corporation, had long chafed at Bill Gates's power over the PC industry. Ellison, a svelte, dapper man fond of stylish suits and known in the Valley as having a runaway ego, was a leader in the push to roll out network computers that would not have to run Windows. The men had not launched a serious bid to this point, but according to a former Apple executive, Jobs had spoken with then–Apple Chairman Mike Markkula in the summer of 1995 about his "secret plan" to revive Apple. Markkula placed the call to Jobs, at then-CFO Joe Graziano's behest. Nothing came of the talks, though a possible combination of Ellison and Jobs—two of Silicon Valley's most colorful personalities—made for great press and industry speculation.

Back in Ellen Hancock's Eyes on the Prize room, she and her team of Apple engineers were busily engaged in early December 1996 analyzing each of their five operating system options. They used the big whiteboard, giving each one numerical valuations as measured against what Apple required of its next operating system. The five basic requirements were memory protection, preemptive multitasking, multimedia, ease of use, and ability to access the Internet. There was a sixth factor that was given equal consideration: how fast the new system could hit the streets. "When we did our numerical scoring, NeXT came out the highest," Hancock says.

About the same time this was taking place, Gil Amelio held court for the press in a wide-ranging interview session on December 16—the same day *The Wall Street Journal* first suggested talks were taking place. He smiled cagily when asked about Apple's operating system strategy and said he would be providing full details at the upcoming Macworld show in San Francisco, beginning on January 7. Just four days later, journalists learned the reason behind that smile. The *Los Angeles Times* published a December 20 article by its technology writer, Julie Pitta, that quoted anonymous sources as saying Apple was expected to announce that day that Apple was rehiring Steve Jobs to advise the company on operating system strategies. Apple, she reported, was also planning to buy NeXT's operating system.

That night, Gil Amelio summoned the media to a hastily arranged press conference at Apple's headquarters in Cupertino. There, on a small stage, was a sight to behold: Gilbert F. Amelio, in his suit and tie, standing side by side with Steven P. Jobs, looking youthful and dashing in his fashionable jacket and white, tieless tuxedo shirt. Both men were relaxed and beaming. Yes, Amelio confirmed, Apple was in fact calling its cofounder out of exile to be an adviser to Amelio. And Apple was buying all of Jobs's NeXT, for $400 million. The final transaction price was $430 million.

Ironically, Amelio chose to pay Jobs far more than what he had refused to pay Gassée; a fitting comeuppance, one might conclude, to a man who had priced himself out of the market one time too many. As Gassée remembers, Apple had come back to him on two occasions that November with money offers to buy Be: the first, for $75 million; the second, for $120 million. The ever-charming Gassée took his crushing defeat like a gentleman, penning a note to Amelio that said that Be was "not in the same league" as NeXT, by virtue of NeXT possessing a proven track record.

Amelio, too, indicated there was really little choice when comparing an untested start-up to NeXT. "I can boil it down to: we picked Plan A instead of Plan B," Amelio said, drawing laughs from a gallery of journalists and employees of Apple and NeXT. More somberly, Amelio said, "In the final analysis, it just comes down to people. This is a very complementary relationship. The pieces fit together better than any other arrangement we looked at." Jobs, in a statement, added, "I still have very deep feelings for Apple, and it gives me great joy to play a role in architecting Apple's future."

Steve Jobs may have been betting on Apple with his heart, but he was not with his pocketbook. In agreeing to sell his company to Apple, Jobs insisted on mostly cash out of that $400 million, or a cool $130 million for his stake in NeXT—not exactly a ringing endorsement for a guy whose technology was supposed to save Apple. The price he got from Apple, moreover, was as much as double what many people in the industry believed NeXT was worth, given the company's failure to attain critical mass.

Amelio says it was NeXT's investors—not Jobs—who insisted on cash. "As it turned out, I wanted to pay cash because the stock price was too depressed," he recalls. Amelio also disagrees that he overpaid for NeXT. "You always want to pay less for something," he says, speaking in his characteristic monotone. "But you also have to figure that it takes something like a hundred million dollars a year to develop an OS that takes five years to build. So the value of an OS is five hundred million. I got, with the acquisition, not only an operating system that I think will prove to be extremely successful, but I got relationships with fifty key [NeXT] industrial accounts I desperately wanted my hands on. And I got some talented people. If you go and assess the value of all those things, you can justify the price."

The news brought Apple to center stage again in the computer industry, at least in terms of media attention. Throughout the long Christmas holiday, people in the industry were abuzz over the possibilities. But there was no unanimity on how Apple would fare with this new deal, as evidenced from the sharply divided comments in an on-line forum hosted beginning on Christmas Eve by *The Wall Street Journal Interactive Edition*.

On the optimistic side were people such as an e-mailer named Noah Schubert, who wrote, "Congratulation to Apple on a home-run deal with NeXT. While much of the hoopla has been dedicated to Steve Jobs' return to the company, what's more important is that Apple finally has a new, modern OS ready to deploy." In that same vein, e-mailer Pat McBride added, "Please Gil and Steve, give us an 'insanely great' OS as soon as possible! We are 'insanely loyal' Apple users, who have enthusiastically 'pitched' and used Apple products for many years. 'Sell' us and we, in turn, will sell the Wintel world." The skeptics abounded, though. "My bottom-line assessment is that a switch [to another company's operating system] is a sign of desperation for Apple. Steve Jobs can't turn it around this time," Wayne Ballantyne, who identified himself as an engineer for Motorola, wrote in his e-mail. Added e-mailer Allen Gilmore, "Apple is a little like a turn of the century railroad e.g. because they are really out of business but just don't know it yet."

Some eighty thousand of the Apple faithful who turned out for Macworld on January 7 apparently were not believing that doomsday assessment, however. The highlight of the show, of course, would be Gil Amelio's big keynote address. Inside San Francisco's Moscone Center, where the show is regularly held, big banners implored "See What's NeXT for Apple." The banners competed for space with others showing a giant photograph of the bespectacled Steve Kahng, the Power Computing CEO, with messages including "Steve says: Defend your OS choice, or you will lose it." That meant that customers should support the Macintosh platform, lest Microsoft Windows be left as the only choice of operating systems on PCs. Kahng, standing in his company's ever-crowded booth, shrugged modestly when asked about the signs and explained, "It was the PR agency's idea."

Down the street, at the San Francisco Marriott, a crowd of alarming proportions was building inside to hear Amelio's speech, scheduled to commence at high noon. It was a glorious day. Just as the clouds had parted when the doctor had delivered his first public utterances nearly a year before, so they did on this day, revealing a deep blue sky. Four thousand people who had been waiting in a dangerously congested hallway corridor for the doors to the Yerba Buena ballroom to open raced to their seats at precisely 11:54 A.M., while another thousand jammed into an adjoining room set up to accommodate the overflow to watch the speech on a large video screen.

In a nearby meeting room, Ellen Hancock had just concluded an interview session with journalists, announcing that a combination of NeXT and

Apple technologies would produce a brand-new operating system called "Rhapsody" (apparently named for the classic song composed by George Gershwin) in the middle of 1998. Until then, Apple would continue with its new plan of releasing updates to System 7 at six-month intervals.

This news was not enough to allay the renewed concerns about Apple, though. Just a few days before, Apple had announced that its fiscal first quarter—the typically busy one at Christmas—had suffered an unexpected shortfall in sales of Mac Performas to consumers, resulting in a likely loss of up to $150 million. That would mean Apple had lost $1 billion in a twelve-month period. Even with the cash hoard Amelio and his executives kept talking about, Apple could not stay afloat if it kept racking up those kinds of losses, not to mention the debilitating impact that the resulting plunge in market share would have on the remaining software developers and to Apple's public image.

At 12:04 P.M., the lights went down in the massive ballroom as symphony music, for a change, washed over the sea of expectant faces. Video images of an alien spaceship descending over New York City from the 1996 blockbuster film *Independence Day* suddenly came alive on two twenty-foot-high projection screens flanking the stage. A deep masculine voice then intoned, "When you've got just twenty-eight seconds to save the entire planet, you better hope you have the right computer." That, of course, was a reference to the film's use of a PowerBook by a zany scientist, played by actor Jeff Goldblum, to upload a killer virus to the alien mother ship. Given all the PowerBook recalls of late, though, the world might not have survived an alien onslaught had a PowerBook been used for the job.

Oh, well. This was showbiz—literally. From offstage stepped the tall, dark, and handsome Jeff Goldblum himself to introduce Gil Amelio as the real star of the day. Dressed in a stylish shirt, Goldblum quipped, "I play an expert in chaos theory in *The Lost World: Jurassic Park*. I figure that will qualify me to speak at an Apple event." With that Goldblum handed the show over to Amelio, who, for the first time at such a gathering, ambled out in a sport jacket and banded-collared shirt. "It's chaos, but I love it," Amelio said, looking like a Vegas comic. Then he launched into what would prove one of the most long-winded, disjointed presentations ever heard in the history of corporate America.

Apple executives who had helped organize the keynote had already begun experiencing misgivings about their boss prior to this Macworld. Although he projected the aura of a down-to-earth, modest man, his behavior demonstrated just the opposite. He was in the habit, for example, of instructing his secretary to fill up his car with gas and keep the fridge of his private Astra jet stocked with goodies, according to a witness. He used that same jet, which had been leased to Apple, to shuttle some friends to an Apple show in Paris during the summer of 1996, forcing staff members including Satjiv Chahil and David Seda to book short-notice commercial flights for as much as $4,000 apiece, according to a former executive.

Just six months into the job, Amelio found time to take a week off for vacation, ignoring advice from subordinates that he participate in a rehearsal of his speech at the Macworld Boston show in August. And in preparation for this Macworld keynote—possibly the most important in the history of Apple Computer—Amelio expressed more concern to the event organizers that a parade of celebrities be enlisted to appear with him on stage than in the substance of his address.

"It all hit me that this guy wants to be famous," says one of the organizers.

Gil Amelio apparently thought so highly of his speaking abilities that he deemed it not necessary to show up at the rehearsal for this address, even though it is common practice in business for top executives to do so. Meanwhile, subordinates such as Satjiv Chahil, then senior vice president for marketing, and Christopher Escher, then vice president for corporate communications, had canceled their Christmas vacations in order to prepare for the show. Chahil used his connections in Hollywood to round up celebrities such as Jeff Goldblum, convincing them to appear for free to bolster the Apple cause. Escher had spent hours fine-tuning Amelio's speech, which was drafted by a speechwriter. Yet, at a rehearsal before the keynote, "we sat there eight hours waiting for him, but he didn't show up," says a former executive.

The lack of preparation showed. Amelio threw out the speech prepared by Escher and chose to ad-lib his presentation, guided only by subject headings displayed by bullet points on a TelePrompTer. He started off smoothly enough, comparing Apple to the Earthlings in *Independence Day* who counterattack the giant alien ship to save the world just as things look darkest. But the speech went downhill from there. Speaking in a halting voice and sometimes losing his train of thought, the private pilot brushed off the latest quarterly disaster as "sort of like hitting one of those air pockets in turbulence. But it will not change our course." Hitting an air pocket? It was more like losing an engine. When the results were officially tallied a few days later, they would show Apple losing another $120 million on sales that had plunged a breathtaking 32 percent from the same quarter a year earlier. This would set off a whole new crisis.

Amelio, however, insisted that his strategy to restore Apple to profitability and then resume growth over a three-year period was on course. "In the past," he added, taking a jab at all those CEO ghosts of Apple's past, "Apple would change its strategy whenever there was a problem. It was a strategy *du jour*." Enthusiastic applause at that. Then, quoting Winston Churchill, Amelio added, "It is very important not to underestimate the problem. It is also very important not to overstate it." Amelio, whose speech was supposed to end at

1:15 P.M., droned on until three. There were welcome respites, such as when he brought out singer Peter Gabriel, formerly of the famous rock band Genesis, to demonstrate a new music program, and when he called attention to a most distinguished visitor seated in the front row: former heavyweight boxing champ Muhammad Ali, who was on hand to promote a Web site about Parkinson's disease, with which he was afflicted.

But the highlight of the show—and it was a show, more than a speech— came exactly two hours into the keynote, when Gil Amelio introduced another distinguished guest: the one and only Steven P. Jobs. Jobs, exuding confidence, style, and sheer magnetism, was the antithesis of the fumbling Amelio as he strode onstage. Wearing wire-rimmed glasses, an Eisenhower jacket, and a banded-collared shirt, Jobs stood serenely and soaked it all in as four thousand screaming Macintosh fans jumped to their feet to give him a sixty-second ovation. Flashbulbs popped from the cameras of a phalanx of news photographers. The return of Elvis would not have provoked a bigger sensation. After ten long years, Steve Jobs had finally come home.

At long last, Jobs waved for silence and cut to the heart of the matter. "We've got to get the spark back," Jobs said. "There's a problem now, and it is called Windows. The Mac didn't progress much in ten years. So Windows caught up. So we have to come out with an OS that is even better. It took [Windows] NT eight years. Fortunately, we have one [from NeXT] that has been battle-tested." Jobs ran through a series of crisp demos, showing NeXT's powerful capabilities. He spoke, in all, just twenty minutes.

Amelio rambled between demos for another hour, closing out by presenting the audience with a final surprise: Steve Wozniak. "Woz" had been a virtual recluse in the industry since the Apple days of yore, having retreated to a life of teaching high school computer classes, driving fast cars, and, in general, enjoying himself. When Jobs stepped back onstage for a reunion with Woz, pandemonium erupted. There was another sixty-second standing ovation, this time so loud that ears had to be covered. Jobs was his usual serene self. Woz, however, seemed overwhelmed by it all, blinking unsurely against the flashing cameras as he stood in a pullover sweater and jeans.

This, incidentally, was not the way the keynote was supposed to end. Just before Jobs and Woz took the stage, organizers say, Muhammad Ali was scheduled to be called out of the audience by Amelio to promote his Parkinson's Web site. But since Amelio had gone way over his allotted time, Satjiv Chahil passed a note up to Amelio to cancel the appearance by Ali, who was seen fidgeting uncomfortably in his front-row seat. "We thought Muhammad Ali was going to faint or something," recalls one of the organizers for Apple. Gil Amelio had stood up "the Champ," one of the world's most admired celebrities. Afterward, Chahil hurried into the audience to apologize to Ali and thank him for his time. The greatest heavyweight boxer of all time, who now has great difficulty speaking, nodded and smiled.

This had been the keynote to end all keynotes. The only trouble was, when the dust had settled and attendees sorted through what had actually been said, precious little of substance had come out. Software developers had wanted to hear specifics on how a Mac/NeXT computer would work. They went away with almost none. Wall Street was not impressed, sending Apple's shares down 37.5 cents in NASDAQ stock market trading to $17.50. And many of the pundits came away more alarmed than before. "At a time when Apple Computer most needed to send a message of confidence and clarity, its performance at last week's Macworld exposition in San Francisco offered little evidence that it had begun digging itself out of its very deep hole," Denise Caruso, a longtime industry analyst respected for her searing commentary, wrote in her "Digital Commerce" column for *The New York Times*. Carolyn Said, columnist for *MacWEEK*, dismissed the affair as "more a pep rally for the faithful than an information-rich battle plan."

Amelio, recalling the Macworld episode with some strain in his expression, admits, "My remarks were not as tight as they could have been." But, he adds, the keynote suffered from two problems. The first was that the people presenting demonstrations, such as Peter Gabriel, spent twice as much time onstage as they were supposed to. In rehearsals, he says, each presenter had been allotted about five minutes, but they took up as long as ten minutes at the show. "My actual speaking was no more than forty to forty-five minutes," Amelio says.

The second problem, Amelio says, was that an outside contractor hired by Apple to write his speech failed to get it finished in time. Amelio had asked for the speech to be submitted to him by December 18, in time for him to rehearse it before setting out on a vacation at Lake Tahoe for the rest of the Christmas break. "I had promised I would spend Christmas with my family, and I did," Amelio recalls. "My family matters to me as much as Apple does, if not more so." But the contractor, whom Amelio did not name, had not finished the speech by then. "December 18 came, and I said to send the speech to me at Tahoe," Amelio says. "The truth of the matter, though, was, the speech was never finished—even five minutes before I got onstage. That won't ever happen again, and I'm embarrassed by it. The people responsible for it simply didn't do their job." Amelio terminated the contractor's speechwriting services but retained the individual for other tasks.

Amelio's much-vaunted turnaround strategy was proving equally devoid of focus. The plan, as of 1996, hinged on Apple's revenue for the fiscal 1997 year decelerating to no lower than $9 billion from its peak of $11 billion. Through the job cuts undertaken in 1996, Amelio estimated that $9 billion would represent a "break-even" point at which Apple could start rebuilding its business to make money again. However, Apple generated only $2.1 billion during its fiscal first quarter, ending December 27, 1996, dropping that breakeven down to $8 billion, or below.

The problem in that Christmas quarter, as Amelio later outlined in an address to his shareholders, was twofold: One, all the quality problems with the PowerBook 5300—the ones that had exploded and the ones that had been the subject of two recalls—had crimped a transition to a new line of laptops, resulting in a shortfall in those sales. And two, Apple had once again missed the mark in U.S. sales of its low-end Macintosh Performa line. Amelio blamed the slowdown in Performa sales on a softening of the overall PC market that Christmas, as well as aggressive competition. Many people in the industry suspected, though, that a third, more ominous factor was chiefly to blame: consumers' general unwillingness to buy products from a company that seemed to be going down the tubes. "When the public smells a loser, it won't buy," Stephen Howard, executive editor of news for MacWEEK, wrote in a column on January 20, 1997. Indeed, Amelio now says Apple has suffered "significantly" in the consumer market. "We didn't know that at the time," he says.

In any event, Apple's disastrous results during Christmas 1996 were a replay of the ones from Christmas 1995. Once again, an Apple CEO was in trouble. With expenses still pegged to his $9 billion break-even plan, Amelio had to cut much deeper into the organization to stanch the red ink—like $400 million worth. That would translate to another round of layoffs, this time jettisoning 2,700 more workers. The self-described "transformation specialist" was none too pleased about this sorry turn of events, as demonstrated when he blew his cool before employees on January 16, 1997. Amelio had taken the stage of the Town Hall theater in Apple's R&D 4 building—the same one where Michael Spindler had endured a verbal firestorm from shareholders a year before—to warn the workforce of his impending new restructuring.

"I do not like the idea of having to try to take out four hundred million dollars of cost," Amelio said. "I have to find a way to do that. It hurts to have to think about doing that. I slept about five hours last night. I have a feeling I'm not going to sleep very well in the next few weeks because I know the decisions that only I can make have to get made. I will step up and do it, but I'm not happy about it."[3] Apple's battered and bloodied workers listened forlornly to this and other parts of the address. But they would not soon forget Amelio's final statement to them nor forgive him for it.

"Dammit!" Amelio spat, glaring into a television camera broadcasting the event, "don't put me in this spot again."

Don't put Gil Amelio in this spot again? This from the multimillionaire who had taken Apple to the cleaners with his compensation package? This from the CEO who would not even bother to rehearse for keynote addresses that were of vital importance to his company? This from a man who had vastly overpaid for NeXT, which had been losing money for years? Employees reacted at first with shock, then with outrage. Many returned to their cubicles to reread the "Let's Make a Deal" values statement that Amelio had asked them to post beside their computers nearly a year earlier. Many drew a big circle around the one that promised "I will take the blame when things go wrong—and give you the credit when things go right."

When asked about that statement, Amelio shakes his head wearily and engages in some damage control. "The problem was, it was out of context," Amelio insists, explaining that the "dammit" phrase was used as part of a story he told about lying awake in the middle of the night talking to himself about Apple's problems. However, it is not clear from the transcript of his talk that this was the case at all. In any event, Amelio adds, "What can I say? I should have worded it differently so it couldn't be misconstrued. It wasn't intended to be the way it sounded. I think a lot of people completely misunderstood the statement and a few people were offended by it, and I apologize for that. I sincerely do."

You have to really admire, and pity, the rank-and-file Appleites who had chosen to stay on to save the company they had loved. They had persevered under bad management for so many years, hoping against hope that somehow their collective efforts would foster a renaissance of the Apple Computer they had known and loved. Unlike Amelio and his ilk, the vast majority were not at Apple for the fame or money. This was still a cause to them, a passion to go on changing the world. "The people who were in it for the money cashed out a long time ago," one marketing manager told me during this period. "The rest of us are here because of the religion."

Indeed, the continued dedication of these rank-and-file workers to what many in the industry believed was a lost cause was an asset to which it would be difficult to affix a value. It certainly ranked up there with the loyalty of the remaining Macintosh customers, who kept buying Apple's computers no matter what. "If you ask me to name a hero of Apple Computer during the past ten years," Apple Fellow Guy Kawasaki told me in early 1997, "I would have to say it was the rank-and-file worker."

Gil Amelio certainly has his talents, or he would not have risen so far. But in blaming his own employees for problems that were out of their control, he displayed a character flaw that was manifested one other time in this address from the stage of the Town Hall theater. It happened when he began attacking the problem of Apple's weak and fragmented marketing efforts, a shortcoming that has handicapped the company for many years. Only in this case, he was lashing out at a marketing plan that he himself had ordered devised.

Shortly before Amelio reshuffled Apple in May 1996, one of Apple's executives had sent the CEO a memo complaining, in part, that Apple's marketing had been fragmented for too long. For example, Apple Pacific had its own marketing department, as did Apple USA, Apple Europe, and practically every product group. But Amelio's reorganization dispersed those marketing functions even more, expanding them into twenty-two different Apple groups from the ten or so they had been before. Now listen to what Amelio had to say about this, with his own marketing director, Satjiv Chahil, seated in the front row of the theater.

"In terms of the internal areas, what would I criticize? I would say that I've been darn disappointed in our marketing efforts, and I think we need to face up to that. We have a fragmented effort and we have twenty-two marketing organizations, everyone running in a different direction. It looks confusing, and guess what? That's what the customers see." Moments later, Amelio resorted to profanity again in assailing what he termed the ineffectiveness of Apple's marketing. "I have told our marketing folks that I don't want any more of this wimpy bullshit." Satjiv Chahil smiled stoically, his face flushing under his turban, as heads turned to see how Amelio's top marketing executive was taking this seemingly personal assault. Chahil would not comment on this, but associates say he was badly shaken.

Amelio says this was another case of his comments being misinterpreted. "I talked to Satjiv right afterwards and he didn't take it that way, but I think some people did," Amelio recalls. "I think I was saying something that was on the minds of virtually every person in that audience, which was that our marketing wasn't getting the job done. I just said it out loud for the first time." But was he not assailing his very own marketing organization? "I didn't design the marketing program we had. I just inherited it," Amelio responds. "The marketing folks had come to me and said, 'This is the plan. We want to do it,' I said. 'Fine, you guys have been doing this for years. Go ahead and implement your plan.'" Chahil, Amelio points out, had nothing to do with this plan.

Gil Amelio lost a lot of points with the workforce that day in Cupertino, but things were about to get uglier. Much uglier.

Amelio went ahead and instituted his new reorg. The first step was a new management structure, the umpteenth in Apple's history. Not surprisingly, given the tenor of Amelio's speech to employees, Satjiv Chahil was neutered as all Apple's marketing functions were consolidated under an Apple executive named Guerrino De Luca, previously head of the Claris subsidiary. Marco Landi was also demoted as Amelio eliminated the COO position to put Landi in charge of just worldwide sales and support.

Interestingly, Amelio also turned his scalpel on one of his strongest allies, the venerable Ellen Hancock, stripping her of the title of chief technology officer. Replacing her in duties overseeing product engineering were two new arrivals to the Apple executive suite: Avie Tevanian, head of software engineering, and Jon Rubinstein, head of hardware engineering. As it turned out,

Tevanian was a top NeXT executive and Rubinstein had been one. Not coincidentally, they were appointed to two of the most powerful positions in Apple Computer after Ellen Hancock had run afoul of Steve Jobs. Steve Jobs was supposed to be advising Amelio, but these organizational moves made it clear that he was actually calling a lot of shots.

Hancock's career-killing move at Apple was to have had the temerity, following the NeXT acquisition, to suggest to Jobs that she be given a few weeks to ponder a basic technical decision: for the Macintosh's new Rhapsody operating system, should Apple use the microkernel contained in NeXT's technology or the one already developed for Copland? "I felt it was a decision that had to be made," Hancock recalls. As she discovered, you never, ever question the great Steve Jobs, at least if he has an iota of power over you. Jobs is rarely wrong, at least in his own mind. Both Jobs and Avie Tevanian told Hancock, in no uncertain terms, that the NeXT deal "assumed" that the NeXT kernel would be used, Hancock says. With Amelio backing them up, that was the end of that discussion. And before she knew it, Hancock was demoted to the powerless position of running the Advanced Technology Group and other minor odds and ends.

Asked to comment on this demotion, Hancock tried to put the best face on it, asserting that Amelio simply wanted more direct control over R and D by eliminating a CTO. But when I pressed her as to whether Amelio was in fact being influenced by Jobs in making personnel decisions, Hancock stared at me and said only, "I will not deny that." She repeated the statement, for emphasis.

Jobs declined to be interviewed for this book but insisted in later interviews with me for the *The Wall Street Journal* that his role in this period remained strictly an advisory one. Amelio, when I asked him if he was really in charge as we sat in his conference room at the end of May 1997, stared at me and replied without hesitation, "There's no question about it. If Steve were here to hear you say that, he would get the biggest laugh of the day. Steve is my adviser. I ask him questions. It's nice to have someone who is smart and who knows the industry who you can bounce your thoughts off of. But at the end of the day, I make the decisions."

Amelio could reshuffle Apple any way he wanted, but the slide was not stopping. The fiscal second quarter, ending March 28, 1997, was headed for yet another financial disaster. When the dust settled, Apple would report an operating loss of $186 million and a net loss of $708 million, including costs related to the acquisition of NeXT and the latest restructuring. In all, since Gil Amelio had taken over Apple and pronounced its problems to be "fixable," the company had bled another $1.6 billion.

So little confidence was left in the Amelio turnaround that Apple executives began leaving again in droves. Of forty-seven executives listed on Amelio's first organizational chart in May 1996, twenty-nine had left Apple a year later. They included Marco Landi, Satjiv Chahil, longtime manufacturing chief Fred Forsyth, and even Heidi Roizen, Amelio's best weapon in attempting to hold on to Apple's fleeing software developers. Roizen couched her departure in a diplomatic way, saying in an e-mail note to her friends and developer contacts that she needed to spend more time with her two children, ages one and three. "I will, of course, continue to cheer Apple on from the sidelines as both a shareholder and a customer," Roizen wrote in the note.

Nobody in the industry really believed that, though. Heidi Roizen was a go-getter of the first order, and if she had truly believed in Amelio's strategy, it is highly likely she would have remained on board to see it through.

Even many rank and filers just could not take the pain anymore. They began dispersing to hither and yon, to the many job opportunities opened up by Silicon Valley's Internet boom. "As for Apple, between you and me, think of it this way: The soap opera was drama for years. Lately it has been farce. Now it seems headed for high tragedy," a longtime Apple source of mine wrote me in an e-mail after he resigned.

The Apple drama intensified even more on March 27, 1997. That is when Silicon Valley software billionaire Larry Ellison announced in an interview with the *San Jose Mercury News* that he was forming an investor group to possibly seize control of the company. It was an admitted trial balloon on the part of Ellison, the chairman and CEO of Oracle, who told the newspaper's computing editor, Dan Gillmor, that he would decide, based on public reaction, whether to launch a bid. And should he gain control of Apple, Ellison vowed, he would clear out Gil Amelio, his managers, and the entire board. "Apple is in desperate need of all-new management and leadership," Ellison said. "I think Apple can be saved. I think Apple should be saved." Should he take over, Ellison said, he and his good friend Steve Jobs would likely be members of a new board.

Larry Ellison was another of those rags-to-riches Silicon Valley entrepreneurs. Having grown up on Chicago's South Side, Ellison had attended physics classes at the University of Chicago before dropping out to seek his fortune in Silicon Valley during the 1960s. After working on a team that developed the first IBM-compatible mainframe, he had cofounded Oracle in 1977 to create relational database software. Tailoring the software to run on computers ranging from PCs to mainframes, Oracle had seen its sales soar to $4.2 billion in 1996 from $131 million in 1987, the first year it went public.[4]

Along the way, though, Oracle hit a serious speed bump: the company lost $12 million in 1991 after suffering growing pains that included bug-ridden software. Ellison quickly righted the vessel, though, instituting a shake-up that included layoffs of four hundred employees and top executives. With the balance sheet back on track, Oracle's stellar growth continued unabated as Ellison went on to become the world's third richest software tycoon, after Microsoft cofounders Bill Gates and Paul Allen, with Oracle stock worth about $6 billion.

All the money in the world, though, could not allay Ellison's seething resentment at Bill Gates's ironclad grip on the personal computer market. Seeing an opportunity to loosen Gates's power when the Internet came along, Ellison, along with fellow Gates hater Scott McNealy of Sun, began championing the idea of stripped-down, sub-$1,000 network computers, or NCs, that could replace the personal computer—and Microsoft Windows—by accessing things directly off the Internet. And what better brand name to put on these machines, Ellison undoubtedly figured, than that of the world-famous Apple Computer?

The news of Ellison's trial balloon to buy Apple rocked both Silicon Valley and Apple's stock price. Apple's shares, trading at a ten-year low of $16.75 the day before the announcement, shot up 11 percent to close at $18.63 when the news was publicized, on trading volume ten times higher than normal. Upon closer examination of what such a deal would entail, however, investors' enthusiasm quickly cooled. For one thing, Ellison was not offering much money. He told the *Mercury News* that his investor group, which would be independent of Oracle, would make an offer tied to Apple's stock price as of March 26, which was $16.75, or $2.1 billion. But, Ellison said, Apple investors would receive 60 percent of their money in cash and the rest in an equity stake in the new Apple.

Another problem was that Ellison did not seem to have a clear plan for how he could turn Apple around. He did not articulate his plan but later hinted in public appearances that he would transform Apple into a manufacturer of network computers, which would fit neatly into his overall NC plan. Indeed, at Oracle's OpenWorld business fair in Tokyo on April 17, Ellison declined comment on whether he would make a bid for Apple but told reporters that "Apple would be a great supplier of NCs." At the same show, Ellison lashed out against Microsoft, saying in a speech that "Windows belongs to one company and one person . . . but information never belongs to one country, one company, one person," according to a Reuters news service account.

The strategy of simply turning Apple into an NC manufacturer was widely viewed in the industry as flawed because it ignored the fact that Apple's very success was based on empowering individuals through computers that they, instead of a big corporation, could control. "Long-term, if it [an Ellison takeover] actually happened, it turns Apple from the computer company of 'personal empowerment' to the network computer company of dumb terminals hooked to a central corporate controlled server/data base," Jim Hill, a Macintosh user from Stockton, California, wrote in one on-line forum. "Your computer gives up control to Oracle servers and data bases. Great for Oracle—bad for us."

Ellison certainly had the deep pockets to pull off a deal. Ellison could also count on wealthy backers, such as Jobs and billionaire Saudi Arabian Prince Alwaleed bin Talal bin Abdulaziz al Saud, a shrewd investor who drew headlines in early April 1997 when he accumulated a 5 percent stake in Apple for $115 million. "I believe there is serious potential for Apple to provide large returns to its stockholders once again, as it did in the past," the prince said in a statement, without publicly throwing his support behind either Ellison or Amelio. Jobs continued to insist in the press that his only Apple role was as adviser.

Back at headquarters in Cupertino, meanwhile, Amelio and his team were trying their best to fend off the barbarians at the gate. "If as a consequence of some suitor coming along, if that were to catapult us in new directions, that would be very bad at this point in time," Amelio told the *San Jose Mercury News*. "Because I think we do have it figured out." During April, Amelio counterattacked on the product front as Apple rolled out a new PowerBook 3400 and a new Power Macintosh 6500/300, lauded by press reviewers as the fastest on earth in their category. "I am now more optimistic than ever," Amelio wrote in a full-page ad Apple took out on April 17 in major U.S. newspapers. "We are simplifying, refocusing, getting back to fundamentals."

That brave talk continued as two of Amelio's top executives—George Scalise, the chief administrator, and Fred Anderson, the CFO—spent time with me one day in April to defend their boss's performance. "I think Apple is near a turning point here, but there is always a lag between financial performance and results," Anderson told me in his eighth-floor office atop City Center 3. Scalise, in his office down the hall, added that Amelio had taken Apple a long way, considering the mess he had inherited. When asked to grade the Amelio team's performance, Scalise, seated behind a desk adorned with neatly arranged yellow folders, did not hesitate. "I'll give us an 'A.' " Scalise said *that* without a smile. Scalise resigned the next month, in May, to become president of the Semiconductor Industry Association, an industry trade group.

In his interview with me at the end of May 1997, Amelio also tried to put the best face on Apple's situation. On this day, he was still smarting from an open letter that month in the respected Silicon Valley magazine *Red Herring*, headlined "Gil Amelio, Please Resign." The letter, written by the editors of *Red Herring*, began, "Please resign. In baseball's jargon, you've been a respectable middle-game reliever, but it's time to bring in the closer. Apple needs a CEO who has the technological vision, the brand marketing skills, and the passion necessary to make the company profitable again. That isn't you. Sorry."

Amelio's position, then, was not unlike that of the ill-fated Michael Spindler when the natives began calling for his head. In fact, I opened my interview by asking Amelio if he ever regretted having taken the Apple job in the first place. Sure, he was making tons of money. But no amount of dollars can restore a shattered reputation, as John Sculley will attest. Pondering the question, Amelio nodded slowly.

"I've tried to live my life by being a doer, by being where the action is," he said. "When I learned in the late sixties the action was in Silicon Valley, I came to Silicon Valley. My philosophy is, I want to be in the arena. I don't want to be a bystander. That's how I got into flying jet planes. I just do it because I wanted to see if I could do it." He paused a moment and added, "The decision might either prove to be the smartest thing I ever did or it might prove to be the most unwise thing I ever did."

Amelio, on this day, could take comfort in two unrelated developments of the preceding weeks. The first was when Larry Ellison, on April 29, issued a press release from his mansion in Atherton, California, announcing that, "for the time being," he was calling off his possible takeover of Apple. The one-paragraph release offered no explanation other than to note, "Mr. Ellison stated that he remains interested in developments at Apple and that he may well purchase stock for investment purposes or otherwise, or revisit in the future his decision regarding an acquisition or control of the firm."

The other development was Amelio's move, announced on May 22, to spin off Apple's much-maligned Newton business into a separate subsidiary. The action was seen by industry analysts as a precursor to Apple selling the business outright by making it more appealing in one neat bundle. Indeed, Apple had considered selling off Newton at several points since 1994—including to Oracle in 1995—and would likely have gotten a better price if it had. But nothing had ever panned out. By 1997, though, Newton's momentum was being outpaced by a fast-selling new handheld from US Robotics called the Pilot, as well as handhelds being designed around Microsoft's new Windows CE operating system for such computers.

The money-losing Newton had turned into such a financial albatross on Apple's balance sheet that many of Apple's executives had pressed Amelio to unload it quickly when he took over in 1996. Amelio was criticized by some of his executives for taking so long to do that, but at least with this new subsidiary he was on the road to pushing Newton out the door for good.

This left Amelio and Apple with the core Macintosh business, the one that has been nearly wiped out by the unrelenting advances of the mighty Wintel empire. In his interview with me, Amelio seemed less confident of the final outcome of his turnaround plan than when I had last spoken with him a year before. For instance, I posed the question of whether his strategy could reverse the perception among many computer buyers that Apple was locked in a "death spiral," unable to pull out of a fatal descent.

Looking me straight in the eye, Amelio replied, "Jim, I don't know how to answer that question. What I tell our people is, we have to be sufficiently compelling in terms of how much better we are than the competition so that will offset people's concern about buying into a risky position or a minority product, as opposed to the majority product." He paused a moment, looking out the window at the sprawl of Silicon Valley below, and added, "So the question is: Are we going to be better? There's no question we are, and we will continue to be better. Will it be enough better? I don't know how to read tea leaves, but we sure as hell are going to give it a good go."

Gil Amelio, himself, would get none. Just six weeks after that interview, on July 9, Amelio was ousted from his job in a boardroom coup that many observers believed was influenced by Steve Jobs. More about this drama is outlined in the Epilogue, but it left Apple's position more precarious than ever as the company scrambled to recruit its fourth chief executive in as many years.

As Amelio and I shook hands at the door, he added a parting thought: "I am convinced we have the right strategy—but we need a few breaks."

In leaving the Apple campus following my May interview with Amelio, I was struck by how orderly it all appeared on the surface. The banana-colored carpet of the executive suite was neatly vacuumed, the windows gleamed, and all the floor secretaries looked calm and professional. Downstairs, in the City Center 3 atrium lobby, the facade of health was maintained by the gleaming marble columns, carefully trimmed palm trees, and procession of employees returning from Apple's cafeteria across a courtyard in the adjoining City Center 4 building. A Macintosh sat against a wall, displaying this peppy message on-screen: "Others can talk about boundaries. We don't believe they exist. Others can talk about high risk tasking. We won't stand and wait. At Apple, we're already moving toward the next frontier. And there's no chance we'll turn back."

There would be no next frontier for Gil Amelio, at least at Apple Computer. The company was immersed in fresh turmoil when the board announced on July 9 that it had ousted Amelio and begun the search for a fourth CEO in as many years.

The news was not wholly unexpected, since Apple's sales, stock, and market share had all declined precipitously during Amelio's seventeen months at the helm. But it raised fresh doubts about the company's viability, coming just a week before the company was to release its results for the fiscal third quarter that ended on June 27. The results actually turned out to be better than expected, as Apple reported it lost $56 million, or 44 cents a share, in the period, compared to analysts' expectations of a loss of about $80 million. Still, Apple continued to lose market share at a frightening rate, as its sales fell 23 percent from the same quarter in 1996, and the loss added to the flood of red ink as

Apple executives declined to predict when the company would be profitable again.

The good news of Amelio's firing was that it was executed with refreshing swiftness by a board known so long for dragging its feet. Rather than let Amelio continue spinning his wheels, a board led by a dynamic new member named Edgar S. Woolard Jr., the now-retired chairman of DuPont Co., decided to move in quickly to try to reverse what was clearly an unsuccessful strategy by Amelio to wait so long to take needed turnaround actions. Woolard was recruited by the board in June 1996, and his addition marked the first time an executive of his business caliber had served as an Apple director. A member of the prestigious Business Council, the sixty-three-year-old Woolard was among select executives who accompanied the late commerce secretary Ron Brown on trade missions around the globe.

It was Woolard who took the lead in notifying Amelio that he had to go. The day after Amelio's forced resignation was announced, Amelio telephoned me at *The Wall Street Journal* to explain what had happened. I had just recently returned to work there following a leave of absence to write most of this book. While spending the previous July 4th holiday weekend with his family at their Lake Tahoe estate, he was working at a Macintosh when Woolard called out of the blue. "Ed said he felt, in a nutshell, that I had done a lot of great things, that I had taken a lot of cost out and rebuilt the product line. But that we weren't seeing the top-line growth at the rate everyone wanted," Amelio told me. "And he said that maybe I had done what I was capable of doing and it was time for something else."

That something else meant that the board wanted someone with stronger sales experience than the engineering-minded Amelio. "I have to confess," Amelio added, "when it comes to consumer sales, that is not my background. If you're looking for someone who is going to pump up sales at Sears, Roebuck, I probably am not the guy." After conversing for an hour with Woolard about this, Amelio spent the next two days burning up the long-distance lines in private discussions with other board members. He argued that his sudden departure would prove too disruptive for Apple at a critical time. Led by Woolard, though, they were insistent he step down. "Was this a boardroom battle? Certainly not," Amelio insisted. "This was a very gentlemanly exploration of options. While I respected and accepted the judgment of what they were doing, smart people inevitably have different ways of seeing things."

When I phoned and asked Amelio if he accepted the sharp criticism that had been leveled against him during the preceding months, he dismissed almost all of it. He contended, for example, that he had accomplished "ninety percent of what I could do," and had done an exemplary job, considering the severity of Apple's crisis when he took over. "If everyone is expecting me to be walking around moping with my chin on the ground, that's not the case at all," Amclio said. "I feel like I'm very proud of what I did in that company. I was the emergency room physician who rescued the patient. Now it is time for the general practitioner to come in and exercise long-term care."

Throughout our forty-five–minute conversation, I was struck by how relaxed and confident Amelio sounded. I believe he was, in fact, relieved at having so much pressure taken off. The obvious financial rewards notwithstanding, it can't be easy to have the whole world scrutinizing your every move, and then pouncing at the first slip-up. He told me on more than one occasion, for instance, how much he was looking forward to spending more time with his wife and their five grown children. "I joke that my family has forgotten my first name," he laughed. He planned nothing in particular after Apple except to decompress with his family for a few months before considering what to do next. He agreed to stay on until September 1997 to assist in the transition.

After that, money would certainly not be a problem. His golden parachute entitled him to severance payments totaling $9.2 million. He also ended up becoming a partner in a San Francisco investment firm, and he co-authored an account of his experiences at Apple called *On the Firing Line: My 500 Days at Apple Computer*, which coincidentally was put out by the same publisher of this paperback.

Despite all his faults, I found myself liking Gil Amelio, just as I did John Sculley. And wondering what the winds of fate would bring next for this downtrodden company. Apparently in hopes of averting its past mistakes in naming a CEO, the board this time promised to conduct a professional search led by a committee consisting of Steve Jobs, CFO Fred Anderson, Mike Markkula, and Edgar Woolard. The well-respected Anderson would temporarily run operations, while Jobs's advisory role would be expanded.

Boy, would that be one of the all-time understatements of Silicon Valley.

17

Thinking Different

Gil Amelio's body was hardly cold when the Mac faithful descended again on Boston in early August 1997 to mark one of the more phenomenal events in the history of the computer industry, the return of Steve Jobs to Apple Computer after years of wandering in the high-tech wilderness.

In the weeks preceding his appearance at this Macworld Expo show, Jobs had demonstrated quite clearly that he was more than just an adviser. He was Apple's de facto CEO. He began running product review meetings. He presided over meetings to hone Apple's marketing strategy. He even sent out a company-wide electronic memo, notifying all employees that their Apple options had been repriced to $13.25—about the level of Apple's stock when Amelio was booted. That was a shrewd morale-boosting move, because it suddenly gave value to options that had been worthless on paper. It was tantamount to a bank telling a homeowner that, instead of his property being worth $50,000 less than his outstanding mortgage, it was actually worth $50,000 more. Surely now there would be less incentive to walk away.

In testimony to Jobs' new influence over Apple, he signed the memo "Steve and the Executive Team" and closed with this slogan: "You cannot mandate productivity, you must provide the tools to let people become their best. —Steve Jobs."

Since it was so clear that Jobs was in charge, I began hounding him for an interview so he could spell out his strategy and intentions for Apple. A number of news publications, including the *San Francisco Chronicle*, were reporting that Jobs' appointment as the new permanent CEO was imminent, but he repeatedly issued denials to me over the phone from his home in Palo Alto, California. "Don't worry, trust me," Jobs assured in his mesmerizing voice, promising to reveal more later after I pleaded for details as to his real role at Apple.

I and the rest of the computer world would not have to wait long.

The full measure of Jobs' power became apparent on the morning of August

6, 1997, when he delivered the keynote address at the final Macworld show in Boston. (This East Coast version of Macworld would move to New York City in 1998.) Anticipation was so high that two thousand people packed into the auditorium of a downtown Boston building called the Castle, and another three thousand were jammed into a room nearby. The uncharacteristically cool and dry weather provided a perfect backdrop for the upbeat mood of Macworld's attendees, who were buoyed by the fact that Apple's stock had surged to nearly $20 after Amelio's departure. The company was still losing money but the losses were narrowing, sales were picking up, and the company's leadership seemed more focused than ever under Jobs and the new board member, Edgar Woolard. It was little surprise that the audience of nerds and wannabe nerds gave a standing ovation and chanted "Steve! Steve!" when the legendary showman strolled out on stage, smiling impishly and looking as cool as ever.

He was forty-two years old, older and far more mature than in those go-go years when he and Apple had ridden a rocket ship of growth. His charisma was as intoxicating as ever, and as he spoke—stalking the stage without notes, peering at the masses through his wire-rimmed glasses, and occasionally cupping his hands as though in prayer—hardly another sound could be heard in the cavernous room. "What I see are the makings of a very healthy company," Jobs said, adding almost casually that there would have to be dramatic changes at Apple, starting with the board of directors.

Bombshell Number One was dropped. Loud applause greeted Jobs' announcement that resignations had been accepted from three of the five board members, including the one-time "king behind the throne" Mike Markkula, as well as Bernard Goldstein and Katherine Hudson. Staying on were Edgar Woolard and Gareth Chang, senior vice president of Hughes Electronics. The applause intensified when Jobs announced the names of the four new board members: Larry Ellison, the flamboyant and powerful CEO of Oracle; Jerome York, former chief financial officer of both IBM and Chrysler, who was well regarded in business for his part in turning around those companies; Bill Campbell, the CEO of Intuit who had earned the nickname "Coach" for his charismatic leadership of Apple's sales force during the mid-eighties; and Jobs himself.

This was astonishing news, because it demonstrated that Jobs was, in fact, willing to attack Apple's root problem of directionless leadership to try to fix the company. "I think change should start at the top," he said. Later, Jobs explained his actions in an interview he finally granted me for *The Wall Street Journal*, after standing me up the night before. Jobs confided that he had been "disengaged" from Apple until the board—at Woolard's behest, Woolard later told me—contacted him shortly before Amelio was to be ousted to ask him to step in as chairman.

Jobs said he contemplated the proposal for about a week before turning it down. The board asked him then to become CEO, an offer he said he also rejected. "I've already got the best job in the world, which is to be part of the team at Pixar," he told me. Jobs added that he was also deeply immersed in family life, enjoying his role as father to toddler children and a grown daughter. "The problem is I have a life. I just can't be the CEO of Apple. I just don't have that to give."

What he would give was his strategic insight, and his presence as the catalyst for Apple to undertake bold changes, such as the ouster of nearly its entire board. In fact, Jobs said that two weeks before Macworld Expo he called the board members together and asked for resignations from all but Woolard and Chang, who were relatively new to the body. None of the outgoing directors opposed the request, not even the venerable Mike Markkula, to whom Jobs broke the news personally. Jobs would not comment on this, but a person familiar with the conversation said that Markkula was shaken and saddened by the request from the man whom he had financed two decades before. "He knew it was time," said this person.

The board shakeup was big news, but it was all but forgotten after Jobs dropped Bombshell Number Two. Gasps of dismay and shouts of "No! No!" greeted Jobs' revelation of his second ingredient for change, a far-reaching alliance with Microsoft, Apple's old nemesis. Under the pact, Jobs said that the two companies would cross-license their patents, in a move to prevent a renewal of the kind of lawsuits that had so badly tarnished relations in the past; Microsoft would commit to supporting the Macintosh for at least five more years with its Microsoft Office productivity suite; Microsoft would invest $150 million in nonvoting shares of Apple stock, in addition to paying an undisclosed sum that two people familiar with the matter said totaled about $100 million, to settle a patent dispute that had been on the verge of litigation; and Apple would bundle Microsoft's Internet Explorer with the Mac, making it the first choice of Apple users over Netscape's rival Navigator.

The Mac devotees were initially horrified at the news because so many still viewed Microsoft as the evil empire that had stolen Apple's technology to dominate the market. "I would not be surprised to see the word 'sellout' used to describe this," fumed one Macworld attendee. "It's just a symbol of allowing Microsoft to dominate one more place."

The sense of unreality deepened when Jobs introduced a familiar guest, Microsoft Chairman Bill Gates, who addressed the gathering via satellite linkup. A chorus of boos erupted as Gates' still-youthful visage appeared on a giant video screen above the stage. Some compared the moment to a visitation by Big Brother. The poignancy was heightened by the juxtaposition of Jobs, standing deferentially on one side, and Gates, speaking front and center from the screen. Less than two decades earlier, it had been Gates deferring to Jobs, when Steve Jobs stood atop the computer industry. "It's very exciting to renew our commitment to Macintosh," Gates droned in his usual monotone.

As Gates spoke, it began to dawn on even the harshest Microsoft critics what this announcement really meant. Apple, fighting for its corporate life, had been given a resounding vote of confidence by the most powerful computer company in the world. Indeed, some actually cheered at the end of Gates' brief remarks. Jobs then told the audience, "We have to let go of the notion that for Apple to win, Microsoft has to lose. For Apple to win, Apple has to do a really good job."

As this book has shown, that was exactly Gates' belief all along. Apple and Microsoft could compete, but they could also cooperate in many areas. This concept, called "co-opetition," simply means putting the practicalities of business above all emotional considerations. Apple had always been an emotional company, and certainly Jobs in his early days was as emotional as anyone. But with Apple struggling to remain relevant, the time for acting on emotion was long past. As Jobs said, "We need all the help we can get."

Later, in our private meeting, Jobs disclosed that he had telephoned Gates a few weeks earlier to intervene in an alleged patent dispute that Apple was planning to file against Microsoft. "I asked Bill if we could work this out, and he was very receptive," Jobs told me. Later that same day, I also spoke with Gates about the alliance in a telephone interview for *The Wall Street Journal*. As Gates remembered, Jobs proposed that Microsoft invest in Apple and form a partnership. "I said, 'Hey, that's a great idea'," Gates recalled. "This is smart business for Apple." And smart business for Microsoft.

As for Apple, Wall Street reacted to the alliance by boosting Apple's shares 33 percent that day. The following day, Apple's stock neared $30 before slowly subsiding on investors' realizations that Apple's problems were far from over. Steve Jobs had pulled off an amazing strategic feat, but it did not alter Apple's fundamental problem, its reduction to a bit player in the PC industry, with a market share so small that it still faced the danger of losing its customers and software developers. Not only that, but this was also a multibillion-dollar company without a CEO. A search committee composed of Jobs, Fred Anderson, and Edgar Woolard planned to oversee an exhaustive quest for a "world-class" chief executive. But the job of implementing a turnaround could not wait until a new CEO would be named, Jobs decided.

He immediately commenced attempting the task by himself.

Over the next year, Steve Jobs would shake his old creation to its very core, in a desperate effort to reinvent the company from the ground up. One of his first moves, for example, was to move Apple's headquarters out of the imposing City Center complex and into the more informal atmosphere of the R and D campus at 1 Infinite Loop. Employees were initially delighted; many had chafed at the Ivory Tower demeanor of Amelio and his predecessors. Jobs even dressed as though he were one of the troops. Letting his beard grow out, he showed up almost every day in running shorts, tennis shoes, and a black pullover shirt.

But Steve Jobs soon demonstrated he had precious little else in common with the average worker. Jobs, for one thing, was an irrepressible control freak, who insisted on signing off on so many details such as product names and packaging that a number of middle managers became afraid to make decisions at all. "You won't find a product manager who feels empowered," one departing Apple manager told me at the time.

One of his first official acts was to send out an internal electronic mail announcing a number of belt-tightening measures, including cancellation of paid sabbaticals. Other e-mails forbade employees on the famously laid-back Apple campus from bringing their pets to work and from smoking even in the parking lots. A fake memo followed, sent out with Jobs' forged e-mail address, announcing that "You've all become lazy and only contribute to Apple's current situation." One of the edicts in the phony e-mail decreed that employees would be charged $3 a day for parking and "only I will be allowed to park in handicapped spaces," a reference to Jobs' well-known habit of parking his Mercedes as close to the headquarters' entrance as possible.

Jobs did not laugh. He retaliated by firing out another company-wide memo, this time threatening to fire anyone caught tampering with the e-mail system or leaking internal documents. A prominent Apple veteran was soon ensnared. Jobs summoned Sandy Benett, the general manager of the Newton subsidiary, into a meeting to inform him that Newton Inc. was being melded back into the company. After Benett told his underlings of the decision prior to an official announcement, word leaked out to the press. Incensed, Jobs ordered Benett fired immediately, according to four people with knowledge of the matter.

After retaining a lawyer, Benett was able to negotiate a resignation, but a chill swept through the rest of the company. "One of my friends at Apple begged me to delete his e-mails from my hard disk," says Dave Winer, a longtime Macintosh developer. Word spread through the company of "Steveisms," some real and some imagined, including an apocryphal report that Jobs conducted spot interrogations of any poor soul he met on an elevator, demanding that they justify their job in thirty seconds or be fired. Jobs laughingly denied such behavior, saying: "Whenever I see people I don't know, I say, 'Hi, I'm Steve Jobs.'"

But Jobs ended up firing or forcing out most of the top executives he inherited, as well as underlings. For example, one of Jobs' personal assistants became a target when he was tardy in arranging the installation at Apple headquarters of the same kind of high-speed digital data line, called a T–1 line, that Jobs had at NeXT and Pixar. When Jobs encountered a delay in receiving e-mail one day, he stormed out of his office, leaned into the cubicle of the assistant, Jim Oliver, and said, "No T–1, you're fired," according to Oliver and another Apple worker.

Oliver left, unsure of whether Jobs was serious or not. "His temper can flare up," he notes. The next morning, Jobs apologized to three other staffers for the incident, explaining that "he just gets extremely frustrated when things don't work the way they're supposed to," one of the workers recalls. Word was relayed by coworkers to Oliver that he could return to work, but he resigned soon thereafter. Jobs never personally apologized to him.

Jobs was gaining such a reputation as a tyrant that disgruntled workers began quitting the company in droves; most of them were pre-Jobs veterans that he didn't want around anyway. "Steve believes Apple was royally screwed up for the past 10 years, and that if you had stayed around from that time you were either incompetent or an idiot," says one former executive who left in protest over how Jobs was treating people. "He assumes everyone is bad until proven good." A group of five engineers interviewing with Jobs for employment at Apple gained firsthand insight into this mentality, when the de facto CEO leaned forward at one point and, according to one, said, "There are 10,000 mediocre employees at Apple that need to be cleaned out." Since Apple was employing barely that number at the time, that statement effectively covered the entire workforce.

Conversely, Jobs seemed to fawn over the employees and managers that Apple had imported from NeXT under terms of the acquisition. "He once told me that five Apple people are worth less than one NeXT guy," one former executive told me. By the early fall of 1997, practically all vestiges of the Amelio management team had been wiped out. Four out of the top five executive positions at Apple were filled by Jobs and his former NeXT underlings, with the fifth occupied by CFO Fred Anderson. Anderson survived the purge, in part, because he sided with Jobs on one of Jobs' more controversial decisions as Apple's new leader, the decision to kill the clones.

To appreciate the impact of this momentous decision on September 2, 1997, step back a few months to the early spring of that year when Jobs was still just an advisor to Gil Amelio. At that time, Fred Anderson was arguing internally that Apple force the clone manufacturers, including Power Computing, Motorola, and Umax Technologies of Taiwan, to pay hundreds of dollars more in royalty fees for the Macintosh operating system and related technologies. Anderson's reasoning was that the clones were growing largely at Apple's expense, taking sales from Macintosh customers who otherwise would have purchased from the mother company. As of mid–1997, the clones accounted for 20 percent of the Macintosh market. Therefore, Apple believed it needed to exact a higher toll for the privilege.

This was practical reasoning, except for one thing: The clones were operating under contracts that had been worked out by both sides many months before. Anderson was pushing to reopen what the clone makers rightly felt were closed deals. Within Apple, Anderson found himself backed by a powerful ally, none other than Steve Jobs himself. Indeed, Jobs used the term "leeches" in a speech before Macintosh developers in May 1997 to describe some of the cloners who, he said, were picking off Apple's highest margin product markets. Emboldened, Anderson convinced Amelio to let him reopen talks with the clone manufacturers on terms and conditions of their contracts. Not surprisingly, those manufacturers reacted with outrage when told they needed to pony up more money.

The talks had made little progress by the time of Macworld Expo in Boston in August 1997, when Jobs announced to the world his clean-up of the board and the peace pact with Microsoft. Almost lost amid the excitement over that news, however, was the near mutiny that had erupted within the show following a fiery speech by a Power Computing executive over what he called Apple's possible total shutdown of the cloning market. In his address before about 700 Mac customers, Power Computing's president Joel Kocher unveiled a Power model that was one of the first to use a powerful new microprocessor called the PowerPC G3.

"Hey, this is a great product," Kocher remembers telling the crowd, which responded with a roar of approval. "Well, guess what? You may not get one." Then he explained that Apple had refused to certify the particular model for sale, and warned that the entire cloning program was in jeopardy.

Kocher's outspokenness earned him some praise in the Macintosh industry, but it also cost him his job. Within the month, he resigned after Power's soft-spoken chairman and CEO, Steve Kahng, insisted his company pursue a more conciliatory style with Apple. While Kahng was widely criticized within his own company for backing down to Jobs, he really didn't have much choice except to negotiate. Power had become a powerhouse in revenues—soaring to some $400 million in annual sales after just two years of existence—but it was not yet making any money. Steve Kahng, in short, could not afford a drawn-out legal fight with Apple.

Steve Jobs surely knew this, since he announced on December 2, 1997, that Apple was buying back Power's Macintosh license for $100 million in stock. Since Power's whole business model was built around the Macintosh industry, the company was left as a purposeless shell to be liquidated scant months later. With the biggest clone vendor out of the way, Jobs that same day took aim at the other two—Motorola and Umax—by announcing Apple would not license any new Macintosh technologies about to be deployed. These included a new hardware design and an operating system for laptops. Since being deprived of these would make the remaining cloners noncompetitive, Jobs had effectively cut off their air, ending Apple's fledgling licensing program after just two years.

"It wasn't the first choice I wanted," Jobs told reporters afterwards, explaining that he would have preferred higher fees for extended licenses. Speaking to desktop publishers at the Seybold conference in San Francisco soon after, Jobs insisted that Apple had no choice but to abandon cloning if it wanted to survive. "If we go down the shitter, the Mac ecosystem goes down the shitter," Jobs told the theater of 4,000 attendees, in reinforcing why he demanded the higher royalty fees from the clones. "I said, 'You guys have to pay a fair price.' They basically told me to pound sand."

This isn't at all what happened, according to executives involved in the licensing discussions for all three of the major clone vendors. For example, Frank C. Huang, chairman of Taiwan's Umax, had shuttled back and forth across the Pacific to meet with Jobs, agreeing to almost every directive the Apple leader set out, including paying higher fees. "But at their next meeting, Steve told Frank he changed his mind. He didn't really want to do licensing," recalls a person familiar with the discussions.

Practically the entire Macintosh industry was stunned and outraged at the shutdown of licensing. In a scathing open letter to Jobs published on the Internet a few days later, Ric Ford, publisher of the highly influential Macintosh news service called MacInTouch, suggested that the Apple co-founder was giving up on the Mac in pursuit of a new foray into network computers. "The current Macintosh is irrelevant to this project, except as a source of funds," Ford wrote. "You will milk the current Macintosh for all the profit you can, minimizing expenses in every way possible."

Steve Jobs fired back a response to the letter, in a one-paragraph missive dripping with venom. Calling Ford irresponsible and wrong, Jobs suggested, "Maybe the folks who read your website have something in common with those who buy the *National Enquirer* [sic], in that they are not really seeking facts or insight but simply entertainment." This was vintage Steve Jobs, the mercurial genius who would not take crap from anyone.

Jobs didn't just bully the little guys. He also mixed it up with the big boys, like Chris Galvin, the chief executive of Motorola. According to several people familiar with the situation, Galvin erupted when Jobs, in a telephone conversation, tried to strike a bargain, granting Motorola the right to continue cloning in return for a promise by Motorola to speed up development of microprocessors crucial to Apple's laptop business. Jobs shouted back, and later hung up on Galvin, one of the individuals says. "They did have very strong words with each other," says one official at Motorola, which later took a $100 million charge on closing its fledgling line of StarMax Mac compatibles.

Neither CEO would comment, and a Motorola spokesman said the two companies are doing business as usual. But two other Motorola officials, who declined to be identified, said the company will likely be less inclined to give Apple the kind of preferential treatment it has enjoyed in the past. "They will be just another customer," one of the officials said. Indeed, both Motorola and IBM issued a press announcement in late September 1997 that they intended to start pushing PowerPC into the so-called embedded market for non-computer devices.

As much as Steve Jobs could antagonize people, he possessed an equal ability to electrify and impress. By the end of that same September, for example, Jobs unveiled a new advertising campaign that was Apple's slickest since the famous "1984" commercial. In fact, this new campaign was created by the same Chiat/Day agency that had masterminded "1984."

By this time, the Apple board had formalized the "de facto" in Jobs' title to "interim" CEO, in public recognition of the obvious. A master at marketing, Jobs used his influence to shape the new Apple campaign entitled "Think Different." Although grammatically incorrect, the slogan paid homage "to the crazy ones, the misfits, the rebels, the troublemakers, the round pegs in the square holes," which included geniuses such as Albert Einstein and Pablo Picasso whose works changed the world. "And it's the people who are crazy enough to think they can change the world, who actually do," intoned the actor Richard Dreyfuss in a television spot for the campaign.

"It absolutely strikes at the soul of Apple, to think different," an unabashedly proud Jobs told me by telephone on the eve of the campaign announcement.

Strategically, Jobs was orchestrating some very shrewd moves for Apple. In what many considered a long overdue action, he streamlined the product line to just a handful of models from what had been a proliferation of forty and more. He revamped Apple's manufacturing operation to follow the "build-to-order" model pioneered by Dell Computer. Indeed, Jobs made that announcement on stage November 4, 1997, at an auditorium in Cupertino, with a backdrop of Michael Dell's face sporting a bullseye. "We're coming after you, buddy," Jobs said to great cheers from an audience of mostly Apple employees.

Given the fact that Dell Computer, by this time, was one of the biggest and fastest growing companies in the industry, while Apple was locked in freefall, the taunt was considered quite a joke to many people elsewhere in the industry. As usual, this attack seemed to be precipitated by emotion on Jobs' part. Just days before, Jobs had fired off an e-mail to Michael Dell, asking him to explain his flip remark when asked by a CNET online interviewer on October 6, 1997, what he would do if he were placed in charge of Apple: "I'd shut it down and give the money back to the shareholders." In his e-mail missive to Dell, Jobs hissed, "CEOs are supposed to have class. I can see that isn't an opinion you hold."

In any event, Jobs was making some positive changes, and more were on the way. With its flexible new manufacturing system, Apple entered the business of selling to customers directly via the Internet, in a website called the Apple Store that generated $12 million in revenues in its first month of business. At the same time, Jobs fortified Apple's shaky relations with the sales channel, in moves such as agreeing to a proposal by CompUSA, the computer superstore giant, to dedicate an entire section in each of its stores to Apple products. The move paid dividends. CompUSA's Mac business ballooned to 15 percent of its total PC sales from just 3 percent before the "store within a store" concept was implemented. Jobs also made sure his sales managers began monitoring the status of Mac products in all stores and resellers every week, to avoid the kind of wild inventory swings that had so bedeviled Apple in the past.

"They are so in tune with the amount of product they are selling," marveled Michael France, senior partner of Mac Center, a big Apple reseller based in Fort Lauderdale, Florida.

It was becoming gradually clear that Jobs was not intent on abandoning the Mac, after all, as so many people had feared after he killed the cloning market. According to those in whom he confided, Jobs said he wanted to keep the Macintosh market as viable as he could for as long as he could, to give Apple time to find new growth opportunities that could rebuild the company into a major industry player. And one of those opportunities, he said, was to parlay the Mac into a consumer appliance.

Shortly after taking the helm of Apple, Jobs huddled with his lieutenants and began debating ways to regain the company's status as a pioneer and innovator. According to people in the meetings, Jobs began thinking of the appliance-like devices such as the so-called Network Computer after concluding that Apple possessed one of the world's great consumer brands, with almost no consumer products. "He figured Apple must become a consumer products company," recalls one person in one of the meetings. "He thinks that if the NC does take off, then Apple can become the Sony of NCs."

Development work began on a product initially called the Macintosh NC, which people familiar with the project say was being designed to contain minimal features of the Mac operating system but run almost all major software programs off a server powered by Oracle database software. As Jobs envisioned it, this product would be initially targeted as a sub-$1,000 alternative to the personal computer in schools, where administrators could benefit from efficiencies in such areas as performing software upgrades from a central location rather than at each PC.

While the concept of a cheap, simplified computer is bound to appeal to some cost-conscious network administrators, many people in the industry question whether many customers will be willing to throw out their considerable investments in PC technology to embrace an unproved one. One major barrier the NC will likely face is the fact that PCs have fallen so dramatically

in price—they are priced under $700 in the U.S. now—that the price differ-
ence between the two has become negligible. As of this writing in the summer
of 1998, the Macintosh NC, believed to be a project code-named Columbus,
is still being kept under wraps, and it remains unclear how successful this tact
by Jobs might prove.

Another uncertainty that has weighed heavily on Apple, at least early on,
has been the difficulty in finding someone to step in as a permanent CEO.
The search was supposed to have been completed by the end of 1997, but as
of this writing the company has opted to leave Jobs in as interim CEO for as
long as he likes. Many names were bandied about. Former Apple Chief Operating Officer Del Yocam was mentioned by some as a possibility, given his
long association with Jobs. But Yocam, busy himself as CEO of Borland
International (now called Inprise Corp.), insisted he was not interested in the
job.

Apple was known to have negotiated with some other candidates, including Joe Costello, the former CEO of Cadence Systems in Silicon Valley. But
Costello moved, instead, to an Internet startup. Even board member Bill
Campbell was approached about the job, since he, too, was an Apple alumnus
and a friend of Jobs as well as his next-door neighbor. The affable Campbell,
though, was content serving as CEO of Intuit Inc., and rejected the overtures,
say people familiar with the matter. He is now chairman of Intuit. And, repeatedly, the board members kept asking Jobs himself to reconsider. He remained
insistent, however, that a return to active duty at Pixar was uppermost on his
mind.

As the weeks turned into months, though, people in the industry became
doubtful that Apple could ever attract an independent-minded chief executive, with someone as powerful—and meddlesome—as Steve Jobs lurking in
the background. Even CFO Fred Anderson has admitted at a press conference that one prerequisite for any new CEO would be a full agreement with
the strategic path that Jobs has formulated. "The worst thing that could happen to Apple would be a 180-degree strategy change," Anderson told reporters
at the Macworld Expo in San Francisco during January of 1998.

In high drama typical of Apple's history, Steve Jobs dropped a bombshell
there that erased, at least temporarily, the industry's preoccupation with the
CEO search. It came in Jobs' January 6 keynote address before some 4,000
attendees assembled in the Yerba Buena ballroom of the San Francisco Marriott; on the same stage, in fact, where Gil Amelio had flopped so miserably
exactly one year before. Since Jobs was known for theatrics, the excitement
was high as the lyrics "I get knocked down/But I get up again/You're never
gonna keep me down," from the rock tune "Tubthumping" by Chum-
bawamba pulsated out of giant speakers.

At precisely 9 A.M., the living legend himself strode out onto stage, nodding appropriately at the chorus of cheers and applause that greeted his arrival in black leather jacket, black long-sleeved shirt, and faded jeans. Wearing a full and bushy beard streaked with gray, the master of ceremony took the Mac faithful through a litany of the recent accomplishments, drawing requisite applause as speech and product demos continued for the next 90 minutes. The address was well delivered, as usual, but audience members seemed to sag in palpable disappointment as Jobs concluded his remarks and prepared to leave the stage.

But he stopped, and added as a seeming afterthought, "Oh, one more thing. Think profit." And with that, he broke the news that sent audience members to their feet with cheers and applause: Apple Computer had earned more than $45 million in the just-ended fiscal first quarter, defying analysts' projections for the company to break even at best. When the official results were announced a week later, they would show Apple earning $47 million on strong sales of new products and belt tightening that had sharply reduced costs. No one at Apple would predict how long the profitability might last, but the news was a welcome respite from all the negativity of the past.

"I can tell you for sure," Jobs said, smirking beneath his thick beard, "that Apple is coming back."

Afterward, I was ushered upstairs at the Marriott for a one-on-one with Jobs. By this time, he had consented to being interviewed by select members of the press, usually including *The Wall Street Journal* and some other major publications. As I stood outside waiting with one of the PR people, an aide rushed out with an anguished look, saying, "He's just walked out of a live interview." As it turned out, Jobs was being interviewed live on the cable network CNBC when he yanked off his microphone and stormed away. The provocation? The hapless correspondent had had the temerity to ask him yet again whether he would become Apple's permanent CEO.

Yet, when I faced him, moments later, Jobs was as polite and charming as he could be, offering me a seat and patiently sitting through a list of questions. Here it was again, this unpredictable shifting of moods that made him such a difficult person to figure out. I even put the CEO question to him, but apparently in such an offhand manner that he didn't feel the need to throw me out. "I'm the CEO of Pixar," he said calmly, munching from a plate of fruit, "and I'm not giving that up." Before I stood to leave, I asked if he had any parting thoughts. He reflected a moment, looked to aides gathered around the room, and said with a smile, "I'm about as proud as I can be of the team at Apple."

From that time through the early spring of 1998, scarcely a week went by without yet another announcement of major change at Steve Jobs' new Apple Computer. Some of the decisions proved wildly unpopular in the Macintosh community. Less than a month after Macworld, for instance, Jobs announced he was disbanding Apple's Claris subsidiary, even though the unit had main-

tained profitability through all of the parent company's turmoils. While folding some of the Claris programs into Apple's main R and D—ostensibly to
bolster the Mac development efforts—skeptics suggested the move represented another callous cost-cutting move by Jobs. "These moves should help
staunch Apple's bottom-line bleeding for one more quarter. I'm just worried
about the quarters that follow," Charles Piller, a technology columnist, wrote
in *The Los Angeles Times*.

Exactly one month later, on February 27, 1998, Steve Jobs provoked more
outrage when he unveiled his final solution for the Newton problem, to kill
the technology altogether. Poor Newton. It had gone through so many trials
and tribulations. First, there was the ignominy of the botched launch of 1993.
Then, four years later, Gil Amelio set it up for sale by spinning it into a separate unit. Scant months later, though, Steve Jobs reversed that process, by
rolling Newton back into Apple. In a terse press release, Jobs explained only
that "This decision is consistent with our strategy to focus all of our software
development resources on extending the Macintosh operating system."

That was all well and good, but many people in the industry wondered
why Jobs did not bother to sell off the technology. At least get something in return for all those hundreds of millions of dollars in R and D the past decade.
Jobs, as usual, left his subordinates to answer all media questions. So, we put
the question to CFO Fred Anderson, whose penchant for slashing operations
and costs was matched in zeal only by Jobs himself. He confirmed in a call
with press and analysts that Apple had considered selling the Newton business, but concluded it could not get enough money to offset the loss of engineers needed for a forthcoming line of mobile devices that would use the Mac
operating system. Presumably, the Columbus project for a sub-$1,000 Mac
NC would fit into this strategy.

"You are better off putting the wood behind one arrow," he said.

Of course, the move made cold business sense. But for the thousands of
enthusiasts who had adopted the Newton, it was one more betrayal by a company with a long history of them. Some staged a peaceful march on Apple's
headquarters. "I think it's just hideous, man," a Newton developer who called
himself Lunatic E'sex, wearing black leather and waist-length hair, told me in
the Newton Source in San Francisco's financial district. Don Crabb, who was
well known in the industry for his frequent MacWeek columns, observed in a
column for the on-line publication, MacCentral, "Sadly, Apple is now so narrowly focused . . . that it is throwing out the very technologies that consumers
need to buy."

Morale among Mac users rebounded sharply, though, on a parade of positive developments that Steve Jobs unveiled over the ensuing weeks. The first
was his disclosure that Apple had earned another $55 million in its fiscal sec-
ond quarter, far more than analysts had been expecting, and the second prof-

itable quarter in a row. While the sales of $1.4 billion were still down 13 percent from the same period a year before, the results clearly indicated the balance sheet was replenishing itself. They also showed his strategy of eliminating competition by killing the clones was paying off, at least so far. Besides cost cutting, he attributed the performance to strong sales of a new line of Power Mac G3 computers, using the same chip as in the Power Computing model previewed at Macworld the previous summer.

The really big announcements came in May 1998, though. Before Apple's annual Worldwide Developers Conference, in the San Jose Convention Center, Jobs drew polite applause from the 4,000 in attendance when he disclosed that the company was abandoning its risky strategy of replacing the Macintosh operating system with the new one called Rhapsody. Instead, Apple would follow the safer approach of combining the stability features of Rhapsody with the graphical friendliness of the existing Mac to create a next-generation system called Mac OS X (as in ten).

For developers, this meant they would only have to make a few adjustments to an existing program for it to take advantage of the new system's enhanced performance. Under Rhapsody, they would have had to rewrite the program from scratch. Since many developers weren't planning to switch to Rhapsody anyway, given Apple's shriveled market share, Jobs' move proved a mandatory one to keep them in the fold. For that reason, the reaction among developers was one of cautious optimism, rather than an outburst of enthusiasm.

"Another WWDC and another multi-year operating system strategy," Richard Zulch, chief technical officer of Dantz Development Corp., joked to his colleagues in the hallway later. When I asked him to elaborate, Zulch smiled wanly and added, "We will find out soon how real this strategy is."

Much more excitement greeted Jobs' other announcement that same month, for this was the one that demonstrated a radical new direction for Apple. We in the press knew something major was up when we received a cryptic invitation over the business wires to attend "a media event" at the Flint Center auditorium of Cupertino College, the same auditorium where Jobs had first unveiled the Macintosh fourteen years before.

More than the media were called out, though. Jobs packed the place with more than 2,000 Apple employees, many of them wearing jeans and ponytails as they filed expectantly to their seats. As we waited for the event to begin, someone began bouncing a beach ball from row to row, amid great cheers. It was largely a symbolic act of juvenile rebellion, though, for those still left at the company had learned that the new Apple of Steve Jobs was no longer a democracy. Indeed, the ball was eventually snapped up by a smiling manager, to mock groans from the employees. Few could have expected differently from a company that didn't even allow smoking in its parking lots.

From the walls of the auditorium, great banners unfurled from the ceiling, displaying the latest examples of Jobs' highly unusual "Think Different" campaign. One featured Lucille Ball and Desi Arnaz, in their "I Love Lucy" prime. The lights finally went down a few minutes past 10 A.M., and out strode Steve Jobs—sans beard. A low murmur spread through the crowd at the sight of Jobs in a rare suit, just as he had been at the unveiling of the original Mac. Perched atop a podium to one side was a mystery computer, its identity concealed by a veil, just as the first Mac had been. "Apple is back on track," Jobs began, to cheers that would continue throughout his presentation. "We are going to roll out the whole product strategy today."

This, then, was what everyone had been waiting for. Jobs had proven he could cut costs. But could he reignite growth for Apple? That, of course, was the million-dollar question. Savoring the moment, Jobs did not hurry it along. Before pulling back the veil of his newest toy, he spelled out a shift in strategy that had been in the works since shortly after he returned. No longer, he said, would Apple manufacture umpteen different models for the market. Instead, it would produce just four: a desktop and portable for the professional market and a desktop and portable for the consumer and education ones.

The Power Mac G3 was the desktop for pros. A PowerBook G3, being introduced that day, would be the professional's portable. The consumer portable would be launched in 1999; Jobs did not give details, but many analysts speculated this was the much-publicized Columbus project for a network computer.

As for the consumer desktop, it was beneath the veil. Its moment was almost at hand, but not quite. He had to show off Chiat/Day's latest commercials for Apple. One showed an Intel Pentium II strapped to the back of a snail. The other mocked Intel's TV spots of workers disco dancing in their clean-room "bunny" suits. In this one, one of the bunnies was shown smoking and on fire, having been scorched by Apple's blazing fast G3. The music from the disco song, "Burn Baby Burn," pulsated in the background. "You guys want to see our ads?" he asked rhetorically, clicking the start button as his employees roared their expected approval. Then he previewed another ad, this one of a steamroller crushing a row of Pentium laptops. "The entire Pentium world has just been flattened," a male voice intoned authoritatively.

At last, it was time for the main event. "I am incredibly thrilled to tell you that Apple is getting back into the consumer market," Steve Jobs said. Then, he reached over to the podium and pulled away the veil concealing his mystery machine. The audience let out a collective gasp as they looked on the most amazing machine most had ever seen. Colored teal and white, shaped like a cone and able to glow in the dark, this was Steve Jobs' reborn Macintosh, dubbed the iMac (as in Internet Mac).

The machine was absolutely beautiful, more resembling a device out of the "Jetsons" cartoon series than the box-like computers adorning most people's offices and homes. With computer and monitor included in the same plastic casing, the iMac fairly reeked of elegance, and bore Steve Jobs' handprint down to little details such as a translucent keyboard that lit up at the user's touch. In recognition of the little computer's strategic importance to Apple, its screen contained the message: "Hello again." The original Macintosh's screen had simply read, "Hello."

"It looks like it's from another planet, but a good planet," Jobs said to good-natured laughs as he led a visual tour of the iMac with the assistance of a video cameraman, whose footage of the back side of the machine could be seen on an overhead screen.

As Jobs ticked off the iMac's technical features, including a fifteen-inch monitor display, a 233-megahertz G3 processor, and 32 megabytes of memory, he predicted that, at $1,299, "We think iMac is going to be a really big deal."

And with that, the incomparable Steve Jobs ended his hour-long presentation, offering this closing thought: "This company can be great again, and I think we're well on the way to it."

In the dark of the auditorium, with cheers echoing from across the great walls, I found myself believing that perhaps Jobs was right. Maybe Apple could reclaim its rightful place as the computer industry's shining light. As I stepped blinking into the daylight outside, though, the effect was much the same as when reality hits as one walks outdoors from a movie theater. Suddenly, one can see more clearly. I began questioning how many people would buy an iMac at $1,299, when fully configured Pentium machines were available for well under $1,000. Granted, the Pentiums didn't look nearly as good as the iMac, but since when do most people buy computers for their looks?

I was not alone in harboring skepticism. We in the press did not discover until reading the fine print of the iMac later that it did not include a floppy drive—the favorite form of storage for most users. Apple officials later explained in interviews that floppy drives were being made obsolete by the Internet, because files could be stored and downloaded on networks. But that day certainly has not arrived in my household, nor, I believe, in many others. In writing this book, for example, I made duplicate copies of chapters on numerous floppies. I could then mail the floppies to my publisher, or keep them in a place of safekeeping. I certainly would not have been comfortable stockpiling this work on a network that some hacker could crack.

"What about little Johnny and Janie, who want to work on their school reports during the day at the school library and in the evening on their home iMac? Or their parents who sometimes have no choice but to bring work home from the office?" wondered the venerable Macintosh analyst Henry Norr, in a column on the MacInTouch web site. "I think [failing to include a floppy is] a horrendous mistake, one that will significantly reduce the appeal of the iMac." Norr pointed out that Jobs' NeXT machine also did not include a standard floppy drive. Indeed, as mentioned earlier in this book, that computer failed to attain many sales in large measure because developers would not support a floppy-less machine.

In the end, of course, consumers will decide the fate of the iMac, which began shipping on greating buying demand in August 1998, as well as that of Apple itself. Even if it does not succeed, Steve Jobs is shrewd enough to have some other tricks up his sleeve to keep his old company afloat for awhile. But, in my opinion, Apple's future remains a limited one over the long term, no matter what he does.

Indeed, the sheer spectacle of his iMac launch was sad in a way, for it underscored how much had been lost over the years. As much as he tried to emulate the excitement of the first Macintosh launch, this was not a product that was destined to change an industry, as the Mac had done. At best, it stood to breathe more life into a sick and tired company. Apple, after all, had shriveled to a $6 billion-a-year company from $11 billion in the span of just three years. With few resources left to compete against Microsoft, it appears to be a company relegated to defending a shrinking niche of the computer market.

Apple Computer had started in a simple garage with a simple goal: To change the world by empowering the masses with the wonders of computer technology. And it was such a noble goal that bright and idealistic youngsters raced to California from all corners of the world to embrace this movement known as Apple Computer.

And Apple, for a good many years, did not let them down. The first Apple II had proven a true technological breakthrough, with its complex, intricate circuitry bound in an appealing box that, for the first time, made the computer as non-threatening as a toaster. This gave birth to the personal computer industry. Then, in 1984, came the Macintosh, the machine with the endearing look and feel that Steve Jobs had designed to free the world's office workers from the tyranny of the staid and unimaginative IBM-compatible computers. And through it all, Apple was like a rocket ship soaring into the heavens, never looking back as its band of wide-eyed mavericks recklessly charted the future, laughing in the wind. They were cool. They were hip. Working 90 hours a week, and loving it. And partying hard, too. At the Friday afternoon beer busts. The Halloween parades. The Pointer Sisters concerts. The beach blasts in Hawaii.

There is nothing so glorious as the promise of youth, and it was this youthful outlook with all its hope and vitality that Apple's culture embraced and nourished. Apple was not like everyone else, because it never wanted to be. The company, through much of its history, was like the teen-ager who is having the time of his life and refuses to grow up. But just as no youngster can defy the laws of aging, neither could Apple defy the laws of business. Apple, since 1987, had been riding the wave of a multi-billion-dollar business from the Macintosh, without ever focusing its considerable talent and energy into making that once-revolutionary machine a computer that could evolve into the future. As a result, Bill Gates, the king of focus, deftly steered Microsoft past Apple to dominion over an entire industry.

It wasn't for lack of talent that Apple failed. So much brain power was concentrated under one roof in Cupertino that Apple Computer arguably boasted a collection of the finest scientific minds in the world. And its executives were among the finest anywhere, at least at other companies. John Sculley, for example, was the Pepsi-Cola whiz kid who surely would have ascended to the very pinnacle of the soda industry had he not answered that taunting challenge from the mesmerizing Steve Jobs atop a Manhattan high rise so many years ago. Like so many others who answered the siren song of Apple, Sculley found himself in a strange new land totally enraptured with the notion of changing the world.

But John Sculley was a born-again technologist who lacked the credentials to gain respect from Apple's powerful engineering community. So even though Sculley was CEO of Apple for so many years, he never really ran the place and the ship became steered by a thousand different captains. One day, it would be Jean-Louis Gassée calling the shots. Another, it would be the sales chief Allan Loren. And both of those men were by no means incompetent boobs. Gassée vindicated himself, after Apple, by starting an exciting new computer company from scratch. Loren went on to become one of the very top executives at American Express, a company which surely would not stand long for someone who is not up to snuff.

Yet, when all these people were assembled at Apple, the freedom was so limitless and the potential to influence so grand that they all fell under the same spell, throwing rational business practice to the winds. Even Michael Spindler, as eccentric and strange as he was, was a world-class strategist whose theories on global marketing were brilliant and ahead of their time. But Spindler harbored such a passion for Apple that it very nearly killed him in the end. He was the Diesel, but in work habit only. Sputtering and spewing like a firehose in front of his whiteboard, Spindler pointed to where he knew Apple must move as industry forces bore down on the company. But he lacked the strength of will to make the ship turn with him.

Deprived of a single-minded leader of the caliber of Bill Gates, Apple, then, was left to run adrift, unable to shift direction even as the alarm bells were sounded of approaching calamity. The calamity being a gargantuan industry commanded by the joint empire of Microsoft and Intel, whose economic forces slowly but surely began squeezing the very life out of Apple Computer. As the controversial human relations chief Kevin Sullivan, puts it, "Apple was like a sandcastle we built on the beach. Once that tide came in, no matter how much we tried to fortify it, in the end we could not keep it together."

So what are the lessons, and where lies the blame? The lessons are simple, even if they may not have been obvious to Apple's executives at the time. Be paranoid, not arrogant. Welcome help from others, don't sneer at it. Seek the long-term reward, not just short-term gain. And, above all else, embrace industry standards. Don't live outside them.

And the blame for what happened to Apple is largely a collective one. The board shares heavily in this by virtue of sticking its head in the sand for so long it had absolutely no clue as to how badly Apple was really deteriorating. The board's prime interest had been profit above all. As a result, it failed to move in and take action when it became clear that its CEOs were unable to do the job.

John Sculley, as fine an individual and accomplished in the field of marketing as he is, erred terribly when he failed to heed all the warnings from some members of his own staff as well as Bill Gates himself to license the Macintosh early on so that Apple would not have ended up so isolated in the world. It is understandable why he did not, given his mild temperament and the fierce opposition he encountered from strong-willed people like Gassée, but that is not an excuse. Sculley was the CEO, after all, and he should have behaved like one. And, while he built the company from a $1 billion enterprise to a giant of more than $10 billion in yearly revenues, Sculley set Apple up for disaster by handing over great power to his subordinate Michael Spindler, who never possessed the skills needed to run a big company.

Even without licensing, Apple could have remained a viable force for some years to come, had Spindler not run the company into the ground by his complete inability to manage the basic business. He allowed research and development to continue spinning out of control, and did nothing as manufacturing and product quality slipped so badly that computers started exploding in flames. Spindler had a chance to save Apple before it was too late, by selling the company to IBM, but both he and Apple co-founder Mike Markkula greedily demanded more money and conditions, killing the deal. In terms of shareholder value alone, this was an enormous missed opportunity. IBM's share price in mid–1997 soared to more than $150 from about $70 at the time of that fateful merger meeting in November 1994, while Apple's shares imploded to $13 from about $40. The shares later rallied to more than $40 under Steve Jobs' management, with volatile swings both ways.

Apple was already in trouble when Gil Amelio stepped in, but he ended up applying Band-Aids on a wound that required a tourniquet. Amelio also cost the company perhaps its last great opportunity to conduct a merger of equals. Had he not fought against the merger with Sun, Apple likely would have advanced much faster into the Internet than it has on its own, and it would have had a strong partner to buck it up in the painful journey ahead.

The jury, as of this writing in the summer of 1998, was still out on Steve Jobs, although he had proven himself the first capable Apple CEO to that point. If nothing else, Jobs should be credited with saving Apple from impending doom under Gil Amelio. Had Amelio continued as CEO, it is highly likely the company would have been near bankruptcy soon, for the business was headed straight off a cliff. Jobs, though, has proven himself a short-sighted manager in the past, as evidenced by his failure at NeXT and his fracture of Apple's engineering teams a decade ago. Many of the moves he has made at Apple, while laudable, were fairly obvious ones to any student of Apple's history.

"I don't think he's doing these things because he's a genius, but because he has no choice," observes Mark Macgillivray, an industry consultant in Sunnyvale, California.

So, finally, what is left for Apple? Gil Amelio had said before that Apple had two roads to take, one toward prosperity, the other toward irrelevance. Apple was already well on that latter road when he took over and it may be impossible for anybody to reverse course any more. The company's share of the PC market rebounded a bit to about 4 percent in 1998; a level still so low that it is hard to imagine many software developers willing to devote the resources to support it for much longer.

Consumers, too, have abandoned the Mac in droves, as evidenced by the miserable sales of the Performa line for two Christmases in a row before the line was pulled. Apple has been forced to retreat into its remaining two strongholds, education and desktop publishing, but these markets are under withering assault by the Wintel competition, too. In short, the real question for Apple is whether it has any real future at all, anymore. The measure of how far it has fallen is reflected in the fact that its fate lies not in its own hands, but in market forces over which it no longer has control. It took many years for the circumstances to build that would begin Apple's inexorable slide. But the company's plunge has taken place so rapidly that it is tantamount to a snowball picking up speed and size as it hurtles down the mountain. Can anyone stop it? Maybe Steve Jobs can. But the odds aren't good that he can do more than slow the fall, perhaps giving Apple a few more years before it is either gobbled up by a bigger company or finally runs out of customers.

Whatever happens in the end, the world owes a debt of gratitude to Apple Computer. This was the brave, if foolhardy, pioneer of the Information Age. So new and exciting, Apple carried the banner of the dawning age proudly on its shoulders, paving the way for so many of the technical innovations we take for granted today. And while the Apple story degenerated into one of the strangest and saddest in American business, the company, nevertheless, has secured a place in history that no amount of managerial bungling can ever erase.

NOTES

Chapter 1. In the Beginning

1. Confidential interview.
2. PC research, Dataquest, Inc., San Jose, California.
3. Ibid.
4. Sculley, *Odyssey*, p. 111.
5. Ibid., p. 198.
6. Ibid., pp. 251–52

Chapter 2. The Glory Years

1. Sculley, *Odyssey*, p. 253.
2. David Diamond, "Geek Cheek," *Wired*, April 5, 1996.
3. Rose, *West of Eden*, p. 117.
4. Kawasaki, *How to Drive Your Competition Crazy*, p. 187.
5. Steven Pearlstine and Lucien Rhodes, "Corporate Antihero John Sculley," *Inc.*, October 1987, p. 48.
6. "Apple Values," *Apple Bulletin*, September 23, 1981.
7. Sculley, *Odyssey*, p. 78.
8. Ibid., p. 6.

Chapter 3. The Licensing Debate

1. Moritz, *The Little Kingdom*, pp. 123–24.
2. Microsoft memorandum, June 25, 1985.
3. Manes and Andrews, *Gates*, p. 189.
4. Ibid., p. 216.
5. Ibid., p. 188.
6. Sculley, *Odyssey*, p. 344.
7. Cringely, *Accidental Empires*, pp. 301–2.

Chapter 4. A "Noble Village"

1. Sculley, *Odyssey*, p. 389.
2. G. Pascal Zachary, "Sculley's New Lineup at Apple," *San Jose Mercury News*, August 3, 1987, p. 1D.
3. Rose, *West of Eden*, p. 179.
4. Kathy Holub, "Stay Hungry," *San Jose Mercury News West* magazine, August 6, 1989, p. 19.
5. Brian O'Reilly, "John Sculley on Sabbatical," *Fortune*, March 27, 1989.
6. Brenton R. Schlender, "Apple Sets Plan to Reorganize into Four Divisions," *The Wall Street Journal*, August 23, 1988.
7. Kawasaki, *The Macintosh Way*, p. 139.
8. Apple Computer, *Annual Report*, p. 8.

Chapter 5. An Engineering Morass

1. Kawasaki, *The Macintosh Way*, p. 161.
2. Apple Computer, "Corporate Background Information," August 1987, p. 15.
3. Cringely, *Accidental Empires*, p. 302.
4. Sculley, *Odyssey*, pp. 200–1
5. Peter H. Lewis, "The Portable Mac: Sharp, but Heavy," *The New York Times*, September 24, 1989, p. 13F.
6. Brian O'Reilly, "Apple Computer's Shaky Revolution," *Fortune*, May 8, 1989.

Chapter 6. The Fall of Jean-Louis Gassée

1. PC research, Dataquest, Inc., San Jose, California.
2. Ibid.
3. "Technologic Computer Letter," Novermber 20, 1989, p. 1.
4. Author's interview with Jean-Louis Gassée on his deposition, *Apple Computer* v. *Microsoft Corporation and Hewlett-Packard Company*, December 16, 1988.
5. "Memorandum of Decision and Order," July 25, 1989, U.S. District Judge William W. Schwarzer, Northern District of California, pp. 4–5.
6. Apple Computer, internal memorandum, January 15, 1990.
7. Sculley, *Odyssey*, p. 328.

Chapter 7. Crossing a Canyon

1. PC research, Dataquest, Inc., San Jose, California.
2. Barbara Buell, Jonathan B. Levine, and Neil Gross, "Apple: New Team, New Strategy," *Business Week*, October 15, 1990, p. 86.
3. Cringeley, *Accidental Empires*, p. 126.
4. PC research, Dataquest, Inc., San Jose, California.
5. Confidential interview.

Chapter 8. Looking for Another Way Out

1. PC research, Dataquest, Inc., San Jose, California.
2. "Assessing the Need for a Discontinuous Jump in Macintosh OS Penetration," Apple internal report, August 30, 1990.
3. Ibid.
4. Confidential interview.
5. Author's interview with Ian Diery, July 29, 1996.
6. Confidential interview.

Chapter 9. Sculley's Waterloo

1. PC research, Dataquest, Inc., San Jose, California.
2. Confidential interview with two sources.
3. "Apple Can't Meet Demand for a Notebook Computer," *The Wall Street Journal*, March 5, 1992.
4. Manes and Andrews, *Gates*, p. 437.
5. Confidential interview.
6. Ibid.
7. Ibid.
8. Ibid.
9. Ibid.
10. Ibid.
11. Ibid.
12. Ibid.
13. Ibid.

Chapter 10. A New Sheriff in Town

1. G. Pascal Zachary and Ken Yamada, "Apple Picks Spindler as Chief for Rough Days Ahead," *The Wall Street Journal*, June 21, 1993, p. B1.
2. Confidential interview.
3. Ibid.
4. Ibid.
5. PC research, Dataquest, Inc., San Jose, California.
6. "PC Industry: The Three Ways to Compete," report by Sanford C. Bernstein & Co., January 1994, p. 33.
7. Kathy Rebello and Paul Eng, "Spindler's Apple," *Business Week*, October 3, 1994, p. 88.
8. Ibid.
9. Author's interview for *The Wall Street Journal* article published January 25, 1994.

Chapter 11. The March to PowerPC

1. Author's interview in February 1994 for article in *The Wall Street Journal*.

2. Dataquest, February 1994 report on worldwide microprocessor market share ranking.

3. Author's interview in February 1994 for article in *The Wall Street Journal*.

4. *Grolier Multimedia Encyclopedia*.

5. Dataquest, February 1994 report on worldwide microprocessor market share ranking.

Chapter 12. From Power Mac to the Cliff

1. Author's interview for *The Wall Street Journal*.

2. Ibid.

3. "Personal Computer Hardware," report by Salomon Brothers, Inc., April 19, 1994.

4. PC research, Dataquest, Inc., San Jose, California.

5. G. Pascal Zachary, "Apple Wants Other PC Makers to Build Computers to Use Macintosh Software," *The Wall Street Journal*, January 18, 1994.

6. Confidential interview.

7. Ibid.

8. Ibid.

9. International Data Corp., Dataquest estimates.

Chapter 13. The Wreck of the Diesel

1. PC research, Dataquest, Inc., San Jose, California.

2. Author's interview for *The Wall Street Journal*.

3. Apple Computer, internal electronic correspondence.

4. Ibid.

5. Ibid.

6. Confidential interview.

7. *Apple Computer* v. *San Francisco Canyon Co.*, *Intel*, *Microsoft*, February 9, 1995.

8. Ibid.

9. Letter from Bill Gates to Michael Spindler, February 23, 1995.

10. Ibid.

11. Author's interview for *The Wall Street Journal*.

12. PC research, Dataquest, Inc., San Jose, California.

13. Apple Computer, internal memorandum, March 15, 1995.

14. "Hoover's Company Profiles," Hoover's Inc., Austin, Texas.

15. Author's interview with Pieter Hartsook, editor of *The Hartsook Letter*, for *The Wall Street Journal*, 1996.

Chapter 14. Spindler's Last Stand

1. PC research, Dataquest, Inc., San Jose, California.

2. Ibid.

3. Confidential interview.

4. Charles McCoy, "Apple Chief Shows Still Waters Can Run Deep—and Angry," *The Wall Street Journal*, July 14, 1995, p. A2.

5. PC research, Dataquest, Inc., San Jose, California.

6. Confidential interview.

7. Ibid.

8. Author's interview for *The Wall Street Journal*.

9. Confidential interview with meeting participant.

10. *Karen Finzi* v. *Laurie Spindler, Michael Spindler*, Superior Court of California, County of San Mateo, January 5, 1996.

11. Charles Cooper, "Spindler Said Suffering Severe Health Problems," *PC Week*, February 2, 1996.

12. *Grolier Multimedia Encyclopedia*.

13. John Markoff, "Changing Guard at Apple: The Board Says 'Enough,' " *The New York Times*, February 4, 1996.

14. Confidential interview.

15. Ibid.

16. "Apple Computer," *Computer Reseller News*, October 30, 1995, p. 40.

17. Confidential interview.

Chapter 15. Mission: Impossible

1. Confidential interview.

2. Ibid.

3. Amelio and Simon, *Profit from Experience*, pp. 303–4

4. Ibid.

5. "Hoover's Company Profiles," Hoover's, Inc.

6. PC research, Dataquest, Inc., San Jose, California.

7. Author's interview for *The Wall Street Journal*.

8. Confidential interview.

9. Ibid.

Chapter 16 NeXT: A Founder's Return

1. David Coursey, "The Incredible Brightness of Be Inc.," *PC Letter*, October 16, 1995, p.1.

2. Linzmayer, *The Mac Bathroom Reader*, p. 257.

3. Transcript of speech by Gil Amelio to Apple employees, January 16, 1997.

4. "Hoover's Company Profiles," Hoover's, Inc.

BIBLIOGRAPHY

Amelio, Gil, and William Simon. *Profit from Experience: The National Semiconductor Story of Transformation Management.* New York: Van Nostrand Reinhold, 1996.

Clapp, Doug. *The Macintosh Reader.* New York: Random House Electronic Publishing, 1992.

Cringely, Robert X. *Accidental Empires: How the Boys of Silicon Valley Make Their Millions, Battle Foreign Competition, and Still Can't Get a Date.* Reading, Mass.: Addison-Wesley Publishing Co., 1992.

Duntemann, Jeff, and Ron Pronk. *Inside the PowerPC Revolution: The Inside Story Behind the Chips, Software, and Machines That Are Changing the Computer Industry.* Scottsdale, Arizona: Coriolis Group, 1994.

Editors of *The Red Herring. The Red Herring Guide to the Digital Universe: The Inside Look at Technology Business—From Silicon Valley to Hollywood.* New York: Warner Books, 1996.

Kawasaki, Guy. *How to Drive Your Competition Crazy: Creating Disruption for Fun and Profit.* New York: Hyperion, 1995.

———, *The Macintosh Way.* Glenview, Ill·: Scott, Foresman and Co., 1990.

Komando, Kim. *1,001 Komputer Answers.* Foster City, Calif.: IDG Books Worldwide, 1995.

Levy, Steven. *Hackers: Heroes of the Computer Revolution.* New York: Dell Publishing, 1984.

Linzmayer, Owen W. *The Mac Bathroom Reader.* Alameda, Calif.: Sybex, 1994.

Manes, Stephen, and Paul Andrews. *Gates: How Microsoft's Mogul Reinvented an Industry—and Made Himself the Richest Man in America.* New York: Touchstone, 1993.

Moritz, Michael. *The Little Kingdom: The Private Story of Apple Computer.* New York: William Morrow and Co., 1984.

Rogers, Everett M., and Judith K. Larsen. *Silicon Valley Fever: Growth of High Technology Culture.* New York: Basic Books, 1984.

Rose, Frank. *West of Eden: The End of Innocence at Apple Computer.* New York: Viking Penguin, 1989.

Sculley, John. *Odyssey: Pepsi to Apple . . . A Journey of Adventures, Ideas and the Future.* New York: Harper & Row, 1987.

Wallace, James, and Jim Erickson. *Hard Drive: Bill Gates and the Making of the Microsoft Empire.* New York: HarperBusiness, 1992.

Young, Jeffrey S. *Steve Jobs: The Journey Is the Reward.* Glenview, Ill.: Scott, Foresman and Co., 1988.

INDEX

About the Author

JIM CARLTON was born in Texas and educated at Kansas State University. For the past twenty years, he has worked as a journalist for a variety of newspapers, including the *Houston Chronicle*, *The Orange County Register*, the *Los Angeles Times*, and, currently, *The Wall Street Journal*. His numerous articles have included investigative exposés of questionable practices in the airline, chemical, and computer industries. He was named a finalist for the 1980 Pulitzer Prize for a series on toxic dumping in Texas, and he has won investigative and feature-writing awards for articles written in California. He lives in San Francisco and covers West Coast technology issues for *The Wall Street Journal*.